African-American Exploration in
West Africa

African-American Exploration in

Bloomington & Indianapolis

West Africa

Four Nineteenth-Century Diaries

EDITED BY

JAMES FAIRHEAD

TIM GEYSBEEK

SVEND E. HOLSOE

MELISSA LEACH

Publication of this book is made possible in part with the assistance of a Challenge Grant from the National Endowment for the Humanities, a federal agency that supports research, education, and public programing in the humanities.

This book is a publication of
Indiana University Press
601 North Morton Street
Bloomington, IN 47404-3797 USA

http://iupress.indiana.edu

Telephone orders 800-842-6796
Fax orders 812-855-7931
Orders by e-mail iuporder@indiana.edu

The paper used in this publication meets the minimum requirements of American National Standard for Information Sciences—Permanence of Paper for Printed Library Materials, ANSI Z39.48-1984.

Manufactured in the United States of America

Library of Congress Cataloging-in-Publication Data

African-American exploration in West Africa : four nineteenth-century diaries / edited by James Fairhead . . . [et al.]. p. cm.
Includes bibliographical references (p.) and index.
ISBN 0-253-34194-9 (alk. paper)

1. Liberia—Discovery and exploration. 2. African Americans—Liberia—History—19th century. 3. African Americans—Liberia—Diaries. 4. Guinea—Discovery and exploration. 5. African Americans—Guinea—History—19th century. 6. African Americans—Guinea—Diaries. I. Sims, James L. II. Seymour, George L. III. Anderson, Benjamin J. K., b. 1834. IV. Fairhead, James, date.

DT634 .A37 2003

916.66204'2'092396073—dc21
`2002152631

1 2 3 4 5 08 07 06 05 04 03

Contents

Illustrations

Maps

Note: The boundaries in these maps do not imply any judgment on the legal status of any territory.

Acknowledgments

As a collaborative effort over several years, this work has involved invaluable support from many individuals and institutions. Many people have assisted in locating materials or in pursuing dead ends. We are especially grateful to Peter Ferguson of the British Library for Development Studies (Sussex, U.K.) for tracking down newspaper microfilm; Michael McSean and Diane Fisher of Michigan State University libraries; staff of Special Collections of Yale University Library; Daniel Meyer and Jay Satterfield of the University of Chicago Special Collections; Marjorie E. Bloss and Talisa Martin of the Center for Research Libraries in Chicago; archivists at the Royal Geographical Society, London; archivists at the Archives d'Outre Mer (Aix-en-Provence, France) for assistance in accessing the Dauvillier Archive; and Ruth Stone and Suzanne Mudge of the Archives of Traditional Music at Indiana University for helping us use materials stored in the Svend E. Holsoe Collection. Martin Ford provided copies of handwritten notes in the State University of New York, Binghamton, copy of Benjamin Anderson's *Narrative of a Journey to Musardu*. Bernard Gardi of Berne History Museum and Chris Wright at the Royal Anthropological Institute library helped locate photographs.

A number of academics have contributed their specialist perspectives in reading and commenting on certain portions or earlier drafts of this work. Their work has been invaluable. In particular, we would like to thank Laura Arnston, Warren d'Azevedo, David Conrad, Elwood Dunn, Christopher Fyfe, David Robinson, William Siegmann, and Elizabeth Tonkin.

This research has benefited from other research programs funded variously by grants from the Michigan State University History Department, the British Department for International Development, and the Economic and Social Research Council. For support during various periods of field research, linked to other projects, but which enabled the material in this work to be assembled, James Fairhead and Melissa Leach would particularly like to thank the Centre d'Étude et de Recherche en Environnement, University of Conakry, and the Direction National de la Recherche Scientifique et Technique, both of the Republic of Guinea, for their authorization and interest in assorted research programs in the country. Botanist Jean Louis Hellié and historian Joël Maxim Millimouno of the University of Kankan kindly assisted fieldwork in the Ziama region in 1994 and 1999, respectively. Fairhead and Leach would also like to thank Annette Sinclair and Sinnet Weber at the Institute of Development Studies, University of Sussex, for assistance in formatting the manuscript. Thanks are also due to Cassandra, Rory, Xanthe, and Francesca, whose births during this volume's long gestation created parental leave and alternative spaces in which to work on it.

Tim Geysbeek would like to thank Dr. M. Kodiougou Diallo, the Vice Rectorat of research of the Université de Conakry, for giving him permission to conduct research in Guinea. The people of Musadu warmly welcomed Geysbeek, especially the late Yaya Dole and his family, who hosted Geysbeek during his short visits in 1986, 1992, and 1993. In addition, Geysbeek sincerely thanks the interviewees who narrated oral histories in this book: Yaya Dole, Bintu Mammadi Donzo, Alhaji Bintu Ibrahima Beete, and Baba Dole of Musadu; Laye Kabine Kromah of Diakolidu; the late Fofin Sumawolo of Lansedou; and the late Lanse Kromah of Macenta. Makula Mammadi Kromah, the late Mustafa Kromah, Muhammad Chejan Kromah, and Muhammad Oppong Sanoe helped Geysbeek record these histories. Faliku Sanoe, Boakai Yamah Ansu Cisse, and Keleti Fofana translated these interviews with some assistance from Geysbeek. Thanks to Djobba Kamara for interviewing Jala Kamara and Kewulen Kamara in Kuankan in 1985 and Alhaji Kaamoo Dole in N'Zerekore in 1990. Martin Ford kindly gave a copy of the interview that he and Faliku Sanoe conducted with Mammad Dole in Bahn, Liberia, in 1985. Dave Partridge of L'Organization Mondiale de la Santé Onchocerciasis took aerial photographs of Musadu and the surrounding landscape in 1993, with Kevin Cexton piloting the helicopter and Stephen Cumings, James Harbeck, Ed and Ruth Vandermaas, and John Wood providing other assistance. Geysbeek finally thanks his son Jamie for helping him to navigate between two word processing systems and to send files through cyberspace, and his wife, Tami, and sons, Jamie, Ryan, and Adam, for encouraging him while he worked on the manuscript.

Svend Holsoe would like to thank Joellen El Bashir, the curator at the Moorland-Springarn Research Center at Howard University, for permission to publish the photograph of Benjamin Anderson, and Ann Shumard of the Smithsonian Institution's National Art Gallery for helping to secure Augustus Washington's daguerreotype of Liberia's President Stephen Allen Benson.

We finally want to thank Indiana University Press for publishing this book, and particularly Dee Mortensen (Sponsoring Editor), Jane Lyle (Managing Editor), Tony Brewer (Assistant Managing Editor), and Jimmée Greco (Copyeditor) for patiently working with us to bring this book to fruition.

African-American Exploration in
West Africa

Introduction

In 1858 America was brewing a civil war, and slavery was the issue. But by then, a few thousand Americans with some African ancestry, whether free or freed from slavery, had already gained greater freedom by sailing across the Atlantic to Africa. Here they had founded the fledgling and controversial nation they called Liberia. Yet their new freedom came with many contradictions. First, theirs was a white-sponsored black republic; most African Americans in the U.S. continued to argue that the emigration program—sponsored as it was by slave owners—was founded less on ideals of white philanthropy than on disposal. Liberia was an African republic designed to solve an American problem. Second, many emigrants who had been slaves in the U.S. now found that they were treating the African populations they encountered in a similar way.

For some among them, an alternative to living these contradictions was to forge stronger and more equitable links with the African nations of the interior, links which would be mutually beneficial and would facilitate large-scale American colonization. This book collates the day-by-day diaries of three pioneering Americo-Liberians who were inspired to live and travel into the far interior: James Sims, George Seymour, and Benjamin Anderson.[1] The first two accounts—of Sims and Seymour dating from 1858—became "lost" soon after they were published. Their reemergence here should transform modern images of this region's past and encourage reflection on what it was to explore Africa.

The accounts of Sims and Seymour provide the first detailed descriptions of the region extending from the coast of Upper Guinea to the savannas in what is today the Republic of Guinea. Together with the narratives of Benjamin Anderson's two journeys of 1868–69 and 1874, these texts document everyday life in the region before its decimation during subsequent decades of conflict associated with African empire building and European and Americo-Liberian colonization. For the first time, a detailed picture can emerge of the political alliances and the commercial and political rivalries that characterized interior politics during the nineteenth century. For the first time, too, we begin to appreciate in detail why Liberia's engagement with these turbulent regions was so faltering.

Since the region has recently been engulfed in conflict, we hope that recalling the more prosperous and populous times that the region has seen will inspire peace. Certainly the details that can be discerned of the region's political alliances of the nineteenth century can help us understand those of the twentieth, and the current patterns of conflict they shape.

Historical sources from this region are curious in their propensity to shock the modern reader. When the Nigerian scholar Khalil Mahmud introduced a new edition of Henry Schieffelin's 1871 book *The People of Africa,* which described the extent of literacy among African adults and children and the scholarly libraries to be found in the West African interior, he noted how it was "truly remarkable that even today, more than one hundred years after the publication of these works, this information is still novel to the great majority of educated and learned men and women in the world. The same old myths are repeated" (Mahmud 1974, xi). The capacity for historical sources to astonish is certainly enhanced, because even among the learned, ignorance of Liberian history has enabled its past to be represented by long outdated myths, of nature, of the rainforest and harmonious "forest peoples," or of a dangerous, unruly world, badly in need of civilization. Liberians and their American sponsors fostered many such images, but the accounts of those who engaged with the interior give lie to them.

The documents here will astonish even the knowledgable in many ways. For example, both Seymour and Anderson visited an area that today is a celebrated tropical forest reserve in Guinea, its international status as a biosphere reserve iconic of present impressions of it as a natural forest Arcadia. Yet unequivocally, Seymour and Anderson both described the lowlands and mountains of what is now in this reserve as open savanna, populous, prosperous, cultivated, and vibrant with trade. This is inconvenient for conservationists dreaming of a primitive African wilderness and for the repressive policies they inflict, premised on their dreams. Such policies engender little but contempt and conflict from descendants of the region's past inhabitants and guardians of its inherited memory, who recall its past prosperity against the tide of modern dogma. They may draw confidence from these texts.

In this same vein of thinking, it is also shocking for many to read the thoughts of Karl Mayer from the 1940s. An American, he surveyed the Liberian forests and populations in 1947, using air photographs covering the whole country, and walked several thousand miles in Liberia to check them. He documented much less forest than modern romantics expect it to have had. And, more significant, such forests as there were, were mostly recent regrowth, following the war and depopulation in recent decades and centuries. The land spoke to him not of a forest wilderness, but of an "overused, worn out country of great antiquity" (Mayer 1951, 25).

The accounts that we reproduce here describe much of the interior already in decline. A Dutch trader living near the coast, some 62 miles (100 kilometers) northwest of Monrovia, managed to glean detailed information about the land more than two hundred years earlier, in about 1630, and described it in a long manuscript. The Dutch geographer Olfert Dapper published his account in 1668. As historian Adam Jones notes, "Had Dapper not published this manuscript, many historians would no doubt have been tempted to speculate that no large states existed in the forest zone west of Asante [Ghana] before the colonial era" (1983b, 23). Once the significance of this manuscript was realized, many Liberian historians had to think again. The account documented the history, economy, and makeup of a kingdom which then stretched from what is now Freetown, Sierra Leone, some 310 miles (500 kilometers) southeast of Liberia, to the Junk River and extended inland from there, perhaps 125 miles (200 kilometers), and was ruled from far inland. This powerful and well-orchestrated state covered the lands that the Americo-Liberians documented here traversed two centuries later. The accounts of Sims, Seymour, and Anderson still discern African state building on a vast scale. By the time they traveled, however, international trade in slaves, gold, ivory, and new weaponry and innovations in—and the expectation of—warfare had helped transform the political and social map. These works help us to consider how.

Yet the accounts we present here speak to a wider audience than just revisionists of regional history. They recall the day-by-day thoughts and experiences of three very different Americo-Liberians during their encounters with the African interior. More than a century later, current works in this genre are still popular. They describe how nostalgic ideals, molded by American politics of African representation, itself rooted in the legacy and social memory of brutal Atlantic slavery, become contorted in interactions with very real Africans who have thoroughly different aspirations, memories, and ways.

In contrast with modern accounts, however, both American slavery and the Atlantic slave trade were a horrific reality when the diaries were written. In one passage, Sims immodestly relates his own single-handed heroism in freeing captive slaves. It is, however, in the tragedy of Seymour's account that even fictive works of the genre are unlikely to be surpassed. Born in Hartford, Connecticut, and an arch-opponent of the Liberian project in his youth, Seymour was eventually converted to the cause of Liberia and immigrated to a colony where realities did not match aspirations. As passionate a Liberian as only a convert can be, but an equally passionate critic of Liberia's exploitation of interior peoples, he decamped to a village in the interior. He then resolved to explore the far interior for the good of the Americo-Liberian colony. Four months later, after documenting his moves from town to town and eulogizing the populousness, hospitality, wealth, and fertility of the regions he crossed, after many moments of humor and only hours from his destination, he was attacked, to die later of his wounds. His American traveling companion, Levin Ash, was captured, enslaved, and put on the market. His head was shaved. Their attack and eventual escape make compelling reading, but more compelling still is the harsh irony: a tour of Africa, pregnant with the optimism of those now freed from American slavery, was dramatically cut short by enslavement.

Compounding this irony was another: African villagers considered these leading citizens of Liberia's "black" republic as "white."

These are works of personal exploration, then, but they also double up as texts appealing to the "authentic" exploration of the era, the stuff of Burton, Livingstone, Stanley, and other contributors to the British Royal Geographical Society's rendition of the world. Benjamin Anderson was proud to have his text shelved in the society's library, and Seymour's journey was reported in its proceedings. Their journeys also compare to the less-publicized travels of persons of African descent such as Blyden, Campbell, and Delany, who returned to Africa to tread paths deep into the interior of the continent from where their ancestors were extracted.

Despite its importance at the time, the text of Seymour's journey was "lost" to Liberians and academics until parts of it were located in obscure American newspapers and put together for this volume. A few historians have recently used isolated parts of Sims's accounts (see, e.g., Akpan 1975; Holsoe 1979a, 66; Saha 1985, 222), but the full texts have also not been available to scholars, let alone to a wider public, and their significance remains unrecognized.[2] The actual works of Anderson have been better known. Yet appreciation of their significance to Liberian history has been limited, awaiting close annotation and analysis in relation to the earlier accounts.

Circumstantial evidence indicates that Seymour's and Sims's accounts quickly became lost. The famous nineteenth-century Liberian writer Edward W. Blyden did list Sims, along with Seymour and Anderson, as one of Liberia's important travelers of the nineteenth century ([1888] 1994, 350; 1886, 26). He also quoted from a part of Sims's journal that the *Maryland Colonization Journal* published in 1859 (1872b, 291). He edited the *Liberia Herald* in 1855 and 1856, was responsible for making sure that exploration stories were published, and knew Seymour personally. Yet there is no evidence that Blyden had access to the full accounts in later years. We can gauge this because, surprisingly, there is also no indication that his friend Benjamin Anderson ever read Sims's and Seymour's accounts.

As these works were also written to advertise the Liberia project, then lagging far behind its founders' dreams, and because, in the case of Seymour's accounts at least, they also exhort the reader to evangelization, parts of them may not be immediately easy or satisfying to read, at least by those more accustomed to modern or "authentic" exploration. Yet some of the importance of these accounts may rest in this contrast and challenge. So as editors, we make no apologies in following the principle of providing the fullest possible text, gleaned from assorted sources and retaining original punctuation, orthography, capital letters, and paragraphing. All that we have added is precision on the day and date, modern village names, and original page numbers, always in editorial square brackets. We derive our texts of Sims and Seymour from their serialization in Liberian newspapers, the *Liberia Herald* and the *Star of Liberia*. But where original editions cannot be traced, we rely on their often re-edited serialization in the American colonization newspapers: those of the Maryland, New York, and Philadelphia colonization societies. Benjamin Anderson published the first of his two accounts in book form. While we derive our text of his first journey from the book *Narrative of a Journey to Musardu, the Capital of the Western Mandingoes* (1870), his second journey was first serialized in a Liberian newspaper, the *Observer* (Monrovia), long before it was published as a book, and this is our principal source.

Before presenting the diaries themselves, we devote a chapter to describing the background to the Liberian colonization, and another to the background of each journey and the evolution of Liberian engagement with the interior. In these, we detail what is known of the travelers. Our first diary account is that of James L. Sims in chapter 3. We then present George L. Seymour's major 1858 journey with Levin Ash, a journey on which they encountered Sims. Chapters 5 and 6 present Benjamin Anderson's better-known journeys to Musadu in 1868–69 and 1874. We also publish the letter in Arabic that the chief of Musadu sent to the Liberian government on the return of Anderson's first journey, which E. W. Blyden translated for the government.

The accounts were written as self-contained texts. Yet considered together, these works clarify the political and economic makeup of the region at the time, and with this knowledge we can better gauge why the journeys unfolded as they did. Our last chapter analyzes the texts together in relation to existing knowledge of the region. This narrative supplements the more conventional notes, with the index designed to facilitate cross-referencing.[3]

Oral accounts can still be heard around the region which speak of the people, places, and events encountered by the travelers. These tell the history of towns such as Musadu and Kuankan, the siege of Musadu that occurred between Anderson's two visits, and stories that people continue to tell about Benjamin Anderson. Usually narrated by griots, guardians of the region's history, or by elders descended from those involved, they provide a stark contrast in style and perspective from the Americo-Liberian travelers' narratives. Including them would have provided alternative entry points, values, and concepts through which to consider the history of the region, a counterpoint to the view of American immigrants. Unfortunately, space constraints have precluded their inclusion here.

Some modern scholars have questioned whether Anderson went to Musadu and even whether Musadu existed (see, e.g., Duignan and Gann 1984, 392; Thomasson 1987, 15 n. 16; Bassett and Porter 1991, 394 n. 105). Their doubts can be attributed to the closure of the Republic of Guinea to outside researchers for many years. Yet doubts—or denials—had been expressed earlier, rooted in regional politics, especially in competing French and Liberian claims to this region in the late nineteenth and early twentieth centuries. In 1890, the question about whether Benjamin Anderson ever went to Musadu surfaced when the explorer Captain Louis Binger published a map which showed that the area of Musadu's location was "unexplored" (Binger 1890). The Liberians complained about Binger's article (Davis 1890), and Binger later acknowledged that Anderson visited Musadu (1892, 137–138). Yet his original claim—in the meantime—must have been welcomed by France, which wanted to annex land that Liberia "claimed."

Ten years later, the French explorer Captain d'Ollone dismissed the travels of Anderson as fabrication. Ignorant of Anderson's second journey and dismissive that a Liberian could or would have made any such journey, he portrayed Liberia as an unknown land which he had explored for the first time. Anderson was still alive, and Liberians and others responded to the claims of d'Ollone. Again, the ensuing debate, which we review at the end of chapter 2, had a crucial subtext: if the territories were unexplored, then presumably the treaties pertaining to them were themselves fabrications, opening the door to further territorial claims which the expanding French colonies were making on Liberia at the time. The travel accounts thus had real political significance—and perhaps in other ways, still do.

1

The Liberia of the Journeys

Liberia and the United States

By 1800 in the U.S., individual states, slaves, freed slaves, and the evangelicals, radicals, and sympathizers who supported abolitionism were promoting emancipation with increasing success. The emancipated organized for further emancipation. The radical thoughts which had inspired white Americans in revolution against their British colonists in the late 1700s left little room for slavery. And even the British whom they had defeated in the cause of freedom were now outlawing slavery. The American white elite had a problem. For the slaveholders and plantation owners in the Southern states this problem was not just ideological. Their plantocracy—plantation economy and culture of white paternalistic supremacy—depended on slavery. When the Northern states and churches began to preach for, politic for, and practice emancipation, the issue of slavery soon divided the Northern and Southern states.

Until the opening salvos of the Civil War in 1861, the Union's unity could only be achieved through hollow compromise—declaring for example, with Orwellian simplicity, that slaves were freemen, but only three-fifths so. Such compromises served to underscore the intellectual unease and political fragility. Compromise could only defer solution. But what solution? One option was racial integration in America, and a second, reintegration of the "black" population into Africa. The latter was termed colonization. As an alternative to integration, the idea of what became Liberia was central to political discourse in North America long before Liberia itself was ever founded (Shick 1980; Beyan 1991; Liberty [1977] 1999).

The colonization alternative was important for many whites who, while calling for emancipation, also feared its consequences for the racial purity they upheld. Thomas Jefferson, the leading light of the revolution, was one such: "Among Romans emancipation required but one effort," he wrote, "The slave when free, might mix, without staining the blood of his master. But with us a second is necessary, unknown to history. When freed, he is to be removed beyond the reach of mixture" (cited in Shick 1980, 3).

For those who felt like this—for Jefferson, more in public than in private it would seem—it seemed logical that the "emigration" associated with colonization would pave the way for slaveholders to liberate more slaves, as it removed the subsequent problem: the impact that freemen would have on "their" society.[1] The idea of colonization became a reality in 1816 when the Society for Colonizing Free People of Color in the United States was founded in Washington, D.C. In the American Colonization Society (ACS), as it came to be called, those championing the relocation of the entire U.S. "black" population united with a second faction: those with a fervor for international evangelization. The 1810s had seen the birth of the American Foreign Missionary Society, and the idea of colonization attracted several white Christians who argued that their mission to civilize, moralize, and evangelize in Africa could best be served by African-American preachers. Indeed, such an idea even provided a religious explanation for the phenomenon of slavery that they now abhorred but which society embraced: in slavery, God was creating civilized black evangelicals who would call Africa to Christianity. Linked to this was the view that the West must replace the slave trade with "commerce, cultivation, and Christianity" to amend for past wrongs (Buxton [1839] 1968, 12; Sherwood 1917; see also Blamo 1971–72, 27; Tonkin 1981; Gershoni 1985).

A second party advocating colonization was made up of slaveholders themselves, who considered "Free Blacks" in the U.S. to be insurrectionists. The first twelve managers of the ACS were slaveholders (Groves 1948, 290–291). With such a coalition of political, religious, and Southern economic interests, the idea of colonization became fundable and gained organizers. The U.S. government, which did not overtly initiate or conduct colonization, nevertheless provided logistical and financial support to the ACS. The organization also needed a place in Africa to "repatriate" people who had been enslaved illegally and whom the U.S. Navy had liberated. Their numbers began to grow in temporary detention camps in the U.S., and a U.S.–sponsored "black" colony in Africa provided the ideal resolution to this problem (Shick 1980, 19–20). The idea that African Americans should start afresh thus suited many constituencies. White slaveholders, emancipation pragmatists, and racists alike could all applaud Robert Finley of the ACS when he argued that black Americans could not achieve political equality as long as they remained in the United States, and that "Everything connected with their condition, including their colour, is against them, nor is there much prospect that their status can ever be greatly ameliorated, while they shall continue among us" (cited in Brown 1857, 99).

The idea of solving social problems by exporting or deporting them was not unique to the U.S. In the 1780s, Britain had planned to send convicts to penal colonies in West Africa (Curtin [1964] 1973). The London-based Committee for the Black Poor began to relocate their poor—African Americans freed by the British during the American War of Independence, who had become refugees in London—to the settlement in Sierra Leone in West Africa. As Curtin notes, this was an era when rational planners felt that these African Americans could produce a "good society," exemplified in the doctrines of the French and American revolutionaries (Curtin [1964] 1973). West African colonization became inextricably associated with developing new societies. When Sierra Leone was founded for the black poor, its detailed statutes, laws, and codes spelt out a particular version of social perfection. Even British plans to deposit two hundred convicts, tools, and provisions for six months in Gambia were couched in terms of social experimentation, albeit more empirical, establishing the colony and then withdrawing all surveillance, to let it form its own government and fare as it could. Cult followers of the Swedish prophet Emanuel Swedenborg, who anticipated a Second Coming in West Africa, were at this time also planning to establish their own brand of utopia, to be located in what later became Liberia's capital, Monrovia. Significantly, the idea of "starting afresh" actually appeared to be possible in West Africa. In several cases, slave dealers and their descendants had been able to establish their own quasi-states on the West African coast. If they could, surely the educated with more civilized motives could do much the same, but based on legitimate trade (Curtin [1964] 1973).

The last party to the colonization alliance was the participating African Americans. In the late eighteenth century, several had petitioned their states to return to their homeland (Shick 1980, 5). However cynical one can be concerning the motives of the white organizers and funders, the possibility to start afresh and to forge a new society appealed as much to the few African Americans who participated as it had to the French and American revolutionaries and to the British and Swedish intellectuals.

Yet to the majority of African-Americans, the idea of emigration—especially under ACS auspices—was abhorrent. It immediately stirred opposition, and throughout the North free African Americans met to pass resolutions opposing the colonization idea (Mehlinger 1916). As David Walker observed, "America is more our country than it is the whites—we have enriched it with our blood and tears . . . and will they drive us from our property and homes which we have earned with our blood?" (cited in Shick 1980, 7). Many resented the religious interpretations which suggested that their destiny lay in civilizing Africa. The logic of the ACS, they argued, was to perpetuate slavery by disposing of the emancipated who might militate for further emancipation. African Americans who supported emigration and those who left American shores were branded as traitors. As we shall see, George Seymour argued against colonization early in his life. In his hometown of Hartford, Connecticut, the dominant sentiment was that "the American colonization society was actuated by the same motives which influenced the mind of Pharaoh, when he ordered the male children of the Israelites to be destroyed" (Mehlinger 1916, 286). For the African-American masses, the ACS was the greatest of all foes to the free colored people and to the slave population. An emigrant was "an enemy to the cause and a traitor to his brethren" (Mehlinger 1916, 286). By contrast, the idea of "total emigration" was the dream within the ACS that Liberian pioneers such as Edward Blyden articulated; Blyden imagined his new country to be only "the gateway to Africa. The great African nationality—the home for the millions in America." Blyden, one should note, was Liberia's most renowned nineteenth-century intellectual and pan-Africanist, a "litterateur, educator, theologian, politician, statesman, diplomat and explorer" (Lynch 1967, vii).[2] But for the majority who considered this dream a nightmare, its specter was all too possible. This was, after all, an era of mass seaborne population movements. In the first half of the nineteenth century, more than 3.5 million British and Germans had immigrated to the Americas.

Statistics on immigration are telling: by 1860, there were more than 4.4 million African Americans in the U.S., of whom 99 percent had been born in America. Among them, 448,000 were free, split evenly between North and South, but they resided largely in urban areas, where the free massively outnumbered the enslaved (Shick 1980, 11). By the same date, only about 13,000 had immigrated to Liberia.

At the risk of generalizing, many of the 13,000 who did immigrate to Liberia used the ACS and were not subordinated to it. They were "not willing to abandon their black nationalist convictions simply because the ACS existed" and had polarized the debate (Shick 1980, 7–8). Yet the profile of the immigrants suggests that such a choice is not the end of the story. Of the 3,000 first immigrants (1820–33), all but 200 were from the slave states of the South and gained their freedom from slavery by agreeing to immigrate. Even by 1852, only 40 percent of immigrants had been free before immigration (Mehlinger 1916). The choice was between being a slave in the U.S. or a free citizen in Liberia.

While the personal motives for immigration surely varied, an underlying desire for many was thus to avoid being a slave or even, as freemen, to avoid being seized as a slave again under the Fugitive Slave Law of 1852 (Liberty

Figure 1. Edward W. Blyden.
Courtesy of the Library of Congress.

[1977] 1999). Du Bois eloquently described the psychological discomfort for African Americans in forever being a “problem,” and this surely influenced the decisions. Black nationalism offered an escape from that “sense of always looking at oneself through the eyes of others, of measuring one’s soul by the tape of a world that looks on in amused contempt and pity.” As Du Bois characterized the “double consciousness” of African-American experience of the time: “One ever feels his two-ness—an American, a Negro; two souls, two thoughts, two unreconciled strivings; two warring ideals in one dark body, whose dogged strength alone keeps it from being torn asunder" (Du Bois 1905, 3).

Many of those who made the journey argued that they had not gone back to Africa but forward to it. They were not there because conditions for black Americans in the U.S. were hopeless, as the ACS argued, but to build a nation run by freed slaves in Liberia. Such ideals would not have precluded a sense of return to a land of forefathers. In critique of their opponents, and more in line with ACS policy, many argued as Seymour eventually did that African Americans had a moral obligation for the redemption and industrialization of Africa. They made the further case that in a material way, through colonization and the control of the African coast, one could stop the further exportation of slaves, which, despite the politics of British abolition, was still being practiced by U.S. and Cuban vessels, among others.

Alternative locations for a black state were forwarded by those who favored emigration, but not under ACS auspices. In 1858, Henry Highland Garnet formed the African Civilization Society in New York City, "To establish a grand centre of Negro nationality from which shall flow the streams of commercial, intellectual, and political power which shall make colored people respected everywhere" (Ejofodomi 1974, 153). Locations were considered in the U.S., in the Caribbean, in South America, and in other parts of West Africa—such as at Abeokuta in what is now Nigeria.

Debates concerning colonization were no less strong than the debates which fueled the Civil War. A propaganda battle ensued to "win the minds of free Americans" (Shick 1980, 7). The ACS published all favorable reports about Liberia and provided a climate in which exaggerated exuberance for Liberia thrived. Critics, on the other hand, forwarded unfavorable reports (see Moses 1998b; Liberty [1977] 1999). As Shick has argued, published reports about Liberia thus tended to exaggerate either the vices or virtues of life in Africa (Shick 1980, 42). The travel accounts reproduced here would fall into those exaggerating the virtues and should be read critically in this respect. Yet in accepting this, readers should bear in mind the many other, potentially more important influences on the authors' experiences and the ways that they narrate them.

Liberia, 1820–74

As with all colonies, narratives surrounding the foundation or "planting" of Liberia have become seeped in events now mythic and in heroism now hagiographic.[3] It is impossible and unnecessary to do justice to these narratives here, but as we shall see, a focus on central people and events may actually misconstrue how the colony survived and why it took the forms that it did. The first attempt at colonization was the private initiative of Paul

Cuffee, seaman, philanthropist, Quaker, and son of an African-American father and Amerindian mother (Fyfe 1962, 112). He had originally made a name in the struggle for African-American rights in the Massachusetts but then turned his private wealth to the cause of emigration to build a black, Christian nation that would block slavery. In 1816, he captained a ship and almost forty American free blacks to Sierra Leone. This private initiative was not sustained after Cuffee died the following year, but it "rekindled the flame of colonization in other states" (Shick 1980, 5; see also Thomas 1986).

In 1818, a leading white American evangelist reconnoitered West Africa's coast to locate a suitable settlement site. Then the ship *Elizabeth,* with ACS backing and a U.S. Navy escort, initiated a settlement on Sherbro Island (now in Sierra Leone). It also failed, due to health and internal division, and its initiators sought refuge in the British colony of Sierra Leone. In 1822, however, survivors among these colonists became the core settlers in Cape Mesurado in present-day Monrovia after an American commodore appeared to have negotiated successfully with political leaders there to acquire land (see Shick 1980).

Cape Mesurado had been a major trading center for slaves and other goods. Over the years, many African polities had disputed its control. Europeans had also competed among themselves and with Africans to possess it, but in vain (Curtin [1964] 1973). In this new attempt, as well, the African leaders who appeared to permit settlement were not really in complete control, and the first settlers were soon besieged. They were saved only by the supportive intervention of one interior warlord, known as Sao Boso, often called King Boatswain, a figure who looms large in the travel accounts. Two years later, the nascent colony was named Liberia, remaining under ACS governorship until it became an independent republic on 26 July 1847.

The settler society from which the diarists originate and to which, in part, they are addressing their accounts had several unique characteristics. Two are most telling. First, mortality was extreme. Over the first twenty-three years more than 4,571 immigrated, but despite births only some 2,388 survived (Shick 1980, 27). Numbers rose, but not much. By 1856, some 9,500 had immigrated (Conteh 1988, 105), but the population hardly attained 6,000. New immigrants would have had more chance of surviving a game of Russian roulette than their first year in Liberia, when more than 1 in 5 would perish from disease. Such a proximity to death, which surely raised personal anxiety and piety, also acquired its own dispassionate vocabulary. Liberian survivors, like logs of wood, were "seasoned" in their first year.

Second, Liberia looked bigger on paper and in its grandiose aspirations than in reality. In 1847, when Liberia became an independent republic with all the paraphernalia of state, it had a population of only 3,300, including about 500 indigenous Africans who had become citizens eligible to vote. Only about 2,000 lived in the vicinity of Montserrado, the rest residing in Bassa

(1,000) and Sinoe (300) (Burrowes 1989, 65). Yet Monrovia, hardly even a village with a few tiny dependent hamlets, could boast a president (J. J. Roberts), a Senate, a House of Representatives, and a Supreme Court. With such small populations, people had to play many roles. Seymour, for example, was a member of Liberia's legislature, a justice of the peace, and a captain in the local militia. Every able-bodied male citizen between sixteen and fifty had to join the defense militia. While maps on paper show Liberia as a vast state, until the opening decades of the twentieth century at least, the new settlers led a precarious existence in the few scattered settlements along the coast where they could gain a foothold. Within the lands claimed, Liberians estimated that there was an African population of two million, dwarfing their own numbers (see Blyden to John L. Wilson, 4 August 1860, in Lynch 1978, 40).[4]

Both Liberia's very survival and its grandiosity may be linked to the character and grit of its originators, but arguably more so to the international interests which depended upon the idea of Liberia and of an independent black republic. Within two years of settlement Liberia could boast its own printing press, and within eight its own newspaper, the *Liberia Herald,* which exemplifies the importance of "the idea of Liberia" in the U.S. and in other international communities. Extracts from this newspaper were reprinted in the American journals of the ACS (the *African Repository*) or in its affiliates: monthly journals of the New York, Maryland, and other colonization societies, from which most of the texts we reproduce in this book have been compiled. Reading these papers today, as then, one is easily beguiled into considering the country to be a well-established, orderly, populous, and prosperous state. Especially now, as historians reflect on the past with written evidence, one risks gaining an exaggerated idea of Liberia's import, the same exaggerated idea of many contemporaries. This is presumably why many visitors—such as the famous English traveler Winwood Reade (1873)—felt rather let down upon their arrival, and why several disenchanted immigrants sought to "set the record straight" when they returned home (see, e.g., Nesbit [1855] 1998). What they wrote was rapidly answered by the ACS in the propaganda war (see, e.g., Williams [1857], 1998).

This war was not limited to print. The ACS funded eloquent emigrants such as Seymour to journey around the U.S. to speak in favor of emigration. Publications and tours concerned recruitment for emigration, but they also served to uphold the rhetorical importance of Liberia to internal debates in the U.S. and internationally. While this was important for Liberia, as certain factions in these debates in the U.S. were providing extensive funding, their importance went far beyond. How the six thousand people in Liberia fared and what they were doing was important to debates concerning the more than four million people of color in the U.S., their future relationship with other U.S. populations, and the global responsibilities for U.S. religious organizations. The Liberian intelligentsia responded well to this position, providing numerous works, pamphlets, news reports, and correspondences, and engaged with intellectuals the world over.[5] Many of the immigrants to Liberia were well educated, and even those who were not particularly so often kept up correspondence with those in the U.S. (see, e.g., Miller 1975; Wiley 1980). In the Northern cities of the U.S., private, segregated "African free schools" had been operating since 1785. By 1849, 45 percent of free black children in the largest U.S. cities were attending school. Slaves and freemen from the South had developed a system of individual tutors who taught in informal settings (Burrowes 1989, 65). Liberia itself established many primary schools and a secondary school. Among immigrants, several held degrees: Alexander Crummell, for example, had a degree from Cambridge University; Samuel McGill and Augustus Washington had attended Dartmouth College in New Hampshire.

The importance of the idea of Liberia did not end at the U.S. border. Liberia featured in U.K. debates concerning British engagement with Africa in the middle and later nineteenth century. Liberian writers such as Blyden and Crummell and the traveler Benjamin Anderson had strong connections with the U.K., corresponding with and visiting British scientific, geographic, religious, philanthropic, and political figures. In 1850, the U.K. appointed a consul in Monrovia, Augustus Hanson, who was the first person of color (from Cape Coast, Ghana) to represent the British government anywhere. Blyden journeyed to Beirut to learn Arabic, to Sierra Leone, to the U.S., and to the U.K. as Minister Plenipotentiary.

The rhetorical importance of Liberia had a major impact on the structure of more than its literary life and representation. It extended into other unique features of this "forever nascent" republic, in particular, its churches and schools. Support from the U.S. to Liberian religious and educational institutions was a major aspect of the national economy. In 1875 Blyden estimated that expenditure made by U.S. donors for religious and educational purposes was fifty to seventy dollars per person annually among some ten thousand Liberians. Blyden's figures may need questioning, but they do highlight the structure and extent of enduring philanthropic generosity, which was linked to financial "dependency" on the U.S. (see Blyden to John L. Wilson, 4 August 1860, in Lynch 1978, 35–43).[6]

Blyden mocked the waste of resources. In Clay-Ashland, the settlement where Sims started his journey with a population then of only two hundred people, there were four churches of different denominations, each with its own school. Ministers were paid from four to eight hundred dollars annually, teachers one hundred fifty to two hundred dollars, and the cost to the U.S. fund-raising public was about four thousand dollars. In Edina, Bassa County, where Seymour first settled, there was a Baptist and a Methodist church. Each had a school, and each consumed about fifteen hundred dollars annually on a population—according to Blyden—of only one hundred people. Buchanan also had a population of little more than one hundred, with three churches and three schools. In 1843, there were some twenty-three churches covering only fifteen hundred communicants, of whom five hundred were not immigrants but were indigenous or recaptured slaves.

Many churches and schools focused on the immigrants rather than on the indigenous populations.[7] As Blyden argued, the concentration of churches was counterproductive. It fostered intense doctrinal controversy within small communities, prevented settler unity, and paradoxically led to a laxity of church discipline, as each denomination lived in fear of the defection of its members. Less than half of the settler population were communicants, so presumably evangelization even of immigrants was not that easy. Anderson was not a communicant, as his obituary alludes, "for reasons peculiar to himself he never consented to unite with the visible Church of Christ" ("Brief Sketch" [1910]). Moreover, the very concentration of religious investment may have provided the lax structure in which social creativity among settlers, for example, in embracing polygyny, could thrive in moral and family life.

Preaching and teaching were thus major earners. It is no surprise then that the literate Seymour, who first settled in Edina, soon moved quickly to the nascent community of Bexley (with a population of one hundred thirty-five in 1843), 6 miles farther in the interior, where he was able to establish a school to secure an income. While preachers were relatively well off, teachers were marginally less so and needed to supplement their incomes. Seymour, for example, opened a blacksmith shop and started a small coffee and cotton farm. Without denigrating the obvious religious and educational zeal of the settlers, the preaching and teaching professions were sometimes not far off from being a scam. At the very least there were strong economic motivations for multiplying and inflating the discourses of African evangelism and education-driven civilization, especially when publishing in the U.S.

While the clergy, teachers, and intelligentsia represented the moral drive and utopian visions which characterized Liberia, they were in strong tension with the merchants, both in their own economic endeavors and in their ways of interacting with African populations. The traders gained the upper hand within the republic's political administration, and trading interests were certainly well represented in the laws passed. In 1847, of the twenty-five hundred immigrants to Liberia, about one hundred had become prosperous traders, labeled by some even as "Merchant princes" (Syfert 1975). Middlemen could make good profits, trading interior produce, mainly rice, dye made from the bark of the camwood tree, palm oil for soap, and ivory, for European imports such as alcohol, firearms, gunpowder, cloth, pots, and pans. The more prosperous traders owned small vessels, and fifty-seven or more of them were plying the coast under the Liberian flag in 1847 (Syfert 1975). Others retailed imports and bulked up goods for international export. There were numerous ways to accumulate trading capital. Many immigrated to Liberia with capital—as Sims attempted—or solicited it from their U.S. sponsors. Others used their manufacturing skills—of sails, coastal sailing vessels, houses, and the like—to build up trading capital, while others worked for Liberian traders or as agents for foreign traders and built up trading skills and their own trading capital on the side. Still others married into wealth. Traders could be extremely wealthy and often incorporated claret, Madeira, and fashionable venetian blinds into their lifestyles. Yet wealth was precarious, and political struggle was a commercial necessity. One trader, Hilary Teage, worth fifty-seven thousand dollars in 1843, was an insolvent debtor by 1847 (Syfert 1975, 109–128).

Laws supported traders, who dominated the "political" class. More than one-third of the eighty-one traders whom Syfert (1975) documented held political office. They used their influence to limit the competition that threatened their profits. They abolished duty free importing by missionaries, whose trade had threatened to undercut them, and they were able to restrict the operation of foreign companies, permitting foreign firms to trade only through Liberian intermediaries (Commissioning Agents). Traders often inflated prices and gained extra profit when selling to ACS agents, who purchased locally the goods they gave to new immigrants—which included provisions for six months. In their interior dealings, traders were able to call on state military action and economic boycotts to enforce commercial arrangements, especially when refusing to pay "transit" duties to certain interior Chiefs. Traders could, for example, enforce price cartels—legally fixing prices paid to interior peoples for rice and camwood (Syfert 1975). Among interior peoples, Liberian traders soon acquired a bad reputation for shady trading practices. Indeed the *Observer* (Monrovia) in 1881 ascribed the indigenous depopulation in the immediate vicinity of the settlements to the economic problems that these traders posed to indigenous peoples ("Trade in Montserrado County" 1881).

Traders and the state also fought a continual struggle to prevent what they described as smuggling by foreign traders. British, French, and other traders escaped Liberian restrictions and duties by trading on the coast away from Liberian settlements. Long-running disputes arose between Liberia and the British government over trading rights (see Liberty [1977] 1999). Many Liberian politicians found it expedient to attribute the persistent financial crisis of the Liberian state to this issue (Akpan 1975). Monrovia commanded major trade routes sourcing African commodities, but much trade switched to other ports, for example Cape Mount and the Gallinas to the north, and to coves near Trade Town to the south. Several of these even continued as slave ports. Liberia could not patrol its shores adequately to prevent illegal trade, and Liberians became preoccupied with creating new settlements on the coast to extend their trade control. The last of the export slave trade ceased from Liberia's shores in the early 1860s when the Liberian government and foreign navies, particularly the British navy, finally succeeded in blocking it. Subsequently, male slaves taken in interior warfare were often executed, as they could not be sold, whereas captured women and children could more easily be put to work on farms (Holsoe 1977, 295–297; Bledsoe 1980, 16–19). In 1868, Anderson observed the execution of captured male slaves.

The country was insecure against invasion by sea and depended upon the security that ships of the U.S. Navy provided, which left the country badly exposed when the U.S. Navy was withdrawn during the American Civil War. This left the shores especially vulnerable to pirates and piratical slavers, who attacked Liberian settlements on several occasions. Furthermore, the extent of Liberian trade along the coast had begun to decline from the early 1850s as European steamships began to make regular runs along the West African coast and to charge lower prices than their Liberian competitors (Akpan 1975, 13; Syfert 1977a, b).

Social Differentiation

Because of Liberia's international connections and its grandiose institutions, it can be shocking to realize that several of the African villages which Seymour, Sims, and Anderson describe as they passed through the interior had populations that dwarfed the entire immigrant population of the Liberian republic. But however small their state, however unified Liberians became in their vulnerability to their indigenous African neighbors, and however indignant they were regarding their treatment in international relations, Liberians experienced bitter internal division and vitriolic debate. Just as the fledgling republic meant so much for so many outside the country, its internal divisions became fuelled by the incompatible hopes, dreams, and doctrines of those outside. Although Liberia defined itself as the "lone star," it was far from alone: it was the focal star in a constellation of external organizations and their newsprints.

Tensions between different religious doctrines in the U.S. were recapitulated in almost every tiny Liberian settlement, with fundamentals, such as correct modes of baptism, being hotly disputed in each. If each tiny church and school was to be the seed of African evangelism, each large church was compelled to sow its distinctive and true seed early on (Shick 1980, 24).

Racial distinctions also mattered. For one thing, there was the distinction between the governing ACS and others—white Americans occupied the governorship until 1841, despite the probable existence of suitable black Americans for the post (Beyan 1989). On several occasions, white governors had to deal with dissent that threatened outright revolt. Even following independence, many aspects of Liberian society were under considerable white authority. Senior missionaries and bishops were white, and Liberian churches depended upon their mother churches in the U.S. because they did not have either the financial base or the numbers required by church law to assert autonomy and elect a bishop. The white Episcopalian missionaries (Dr. Savage, Rev. L. B. Minor, and John Payne), many of whom had been slaveholders themselves, could not become citizens of the black republic. They stayed in the Episcopal mission established in Cape Palmas, outside the republic's borders, until this was annexed in 1857 (Scott 1858, 25 ff.). At several moments, leading Liberian clergy such as Crummell sought autonomy from the "mother church" in the U.S., leading to bitter and enduring rifts (Ejofodomi 1974, 161–186; Dunn 1992).

Racial difference, however, goes far beyond black and white. Indeed, considering race as a black and white issue was common for white racists, blinded by their own singular prejudice to the prejudices, differences, and experiences of their "other." In America, as Blyden noted, only a few white people could understand the bitterness that existed between colored and black people (Lynch 1978). And the distinctions between blacks and "mulattoes"—to reproduce with unease the terminology in Liberia at the time—which were very strong in the U.S., became even stronger in Liberia.

Stereotypically, mulatto slaves often had greater opportunities in the U.S., gaining education and training and becoming favored house servants. Many were freed by their parent-owners and constituted a large proportion of free "blacks." White masters regarded mulattoes as superior in intelligence to "full-blooded" blacks, and their lives were different than those of most black field hands. Within Liberia, as in the U.S., mulattoes tended to be better off, better educated, and better acquainted with the trappings and doings of "civilized" (white) society. According to elements of black opinion, the superiority and social arrogance which mulattoes displayed in the U.S. immigrated with them. William Kellogg, speaking of mulattoes in 1852, played into such stereotyping. As a mulatto himself, he argued that it would be better to remain in "the hands of my superiors than [fall] into the hands of my inferiors" (cited in Shick 1980, 15). He would only consider immigration to a mulatto colony separate from a black one. Yet despite perhaps being better treated in certain respects, mulattoes, as offspring of illegal and illegitimate "mixed unions," were abhorred by many elements in white (and black) society, which victimized them for their complexion and for the "immoral" acts that their very existence was seen to represent.

Racial debates in Liberia were linked to "scientific" debates concerning racism raging in the U.S. and Europe, which also related race to health and intelligence. And in Liberia, the high mortality rate fueled this racist discourse. Speculation was rife not only about what caused the fevers, but also about why some survived and some did not. Observations of differential resistance, however unsystematic, fed easily into the scientific racism of the age.[8] Blyden argued viciously that mulattoes had higher death rates because of their "unhealthy mix of Caucasian and Indian blood, incapable of withstanding the climate." Moreover, inferences concerning bodily health spilled over into those concerning social health: "The mulatto, conceived as he was as a general thing in violation of all moral and social laws, has brought to the Negro race nothing but physical degeneracy and mental and moral obliquity" (Blyden to Coppinger, 19 October 1874, in Lynch 1978, 176). By the 1860s, Blyden was arguing that mulattoes should not immigrate to Liberia: "I have spent twenty years of my life in teaching mongrels who do not live in this climate, or if they live become obstructive. . . . When we complain and protest against their doings, they cry out 'persecution on account of colour'" (Blyden to John C. Lowrie, 9 May 1876, in Lynch 1978, 205). That his wife was mulatto did not make for a happy marriage.

Racial differences and hatreds soon became entrenched within Liberian politics. The political leadership of early immigrants was primarily mulatto. Indeed, early immigrants were largely mulatto, and as first-comers, they came to dominate trade, wealth, and politics. As the colony grew, political debates increasingly divided along color lines. The political division between the True Liberian (Republican) Party and the Old Whigs became racialized, with the former dominated by mulattoes and the latter by blacks. Blacks tended to argue for integration, or assimilation, with other Africans, whereas mulattoes, they argued, frustrated this. Blacks believed that mulattoes in the Republican Party elite opposed the development of schools up-country, resisted the extension of national boundaries, restricted West Indian immigration, limited the access of blacks to college and government, and provided very little support for interior exploration.

It is certainly the case that many light-skinned mulattoes continued to secure appointments to high office. While they may not have been a clique based solely on color, but rather a close knit, political aristocracy, many of those marginalized from power and from mulatto society interpreted this political and financial monopoly as a color issue (Shick 1980; Sawyer 1992).

The color division came to be expressed in the nascent state's geography and economy. The capital, Monrovia, with its grip on trade, was mulatto dominated. Other settlements, such as those that were gradually established a little farther up the Saint Paul River, became dominated by blacks and were oriented toward farming. These settlements attracted many black settlers. Mulatto immigrants, especially, avoided farming. They had little experience with tropical agriculture and found farming socially demeaning, associated as it was with slavery. Immigrants who did farm generally reproduced a Southern U.S. plantation, writ small, using laborers and bonded laborers to work on sugarcane and coffee plantations. As they became more numerous, such black farmers became politically more assertive. This was especially so when farming experienced a boom in the 1850s to 1870s due to good prices for food and plantation products.

By 1870, color had become a key issue in politics. The 1870 election brought President E. J. Roye to power, which was the first time that the "mulatto aristocracy" had been voted out of office.[9] Enmity soon spilled over into violence. Following his election, Roye had to raise a loan to keep the country solvent, and he negotiated this with Britain. Simultaneously, he introduced legislation to extend term limits for presidents. The loan was corrupt, his political opponents argued, and so was the legislation, which Roye designed to keep himself in power. The mulatto-dominated capital took up arms. Before Roye could muster the political and militia support from his power base in the interior Liberian settlements he was deposed and jailed. Blyden claimed that "a mulatto" shot Roye, while others stated that Roye drowned after he escaped from jail. Meanwhile W. S. Anderson, whose 1870 journey is reviewed in chapter 2, had been one of the state Commissioners who visited the U.K. to negotiate the unpopular loan (Blyden to William Coppinger, 19 October 1874, in Lynch 1978, 177; Lynch 1967, 49–53; Sawyer 1992, 165–168). Several prominent blacks, such as Blyden, were lucky to escape with their lives from mob violence, and Blyden fled the country to Sierra Leone.

Such bitter racial division was elaborated in other forms of association. Mulattoes, for example, appear to have been more fully engaged in Masonic orders (see Blyden to John L. Wilson, 4 August 1860, in Lynch 1978, 38–39)—although Roye was also a member of the Masons. As Blyden put it, "Every Mulatto in Liberia, from Cape Mount to Cape Palmas is a Mason—as soon as a new one arrives in the country, he is initiated" (Blyden to William Coppinger, 21 October 1875, in Lynch 1978, 196.) The Independent Order of the Sons of Ham was founded in 1849, and the Masonic Grand Lodge of Liberia in 1851. By the end of the century, eight Masonic orders existed (Shick 1980, 56). Social cleavages also emerged between settlers from different regions in the U.S. and between these settlers and those from the West Indies. People tended to settle in urban quarters or in towns that were specific to their origins. This settlement pattern was due to the sponsorship of particular state colonization societies, which were granted particular settlements in Liberia (see, e.g., Johnston [1906] 1969, 147; Reeve [1923] 1969, 40; Huberich 1947, 397, 1402–1408; Fraenkel 1964, 71, 83–88; Breitborde 1979, 112–115; Tonkin 1981, 312).

Alexander Crummell summed up the deep enmity: "Never have I in all my life seen such bitterness, hate and malice displayed as has been exhibited by the two factions of the state" (cited in Ejofodomi 1974, 113). These were hard words, indeed, from someone so victimized by discrimination in the U.S. Crummell found it "the saddest of all things to come here to Africa, and find one's black face a disgrace both in his ecclesiastical and social relations, with half caste people" (cited in Ejofodomi 1974, 113). The racial tensions in the colony probably influenced the strong sense of skin-color awareness exhibited in the travel journals. The earlier travelers whose diaries we reproduce, Sims and Seymour, appear to have been mulatto, whereas Benjamin Anderson was black (Blyden to William Coppinger, 19 October 1874, in Lynch 1978, 177; Blyden to John C. Lowrie, 9 May 1876, in Lynch 1978, 205).

A further arena of social distinction arose between the immigrants from the U.S., usually second to fifth generation Americans, and slaves who had only recently been captured and who were liberated into Liberia by American warships which were intercepting illegal slave cargos. The policy of locating liberated slaves in Africa, rather than the U.S., underlay U.S. government financing of the Liberia project, as we have seen. Their numbers remained rather small—only about 6 percent of immigration in the early years until 1846. In that year, however, 756 so-called recaptives disembarked from one captured slaver. As color politics became intense in the U.S. between August and October 1860, the U.S. exported a further 5,500 captives, many having been temporarily lodged in Florida. Recaptured Africans came to be called "Congos" rather pejoratively, alluding to the origin of a minority among them (Liebenow 1987, 49; Sawyer 1992, 186–188).

Before the huge influx, recaptured slaves were incorporated into the colony largely as "apprentices." American settlers generally had a number of Africans attached to their families, acting as servants who performed drudgery. The streets of Monrovia were "full of them," wearing cloth, like togas, and ornaments of teeth, rings, horns, and small bags. Known as apprentices, they were often African children who had been sent by their families to learn the fashions and language of the "white man." The state regulated this institution, sensitive to the accusation that apprenticeship was actually slavery. Youth under eighteen were only allowed to live with settler families if they were bound for a specified term of years by an "apprentice" contract which spelled out mutual responsibilities and which could be enforced through the courts. Nevertheless, the institution had some echoes of American slavery. Apprentices, for example, could not keep their own names and were given Christian ones (Nesbit [1855] 1998; Williams [1857] 1998; Fraenkel 1964; Akpan 1973; Shick 1980; Tonkin 1981).

The settlement's early savior, King Boatswain, or Sao Boso, had sent his child and eventual heir, Momolu Sao, to be educated as an apprentice in Monrovia. When the latter inherited the chiefdom, he permitted a Liberian school to be built in his capital, Totokwele. When Seymour made his first journey to Pessay in 1855, he returned to Bexley with twenty children, probably also sent by intervening Bassa towns whose leaders had expressed a willingness to send some of their children to school when Seymour was on the way. When W. S. Anderson visited Kpayekwele in 1870, he returned with one of the chief's children to be educated. Clearly, placing some children in Monrovia to become apprentices and to gain a settler education soon became a strategic option for interior peoples—or at least, for certain families.

The apprenticeship system remained rather small until it began to absorb recaptured Africans, who—on arrival—were placed among settler farmers and householders as apprentices. With the huge influx of recaptives in the 1860s, the capacity of Americans to accommodate them was far exceeded, and recaptives were instead directed to settle for themselves in interior (black) settlements in the colony which were dedicated to farming. Plantation owners employed many in interior plantations and industries, such as sugar refining. In this way the recaptives became important to the expansion of the frontier. When Benjamin Anderson journeyed in 1868–69, he employed several as porters.

Given all these bitter divisions, it is inappropriate to speak of Liberia's "Americo-Liberians" as a single category, and more improper still to consider Americo-Liberians as comprising a single "ruling elite." True, in these decades, many shared the common experience as immigrants, and they had much else in common. Yet they were not acting as a homogeneous group either in their own settlements or in their perspectives and relations with interior people.

Liberian Images of the Interior

Liberians not only distinguished among themselves, but also among the Africans with whom they interacted. In particular, Liberians contrasted their problematic engagement with immediately neighboring populations—often imaged as hostile, disorganized, heathen, crude, and naked—with the images of civility, piety, and literacy of peoples in the far interior. Information about the interior was derived from several earlier travel accounts by white explorers. Major Alexander Laing had journeyed to Falaba in what is now Sierra Leone in 1822. Several journeys had been made to Timbu (Timbo), the Fula capital of an Islamic state in the Futa Djallon of Guinea, including one by Blyden.[10] Timbu had formed an Islamic state during the early to mid-eighteenth century. Though this region erupted into civil war later that century, Timbu continued to be an important religious center and maintained its links with key Muslim towns such as Kankan (see Kaba 1973; Last 1987, 10–12; Person 1987, 273–279; Sanneh 1989, 100–102).

In 1860, a further French expedition was sent to Timbu (Lambert 1860). Mungo Park and Rene Caillié made journeys toward and to Timbuktu from 1795 to 1797 and in 1828, respectively. Information concerning the interior could also be gleaned from the many less-literate travelers reputed to have made inland journeys. The trader Harrison told stories of his visits inland from Cape Mount in about 1795 to the Governor of Sierra Leone, Thomas Ludlum, and presumably told others much more. The short, secondhand account that Ludlum wrote was published in the *Sierra Leone Gazette* (April 1808, see Hair 1962).

Many Liberians also appear to have made smaller visits to the interior.

More than a dozen trips were made some 50 miles inland to Bopolu.[11] Journeys were also made to other destinations, although few are well documented. Within five years of the first settlement, a Liberian "had travelled 140 miles into the interior," where he "discovered a country inhabited by a numerous people, far advanced" (Wilkeson 1839, 28–29). Nothing more is known of this account. In 1831, Governor Joseph Mechlin journeyed to the source of the Junk River, "some 40–50 miles" inland (Mechlin 1831). In 1843, the then-Governor—later president—J. J. Roberts journeyed about "80 miles" inland up the east bank of the Saint Paul. He made an overland circuit back, accompanied by Gabriel Moore, to visit Gola chiefs and sign treaties. The distances given for Mechlin's and Roberts's trips are too far (Roberts 1845; see "Interior Roads" 1873, 334).[12] Anderson, during his 1874 journey, noted that the chief of Sanoyea had "a paper made by our people in 1854" which D. J. Beams, who had presumably gone there, had signed. This "paper" was presumably a treaty that the chief signed with the Liberian government.[13]

The journeys by Roberts, Beams, and others formed part of Liberia's attempts to sign treaties with leaders from the interior to promote peace and trade (Foote 1854, 177–179). Yet Liberians also made trading trips into their interior. One journeyed from Marshall in April and May 1851 ("Tour into the Interior" 1852). When Sims entered Barlain territory, some 90 miles inland, he noted casually that "Several Liberians who visited this country in 1856 told me an amusing story of a rooster" (chap. 3, 103). Missionaries were a third category of traveler. White missionaries made several journeys inland. In 1850–51, an unnamed missionary journeyed to the inland villages of "Queahs and Condoes" ("The Country Adjacent to Liberia" 1851). Others traveled inland from Cape Palmas, including the white missionaries J. Leighton Wilson in 1836 (Wilson 1836), Savage in 1837 (1839), L. B. Minor in 1841 (Hening [1850] 1853, 158–166), and C. C. Hoffman in 1861 (1862). In 1856, Rev. George Thompson of Mendi Mission, Sierra Leone, explored "100 miles up the St. Pauls" (1856). African-American immigrants such as Crummell also conducted missionary tours from Cape Palmas.[14] Other journeys apart from Seymour's were also made inland from Bassa, including that by Thomas E. Dillon to Gibi (1871).

In short, Liberians and others had made repeated journeys to the regions inland from their settlements along the coast. As the *New-York Colonization Journal* noted in 1860, "There is quite a tendency among intelligent members of the Republic of Liberia to visit the interior to ascertain the resources of the country" ("Exploration of Africa" 1860). All these journeys were, however, overshadowed by the lure of Musadu and the much more ambitious journeys made toward there, which we document here. These took on an air of "exploration" and were published in installments alongside the works of David Livingstone and others in the American colonization newspapers.

The interior was also known for the traders who reached the colony, bringing ivory, cloth, camwood, gold, and ironwork. Certain Liberians took much time to inquire about the interior. The most notable was Blyden, who journeyed to Beirut, Lebanon, to learn Arabic in 1866 and on his return sought out traders with whom to speak.

Despite these journeys and accounts, there was certainly ample opportunity for speculation, especially concerning the far interior, as d'Azevedo has argued (1994, 1995). Liberian interpretations of early accounts and of Africans arriving from the interior were framed by several powerful ideas about the interior and its people, which were rooted in rumor, mythology, and the science of the times. First, the idea that there was an intelligent, civilized, industrious, and mercantile people, the "Mandingo," who inhabited the interior and who contrasted with "local Africans," was scorched into the collective memory at the colony's foundation. In the battles associated with the original settlement, Liberians were on the brink of defeat when the interior warlord King Boatswain came almost miraculously to their assistance. Liberians thought King Boatswain to be a "Mandingo," or a Manding warlord, a representative of Mandingo power in the far interior. The idea that the Mandingo nation was a more-advanced civilization than other interior civilizations was also held by a second Liberian savior, Major Laing. His chance arrival by boat on 30 November 1822 helped broker a final truce between Liberians and their hostile neighbors. He had just returned from a long journey inland from Sierra Leone (Laing 1825; Wilkeson 1839). His effusive accounts of the interior, coupled with Boatswain's gallant intervention, sharply contrasted with Liberians' experience of their near neighbors.

Positive images of the interior and its inhabitants were not, however, dependent only on past travels and these chance events, but had a much longer history within which these events were understood. Many Liberians themselves (and African Americans in the U.S.) were generally proud to claim to be of "Mandingo" origin (d'Azevedo 1995, 77). At the time, it was common to link cultural superiority with racial character, so it was not surprising that many civilized African Americans, with a civilizing mission, located their superiority in their ancestry as well as in their Christianity. Mandingo ancestry connoted superiority. Scientific racism, exemplified in the work of the leading phrenologist George Combe, would have it that "Negro people of the Western Sudan were not really Negroes at all." They were physically like other "Negro" people, but "'their state of comparative civilization'" showed they had reached heights impossible for the "'inferior' Negro race" (Combe [1819] 1845, in Curtin [1964] 1973, 370).

Some traced this superiority, associated by observers with slightly lighter skin, to mixture with "Caucasian" blood. In 1850, for example, the American Thomas Bowen noted that

> The Mandingoes, whose country lies three or four hundred miles to the northeast of Monrovia, are one of the finest tribes in Africa—tall, erect, muscular and intelligent. . . . Like other tribes in the interior, the Mandingoes are sufficiently mixed with Caucasion blood to give them a semi-European cast of countenance, which is sometimes accompanied with a yellow or mulatto skin. (Bowen [1857] 1968, 41)

Bowen appears to have read Macbriar's *Sketches of a Missionary's Travels* (Macbriar 1839), which made the same point.

Others accounted for the superiority in terms of separation from, not integration with, Caucasians. Several missionaries and scientists drew on romantic traditions concerning a spiritual (and racial) purity in the West African interior. Seymour spoke merely of the "pollution of coastal tribes," while Blyden argued that

> Interior people have the advantage over us in never having been under foreign masters, in never having imbibed a sense of inferiority or a feeling of self-depreciation. They had never had to look up to white men for anything, so as to form in their minds comparisons between themselves and others disparaging to themselves. They are entirely free from the mental and moral trammels which the touch of the Caucasian has imposed upon us. (Blyden 1871c, 321–322)

Blyden found that the interior peoples were "more independent than our independent republic." The Islamic Mandingo societies beckoned as a prototypal African civilization, "to be enjoined in common mission of pagan redemption and African progress."[15]

D'Azevedo suggests that this romantic image of the interior was linked to the ancient legend of Prestor John. Prestor John, who was said to be a medieval Christian king who would defeat Muslims and bring help to the Holy Land, became identified with a real king of Ethiopia (d'Azevedo 1994, 200; see also Severin 1973, chap. 2). Yet in Sierra Leone and Liberia at least, it is possible to trace the influence of a more specific—if rather bizarre—evocation of such romance linked to the preaching and speculation of the Swedish "prophet" or "heretic" Emanuel Swedenborg in the 1760s. In a revelation he claimed to have heard that God had established not just one true Church of Christ but a series of equally "true Churches," located wherever people had the most perfect knowledge of God. The decline, fall, and last judgment of one true Church, his revelation went on, was to be matched by the foundation of another in a previously heathen but "pure" nation. In the due course of time the Adamical Church had thus ceded to the Noahtical Church; the Noahtical to the Israelite, and the Israelite to the Christian. Important to West Africa, Swedenborg noted that following the last judgment of the European Church in 1757, a new church was being founded; this was to be in the celestial reaches of the West African interior where people lived a more spiritual life: "The Whites had cultivated only their understanding, but the black have cultivated their will and affections" (cited in Curtain [1964] 1973, 27). Europe had become corrupted, and the Church of the New Jerusalem was even then being established in the African interior—taught by angels, although the doctrine had not yet reached the coast (Lindroth 1955; Curtin [1964] 1973).

Swedenborg's views became widespread among Sweden's academics, especially its natural scientists. They founded a Swedish Swedenborgian colonization society, with the royal blessing, and several aimed to establish a Swedenborgian utopia in West Africa. A leading light, Carl Berns Wadstrom, linked up with leaders of the British antislavery movement, Thomas Clarkson and Grandville Sharp. And when ships left to found the Sierra Leone utopia, eleven Swedenborgians—"gentlemen of rank, great learning and abilities, several of them members of universities, and philosophers"—were due to sail with them (Lindroth 1955, 196). They missed the boat (Curtin [1964] 1973, 103). Wadstrom and others nevertheless published a prospectus for a new Swedenborgian colony to be located where Monrovia is today, among Africans whom they believed to be living in a simple, uncorrupted state of nature (Curtin 1968). Their republic was to be paternalist, with Africans beginning in servitude but gradually advancing to full citizenship.

The Swedenborgian passion for an African expedition continued. Soon cult follower and botanist Adam Afzelius, together with alchemist Nordenskiöld, did get to Sierra Leone. The latter made an inland trip but died. It is reported that Afzelius met travelers who "were beautiful and comely (very different from the Negroes of the coast), their voices were sweet and sonorous, their gestures and manners, mild and engaging, and that they had frequent and open communication with the spiritual world and its inhabitants" (Servanté [1805] 1857, 313).

The Swedenborgian connection continued in West Africa. The Rev. C. C. Hoffman, leader of the Domestic and Foreign Mission Society of the Episcopal Church of the U.S. in Liberia and himself a traveler into the interior (1862), was reputed to be a brother-in-law of the leading Swedenborgian, Dr. J. J. G. Wilkinson (Blyden to William Coppinger, 28 February 1891, in Lynch 1978, 420). In the 1890s, Wilkinson was to dedicate his book to Liberia's leading intellectual, Blyden (1892; see also Lynch 1967, 82).

Such positive images of the Mandingo interior people help us understand why both Seymour in 1858 and Benjamin Anderson a decade later wanted to get to Musadu. As Anderson's book title proclaims, Liberians considered Musadu the capital of the western Mandingoes. At the time, the Mandingo nation or confederation was thought to be huge. Liberians, including scholars such as Blyden, believed that Arabic was the language of scholars for thousands of Manding and Fulbe Muslim teachers (see, e.g., Blyden 1871c, 331; Dennis 1873, 348–349). Coastal traders from Gambia to the Niger Delta had encountered those who spoke the Mandingo language.

Bopolu, the home of King Boatswain, became imaged as a gateway to "great Mandingo empires" (d'Azevedo 1994, 221). But although the settler community heralded the Mandingo of Bopolu during the first half of the century, attempts in Bopolu to block settler penetration beyond its realm, as d'Azevedo argues, made Musadu and the more-interior Manding seem more attractive to Anderson (d'Azevedo 1994, 221).

President Benson's advice to Seymour indicates the importance attributed to Musadu: he instructed Seymour to

> attempt to reach no further . . . than the capital of Mandingo Country, Moosá-doo, which means Moses' town. This is described by Mandingoes who have visited us, as being a very large and populous town; and as its inhabitants are great itinerants, as well as intelligent, having a literature of their own, I have no doubt but that accurate information can be obtained there for the country lying beyond, for several hundred miles, even to and beyond the great Niger, which would be of much service to us in preparing him [Seymour] for the next exploring tour, to commence earlier in the dries; when I do not entertain a doubt that he will reach at least a branch of the great Niger. (1858b, 130)

The eventual arrival of Anderson in Musadu did little to dispel these perspectives; rather, it reinforced that "Musardu is two thousand two hundred and fifty-seven feet above the level of the sea, with a healthy climate, and cool and limpid streams. Musardu is the capital of the Western Mandingoes, the most famous, most cultured, and most enterprising tribe in Western Africa" ("Liberian Methodist Mission" 1873, 193).

The interior was important for Liberia in many ways. First, development on the coast depended on trade relations with the far interior. Second, as mass immigration from the U.S. was anticipated, the far interior would be important for establishing settlements. Third, many Liberians aspired to assimilation between immigrants and Africans into "one people," a "manly, noble and complete African nationality" (Crummell [1862] 1969, 81). But while assimilation of Africans into Liberia was a goal, at least of black immigrant factions, this did not imply respect. Assimilation involved the regulation, education, and labor discipline associated with civilization. Citizens needed to be Christian. Such Christian paternalism imaged African culture as backward, as a world "without history," geographically cut off from the motor of civilization. Society was to be reconstructed, with agriculture, education, and medicine integral to evangelism. There was segregation in several churches (Ejofodomi 1974, 121, 131). Christianity was integral to the modernizing project, to "bring light to dark places." In one instance, Seymour actually asked for a battery to be sent from the U.S. so that he could assist his missionary activity by using technological superiority (1857a, 197–198). For Africans to become citizens, they had to prove that for three years they had abandoned all the forms, customs, and superstitions of "heathenism" and conformed to the forms, customs, and habits of "civilized" life, something acquired through the apprentice system (cited in Ejofodomi 1974, 122).

Some have argued that the paternalism of the ACS and the society that spawned it toward black Americans was transposed to become the paternalism of the new colony over interior peoples. Certainly, civilization in Liberia was defined much as leading Southerners defined it, including its trappings in dress, worship, and architecture (Beyan 1989, 144). Yet considering these aspects of life merely in terms of "settler domination" may be to overlook the interplay of African and European cultures, both in the U.S., where African cultural influences extended, and in Liberia, with the interplay of disparate African influences as recaptives and interior African populations interacted with settler ways. This interplay would be important for understanding elements of both syncretism, for example, in emergent practices of settler polygyny, or (arguably) in the appeal of the secret fraternities of the Masonic lodges, and distinction, for example, in the issue of dress.

Liberians hotly debated the issue of polygyny. Some, like Blyden, were reputedly pro-polygyny, considering it a blessing to prevent depopulation. In general, informal unions with "Congo" or interior women (once bridewealth was paid) were socially countenanced, and children, legitimate. Some, like Crummell, were opposed to polygyny, maintaining a more "American" stance, arguing that it demeaned women and hence society (Crummell 1871, 15).

The issue of distinction and dress also warrants exploring in more detail. Many of the social lines among Liberians were hard to interpret for many Africans. Interior people referred to the settlers as "white men" (see Curtin 1972, 232–233). This is not surprising. During the long course of the slave trade, the coast had had a history of "white" settlers, many of whom had settled for long periods in African villages and had established families. The children of mixed marriages brought up in the ways of their fathers were naturally considered white in many respects (just as in Europe and North America, children of mixed union are still often considered black). Yet African skin colors themselves spanned a range which overlapped with many of these "white" people. It is only reasonable that it was clothes, writing, and religion, not skin color per se, that signified African distinctions between black and white.

Inasmuch as people linked color to personal identity, identity therefore hinged on writing, language, clothes, and religion, which gave these elements added significance. If being "civilized" was somehow synonymous with being "white," it was something that one could "become" or, presumably, could lose. Most visitors to Liberia remarked on the extreme care that Liberians took in dressing, on their tendency to "overdress," almost in exaggerated, pompous distinction to African life. Yet in this act of distinction from Africans, they simultaneously created themselves as "white" in local eyes. Dress codes thus became integral to racial and religious identity in a curious type of Christian materialism. Blyden wrote:

> There are now scattered through these forests, intelligent young men trained in the schools who, ashamed to come among the Americans in native dress, and thinking it useless to instruct their own people unless they can secure them American dress, hide themselves in the woods in utter uselessness. A Christian, to their mind, is a man with a beaver hat, Wellington boots, broadcloth coat and pants, or a woman with a crinoline, a "love of a bonnet," a long muslin or calico dress; and they consider it useless to offer their people Christianity unless they can also have these things. (Blyden to N. H. Hare, 14 September 1872, in Lynch 1978, 115)

These forms of distinction interlocked with intra-African racial discourse. It appears that the strong distinction of interior Mandingo peoples from coastal Africans was (even then) also common to African discourse and was not just an external imposition. This was captured in the rather telling remark that a villager made to Sims in Passilla, that "everybody who 'Sarvy book,' except the Mandingoes, are 'white,'" and that "the Mandingoes would be white too if they would only dress like white people" (in chap. 3, 95; see also Tonkin 1981, 318–319). Sims, like other African Americans who journeyed to Africa, found that the local people considered him "a stranger in the village," even though he had the same skin color (in chap. 3; see also Griffin and Fish 1998, xiii).

For many of those living in it, the survival of the fledgling community, once "planted," was itself a miracle. And in truth, the high death rates, the internal division, and the marginality in West African coastal realpolitik would normally have been insurmountable. Yet the external forces that "needed" Liberia (who represent one-half of every major debate of this issue in the period) could not let Liberia fail. Liberia in this early period was a state which was independent in administration from the ACS in the U.S. from 1847 on, but was continuously dependent on immigration and finance. The dream and the reality were continuously restated in the colonization journals, riding roughshod over the "unforeseen" problems. Ethical dilemmas—especially in sending people to a region of such high mortality—were off-loaded onto "God's will," a will experienced bravely by the immigrants and ACS envoys alike.

The travel accounts we publish here should be read as speaking to the debates of their time. They most certainly present the Liberian interior in optimistic tones, "a heart of lightness." Yet it would be an act of extreme ignorance to dismiss these accounts as merely propaganda for immigration, reflecting as they do, passionately and critically, the other key debates of their times that we have tried to review here, as well as the experiences of travel.

2

Journeys in the Interior

Many authors have suggested that the Liberian settlers hardly traveled inland. Considered in this light, the accounts in this book would appear as exceptions in a country otherwise disinterested in—or incapable of—forging strong and enduring links with its hinterland. Yet the background to each of the major journeys, considered in the light of the shorter exploration, trade, and missionary travels noted in the last chapter, makes it clear that these interior travels formed part of a more active, if often frustrated, engagement between the nascent colony of Liberia and its hinterland.

Both interior African politics and American and European interests were important dimensions to this faltering engagement. African politics was key to travel in the interior. Before the death in 1836 of King Boatswain, the "interior Chief" who had supported the colony at its foundation, Liberians were able to make several journeys to his capital at Bopolu. Conditions for travel deteriorated during the succession disputes following his death until the eventual ascendancy of his heir, Momolu Sao, whose Condo confederation also came to exert a grip over interior politics from the 1850s until the late 1860s. Liberians started to reestablish contacts with the interior peoples a few years after Thomas Bowen visited Bopolu in 1850, and Liberians apparently also started to become more informed about Musadu from the mid-1850s. Conditions were improving for travel because certain political alliances had been formed. As is documented in chapter 7, these alliances (and the interests of the travelers' guides) heavily influenced the routes which the travelers took. Inversely, the routes the travelers took and the links between the journeys and Liberian state policy also had some influence on the interior political balance.

The journeys were also strongly influenced by external interests: by the ACS and its private donors, who partly funded the journeys, and by the U.S. government, which—in the guise of the U.S. Minister Resident—was clearly party to the formation of much Liberian national policy. This is well evidenced in the events surrounding Anderson's proposed third trip to Musadu and beyond in the late 1870s. External involvement was not limited to the United States. Several British and French commercial and imperial interests had their eyes on the resources of the interior and also sought to finance interior exploration.

George L. Seymour, 1855–58

Seymour was born in Hartford, Connecticut, on 16 August 1819. As a youth, he learned how to farm, build, smith, read, and write (Seymour 1842, 125). In 1845 he was described as "a free colored man, brought up and educated in Hartford," suggesting that he was freeborn ("A Colored Colonists Views" 1845, 342). His father appears also to have been named George.[1]

Seymour was originally "bitterly prejudiced against going to Africa, and felt very indignant to the white man, whoever he might be, that would suggest such a thing to him." He considered that the "scheme of colonization" was a "nefarious plan to expatriate the free people of color from amongst us, and turn them out to Africa to DIE!" (cited in "A Colored Colonists Views" 1845, 342). The colonization plan was a "Compromise with slavery" (Seymour 1851, 267). However, he "met with a colored man who had been some years in the colony of Liberia . . . which induced him to determine to go to Africa and try the experiment for himself. But still such were his misgivings that he would not consent to go till he obtained a promise from the benevolent gentleman . . . who urged him to this course, that if he were disappointed or dissatisfied when he had been in Africa a while, that gentleman would furnish him the means of returning" ("A Colored Colonist's Views" 1845, 342). This gentleman was Anston G. Phelps, President of the New York Colonization Society. Phelps's investment paid off. Seymour became enamored with Liberia. He was soon encouraging others to move there and wrote many letters supporting the colonization scheme. Dozens of people from Hartford migrated to Liberia. In a letter dated 21 March 1851, Seymour wrote sentiments that he repeated later in life: colonization "affords protection [from slave dealers] to some 100,000 natives"; and his move to Liberia was part of the "designs of Providence in the return of the exiled sons and daughters of Africa" (1851, 267).

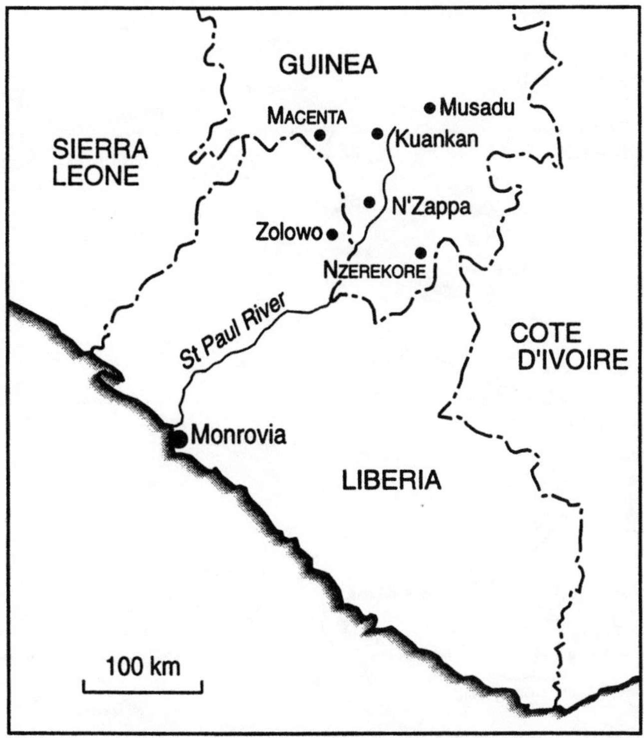

Map 1. The journeys in regional context.

Seymour went to Liberia at the end of 1841 and wrote, on 21 December, about his fifty-two-day voyage during which he came down with a fever. He exclaimed that the "colored man" was on "one equal footing here" (Seymour 1842, 125). He later encouraged his sisters to follow him (Seymour 1845, 343). After landing at Monrovia he moved to Edina, which was on the coast near Buchannan. In 1842, he then moved 6 miles (10 kilometers) inland to Bexley, where he lived for thirteen years. There he established a school, opened a blacksmith shop, and started a small farm where he raised coffee and cotton (Seymour 1843, 233; 1845, 343; Bennedict 1843, 233–234; "Liberia Interior Exploration" 1859). During his first four years in Liberia, he became a member of Liberia's legislature, "a Preacher of the Gospel, a Justice of the Peace; and a captain in the local militia." He farmed, and sought to purchase a "steam saw mill" for felling timber, and hoped to grind sugarcane to make sugar and molasses ("The New York State Colonization Society" 1846, 181–182).

Seymour first returned to Hartford in 1846 to encourage his family to

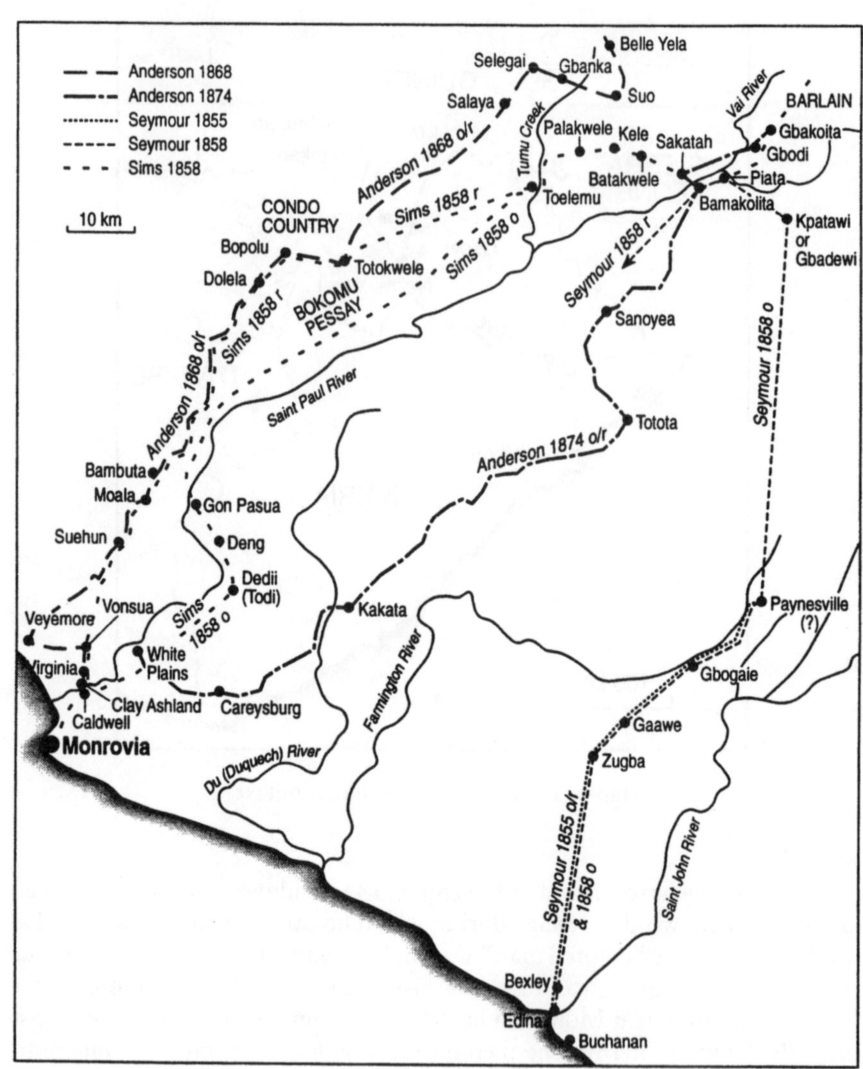

Map 2. The journeys in southern Liberia.

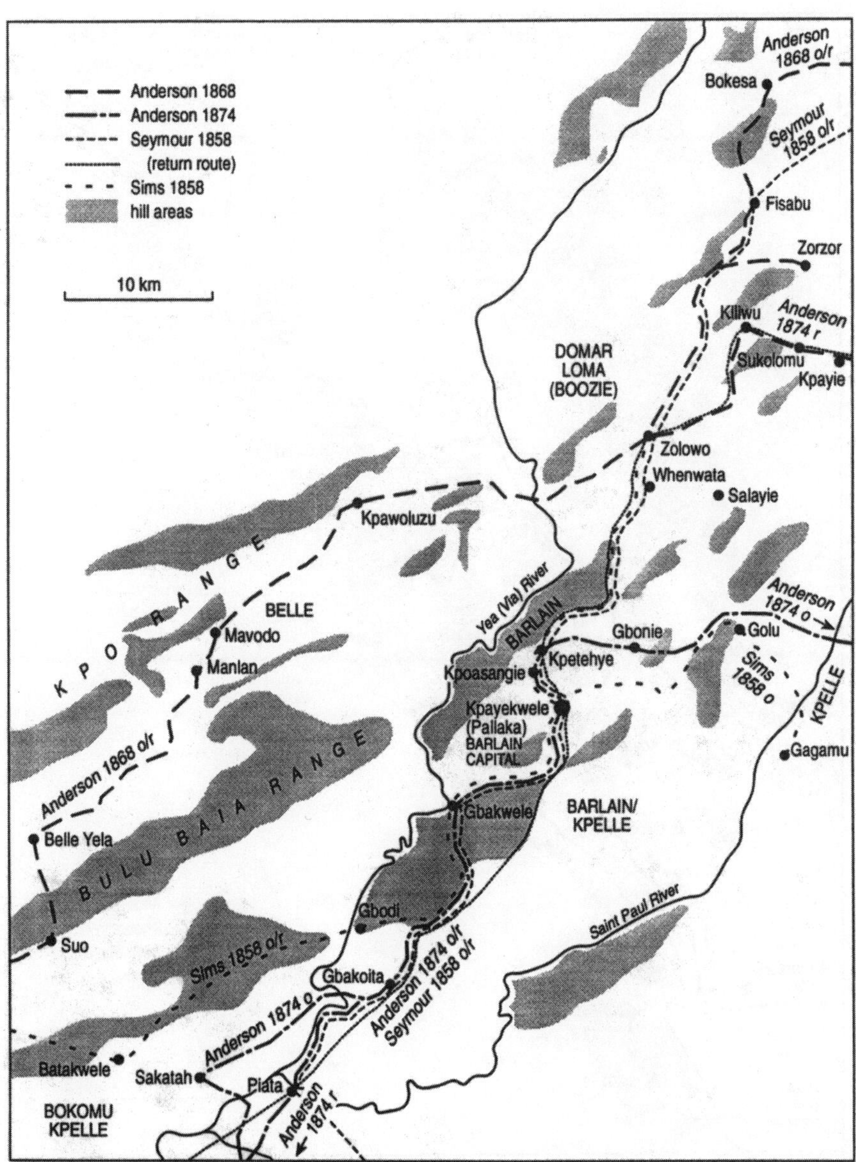

Map 3. The journeys in northeast Liberia.

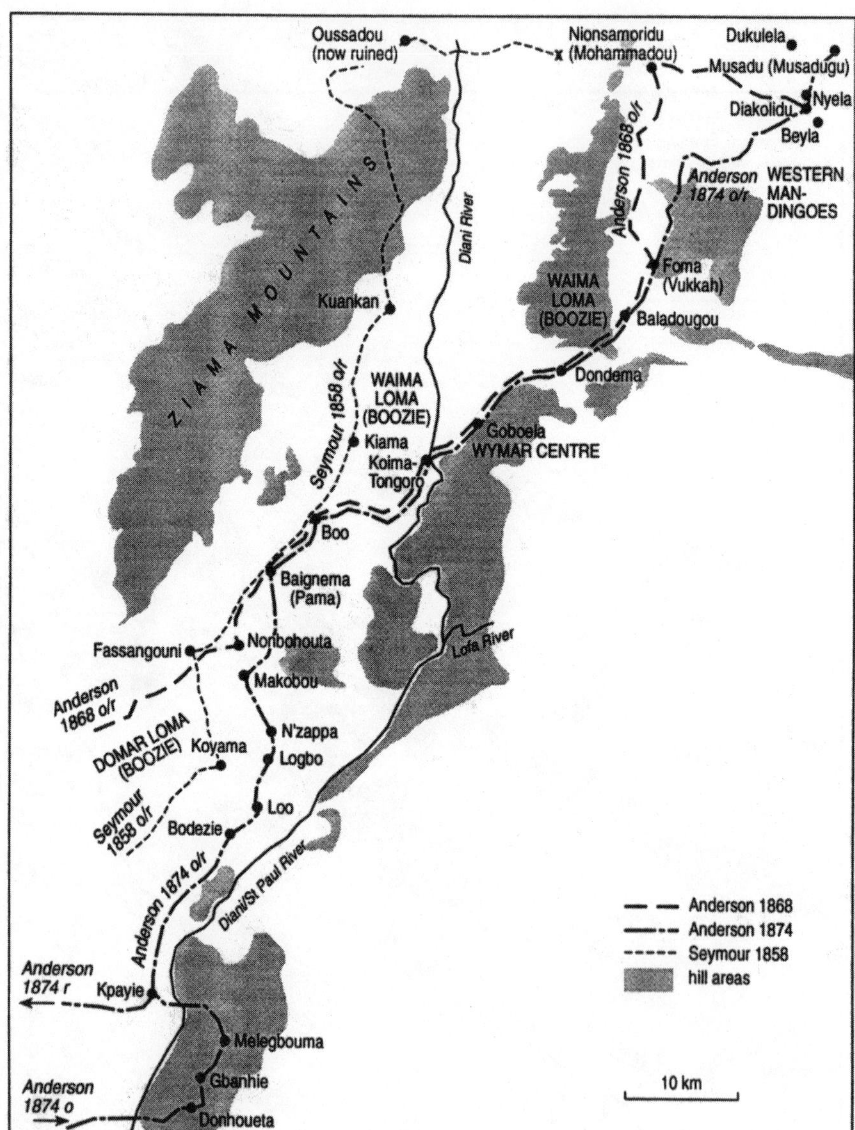

Note: In 1858 Waima Loma formed part of 'Upper Condo'.

Map 4. The journeys in the north, Guinea.

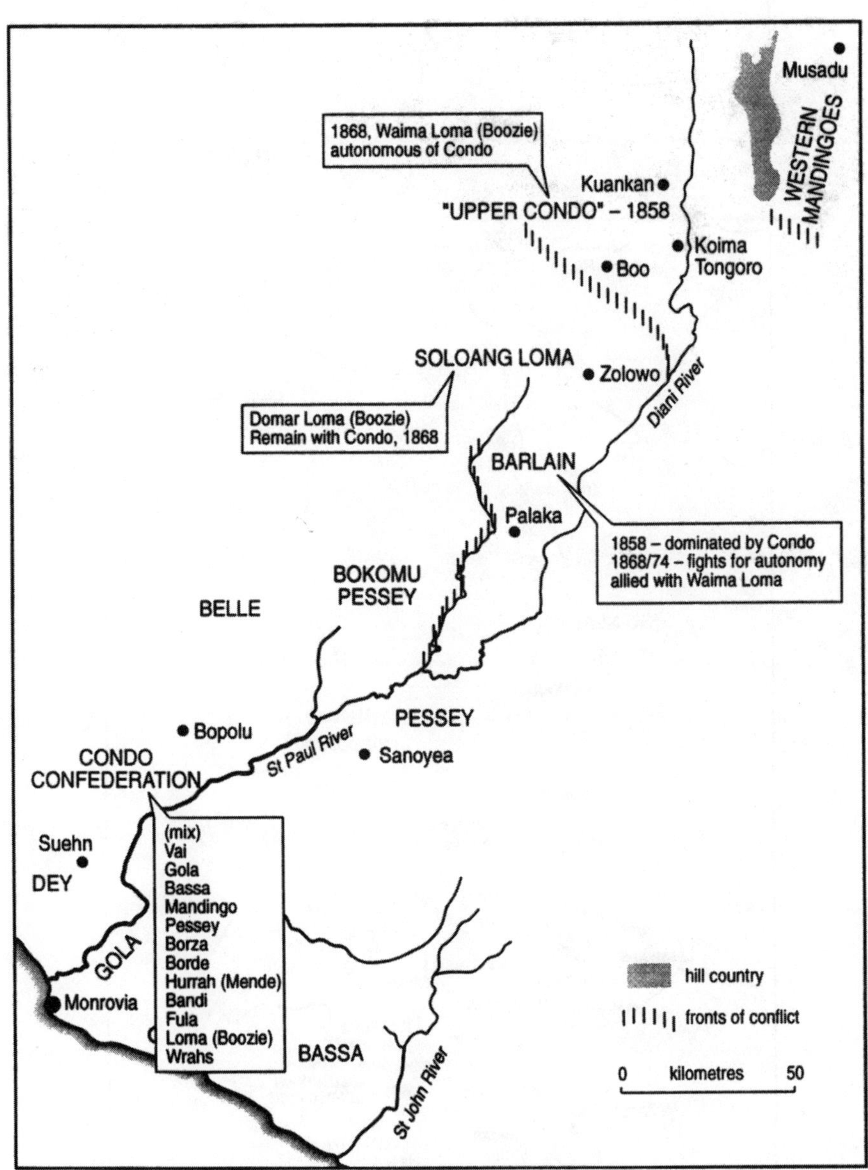

Map 5. A political map of the region.

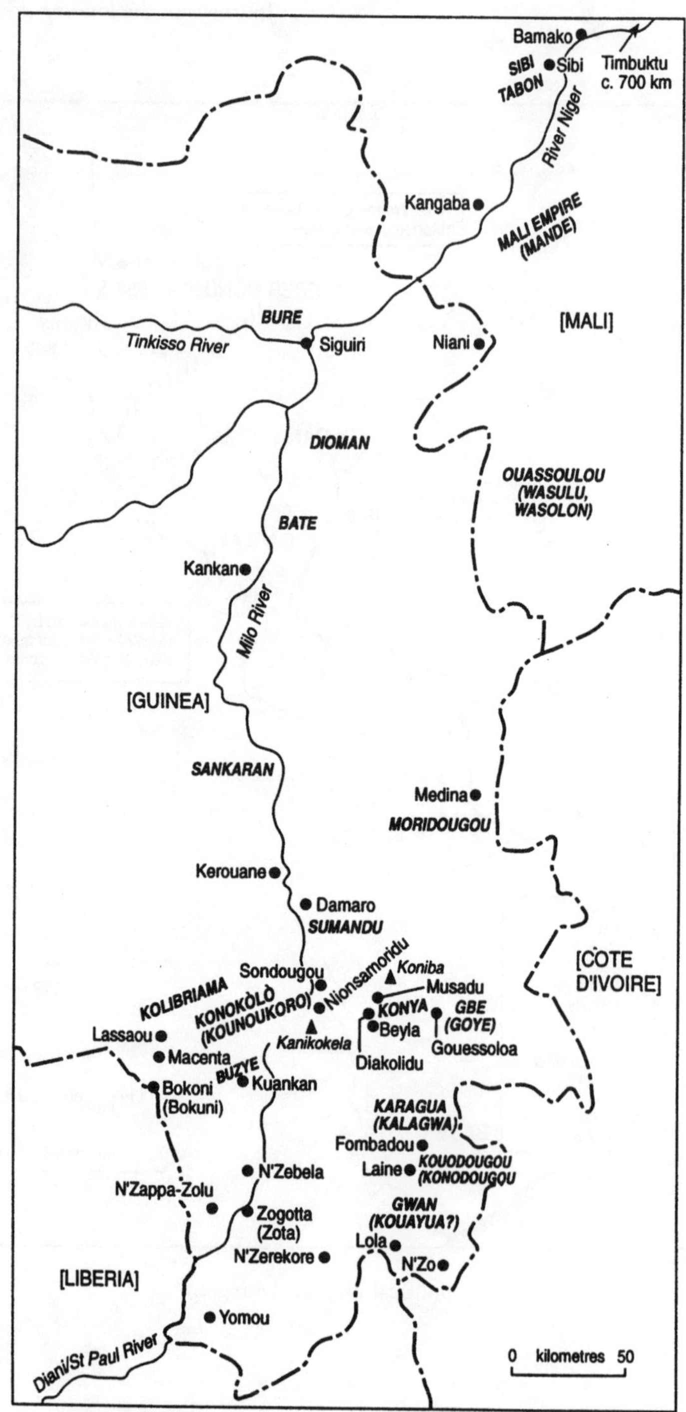

Map 6. Valleys of the Niger, Milo, and Saint Paul rivers.

join him and was partially successful (Seymour 1845, 343; Washington 1851, 261). He also traveled to New York and Boston to address the annual meetings of the New York State Colonization Society and the Massachusetts Colonization Society. On these visits, he met notable people such as John Latrobe (President of the Maryland Colonization Society and the American Colonization Society) and Simon Greenleaf (once regarded as the principal drafter of the Liberian Constitution in 1848) and spoke about his own work.[2] He reminded his audiences that Africa was the only place where the "colored people" could find total freedom and equality, and that "Colored missionaries" were the only people who could "evangelize Africa" ("The New York Colonization Society" 1846, 181; "Annual Meeting of the Massachusetts Colonization Society" 1846, 227).

Seymour continued farming when he returned to Liberia (Seymour 1848, 182–183) and married Mary Cole from Connecticut, in Bexley, on 26 August 1848 ("Married" 1848, 43). In 1852, he was put in charge of constructing a mill for the Liberia Saw Mill Company (Benson 1852, 34). Much timber was available to be cut, and he thought that this would be one way to increase commerce in the region. In October of the same year, Seymour's sister, Mary, her husband, George Cisco, and their three young children went to Liberia (Brown 1980, 17). From 1853 to 1855, Seymour represented Bassa County in the Liberian House of Representatives as a Republican under the administration of Joseph Jenkins Roberts ("According to the Official Returns" 1853, 79; "Meeting of [the] Connecticut Colonization Society" 1855, 238).

From 30 April to 18 May 1855, Seymour made his first significant foray into the interior.[3] He started from Bexley, traversed through Bassa country, and went as far as a Pessay or Southern Kpelle chiefdom that King Darby ruled.[4] Seymour took note of the wood, iron, tobacco, kola, ivory, timber, and crops in the region and wrote that there was a "receptiveness to evangelism" among the Africans. He recorded the antagonism that existed between the Bassa peoples living nearer the coast and the Southern Kpelle inland of them. The Southern Kpelle complained that Bassa Chiefs prevented Southern Kpelle trade with the coast, which had to pass through Bassa lands, or taxed it excessively. Seymour persuaded several Bassa Chiefs to sign an agreement stating that they would keep the road open from Southern Kpelle country to the coast. Opening this route was important for the commercial development of Liberian settlements in Grand Bassa, and it is probable that this was a main goal of his journey. Southern Kpelle country was, as Seymour so often noted, a source of much camwood, for which there was a lucrative export market at that time and on which the Liberian settlers in Grand Bassa depended. An indication of this trade is given in 1857, when Seymour directed a large trading caravan to Bexley from the Southern Kpelle country (and beyond?), consisting of nearly two hundred fifty people and loaded with camwood, rice, and other goods ("A Liberian Caravan" 1857, 364; Seymour 1857a, 197–198).

This trip was, however, a turning point in Seymour's life. In his words, he was greatly "affected" by the spiritual needs of the Bassa and the Southern Kpelle and by the great industrial and commercial opportunities that this section of the interior afforded the Liberian republic. One writer noted that Seymour "seems now disposed to devote himself more entirely" to his missionary activities "than he has been able to do heretofore" ("Exploration in Africa" 1855, 1).

His 1855 journey report reveals his religious and radical political views. He "sorrowed at the destitute condition of the simple people, as regard their knowledge of divine things," that is, Christianity. Nonetheless, he rejoiced that they responded positively when he preached, and that many of the people wanted to send their children to school and "imitate the better aspects of life." He also believed that the "aboriginal inhabitants" had as much potential as the Americo-Liberians to effect positive change in Africa and said that they might take the place of Americo-Liberians if they converted to Christianity (Seymour 1856, 172). Such notions echoed the ideas of the dark-skinned Americo-Liberians who started to challenge the dominance of President Roberts's mulatto merchants, Liberia's rulers (see Sawyer 1992, 153). In this, his critique was made more pertinent by his own status as a mulatto.

Seymour also chided the Liberian "petty country merchant" who charged exorbitant prices and caused many well-meaning Africans to go into debt. He believed that the settlers should invest more of their time in agriculture and industry, or their overemphasis on commerce would ruin the republic. As things were, he worried that "a domestic slavery will be introduced into the Republic in order to support the indolence and luxury of the few and to secure and maintain this state of things the poor savage must be kept in ignorance," and that this would brand immigrants "with the stigma of a vicious and wicked people" (1856, 173).

Seymour thought that missionaries should live and build settlements in the interior and establish mission stations nearby. In June 1855, he set an example and moved near Darby's town, where he established his "Pessay Mission," which he also called the "Interior Mission" or the "Interior Liberia Mission." He named the settlement "Paynesville." Seymour's philosophy for the mission was that "faith and works go hand in hand." While he was fully committed to preaching the gospel, he also wanted to teach skills such as blacksmithing, cabinet making, and building. This coincided with his view that the advancement of civilization, extension of trade, building of new settlements, abolition of the slave trade, and spread of Christianity would pacify the "warlike character of the tribes" and be good for Liberia (see also Seymour 1857a, 197–198; 1857b, 15; 1858c, 200–201; 1859a, 122). In 1856,

Seymour, Peter Adams, Effey Seymour, and others proposed to merge their mission with the Union Mission in the U.S., though nothing came of this overture.

Soon after Seymour returned to the Paynesville mission, he began to lobby the government to back a longer journey to the interior. Fortunately, his old friend from Bassa, Stephen A. Benson, had just become the President of Liberia. One of Benson's goals was also to exert a greater presence in the interior (1858a, 131; see also Martin 1969, 22–28; Sawyer 1992, 153–154). One supposes that Benson and Seymour might have talked about interior policy and potential on several occasions. Yet, although the Liberian government was content at this point with merely exploring the hinterland, Seymour was more of a visionary and was thinking ahead toward settlement.

During late 1856, Seymour drafted and circulated a petition in Bassa that encouraged the government to extend contacts and roads into the interior. He forwarded this petition to the legislature, and the legislature passed the measure into law on 3 February 1857. It was titled an Act Authorizing the Appropriation of Three Thousand Dollars for Exploring and Opening Roads into the Interior of the Several Counties, was passed in December 1856 and January 1857, was dated 3 February 1857, and was published in the *Liberia Herald* (4 February 1857).[5]

This appropriated three thousand dollars to enable exploration of Montserrado, Grand Bassa, and Sinoe counties by three Commissioners of interior roads and explorations. The Commissioners were to explore, to keep a correct journal, to survey and map highways, watercourses, towns, and villages, and to describe the resources, population, and production of the country. They were also to settle disputes, to purchase territory and negotiate treaties with Chieftains, and to secure the preemptive right to their lands and territories.

Benson then supported Seymour in 1857 to travel beyond Liberia's borders to "the capital of the Mandingo Country, Moosá-doo." Benson planned to send Seymour to "Moosá-doo," or Musadu, on his first trip, and then to have him find the sources of the Niger on a subsequent mission (Benson 1858a, 131). The stated purpose of Seymour's 1858 trip was to establish trade links and to gain information to enable subsequent exploration (see Liebenow 1987, 26).

The estimated cost of Seymour's journey was $300. Despite the act, the Liberian government could not "prudently make any considerable expenditure," so President Benson officially sanctioned a "subscription" list whereby "contributions from [Liberia's] citizens and others" would "assist [the] Government in putting this important enterprise on foot." Seymour went to Monrovia at the end of 1857 to raise money. Thirty-three Liberians gave a total of $122.76. These included notable merchants such as the McGill brothers, Daniel Warner, Augustus Washington, and C. M. Waring and Company, all

Figure 2. Stephen A. Benson, President of Liberia, 1856–64. Photographed by Augustus Washington. *Courtesy of the Library of Congress.*

of whom probably looked at Seymour's trip as a business investment. While the government might have given some money, most of the rest was "contributed by a few liberal gentlemen in the city of New York (Benson 1858a, 131)."[6] Seymour had several potential benefactors, such as Anston G. Phelps, President of the New York Colonization Society, who had personally encouraged him to immigrate to Liberia (Seymour 1845, 342; 1851, 267).

Augustus Washington's support of Seymour exemplifies the combination of commercial and personal links on which the journey depended. Washing-

Figure 3. View of Monrovia from the Anchorage. Wood engraving by an unidentified artist after the daguerrotype by Augustus Washington. *Source:* Twenty-fourth Annual Report of the Board of Managers of the New-York Colonization Society *(New York, 1856).*

ton was born in 1820 in Trenton, New Jersey, of African-Asian parentage, and lived there until he was sixteen. He attended a private school with white students, and then moved to New York where he taught from 1837 to 1841. Washington became a proponent of the abolitionist movement and "African missionary work" (Moses 1998a, 182). He strongly advocated sending "Afric-Americans" to Liberia after earlier opposing this idea, like Seymour (Washington 1851, 259). At other times, he sought to create a separate state in the U.S. for black Americans. He published his views in the *New York Tribune* and the *Colored American.*

Washington had moved to Hartford, Connecticut, in about 1842 and attended Dartmouth College the following fall as the school's only African-American student. He abandoned his studies because he could not afford to pay all of the fees and instead became a successful daguerreotypist and a teacher. He met his "excellent friend" George Seymour in Hartford and eventually traveled to Monrovia in 1854 with his wife, Cordelia, and his two young children, sponsored by the Connecticut State Colonization Society through a grant of two hundred dollars. Washington immigrated with five hundred dollars, investing this in trade, photography, property, shipbuilding, newspaper editing (for the *New Era*), and plantation farming. He had horses, cattle, and a steam mill on his farm, where he employed fifty poor settlers and Africans. He also traveled to Sierra Leone, the Gambia, and Senegal to market his goods and to take pictures. He was elected to the legislature and had become the Speaker of the House by 1867, and from 1869 to 1874 served as a Senator. He returned to the United States for short visits in 1855, 1858, and 1868 and died in 1875 (Moses 1998a, 181–183; Shumard 1999).[7]

By 1858 Seymour had raised the funds and prepared his journey. He probably became a Commissioner under the new legislation cited above, a position that involved keeping a journal and a map, which he mentions that he drew but which has not been located (Seymour 1856, 11). Following a preparatory trip to Monrovia, he returned to Paynesville in mid-January 1858 and began his interior journey from there. He spent March and early April on Commissioner's business, resolving a dispute that had developed between two chiefs, Borwandow and Darby (Seymour 1858d). He had returned to Paynesville by mid-April, and on 28 April 1858 Seymour headed into the interior, accompanied by Levin Ash and William Taylor.

Relatively little is known about Ash and Taylor. Ash came from Indiana and had helped Seymour found the interior mission in Paynesville.[8] After their 1858 journey he returned there with Seymour ("Seymour's Travels in Western Africa" 1860, 494). Seymour wrote that Taylor was from Philadelphia; perhaps he was the William H. Taylor from Camden, New Jersey, who, at the age of twenty-four, sailed from Baltimore to Buchannan on 1 May 1852 ("List of Emigrants" 1852, 181). Before they departed for Musadu, Seymour wrote that both Taylor and Ash planned to return to the United States to report about their trip and "awaken the interest of their brethren for the interior of Liberia" ("Explorations East of Liberia" 1858). The Liberian materials do not explain what happened to Ash and Taylor after the journey, except that Ash accompanied Seymour back to Paynesville.[9]

They were gone for eight months and should have made $200 just for the time that they were gone. Being paid by the day and by the mile gave them an incentive to delay their journeys and to exaggerate mileage to make more money. Although we do not know how the Commissioners calculated miles, the mathematical book that Benjamin Anderson used on his first journey cited the popular notion that 1000 paces equaled 1 mile (Davies and Peck 1867, 372). Seymour wrote that Quanger, or Kuankan, was 384 miles (618 kilometers) from Grand Bassa and 280 miles (451 kilometers) from Monrovia. At 10¢ per mile, Seymour, Ash, and Taylor therefore would have earned a $61.40 travel supplement in addition to the $200, calculating 10¢ per mile from Grand Bassa to Kuankan, and another 10¢ per mile back to Monrovia.

Three months into the journey, Seymour, Ash, and Taylor met James L. Sims in Solong (Zolowo). Seymour and Ash left Taylor there, where he stayed for some time. After Seymour returned, he commented that he and Ash had returned to the coast, but that Taylor was at Zolowo. Seymour wrote that they left Taylor

> in a state of ill-health, in company with another young Liberian [James L. Sims], who had personal interest to attend to of considerable amount; but I learned that Mr. Taylor did not succeed so well in his trade. Therefore he had not returned to the coast at my leaving Monrovia last; yet I learned that he was well, and would likely return to the coast soon. (Seymour 1860c, 278)

Seymour and Ash continued for another 80 miles (129 kilometers) or so and ended well into the land of present-day Guinea, some 25 miles (40 kilometers) west of Musadu. They had traveled through Barlain Kpelle country, passed "King Carmer's," or Jaka Kaman Kamara's town of Kuankan, and apparently reached the northern edge of Loma territory. They were probably only one or two days' walk away from Musadu when they were attacked, wounded, and forced to abandon their mission.

Seymour and Ash were attacked about 25 miles west of Musadu. The question of who attacked them remains open and interesting. Seymour suggests that he was attacked because he was impatient. He also infers that Jaka Kaman was in part responsible. Benjamin Anderson also noted, when passing through the region ten years later, that "it is a fact notorious throughout the country" that Jaka Kaman "was a principal actor, and that the whole plot was concocted at the town of Boe" (chap. 5, 225). Indeed, Jaka Kaman's rival, Dowilnyah, told Anderson "that five principal chiefs were concerned in the assault on Seymore." Jaka Kaman, however, blamed the attack on "King Barbenier" (chap. 4, 153). Earlier on his journey, Seymour had in fact been warned that the "Bababeenias," as Sims termed them, were "very cruel and pugnacious" and caused problems on the road to Musadu (chap. 3, 119). We know this from Sims, who met Seymour earlier in his journey and helped Seymour negotiate to continue on with his journey with the chief of Zolowo, whose warning it was. From Seymour's account we can infer that the Barbenier territory was east of Oussadou, between it and Nionsamoridu.

The account also reported from Captain Dauvillier's 1905 biography of Samori Touré (Archives d'Outre Mer de France, Aix-en-Provence, APC 105, carton 5, dossier 14, Papers of Dauvillier) stated that early in his life, Samori

> established himself as chief of brigands, initially with two or three of his acolytes, to waylay passers by on the paths between Nionsamoridougou and Kuong-Kan (Bouzie) [Kuankan]. His affairs prospered, his band increased, and he had, by the end of the year, about 200 inhabitants under his orders, attacking, pillaging the small villages and terrorising the whole country.

This region of Samori Touré's operation is the exact location where Seymour was attacked. From Dauvillier, we can also infer that Samori was operating in this way in about 1858. This picture gains independent support from the more recent work of historian Yves Person, who cited an oral account that in about 1858–59 Samori became a brigand in this region (1968,

1:268 n. 92; 1970, 84–85). It is also feasible that Barbenier derives from *Gben-ya,* "the place of Gben," which is the name of the northern hills of the Vukka range between Oussadou and Nionsamoridu, the land that encompassed the natal home of Samori and his parents. It is also known that Jaka Kaman, who was considered responsible for attacking Seymour, personally favored Samori and defended his interests as a trader (Person 1962, 172). In short, bandits were certainly operating on this path at this time, and Seymour may have fallen victim to them.

There was a possibility, in slaving areas, for strangers who were traveling to be kidnapped. This was particularly true in Muslim areas such as this when the strangers were not Muslims. According to Muslim law, Muslims could not enslave other Muslims, although Muslims did not always obey this prohibition (Fisher and Fisher 1970, 5–8). While it is likely, as Seymour and Ash believed, that they were targeted for kidnapping or execution for leaving Oussadou without Jaka Kaman's permission, some element of capture for the purpose of enslavement may have also been a motive. Yet given that certain bandits such as the young Samori were themselves linked politically to Jaka Kaman, "being victim to bandits" does not rule out the kind of political intrigue that both Seymour and Anderson picked up on. Rather incredibly, then, there is reasonable evidence that Seymour may have fallen victim to the young Samori Touré, a name which came to dominate West African history in the closing decades of the century.

After their escape, Seymour and Ash took three and a half months to return to Monrovia, reaching there in December 1859. Ash might have arrived first, telling the English traveler Harriette Brittan about their journey (Brittan 1860, 315–316). When Seymour returned to Monrovia in mid-December 1858, he gave President Benson "about 100 pages of foolscap of the journal of Seymour" ("Discoveries in Africa" 1859, 3). This same source also said that the *Liberia Herald* was publishing Seymour's journal, and that his journal "is to appear hereafter in a pamphlet from Monrovia." One issue of the *Liberia Herald* publication has survived (fig. 11), but the records do not indicate if Seymour's journal was ever published separately. The Royal Geographical Society and the Presbyterian *Home and Foreign Record* published summaries of Seymour's journey and praised the efforts of Seymour and Ash (Earl de Grey and Ripon 1860, clxvii–clxviii; "Seymour's Travels in Western Africa" 1860). However, it is only with the publication of Seymour's 1858 journal in this volume, culled from the *New-York Colonization Journal,* the *Liberia Herald,* and the *Philadelphia Colonization Herald,* that Seymour's journal is now available to readers in a broad medium.

After Seymour arrived in Monrovia in mid-December 1858, he spent little over a month there before returning to Paynesville. Yet rather than take his usual sea route to Bassa, and inland from there, he preferred to try an overland route, "along the interior frontier of Liberia from Careysburg to Paynesville, between the St. Paul's and Junk Rivers."[10] The route from Bassa had become closed during his absence. He went with his son, his travel companion, Levin Ash, and another man. He left on 19 January 1859, and his journey passed "through eighteen towns, crossed three small rivers, sixty-four creeks, and passed eighty-two swamps." These included Tow, before the Farmington River, and then the villages of Pey, Iovan, and Wheor, through what became Liberia's giant Firestone plantation. This was a lightly populated, forested landscape. Once in Dogray, the first village in Southern Kpelle country, he negotiated a peace between them and the Gibi people, whose land he had traversed. He then traveled through Manicoys to Paynesville, journeying through five small towns on a half-day's journey.[11]

At home, Seymour soon sought to align himself with the Presbyterian Church. He had earlier been affiliated with the Methodist Church but established the Pessay Mission in Paynesville as an independent organization. On 5 May 1859, Edward Blyden and other elders of the Presbyterian Church determined that Seymour could join their organization, and that Seymour's Pessay Mission could be put "under their control." The Liberian presbytery sent a letter to the United States asking the Presbyterian Board of Foreign Missions to accept Seymour and the Pessay Mission under its auspices ("From Liberia: Presbytery of Western Africa" 1860, 275–276; Seymour 1861, 61).

Seymour appears to have remained at Paynesville. In the last month of 1859 and into January 1860, he was again settling a dispute there between the Bassa and the Southern Kpelle. These groups had closed the road to the coast because they were arguing about rights over the camwood trees. Further trading difficulties had started in 1858 while Seymour was away with Ash, suggesting perhaps that the chiefs only abided by their agreement to keep the road open while Seymour was living in the area and was able to adjudicate associated problems. In any case, Seymour helped resolve the difficulties by the end of January 1860 (Seymour 1860c, 276). He hoped the Liberian government and the Southern Kpelle would form some kind of "union," and that it would be possible to build a road from the Saint John River to Paynesville (Seymour 1861, 61)

On 25 January 1860, Seymour lamented that the wound he received when he was attacked in the interior had "impaired" his health and had "reduced [him] to much less than an able-bodied man" (Seymour 1860c, 276). On 17 August he wrote: "I have been so unwell that I almost despaired of life once or twice" (1861, 61). Seymour died in September or October 1860, at the age of forty-one. The *Home and Foreign Record* received a letter dated 1 November informing it of Seymour's death ("Seymour's Travels in Western Liberia" 1860, 302; see also "Africa" 1861, 45).

James L. Sims, 1858

Little is known of James L. Sims's life and the circumstances surrounding his journey. He was born "free" in 1832 and grew up in Manchester, Virginia, where he learned how to "read & write" and became a "barber."[12] Internal references in the text suggest that Sims was well read.[13] When he was twenty years old, he moved to Liberia, sailing from Norfolk, Virginia, on 27 November 1851 aboard the *Linda Stewart.* A seventeen year old from Manchester named Richard Sims also sailed with James. Richard was also freeborn and literate, and the two might have been brothers or otherwise related ("List of Emigrants" 1853, 29). After Sims returned from the interior, the *Philadelphia Colonization Herald* published this description of him:

A LIBERIAN EXPLORER

In the development of traits which contribute to national greatness, the young Republic of Liberia has manifested several, which have proved eminently significant and useful. Recent intelligence from that prosperous and progressive commonwealth has furnished the report of the explorations of Mr. James L. Sims, who lately returned from a journey into the interior east of Liberia, far beyond her territorial and political jurisdictions [i.e., beyond 40 miles from the coast]. He represents the country as beautiful and productive; the climate refreshing and salubrious; the soil as rich and unsurpassed, and the natives peaceful, happy and industrious.

Mr. Sims is a native of Virginia. He removed to Liberia in 1852 from Manchester, in that State. He soon became popular, and has always been noted for his courtesy and intelligence. At the expiration of a year's residence in his adopted land—during which he was engaged in the grocery business—he visited the United States. The vessel in which he embarked was wrecked, but after much delay, it made St. Thomas, West Indies, whence Mr. Sims took passage in a ship to Newport, R.I., and then to New York, Philadelphia, and to Richmond.

Having settled his father's estate—whose death was the occasion of his visit to America—he purchased a stock of goods and proceeded to Liberia, landing in July, 1854. The former were despatched by the brig *Harp,* which went ashore in front of Monrovia, and were lost or much damaged. They were not insured, and his means were thus nearly all swallowed up by the sea.[14]

After a brief sojourn at Cape Mount, he started from Clay-Ashland, one of the Liberian inland towns, January 1858, on a journey into the interior, accompanied by twenty-seven natives, and provided with articles calculated to enable him to travel among the aborigines. He succeeded admirably in his mission and returned in the following October, in good health. He is now in the service of Vice President Yates, having charge of one of his farms on the St. Paul's River. Mr. Sims is about twenty-eight years of age, tall and thin, and of a dark brown complexion.

> We give an extract of his journal, on the first page. It is a fair specimen of the style of his entire report. ("A Liberian Explorer" 1860, 2)

Sims apparently gained private finance for his own trip, which was a trading endeavor. In addition to the significant investment required to hire over two-dozen porters, Sims hinted in his journal that one reason why he traveled into the interior was to trade ivory (chap. 3, 111). Unlike Seymour and Anderson, he appears not to have had the public backing or support of the Liberian government: there is as yet no evidence that Sims was a government Commissioner under the legislation that Seymour forwarded, although this cannot be ruled out. Sims's account is humorous and attentive to the intrigues and sentiments of the people he met and to the intricacies of everyday life, which contrasts with the missionary zeal of Seymour's account and with the scientific trappings of Anderson's "exploration." Sims built a house in the town he traveled to and lived for some months there, observing life much as an anthropologist might today.

Following his return, in 1859 the Liberian legislature authorized President Benson to withdraw fifty dollars from the Treasury to publish three hundred copies of "James L. Sims' Journal of travels to the interior of Liberia." This was to be done as a "testimony of his country's approval, and high appreciation of his enterprising efforts, and laborious investigation, in the acquisition and dissemination of useful knowledge in Liberia" (*ATL* [1857–61] 1862, 67–68). No record has survived, to our knowledge, about whether the government published Sims's journal. The government did, however, publish it in their newspaper, the *Liberia Herald.* The *Star of Liberia* was the other Liberian newspaper that published Sims's journal. The *Maryland Colonization Journal,* the *Philadelphia Colonization Herald,* and the *New-York Colonization Journal* published near-complete extracts of Sims's journal from the *Star of Liberia* and the *Liberia Herald.* Copies of the relevant issues of the two Liberian newspapers have not survived to our knowledge, so the republication of Sims's journal that appears in chapter 3 is the most complete version that we have been able to cull from the colonization journals.

Other Journeys

National pride was at stake in Liberian exploration. As President Benson argued, "[we should] not wait for foreigners to come to our own country and do for us what we can do for ourselves" (1858a, 131). Foreigners were indeed interested in interior travel. Benson may have been referring to an unknown missionary who "passed through thirty villages of Goulahs, Deys, Queahs, and Condoes" on a "two hundred and fifty mile journey" in 1850–51 ("The Country Adjacent to Liberia" 1851), or to the white Sierra Leone missionary, Rev. George Thompson, who made a tour 100 miles up the Saint

Paul in 1855 (Thompson 1856), or to the white missionaries in the Cavalla region such as Rev. C. C. Hoffman, who had a keen interest in the interior and eventually published short accounts of his journeys in the Royal Geographical Society proceedings (Hoffman 1862).

Another white traveler on the scene who wanted—but failed—to go to Musadu was Ben. E. Castendyk.[15] Castendyk was "resident at Baltimore [U.S.], but born in Bremen (Germany)." He was probably linked to the white missionaries located near the Cavalla River, through the Bremen connection. He seems to have been the nephew of Pastor Georg Treviranus, who was a leading light in German (Bremen) and Swiss (Basel) missionary activities in Ghana, itself linked to Liberia. Treviranus had married into the Castendyk family in Bremen.[16]

Castendyk traveled from New York on the *Mendi* on 24 May 1859 and arrived at Monrovia on 12 July after forty-six days at sea. Fortuitously, he was traveling with Dr. Martin Delaney, himself on an exploratory trip to what is now Nigeria, where he hoped to locate the site for an alternative African-American colony that was independent of the white-inspired colonization project (Delaney 1861). Delaney described Castendyk as "a german gentleman travelling for pleasure."[17] Within two weeks, Castendyk had accompanied Delaney up the Saint Paul River, along with the U.S. consular agent for Liberia, John Moore, and a Liberian government surveyor. They rowed up the Saint Paul in a canvas-covered boat, loaned by Vice President Yates, "to examine the planting district." While Delaney soon traveled on along the coast, exploring up the Cavally River with Alexander Crummell en route, Castendyk remained to plan an ambitious expedition, citing former President J. J. Roberts (then serving as British consul) as a referee. He wrote to the President of the British Royal Geographical Society, Sir Roderick Murchison, about his plans. After a repeat journey up the Saint Paul for 20 miles, he planned to leave the river to his right to "take a northern route to try to reach Musaduh, the capital of the great mandingo kingdom." Although the "Carriers had been engaged, and goods obtained," he was, however, prevented from leaving. "The appearing of hostilities between the different tribes through whose countries I would have to pass, overthrew all my hopes to see Mussaduh and to cross the Niger in a higher latitude than Sierra Leone city." He chose a second route, leaving as the rains diminished in October or November 1859, but he was then thwarted by disease. He must have left Liberia in late January 1860. On 23 March 1860, he wrote from Boston two weeks after arriving: "The African diseases to which Europeans or any other white men are generally subject have prevented my progress beyond a distance of about 175–200 miles, penetrating the interior easterly. I was brought back to the sea coast by an expedition, which my friends at Monrovia sent in search of me, in a state" (Castendyk to Murchison, 23 March 1860, Archives of the Royal Geographical Society).

Following the journeys of Sims and Seymour, Liberians continued to make shorter journeys into the interior. At around the same date Amos made a "tour of observation of the Falls of the Sinoa river," and Miller toured the Gola country (Earl de Grey and Ripon 1860).[18] In 1860, Alexander Crummell, the Cambridge-educated Liberian pan-Africanist, journeyed up the Cavalla River.[19] Hoffman repeated the same journey the next year (1862). In 1868, an indigenous Liberian Christian convert, Gabla Church Brownell, made a long tour from Cape Palmas to Mount Gede (Brownell 1869). W. S. Anderson ventured about 90 miles inland up the Saint Paul River in 1865 but did not publish this account (see Anderson 1866). And Benjamin Anderson noted how a Liberian trader named Sanders Washington helped him in Bessa's town in 1868.

Benjamin Anderson's First Journey to Musadu, 1868–69

In the mid-1860s, Liberia's President Warner, in conjunction with Henry Maunsell Schieffelin and other supporters of the colonization movement in the United States, started to make plans for more "scientific" exploration to the interior. Warner was continuing where his predecessor Stephen A. Benson had left off in 1858 when he sent Seymour and Ash to Musadu (d'Azevedo 1994, 239 n. 45; 1995, 70). Benjamin Anderson, who was only thirty-three in 1868, combined the skills needed as a veteran soldier, a politician, and a surveyor.

Benjamin Anderson was freeborn to Israel and Henrietta Anderson in Baltimore on 4 January 1835.[20] Much of our information about Anderson comes from an unpublished four-page obituary titled "Brief Sketch of the Life and Character of the Late Hon. Benj. J. K. Anderson. M.A., Ph.D., K.C."[21]

He was a "pure" or "full-blooded Negro" (Büttikofer 1890, 29). He was brought up in the brickyards of Baltimore, where he learned to make bricks, and attended "primary schools." Yet "so strong was the race prejudice against Negroes obtaining an education, even in the North, that while attending school he was very often sneered and beaten by white men which he as often resented [retaliated] by flogging some white lad, for which reasons his mother thought best to leave America with him fearing that something serious might happen, and thus cost his life" ("Brief Sketch" [1910]).

At age seventeen, Anderson thus departed from Baltimore for Monrovia with his mother and possibly his sister on the *Liberia Packet* on 31 December 1851 ("List of Emigrants [*Liberia Packet*]" 1852, 118; Brown 1980, 8).[22] The *Liberia Packet*'s emigrant list states that three of its passengers were "Benj. Anderson," age sixteen (born in 1835), "Judy Anderson," age nineteen (born in 1833), and "Henri'a Anderson," age thirty-five (born in 1816). All three were born free. No occupation was listed for "Ben," as he was

Figure 4. Photograph of Benjamin Anderson on a postcard honoring Liberia's independence day celebration. Frederick Starr mailed this postcard to Liberian immigrants in the U.S. in 1918. *Courtesy of the Frederick Starr Collection, Howard University, Moorland-Spingard Research Center.*

otherwise called (see Blyden to Coppinger, 3 October 1887, in Lynch 1978, 380). Henri'a or Henrietta was a "laundress," and Judy was a "drayman," or "puller of carts."

The *Liberia Packet* docked in Monrovia in April 1852 ("Brief Sketch" [1910]). The voyage took so long, about two months longer than usual, that two passengers died. None of the emigrants were allowed to disembark immediately after they arrived in Monrovia, "in consequence of their being down sick with the fever" ("List of Emigrants" 1852, 118).[23] The immigrants were housed and given weekly rations during their first six months at the "recepticle," which was 8 miles away from central Monrovia up the Saint Paul River, and then moved to Virginia up the Saint Paul River (Dennis 1852; "Brief Sketch" [1910]; see also Nesbit [1855] 1998, 90–91; Washington [1854] 1998a, 206). Anderson had moved to Carey or Mechanic Street in central Monrovia by 1868 and still lived there ten years later (B. 1878).

As the "Brief Sketch" elaborates, "They had as fellow passengers on the voyage the late Hon. Asbury F. Johns of this City, who became interested in young Anderson, and engaged his services as clerk in a business which he was to establish on his arrival to Liberia. He accordingly was employed by Mr. Johns with whom he worked quite a while receiving as wages four dollars per month with which he assisted in supporting his mother."[24] Asbury Johns, age thirty-two, was an accountant when he sailed to Monrovia (Brown 1980, 35). Within three years of his arrival, he had become one of Monrovia's "wealthy merchants" (Peterson [1854] 1998, 48).

Benjamin Anderson soon joined the militia after he migrated to Liberia (Shick 1980, 85–87), becoming Ensign ("Brief Sketch" [1910]). In 1856, he accompanied Edward W. Blyden to Sinoe to quell a Kru uprising against the settlers and was wounded in the left knee (Blyden 1900, 8).[25] The "pot slug" shrapnel that was not removed caused him "considerable trouble and inconveniences" in later years. A year later, Anderson fought in Cape Palmas for its annexation to Liberia ("Brief Sketch" [1910]).

When Anderson was not away on "military expeditions" during the 1850s, he attended school in Monrovia and worked. He attended the Monrovia Academy or the M.E. (Methodist Episcopal) Seminary that Rev. James W. Horne founded in 1853 ("Brief Sketch" [1910]; Blyden 1874b, 359).[26] This is where Anderson received his training in mathematics and surveying. As the "Brief Sketch" notes: "He was a clever student, showing special adeptness in mathematics, for this reason Prof. Horn very often entrusted him the instructions of the junior classes." In 1861 Anderson married Mary Ware, and they had one daughter ("Brief Sketch" [1910]).

The *Liberia Herald* listed him as a member of the First Military Regiment in 1861 (3 July 1861). During the "early sixties," Anderson went to Cape Mount and Maryland, leading the "Grenidier Guards, a Company of Soldier from the territory of Grand Cape Mount." He became captain of a Monrovia company known as the Young Guards, the "sister to and rival of another Monrovia Company known as the Montserrado Regulars," then commanded by James S. Payne. He rose to the rank of colonel by 1875 ("Brief Sketch" [1910]).[27]

Anderson had a political as well as a military career. In 1861, Anderson became the Comptroller for the Department of Treasury. In April 1863, he became Secretary of the Treasury of the Republic and member of the cabinet under President Stephen Benson, but was replaced soon after Daniel Warner became president in January 1864 (*Report of the Special Committee of the House* 1864, 26, 29; Chavers 1864, 1).[28]

On 18 January 1864, ten days before Anderson left his cabinet position, the House of Representatives established a Special Committee on Public Accounts to investigate charges that had been brought against Anderson's Treasury department. He answered questions about money that the government received from the American Colonization Society, money that had been withdrawn from the Treasury, the amount of currency that was issued during the last quarter of 1863, and the date by which he would complete his December report. Anderson judiciously answered all of the questions. He also said that he would complete his report by the end of February, but he did not do so until 7 April. The committee's final report of 19 February listed several complaints: Anderson was frequently absent from his office; he did not give his associates access to the books when he was gone; there was "much irregularity and looseness in keeping the Public Accounts"; there were "considerable errors in additions"; there were inaccuracies in the disbursements for recaptured Africans; and large amounts of money went to people (like President Benson) without being reported. Nevertheless, Anderson does not seem to have profited from this job, as his total assets at the end of the year were a modest $34.50 (*Report of the Special Committee of the House* 1864, 1–8, 26–29; Chavers 1864, 1, 7). Two of the three committee members, Augustus Washington and Henry W. Dennis, later assisted Anderson in 1868 and 1874 when he went to Musadu.

Aspects of Benjamin Anderson's political philosophy can be inferred. Anderson served as the Secretary of the Treasury under Edward James Roye (1870), James Spriggs Payne (1876–78), and, according to the "Brief Sketch," Daniel B. Warner and J. J. Roberts, as well as being Secretary of the Interior under Hilary Richard Wright Johnson (c. 1886). The Liberian government encouraged or funded Anderson's trips to Musadu during the presidencies of James S. Payne and J. J. Roberts. These presidents represent the entire spectrum of political culture during this contentious period in Liberia's history. At one end was J. J. Roberts, the archetype mulatto from the elite element of the ruling merchant class who was Liberia's first president and the most influential person in the Republican Party until he died in 1876. Roberts was "outward directed" in his approach toward the United States and Europe with regard to ideas about civilization, religion, statecraft, and trade and had condescending views of the indigenous peoples. E. J. Roye, Daniel B. Warner, and Stephen A. Benson, by contrast, were darker-skinned settlers who believed that Liberia should be oriented along the lines of a "strong black civilization." They encouraged expansion into the interior and felt that the Liberian state would not become successful until local Africans became an integral part of the economic and political process. They entailed the "stronger element of cultural and racial nationalism" that Blyden championed for all peoples of African descent (Sawyer 1992, 153). Dark-skinned planters who lived up the Saint Paul River, the dark-skinned merchant faction that Warner and Roye represented, many less-fortunate mulattoes, and recaptives from other parts of Africa who docked in Monrovia came to support the True Whig Party that was established in the late 1860s. The party selected Roye as its standard-bearer for the 1869 elections, and Roye narrowly defeated President Payne. Yet Roye was turned out of office in 1871 in the biggest political scandal of the era, and the Republican Party returned to power for the last time under Smith, Roberts, and Payne. Eventually, Anthony W. Gardner's electoral victory of 1878 forever doomed the Republican Party (Sawyer 1992, chaps. 5, 7).

Notwithstanding the statement in Anderson's obituary that Anderson was a "loyal member of the 'NATIONAL TRUE WHIG PARTY,'" Professor d'Azevedo has convincingly argued that Anderson thus "does not seem to have been formally allied with any political group" (d'Azevedo 1995, 70). He held cabinet positions in three Republican administrations and two True Whig administrations. He went to Musadu under the helm of two Republican presidents (Payne and Roberts) and was slated to visit Musadu for a third time (en route to Medina) under a True Whig president (Gardner). Anderson had some leaning toward the Republican Party in 1872 when he tried to capture that party's nomination for an empty House of Representatives seat, but his popularity in these circles was not great and he was soundly defeated. To quote from d'Azevedo:

> Anderson may have been a constituent of the emergent Liberian middle class with its economically progressive and socially anti-elite orientation. His "friends in Monrovia" might have well been among the eager young businessmen, technicians and office seekers pressing for a policy of Liberian national expansion through interior trade and diplomatic alliances.[29] (d'Azevedo 1995, 65)

When plans for a new interior expedition were drawn up, Anderson became involved. In the introduction to his 1870 published account, Secretary Joseph Henry of the Smithsonian Institution wrote that Anderson "volunteered to undertake the exploration" (chap. 5, 157). It was Anderson himself, according to Sir Harry Johnston, who knew him, who went to the United States to solicit funds for this trip once he had finished his tenure as Secretary of the Treasury (Johnston [1906] 1969, 251–252; see also Fisher 1971, 1; Schulze 1973, 3; d'Azevedo 1995, 88, 94 n. 106).[30] He was successful in soliciting funds from Schieffelin, who gave two hundred dollars, and from Caleb Swan, who gave one hundred dollars.[31] For this, the *African Repository* later dubbed Anderson's journey as the "Schieffelin expedition" ("H. M. Schieffelin, Esq." 1867, 269; see also Henry 1870, v; "Colonization" 1886, 12; King 1888, 112).

H. M. Schieffelin (1808–90), from New York, was "a great friend and benefactor" of "Colonization, Missions, Liberia and humanity in general", as Blyden noted (Blyden 1891, 5). He became a Vice President of the American Colonization Society in 1851 and was elected to the New York State Colonization Society's Board of Managers in 1865. Significantly, he became Liberia's first Chargé d'Affaires to the United States in 1865 and held that post for ten years, spanning both of Anderson's journeys (Henry 1870, in chap. 5, 157; "Colonization" 1886, 12; King 1888, 112). His support for Liberia was diverse. He bolstered the image of Liberia by editing *The People of Africa* (Schieffelin [1871] 1974), which comprised a series of articles by Blyden and others on Islam and the interior regions of Liberia and Sierra Leone, and also edited the letter of Musadu's chief, Vafin Dole, to President Payne in 1868 (chap. 5, 231). He funded several projects in Liberia, including a soap factory, a coffee huller, a cotton gin, and a small steam mill (Henry 1870, chap. 5, 157; "Necrology" 1891, 3; Mahmud 1974, v). He paid the cost of surveying the Saint Paul River and the road to Careysburg to improve transportation and to increase business opportunities ("H. M. Schieffelin, Esq." 1867, 269). As the Colonization Society Vice President, Schieffelin sought to advance educational opportunities in Liberia, sponsoring individuals such as Blyden in school, giving money to Monrovia College, and granting the Liberian government three hundred dollars per year for schooling from 1874 ("Fifty-seventh Annual Report" 1874, 45; "Death of Henry M. Schieffelin, Esq." 1890, 126; Blyden 1891, 5). The New York Colonization Society, through Schieffelin's efforts, also paid for the survey of land near Arthington and the establishment of the Manual Labor Institute (*ATL* 1872, 11). Liberia named settlements after Schieffelin in his honor, both in Grand Cape Mount and along the Junk River ("H. M. Schieffelin Esq." 1867, 268; *A Brief History of Montserrado County* 1965, 125; see also "Our Liberia Letter" 1881, 78–79). For someone so interested in Africa, he nevertheless preferred to experience it through others. The American Colonization Society's obituary said that Schieffelin "never saw and never expected to see" Africa ("Necrology" 1891, 3), though Blyden wrote that he died in Egypt (Blyden 1891, 5).

Anderson could not convince any other "American," as he put it, to travel with him. He complained that he failed in "every effort" to find "another civilized person" to accompany him, because "the undertaking was considered of too dangerous a character" (chap. 5, 163). The experience of Seymour and Ash would have contributed to this sense of danger. Furthermore, Americo-Liberians had acquired a dubious reputation in their trade dealings with interior peoples. Yet Anderson had had some experience of travel, having accompanied the militia force to Sinoe, Cape Palmas, and Maryland.

Anderson headed for Musadu on 14 February 1868, under the presidency of the newly elected James S. Payne of the Republican Party. He spent his first four months traveling between Vannswa, Bessa's town, and Bopolu, trying to overcome attempts by the Gola, the Manding, and his own carriers to stop him from going farther into the interior and eventually reaching Musadu. Only in mid-June did he finally leave Bopolu and travel through Southern Kpelle territory and beyond. He then traversed Belle land during the first week of July and spent the next three months inching his way through Domar Loma terrain. Anderson reached Waima Loma areas in early November and ascended to "Mandingo country" one month later. The Liberian explorer finally walked into Musadu on 7 December 1868. Anderson described Musadu, the gold fields, the town's rich past, the "strangers" who came from Senegal, and the impressive military review that King Vomfeedolla, or Vafin Dole, staged for him. Dole prepared a letter in Arabic explaining the problems that the powerful Chief Ibrahima Sissi had been giving his town, and he asked Anderson to deliver the letter to the Liberian government when he returned to Monrovia. Anderson, or *Musadu tibabu fin* (the black European of Musadu) as he was known in Musadu (Delafosse 1903), departed for Monrovia fourteen days later on 25 December. He wound his way back home along nearly the same route that he took to reach the Mandingo capital. He arrived in Monrovia on 25 March 1869 after spending a curious month-long sojourn in the Bopolu area at the end of his journey and was given a hero's welcome.

Schieffelin published Anderson's 1868–69 travel account through the Smithsonian Institution in 1870 (chap. 5).[32] Schieffelin sent Anderson four hundred copies of the book. Anderson gave most of them away as gifts and sold a few. Blyden noted that the President of the Royal Geographical Society of London placed Anderson's book alongside the works of Africa's other great explorers: Heinrich Barth, David Livingstone, and Alexander Gordon Laing (see Blyden to J. C. Braman, 10 October 1881, in Lynch 1978, 300). This claim is borne out by the *Journal of the Royal Geographical Society,* which stated that "The President" of the society, Sir Roderick I. Murchison, gave a copy of "G. F. [*sic*] Anderson's" *Journey to Musadu* to the library sometime between the date that the book was published in the early weeks of 1870 and May 27 of the same year ("Accessions to the Library" 1870, xciii). This is the only reference that the Royal Geographical Society made to Anderson's trips. Anderson's 1868–69 journey was overshadowed by David Livingstone's travels in the Lake Tanganyika area and his efforts to find the source of the Nile and trace the tributaries of the Congo River (Murchison 1870, clxxv–clxxvii).

Commentators nevertheless declared this trip a great success because

Anderson reached Musadu, gained much geographical knowledge, learned about the sources of gold, and allegedly persuaded Musadu's chief to sign a treaty which ceded the area to Liberia (see, e.g., Johnston [1906] 1969, 250–254; Karnga 1909, 32). Yet as we shall see, these writers seem to have overemphasized the importance of gold and contrived the issue about Musadu's chief signing a treaty. According to Seymour's legislation of 1857, the Liberian government empowered commissioned travelers to make treaties to purchase land. The first appearance of territorial claims made during exploration is marked on Anderson's 1879 map of Liberia (fig. 27) as having been acquired by treaty in 1868–69. These territories consisted of regions which Bopolu's leaders seem to have considered under their control and were presumably negotiated during Anderson's first journey—although they possibly related to Blyden's journey to Bopolu later in the same year.

Others have been less complimentary. Someone claimed that Anderson "grew fat on short allowances" during his sojourns to Musadu. Speaking of his 1868–69 trip, the writer continued: "After having successfully struggled with difficulties and overcome privations and inconveniences to which Stanley would have devoted a long and thrilling chapter, he returned to the coast not only safe and sound but ridiculously corpulent" ("Elephant Taming in Liberia" 1880, 86).

According to President Barclay's eulogy, Anderson "endeavored by public lectures and earnest appeals to interest our principle men in [an] effort to secure our territorial interests in the Mandingo Plateau" after he returned, "but without much avail" (Barclay 1911, 31). Yet President Payne reportedly established the Interior Department of Government in 1869 because of the information that Anderson brought back (Dunn and Holsoe 1985, 137).

When Benjamin Anderson reached Musadu in 1868, the "old men of the town" told him that "Musadu was only the ruins of a former prosperity" (chap. 5, 211). They blamed Blamer Sissa (Ibrahima Sissi), who "stripped Musadu of everything valuable, and even carried off nearly all the pretty young women" (chap. 5, 214). Just before Anderson headed back for Monrovia, Vafin Dole, the chief of Musadu, had a scribe write a letter to the Liberian government on his behalf, in which he detailed how Ibrahima Sissi "laid waste and destroyed all the treasures of the country" on three separate occasions earlier in the 1860s (chap. 5, 235). E. W. Blyden translated Dole's letter, written by Dole's scribe Mohammed Barta (Bility), after Anderson returned to Monrovia. Schieffelin published Dole's letter through the Smithsonian. Some copies of the pamphlet appeared separately (Barta 1870), and other copies were added as an appendix to Anderson's 1870 book. Schieffelin also published a copy of Dole's letter in the book that he himself published in 1871 (Schieffelin [1871] 1974, 129–136). We reproduce this letter as the appendix to the republication of Anderson's 1868–69 journey as Schieffelin originally intended (chap. 5).[33] It is the only known surviving document to be written by an African in this region of southeast Guinea before the twentieth century.[34] This letter, like the accounts of Sims and Seymour, was published shortly after the time that it was written but became "lost" in the intervening years, and has not, until now, effectively become part of the historical record.

William Spencer Anderson, 1870

In 1870, E. J. Roye was elected President of Liberia—after a contest in which race was a primary issue and in which a "mulatto aristocracy" was ousted from power. He had "scarcely been inaugurated before he resolved to explore a more direct road to Musadu" (Schieffelin [1871] 1974, 150). Seymour had attempted the "eastern" route, traveling from Bassa to Barlain and then north; Benjamin Anderson had attempted a "western" route, putting himself in the care of leaders from Bopolu and their interior Condo allies. The more-direct route was the "great Barlain road" along the southeast side of the Saint Paul, through the Southern Kpelle and Barlain to Pallarker (Kpayekwele), and then northward. President Roye commissioned William Spencer Anderson to pursue this direct route. Anderson had already made a substantial exploration trip in that direction.

W. S. Anderson had emigrated from Delaware to Monrovia in January 1853 at age twenty, a freeborn barber and member of the Protestant Episcopal Church ("List of Emigrants [*Linda Stewart*]" 1853, 26). Once in Liberia he had started a sugarcane plantation and had traveled even to Bopolu to seek laborers for his farm. He became, by one account, "the largest sugar and coffee grower in Liberia" (Dunn and Holsoe 1985, 17; see also Anderson 1866, 338–340; Schieffelin 1866; Johnson 1867b, 215; "Liberia" 1873, 43; Shick 1980, 112–114). He also became a member of the House of Representatives for the Whig Party in the late 1860s, and the Speaker of the House of Representatives during President Roye's administration. More details of his life and agricultural activities are given in Shick (1980, 112–114).

W. S. Anderson was charged to "open up the road" and to secure a permanent highway to the interior both by erecting stations at proper distances for protecting caravans and by purchasing territory and negotiating treaties. He was "supplied with goods for presents to the chiefs and to meet expenses" and also was "furnished with forty men well armed as a guard," (Schieffelin [1871] 1974, 150). Another source suggests only twenty-five guards and thirty-five baggage carriers. This was therefore another substantial journey and is only known through summaries ("Barline Country" 1870; "The Barline Country" 1870; Blyden 1870; "Hon. W. S. Anderson's Address" 1870; Crummell 1871, 14–15; "Eastward Empire Points the Way!" 1873).

Linked to the expedition, contracts were made to build fortified block-

Figure 5. The old blockhouse at Bandajuma, Sierra Leone. The building indicates the idea behind the blockhouse scheme. *Source: Alldridge,* The Sherbo and Its Hinterland *(London, 1901).*

houses at the stations. One was soon built about 30 miles to the northeast of Careysburg, on the banks of the Du River, "the first of the chain of the blockhouses, only serving as a resting place for the weary travelers to and from the interior, who are not too timid to venture with their caravans *in search of a market* for the sale of their oil, wood, rice, fowls, cloths, cattle, &c" ("Eastward Points the Way!" 1873, 332). Benjamin Anderson was Secretary of the Treasury at this time, and it was he, apparently, who persuaded the government to start building ten blockhouses in 25- to 30-mile intervals from Careysburg "to the Mandingo country." Benjamin Anderson stayed in the first blockhouse when he set out for Musadu in 1874 (chap. 6, 244; Seys 1870; see also Sabin 1974, 187; Dunn and Holsoe 1985, 150; d'Azevedo 1995, 65).

Although several commentators have suggested that the Liberian government did not follow up on the cordial relations that Benjamin Anderson had established with Musadu, it seems likely that W. S. Anderson's journey in 1870 was just such an attempt. Indeed it was an ambitious one, with all the trappings of state, conducted by a Commissioner who combined exploration ability with political eminence (Schieffelin [1871] 1974, 150).

W. S. Anderson departed when the legislature recessed in 1870. The trip lasted from about May to August. The stories that Anderson told about Kpayekwele's stone wall, agriculture, trade, industry, and music captivated his audiences and reinforced images about the prospects of trade with the interior that Benjamin Anderson brought back the previous year.

But for reasons unknown, W. S. Anderson only reached Kpayekwele. Anderson wanted to go to Musadu, "the country of our first explorer," but claimed that "means are exhausted" ("Eastward Empire Points the Way!" 1873, 332).[35] It is probable that the reasons were linked to interior warfare and to the concerns of interior peoples (such as those of Bopolu) of being bypassed in interior trade relations (see chap. 3). Yet ill health, lack of resources, or Liberian politics back in Monrovia may also have led to the journey being called off. A copy of his journal does not seem to have survived, and there is no indication that this was published.[36] From the summaries of his trip, we glean the following.

He reached Kpayekwele, the capital of the Barlain country, which was eight days from Careysburg.[37] This was the walled town of Pallaka that James Sims and George Seymour had visited twelve years earlier, and that Benjamin Anderson visited four years later on his second journey to Musadu. It was itself four days from Musadu. He took the route to the left, or southeast, bank of the Saint Paul River, which was a convenient route to Musadu, free as it was "from the interference of the semi-civilized Muslims."[38] He traveled through Queah and Southern Kpelle countries via Beah Twi, Karpestown, Wah Gie Place, Shillipah, Nyiya, Woomah, Powle, and Palingah before reaching Kpayekwele, which he called Pallarker.[39] The town was very "old, parallelogram in shape, and enclosed by a wall built of stone and clay, six feet thick and eighteen feet high, surmounted over the gates by watch-towers, where guards are regularly stationed. It has never been taken" (Blyden 1870, 282–283). One of W. S. Anderson's companions was Allen Hooper, a coffee grower. He was so "entranced by the visions that met his gaze" that he stayed two years at Pok-bah town and planted considerable coffee to encourage the natives to grow coffee ("Eastward Empire Points the Way!" 1873, 333).[40] Whether Anderson himself passed this village is not certain.

Advertising the town and region for missionary and immigrant settlement, the reports of his journey describe the country as populous, wealthy, friendly, hospitable, and healthy—drier and freer from "miasmatic influence" than the coast. Moreover, W. S. Anderson is quoted as saying that that the "Pessa and Kpelle are pagan, no Mussulmans, not even a priest, in any of the large towns, quite an unusual thing for this part of Africa," making it "more susceptible to religious and intellectual culture than our Coast tribes."[41]

According to W. S. Anderson, the inhabitants are tremendous cultivators, "planting even on the tops of mountains." Rice and corn are grown, and "Palaka country alone produces corn enough to supply the demands of the entire Republic of Liberia." The valuable camwood forest begins "six days' walk from Careysburg, N.E. by E., and extends with slight intervals to a great distance beyond Palaka." Palm trees abound in certain sections, and everywhere plants are "well watered and extensively cultivated." People "make their tobacco-pipes, earthen ware, knives, hoes, and every other agricultural implement. Musical instruments are made from elephant tusks, and their mats of the stalks of a plant that grows in the swamps. They have fine cattle, sheep, goats, and fowls in abundance. The forests abound in quite a variety of game" ("The Barline Country" 1970, 317). Anderson also reportedly said that "The markets are supplied with every variety of exchangeable commodity desirable, and attended by thousands from all parts of the surrounding country" ("The First of August Demonstration at Clay-Ashland" 1870, 341). "Rice is cheap, at six cents a bushel. Those in Palaka are broadly self sufficient but buy country cloth and salt from the Boson people" ("The Barline Country" 1970, 317).[42]

W. S. Anderson was said to have entered into treaty stipulations with Pallaka, signed by the chief and headmen.[43] In one description, it is said that "he secured by purchase and treaty stipulations to our government an area of about two hundred and fifty miles, no less than one hundred and fifty thousand inhabitants." According to Svend Holsoe, Anderson "brought back several treaties with local rulers who agreed to facilitate trade through their region to the coast" (Dunn and Holsoe 1985, 17). He also left a Liberian flag flying from Pallaka's walls. The people of Pallaka were "anxious to enter into relations with Liberia": they presented him with too many presents of bullocks, ivory, cloth, and so forth to carry, and the chief entrusted Anderson with his son to be educated in Monrovia and was keen to have schools established in his country. When Anderson returned, he took the same route, giving assurances that Liberians would return.

After his return, Anderson visited London to help negotiate the infamous financial loan agreement of 1871. He was arrested when he returned to Monrovia. In 1872, a wealthy planter named Jesse Sharp killed Anderson as he emerged from a courthouse. The court had decided a case in Anderson's favor, and Sharp shot Anderson because he was "so dissatisfied with the decision" (Dunn and Holsoe 1985, 17; see also "Affairs in Liberia" 1871, 252; "The English Loan" 1872, 137; "Interior Roads" 1873, 335). Anderson died on 27 September 1872 ("West Africa" 1872). Blyden attributed the murder to more sectarian motives: as a black, Anderson fared badly following the mulatto coup d'etat of Roye in 1871 (see Blyden to William Coppinger, 19 October 1874, in Lynch 1978, 177; Blyden to John C. Lowrie, 9 May 1876, in Lynch 1978, 205; Blyden to William Coppinger, 3 September 1877, in Lynch 1978, 259).

Benjamin Anderson's Second Journey to Musadu, 1874

After his 1868 journey, Benjamin Anderson lobbied for a more systematic policy toward the interior. In January 1870, President Roye of the emerging True Whig Party appointed Benjamin Anderson to be his Secretary of Treasury (Seys 1870; see also Sabin 1974, 187; Dunn and Holsoe 1985, 150; d'Azevedo 1995, 65). Four months later, Anderson persuaded the government to start building blockhouses in 25- to 30-mile-intervals from Careysburg "to the Mandingo country" (see chap. 6). Then Roye "dismissed" Anderson in November for reasons that are presently not entirely clear.[44] From mid-November 1871 to April 1872, Anderson's friend Blyden tried and failed to get Sierra Leone's Governor, Arthur Kennedy, to allow Anderson to use Freetown as a base from which to find the sources of the Niger River (Lynch 1967, 89; Fisher 1971, iii). Interior exploration was becoming increasingly popular in the region. Eventually Blyden—who had sought asylum in Sierra Leone—journeyed to Falaba and to Timbu on behalf of Sierra Leone in 1872 and 1873 (Blyden to J. Pope Hennessy, "Report of the Expedition to Falaba," January–March 1872, 26 March 1872, in Lynch 1978, 101–109; Blyden to Alexander Bravo, "Report of the Expedition to Timbo," January–March 1873, 10 March 1873, in Lynch 1978, 117–139). Anderson was reported to be contemplating a tour into the interior in 1872 ("Personal" 1872, 311). Again, in October (1873), another notice was posted which stated that Anderson would "probably be sent upon another tour of exploration by the Government" ("Progress in Liberia" 1873, 311).

These attempts to follow up links with the interior might well be connected with the idea of building a railroad from Monrovia through the Kong Mountains to the Niger River and even to Cairo, which began to be discussed after Anderson returned from Musadu in 1869 ("Railroads in Liberia" 1869, 209; T. 1871, 7; "Roads to the Interior" 1873, 217; Haven 1877, 110; Allen 1878, 71; Lynch 1967, 146–147). Anderson's reports of gold also stimulated the establishment of the Mining Company of Liberia (Schulze 1973, 146).

In late 1873, the legislature granted a concession to two English engineers from London to construct "Railroads and Tramways . . . throughout Liberia," but the men did not pursue the matter ("Propositions to the Republic of Liberia for Concessions of Lands" 1874). These engineers were most probably linked to Robert Arthington (1823–1900), a Baptist living in Leeds, England. He had inherited two hundred thousand pounds from his father in 1864 and invested it in British and American railways, building a huge fortune.[45] He had written in October 1871 that he would fund a journey "to make a thorough survey of the country between the northern border of Liberia and the Niger—Joliba—as early as possible," and that he was ready to contribute two hundred pounds (one thousand dollars U.S. at the time) for this ("Exploration" 1872, 46–47). In 1873, Arthington restated his aim but this time wrote off Liberians as incapable of authentic exploration:

> I am very desirous to advance the travel and traffic line by direct communication between Liberia and the Niger, (or Joliba). . . . I want a survey of the ground between the Liberia and the Niger to be made, which shall stand for all time, and be accepted as satisfactory by America and England. I do not, therefore, think that it would be prudent to intrust the matter chiefly to a Liberian, though he may be skillful in surveying, &c., or if that be needed, in taking observations for astronomical geography. (Arthington 1873, 255; see also Blyden 1873, 373–376)

We can presume here that Arthington rejected the ceding of control to Anderson, believing that only a white expedition leader would be satisfactory. Whether Africans or African Americans could explore Africa was, clearly, an open question in certain circles. It is conceivable that an Englishman did travel to Musadu in connection with this. According to G. A. Crüwell, who visited Liberia in 1874, "a young Englishman went up to Musardo without an armed escort and returned to Monrovia, all in three weeks, not very long ago. But he could not have seen much of the country at the rate he is to have, and must have, traveled" (Crüwell 1878, 44).[46] No records relate to this.

Anderson's personal and political life remained busy. In 1871, Anderson got married for a second time, this time to forty-one-year-old Josephine Amelia Tredwell.[47] In July 1872, Anderson became one of six persons who vied for the Republican nomination of a seat that opened in the House of Representatives ("Affairs in Liberia" 1872, 309). S. J. Campbell won the election, and Anderson was decidedly defeated. He received only thirty-two votes, or about 6 percent of the five hundred twenty votes that were cast ("Election" 1873, 22). It is not clear if Anderson simply allowed his name to be put forth for nomination, or if he actively sought the position.

On 4 February 1874, the Liberian legislature passed the 1874 interior law which again provided financing for and set more systematic goals for further and comprehensive exploration (*ATL* 1874, 6–10).[48] The law, again, speaks for itself:

> Whereas it is of the highest importance that the most friendly relations be stabished [*sic*] between the Republic of Liberia and the native Chieftains in the interior of the Republic of Liberia proper, as far back as two hundred miles at least from the sea-board;—and whereas the making of Treaties of alliance by the said Chieftains with this Government would be the most certain means of establishing and securing their friendship, together with the opening of free and uninterrupted [p. 7] trade, as well as to protect the highways;—and whereas Deeds of cession and Treaties of alliance formerly executed to the Republic of Liberia by said native Chieftains, would secure the double effect of strengthening friendship as well as extend the interior bound-

ary of this Republic;[49]—and whereas the appointment by this Government of discreet and proper persons to be termed Commissioners to the Interior would secure these desirable objects;—and whereas the expense of carrying out this measure would be trivial when compared with the benefits which would accrue to the Government and its citizens, as the Government would gain prestige, territory and pecuniary benefits; Therefore,

It is resolved by the Senate and House of Representatives of the Republic of Liberia in Legislature assembled:—

Sec. 1st. That four discreet persons be appointed by the President to be termed special Commissioners to the Interior, and in addition thereto, four other persons shall be appointed in like manner to be termed Assistants to the said Commissioners to the Interior, all of whom are to be appointed as follows, viz;—one Commissioner and one Assistant for Montserrado County, and one Commissioner and one Assistant for each of the leeward Counties. viz.:—Bassa, Sinoe and Maryland;[50] and each Commissioner shall be furnished by Government with six baggage carriers together with such other outfits as the nature of their mission may demand; whereupon, they, the said Commissioners, shall go into the interior immediately in the rear of their respective Counties, pursuing a course that will lead directly interiorwards. And as soon as the interior boundary of this Republic is reached, and at that point or distance in coming in contact with the natives, the said Commissioners shall then and there commence to communicate, express and state in the most clear and positive manner, the object of their visit and mission to the section of country which they may be in, and shall continue to go interiorward, making Treaties, and making known to the Chieftains or Chiefs the object of their mission, and the object of the Government in sending them in the interior, until they shall have gone not less than Two hundred miles, and as far beyond that as practicable interiorward from the boundary line, which shall be to this effect, to wit:—Division first; that the Government of the Republic of Liberia is desirous to open and keep open the highways leading from the interior to the frontier, without interruption by any person or persons, clan or tribe whomsoever, and so to be kept open—which influence the Government desires to extend the entire distance to [p. 8] which the said Commissioners may go. And they the said Commissioners are hereby positively directed to state to the Chiefs and natives generally with whom they may come in contact, and shall then and there state to them the kind of produce and commodities which are or may be most desirable in the Liberian market, as follows, viz:—Palm oil, Camwood, Ivory, Raw-cotton, Gum, Benny-seeds, Dried-pepper in quantities, Dried-Coffee in the hull, Cattle, Gold, Hides and skins of every description, Rice, Ground-nuts, together with all such other articles that may be pressed into general use. And to this end, they the said Commissioners shall agree and stipulate with the said Chiefs of Chieftains ruling and district or territory as aforesaid, that the Liberian Government will agree or stipulate on its part to pay or cause to be paid to any Chief or Chieftains so ruling districts or territories as aforesaid, who will or may agree on their part to keep open and protect the highways so leading to the frontier as aforesaid, an annual stipend to the amount of Fifty dollars (50,00) one half of which amount shall be paid in advance by the Government through the said Commissioners. And further, it shall be, and it is hereby made the duty of Commissioners to present the Liberian flag to each Chief so agreeing and stipulating with this Government.—Division second;—And they, the said Commissioners, shall be, and they are hereby positively required to use their best endeavors to make and ratify peace between any Chief or Tribe who may be in a belligerent attitude towards the other, and whenever it appears practicable that peace can be made, the said Chief shall be required to ratify the same in strict accordance with their own customs.

Sec. 2nd. And it shall be, and it is hereby made the duty of the said Commissioners to propose to any Chief or Chieftain, residing beyond the internal boundary of this Republic, the privilege of becoming allies to this Republic; and further, that the said Chiefs or Chieftains may have the privilege of executing deeds of cession, ceding their territory to the Republic of Liberia, which deeds of cession shall be drawn, worded and constructed on the common law principle; and shall in every case contain a clause to read in these words: "that said Chief for himself and his successors in office, do covenant, promises and agree that the territory or section of country now ceded to the Republic of Liberia, shall never be alienated, sold or transferred to any person or persons, nor to any other nation or government whomsoever,"—and further, the boundaries and extent shall be named and described as nearly as possible, all of which shall be managed, done and effected by said Commissioners in a most [p. 9] careful and proper manner,—and copies of the said Treaties of alliance and Deeds of cession shall be by said Commissioners properly and speedily forwarded and returned to the State Department to be filed in the archives.

Sec. 3rd. The Commissioners shall also devote themselves in a measure to such matters as refer to the physical nature and condition of the country through which they may pass, by noticing and noting the degrees of temperature as indicated by the thermometer, as well as to make close observation of rivers, lakes, mountains, prairies, etc, all of which shall be made a matter of report.

Sec. 4th. And it is further resolved, that the said four Commissioners with their Assistants shall continue in service for the term of one calendar year from the date of their commission, for which calendar year's service, the said four Commissioners shall receive a salary of Five hundred dollars ($500,00) each; and the said four Assistants shall receive a salary of Three hundred dollars ($300,00) each; and further, there shall be allowed for the purposes above stated, a contingent sum of Two thousand dollars ($2000,00) making for this object a sum total of Five thousand eight hundred dollars ($5800,00)—That the said Commissioners for Montserrado County shall be sworn by the President and the other Commissioners shall be sworn by the Superintendents of their respective Counties from which they may be sent.[51]

Sec. 5th. It is further resolved, that the above named Commissioners shall lay before the different Chiefs with which they have succeeded in making

Treaties, the great necessity of the education of their children, and to get them [each town or tribe, wherever they may have entered into treaty stipulations,] to agree, if possible to pay one-fourth of the Teacher's salary, assuring them that the Liberian Government will furnish Teachers and pay them three-fourths of their respective salaries, which salary shall not exceed Three hundred dollars [$300,00] per annum.

Sec. 6th. On the return of the Commissioners from the interior, the President is hereby authorized and required to appoint suitable persons to reside in the influential towns as Agents of the Government, to guide and stimulate, with the consent and co-operations of the Chiefs, the industry of the people; to instruct them in the elementary branches of an English education, and also to assist in settling all difficulties of a legal nature; and the said Agents or Teachers are required to keep a correct diary, and to make quarterly reports to the President or to the Superintendents of different Counties of their doings as Agents and Teachers of said Government.

Sec. 7th. And it is further resolved, that the President shall invite from the interior routes opened, and from the different districts of the Coast, one or two of the leading Chiefs [two from each County] to be present each year at the meeting of the Legislature, to sit in each branch as referees and advisors on all matters effecting or appertaining to the particular locality to which said Chief belong, and the expense of said Chief, so invited shall be borne by the Government.[52]

Sec. 8th. And is further resolved; that a copy of this Resolution, shall be circulated as far as possible among the Natives within our jurisdiction.

The President is authorized to draw out of the Public Treasury all amounts necessary for carrying out the provisions of this Resolution.

Any law to the contrary notwithstanding.

Approved, Feby. 4, 1874.

Anderson's second trip to the interior was directly linked to this act. President Gardner commissioned Benjamin Anderson to be the Chief Commissioner of Montserrado County according to the provisions of the 1874 interior law, although by the time he left, J. J. Roberts was once again president. The Liberian government paid the expenses of his journey and eventually included an additional three hundred dollars to reimburse him for personal monies that he spent (see chap. 6).

Anderson also certainly had some private financial interest in this expedition. This is confirmed in the text when Anderson was forced to use his own goods as presents. Some have claimed that Anderson's main reason for going to Musadu in 1874 was to find gold (Johnston [1906] 1969, 490; Karnga 1909, 32; Cassell 1970, 286). Someone even claimed that "the Colonization Society" had planned to "build a city" at the mines of "Bila," or Beyla, scarcely 6 miles (10 kilometers) from Musadu ("Discouraging Features" 1921). It is also possible that American and British commercial interests had their eyes on the interior gold fields.

In contrast with Anderson's first journey, but in keeping with the journey of W. S. Anderson, the 1874 trip was a larger affair. Benjamin Anderson credited James B. Dennis of Careysburg with encouraging as many people as possible to accompany him. As commissioner, Anderson traveled with an Assistant Commissioner (Capehart) and eight other "Americans," as well as five "Congoes" and a Gola. However, only one "Congo" and two "Americans" completed the journey.

Anderson had planned to leave for Musadu at the beginning of the dry season in late 1873. The interior law, however, was not enacted until 4 February 1874, and fighting was reported in the Bopolu area at the time following the death of its chief, Momolu Sao, in 1871. A different route had to be envisaged. Anderson set out on 6 May 1874, once he had been commissioned and once hostilities had subsided ("West African Exploration" 1873, 346; "Progress in Liberia" 1873, 312). He took a more southern route to Musadu this time, following the route that W. S. Anderson took.[53] He bypassed Bopolu and Condo interests, heading directly into Southern Kpelle, south of the Saint Paul River. Anderson tried to resolve several wars that the Southern Kpelle were fighting and got some of these chiefs to sign treaties which reportedly ceded their land to Liberia. He then crossed into Barlain (Gbalein) Kpelle territory. Five months later he reached the Waima Loma. Anderson's pace increased from this point on, and he arrived in Musadu on 7 November 1874. He stayed for only ten days and departed on the 16th. Even though Chief Dole chided Anderson because the Liberian government failed to respond to his first letter, Dole and the people of Musadu graciously hosted Anderson and his contingent. The people of Musadu explained how a young warrior named Sargee (Saji Kamara) had besieged Musadu the previous dry season, and how Ibrahima Sissi—their former nemesis—rescued them. Anderson had frequent contacts with Sissi's military representative, who commanded a force to protect the region. Anderson gave away five new Arabic Bibles and presented a Liberian flag to Vafin Dole. Then he made a much quicker journey back to Monrovia and arrived in just over one month, on 18 December.

Anderson gave the Liberian government a manuscript copy of his report after he returned to Monrovia. Anderson later wrote that the members of the government "gave themselves no further trouble about it" because it was "absorbed . . . in our little pigheaded politics" (Anderson 1903b, 7). The government did not establish any more contacts with Musadu or publish Anderson's journal, map, meteorological, or astronomical calculations, or longitude and latitude tables.

Because Anderson's 1874 trip was not expeditiously published in book form, Anderson's 1868–69 journey became the best known.[54] Several authors thereafter failed to mention Anderson's 1874 expedition.[55] Anderson gave public lectures about his journey in Monrovia. In attendance at one meeting was an "English gentleman," James Irvine, who was so impressed that he aimed to have Anderson's "Report" read before the British Association at Glasgow in 1876 (see Blyden to John C. Lowrie, 4 September 1876, in Lynch 1978, 228).[56] Yet the journey received no international publicity.

Anderson appears to have suffered personal financial loss on this journey, which the government saw fit to compensate. On 22 February 1875, the Liberian legislature voted to give Anderson three hundred dollars "in addition to the salary allowed him by law. . . . [He] was deserted by his regular carriers, together with the Assistant Commissioner [Capehart], and much of the Government's means being lost in consequence, and he [Anderson] the said Chief Commissioner [was] obliged to make use of his own money for Government service" ("Resolution for the Relief of Benjamin Anderson" 1875, 33).

Later commentators said that Anderson's 1874 journey was a failure because he did not reach the gold mines that he discussed in his first narrative, and because he did little to advance the geographic knowledge of the region. They did concede, however, that Anderson helped advance Liberia's "political influence" (see, e.g., Johnston [1906] 1969, 490; Karnga 1909, 32; Cassell 1970, 286). Some were disappointed that Anderson did not travel farther into the interior to search for Musadu's source of gold. Their motivation—whether political or not—is not clear. When President Gardner opened the legislature in December 1879, he noted that Ibrahima Sissi's Medina had "Gold in great abundance," and that "Anderson for some reason unknown to him declined the invitation" to go to Medina (Gardner 1879).

The main goals of Anderson's second mission were, however, to establish trade links with Musadu and other towns along the way, and to try to persuade the towns' leaders to cede their lands to Liberia. He failed on the second objective in part, as no contemporary information has surfaced which suggests that Musadu signed a treaty. In 1879, when the Liberian newspaper, the *Observer* (Monrovia), was publishing the 1874 journey, it also carried an article that outlined the treaties that Anderson signed with chiefs in the interior in 1874 which follows in the next paragraph ("Official Notice" 1879).

TREATIES
ADDENDUM
OFFICIAL NOTICE.

DEPARTMENT OF STATE,
Monrovia, Sept. 5th, 1879.

For the information of our citizens and others whom it may concern; notice is hereby given that the following Districts were formally ceded to the

Republic of Liberia, in 1874 by the Kings and Chiefs holding dominion over the same.

Beahway and Nyawora Countries King Dogbar. Chief Town 64 miles from Monrovia. Bearing N. 55 deg. E. Lat. 6 deg. 59 min.[57]
King Pockpar's district, Interior Pessy Country. Chief Town 81 miles from Monrovia. Bearing N. 64 deg. E. Lat. N. 6 deg. 58 min.[58]
King Kryneseh's district, Pessy Country. Chief Town PAH-YE 123 miles from Monrovia. Bearing N, 36 deg. E. Lat. N. 7 deg. 58 min.[59]
King Dorviluyah's district, Nymar Boozie country. Chief Town Gubbewallah 135 miles from Monrovia.[60] Bearing N. 8 deg. E. Lat. N. 38. deg. 9 min.
King Bopowa Keang's district, Ya Poroh Country. Chief Town SAKATAH 156 miles from Monrovia. Bearing N. 62 deg. E. Lat. 7 deg. 32 min.[61]
King Bamarquella's district, Nyarly Country. Chief Town PYE 175 miles from Monrovia. Bearing N. 64 deg. E. Lat. 7 deg. 33 min.[62]

Whether this article reports accurately is open to some dispute. The case of King Dowilnyah (Dorviluyah) of the Waima Loma exemplifies the problem. Dowilnyah signed his treaty in Gubbewallah on 20 November when Anderson passed back through the town on his way home. A copy of this particular treaty is in the Svend E. Holsoe Collection at Indiana University. Yet claims that Dowilnyah "formally ceded" his land "to the Republic of Liberia" are suspect. Holsoe writes: "According to the agreement, they [the Liberians and the Waima Loma] were to live in peace with each other and Dowilnyah would not hinder trade through this country" (1976–77, 5). It is possible that the incorrect interpretation of Dowilnyah's treaty report in the *Observer* (Monrovia) indicating cession of land might be applicable to some of the other agreements that the chiefs are said to have signed. Anderson would have tried to get the best arrangement possible from each chief, with the ultimate goal of land cession, but that did not happen in every case—at least in the situation with Dowilnyah. The 1879 map that Anderson published does not include the towns that Dowilnyah ruled as being in the area "ceded to Liberia in 1874 by treaty." These are indicated as independent, like Musadu (fig. 28). This designation is, however, given to the lands covered by the other treaties, perhaps indicating Anderson's honesty in drawing up the map. Such Domar and Waima Loma lands that had been "acquired by treaty" were done so in 1868–69, and—as we mentioned earlier—appear to have been acquired from Bopolu. No Waima Loma towns are marked in the Waima areas ceded to Liberia.

Holsoe's summary of the treaty with Dowilnyah is similar to Sir Harry Johnston's analysis about the treaties that he saw in Monrovia. Johnston wrote:

> Anderson made treaties with the chiefs by which they placed their countries within the limits of Liberia. These treaties, the originals of which, written, in

> Arabic, are still in the archives at Monrovia, do not seem to have been much more in intention than treaties of friendship. But as a result of them a somewhat eccentric hinterland boundary was fixed for Liberia. ([1906] 1969, 254; see also Karnga 1926, 43–44; Richardson 1959, 103)

It is possible, however, that Johnston was also basing his analysis on the treaty with Dowilnyah. According to a statement that Anderson allegedly made to the Secretary of State, only one Southern Kpelle chief ceded his land to Liberia. This seems likely, as a half a dozen chiefs in this area had been fighting for years, and some would have seen some sort of political link with Liberia to be to their advantage. King Dogbar reportedly ceded his land to Liberia sometime between 12 and 18 June or 10 and 14 December 1874, on Anderson's outward or return journey. This acquisition was noted in a secondhand report: "Captain Benjamin K. Anderson, Chief Commissioner for Montserrado County, has informed the Secretary of State of the acquisition of a fine territory in the Pessay country, the Chief and people incorporating themselves with the citizens of the Republic" ("Interior Annexation" 1875, 72).

Anderson wrote that the people of Musadu wanted to sign a military and economic agreement with Liberia. However, it is improbable that Vafin Dole signed a treaty. Anderson did not place Musadu in the territory that Liberia claimed in his 1879 map. Writers later claimed or implied that a treaty was signed which placed Musadu within the territorial limits of Liberia. These writers sometimes mixed the sequence of events and variously stated that this agreement occurred in 1868, 1874, or the late 1870s, when the Liberians had contacts with Ibrahima Sissi's envoy, as we document later in this chapter.[63]

The 1874 interior law required Anderson "to present the Liberian flag to each Chief so agreeing and stipulating with this Government" (*ATL* 1874, 8). A strict reading of this law implies that Anderson gave flags to every chief who signed a treaty. Anderson, however, apparently gave flags to chiefs who signed treaties of friendship that did not constitute cession of land. He not only gave a flag to Dowilnyah, but also to Vafin Dole in Musadu.

Anderson's Plans for a Third Interior Journey, 1879

Soon after his return in 1875, Anderson was diverted to Cape Palmas to fight in the Grebo war. On the battlefield, he "did effectual work" with the eighteen-pound cannon and was given the commission of Colonel of the Artillery. He also commanded the garrison at Harper, near Cape Palmas, for six months. While away, Anderson heard that his wife, Josephine, and "little daughter" had died. Some time later, Anderson married Eliza A. Pointer ("Brief Sketch" [1910]).[64]

Liberian plans for extending trade and political relations continued. Liberia's colonial economy had thrived during the 1850s and 1860s, when Liberia's leading shippers and plantation owners became wealthy as they received good prices for the palm oil, camwood, coffee, sugar, ivory, hides, cotton, and rice that they exported. The economy, however, had moved into recession as the prices for these goods dropped, and as European businessmen with new steamships undermined the Liberian sail ships. Liberia fell further into debt, and the government turned to the interior, especially to the promise of goldfields, for a solution (Sawyer 1992, 156–175).

In 1877, President Payne told the legislature that "block-houses and trading depots" should be built at regular intervals, but again the government did not pursue these objectives because of the lack of funding (Payne 1877, 7). As a key figure promoting interior trade, President Payne again made Anderson Secretary to the Treasury by June 1877 or earlier (see Blyden to John C. Lowrie, 12 July 1877, in Lynch 1978, 242).[65] Again, however, Anderson became involved in a scandal. On 21 December 1877, the House and Senate "suspended" him for failing to submit the annual report for his department in September. The House then impeached President Payne three days later and suspended him from office on 1 January 1878, six days before the True Whig Party candidate Anthony Gardner was sworn in as president. Vice President Charles Harmon became the acting president during those last days. The House of Representatives issued six articles of impeachment against Payne. The first article charged Payne with refusing to suspend Anderson from office because he knew that Anderson "had been guilty of misdemeanor and official misconduct in office" ("Papers in the Case of Impeachment" 1877). Payne denied all of the accusations, and eventually the High Court of Impeachment, the Senate, dropped all of the charges against the former president.

In his inaugural address on 7 January 1878, President Gardner recommended that Anderson make a third trip to Musadu "for trade and evangelism." Gardner extolled Musadu's "great mart of Cattle, Beni seed, Rice, Cotton, Country cloths, and Gold," and said that "Musardu will soon become a dependency of the Republic of Liberia" (1878). Yet the very next day, the House of Representatives "preferred Articles of Impeachment against Honorable B. J. K. Anderson (suspended) Secretary of the Liberian Treasury, for malfeasance in office and using the public funds without the authorization of law" ("Impeachment of Honorable B. J. K. Anderson" 1878, 3). One month later, the Senate found Anderson guilty on three counts and ordered the Department of Justice to "institute criminal proceedings against Mr. Anderson" ("Impeachment of the Ex-Secretary of the Treasury" 1878, 2–3). Whether this order was executed is unknown. One can note, however, that economic instability, political revenge for Payne's treatment of former President Roye, and the struggle between the Republican and the True Whig Parties may have had as much or more to do with these proceedings as anything that the individuals did in office (Sabin 1974, 213–215; Massing 1980, 93; Geysbeek 1999).

Interests in building a railway had continued. In January 1879, the Senate granted, at President Gardner's request, a concession to Henry Charles Criswick and Robert Burnell to construct "a Railway from the town of Monrovia to the town of Musardu in the Republic of Liberia" (*ATL* 1879, 9–10; see also Gardner 1878, 5–6; "The Railway Scheme" 1878; "The Musahdu Railway" 1879).

Yet other events in 1879 further heightened Liberian attention to the interior policy. This new focus was prompted by perceived threats that the French wanted to take Liberia. Peter Murdza provides a good overview of events. Liberia's representative in France, Leopold Carrance—an ardent supporter of Liberia—mistakenly gave the impression that France wanted to make Liberia a French protectorate. Murdza wrote that Carrance was attempting to stimulate official French interest in Liberian affairs from Paris. Not intending a French takeover, he nevertheless used terms such as "protectorate" in his proposals, and rumors spread in Liberia of French plans for annexation. American inquiries eventually absolved the French government of any wrongdoing, blaming Carrance for the misunderstandings, but this failed to dispel Liberian suspicions (1979, 166–167, 208 n. 14).

To counter the threat, the government probably encouraged the *Observer* (Monrovia) newspaper to start publishing Anderson's second "journey" to Musadu in thirteen installments, and the State Department published the treaties that Anderson made with various chiefs in the same newspaper in September.[66] The government also commissioned and published a revised version of the map that Anderson sketched in 1874—purposely including the land that Liberia had claimed since independence. Even in September 1876, Edward Blyden had lamented the fact that the Liberian government had not published the "valuable map" that Anderson made after he went to Musadu in 1874 and asked the Presbyterian Board of Foreign Missions to publish his map in their periodical, the *Foreign Missionary.* Anderson traced the routes that he took to reach Musadu on both of his journeys and indicated the key areas where the government had signed land treaties since 1847. Secretary of State G. W. Gibson verified the accuracy of Anderson's map on 3 October 1879.[67]

Serious planning on the railroad began in December 1879 when Anderson led two U.S. naval officers up the Saint Paul River to conduct a survey and map their results ("Survey for a Rail Road" 1880, 14; Lynch 1967, 146–147). Nothing, however, came of these plans, even as the British and French started to build railroads on either side of Liberia, in Sierra Leone and the

Ivory Coast. Neither private investors nor the Liberian government had the will or capital to build ("The Railway Scheme" 1879; Lynch 1967, 147; Murdza 1979, 236–237; Sawyer 1992, 171–172).[68]

By September 1879, Liberia's controversy with the French, at least at an upper diplomatic level, was over. Secretary of State Gibson's letter that Murdza cited, above, indicates that even though Gibson and the French were on good terms by early September, many Liberians still remained suspicious of the French. Yet Gibson's letter also provides some telling insights about Liberia's desire to colonize the hinterland with France's help.[69] Liberia sought to control the markets of the "rich interior country" and felt that its citizens—being of the same racial heritage of the indigenous Africans—would have a better chance of developing "sympathies" and common "interests" with their African relatives, whom they wanted to peacefully subdue. The Europeans, Gibson argued, wanted to conquer Africa by force. Any European nation, like France, that worked alongside the Liberians would accrue long-term benefits. On 2 September 1879, Gibson wrote to Carrance:

> Your views of a French Protectorate for Liberia are forceful and highly appreciated. . . . This matter is receiving increasing attention and consideration, especially in view of the fact that our government is now actively engaged in annexing large tracts of inland territory with the view of reaching as soon as possible the waters of the Niger, so as to turn the trade from that rich section of country into Liberia. Active negotiations are now in progress, and we have already annexed an extensive region of [the] country to the distance of nearly two hundred and fifty miles from the coast. This will add immensely to the value of our commerce [p.5], and afford a rich market for the French and the other foreign manufactures.
>
> It is in the power of the French government to aid us in acquiring and controlling this rich interior country, for which consideration special concessions would be made to her merchants and citizens that would prove profitable to France and beneficial to Liberia.
>
> There is no doubt that Liberia being composed of Africans, and with a little aid from France, [could] do more toward securing a permanent hold upon the interior [p. 6] trade of western Africa, than any foreign nation. What England, France, and Germany acquire expensive naval and military force to accomplish, we can effect by Race sympathies and Race interests. The European nation therefore that will come to the aid of Liberia in carrying out the measures above-named, will secure a lasting benefit in the African trade not found to be so valuable to the world. Upon this subject I hope to make your further communications hereafter. (Gibson to Carrance, 2 September 1879, in Frederick Starr Research Collection)

Revived interest in the interior was thus not only countering perceived French encroachments on territory that it "claimed," but was also showing Liberians' capability as intermediaries. Liberia began to pursue the contacts that Medina's Chief, Ibrahima Sissi, had made with Liberia and again sought to send Anderson and others to Medina to annex more land, to encourage the formation of the commercial "Liberia Interior Association," and to build a railroad from Monrovia to Musadu and beyond.

Thus during the last months of 1879, President Gardner was communicating with Ibrahima Sissi of Medina, the new power in the region of Musadu, in the hope of extending commercial, political, and religious ties to Medina, the political center which by then had assumed ascendancy over Musadu. Liberians had become aware of the power of Ibrahima Sissi following Anderson's first journey to Musadu in 1868–69 and from Vafin Dole's letter of 1868, which told how Sissi pillaged Musadu in the 1860s (see chap. 5). Although the residents of Musadu were seeking to distance themselves from Sissi when Anderson first went to Musadu in 1868, Musadu's townspeople made a U-turn and called Sissi to their aid five years later when a second interior warlord, Saji Kamara, laid siege to the town. When Anderson returned to Musadu in 1874, one of Sissi's commanders, Dah Cidee, was still in the vicinity to protect Musadu and the surrounding towns. Subsequently, Sissi had gained an even wider sphere of influence. But even as he did so, the new war leader, Samori Touré, was also building up an influence that would come to dominate regional politics in the late nineteenth century. In 1878, though, Sissi's army was still able to push through Samori's lines (Person 1970, 86–87).

Liberia, like Sierra Leone, was becoming more important to the interior wars, providing an export market for the gold, ivory, and other produce that helped financed the supply of arms and ammunition with which to fight. In August 1879, Ibrahima Sissi sent a delegate, his son Fomba, to Monrovia. The *Observer* (Monrovia) newspaper reported that Fomba Sissi's visit to Monrovia was "the most important domestic event of the year [1879]" ("Eighteen Hundred and Eighty" 1880).

Fomba met with President Gardner at the Executive Mansion on 13 August, along with the United States Minister to Liberia, John Smyth, whose dispatch is the only source concerning this meeting (Smyth 1879a). Fomba said that the chief of Medina desired to live in peace with the Liberians and to carry on trade with them instead of with the people of Sierra Leone. Trade with Monrovia was only a third of the distance and took a third of the time. He sought Liberian help to keep the roads open and to stop interference with three intermediary predatory chiefs, whether through conciliation or force. Fomba proposed that Liberia would benefit from the acquisition of gold, food, cattle, goats, and horses that abounded in Medina. He boasted an army of ten thousand horsemen and many more foot soldiers. Asked for his advice by the Liberian President, the U.S. Minister encouraged the formation of a treaty, which the President agreed with, asking Fomba Sissi to inform the king to accept the offer. He directed Minister Blyden to write a letter in Arabic to Ibrahima Sissi, proposing a treaty. Fomba Sissi agreed that a Liberian Commissioner should be sent to negotiate the treaty. He stipulated, however, after an unknown person's name was raised (probably Anderson's), that it would be necessary to send men who were sober, and who did not drink spirits. Such men talked "two ways," and "the King and his people talked one way" being Muslims—a people with a book who had sense. The U.S. Minister, in his dispatch, anticipated that such a treaty would make Liberia the conduit for trade beyond Musadu, in the heart of central Africa.

By September, Liberia was making plans "for the annexation of the interior kingdom of Medina," as detailed in the *Observer* (Monrovia), which interpreted Sissi as wanting some form of union with Liberia:

> Measures are on foot for the annexation of the interior kingdom of Medina, lying about three hundred miles to the North of Monrovia, to this Republic. This, together with the Bopora and Barline districts, will likely be organized into a county, having the privilege of electing and sending members to the Legislature in common with the other counties. The Medina-Bopora County will form the richest and most populous one in the state, having a population of about five hundred thousand souls. A large portion of the community have, and are acquainted with the Old Testament scriptures, in Arabic, and the Koran. They are temperate and chase people. Polygamy exists, but adultery and fornication are rarely known among them, so severe is the punishment inflicted for these offenses. Drunkness is unknown among the Mahommedans of this region. The annexation of this extensive section of Country to our present domain, will greatly enhance the importance of Liberian Commerce, and open a new outlet for the largely increasing quantities of European and American Manufactures that are pouring into our markets. It is proposed to keep the roads for the free transportation of trade between Monrovia and Medina; by the establishment of military and trading posts on the route, and thus draw in the immense traffic from that place, and more than a hundred miles beyond, this region is rich in gold, iron and other valuable mineral products, besides ivory, cattle, groundnuts and cotton, which latter is manufactured into the thousands of cloths that are annually brought down to the coast. What an opening is here offered for a railroad! It will yield an immense profit to any Capitalists who will penetrate with the steam car this virgin market of interior Liberia. The Government will make a liberal concession to any reliable company that will undertake this enterprise.
>
> The annexation of this Section of country is a matter in which every Liberian citizen should feel the deepest interest; and it is hoped that they will see the importance of coming forward to aid the government in carrying out this desirable measure. Not only Liberian citizens, but foreign mercantile firms transacting business in this country, should also aid in facilitating the accomplishment of this object, as they too will largely share in the pecuniary advantage therefrom.
>
> It will require about fifty thousand dollars for the first year, to meet the

> expense of establishing military posts on the road and of subsidizing the leading chiefs. After which the annual expense will be comparatively trifling, as the posts will soon become nearly self-supporting establishments.
>
> Not only will the accomplishment of this object greatly add to the population, wealth and political strength of the Republic, but will bring us in contact with the healthy interior where horses thrive in abundance, and cattle are innumerable. The Liberian Explorer, Hon. Benj. Anderson, visited the Musahdu country a few years ago on a government mission and saw, on one occasion, a company of fifteen hundred horsemen, which was only a portion of the cavalry under the command of the chief to whom he was sent.
>
> Here too will be presented a large and inviting field to Foreign Missionary Boards, who seem anxious to make advances interiorward, with the bible in their hands, with the view of aiding in the work of Africa's redemption.
>
> Liberia, the result of persevering Christian philanthropy through many years of toil and anxiety, on the part of the friends and supporters of the American Colonization Society, will then begin to be what her friends have long sought to make her—"the open door to Africa." ("Notes: Measures Are on Foot" 1897)[70]

Fomba left Monrovia on 7 October carrying the letter that Blyden wrote, which said that Gardner wanted to improve trade links between both realms and that he planned to send a "Messenger," or Commissioner, to "negotiate a treaty of Friendship, Peace and Union" (Smyth to Evarts, 18 November 1979, in U.S. Consulate Despatches 1863–1906). Supporters of Liberia in the United States and some Liberians misconstrued this to mean that Liberia may have annexed Medina, but the letter clearly stated that such a treaty would not be made until a commissioner was sent. Again, this letter comes to us via the U.S. Minister who resided in Liberia.

On 10 December 1879, President Gardner devoted a portion of his annual speech to the legislature to Medina (1879). He outlined the commercial and military advantages that Liberia would gain by forming an alliance with Medina and said that "Dr. Blyden, Dr. Priest and Hon. B. J. K. Anderson" were planning to go to Medina in January or February 1880, after Fomba returned to Monrovia. Gardner also hoped that a move toward Medina would strengthen himself and the True Whig Party. Internationally, Smyth told Gardner that the redirection of Medina's trade from Sierra Leone to Monrovia would be a clear victory over Great Britain, which was itself extending its influence past Sierra Leone.

Unfortunately, however, Fomba could not get back to his father in Medina and was forced to return to Monrovia a few weeks later, having been obstructed at Bopolu. Later, the *Observer* (Monrovia) noted that the path had become clear again and that Fomba was to return to Medina with large presents. The government planned to dispatch the proposed expedition "soon or the rains will be upon us and then the Government will have to forego this practicable and very desirable enterprise. May Heaven speed FOMBA'S steps!" The *Observer* published this notice on 22 January 1880 ("Notes: The Notable Fomba Sissy" 1880).

While the government evidently hoped to send them to Medina before the rainy season began in April, giving Fomba enough time to make a trip to Medina and back, this was not to be. The rains came. After the rains, in September 1880, Fomba returned to Monrovia again with what he said was a letter from Ibrahima. The Monrovians, however, began to distrust him ("Notes: Foumba Sissy" 1880). Moreover, the army of Samori Touré's expanding empire had started to pressure Ibrahima at the end of 1880 and defeated him in the early months of 1881. Samori spared Ibrahima's life but executed the leading men from Konya who had come to his defense—including Musadu's Chief Vafin Dole, whom Anderson had met in 1868 and 1874. Samori traveled north and destroyed Medina in April 1881 (Person 1968, 1:342–343).

During these events, Anderson had helped found and became a Director of the Liberian Interior Association, which was formed to promote "trade with the Interior. To suggest and provide methods of carriage and transportation. To promote . . . commercial, agricultural and political interests in the interior, and among the tribes of that section." The association offered to raise the fifty thousand dollars which had not been raised either by the Liberian government or by loan from the U.S. John Smyth, the United States representative to Liberia, recommended that the U.S. reject Liberia's request "of $50,000 for the establishment of military posts back to the kingdom of Musardu" because Liberia was already too far in debt and could even not meet its current obligations (Smyth 1879c, 2). The company proposed to sell ten thousand shares of stock at five dollars per share. It strived to develop private links to the interior because the government was not interested. Yet it was not until 3 October 1881 that Anderson joined the organization's officers for a meeting with President Gardner, where they formally presented the goals of the association to the government and "solicited the countenance of the Executive authorities" ("The Liberia Interior Association" 1881).[71] By then Sissi had fallen, along with Musadu and Medina, to Samori Touré, heralding a period of incessant war in the region.

One observer's thoughts concerning these fanciful ideas about Medina and investment in interior trade proved to be prophetic, for the government's plans to reach Medina faded away:

> There are a certain class of persons with more zeal than discretion who seem to delight in nothing so much as puffing Liberia. . . . We have friends who are struck with the fact that Liberia is to be a good commercial centre. They circulate such tales as the "Annexation of Medina" and tell about "Thousands of acres covered with gold and iron" (probably meteorite deposits); and ask the public to invest. . . . The result of this is that our credit is destroyed abroad while at home we live on stilts, constantly encouraged

to go beyond our means; because we hope in some of these wild schemes.[72]
("Liberia's Friends: 'Succumbed to Friendship?'" 1880)

Journeys to the interior became moribund. There is no record that any Americo-Liberians or westerners attempted to travel to Musadu or its vicinity before the close of the nineteenth century. Of course, the Manding and other Africans continued to travel between Liberia and Musadu.

Anderson's Later Life and the d'Ollone Controversy

Anderson continued his life as a teacher, surveyor (with his son, Benjamin John Knight Anderson Jr.), and expert on the interior, and again served as Secretary of the Interior in the 1880s.[73] In 1885, Anderson joined Commissioners H. W. Grimes and Edward Blyden in Freetown to complete negotiations on the quarter-century-old boundary dispute between Liberia and Sierra Leone. Before 1883, President Gardner had honored him as Knight Commander of the Order of African Redemption. This was the highest honor that Liberia's Chief executive could bestow ("Brief Sketch" [1910]).[74]

In 1903, Anderson was writing a trigonometry book when news erupted that the French explorer Captain Henri d'Ollone challenged the authenticity of his journeys in the French press. In 1901, Captain Henri d'Ollone of the French infantry published the findings of the "mission" that he and H. Hostains went on from 1898–1900. He claimed that Anderson "fabricated" his accounts based on the testimony of slaves who had come from the interior (1901, 257, 282). Some French supported d'Ollone's claims (e.g., see Franklin 1901, 525–526). D'Ollone's claims fueled French diplomats who wanted to renegotiate the 1892 treaty which set Liberia's boundary at Nionsamoridu—just 17 miles southwest of Musadu (Murdza 1979, 490). The controversy ignited when d'Ollone republished his claims in 1903 in the *Annales de Geographie* (1903). He argued that Anderson's map was an improbable series of zigzag lines with acute angles rather than the sinuous route of an explorer, and that Anderson mentioned only villages, not mountains, peoples, and watercourses. Mistakenly thinking that Anderson had traveled only once to Musadu, and knowing that he returned the way he came in 1868, d'Ollone ridiculed the two routes which appear on Anderson's maps. He found inconsistencies in Anderson's location of Zolu, not realizing that there were two. D'Ollone had not found natives who had heard of Anderson. American support and publication, he insinuated, was linked to the unofficial American protectorate's interest in extending its frontiers. D'Ollone continued:

> Add to all that, that Anderson, who many think to be an English person, or an American, is simply a black Liberian; that none of his brethren have ever dared adventure more than 10 km from the sea or navigable river, for fear of being eaten by the natives, aggressive cannibals; that he had only very

Figure 6. Captain d'Ollone, on the right.
Source: D'Ollone, De la Côte d'Ivoire au Soudan et à la Guinée *(Paris: Librairie Hachette, 1901).*

> ordinary education, little in relation the use of instruments that he would have had to carry to make the astronomical calculations and which he makes a lot of in his book. (1903, 140)

On 6 June, the *Bulletin du Comité de l'Afrique Française* published an editorial which supported d'Ollone's accusations in "L'hinterland du Liberia" (1903, 193–194). The French correspondent for the *West African Mail* in

Paris apparently read this and wrote an article two days later titled "French Claims to the Liberian Hinterland" (1903) that the *Mail* published on 8 June. He suggested that a "Liberian question" would soon arise, saying that it was "now a well-established fact that Anderson never accomplished his so-called travels," and that the French have, for the first time, methodically explored and scientifically mapped out regions which Liberia claimed but neither knew, ruled, nor influenced. The correspondent gave new precision concerning rivers, which "takes from Liberia almost the third of her territory and incorporates it within the Ivory Coast" (55).

For six months, the Liberian and Sierra Leonean press published several articles to refute d'Ollone's accusations. First, an anonymous reply, "A Gross Injustice?" (1903), appeared in the *Sierra Leone Weekly News* and in Liberian papers. It was probably written by Edward W. Blyden, who was living in Sierra Leone at the time (see Lynch 1967, 168–172). He writes that a misinformed Frenchman was hatching up a French claim over the Liberian hinterland in violation of the Franco-Liberian Treaty of 1892 and was robbing "the only African explorer of West Africa of whatever honor is due to him and his race."[75] He notes that Anderson's book was accepted by the Royal Geographical Society, shelved alongside the greats, by the Smithsonian Institution at Washington, and by the traveler Winwood Reade, who traveled into Liberia in 1870 and knew Anderson. Mr. Anderson, he defends, is a "pure Negro" Liberian citizen, and the only African recognized as a trustworthy geographer and cartographer who is still alive and can defend himself and his country (Reade 1873, 254).[76] French pretensions to the parts of Sierra Leone explored by Professor Blyden were, he notes, thwarted by evidence of printed documents and of living witnesses, and Liberia should appreciate and look after her hinterland.

Anderson, then sixty-eight, vigorously responded and provided new information about his journeys (Anderson 1903a). He presented an itinerary, meteorological tables of the 1874 survey, and astronomical observations which appear below (figs. 7 and 8), suggesting that the abstracts from the original manuscript journal of the expeditions of 1868 and 1874 speak for themselves and cannot be invented. He noted the existence of the letter written from the "King Vomfeedolla of Musahdu" to the Liberian government, "acceding to our mutual treaties and agreements," and of the large and inscribed Arabic bibles, the Liberian flags, and other gifts that he had left in Musadu.[77] And he wrote that he was well known under his nickname "Musahdu," that his 1874 journey was published in the *Observer*, and that "civilized" witnesses who accompanied him were still alive.[78] French claims were linked to territorial aims.[79]

The Paris correspondent defended himself, deflecting criticism onto d'Ollone's work, which Liberians did not know ("Our Paris Correspondent on the Dispute" 1903). He also pointed out that d'Ollone was unaware of

The Liberia Recorder.

THE LATITUDE OF MUSAHDU, MANDINGO COUNTRY.

Observations made with the Sextant, artificial horizon, and marine clock. At Musahdu Friday 11th of December, A. D. 1868; the sun's declination South 23° 04' 41" (considered invariable). The sun's correct central altitude 49° 45' 13" and 13° 18' 29": the elapsed time between the observation one hour exactly:

From 9 hr. 12 min. 00 s. to 10 hr. 12 min. 00 s.

Elapsed time a. m. 1 hr. co - dec. 10.° 88430
Declination S. 23° 04' 41" 10. 03617

(A) 6° 54' 08" cosec = 10. 92047 cos 9.09648 cosec. of declination cosec. 10.° 40743
½ sun's alt. 44 31 51 cosin = 9. 85307 cosec 10.15410 cosins of A = cosin 9. 99684
½ diff. alt. 5 13 22 sine = 8. 95915 sec 10.00187 B 23.° 13.' 00" Scosec = 10. 40427
C 32 42 17 sine = 9. 73263 cos 9.92504 cosin 9. 92504
Z sect. 10.07779 Z 33.16.43 N sine 9. 24228

E 10.03.43 N alt. sine 0

Barometer 27.80.
Thermometer 82°
Nautical Almanac for 1868 } Latitude North According to Bowditch 8° 27' 11" N alt. sine 9° 18732

Astronomical Calculations.

LATITUDE OF BONYA, PESSY COUNTRY.

Observations made with the sextant, artificial horizon, and marine clock at Bonya, Tuesday, August 25, A. D. 1874, the sun's declination (North) —10°44'47" North (considered invirable):—

Barometer 28.54
Thermometer 72°
Time by clock. Altitudes of sun's Lower Limb.

Preparation.

Sextant's index error
off †33' 30"
on — 30 40
2' 50" additive

1st set
hrs. m. s.
2 55 45 . . 89° 35' 00"
2 58 00 . . 88 38 40
3 01 00 . . 87 03 50*

Altitudes corrected

	1st observed altd.	2nd observed altd.
	87° 03' 30"	65° 53' 50"
Index error	2 50	2 50
	2)87 06 20	2)65 56 40
Double Reflexion	46 33 10	32 58 20
Parallax & Refraction	—0 54	—1 06
Sun's semi-diameter for nautical epherneris	†15 52	†15 52
True altitude of sun's center	43° 48' 08"	33° 13' 06"

2nd set
hrs. m. s.
3 32 45 . . 71° 52' 50"
3 30 30 . . 70 04 00
3 36 10 . . 68 49
3 41 50 . . 67 25
3 45 00 . . 65 53 50*

Difference of time hrs. m. s.
3 45
3 01
44m = 11°

CALCULATION.

90° — 43° 48' 08" = 46° 11' 52" = Z
90 — 33 13 06 = 56 46 54 = Z
90 — 10 44 47 = 79 15 13 = D
} Elapsed time 44m = 11° = a' : ½a' = 5° 30'

Cotg ½ a 5° 30' = 11.011602 sine = 8.° 981573
Cosine D 79 15' 13" = 9 270590 sine = 9. 992316

PSS 88° 58' 15" = tang 11.741012 sine = 8. 973889 = 5.° 24' 12" = ½ O
2

10.° 48. 24 = O

Z = 56.° 46' 54"
Z = 46. 11. 52
O = 10. 48. 24 sine colog 56.° 53' 35" = 0.0769 36
sine colog 0. 06 41 = 2.7112 87
2)113. 47 10 sine 10. 41 43 = 9 2685 45
sine 46. 05 11 = 9.8575 65
56.° 53' 35"
10 48 24 2)21.9143 27
46 05 11 83° 42' 07" tang ½ A 10.9571 63

hrs. m. s.
78.° 25' 59" = 5 13 44 log rising 4.90285
sine 46° 11' 52" 9.858377
sine 79 15 13 9.992316
56695 = log 4.753543
838139 = nat cosine 33° 03' 21"
nat sine of 1405089 = 8° 04' 36"

56 53 35
46 11 52 167 24 14 = ZSS'
88 58 15 = PSS'
10 41 43 78 25 59 = ZSP
} D — Z = 79° 15' 13"
46 11 52
56 53 35
56 46 54 83 81 39 = natural cosine 33 03 21
06 41"

Latitude North 8° 04' 36" of the town of Bonya.

The Latitude of Monrovia 6° 18' 30" N. Longitude of Monrovia 10° 48' 30" W.
" " Musahdu 8° 27' 11" N. " " Musahdu 8° 24' 30" W.
From Monrovia to Musahdu, course North 47° 45' 30" East. Distance 191 and eight-tenths nautical miles.
The figures for the longitude of Musahdu are calculated by the method of lunar distances and are too numerous and complicated to be inserted here.—†Means plus.

Figure 7. "The Latitude of Musahdu" and "Astronomical Calculations" by Benjamin Anderson. *Published in the* Liberia Recorder *29 August 1903.*

12 The Liberia Recorder.

An Itinerary Table of the Exploration or Journey from Musahdu to Monrovia, made in 1874.

PLACES.	DATE AND WALKING HOURS.		ESTIMATED DISTANCE.	
From Musahdu to Vukkah	November	Tuesday 17th, walking from 7 a.m. to 6 p.m.	one day	30 miles
" Vukkah to Pellawarrah	"	Wednesday 18th, walking from 7 a.m. to 4 p.m.	one day	25 miles
" Pellawarrah to Gubbawalla	"	Thursday 19th, walking from 8 a.m. to 2:30 p.m.	one-half day	15 "
" Gubbawallah to Pynyah	"	Saturday 21st, walking from 7:30 a.m. to 5 p.m.	one day	25 "
" Pynyah to Tormu	"	Monday 23rd, walking from 6 a.m. to 4 p.m.	one day	30 "
" Tormu to Pahya	"	Tuesday 24th, walking from 6 a. m. to 2 p.m.	one-half day	15 "
" Pahya to Tolu	"	Monday 30th, walking from 8 a. m. to 4 p.m.	one-half day	15 "
" Tolu to Pattahya	December	Tuesday 1st, walking from 7 a.m. to 3 p.m.	one-half day	20 "
" Pattahya to Pallahkah	"	Wednesday 2nd, walking from 6 a.m. to 12 m.	one-half day	15 "
" Pallakah to Jowah	"	Thursday 3rd, walking from 8 a.m. to 3 p.m.	one-half day	20 "
" Jowah to Bockquetah	"	Friday 4th, walking from 7 a.m. to 3 p.m.	one-half day	20 "
" Bockquetah to Pye	"	Saturday 5th, walking from 6 a.m. to 1 p.m.	one-half day	15 "
" Pye to Barmaquirlla	"	Monday 7th, walking from 6 a.m. to 1 p.m.	one-half day	15 "
" Barmaquirlla to Sinoyo	"	Tuesday 8th, walking from 6 a.m. to 1 p.m.	one-half day	20 "
" Sinoyo to Danpellah	"	Wednesday 9th, walking from 6 a.m. to 4 p.m.	one-half day	20 "
" Danpella to Dogbar	"	Thursday 10th, walking from 6 a.m. to 12 a.m.	one-half day	20 "
" Dogbar to Encampment	"	Monday 14th, walking from 6 a.m. to 3 p.m.	one day	25 "
" Encampment to Hind's Creek	"	Tuesday 15th, walking from 5 a.m. to 5 p.m.	one day	30 "
" Hind's Creek to Simpson's Town	"	Wednesday 16th, walking from 5 a.m. to 3 p.m.	one day	25 "
" Simpson's Town to White Plains	"	Thursday 17th, walking from 6 a.m. to 5 p.m.	one day	30 "
" White Plains to Monrovia	"	Friday 18th,	one day	25 "

Musahdu is North 47° 45 30″ East from Monrovia, direct line } About 16 days walk. Zig-zag miles 460

Distance 191 and eight-tenths nautrical miles—direct as the bird flies.

Sundry Abstracts from the Meteorological Observations Made During the Exploration from Monrovia to Musahdu A.D. 1874.

STATION.	Date 1874.	Hour of Day.	Barometer	Thermom't'r	REMARKS.
Pahya, Weimor Boom Country.	Monday, 21st Sept	6 a. m.	26.61	72°	Sky overcast, clear, breaks East.
Pahya is a large town surround-	"	4 p. m.	28.54	88	Clear, Sunshine.
ed by 3 concentric thick walls	Tuesday, Sept. 22	10 a. m.	28.62	78	Sky overcast, sun out at intervals, observ'n
made of adobe and flat granite	"	noon	28.54	86	Clear sunshine.
rocks mixed, the walls being 26	Wednesday, Sept. 23	6:30 a. m.	28.53	72	Sky overcast.
feet high, 8 and 9 feet at the	"	3 p. m.	28.48	82	Thick cumuli, thunder.
bottom and tapering off towards	Thursday, Sept. 24	6 a. m.	28.58	72	currus and light thin clouds.
the top. Here the prairie lands	"	2:30 p. m.	28.52	82	Cloudy.
begin and the trees are disap-	"	7:30 p. m.	28.62	76	White clouds, wind W. N. W., moonshine.
pearing.	Friday, Sept, 25	7 a. m.	28.63	64	Mackeral sky.
	"	9:30 a. m.	28.66	82	Sunshine and white cloud.
	Saturday, Sept. 26	10 a. m.	28.58	86	Sunshine.
* * * * *	Sunday, Sept. 27	6:30 a. m.	28.58	74	Overcast, cattle and horses appearing.
	Sunday, Oct. 25, passed	Boe, Zigga—P	orra Zue's m	arket, going	on and coming to Gubbah-Wallah.
Gubbawallah.—This is anoth-	Monday, Oct. 26				Resting and talking with the king.
er large walled town on the St.	Tuesday, Oct. 27	6 a. m.	28.24		Thermometers all broken.
Paul's River itself—where this	Wednesday, Oct. 28	8 a. m.	28.22		Clear, sunshine.
river is about only 20 feet wide,	Thursday, Oct. 29	6:30 a. m.	28.18		Foggy.
with a suspension bridge on	"	2:30 a. m.	28.16		Clear
wicker work swinging over it.	Friday, Oct. 30	6:30 a. m.	28		
	Saturday, Oct. 31	6 a. m.	28.20		Thunder from east, tornado.
Pellaharrah	Tuesday, Nov. 3	2 p. m.	28.20		Travelling, left Pellabarrah.
Battatah	Wednesday, Nov. 4	9 a. m.	27.84		" " Ballatah.
Vukkah	"	1 p. m.	27.86		Direction N. N. E. having arriv'd at Vukkah.
Musahdu	Sunday, Nov. 8	7 a. m.	27.80		Clear sunshine.

Figure 8. "An Itinerary Table" and "Sundry Abstracts" by Benjamin Anderson. *Published in the* Liberia Recorder *29 August 1903.*

Anderson's second journey. Then he interviewed d'Ollone, who again suggested that Anderson's map was wrong ("The Franco-Liberian Controversy" 1903). Royal Geographical Society ratification had been uncritical and was important. Anyway, the correspondent argued, if "one of them went 30 years ago, why do they not go there today?" Yet the editor of the *West African Mail* added that Anderson had made out "an unanswerable case," and that d'Ollone's denial was based only on the map and did not explain the Musadu letter, Anderson's abstracts, or even earlier French acceptance, for example, by the geographer Réclus.[80]

Then, in October 1903, the famous French administrator, traveler, and "Africanist" Maurice Delafosse stepped in, having been the French representative in Monrovia during the time of the Hostains-d'Ollone mission (Murdza 1979, 170, 206 n. 1).[81] He stated that Anderson did go to Musadu, which was evident from his original book, its unauthorized reprints, the reasonably accurate town coordinates, and his reputation in the interior among the Manding who speak of him as "'the Black European of Musadu'" (1903, 805).[82] Mandingo visitors to Monrovia spoke of Anderson's journey and called on him. Had d'Ollone troubled to visit Monrovia, Delafosse remarks, he would have found Anderson's accounts and other letters sent to Liberian authorities by different chiefs referring to Anderson's second visit. Moreover, he writes, "two other Liberian explorers, Seymour and Ash, had visited Zigaporasu [Koiama Tongoro] (between Zolu and Beyla) about 1850, although without any political or scientific result" (1903, 1895).[83]

In November 1903 the editor of the *Sierra Leone Weekly News* introduced a second reply from Anderson, arguing that his 1874 travels should be published while he was alive to receive his own final corrections and recommendations (Anderson 1903b). Anderson's letter was indignant, admitting also that he had at times been taunted with similar doubts by his own people. He lambasted Liberia for not engaging with its hinterland and for not formally publishing what he had acquired and possessed. It should be Liberia that defended Anderson, not Anderson himself. Anderson then wrote a third letter which provided important information from his journal, some of which did not appear in the earlier published versions of his two trips. The letter, which follows in full, was titled "Prof. Anderson's Reply to Captain d'Ollone: THE OBJECTIVE POINT." It was published in the *Liberia Recorder* on 19 December 1903 (1903c). Anderson wrote:

> To go from Monrovia to Musahdu is no great geographical feat; nor any wonderful thing to accomplish. It was therefore physically possible for us to step out the door of our house in Mechanic Street, Monrovia and go straight to the waterside, get into a canoe with bag and baggage and paddle our way through the windings of Ayers Creek until we get into the St. Paul River.[84] Once there, you can choose whatever bank you wish to follow; say we choose to meander or survey on the eastern or left handside: the course of the river here is north, north-east—on you go until you are interrupted by the rapids at Millsburg when you will have to get out and walk around in order to resume your voyage;—-having got beyond these rapids the river assumes its ordinary placid course, 6 or 7 miles until you come to another series of rapids a little more precitptious [*sic*] than the first, owing to a higher elevation of land: your work now *earnestly* begins of meandering with the compass but better still with the transit instrument, sticking in your latitude and longitude as the weather permits at choice points and noticing the rise of the land with your asteroid as best you can. By and by you reach questionable and forbidden ground—-between the Condo and Pessey countries—-where the lords of the soil may wish to know by what authority you do these things, of continually gaping up in the skies at the sun with your sextant and careering through their country with compass in hand.[85] This conduct is sure to excite the suspicion of barbarians generally, and our case was not an exception. But whoever would undertake single handed, to *methodically* explore this region especially if he was a white man, would find himself in a few moments—

fitted with a jacket of poisoned arrows as numerous "as the quills on the fretful porcupine" [Shakespeare, *Hamlet* 1.5.20]; unless the natives give him permission to do so. A dash or presents of [*sic,* or] gift however, explains away every difficulty and the exploration proceeds, passing village and settlement through hill and dale and heartily wooded forest; the main stream receiving numerous arteries or branch creeks, that intersperse this region on the right and left like a network and drains the country into the valley of the St. Paul River.

As the physical features of the country partake of a rough and hilly variety, so also are the streams innumerable that intersect it everywhere in the rainy season of July, August and Sept. Supposing the weather permits you to cling to the right bank of the St. Paul River without interruption, you will soon find yourself in the Barline country of the divisions of the Pessey section and once known as the principle mart of trade. Pallikah is close to a branch of the river [the Via]; passing on you come to Barmaquirlla [Gbakwele] near the St. Paul River; you can then cross over into the Domar Boozie on a raft if you like.[86] The river here at this point flows smoothly on but divides itself into two branches, one to the east and the other to the north-east. You are now supposed to have changed banks so as to be on the left bank and to have left the Domar-Boozie and come into the Wymar-Boozie.[87]

The river begins to grow narrow and more rapid and the cataracts increase as the land is steeper in its slopes. We finally arrive at the largest and last town in the Wymar-Boozie country standing on the left bank of the St. Paul River on the confines of the great Boozie and Mandingo country, named; Ziggah-Porah-Zue [Koiama Tongoro] where the great market is held every Sunday and where the communication from bank to bank is by a bridge of wicker work about 100 ft. long: the river here narrowing to a width of 75 to 100 ft. The bridge is made of strong twigs and grass rope very skillfully plaited together and elevated by means of tall trees to a height to prevent the rise of the river from interfering with it: this bridge is used for the crossing of the women, children and foot passengers generally, while the horses and cattle are swum across.[88]

Leaving Ziggah-Porrah-Zue and crossing with the suspension bridge to the right bank, we go on through several villages until we come to Vukkah [Foma]. This is a village seated on the high ridge of hills or mountains that separate the heavily wooded section of the Boozie country from the almost treeless plains of Manding; here perched upon these elevations you can look down on an extensive plateau nor prairie where the undulations of the land are of a more gentle character than the abrupt corrugated hill and dale of the Boozie country; you are where you can see the large towns and villages dotting the scenery for miles with herds of cattle here and there to relieve the prospects, every now and then, is seen some one on horseback with his large white toga or gown fluttering in the wind as he goes galloping on a visit of pleasure or business of his own to a neighboring village or town.

We may now descend into the Mandingo country proper, passing through the outlying villages and farms until we come to one of the large towns Mahammedu [Nionsamoridu], where the great market of the country is held every Wednesday. The roads on each side is hemmed in where they are taken up in farming by cane-brake and long grass. In the dries this is a source of trouble and danger for if this stubble once takes fire, the conflagration spreads far and wide.

You can now walk on until you come to Musahdu, where the St. Paul River has dwindled into an insignificant stream from 50 to 75 ft. wide; flowing hard by the western gate of that town, out of which early in the morning the young boys ride their horses for the purpose of watering and cleaning them.[89] Standing erect with their feet on the horses' back in order to show their equestrian skill in riding, they can gallop them back in the same position. We are now at Musahdu without the least trouble of trudging behind other people or crossing their paths to get there.

Our natives have several ways of reaching Musahdu, and they have two or three short cuts where they cross the river at points of least obstruction. My original intention in my second journey to Musahdu was to follow at any cost, the trend of the St. Paul River since its source originates in the Mandingo country at the foot, as I learned, of a series of high hills. The St. Paul River is therefore one of the principle reservoirs of watershed with the parallel stream of the Mahfah, Little Cape Mount [Lofa River], Farmington, St. John's River and a number of others; even the little Duqueh penetrates far in the interior.[90]

Our natives, however, do not perform their peregrinations by water but by land; and we had to conform to their wishes and ways, and the more so, as the rainy season was a most intense one, and travelling by water very dangerous on account of the numerous rapids and the destructive velocity of the stream. To follow out our original intention; the exploration would have to be carried on in the dries.

When we reached Vukkah the king of Musahdu, Vomfeedolla [Vafin Dole] sent an escort to bring us on to the capital. The very surroundings of the scenery, the long gentle rolling and sloping plains, interrupted by some more elevated terrace or table land and this again, by a number of pinnacle-like formations standing out in bold relief against the sky, gave such a varied outline as to defy any effort at a verbal description. Nothing but the pencil or photographic art can do justice to these magnificent efforts of nature.[91] The effect on the mind is, to transport it from the gloomy feeling which a dense damp and somber forest naturally produces, to the pleasing and agreeable sensations which the sudden opening of a vast panorama, lit up and tinctured by the morning glories of the rising sun, must naturally change it into.

Captain d'Ollone abruptly asserts that Anderson has never been to Musahdu. No one doubts that Captain d'Ollone is a scientific and competent explorer, but, whether he be by the logic of his facts or the logic of his figures, neither one nor the other can prove that Anderson has never been to Musahdu. He says, "Our expedition started at Bereby, a French Station on the Ivory Coast and finished at Beyla, a French Station in the Soudan, from whence the expedition proceeded through the Soudan and French Guinea to the coast again. In our case [p. 7] the departure and arrival of the expedition are established without possibility of dispute. . . . Now the map of our route is almost different from Anderson's." Why, to be sure! and it must be necessarily and scientifically so; since Anderson's initial point of departure was Monrovia and not Bereby, and his objective point finished at Musahdu and not Beyla.

Both the points of the start and the finish of each expedition are far and wide apart; not only must the two routes be different but they cannot even be parallel.[92]

"But as the map of our route is absolutely different from Anderson's, therefore Anderson's map is *fausse*"—*wrong*. This is rather hasty, as he had not seen the calculations upon which the map was founded.

"taking [*sic*] the line between Monrovia and Bereby as a base of a triangle and Musahdu as the vertex, the two journeys must run into each other. We see the grand humor of contempt that runs through all the Captain's remarks with reference to us. He has the egotistic conceit that no black man can explore Africa in comparison with himself; comparisons are invidious things, but there is no rivalry in my case for, I went to Musahdu before he was born, judging from his picture.[93] And as for the peculiarity of Anderson's itinerary, they would have been overlooked out of a friendly feeling."

A simple truthful itinerary is merely a formula and has no peculiarities, it is simply a plain form of facts. "And on the assumptions that Anderson had little topographical knowledge, a case by no means uncommon amongst travelers," Anderson's exploration was not strictly a topographical survey; it was what is called by engineers, a flying or trial route survey, afterwards to be followed up by a more deliberate exact examination in which the topographical features and kindred subjects would be considered.

"As regards the voyage of 1868, there are only presumptions against Anderson, but they are strong."

Anderson's facts stand up in his record as against all *presumptions* to the contrary.

The gist of the controversy is this: that "Anderson has never been to Musahdu."

It is for the French record to abolish that fact and make it a fiction.

"Nothing proves Anderson's voyage but his map." The surface of a paper map is no proof but the calculations upon which it is founded, is fundamental proof, they may even disagree with the calculations subsequently made, still they are the proof of that map; the exactness of position lies, which were the best observations, we raise no question as to this, but even this does not disprove that Anderson has been to Musahdu.

As to the modifications which it appears our map will have to undergo to render it less in exact, we know it is easy to invent a map; the maps of the ancients are conjectural specimens or guest [*sic*, guess?] maps of that kind. And all this before, the modern science of exact astronomical calculations came into vogue, but give them precision and certainty. But it seems now to be a foregone and abiding conclusion with the Europeans, that a Negro is incapable of knowledge of this kind or it seems to be devilish provoking to some body if he attempts it.

When our map was gravely charged with a fictitious origin, we knew at once what such implications meant and what they were intended to be the forerunner of. Were our map ever so correct, it must now of course, to answer the purpose of future designs, be pronounced *"fausee"—wrong.*

"Il paraitrait que depuis on aurait fait subir a cette carte originale quelques modifications pour la rendre moins inexacte."[94]

As a matter of course it will have to undergo not *such modifications,* but it will have to be entirely substituted, in order to make it suit the ulterior designs or future appropriations. There is no need, however for any further comment on this.

These things, *futuri esse.* We wait to see the policy of the Government.

Captain d'Ollone would have done us a service had he sent us a copy of his late geographical exploits in the Soudan which certainly, would have pleased us much more than his unavailing efforts to negative what we have done.

B. J. K. ANDERSON.

Finally in 1904, the *Liberia Recorder* published the Arabic text and Edward W. Blyden's translation of the 1868 letter from Vafin Dole.[95] After that, only a few lone voices continued to question the validity of Anderson's trip after 1903 ("Franco-Liberian Relations" 1904, 98; Arcin 1911, 528). The French, nonetheless, continued to press for more land and appropriated more in 1907 (see Fisher 1971, vii; Murdza 1979, 407 n. 31, and Leopold 1991, chap. 2).

Perhaps to honor Anderson during this affair, the Liberia College conferred an honorary Ph.D. on Anderson ("Brief Sketch" [1910]). Anderson did not complete his trigonometry book "owing to a very severe attact [attack] of illness which he had interfering very materially with his mind." Three years earlier, Maurice Delafosse wrote that Anderson sometimes did "not make good sense," suggesting that Anderson underwent some form of dementia during the latter years of his life (1900, 187). Anderson died on 27 June 1910 ("Brief Sketch" [1910]).

Interior Memories of Anderson

In Musadu and elsewhere some people retain memories of Anderson's short visit, two or three generations removed from those with firsthand memories, and after the major disruptive wars associated with Samori Touré and French occupation. We know of several accounts that Svend Holsoe, Martin Ford, and Tim Geysbeek collected from 1965 to 1993 in Liberia and Guinea that appear to speak of it. One of Vafin Dole's grandsons, Yaya Dole, said that the American visited Vafin Dole in Vafin's yard, as Anderson himself notes for 1868 (see chap. 5). Understandably, such accounts recorded in Musadu are the most detailed and accurate. Many of the stories link Anderson with the large cotton tree that is situated on the southern edge of town near the Dion river (fig. 9). Some claim that Anderson stayed at, or slept under, the cotton tree. Others say that a written document, a talisman, or a piece of the American's "property" was put into or attached to the side of the tree, perhaps referring to the flag that Anderson left flying on his departure. A hand mark is connected with the cotton tree by one narrator, but another refrains from detailing this, as a law forbid aspects of this to be told outside Musadu.

The traditions mention a written document, talisman, or property, which may refer perhaps to the Bibles which Anderson left. Alhaji Beete of Musadu told Geysbeek and Baba Dole in 1993 that "the American . . . wrote about the difficult times that we experienced," a faint memory perhaps of stories about Ibrahima Sissi and Saji Kamara that Anderson recorded in his journal. Oral traditions also provide names of two or three people who interpreted for Anderson: Fode Lua, Mamabine Mammadi, and Mafine Kaba. In the earliest account Alhaji Seku Salifu told Svend Holsoe in Monrovia in 1965:

> The Americans . . . went to Musadu and they left their handmark there. . . . Someone came here before. Some white man, some American. Yes, I don't know his name. He put a hole in the cotton tree, a talisman. He wrote and put it in a bag and put it in the cotton tree. The four cotton trees, the four together, it is the one in the middle.[96]

Nearly twenty years later, a Sumawolo from Musadu who lived in Bahn, Liberia, told Martin Ford a popular story about how some "Americans" went to Guinea to visit Musadu and collect some old stories (1984). Even though the story is confusing, to the extent that Sumawolo unknowingly talks about the French who built the iron bridge that presently crosses the Dion River, Sumawolo's story still gives one a sense of how the people associate Musadu with one or more "American" visitors from Liberia. Sumawolo said:

> The Americans, some Americans went to Musadu. They ask the people to tell them the story. Old, old things. One old man there, they call him Vafin Bility. He was the only person that could know more history at that time, so they went to the man. The old man explained a lot of history to them. . . . Then the American told the people in this particular town, "we have our property here, our grandfather left our property here.[97] It is under a big cotton tree." So they went, they fix a bridge, and put it there and tell the people they have their property there. So they left. They went back. (Sumawolo 1984)

In 1986, Yaya Dole told Mustafa Kromah, Chejan Mohamed Kromah, and Geysbeek in Musadu:

> The first American who came here stayed under the cotton tree. That is where he slept. He set up a tent and slept there. At daybreak he would go to my ancestor Vafin Dole's house and talk. That happened in the presence of the important people. The youth would sit there like I am here and say, "Yes sir,

Figure 9. A cotton tree that the Manding associate with Benjamin Anderson in Musadu. *Photograph by Tim Geysbeek, 1986.*

> yes sir, yes sir." That is how they used to answer him: "Yes sir, yes sir, yes sir." That is what the youth would say. Fode Lua, who used to narrate the old history, would go with the American when he needed my father. He would tell him what to say and explain it to the people in Yakodu [Diakolidu]. That is what they did. My ancestor Vafin used to explain things to them. (1986)[98]

Finally, in 1993, Baba Dole and Tim Geysbeek visited Alhaji Ibrahim Beete (Bility), one of Yaya Dole's friends in Musadu. Beete said:

> An American came and asked about all of the places in Mamadigbè's garden. A nail was pounded into the cotton tree there. They used to knock the cotton tree and listen and listen. They said that the property of their ancestor is in the cotton tree. I don't know whether or not that is true. They stayed there for three or four days. They wrote about all of those things.[99] Mamabinè Mammadi used to interpret for one of them.[100] Mafine Kaba used to interpret for one of them, the American. They wrote about the difficult times that we experienced. (1986)

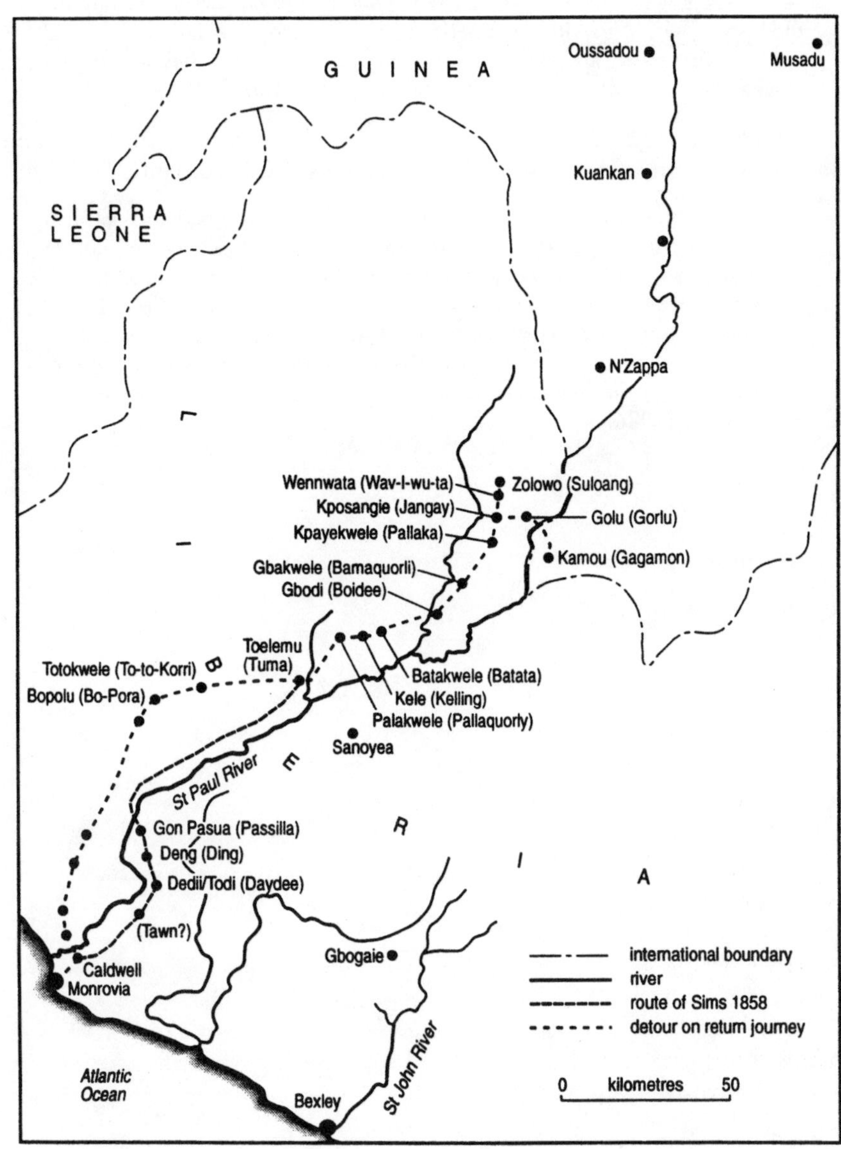

Map 7. James L. Sims's journey, 1858.

3

James L. Sims, 1858

SCENES IN THE INTERIOR OF LIBERIA: BEING A TOUR THROUGH THE COUNTRIES OF THE DEY, GOULAH, PESSAH, BARLAIN, KPELLAY, SULOANY AND KING BOATSWAIN'S TRIBES, IN 1858.

By James L. Sims.

I left the settlement of Upper Caldwell [Caldwell, 6°23'N, 10°46'W], on the St. Paul's river early on the morning of the 8th of January, 1858, accompanied by twenty-seven natives, including prince Eda, a native of Barlain, and Gotorah my interpreter.[1]

The morning was a beautiful one, and as we wound our way along the narrow paths, birds of every plumage poured forth their sweetest notes, which were answered by the merry shouts of the natives, or a peal from their rude wooden horns. About ten o'clock, we arrived at a small collection of houses, known as Governor Tom's town. Here, in a very few minutes after our arrival, Gotorah managed to get up a row. The Governor, it seemed, wanted us to pay a bar of tobacco for the privilege of passing through his town; but Gotorah without informing me of what was going on, refused to pay anything; whereupon the Governor came to me, followed Gotorah, who declared that "if I mind these people I would not have tobacco enough to put in my pipe when I got to Barlain."[2] The Governor intimated that Gotorah was officious; this was more than a Vey prince could swallow; so Gotorah informed all present that the American man was under his care and protection, and to demonstrate his position, he drew the ramrod from his gun and applied it with such a vigor about the head and ears of Governor Tom, that his Excellency took to the bush, followed by an assurance from Gotorah of a severer chastisement if he again dared to make "'Merica man" pay for passing through his miserable old town.[3] We left Governor Tom's town, (to the great satisfaction of all concerned,) for Tawn, where we arrived just at sun down.

Tawn contained about one hundred houses. The inhabitants are a mixture of nearly every tribe to be found in Liberia. The agricultural resources of Tawn were not calculated to make a very favorable impression. Notwithstanding, the soil, judging from the quality of the few articles growing, was extremely fertile. Tawn is a kind of depot where people, going to the interior, generally pass their first night after leaving the settlements, as there are no more towns nearer than sixty or seventy miles.

Having been informed of this, I ordered my goods to be stowed away, and a house provided for myself. This being done, I retired to reflect on my first day's journey to the interior, and to dream of the future.

Early next morning [Saturday, 9 January 1858] we were on the path; just at sun rise, we entered a dark gloomy forest; the path was hugged on both sides by an impenetrable jungle, led through dismal swamps, and over steep and rocky hills. So thick were the tangled vines and bushes over head, in some places, that the sun would be entirely obscured for hours at the time: on we went. Twelve o'clock came, and not a house nor a farm could be seen to relieve the monotony of the scene. Robinson Crusoe, on his lonely isle, never [p. 66] wished more sincerely for the sight of a sail than I did for an opening in the bush.[4] About four o'clock, to my great joy, we reached a large open field, with a few fruit trees, and a stream of delicious water. To us, this place was a little paradise on earth. I felt like one just released from a long and weary bondage. After resting awhile, we again took the path. One hour's walk brought us suddenly to the banks of the St. Paul's; just at this point a solid bed of rock, extending all the way across the river, and nearly half a mile up, dissipates all hopes of the St. Paul's ever becoming a highway to the interior.[5] At sun down we came to a small river, tributary to the St. Paul's—this we had to ford, which was not a very easy task, as some of the men had very heavy burdens; and the rocks at the bottom, on which we had to walk, were very slippery; this, together with the great velocity of the stream, and the growing darkness, rendered our situation anything but agreeable. However, the whole party crossed over without any serious accident; and here, on the banks of the river, we passed our second night.

Next morning [Sunday, 10 January], by the time it was light enough to distinguish one from another, we were plodding our way through the country of the Goulahs.[6] Our course now lay in an easterly direction, through a country well timbered, and watered by beautiful sandy streams. We entered Daydee [?Todi, 6°32'N, 10°33'W], a Goulah town, a little before sun down, just in time to see the industrious people return from their farms. Daydee is a pleasant little barricaded town about the size of Tawn. The king met me at the gate and conducted me to a large house in the centre of the town, where I was soon surrounded by gaping crowds of men, women and children. The king was very kind: He gave me the largest and best house in the town to sleep in, and several others did the same for my "carriers." The good people of the town brought us rice, palm oil and chickens, which were purchased for a trifle—the prices being fixed by the king.; [*sic*] however, he would not allow me to pay for any thing that I intended to eat myself.

Next morning [Monday, 11 January] I gave the king a bunch of white beads in return for his kindness, and another bunch to be distributed among his people who had given up their houses to my carriers. We left Daydee, and arrived at Zama about four o'clock. Zama is quite a large town, and I think, boasts of a population between six and seven hundred natives. Nothing seemed to surprise them more than to see a single Liberian venturing so far alone, and when I pointed to my carriers, saying that I was not alone, they laughed and said that if I should happen to have any fighting to do, I would soon see whether I was alone or not. Here we passed our fourth night.

The next day [Tuesday, 12 January] we reached Ding [Deng Gola, 6°38'N, 10°34'W], a town about the size of Zama. Here, as in all the Goulah towns I had seen, the people appeared to be surrounded by plenty of all of the necessaries of life. Their farms were well cultivated, and their towns literally stocked with fowls, goats and sheep. The Goulahs are generally very industrious, but much addicted to gambling. They differ in color from jet black to a light yellow.[7] I remained at Ding two days, during which time I visited several of the dependent towns, which afforded me an excellency opportunity of examining the soil, streams, and forest in its vicinity, none of which can be too highly praised.

Friday evening, the 15th of January, we entered Passilla [Gon Pasua, 6°40'N, 10°36'W], situated on the banks of the St. Paul's river. This town consisted of some two hundred houses and a mixed population of Goulah and Passah people—who crowded around me in such a manner that I was nearly suffocated[.][8] I was not a little surprised at this, nor could I conjecture what it was about my person, unless it was my clothes, that attracted their attention; as nearly [p. 67] one half of the people in the town was of a lighter complexion than myself. But the great secret was simply this—I was a "white man"—white because I was a "Merica man"—"Merica man, because I Sarvy book," and every body who "Sarvy book," except the Mandingoes, are "white."[9] They say the Mandingoes would be white too if they would only dress like white people. I did all that I could to convince them that I was not white, but I was unsuccessful; they would have it that I was white, and therefore I had to undergo, and submit to the most minute inspection. The inspectors were chiefly ladies, and very inquisitive ones too. After a while I succeeded in reaching the king's residence. Jollah Goondo (the king) was a fine looking old man of a yellow complexion and curly hair. He is short and thick in statue with very good features. At his right hand was a venerable looking old Mahometan priest, who as I approached them, rose and putting his right hand around my waist and his left hand on my right shoulder, exclaimed, "Allah Akbah! Allah Akbah!! Allah Akbah!!![10] He then pointed to the mat, on which the king was sitting, and motioned me to a seat. The king then proceeded to question me, he asked where I was from? where I was going—what I was going for? and many other questions, all of which I answered to the best of my ability. I also informed him that I intended to travel no farther in the Goulah country, but should cross the river and proceed to Tumah, in the Pessah country, as soon as I was sufficiently rested, and that I wanted him to send a messenger before, to ascertain whether I would be allowed to pass. He consented, and after the price was agreed upon, I was conducted by one of the king's sons who carried on his shoulder a Danish gun, about seven feet long, to one of the king's own houses, which he said belonged to me as along as I remained in the town. A few minutes afterwards, the lad returned with a white fowl in one hand and a bowl of white rice in the other, which he said were presents from the king.[11] I informed him that it was very acceptable, as I had eaten nothing since I left Ding.

The next day [Saturday, 16 January] was occupied in looking at the town, visiting the farms and swimming cross the river—which at this point is not more than three hundred yards wide. I saw, in strolling through the town, two men in a blacksmith shop, busily engaged in making knives and bill-hooks. In another part of the town I saw several women making pots, bowls and water coolers of clay; further on were several men tanning and working leather; setting on a mat, under a shed, not far from the king's residence, was the old Mahometan priest, employed in writing charms for the superstitious Goulahs. I saluted him in Vey which he very readily understood. Gotora being present I managed to get up a conversation with the follower of the "false prophet." After asking my name, age and place of my birth, he proceeded to give me a sketch of his life. "My name," said he "is Ibrihims, I was born at Jani (Jenne) and was sent at a very early age to Timbuturu (Timbuctoo) to receive my education. Timbuturu is a very large town, twice as large as Jani; a great many white people come to Timbuturu from beyond the sand country. I left Timbuturu before I had finished my education and went back to Jani. A few years after my return home, I went to Timbu in the Futa country. From Timbu I went back to Timbuturu, and from Timbuturu back to Timbu, from Timbu to Sierra Leone, from Sierra Leone to Drukora (Monrovia) and from Drukora I came here."[12] Just as Ibrihims concluded this part of his narrative, a woman, as bright as a mulattoe, came up, and informed me that the king was about to take his morning walk, and desired that I would accompany him. I found the king standing in front of his house, dressed in a Mendingo costume, and surrounded by the dignitaries of the town, who very [p. 68] respectfully gave way as I approached. After giving sundry orders to his wives, whom it seemed formed the major part of the inhabitants of Pasilla, the "royal train" moved off. We visited the farms, which consisted chiefly of corn, cassadas, a small patch of sugar cane and cotton.[13] The land, as usual, is very good. After looking at the farms, we took a stroll down the river; while on our way up, as some of the party cried out, "Moa, Moa," (water cow) I turned around just in time to see a large hippopotamus plunge into the water from the opposite bank.

On Monday the 18th—the messengers, whom the king had sent to Tuma [Tulema, 7°7'N, 10°5'W], returned with six men from the head-man of Tuma who informed me that I would be permitted to pass unmolested, and that the head-man had sent me a present of fowls and rice. Nothing was left for me to do but to dash (pay) the king and commence my journey for Pessah. But it was destined that I should have an adventure before leaving Goulah. It is said by some writer that when the sun goes down all Africa dances.[14] This assertion may at least, be applied to all Guinea, if not all Africa: for the golden rays of the departed orb were still visible on the western horizon, when the lads and lassies of Pasilla came forth to indulge in this, their favorite amusement; they sang and danced until about 9 o'clock when one by one they glided away—leaving me alone. In a few minutes after this, everything was as still as death; not a living soul could be seen but myself. Nothing could be heard by the rustling of the leaves of two trees that stood in the town but the moon shone forth in all her splendor which made it a time of sweet reflection. I went into my house and laid down, but I did not sleep. I was soon lost in a reverie. The labors of those intrepid men who first made known to the civilized world, the habits and customs of the people of this benighted continent came vividly before me. At length, finding that I could not sleep, I got up and went out. It being very cool, I threw a large Mandingo cloth around me and started down towards the river;[15] as soon as I had entered a little skirt of bush, between the river and the town, I heard somebody call on the opposite bank. I hastened down to the landing, where I found two large canoes tied to the root of a large cotton tree, and asked in the Vey tongue "Who's there?" "Me Dwarrow" was the reply in the same language.[16]

> "Where are you from? I continued.
> "From Passah."
> "What have you got?"
> "Jung," (Slaves.)
> "How many?"
> "Mormandi a-kor-dunda," (twenty-one.)
> "Where are you going with them?"

"To the Frenchman, at Cape Mount."

"Very well; wait until I go and get a paddle."

"Make haste." And I did make haste. From the very moment that he mentioned the word "*Jung,*" I wanted to be at his throat. And was determined to liberate the slaves at all hazards. I was not long in retracing my steps to the town, where, after a fruitless search for a paddle, I found a pole about ten feet long, which I took and bound ten or a dozen pieces of bamboo, about a foot in length, across one end; with this I returned to the land, untied one of the canoes and started for the other side. Although I had not arrived at any definite conclusion how to act, I pulled with all my might. On drawing near the bank, I saw a number of men and women with their right hands tied to their necks; behind them, stood two men armed with muskets and cutlasses. I saw at a glance that the two armed men were Veys. After saluting them, the following conversation passed between us, which was commenced by myself in the following manner:

"Hallo, what's matter, you live paff [past?] night time?"

"Who you be live talk English? What side you sarvy (learn) English?"

"O, I live Cape before. I sarvy talk 'Merica proper; what side you buy dem people?"

"I buy him Pessah country."

"What's matter you no sleep some dem town behind you—how you live paff so night time?"

"O, you see dese people no want left he country; I look too much troubly, last night; one dis people take axe, he broke he hand off."

"Where he now?"

"O, I take my knife I done kill him, he no use, France man no want man got one hand, my money done lose too."

By this time I had matured a plan by which I would be able to carry out my wishes.

"How many will your canoe carry?"

"Ten or a dozen; it would be better to let me cross the men first with yourself and leave the women in charge of your partner."

"Very good."

"You get in first and set in the head, so you can look out for the rocks."

"Very good too."

"Are all the men in?"

"Yes."

"Push off."

I pulled out midway in the river and took out my knife, and then, with my left hand, I kept up a continual noise in the water, while with my right, I cut loose the man that sat next to me; as soon as he discovered that his hand was free, he would have jumped over board, but I gave him a light tap on the shoulder, which made him look around. I gave him the knife and motioned to him to cut loose the man next to him. The Vey man, who all this time had been keeping a vigilant look out ahead, drew his cloth around him and laid down. All the better for us. All of a sudden the whole thirteen of the slaves stood up, not one of them was tied. This was all I wanted. "Look out Dwarrow," and over went the canoe. The slaves, as I expected they would do, swum back to the landing from where I had just taken them. Dwarrow, who was prevented from swimming by his heavy Mandingo cloth, and I held on to the canoe, crying out to his partner on shore to look to the women. The canoe by this time had drifted very near a ledge of rocks some distance below the town: seeing the danger, I let go and swum ashore; and after feeling my way through an almost impenetrable jungle, I entered the town by a circuitous route.

Here is direct palpable proof that the French slaver, Regina Coeli, Capt. Chevelier, at Cape Mount, in 1858, was openly engaged in the slave-trade, in defiance of the laws of Liberia, and the feelings of the people.

Pessah Country

Tuesday morning, 19th. [January]—By the time it was light we were ready for traveling.[17] The king and nobles were all assembled in front of my house, so as to be ready at a moment's warning to accompany me to the landing. The women and children brought me presents of eggs and groundpeas. A man was sent to bail out the canoes, and prepare them for crossing us; we shook hands with the kind people of Passilla, seated ourselves in the canoes, and amidst firing of guns and the deafening shouts of the natives, we bid adieu to Goulah. A few minutes more, we crossed the St. Paul's, and were hurrying on through the country of the Pessahs.[18] The Pessah people, called by us *Pessies,* and sometimes Pessahs, are, without exception, the largest tribe in this part of Western Africa; and a greater number of these have been sent into slavery than any other tribe in Liberia. Their country commences immediately in the rear of, though some distance from, Cape Mount, and extends in a direction nearly the whole length of the Republic. It seems that they were never a warlike people, until driven into it by the slave-hunters. Situated as they were, they could have no intercourse themselves with foreigners—thus their only weapons of defense were a few rude knives and bill-hooks of their own manufacture. This, together with their simple habits of life, rendered them an easy prey to their more powerful and warlike neighbors—the Veys, Goulahs, and Kroos. These avaricious people, armed and equipped by the slavers, carried death and desolation into the very heart of the Pessah country. Thousands and thousands were slain; thousands and thousands were carried into slavery; whole districts were depopulated, and in fact, a regular war of extermination has been kept up against the Pessahs, ever since the days of Pedro Blanco.[19] On the other hand, the Manni-Mohammedans, in the rear of the Pessahs, carried on a slave-hunting war as disastrous to these unfortunate people as the one so vigorously prosecuted against them by the Veys and others living near the coast. What wonder, then, is it that they are, though powerful in numbers, weak and feeble, poor, miserable, and degraded? Such they are, and such they will be until the influences of civilization shall regenerate them.[20]

It is not an unusual thing to hear the natives about the settlements say: "Before you Americans came here to live, a Pessah man dared not come to the beach; but now they can come and go just whenever they please."[21]

We passed several half towns during the day, at each of which, as we passed through, the little children fled, screaming as though something frightful was after them; the women ran into their houses, and closed the doors, as though the plague was passing through the town. At night we camped beside a rivulet, the Tuma being yet some two miles distant.

Next day [Wednesday, 20 January], about twelve o'clock, we reached the Tuma—a small stream not more than one hundred and fifty yards wide. The town takes its name from the river, and has about two hundred houses.[22] The headman, who [p. 209] said he had never seen a Liberian before, seemed to be overjoyed when I told him that I intended to pass the night in his town.

Next morning [Thursday, 21 January] we crossed the Tuma on floats, which consisted of several logs of cotton-wood firmly bound together. About an hour after crossing the river, we came to the farms of the Tuma people. Some forty or fifty women and half-grown girls were busily engaged in gathering up the sticks and rubbish, while the men removed the heavier timber. Perched upon a stump in the centre of each farm, might be seen a little fellow with a drum, which he thumped most furiously, to which the people sang and kept time while working.[23] On leaving the farms, we entered a beautiful country—a country of hills and valleys, shady groves and meandering streams. Here, too a bird,

> "With purple beak, and rainbow colors flung
> At random o'er his plumes, among the rest,
> Was one pre-eminent; his supple tongue
> A gift like human eloquence possessed,
> And with such art and copious numbers sung,
> That all who heard, a prodigy confessed."

A little after sun-down, we arrived at a considerable town called Dagla [?Dokota, 7°10'N, 10°5'W]. On entering the town, a multitude of people gathered round me, exclaiming: "*Quee-ar-pie! Quee-ar-pie!*"[24]—An American has come! An American has come! They conducted me to the King, who was seated on a leopard skin, before a large fire, surrounded by the principal headmen, and a number of women. A few minutes after I had been ushered into his royal presence, a deputation of five men was sent to me from the people, requesting me to come and take a seat in the palaver-house, so that everybody might have an opportunity of seeing me. A refusal would have been considered most uncivil. But the good old King, who saw that it would be anything but pleasant to me, said: "No; the American is hungry and tired, go and prepare water for him to wash, and something for him to eat." These orders were instantly obeyed. A large brass kettle of warm water was produced, which the King took, and first dipped the tips of his fingers in, and then drank some. This was to let me see that nothing had been put in it to injure me. Next, a large bowl of rice was brought, and a chicken, which the King handed to Gotorah, saying: "This is for your father; go and cook it; we don't know how to cook for Americans."[25] That night the drivers* (*A species of black ant, very ferocious, which go in millions, and with sharp forceps bite severely. When they enter a house, the custom is to leave it till they depart.) very unceremoniously entered my house; being very disagreeable companions, I left them to look out for somebody else, and the house for itself. I slept the balance of the night on a mat in the palaver-house. It was at this town that I saw, for the first time, tobacco growing in Africa. The *quality,* however, was *very inferior.*

On the 23d, [January, Saturday] we arrived at a town, much larger than any we had yet seen, called Pallaquorly [Palakwele, 7°12'N, 10°3W]. This town did not contain less than two thousand inhabitants. The headman appeared to be a man of about forty years of age, jet black, with European features. He was tall, stood erect, and was of the most dignified appearance. On being told that I was going to Barlain, he asked why I wanted to go there. "What is there that is not here?" he continued. "I have ivories, cattle, horses, and camwood, if you want them." I told him that my object in going to Barlain was more to see the country, than anything else. On hearing this, he turned round to an old man that was sitting not far from him, and said: "There is something about these people that I cannot understand." I met with [p. 210] two Albinoes in this town. They were slaves of the king's favorite wife. There were a great many people here of a dark olive complexion, and good hair. Several Manni people lived here also, and exercised great authority with the King.

On the 25th, we arrived at Bata-ta [Batakwele, 7°13'N, 9°56'W], a larger town than Pallaquorly. The day after our arrival at this place, was a day that I never shall forget. A man, in passing through one of the farms, saw a woman at work, as he thought, alone.[26] He seized her and attempted violence upon her.[27] Her cries soon brought to her several men at work in another part of the farm. The offender drew his sword, and killed one man; but he was overpowered and captured. He was taken to the town, tried, and condemned *to be cut into pieces.*

Jan. 26th. About 9 A.M., the prisoner was led out, bound, and preceded by the executioner. Behind him was the multitude—all men, not a woman to be seen. I was standing near the place of execution when the prisoner came up. He was entirely naked. Great drops of sweat rolled from him, as he stood, trembling, imploring for his life. Finding his cries were not heeded, he became silent, when, all at once, his countenance assumed an expression of demoniac malignity I shall never forget. But the grim executioner was not to be deterred from his work by savage looks. He cut off the fingers, then one ear, and then his nose, when I was compelled to turn away. The King, seeing this, ordered the executioner to behead the man at once. He raised his knife; it fell, and the culprit's head rolled in the dust.

As soon as this execution was over, I collected my men together, and started.[28] After traveling about three hours through a dark, dreary forest, we found ourselves suddenly in the midst of an open plain, and before us stood the "cloud capped" mountains of Pessah. Our route lay directly over these mountains. After a sore struggle, we ascended one, the summit of which commanded a view of all the surrounding country. The sight was lovely beyond description. As far as the eye could reach, east and west, was a chain of mountains. Before us, mountains! mountains! Some of these mountains are clothed, from base to summit, in a livery of verdure; others, with their dark iron fronts, looked as sterile as mounds of sand.

After walking about half an hour, we descended into a deep valley. Before we could reach the next mountain, a heavy rain came up. We were all wet and chilly, when we reached the desired haven. We climbed up to the top, where we found a few huts. These little huts, however, contained all that was needful—kind hearts, that were always ready to give a drink of cool water and a shelter to the weary traveler. The few remaining inhabitants gave me a hearty welcome. One old woman, however, could not be prevailed upon to shake hands with me. "He looks like any other man," said she, "but I am afraid of him." This good old lady resigned her house to me, it being the best in the town, though not until she had swept it out, and put new mats on the bed and floor.

Next morning [Wednesday, 27 January] as the sun rose, the country presented the loveliest scene my eyes ever beheld. A heavy mist or fog hung just below the summit of the mountains, and stretching out on every side to the horizon, looked like a vast ocean, and the tops of the mountains, peering one above the other, had every appearance of a group of islands.

After settling with my kind hostess, we took our departure for Kelling [Kele, 7°13'N, 9°59'W] which place would terminate our travels in Pessah. Kelling stands on the summit of a rocky mountain. It is an old, dilapidated town, with but few inhabitants. It was taken in war by the Barlains in 1855, which put an end to a long and bloody struggle between the Barlains and Pessahs. As usual, I was cordially received. The King gave me a house to sleep in, and two others for my men.

Leopards are numerous in this part of Africa, and the people of Kelling were not without their share of troubles from these sheep-stealing prowlers. A single leopard would in one night butcher a dozen sheep, suck the blood, and leave the flesh for the owners. One had gone so far as to knock a bull down. As the town was not enclosed, the people feared lest some more dainty than the rest, might take a liking to a bit of *nu-sjewa,* (human flesh).[29] They [the leopards] are taken with large traps.[30] When one is killed, the skin and front teeth belong to the King; the flesh is eaten by the people. So, to prevent the leopard from eating them, they thought they would just eat the leopard.[31]

[P. 84] On the 28th [January, Thursday], we took our departure for Barlain. We traveled some four or five hours over a rugged, mountainous country.[32] Late in the afternoon we reached the Yea river, which is about two hundred yards wide, and separates the Barlain from the Pessah country. We crossed the Yea on floats, constructed like those on the Tuma. Several Liberians who visited this country in 1856, told me an amusing story of a rooster, which they affirmed, upon the authority of the Barlains, had been haunting the banks of the Yea for a number of years. They gave me a description of him, and said I would find him, unless he had deserted his old home, at the landing, on the Barlain side of the river. At the time of my arrival at this place, I had forgotten all about it; but I had scarcely pulled myself up the steep bank, when a white rooster strutted out of a little skirt of bush, near the path, ruffled up his feathers, paraded up and down the path several times, and re-entered the bush. From the description given me of the rooster, seen by the Liberians two years before, I was obliged to come to the conclusion that the one I saw was the same. And what was more striking, there was no town or village within a mile of this place. According to the superstitious notions of the people, this rooster has been at this place for several hundred years. He is a good genius of the river, and to kill him would cause the most serious consequences.[33] The river would dry up and the whole country would be cursed with thirstiness and famine, so the natives say.

That night we reached Boidee [Gbodi], where we passed our first night in Barlain. I was received with every demonstration of joy. The head man, who was a relative of the king of Barlain, said I should have a escort of ten men from his town to accompany me to Pallaka [Kpayekwele, 7°28'N, 9°37'W]. I slept but very little that night. Drums were beating, guns were firing, and songs were sung until near day-break, in honor of my arrival.

Very early next morning [Friday, 29 January], we pursued our journey through a lovely country to Seewau-ta. This was the largest native town I had seen in Africa—and everything exhibited a degree of civilization that is not to be found amongst any other tribe in Liberia. Their houses were larger and more comfortable than those of the Pessahs or Goulahs. I counted five looms for weaving cloth; the blacksmiths displayed much art in working iron and copper, and the women produced earthen-ware beautifully ornamented [p. 85]. The country in this neighborhood is beautiful and exceedingly fertile. Cultivation is conducted with some skill and great diligence; rice is raised in immense quantities; large fields of indian corn may be seen together with small quantities of sugar cane; great attention is paid to cotton also.

I left this place on the 1st of February. My company had swelled by this time to nearly one hundred men, principally Barlain people, who wished to congratulate the king on my arrival. That afternoon we passed the remains of several small towns that had been destroyed by war. At length we came to a spot where once stood, as I was informed, the largest town ever built in Barlain. A part of the wall was still visible, but with the exception of this, no vestige was left of the unfortunate thousands who perished in a single night by fire and sword. The event is still fresh in the memory of the Barlain people, and now whenever they pass through this once beautiful and inhabited country, but now desolate and depopulated, their countenances betray the feelings of emotion, caused by the recollections of that night of blood when that town was destroyed. The following melancholy account of the destruction of this place may serve to show the cruel, and barbarous mode of warfare practiced by some tribes in this part of Africa.

The town was situated on the bank of a branch of the Yea river, was enclosed by a thick clay wall, several feet high. The people had, by a long and uninterrupted trade with king Boatswain's people, who carried on a direct trade with the Liberians, accumulated large quantities of foreign goods. This excited the avarice of the Kpellays, a savage, barbarous tribe, inhabiting a mountainous country north-east of the Barlain. About this time disturbances broke out between the Barlains and Pessahs. Nothing could have transpired more favorable to the designs of the Kpellays than this. Accordingly a Kpellay chief, with several hundred men offered their services to the king of Barlain to fight against the Pessahs. The unsuspecting Barlains gladly accepted the offer, and quartered their supposed allies, at their own request, [at] Du-gla-ta,—the town alluded to above.[34]

One night whilst the inhabitants were asleep, little dreaming of the storm that was gathering over them, they were aroused from their slumbers by the savage war-cry of the Kpellays, who fell upon their sleeping victims like "furies from the bottomless pit." Men and women, old and young, were mercilessly put to the sword. The goods were removed, the town set on fire, the wall beat down, and even the cattle and sheep shared the fate of their owners.

"Hapless children of men, when shall the cherub hope smile on you from heaven, and with a compassionate voice, call you to the pleasures of reason?" If a correct account could be given of all the wars fought in Africa, during the last century, together with the suffering and desolation that inevitably must have followed, it would be a tale too horrible for "ears of flesh and blood"; and if all the blood that was shed in these wars could be collected in one body, it would float a greater number of ships than humanity would be willing to conjecture.

We slept that night at the farm of an old gentleman, who gave us a hearty welcome and seemed to be much surprised at seeing how contented I made myself—stretched out on a mat on the hard clay floor.

Next morning [Tuesday, 2 February] at sunrise we were standing on the banks of a small river, simply called Nyar, (water.) Now that we are in the country of the Barlains, fording and swimming rivers are done away with. These "partially civilized" people have invented a way of crossing rivers that I was not prepared to see. It is done simply by ascending a platform [p. 86] about ten feet high, and walking over a suspension bridge, as many do in some parts of America; the only difference being in the materials of which they are constructed. These are built of vines. I shall give a description of them in another place.

After crossing the river we set out with light hearts for Bamaquorli [Gbakweli, 7°24'N, 9°51'W] a large town, within three hours walk of Pallaka.[35] We passed two towns still larger than any I had yet seen. One of these was surrounded by a strong-stockade, the other by a clay wall eleven feet high, and a stockade out-side of that; each of these towns had four gates, which are barred and locked at night. A great many cows and sheep were feeding near the towns, some of which were the largest I ever saw in Africa.

We arrived at Bamaquorli about four o'clock. It happened to be market day. Every body in Africa and out of Africa knows what a "great noise" can be produced by an assembly of some three or four hundred women. Long before we reached the town we could hear their voices, as the voice of a "vast multitude"; but on reaching the spot we did not find over seven or eight hundred persons, men, women and children.[36] The market was held in the open air, beneath several large cotton trees. The principal articles for sale were rice, palm oil, country cloths, salt, powder and a few other articles of their own manufacture.

On entering the town, my men let loose a volley of about forty muskets. Du-gla Mannu, the king, a little short man, with a long grey beard, soon marshaled his forces and burnt powder pretty liberally for nearly an hour. It was agreed upon that I should remain here until next morning, for the double purpose of giving all the people a chance of seeing me, and myself an opportunity of seeing the Mama dancers. Mama is the chief priest of a secret fraternity, and though he is never seen by any body who is not a member of the order, is present every where. All the kings, princes and headmen are his agents to whom he reveals his pleasure.

Every king and headman of a town has two or more dancers, generally known as the Mama dancers. They are generally young boys, fantastically dressed, who have the honor of acting as pages to Mama on great occasions. Besides this, whenever a Mama meeting is to be held and Mama is expected to preside in person, notice is given by the dancers, who with drums go to the king's residence and dance. The symbol of Mama is an elephant's tail.

The sun is down—the dancing is over.[37] From the eastern part of the town comes the sound of voices, floating on the evening zephyr, sweet, plaintive and mournful. The followers of Mahomet are at prayer. About one-third of the inhabitants of this town are Mahometans, who have settled in Barlain for the purpose of trafficking with King Boatswain's people, and some of them are very often seen in the settlements. The country of these people is called Manni.[38] They are scattered all through the Pessah, Barlain and King Boatswain's countries and subsist solely by trading. When they have accumulated a considerable amount of goods, they invariably return to their own country: they are as restless as Tartars, and in making bargains will "cavil on the ninth part of a hair."[39] They are the same people whom the American missionary, Mr. Bowen, saw at Sama, and through some mistake, calls them Mandingoes.[40]

We did not leave Bamaquorli the next day [Wednesday, 3 February] until near twelve o'clock, and arrived at Pallaka, the point of our destination about four o'clock. I was kindly received by king Bassee Darn, who had already prepared a very comfortable house for me, having heard several days previous to my arrival that a Liberian was coming to see him. Pallaka, which contained about four thousand inhabitants, half of whom were Manni-Mahometans, [p. 87] and was surrounded by a clay wall nine or ten feet high, had every appearance of being a very old town.[41] The wall in some places was in a very dilapidated condition. The town is situated in a valley with high mountains on the east and west. In front is a beautiful little river with a vine bridge over it. Between the river and the town were several very large cotton trees, and a large border of black granite rock. In the centre of the town was a market square. The people were the most industrious and apparently the most happy I ever met with;—it seemed that the whole country was one immense rice farm. The Mahometan women had several establishments for manufacturing earthen-ware, while the Barlain women made rice, palm oil and other necessaries for market. Two days after my arrival [Friday, 5 February] I had a conference with the king. He allowed me the privilege of living at Pallaka as long as I felt disposed to do so, and besides I was allowed to build a house in the town, and was to have the enjoyment of privileges allowed the Mahometans. I must not close this chapter without giving a description of the king of the Barlains. Bassee Darn was about ninety years of age, but did not appear to be over sixty. He was short, but corpulent, and would weigh, perhaps, over two hundred pounds—good features and sharp, keen eyes. He had, without any exception, the smallest hands and feet I ever saw to a man of his size. He was very black but had curly hair. The most striking feature in the character of the king was an excessive love of money. He was avaricious in the extreme. I was told that he built a large house somewhere in the bush where he kept the most valuable part of his money, but nobody but himself and two or three of his favorites knew where the house was. But the redeeming points of the old king were hospitality, and an abhorrence of cruelty. He was much beloved by his people.

[P. 213] The first thing I did after my arrival at Pallaka, was to build me a house, which I completed in about a month, with the assistance of several Veys, whom I found in Pallaka.[42] It was a small structure, being about thirty feet long, with a piazza, which the Barlains never have to their houses, and slab doors and windows; the railings around the piazza were nailed, as were the slab doors and windows. Varni, my Vey carpenter, procured me a piece of timber for a table; the King added two chairs, which he had purchased from the Vey traders; these, together with my chests and boxes, presented a somewhat civilized appearance. But what excited the curiosity of the simple people, was the nails; people came from all the neighboring towns to see the "iron house," as they called it. And so great was my reputation exalted by what they considered my architectural skill, that had his Majesty, the King of Barlain, been acquainted with the European method of bestowing honors in monarchial government, he would have created me a knight of some order. There is no country in the world, perhaps, that affords more game than Barlain; deer, wild hogs, ground hogs, "bush" cows, and many other wild animals, too numerous to mention, infest the forest of this delightful country. The usual mode of taking these animals by the Barlains is very simple. A path is cut round several acres of forest where wild animals mostly visit, and the place is surrounded with strong nets, strong enough to hold an elephant, if he should happen to get into it. And then all the men, women and children that can spare the time, gather themselves on one side, and whoop and halloo in such a way that everything in the enclosure, snakes and all, are very soon on the move, seeking safety in flight. But it is fleeing from bad to worse: a few leaps, and the animal is sufficiently tied up in the nets to prevent his escape. The women are left to keep up the noise, while the men go round and kill whatever may be caught. I always accompanied them on these occasions, and have seen from twenty to thirty animals of different kinds taken in a day. Whatever is caught is carried and laid at the feet of the King, who deals out to every man his share; his own and mine, however, were always the largest. Whenever there was no hunting of this kind going on, I used to amuse myself by bird shooting in the farms; some of which were as much as three or four miles from town.

Barlain is a small kingdom about two hundred miles east of Monrovia. It is separated from the Pessah country by the river Yea [Vai], and from Bousa [Loma] by the Bousa mountains. The people speak the Pessa language, but strenuously deny all relationship with them; yet they certainly are Pessahs, though of a higher order. They are the most industrious peo-[p. 214]ple in this part of Africa, and, with the exception of the Manni-Mohammedans, are the most civilized. Like all other tribes in and around Liberia, there are to be found among them some who are of a deep yellow complexion, and some who would pass in any country for mulattoes. They have good features, and generally very pretty hands and feet. They are very hospitable to strangers, and even kind to their enemies, and, as a general thing, they are milder and more placid than any of their neighbors; but regularity of life, industry, honesty, and a "reverential regard for their parents and rulers," are the most prominent traits in the character of the Barlains.

The soil is exceedingly fertile, producing the finest sugar cane, tobacco, corn, cotton and ground-peas I ever saw in Africa. The people spare no pains in cultivating these articles; consequently, there are no beggars to be met with in Barlain. Besides the above named articles, plantains, bananas, pine-apples, pawpaws, and almost every fruit known in the settlements are plentiful. I think, too, the palm-oil made here is superior to that made near the beach. In short, Barlain is one of the most productive spots I have met with, and it is certainly

"—A goodly sight to see
What heaven hath done for this delicious land,
What fruits of fragrance blush on every tree,
What goodly prospects o'er the hills expand."

Nature has certainly dealt out her blessings in some parts of Africa with a lavishing hand. India is not the only place where "every prospect pleases."[43]

The principal mountains in Barlain are the Pessah-pru in the west. I have very good reason to believe that there is limestone to be found somewhere in these mountains.[44] One day a Manni man brought me a piece of something which looked very much like limestone, and knowing no other way to prove it, I burnt it; it turned out to be the genuine article. The man said he had seen the same kind of stone at Monrovia, and knowing that it was worth something (Mohammedan like) he would not tell where he found it.

There are several small streams in Barlain that abound in fine fish, such as the trout, cat-fish, torpedo and perch. The only rock to be met with is, for the most part, the same as that used in the settlements for building. There are several kinds of birds here that I have not seen on the coast.

The largest towns in Barlain are Pallaka, the capital, Gorlu [Golu, 7°30'N, 9°29'W] and Wau-i-wu-ta [Wennwata, 7°35'N, 9°35'W] (Wau-i-wu's town.)[45] Pallaka and Gorlu each contained about four thousand inhabitants. About one-third of this number are Manni-Mohammedans. They have made but few proselytes, their aim being to enhance their worldly interests. The centre of attraction in Barlain is Jangay [Kposangie, 7°29'N, 9°38'W] the great market town.[46] Here the beauty and the industry of the interior natives are to be seen every Saturday, the Jangay market day. There are six other towns in Barlain where market is held on different days; and to distinguish one from the other, they have adopted a name for every day in the week. Thus Jangay market day is called *Siveru-noisu* (Saturday market,) Bamaquorli market is called *Mannissa-noisu* (Sunday market,) and another is called *Tenni-noisu,* or Monday market, and so on, until we have the seven days.[47] Notwithstanding I believe the names of days were instituted to distinguish the different markets, the people have discovered the utility of it for other purposes—as, for instance, you ask a man, "When are you going home?" *"Nair de monnissa."* (I am going Sunday,) or any other day he may choose to name. I think it worthy of notice, too, that they should name only seven [p. 215] days, and give a name to each day, and not to the towns where the markets are held. But the Jangay market is worthy of a description. It is a large square behind the town, enclosed by a strong stockade; the people sit in the open air beneath several large shady trees, with a few little booths scattered about for the benefit of those who may have dry goods for sale in rainy weather. People from all parts of the interior flock to this market, not by hundreds, but by thousands, and everybody is sure to put on his best. Besides Barlains, may be seen Bousas, Kpellays, Ba-ba-beenias, Basees, King Boatswain's people, and the handsome Mannies towering above the rest, with their gay robes and short trowsers, sandals and beautifully worked caps, cheating and lying, getting everything cheaper than anybody else can buy it, and getting more for their articles than any others can get for theirs of the same kind.

⁂

[P. 217] Besides the products of the country, such as palm-oil, rice, goats, sheep, fish, fowl, cotton in the seed, spun cotton, cloth, knives, earthen ware and hundreds of other little things, the market is crowded with guns, powder, iron pots, salt, calicoes, coral beads, writing paper, and most every thing that is to be found in a trading factory on the coast.[48] The Manni people sometimes bring down large quantities of mineral salt. The market is admirably conducted under the supervision of an officer, whose business is to settle disputes and collect whatever may be gratuitously given towards keeping the market in good repair. No domestic cloth is allowed to be sold until mid-day, from which time until dark it is really amusing. As soon as the officer gives notice that market is open for the sale of "country cloths," the Mahometans commence. You will see one with a beautiful cloth in his hand, crying, "Twenty sticks of salt! twenty sticks of salt!" Two hours later, you will hear him crying, (for the same cloth,) "Fifteen! fifteen! fifteen!"—by and by it is, "Ten! ten! ten!"—and about dark it is, "Who'll give me three? who'll give me three? who'll give me three?" At length the poor fellow, seeing that he can't cheat any body, rolls it up and carries it home; but he is sure to carry it during the week to some of the lesser markets, and if he fails there, he will send it to the beach and take whatever he can get for it.

The next object of attention—if not the first—is the bridges, which are constructed in the following manner. First, on both banks of the river, opposite each other, is erected a butment eight or more feet high, and about five feet wide; next, a layer of vines, the bigness of a man's finger, is stretched across from one butment to the other as tight as they can be drawn and made fast. Other vines are then interwoven in this layer, which forms a sort of net work—this is the floor. A number of vines are then firmly bound together and stretched across for hand railings; vines are then tied, about an inch apart, all the way across, to one of the railings, and carried under the floor and tied to the other railing. The same materials are then interwoven in the sides in the same manner as in the floor. The bridge is now formed. Lastly, strong vines are suspended [p. 218] from the trees (a place where there is a number of large trees is always picked out) on either side of the river and both sides of the bridge, to the railings. Thus the bridge is strongly supported by the butments and the suspending vines from the trees, and will bear the weight of as many people as can crowd themselves on it. They generally last, with a little repairing, from three to four years. The great *Sali-Shirong* (or devil, as we call him) of the country always superintends the building of bridges, consequently no woman knows how they are constructed, but believes that the devil builds them.[49] No woman would under any circumstances show her face when the sepulchral voice of the *Sali-Shirong* is heard in the town, or any where in the neighborhood. The word *Sali* in the Pessah language, literally means medicine, and the word *Sali-Shirong* means medicine-man or doctor. These doctors are much feared by the people on account of their supposed power over life—it is thought that they are able to kill or cure without being present, or even in the same town where the patient may be. Besides this, the doctors possess the power of cursing the country with pestilence or famine. The principle *Sali-Shirong* is called *Ngamu:* and like "Egugun," the great devil of the Yoruba people (as described by an American traveller) is a "tall fellow," (about ten feet) "fantastically clad from face to foot," and is, with some tribes, "a personification of the executive or vindictive power of the government, but all women are required to believe that he is a terrible spirit who takes vengeance on violators of the law."[50] The women have a *pollondoi,* or devil bush also; the head woman is called Zo, and is, generally, the oldest woman in the country, and none but old women are allowed to associate with her while performing the rites of the devil bush. Zo would no sooner pry into the secrets of *Ngamu,* nor *Ngamu* into those of Zo, than a boa constrictor would, knowingly, crawl into a bed of drivers. All the tribes I met with have some notions of a supreme being, "the unknown, the cause and preserver of all things," they have a name for God, but are ignorant of his true character. These people have a number of idols, which they worship merely to protect them from evil. Every man has two or three which he carries every where he goes. These little idols are generally from three to four inches long, made of clay and decorated with cowries.[51] Whenever a man is about to take a long journey, he makes a sacrifice to his idol and earnestly implores its protection. Whenever a man is taken sick, he attributes it to the displeasure of his idol, to whom, immediately on his recovery, he makes a "grand" sacrifice. The most acceptable oblation that can be offered to one of these idols is the juice of the Khola, which, after being chewed, is spit upon the idol; sometimes the blood of goats and chickens (white) is sprinkled on the greegree; and on particular occasions a libation of palm wine is added.

Slavery exists in Barlain, but in the most modified manner; the master and slave labor together in the field during the day, and sleep together on the same mat at night: the slave calls his master father, and if the children of the master be younger than the slave, they must call the slave father; nor is any man allowed to call a bond-man a slave; he would be made to pay for it. The slave has a voice in all palavers as much so as the richest man in the country. Another beautiful trait in the character of these people is, that they will not make slaves of their own people.

I wish to say something here about the "great Mama palaver" which originated in the interior about the year 1854. It was thought at one time by the Liberians that this secret league of the natives was propagated by the crafty and warlike prince Boombo, during his visit to Bassee [p. 219] Darn, King of Barlain, in 1856.[52] The Liberians were under such serious apprehensions, too, in regard to Mama, having heard that it was a secret move by which Boombo had managed to draw all the interior tribes into an alliance with him for the purpose of attacking the Republic; but the Mama fraternity owes its origin to motives entirely different.

The following is a correct account of the origin of Mama. It is well known by most Liberians that the natives living between the settlements and the interior natives have always made it a practice of preventing the interior natives from coming to the "beach," and, in fact, they have tried, and partly succeeded, in cutting off all intercourse between the Liberians and the Barlains, Bousas and other tribes whose countries are rich in the production of camwood, palm-oil, &c., and from whom alone ivory, cattle, cotton and gold dust can be procured. Whenever the people from the interior attempt to come down to trade with the Liberians, they are stopped and forced to do their trading with the natives above named, who pay them whatever they please; and if any complaint is made, they are taken (the interior natives) and made slaves. These pirates then take the stolen produce, bring it to the beach, and make the Liberians pay almost as much for it as it is worth in Europe or America. This is an every day occurrence. The King Boatswain people are the ring-leaders. I have seen, at Bo-Poro, from eighteen to twenty men robbed of all they had, (some three hundred dollars worth of produce,) and sold into slavery, because they refused to pay one-half of what they had for the privilege of passing through the town. Similar depredations gave rise to Mama. At length the interior people became tired of such treatment, and resolved to make war on the King Boatswain, Goulah and Pessah tribes; but the latter, having the opportunity of procuring guns and powder any time from the beach, had a decided advantage, and after a hard fighting, succeeded in shutting their enemies up in their own country. Things, with the interior natives, now became desperate. They saw that their bows and arrows and short cutlasses were but toys in their hands, when standing before powder and balls, rifles and genuine Kentucky bowie knives; consequently, they had to resort to stratagem. Accordingly, Mama, a Bousa prince, convened all the different tribes in his neighborhood, who, after deliberating on their almost hopeless condition, swore an eternal alliance with prince Mama against every tribe which was not a member of the league. By this means, prince Mama soon became very powerful; the fame of the secret league was soon spread far and near, and people came hundreds of miles to "take the Mama gree-gree." Now to show the intentions of the interior natives in getting up a secret fraternity, I will present to the reader some of the leading oaths that every man is obliged to take before he is allowed a voice in the "Mama bush." First, the man must swear that every Mama's cause shall be his cause—and that he will defend a brother Mama, if it is necessary, unto death; and that he will use all his influence in opening a road by which the interior people may have intercourse with the Liberians. Besides the oaths above mentioned, no two tribes or men who are Mamas can fight. Mama became the watch word; and a sort of masonic sign, which nobody but a Mama man knows, is now a protection to a member of the league amongst all the people living beyond the Dey country. Memmoru, king of the King Boatswains, became a member in 1857, and, to his astonishment, found that, without breaking faith with Mama, he could no longer prevent the interior natives from coming to the beach and trafficking with the Liberians.[53] So great was the excitement in the King Boatswain country on the return of the king from Barlain, whence he [p. 220] had gone to be initiated, that the people threatened to depose him. All his head-men, after learning the nature of the Mama, refused to join, and there are but few Mamas in the King Boatswain country now. Had Memmoru known the nature of the oaths that he was about to take before entering the

Mama bush, he would never have taken it. By this means, and this means only, the interior natives are enabled to visit the settlements. Mama has done good in more ways than one. Every king who becomes a Mama man is obliged to admit all in his dominions who wish to become members—free or slave; and yet nobody can hold a Mama man in bondage. Consequently, thousands and thousands of slaves have been made free men, by the institution of the Mama. There are several powerful chiefs yet in the King Boatswain country, who would not join the league, and who still interfere with travellers. Barlain is now the strong-hold of the Mama people, and Mama himself, who died in 1856, is supposed to be living in splendor somewhere in or near Pallaka, a report to that effect having been promulgated by his followers.

According to tradition, Barlain was once inhabited by the Kpellays, the most uncivilized, with the exception of a portion of the Pessahs, I have yet seen. King Bassee, great grand-father of the present King, drove the Kpellays out and took possession of the country. The Kpellays, however, have been waging a very destructive war with them ever since. However, there have been no wars in Barlain now for several years. The last fight they had with the Kpellays, if what they say be true, was bloody in the extreme. The fight took place in front of Pallaka, between the town and the river. They fought from the rising of the sun until the going down of the same.

"Long time the victory in even balance hung."

However, the Barlains prevailed. The Kpellays were put to flight: a youth hewed himself a passage through the ranks of the Kpellays, and cut away the bridge which cut off the retreat of the enemy. The Barlains pursued them to the banks of the river, where many of them, seeing no way to escape, plunged in and perished. Several bush fights took place after this. At length, "grim" visaged war smoothed his wrinkled front in Barlain, and "capered nimbly" over (perhaps) to Russia,[54] where "brain spattering" was carried on in a more civilized manner.[55]

Visit to Kpellay.

I have said that the Kpellays inhabit a mountainous country to the northeast of Barlain.[56] They are a tall, handsome race of people, rather grave looking, and might pass for Mannis or Mandingoes. I had begged of King Bassee Darn several times to allow me to visit Kpellay, but he always refused, alleging that my person would not be safe amongst such savage people. Some of my friends hinted, confidentially, that the Kpellays were great elephant hunters, and, consequently, were owners of several very large tusks, which they would be willing to exchange for cloth, tobacco, &c., and that Bassee Darn was afraid that I would like Kpellay better than Barlain. I saw very plainly that I would never be able to go with the king's permission: so I concluded to go without it. I told Gotora and Fasseena of my intention—they approved of it, and on the 1st of March we started for Zeppea [N'Zappa, 7°57'N, 9°16'W]. To allay suspicion, we took nothing with us but our guns, one of which I intended to present to the king as a "dash." On the 4th, about mid-day, we ascended one of the Kpellay mountains, and after a walk of about two hours, reached Kamo [?Gagamu, 7°25°N, 9°25'W], a town of perhaps two thousand inhabitants. Du-gla-ma-kinna, the king, was seated under the palaver house, on a leopard skin tastefully adorned [p. 221] with cowries and bound with red leather. Kamo, though of considerable size, is a miserable collection of circular huts; the people, however, are very industrious; they raise more rice than the Barlains: cotton is pretty extensively cultivated also. Ilisu [?Yélé, 7°30'N, 9°19'W] is a town not so large as Kamo, but is of more importance, on account of its being the market town. Kpellay is noted for the great number of elephants that roam over this beautiful country. Nearly all the ivory bought in Montserrado county is brought from here. The Kpellays are very expert in taking the elephant, though their mode of attack is perilous in the extreme. The hunt is generally attended with much ceremony. The company, before leaving for the bush, is drawn up before the house of the king, who makes a sacrifice of a white fowl to his gree-gree, as a sort of bribe to the "fickle goddess" Fortune.

The next in order is a sort of scalp dance, in which all the leading hunters make all sorts of grotesque gestures, showing how they intend to hand, draw, quarter and eat the first elephant that should be so unfortunate as to be caught napping or grazing. The ceremonies being ended, the "mighty hunters" take their departure for the bush. So soon as they come upon the track of a elephant, the party separates; and whoever happens to be so fortunate, or unfortunate, as to get the sight of the "big meat," has the most dangerous part of the work to perform.[57] The hunter noiselessly approaches the elephant from behind while grazing, slaps him on the side with his open hand, and slips under the elephant to the other side, and as the elephant turns round to see what it was that touched him, the hunter discharges a triple load of pot legs and iron slugs behind his ear. Very often the elephant falls dead on the spot, but sometimes he will walk off a considerable distance, where, however, he is soon surrounded by the dispersed party.

The danger in this mode of taking elephants is this—if the man, who approaches the elephant and strikes him on the side should happen to stumble or make a mis-step whilst passing under the elephant, he would either be crushed to death by the elephant treading on him, or be beat into a jelly by his trunk. Several have lost their lives in this way.[58]

We remained in Kpellay four days, the most of which time was spent at Kamo. A great many people came to see me from the adjacent towns, who brought me presents of rice, fowls and ground nuts. The Kpellays are, physically, one of the finest tribes in this part of Africa—tall, erect, muscular, with Semi-European features. They are warlike and vindictive in the extreme. The most of their time is spent in piratical excursions against their neighbors. Prisoners taken in war by them are cruelly treated, and some are put to death in the most barbarous manner. The languages [*sic*] of the Kpellays seems to be a mixture of Bassa, Pessah and Vey.

The soil here appears to be as good as any, and the beauty of the scenery in some places is indescribable. A number of beautiful birds is to be seen in the forest, and a tribe of the sauciest little red monkeys I ever saw. During our stay at Kamo, Fasseena gave us the slip and went over to Bo-Pora, where he remained until my return home. Early in the morning of the 9th of March, we left Illisu for Pallaka, where we arrived on the 14th. On my return, I was informed that the king had concluded to spend several months at Ngarella, (water side,) and that the king was having a house built for me like the one built by myself at Pallaka.[59] I was glad of this, because there was some talk of war, and the walls, etc. round about Pallaka were not in a very satisfactory condition. However, no war came, and on the 20th of March we took up abode at Ngarella.

Gree-gree Poison

[P. 1] There is nothing, perhaps, more disagreeable to a traveler among uncivilized nations, then the revolting and inhuman practices of, and the superstitious reverence paid to their priests, or gree-gree men.[60] During my stay in the interior, I was eye-witness to several scenes which I shall never forget. I must record one of them here.

An old woman at Pallaker, who had planted a pretty extensive field of rice, and who had not slaves enough to prevent the birds eating it, applied to a gree-gree-man for a gree-gree to place in the field, that would act in the stead of slaves. The old rogue of a priest, as a matter of course, gave her something, for which she was obliged to pay before leaving the spot. It was a little bundle of something, about an inch long, besmeared over with the juice of kola-nuts. She was instructed to bury it in the centre of the field, and she was assured in the most priest-like manner, that as long as the gree-gree remained buried there, the birds would not only no longer be prevented from eating the rice, but would be deprived of the power of flying across that particular farm. The rice was planted, and so was the gree gree, and the time came when "seeds feel the influence of the sun, and unfold themselves in the bosom of the earth, spring up and grow." But this was not the case with the mother. But this was not the case with mother Palla's rice; for despite the vigilance of the gree-gree, the birds bore off every grain of it in their little maws. Perhaps the little thieves were at work whilst the gree-gree was asleep. However, the rice never came up, and the old lady very naturally applied to the priest for an explanation of the failure of her rice crop. But the old priest was prepared for her, and had been since the day he gave her the gree-gree. He asked her if she had put the gree gree in the centre of the farm, and on being told that she had, requested that she would give him until the next day to consult his *Sali,* at the expiration of which time he would explain to her the reason why her rice did not come up, and besides, perhaps he would be able, through the efficiency of his gree-gree, to make the rice come up.

The next day came, and the old woman was again seen at the door of the *Sali pellimu.*[61] The old hypocrite, with a face as long as that of a used-up Montserrado politician, told her the following diabolical tale, "The rice you planted," said he, "has been picked up, not by birds, but by a witch; and that witch is a woman who lives in this town."[62] Of course, the old woman believed every word that had been told her, and went and reported it to the King. In a few moments afterwards, the whole town was in an uproar, for everybody had heard that a witch was in their midst. The cry naturally arose, "Who is she? who is she?" Women looked at each other, as they passed, with suspicious eyes. Men were afraid of their own wives. At length, the people assembled, and demanded that the gree-gree-man should tell who the witch was, in order that she might be put to death. He went and consulted his gree-gree, and came back and told the people that the witch was a white (yellow) woman, a virgin, and was standing in their midst. There was but one woman in the crowd that answered to that description; her name was Kuldu, a pretty yellow girl of about eighteen or twenty years. The gree-gree-man had a spite against her for some time, because she had refused to be his wife. Although she was a general favorite in the town, everybody looked upon her now as they would upon the most hateful thing the imagination could conceive. Curses and imprecations arose from every quarter of the town, and her own mother fled from her, as though she had been the evil one himself.

The innocent girl was taken into custody by the gree-gree men, who were paid and feasted by the people for the inestimable service they had rendered the community at large in detecting the wretch. Within three days after this, a poisonous decoction, more fatal than the deadly Upas, was coursing through the veins of the unfortunate Kuldu.[63] The third day after Kuldu had been declared to be a witch was closed, the sun was already half hid behind the western mountains, when my attention was attracted towards the western gate of the town, by seeing several women start out of the gate, and run back again. I started towards the gate, but the women made signs to me to go back; however, I paid no attention to them, but went out. A few yards to the left-hand side of the gate, behind the wall, was a form stretched out at full length upon the ground, wrapped in a country cloth. I went and gently raised the cloth from the head of the prostrate form—it was Kuldu. Her once yellow face was now black, swollen, and emaciated; already had the film of death gathered over her once bright and sparkling eyes. One minute more, the sun is gone, and with it fled the spirit of Kuldu!

The name of the man who prepared the poison, and administered it to Kuldu, was Ka-ta. The arch-devil was found dead one night in his own house, about a month after he had poisoned Kuldu. The incidents connected with his death were of so striking a nature, that I am compelled to relate them here. A Mohammedan, with whom Ka-ta had contracted a debt, applied to him one day for a settlement, but as a third person was not present when the debt was contracted, Ka-ta, of course, knew nothing of it.[64] The Mohammedan carried the palava to the King, who, after hearing both sides of the question, decided it in favor of the follower of the faithful. Ka-ta appealed to the higher powers—the gree-gree-men, who, as a matter of course, decided in favor of Ka-ta. A quarrel ensued. The Mohammedan swore by the Prophet, that Ka-ta should not live to see another moon. Ka-ta swore by his Sali, that the Mohammedan should not live another week. They parted; Ka-ta retired to consult his gree-gree, and the Mohammedan his Koran.

The resources of these two men to work mischief were not trifling, and that something serious would grow out of the matter was evident from that fact; and I was selfish enough to be partial towards the Mohammedan, for the poisoning of Kuldu was still fresh in my memory. However, nothing of importance occurred for about three weeks, when Va Fulli, the Mohammedan, suddenly disappeared from Pallaka; but as everybody knew the roving disposition of the Mohammedan, his sudden departure, or his absence from town, was not particularly noticed. The day after Va Fulli's departure, Ka-ta was missing; still the people did not seem to evince any uneasiness, nor do I believe anybody noticed it but myself. For two days Ka-ta's house was closed. So on the evening of the second day, I went to the King, and inquired after Ka-ta; the King said he thought Ka-ta had gone to his farm. But that very night, though a dark and stormy one, brought Ka-ta to light. About eight o'clock, strong evidence of a fearful tornado was prognosticated by dark clouds overhead, and total absence of them on the horizon.[65] About a quarter past eight, the tornado was raging with all its fury. I never witnessed such a tornado. Loud howled the winds; the lightning blazed through the darkness of the clouds; heaven and earth were in uproar. During the tornado, trees of great size were uprooted, and carried to a considerable distance, and several houses in the town were unroofed, and Ka-ta's was among the number.

As soon as the tornado was over, the people went round in crowds, to see and console those who had suffered from its effects. The King, always ready to do a good turn for his people, was at their head. When they arrived at Ka-ta's house, the greater part of the mob was ordered to keep a distance; the door was broke open, and the King, preceded by a boy with a bamboo torch, went in, where, to his surprise, he found Ka-ta lying on a mat dead. The dead body, already in a state of putrefaction, was a hideous sight swollen almost to bursting, the two eyes protruded, and his fists clenched, as if he died in the act of grasping at something. The King came out, and went to his residence. Soon after, the town-crier went round, and gave out that the King's orders were that every man and woman in the town was to go into their houses, and there remain until morning; and further, whoever disobeyed should be punished with death. I know of but one that disobeyed; he, however, was not put to death. At nine o'clock there was not a cloud to be seen. The moon, amidst her starry train, shone resplendent; and by her light, the man who disobeyed the King's orders saw several men take the dead body of Ka-ta, wrap it in a mat, and carry it out of the town; but what they did with it after that, nobody knows but themselves. The next day, Va-Fulli made his appearance in town. It is useless for me to say that Va-Fulli poisoned Kata; all the people at Pallaker knew it, but who would dare tell him so? I told him so one day, and he acknowledged it, and said he could poison everybody in the town in half a day, if he chose, and would do it if they gave him cause; and furthermore, said he, "The Koran tells me to do so." The Mohammedans are much dreaded by the people among whom they have settled.

Cases of poisoning, such as those of Kuldu and Kata, are every-day occurrences in the interior. But none but the gree-gree men and the Mohammedans are guilty of these crimes.

After leaving Bananella, we entered a good open road, some six or seven feet wide.[66] We continued in this path until we came to a brawling little river, darting swiftly through narrow passages in the ragged rocks, and, some distance further, fell with a thundering noise over a ledge of rocks to a considerable distance below, and formed a sheet of milk-white foam. A vine bridge is suspended over this noisy little stream. About sunset, we came to a sudden fork of the road; and as we turned into it, a view burst upon us, the soul inspiring beauty of which must be seen to be fully appreciated. Before us was a circular range of high mountains, some of which were clothed in a livery of the richest green, while others were cultivated to their very summits—far above the clouds. In the centre of this circle of mountains, another mountain rears it head, upon the summit of which stood the city of Suloang [Zolowo, 7°39'N, 9°33'W],[67] surrounded by a splendid wall of clay; and its hundreds of tall, circular, thatched roofs glistening in the setting sun, presented a sight well worthy of an artist's pencil.[68] We entered Suloang a little after sunset, and I was conducted to the house occupied by my countrymen.[69] I found them all, with the exception of one, in good health and spirits. The reports brought me, from time to time, about them, had been somewhat exaggerated; nevertheless, their situation was anything but an envious one. It is well known that none of the kings living within seventy-five or a hundred miles of the beach, will, if they can possibly prevent it, allow strangers to visit the countries interior of them. This, as they supposed, well conducted policy, is to keep the Liberians in ignorance of the vast riches of the interior. Again, when they have to contend with a Liberian who is determined to push his way through at all hazards, to the interior, they will invent frightful stories, about men with tails, and a tribe who have their eyes on the top of their heads; and finally the poor traveler will have to contend with the Ghirzu, a frightful something, partaking of the shape of both man and beast. Many such ludicrous tales were told to the Liberians at Suloang, but as they appeared to be determined to go, King Bahmo lost all patience with them, and told them plainly that they should not go unless they would agree to leave nearly the whole of their goods with him; and he nearly succeeded in getting the whole of them. We did not see King Bahmo on the day of our arrival. He was absent on a visit to one of his half towns; news was speedily carried, however, that another "white man" had come. His Majesty, with the well known African hospitality, sent me a fowl and a bowl of white rice for my supper. The bearer brought a message from the King, which was translated by Gotora, as follows: "De King say he self no live here, but him big Sissa live here, and him big Sissa be head man dat time King self no live here.[70] Any ting you want him big Sissa give you." Towards evening, the next day, I was informed that his Majesty had arrived, and that he desired so see me; of course, I lost no time in presenting myself. He was seated on a mat, with several of his principal men at his left hand; he wore the usual costume of the Mohammedans, and appeared to be about fifty years of age. He wore a moustache that would have made a French colonel die of grief. King Bahmo was "black but comely," with a countenance indicating shrewdness and intelligence.[71] During our conversation, he stated that he had no objections to the Liberians passing through his country, but he was apprehensive of the Bababeeias, whom he described as being very cruel and pugnacious. However, before the conference ended, he had agreed not only to let them pass unmolested, but to render them some assistance. A bumper of delicious palm wine closed the interview. The country of Suloang is, without exception, the loveliest spot I ever laid eyes on. The wildness and beauty of the rugged but majestic mountains, and the tree bordered streams, render the whole scenery picturesque in the extreme.

At Suloang, the heavy forest and dense undergrowth begin to diminish, giving way to an open country, interspersed by little prairies; consequently, fire-wood is scarce and very dear. The people of Suloang are tall, black, and handsome, somewhat resembling the Mandingoes; they belong to the Bousa family, and like the Bousa their language is one of the sweetest and most musical I ever heard. I am under the impression that nearly all the tongues spoken in Guinea are dialects of one great language. The affinities of the Bousa language extend over a great part of the interior.

About the first of August [Tuesday, 27 July], Messrs. Seymour and Ash left Suloang for Musa-du (the city of Moses), the capital of the Mohammedan kingdom of Manni. Most Liberians have been laboring under the impression that all the Mohammedans who visit the beach are Mandingoes; this is a mistake. All Mandingoes whom I have met with in Liberia were Mohammedans, but I have seen Mohammedans who were not Mandingoes. The Mohammedans in the interior of Liberia resemble the Mandingoes in features, but speak an entirely different language. The Veys belong to the Manni family; their language and traditions are proof of this. The Mandingoes are very gay in their manners, while the Manni people are, for the most part, grave, serious, and thoughtful, and rigid adherents of the Koran. The American missionary, Mr. Bowen, speaking of these people, says: "I was told of a class of devotees in the tribe, who abstain from war and traffic, and refuse to shake hands with another man's wife."[72] This is strictly true. I have seen several at Palaka, who would not allow another man's wife to enter their houses.

On the 15th of August, I bade adieu to Suloang—Suloang, whose "melancholy loveliness, once seen, can never be forgotten." I arrived at Palaka on the 20th. The rain commences in the interior about the middle of this month, and as it deprives the people of the pleasure of indulging in drumming and dancing, they amuse themselves by giving night entertainments. These night entertainments are admirably conducted; men and women—expert singers—fantastically dressed, and with musical instruments, sit in front of the audience, and rehearse the traditions of the country, together with other legendary tales, some of which are wild and thrilling in the extreme. A Bousa man, named Sukea, was the favorite performer. His favorite theme was a story called "Yandomah," which is not inferior to any of the stories contained in the "Arabian Nights."[73]

On the 15th September, I bid a final adieu to Barlain. Notwithstanding the rains had fairly set in, I thought I would like to return home by way of the King Boatswain's country; and accordingly, with the consent of my faithful Gotorah, I set out for Bo-Pora [Bopolu, 7°4'N, 10°29'W], the capital of that piratical kingdom above mentioned. On the 27th we reached To-to-korri [Totokwele, 7°3'N, 10°24'W].This town is the favorite residence of Memmoru Sowe, the King of the Boatswains.[74] It has several two-story houses, which are finished off in a manner which one is hardly prepared to see among these pirates. Bo-Pora is still another day's walk south-west of To-to-korri, and is situated in a valley, surrounded by mountains on every side.

Prince Boombo was also at Bo-Pora, on a visit. He appeared to be very glad to see me, and insisted on my spending two days with him. I complied with his request; and during the whole of the first day, I had to perform the duties of an amanuensis to his Highness. I penned several letters for him, one of which was directed to a relative of his, a respectable trader in Sierra Leone.

The King Boatswain tribe is composed of Veys, Golahs, Kausaus, Pessahs, Bousas, and several other tribes. They have composed a language for themselves, which is partly original, and some words from each of their respective tongues; they have assumed the name of Condors. There is little or nothing to be admired in the character of the King Boatswains. They are a set of roguish, kidnapping knaves, robbing all the interior natives who attempt to come down and trade with us, and making slaves of all who resist. Memmoru Sowe, king of Condor, is nothing more nor less than a generalissimo of banditti. Nearly all of them are Mohammedans.

Sowe Boatswain, the founder of the King Boatswain kingdom, died some fifteen or twenty years ago, leaving two sons.[75] Lansana, brother to Sowe Boatswain, according to African usage became king of the country, and guardian of the two orphan princes. King Lansanna survived his brother but a few years; but, strange to say, on his death-bed, made his people swear allegiance to Memmoru, who, being the youngest, had not a shadow of right to the kingdom. Memmoru was living, at the time of his uncle's death, at Monrovia, with one of our most respectable citizens, who had spared no pains in trying to inculcate in him religious and moral principles.[76] As soon as Memmoru heard of what had taken place, he hurried home to take possession of the kingdom, and the vast riches which his father had acquired by honest trade with the Liberians. He was received with open arms by all except his older brother, who, notwithstanding, never made any attempt to recover what rightfully belonged to him, but always appeared morose and dissatisfied. Memmoru became apprehensive of him, and had him assassinated.

At the time of my arrival at Bo Pora, Memmoru was preaching a crusade against an inoffensive Pessah town, with as much fervor as ever Peter the Hermit preached against the infidels of Jerusalem.

On the 1st of October, we bid adieu to Bo-Pora. Nothing worthy of note transpired until the night of the 11th. It was dark and rainy; about 9 o'clock a number of lights was seen ahead of us, but nothing daunted, we went on. Soon, voices could be heard; we hurried on, and soon found ourselves in the midst of a large town. A few minutes after our arrival in the town, we were somewhat frightened by the crashing of a huge bell; by and by several persons met us with "How do you do? how do you do? And so you have got back." The spell was broken; the town was Clay-Ashland, and we were home again.

Observations on the Different Tribes

The most important tribes in the interior of Liberia are the Condors or King Boatswains, Barlains, Bousas, and the Manni people.[77] As regards the Condors, owing to their savage and warlike mode of life, a careless observer would without hesitation, pronounce them to be ready and fit only for destruction. But I am of a different opinion. They are a powerful tribe, and are feared and respected for hundreds of miles around. Their present degradation is owing to the avaricious character of some of their chiefs and headmen. The most of them are friendly towards the Liberians, and embrace every opportunity to imitate civilized habits; they are in favor of the Liberians building settlements in their country, and only submit to the rule of their tyrannical chiefs through sheer necessity. Taking all things in consideration, it is my opinion that the Condors will be the first to embrace civilization.

The Barlains are decidedly a superior tribe to any in the immediate vicinity of the Republic. They are an agricultural people, and punish idleness as a crime. Theft is a capital crime. They, too, are anxious for an American settlement to be established among them; and that a settlement in Barlain could not fail of success is incontestible, for several reasons. 1. The Barlains and other tribes in their neighborhood are in favor of such a scheme. 2. The soil is of extra fertility, well adapted to the raising of sugar-cane, pepper, ginger, ground peas, and unsurpassed for the production of cotton. 3. One-third, if not more, of the forest of Barlain consists entirely of camwood. 4. Any quantities of iron may be purchased at the market-place at a very reasonable price, and it might be made a special article of trade, and enough might be purchased with ease to supply the wants of the Republic at least; with these advantages, I think the settlers would soon find themselves in a very prosperous condition.

The Bousas are noted for the immense quantity of cotton raised by them, which is woven into cloth. Cloth is the only article of trade produced by the Bousas. These cloths are brought from Bousa, on the backs of slaves, to the beach, where they are disposed of for calicoes, guns, powder, salt, etc. This is another proof of the advantages an American settlement in the interior would have; for it is hardly to be supposed that the Bousas would prefer going to the trouble of converting their cotton into cloth, carrying it to the beach, a distance of three hundred miles, when, if there was an American settlement in Barlain, they could carry their cotton to the settlement, and dispose of it for the same articles; and, besides, this would be an encouragement to them to enter into the raising of cotton on a larger scale. We have no conception of the amount of cotton that could be purchased in Bousa in one year. The longest tobacco I have ever seen, I saw at Suloang. And as very good tobacco has been produced on the St. Paul's river, I have no doubt but that as good as any in the world may be raised in the interior. As a matter of course, the natives are unacquainted with the mode of curing tobacco; consequently, they use it in its green state, that is, they do not smoke it, but make the following curious use of it.

The green leaf is plucked from the stalk, and roasted in the fire, which renders it soft and pliable; the juice is then squeezed out, which is taken and held in the mouth until it becomes cold. I suppose they derive the same benefit from it that their civilized brethren do from chewing it. But the most remarkable feature about it is, they can converse with their mouth full of tobacco juice as well as though they had nothing in it; but, like every thing else, I suppose, "practice makes perfect." The Bousas cultivate another species of tobacco, called *tangon* plant, the leaves being about the size of a man's hand. This they smoke. So soon as the plant has attained its growth, the leaves are broken off and dried in the sun; when dried and ready for use, they have the appearance of ten leaves after being boiled. It has the scent and taste of any other tobacco.

The Manni kingdom is situated about one hundred miles interior of Barlain; I made special inquiries about this place from persons living there, and others who had visited it. Musa-du is the capital; the present king is named Vai-Mami or Vey-Mami.[78] Musa-du is said to be a city several miles in circumference. A Veyman who had visited both Musa-du and Timbu, the capital of Futa, said that Musa-du was the largest. The Manni people raise a great many horses and cattle, which they bring down to Barlain for sale. There are no trees in Manni, the whole country is prairie; for firewood the people have to substitute cow dung, and a kind of moss which grows abundantly in that country. As regards the religious and moral character of the interior natives, it is useless to comment. However, I will make a few remarks. About one third of the population living within five hundred miles of the coast are Mohammedans, and one half of that number mere hypocrites; the rest are Pagans, all of whom, however, have some idea of a Supreme Being, whose dwelling-place is known to himself alone; and whose anger, when kindled, may be appeased by sacrifices, the shedding of blood, the juice of kola-nuts, and penitence; and whose viceregents or representatives are the gree-gree-men. All this is well known to most people. The morals of the interior natives are far superior to those of the natives living near the beach, who have had intercourse with foreigners. In regard to the social intercourse of the everyday habits and customs of the African, I believe the whole continent to be synonymous. From the information given of the moral character, the manners and customs of the people of Africa, by travellers and traders, an unprejudiced person can but allow that Africa is Africa all over—Moors, Arabs, and Negroes; and that a Guinea Negro, one free from the contamination of foreigners, is no lower in the scale of humanity than his brethren of the Caucasian; and that there are white men in America and Europe who can do things with as much brutal apathy as the blackest and most woolly-headed Negro that ever sweltered beneath the burning rays of an African sun.

4

George L. Seymour, 1858

EXTRACTS FROM THE JOURNAL OF THE JOURNEY OF GEORGE L. SEYMOUR TO THE INTERIOR OF LIBERIA, 1858

More than a year ago, we published some interesting letters, dated at Paynesville, in the Pessay country, 100 miles east of Monrovia, written by George L. Seymour, Esq., a Liberian, whose zeal and enterprise had induced him to emigrate from the sea coast to the interior, and who made an earnest appeal to his colored friends in America to enter into the inviting mountain country where he was settled, and extend a knowledge of Christianity among the native tribes.[1]

After a year's residence, and the opening of a small farm, and school, and blacksmith's shop, Mr. Seymour heard so much about the country still farther interior, that he desired to make a tour of exploration. An appeal was made for aid to defray the expenses and over two hundred dollars contributed in Monrovia and Buchanan, for that object.

Mr. Seymour, after overcoming obstacles which delayed his journey more than a month, began his journey late in April, and was absent nearly eight months, during which time he travelled, going and returning, about seven hundred miles.[2] We find a series of articles in the Liberia *Herald,* descriptive of the people and places visited by him, full of interest. Hoping hereafter to give them *in extenso,* we for the present furnish a brief synopsis of the journey as far as yet published, prepared by a friend in this city.

Our readers will see that Liberia has interiorward a fine country, and an intelligent and industrious native population. They will, perhaps, learn more than ever to appreciate the advantages which our colonization of Liberia affords to efforts designed to explore and occupy the religious desolations of Africa.

1858, April 28 [Wednesday].—Left the new settlement of Paynesville [? c. 6°32'N, 9°45'W] (100 miles S. E. Monrovia) for Bandae's town [?Gbandela, 6°52'N, 9°44'W, or Gbondoi 6°55'N, 9°37'W], passed through several small towns, over beautiful streams of water and heavy forest; rice, corn and cassada, in rich profusion; parted from King Darpley half way, and arrived at Barbondaw late in the afternoon; found Jourporpar, another Pessy king waiting to pass us on to his town 15 miles farther—had a good supper of rice and fowl in clay bowls.

April 29 [Thursday].—Rose early, town summoned to prayers, waited all day for our baggage from Paynesville.

April 30 [Friday].—Travelled N. E., over hill and dale, beautiful country, well watered, and no obstruction to a cart path, passed four towns, all had a variety and plenty of vegetables; but few swamps, timber in abundance—arrived at King Jourporpar's town of 85 houses and 425 inhabitants; the finest cattle I have seen; the people have plenty of rice, meat, and palm oil. The king has pleasant features, a good countenance, dark complexion. Cotton spinning and weaving carried on here. The king sent a letter by them to Monrovia for a missionary to come and live there.

> [P. 304] *Dear Sir*—I am a man of authority in the Pessey country, but I and my people are very ignorant as it relates to the things of God.[3]
>
> I have been informed that there is a God and a Savior; but there is no one to instruct me and my people in the way of salvation, or my children in letters. I have a town over which I preside, counting eighty houses, and about four hundred people; and we reside about one hundred and fifty miles from the sea-coast. I am willing to do all I reasonably can to encourage some Christian man and family to reside in or near my town, for the purpose of imparting the necessary instruction. Will one come? Will any one have compassion on us? Does no one love our souls? Must we be lost because no one cares for us? Is there not a heaven for us as well as for Americans? I am poor and ignorant, and can say no more, but hope some one will give me a favorable answer.
>
> JOURPARPAR.

May 4 [Tuesday].—We left the king with regret for Portarwee, 26 miles N. E., and passed through a delightful country, through rice and cassava farms; the country well watered with cool streams, on rocky and sandy beds; passed a high hill with excellent farms around it, one had 100 acres of rice;

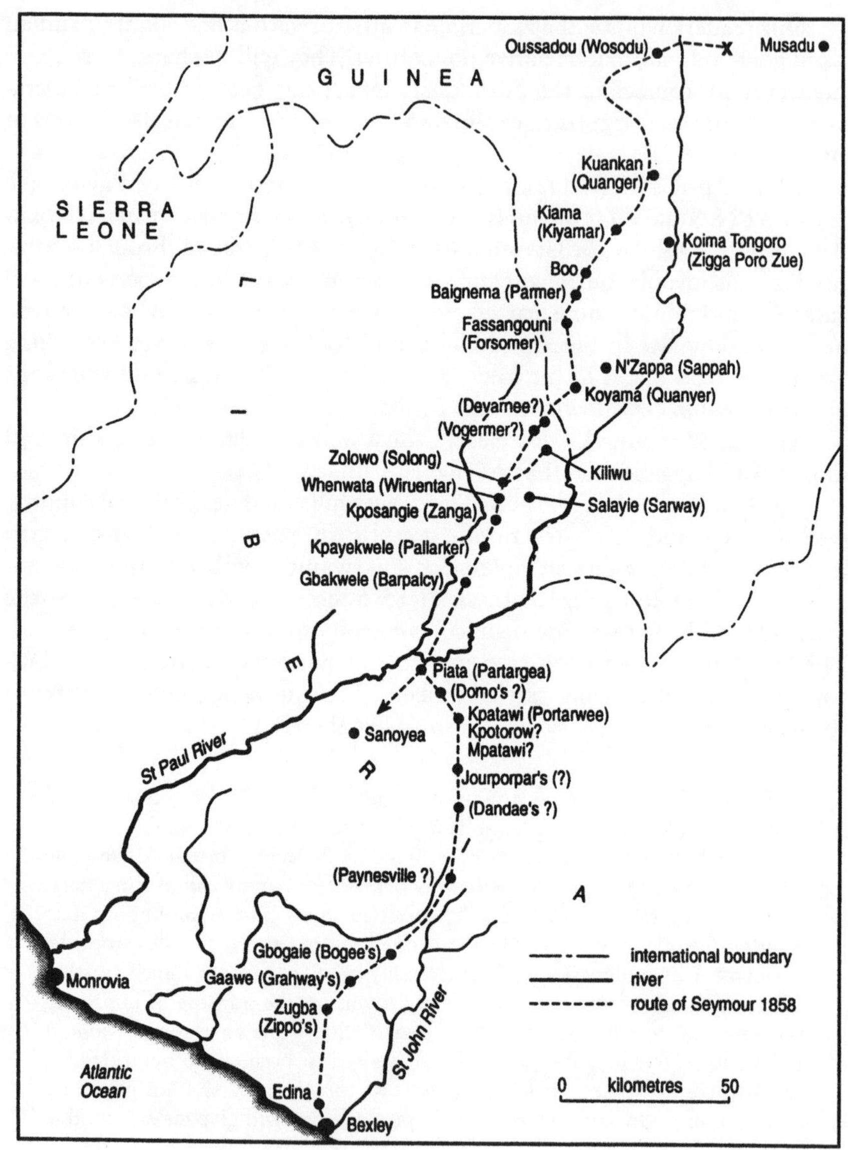

Map 8. George L. Seymour's journey, 1858.

afternoon arrived at Portarwee [?Kpatawi, 7°7'N, 9°40'W] on a hill 500 feet high, it has the largest orange tree I ever saw.[4]

May 5 [Wednesday].—The next morning, Mercury 71 degrees, the valley was covered with a mist as white as snow, the surrounding hill tops as they appeared above the snow-white mist presented a beautiful sight.

May 6 [Thursday].—Passed some fine farms, and came to King Domo's town; he is about 75, copper-colored, a very dignified person, hair very white. The Queen is a fine woman, dark color, easy manners, pleasant address, and we felt we were among a superior people.

May 8 [Saturday].—Ascended a mountain in the town almost entirely under cultivation, and I could but pray for the day when Liberia's Lone Star might float over these verdant fields; no part of North America can boast such beautiful scenery, and such richness of soil.[5] We saw to-day the fattest woman any of us had ever seen; passed furnaces in good condition for smelting iron, which is of very superior quality.[6]

We saw industry, cleanliness, economy, and mechanical genius, far surpassing any I had ever seen among the natives of the coast, or many of the immigrants from the United States. There is an active barter trade carried on with this whole region—which the people of Liberia have no idea of—and as soon as the interior of Africa is properly known, the old stigma of indolence and ignorance with which the people have been branded for so many ages will be entirely removed.

May 14 [Friday].—Left King Domo's town, passed through many towns, and in 18 miles came to Partargea [?Piata, 7°13'N, 9°46'W], about 3 miles from the St. Paul's river, on a beautiful elevation, with a fine view of some mountains to the N. E.[7] The town has 60 or 70 houses, and 300 or 400 inhabitants; good wagon roads may be made all through this country.

May 15 [Saturday].—Went to St. Paul's river, a beautiful, bold stream about 200 yards wide, its course very serpentine; on the north side is a cone-shaped mountain in the centre of the plain, which we named Mount Stephen, in honor of President Benson; they should have named it Mount Benson, about 200 miles from the coast.[8] It would be a good place for the Capital of Liberia.

The religion is Mahommetan, and here the faithful missionary will find ample room for his work.

May 17 [Monday].—Left Partargea, and crossed the St. Paul's river, and halted at a town 3 miles from Partargea; here is abundance of fine fish; ascended some high lands from which we had a fine view of the river and country below; here we counted 93 farms all under very good cultivation.

May 19 [Wednesday].—Went to the top of a mount they called Mount Elem.

May 22 [Saturday].—Left the town of Carterpool, passed through several towns, and then reached the [Via] river—came to the town of Barpaley

[Gbakwele, 7°24'N, 9°51'W], crossing a new bridge for foot passengers, with hand rails on each side; from this town we passed to the large town of Pallarker, the residence of King Barsedon.[9]

We rested a little in Pallarker, and then passed on to a suspension bridge over a tributary of the St. Paul's; this bridge is a wonder; where did they get the idea of one?[10] From the bridge we passed to another town of King Barsedon called Zear, or waterside; it is well fortified.[11] The king is a stout-built man of ebony hue, quite fleshy, his head shaved on the top, hands and feet quite small, about five feet high; he commands a large force, and rules over a large territory; men and women are generally larger here than on the sea coast. We met here many young men who spoke some English, and had resided some time at Monrovia.

May 26 [Wednesday].—The King Barsedon and his attendants went out with their game nets to catch animals near his farm; on his return he brought in several of the antelope tribe. He had the hide of a lion, killed some distance in the interior. Leopards are said to be troublesome in this section.

The king is very avaricious, and was much dissatisfied with the present I gave him. A young Liberian who had been here six months, was a great favorite with him.[12]

May 28 [Friday].—Left Zear for the Mandingo town of Pallarkar, about 300 people.[13] The king would not let his "boys" carry our baggage, and we had to carry it ourselves for some distance, three miles, as none of the Mandingos would carry it against the wishes of King Barsedon, until we were out of sight of Zear.

At Pallarkar we saw five looms for weaving cotton cloth, also five potteries, which made very neat ware, pots, bowls, and oil jars, to hold eight or nine gallons, and some very neat pipes for smoking. A market is held for two hours, abundantly supplied by the females from the surrounding towns. The people are more intelligent, and the kindest people we have seen.

The head man, named Vomba, has resided in Monrovia six months at a time, and is much respected; the town is about 15 miles from the St. Paul's, the path going over hill and dale.[14] The women have silver bracelets, some costing over $60, and they show to great advantage on the delicate wrists of the beautiful Mandingo damsels, whose teeth are white as snow, hair tastefully plaited, clad in white or colored cotton cloth, with a part of the body naked, displaying symmetry, and beauty of form, which creates a charm of no ordinary character.

Pallarkar is about east by north from Monrovia, about 175 miles distant, and 235 miles from Grand Bassa. A good cart path may be made the whole distance, upon which could be established Mission stations on a field white for the harvest, but no laborers among the countless thousands.[15] The solicitation of the natives for missionaries is general. Quite a number of long horned cattle are frequently coming to, or passing from the town to the interior. We made a visit to the potteries where they make beautiful ware, and fine smoking pipes, which are traded off into the interior in considerable quantity.

June 1 [Tuesday].—Mr. Taylor and myself went to visit a small town a mile from Pallarker; it is a perfect garden, where they cultivate every variety of vegetables; near here some mountains are visible, and also some E. S. E. from Pallarkar. We have not seen a barren piece of ground the whole 230 miles we have come. It is a month since we began our tour.

June 2 [Wednesday].—We took a walk of five miles over hill and dale, and streams of pure cool water, and cheered by the music of the numerous birds; it is a delightful country, all the people in their farming labors. Here should be the future Capital of Liberia. The St. Paul's river, can no doubt, be made navigable the whole distance to its mouth.[16]

June 3 [Thursday].—Went to the market, which is conducted solely by women, who are very sharp at a bargain. The Mandingoes are very strict in the management of their children, who are required to obey and to labor when young; they and their children are very cleanly, they are all industrious; it is not correct to say Africans are an indolent people.

June 3d, 1858 [Thursday].[17] A company of about fifteen play-actors or dancers came into the town of Pallarker, about one hundred and twenty miles north-east of Monrovia. Four were dressed in white pantaloons, gathered at the ankles in Turkish style. The Mandingoes were assembled in great numbers. After they had played an hour or more on their rude instruments, they left Pallarker, beating their drums in a slow march. The people are very fond of music. They go to wars, dance, and cut and plant their farms with music.

June 4th [Friday]. I left Pallarker early, with brother Ash, for Zanga [?Kposangie, 7°29'N, 9°38'W] the market town, twelve miles, leaving Mr. Taylor to take care of our baggage; for, as I have mentioned, the Mandingoes were unwilling to aid us, unless King Barsedon consented.[18] We travelled on through a beautiful piece of woodland, with now and then a farm, with corn and rice in different stages of growth. The view had a charm that destroyed any feeling of fatigue. We ascended a lofty hill with some difficulty, and expected to go down on the opposite side; but it proved to be high table-land, with good water, which makes delightful places for the small towns.

After passing the summit of the hill, the view of the hills and mountains were of unsurpassable beauty. We continued on this table-land, or ridge, with deep vales on each side, to the market town.

In the vales and on the hills were seen the Royal Oil Palm, the hope and strength of the country. It is universally tall, but the African goes up, with his hoop, sixty, eighty, even ninety feet, going round the tree and cutting out all the ripe nuts, and then descending in the same manner. One vale was delightful indeed, and seemed to be mostly occupied by palm-trees. It could be selected as a mission-station to great advantage.

The oil is the purest I have seen in the country, and they dispose of all they make.

The soil is red, yellow, and white clay and sand, and white, red, and black gravels mixed with iron ore; the rocks are of a gray sand mixture, very hard, with flesh-colored veins. Rocky Hill was capped with huge blocks of superior building-stone. The timber appeared to correspond with that near the coast. We passed several streams of cool, clear water, flowing over beds of rocks, gravel, or sand. The heavy forest has very little undergrowth, and not tangled with vines and briers. I was compelled to take off my shoes to pass a small stream but once between Pallarker and the market town, a distance of twelve miles, and the path was wide and firm. We were in company with many persons going to Zanga, the large market town, so we had no difficulty in finding the way; in fact, the path is one of the large roads to the interior—of course, much worn. Zanga stands on a hill. It has about one hundred and fifty-six houses, and about six hundred inhabitants.

The name of the head man is Varsheardupar.[19] There are sixteen head of cattle in the town. We were a wonder to the inhabitants, being the first civilized men they had seen; and they flocked around us to gaze upon us.

On our way to Zanga, we met a young man who could speak English, and learned he had lived with Mr. Hines, of Monrovia, where he received instruction in English.[20] I got him to turn back with us, and he rendered us much service as interpreter.

June 5th [Saturday]. Sitting in the house, with my journal, I heard a great noise of market people, about eight. I made a visit to it, and found about two thousand persons of different tribes, mostly Pessys, and some Mandingoes, and Booseys, and Wamo people, with two or three broad stripes each sides of the face, all actively engaged in exchange and barter.[21]

On the ground were about two hundred country cloths, about one hundred and fifty gallons of palm-oil, and jars, pots, bowls, etc., and amber dishes to hold a solution of tobacco, held in the mouth in place of chewing, which is the practice among the interior tribes; also, about two hundred sticks of salt were there. It is a long bamboo tube, holding a quart; a hundred of them is the market value for a full grown slave. I was told this market was small, compared to some further in the interior. The people began to disperse by nine, and by two were all gone. They are clad in their best, and most all in home-spun; and every variety of stripe may be seen, with now and then a plaid on. Head handkerchiefs are very common in this part of the country, no doubt the fashion went over from Africa to America. Many men had on hats and caps, as if they felt the importance of showing off to the best advantage. Some come a day-and-a half walk to market. Oil, soap, rice, iron, cloth, etc., are exchanged for salt, colonuts, pots, and jars, etc.

Zanga is near a branch of the St. Paul's. I brought specimens of the rock in the vicinity. The weapons are similar to those further back in the interior—muskets, spears, arrows, cutlasses, knives, etc. The people are very kind to us, and appear glad that we are going through the country. This is a delightful spot for a mission-station, and they would be rejoiced to have one.

I have seen persons in confinement—some for misconduct, and some as slaves—and some on the road to market. Slavery is said to be mild and partriarchical, by those who have traveled in Africa. So I find it to be, as I have hinted elsewhere; but civilized influences would check the traffic, and I feel it to be the duty of the Liberian Government to extend her influence beyond the limits of her own territory.

June 6th [Sunday]. We had a short service for the people of Zanga, who attended with great stillness and order. Our health has constantly been very good.

June 7th [Monday]. Brother Ash and myself took a short stroll in a path near the town, and went to another part of the St. Paul's branch which passes the town of Pallarker, and saw a most beautiful fall; we heard the sound a considerable distance. The hard granite is in square blocks ready for buildings. It is a fine place for a high-school or college. It has been named Ash's Falls. It is an absurd idea that Africa is a dead-level plain, it has great variety or beautiful mountain scenery and fertile vales, and is very healthy.

June 8th [Tuesday]. James Hines and myself left Zanga in the afternoon, to visit a mountain six miles distant. We arrived near sunset, as we walked slow, to view the country. We passed through several towns—one quite large—and rice and corn fields. The ascent of the mountain was tedious. We arrived at a farm on the side where we refreshed ourselves with some pure cool water in a clay jar, under the shade, for those at work on the farm. We ascended to the top of the mountain, and arrived at Sarway, the town on its very summit. It is small, but very comfortable, but surrounded with colar, plantain, and banana trees, all in a thriving condition. The name of the head man is Saqually.

The mount is about one thousand two hundred feet above the sea, and has the most extensive view I have yet seen. We named it Mount Roberts (in honor of our Ex-President). Some of the mountains near are cones; others are continous chains. To the south-west lies the beautiful plain of Benson's View. In this plain several towns are to be seen from Mount Roberts, also the Royal Palm tree in its majesty; and on Mount Roberts arbor cotton is in a most flourishing condition—superior to any cotton we have seen. The people have cut down most of the heavy forests, except here and there on the mountain sides. From the top of Mount Roberts, one hundred and eighty-two farms, and seven towns are visible. Benson's View is a most delightful location for an American settlement. It should be occupied by the missionary. The inhabitants, willing, peaceable, numerous, and the country well watered.

A branch of the St. Paul's passes through a part of this plain, and numberless small streams. Oil is taken to the large market, and jars and pots of it abound. I saw several looms in Benson's View, and everything gives evidence of industry. Nothing is wanted but good religion and civilization to complete their happiness. The civilized world owes this part of Africa a heavy debt, for many of her sons have been carried off to Christian lands. About half-way down Mount Roberts, is a beautiful spring, from which they get supplies of the nectar of life.

⁂

June 9th, 1858 [Wednesday].[22] The St. Paul's river is about half a day's walk from Mount Roberts, south-east. The towns in the plains have either sweet or bitter oranges. The air of this region is healthy. From the top of Mount Roberts, we saw, at sunrise, the whole of the plain below covered with a white mist, like a thick mantle of snow, with the tops of the green hills above it like islands, and creating a charming contrast in colors. Before 9 o'clock, the golden rays of the sun disperse the mist, and reveal the beautiful landscape of mountain, hill and vale. In the afternoon we returned to the town of Zanga.

June 12th [Saturday]. The people began to arrive about 7 A.M., and before 10 o'clock the market was crowded with persons, standing or sitting, with various articles of exchange from the interior. There was the greatest confusion of noise in talking. They have great curiosity to see us, and, not being accustomed to mulattoes, some regard us as dead men come to life. They were, however, very kind to us, and many would hail us with "Good morning." Society is much improved by these markets, and it would be a good place to send light and knowledge through the country.

June 14th [Monday]. Left Zanga, at 8½ o'clock, A.M., and crossed the Pallarker branch of the St. Paul's; traveled several miles, and arrived at a small town on a hill, and halted a few moments for the baggage carrier to overtake us. We passed through cultivated fields, up and down hills, and through vales, which, with the distant mountains, presented a beautiful sight.

After a walk of nine miles, we came to the town of Wiruentar [?Wennwata, 7°35'N, 9°35'W], one of the half towns of King Barmo's.[23] It was surrounded by a strong mud wall, of twelve feet high, and four feet thick, and has nine hundred inhabitants. We were treated very kindly. Their gardens had several kinds of salad and greens, and we saw a large sweet-orange tree, full of fruit, some of which we ate; and one woman presented us a basket of clean rice.[24] There are cattle, sheep, and goats; and fowls are plentiful. This is the first town on this road, in the Boosey country. We crossed Sims Fork,[25] the largest branch of the St. Paul's, the dividing line between the Barling and Boosey countries.[26] We crossed over a suspension-bridge. The farther we penetrated the country, the more kind and hospitable the inhabitants were. We met several cattle-drivers, with their animals, through the day; and the farther we went north-east, the more visible were the signs of perfect independence.

We left this walled town, and walked through groves of colar trees, about eight miles, passing rice-farms and beautiful streams of water, and sometimes through the site of old towns, sometimes near, and sometimes leaving Sims Fork, which winds among the hills, and, with dashing frenzy, rushes over the rocky obstructions, with a roar which is a relief to the serene stillness of the afternoon.

From a slight elevation, we saw the city of Solong [Zolowo, 7°39'N, 9°33'W] of about 2,200 inhabitants.[27] We entered by four gates. The walls are twelve to sixteen feet high, six feet thick; gates, large and heavy. This is a beautiful location for a mission-station. The people are kind and agreeable, and good livers. There are ten looms here, and it is pleasant to hear the shuttles. There are smiths shops at two of the gates. There is an extensive trade carried on in bullocks, cloths, and slaves. On entering the town, we were conducted to a large, comfortable dwelling, in which we were well accommodated. We had the pleasure of eating a good supper provided by the King's sister, who appears to be the third in the kingdom. We had cocoanuts presented to us, as a token of friendship, we being the first civilized men in this part of the country.

The city of Solong is on elevated ground, and makes no mean appearance. The whole city and inhabitants display an advanced state of society. The young women of Solong are beautiful indeed, and very kind, and would make you feel at home among them.

June 15th [Tuesday]. King Barmo arrived in the city about 9 A.M., with great dignity of personal appearance, but with little display.[28] His voice is soft and musical. He is tall and well proportioned, about fifty years of age, about five and a half feet tall, of true ebony hue, beautiful teeth, and pleasant countenance, commanding great respect from his headmen—dressed in a large white cloth, a large brass ring on each ankle, brass rings on his hands, and a short sword. He furnished us a good breakfast of rice and fresh beef. We had prayers as usual, at which many of the people were present. It is likely the first thing of the kind among them; and they were very attentive. After breakfast, the King received his dash, with which he appeared tolerably well pleased. We stated our object, and he withdrew with his suite. In an hour, he returned with expressions of acceptance of what he had received; but he told us he could not give us boys to take our baggage, on account of the war in which he was engaged with King Barsedon. King Barmo has many women. He is very kind to them, if they behave well; but if not, they have great reason to fear. His children are numerous, and some of them very beautiful—the females, in particular.

The women do not stuff their children like the Bassas, Pesseys, and Barlings, but give them cold water to drink, and wash them in it; they are then oiled and laid in the sun to dry, which accounts for the beauty, strength, and brightness of their eyes. The children get no other food, when young, but breast-milk and cold water. The men and women of the Boosey tribe, of this part of the Condo country, are good, portly, well-framed people, and appear to attain great age. They have beautiful, clean, white teeth, of which they appear quite proud, and take great care.

June 17th [Thursday]. Brother Ash and myself took a tramp to a mountain west of Solong. In about two hours, we arrived at the foot of a short chain of mountains, the loftiest peak of which is called Mount Nancy, on the north-west side of Benson's view. From the top, we had the most delightful view. The summit and sides are mostly planted in rice. From the top of Mount Nancy we counted one hundred and forty farms, and seventy mountain peaks, the city of Solong, with five considerable towns in the south-east. The palm-tree makes a large part of the remaining forest, and can be counted by thousands. Their oil is plentiful. The city of Vogemer, and three towns [are] visible to the north east. Mount Nancy is about 1,300 feet above the sea; and, on the north-east side, a short distance from the summit, is a springy marsh, which sends down streams of good water through the plains of Benson's view, which is well watered throughout. It is the place and position for a Liberian city. Granite rock is plenty, clay for bricks, and wood to burn them; and a country swarming with inhabitants, inviting the missionary to reside among them. They are peaceable and kind, and give great hopes of future mental and moral improvement; and I cannot conceive Liberia is guiltless, if her church remains inactive towards her native bretheren of the interior.

June 26th [Saturday]. We went to a little town, on a hill, about four and a half miles from Solong; having a beautiful view of the surrounding country-mountains, hills, vales. Cultivated farms were to be seen. The people plant cotton at the same time they plant rice. The farms are of great extent; for it is common to see a hundred-acre farm in one cutting. Their manly industry is proverbial.[29]

June 27th, Sunday. We employed ourselves in reading and resting, and talking to a company of men in Solong, who listened with attention.

June 28th [Monday]. Continued to transcribe my Journal. It is the last day of the second month of our tour; and we have not seen a day that it rained all day, and but one very cloudy, but on the contrary, the weather has been very pleasant, the same as in the dry season—occasionally raining in the night, but so little as not to interfere with traveling. The winds of the interior are very mild, and they distribute the fragrance of the forest through the air. I noticed the dew fell much sooner and heavier, near the city of Solong, in the shade of the mountains than it did elsewhere.

July 6th [Tuesday]. I went with Mr. William Taylor to the walled half-town Wireuntar, to see the execution of a murderer, who had killed a little boy. Stopped on our way to look at the falls in the Sims Fork branch of St. Paul's; found it grand and imposing. It is almost a perfect dam, and would require but little labor to make it complete. It is called the Boiling Ffalls [*sic*]. It is a beautiful mill-seat, and a charming spot.[30] We remained at Wireuntar until the 10th [Saturday], the day of the execution, walking a few miles round the town to see the country, which was beautiful indeed.

On the morning of the 10th, the people were stirring early, and there was a large assemblage of headmen and chiefs, and gentlemen who were in attendance on the occasion; and for them a bullock was killed for a dinner, on the same ground where the execution was to take place. After the animal's throat was cut, it was quartered—hide and all. The law of the Marmar fraternity is very strict, in relation to bloodshed. As I have mentioned before, there is no redemption. Abut [About] 3 P.M., the young man was brought to the place of execution, which was a grave-yard not far from the town, shaded by colar and other trees. The ground was cleared as neatly as a dooryard. There was a large assemblage of persons in court-order waiting for the order for execution.

The young man was compelled to sit on the ground near the grave dug to receive his body. He was questioned how he would be despatched, but changed his mind, and said he would be cut up. He then spoke as loud as he could to inform the murdered boy he was coming. Then the executioner sprung upon him, and, in an instant, cut off the left hand, and then the other, and then the heel tendons, when the King ordered his head to be cut off, which was done, in two strokes. His body was quartered, and thrown into the grave; and the blood mingled with that of the bullock, as they were both butchered on the same spot.

As in the United States, the execution was a matter of levity with some; but by far the greater number were sober and sedate. After they buried the body, all dispersed; and we, in company with King Barmo, returned to the city of Solong, with deep impressions of solemnity, on account of the bloody sight.

July 15th [Thursday]. Brother Ash and myself went to a peak northeast of Mount Nancy, named Mount Joseph.[31] On the side towards Solong, are steep bluffs, about four hundred feet above the plain of Benson's view. It has a fine spring, which gives about fifty gallons of soft, cool water per hour.

July 19th [Monday]. We went to a half-town north-west from Solong, to look at a hole in the side of a mountain, reported to contain a leopard, a snake, and a porcupine. We ascended Yates ridge. From the top, we wound round and down to a crystal stream, which we followed up till we came to a small hole in the hill, which we found contained nothing. We followed the stream down the descent to the plain below. This part of Africa presents one of the greatest varieties in nature. Mountains, hill, vale, plains, rivulets, streams, creeks, and rivers are seen always—and all these waters beginning at some mountain spring. On both sides of Yates ridge, in the valleys, are rice farms, with cotton, corn, and casava, presenting a cheerful appearance. This ridge is about a mile north-west from Mount Nancy, and between them a Liberian settlement could be established to great advantage. It has iron near it, with a variety of other deposits. We saw rice heading, to-day, for the first time in this part of the country; and in the small towns are to be seen men, women, and children working in cotton, picking out the seed, carding or bowing, and spinning it. This part of the Booseys do not manufacture iron, but obtain their supplies from the upper Condo country, of the upper Booseys. We returned to the half shire town, much fatigued, and hungry.

1858, July 23rd [Friday].[32] Brother Ash and myself walked from the city of Solong, five miles, and came to the barricaded and walled town of Kiemer, north-east of Solong. It has about one hundred and eighty dwellings, and nine hundred inhabitants. The head man is named Worobar. It has two single, and one double loom; and industry is the order of the day. From Kiemer we went to Kleemoo [?Kiliwu, 7°44'N, 9°28'W], a walled town, about twelve miles north of Solong—four looms; nine hundred and fifty inhabitants; name of the head man Yeekbyssee. The country is beautifully diversified, with mountains, hills, and vales, and mountain streams tumbling down among the rocks with a wild rush, every stream being a good mill-race. The *great Misardo path* runs through these towns, and is the highway for the Mandingoes to this part of the country, one of whom we met on his way to the great market of Zanga. He was about twenty-five, dark color, but beautiful features; a fine set of teeth; tall and well proportioned; and good hair. The Booseys, and people from the north, have much better hair than those more south. In these two towns are several head of fine, long-horned cattle;[33] but we have seen no horses yet, nor any of the shining dust.[34] We have enjoyed many a good mess of tomatoes at Solong; but who planted them we do not know. The people make no use of them.

July 26 [Monday].—This day of Liberian Independence was not forgotten by us, and we fired a salute on the occasion; and Mr. James L. Sims, who is also on an exploring tour, acted as Marshal for the day. Our dinner was rice and wild hog's flesh, well cooked. We made arrangements to go tomorrow to a town farther in the interior.

July 27th [Tuesday].—Brother Ash and myself set out for Carmer's town, said to be within four days' walk of Misardo.[35] After traveling twelve miles, and going over a very high hill, or mountain, going through old farms, with the thick, wet grass closing on each side of the path, we came to the town of *Vogermer,* barricaded and walled—about twelve hundred inhabitants, and six looms; spinning of cotton going on at a brisk rate; several cattle in the town, and one large bull of the long-horned tribe, with a good number of sheep and goats. The mountain streams are numerous, and, dashing through the sharp windings among the hills, made a delightful contrast with the other sounds. The rocks were of a pure white, and very plentiful. I took specimens.

There is a large stream near the town whose bed and sides are granite. It forms beautiful waterfalls and mill-seats. The inhabitants of Vogermer were perfectly amazed at us, and crowded around to have a look at the strangers, and, after they had turned away, would come and look again. They were very kind, and no way disposed to interfere, or take hold of our things without permission. There are mountains near the town, which give the place a beautiful varied appearance. In the town I saw the arbor cotton in perfection, spreading from the main stalk eight or ten feet, spreading on the arbor like a vine, and so high as to admit a person under it to pick the staple. It was full of young bowls and blossoms, and seemed inclined to shoot from the parts of the husk lying on the arbor, in straight stalks. There were several Mandingoes in the town. They had gardens, as is usual in large towns, with cotton, corn, egg-plant, etc. We were furnished with a supper of rice and dried meat.

July 28th [Wednesday].—After breakfast, we left Vogermer, and traveled about five miles, and came to a small town, surrounded with corn, plantains and bananas. We ate our dinner here, of two large fowls and rice. The people were very kind to us, and seemed willing to furnish us anything we wanted at our own price; but we were compelled to decline all but necessary purchases. We very readily found some one to aid us on with our baggage. We passed on over hill and dale, and streams of water, on a good path over sand and gravel, with some clay spots, and saw a lofty hill of one solid rock, with scattered weeds or bunches of grass upon it; the sight was beautiful. We passed on, and climbed up a lofty part of the same ridge, about two hundred feet; but on the opposite side we descended but about one hundred feet, and this has been the case through the country. There are, therefore, the highlands of the interior, where plenty of health and life can be enjoyed. We soon got out of the hills, and came to a large spot of flat swamp—water on it half-knee deep; the bottom, of sand. It was about three hundred feet wide where we crossed it.

We soon arrived at the city of *Devarnee* (about fourteen miles from Vogermer), inclosed by a barricade and mud wall, with three hundred to four hundred dwellings, eighteen hundred inhabitants, and nineteen looms. The gardens are beautiful, clean, and well filled with tobacco, cotton, eggplants, yams, etc., etc. They manufacture pots, jars, etc. Some Mandingoes reside here also. As usual, a great crowd followed us. They are very kind, and gave us bananas to eat, the first thing; and some brought a fowl, which was cooked for our supper, with rice. A kinder people I never met with; and, in fact, their kindness is to be complained of, in some cases; and, if a person has not some stamina of moral character, he will accommodate himself to every sort of kindness. The wall of Devarnee is a much larger circle than the wall of Solong. The headman is large, portly, dark, well proportioned, and seemed disposed to accommodate us to every thing to our choice. We slept in a large kitchen. The large doors were closed with large, strong bamboo mats; and we have not slept so sound and comfortable on our journey. We sang a hymn or two, and, as usual, the people listened with attention, and thanked us for it.

To-day is the last of the third month of our tour. The month has been mostly very pleasant—a few days cloudy, with mist and rain in the night. On the whole, it may be called pleasant.

July 29th [Thursday]. We left Darvarnee early; and, as we passed out of the last gate, the throng increased, until there was an uproar behind us not unlike cities in the civilized world. We have seen some of the finest-looking people, in this city, we had ever seen—the men, well formed, muscular, and handsome, dark skin, good features—and would, no doubt, if cultivated, acquit themselves well in any profession. The women are not to be surpassed; and their lively, intelligent countenances bespoke that they were of no ordinary grade. They are all very industrious—cotton-picking, carding, spinning, and weaving being their great business. They rise early, and you may see them at the water-side as soon as it is light. They are all furnished with large cloths, which keep them warm, and are not shriveled up with cold as some people I have seen.

In about three miles, we lost sight of the mountains and hills, and came to a beautiful, fertile plain, in appearance, similar to the country near the seacoast. We passed rice farms, with cotton and corn, and several pea-nut-farms all looking as if the people considered good-living as the first object of man. At a small town, having refused to purchase more rice and fowls than we wanted, *they gave them to us;* thus, as we penetrated the interior, we found kindness and hospitality somewhat cultivated among the inhabitants. When they were informed that we were on our way to *Misardo,* it was not a wonder with them as with the people back; but they seemed glad we were passing through the country.[36] We arrived at a farm with a few houses, and ate our breakfast, and prepared our sandals, the only thing we could use on the path with comfort. We concluded to stop here for the night, as there was a heavy mist, and we were told we could arrive at Camer's the next day. We were treated very kindly by all; and I had a beautiful Weamo woman offered me; but of course declined the offer, as too generous for reason and right.

The only change in the wild vegetation to-day, was a berry, now and then, we had not seen elsewhere. The palm is as abundant as in other sections of the country. In fact, Africa is a land of palms; and the bamboo is as plentiful in places, as near the seacoast; and the people act wisely, and make their wine of the bamboo, and save their palms.[37]

July 30th [Friday]. After breakfast of rice and fowls, we left the small town early, and soon entered a swamp. After we got out of it, the path was good; and, in six miles, we came to the city of *Quanyer* [Koyama, 7°54'N, 9°22'W], fourteen miles north of Devarnee, with a barricade and wall, four hundred dwellings, and about nineteen hundred inhabitants, and eighteen looms. It is presided over by King Kullamoo, a young man of some degree of manliness, who would be an ornament to society, if educated. Some of the people are as handsome as I have ever seen among the country people, and will bear a good comparison with most of our Liberia ladies in beauty. Some are very light color, while the dark ones are none the less handsome. The hair of either is beautiful. They have hand-bands of a neat black braid, worn around the forehead, and often down a little above the eyes. The people are very kind indeed. The King made us a present of a goat for our dinner, which we had cooked, and ate of it plentifully. We met here a young man named John Hooper, who informed us he received his instruction in English of Mr. Hooper, at the Liberian mission, White Plains, St. Pauls river; and who can tell how much this city owes its nobleness of character to the influence of this young man![38] He speaks in the hightest terms of Mr. Hooper, who may be satisfied that he has conferred a favor on Liberia, that in this one instance is worth sums untold to the world; for the influence of the young man is as visible as if he had been an accomplished missionary.

Quanyer is a place for a mission-station, but the persons wanted here are Liberian missionaries. The country as far as we can see is level; the soil rich; the rice fields and ground-pea lots most flourishing. Most of the roads to the city are so wide and clean, a horse and buggy could travel them with comfort. In the small town where we slept last night, we saw some good sized onions. On this side of the mountains, the water is running to the south-east, and on the side towards Liberia, it runs to the south-west. The people are very clean in their cooking. They have covers to all their pots; and they wash them clean. The covering of pots we first noticed at Potayea, on the St. Pauls (which we left 4th [*sic,* 14th] May), and likely it extends to the desert; for I regard it as a custom introduced by the Mandingoes, for as I have stated, many of them reside at Potayea. There are a good number of cattle at Quanyer, and a daily market for oil, rice, peas, corn, cotton, and snuff. There are many gardens in the city, and about it, attended to with care. Those outside are along the wide, well cleared paths, which seem attended to for the comfort of the people.

July 31 [Saturday].—We left Quanyer about 7 A.M. The young men were instructed to inform King Seiyea that he must receive us with kindness, and aid us, as we were going on to Misardo, from his brother King Carmer.[39] We parted from King Kullemoo with the best of feeling; for he appears to possess the feelings of a man. We travelled for six miles, and came to the city of Blackabelley [?Belebezoo, 7°56'N, 9°21'W]. The headman was a giant of a Weamo man, and would make two and a quarter common men.[40] He was about sixty, with large grey moustache, a fashionable appendage in this part of the country. Blackabelley is walled, and contains about seventeen hundred inhabitants. It has twenty four looms, seven or eight in constant operation. We saw more Weamo people here than at any other place. Two or three hundred people flocked around us, to get a good view, and formed a complete circle, which was easily broken; for if we had been lions or tigers, they would not have been more afraid of us. The headman offered us a house; but we declined the offer, as we had walked too short a distance to stop. So we passed on, with a crowd at our heels, and passed through by the market-place, in which were similar articles to those in other towns—many expressing regret that we should pass through without stopping for the night. Many ran to the wall, near the gate, to get a view of us; for it is evident that we were the first civilized men they had seen.

We pursued our journey, passing rice-farm after farm, in which the lofty corn was seen, and farms of no small extent on either side of the path, with here and there a hill in the distance, with the palm to enliven the picture; for they stood very plentiful in places. We met several persons, who seemed glad to see us. The path in the plain is not so good as in the mountains. In some places, the water stands, but in all cases it has a sandy bottom. We crossed a pole bridge, and came to a cleared road, three miles long, which led to Forsormer [?Fassangouni, 8°2'N, 9°23'W], the residence of King Seiyea, King Carmer's brother.[41] This road is well shaded from the sun by colar-trees, etc. We had passed many patches of a large kind of grass, called by us cane-grass, from its similarity to sugar-cane. It grows ten to thirteen feet high, and is sometimes used in making light fences.

We arrived at the city of *Forsormer,* about twenty miles north of Quanyer, and by the time we arrived at the royal residence, we were surrounded by two or three hundred people, the greater part Weamo people. King Seiyea received us with great kindness and enthusiasm. He soon had water provided for us, and I was compelled to wash in the open space between the wall and the house; but I took care not to expose my whole body at once. After we got composed, one brought us bananas; and we sent a gun-flint to market, and bought six good ears of boiled green corn, a great deal better than that near the coast. The King got a fowl cooked for us immediately, and, by the time we had ate that, he had a small sheep brought, which he presented to us, and said that, as we had come all the way from the coast, and arrived safe at his town, it was as little as he would think of doing for us. He is a large, muscular man, well proportioned, dark but good features, with Weamo mark; very active in motion. He was wrapped up in a large cloth. He commands respect among the people, and his orders are promptly obeyed by all.

The city has four or five gates, as usual. The barricades are upright sticks, about twelve feet high; and a wattled work of small sticks on the top makes the whole about twenty five feet high. Forsormer contains about seven hundred dwellings, and about three thousand inhabitants, and forty looms, most of which are at work most of the time. Working in cotton appears to be the great business of the inhabitants, and those who work at other trades—pots, jars, leather, etc.—have their cotton spinning as well as others. The females do most of the spinning; the males do the weaving. A few guns are seen here; yet they have formidable weapons—as spears, arrows, cutlasses, etc. Different trades are carried on here—tanning, carving, dying pots and jars, making hats for rain or sun, etc. In their daily market, civilized persons could procure a good supply, every day, for table use. I will venture the remark, that the civilized world cannot add to the happiness of these people unless they advance mentally; for they have all the common wants of life in abundance. The people in this part of the country make very little use of tobacco, except as snuff, of which they hold half a teaspoonful in their mouth a few moments, and then spit it out. In a company of one hundred and fifty persons, there will not be more than three or four pipes among them. The snuff is made of the small Cuba tobacco, well dried in the sun, pounded and sifted very fine. Their bows are four or five feet long, very strong, with cotton strings. At each gate of the city are smiths' shops, and watch houses. These large towns are kept very clean, all the sweepings of the house and streets being carried outside the walls. Our dwelling is on the north side of the large square, in which the children run and play; and they play and skip about in high glee. The square is perfectly clear of grass; and around it, at almost every dwelling, cotton spinning is carried on with activity.

1858 August 3rd [Tuesday].[42]—We left the city of Forsormer, walked about 15 miles and arrived at the city of Parmer [Kpama, 8°8'N, 9°16'W], governed by King [Patebo], the common trades and occupations are carried on very briskly, with a daily market kept by females.[43] In coming to Parmer, we passed a grassfield, in which the grass is about two feet high, except the cane-grass which is large and tall.[44] After we left Forsomer, we came in sight of some mountains which appeared a solid barren rock, so steep, the ascent would be difficult. We saw other ridges covered with cane-grass and scarcely any tree but the palm. The rice farms are very large and lay on either side of the path. We met many persons [on their way to] market with some dozen head of cattle, some very fine ones.[45]

Leaving Parmer, in about five miles, we came to the city of Boo [8°12'N, 9°13'W], some nine hundred dwellings, and three thousand six hundred inhabitants, about fifty looms, which probably make two thousand yards of cotton cloth per year, consuming about five hundred pounds of cotton.[46] A daily market is here, as usual. The inhabitants were enthusiastic to have a look at us, and, to gratify them, we concluded to stop a day or two. The voices of two or three hundred of them are like the chattering of so many black-birds. The beauty of this country is past description by language. The people are independent. I saw in the town some persons of very light color, with the Weamo mark. The people are generally large. I think the Weamoes are the Booseys proper, as the Barlings are Pesseys. Some of the Booseys have their hair platted up in complete order all over the head. The females use artificials, and make a braid of palm thatch, worked into the hair, as our civilized ladies use false hair, and these artificial braids show to great advantage; and it is not uncommon to see two to five braids on one side, or both and sometimes down the centre of the forehead.[47]

I am compelled to give my opinion in favor of the native African ladies, as to good looks, of which they appear as proud as any people in the world; and to this good appearance they add brass, silver and gold earrings, and bracelets, and finger rings. I have seen twenty or thirty dollars' worth of the pure stuff on the delicate wrists of a female; and these ladies of the African courts, mantled in their snow-white clothes, show to great advantage and are industrious and active, to a degree that should make Liberians blush, who think they cannot make their own dress. The two largest towns or cities should be occupied as mission-stations; the people are willing to have mission-stations among them. They are three hundred and forty three miles from Grand Bassa, and two hundred and forty-six miles from Monrovia. There are a large number of cattle and sheep in these large towns. In Boo, they had two bands of music, one band with five ivory horns; the other, of six horns, and each band with two drums—one single, and one double. I saw the grave of the former head man of the city, and was informed that several head of bullocks were butchered and put into the grave with the corpse. They appear to have some gree-grees, but do not act as bigoted as the Bassas, or others with whom we are acquainted.

August 4th [Wednesday].—I went with some boys to visit one of the barren mountains west of the city. We passed many well cultivated rice and corn farms of great extent. The palms are [------] trimmed in farm cutting.[48] On we passed, over ridges and rocks and water, and over a bridge of palm-tree trunks and arrived at the foot of Mount Jane on our left, and Mount Rebecca on our right.[49] I was soon left alone to climb the rocky path, which led near a mountain stream of the best water in the world ever used. The stream descends from an elevation of near two hundred feet, from a small bamboo swamp in the gap of the mountain, the rocky sides of the two mountains forming a reservoir, which, if completed, would contain several millions of gallons for the use of a large city; for I fancy [------] enterprise and energy expanding to these very mountains.[50] I went to an elevation in the path, cutting my way through grass and bushes, until I fell in with the tracks of wild cattle, so fresh and plentiful I was convinced the herd was tolerably large. With difficulty, I hitched up the ascent, step after step and at length stood on the summit of Mount Jane, and on it were wild cattle paths and manure to an extent that convinced me a good business could be done in hunting them. On the top of the mount is a heavy coat of the grass with which they cover their houses, with a clump of cane grass in a few spots.

From the top, the prospect is beautiful; for on either side is a plain, and on each plain a large town is visible.[51] No part of the country can be called barren, except the naked rocks. The plain is covered with small bushes and grass, and it gives the country the appearance of an old farm, with palms standing scattered all over it. The grass is cut down and burnt, and the land planted in rice, corn, cassava, ground-peas, etc., all of which looks as thriving as if it was land from which heavy timber had been cut. Liberian settlements could be established here with advantage to the native population.

Men and women plant rice. The rice-birds are quite bad, and females as well as males use the sling with great dexterity. The large rain-hat is much in use in this section of the country. It is formed like a round shallow dish-cover, and is about two feet eight inches across, made perfectly water-tight, and will shelter the person very well, if there is but little wind.

We obtained some mineral salt in the city of Forsormer. It is a beautiful article, white as snow, and has the appearance of crystalized ice, or clear white rock. The people here seldom go to the sea coast; they congregate in large towns, and have no small half towns, which accounts for the large country cities. They are planting rice in this plain, while at the same time some fields of rice are heading. Their smith's shops are at each of the five gates of Boo. In them they make fire-tongs, a dog-bell, a spear, a rice hoe, and so on, palm-nuts being used for charcoal, and they appear to make a great heat. The city presents a scene of great activity. Different trades are carried on, in connection with other cities and towns. In one part you may see cattle tied for sale, or brought in from the interior. All appear to be doing something—in one place, hat making; and through the city rice pounding and eating.

There is a weekly market held at this city, not so large as the one held at Zanga, in the Barling country, yet of no less interest.

August 6th [Friday].—We left the city of Boo, and had a good path over flat country, through rice farms—in places a good deal of water. In twelve miles we arrived at the city of Kiyamar [Kiama or Irié, 8°16'N, 9°6'W]. The water runs to the east. It appeared to begin at the barren mountains, six to ten miles to the west. We came in sight of prairie-looking fields, having the grass for covering dwellings very abundant, with here and there a clump of cane grass. We arrived at a considerable stream running east, over which is a good bridge. It is said to pass near the city of Moosadoo.[52] Eight miles from this bridge, we crossed an extended plain, which looked like one extended rice field. We came to the city of Quanger [Kuankan, 8°27'N, 9°8'W], the residence of King Carmers, the King of Upper Condo country.[53] The city makes an imposing appearance. It has one thousand five hundred dwellings, and four or five thousand inhabitants, and seventy-five looms. It has a daily market, which presents a scene of great activity. There are a large number of cattle in it every day; we counted one day sixty seven head—some very fine and large, and all in good condition—also two stud-horses, two mares, and two colts. The price of the horses is from forty to sixty dollars. The inhabitants are very active in their different occupations, cloth-manufacturing being the principal. The king has a large house, sixty by twenty-one feet. The dwellings are all covered with grass, of which there are two kinds—one very fine, the other we have called the house-grass—neither of them appears so durable as the leaf or bamboo covering.

August 8th [Sunday].—Kagular, the King's son, gave us a small bullock, which we killed, and returned him one half. Before receiving it, I informed him I could not make him a suitable return. His manly reply was he did not care whether I gave him anything in return or not. The animal must be killed, as we were the first Americans at his father's town. He afterwards brought us a peck of beautiful clean rice, and some oil, with which we fried the liver and heart. King Carmer is the rightful sovereign of the upper part of Boosey country; thus, his residence is regarded as the capital of the upper Condo country. As the people all congregate in towns, when one of them is taken, the spoil in slaves is great, which accounts for military expeditions returning with their thousands of victims. There is a Mandingo chapel in the city, but the worshipers of the Prophet appear no way zealous in the performance of religious rites. It is said King Camer is a Mandingo; he is now in the town of Jolado, assisting in war a brother Mandingo.[54]

The peaks of some of the mountains I have mentioned are quite lofty, and the surrounding country is very beautiful. The plain, which is a little rolling, stretches out in a beautiful site for a large city; the only objection is a lack of timber. The mountains form a beautiful border to the plain, and the city of Quanger appears the great centre of attraction. It is only for Liberia to call in the aid of art, and the thing would be accomplished. The plain is well watered, and the soil fertile. Quanger is about three hundred and eighty four miles from Grand Bassa, and about two hundred and eighty-seven miles from Monrovia, and about fifty two miles from the city of Forsormer.[55]

I brought specimens from Mount Jane of a sap which hardens from a tree that I think may be found near the coast. The people here do not make use of the black stain used by the lower Booseys, Barlings, and Pesseys, they use ornaments of iron, brass, copper, silver, and gold, rings and bracelets. Firewood is scarce about this large city, but they have a wood market, and it would do a person good to see the activity of the little boys, who are the principal traders in this line. Quanger is about fourteen days' walk east from Sierra Leone.

The birds are changing their plumage. There is a black bird, with a beautiful yellow spot on the butt of its wings; and a large raven bird of dusky red. The horn-bills, crows and hawks are hardly seen here, as they require forests for their accommodation. The sheep and goats here are much better than I have seen elsewhere. The goats have bags larger than those of the cows.

Bullocks, buffaloes, hogs, hippopotami, are among the wild animals of this part of the country.

The city of Quanger is about fifty-two miles from the city of Forsormer. Quanger has five gates; and from them roads lead in various directions to twenty three cities and towns. There are several other towns, the names of which I could not ascertain, as there appears no good understanding between this city and King Jabo's.[56] With this view of the surrounding country, the world may see that it is a good mission-station, and should be occupied as soon as practicable; and if Liberia will furnish men, the Christian church will furnish the means.

There are different kinds of musical instruments in Quanger—drums, horns, bells, etc., the last made from iron, upon which they beat a stick, producing a sound similar to the triangle. The Booseys and Mandingoes are mixed up in this city, as are the Pesseys and Booseys near the city of Solong. This connection of different tribes is controlled by the influence of domestic ties; for they intermarry to a considerable extent, which has a powerful check on their disposition to war. And as intermarriage and commerce are increased, so in proportion is the bond of union.

The upper line of the Boosey country terminates at the mountains north of the plain we called Washington's plain, bounded by Lewis' mountains, a distance of about one hundred and twenty miles north and south.[57] The distance east and west is unknown to us, but probably two hundred to two hundred and fifty miles. The tribe occupying this section being numerous, we may safely set them down at one hundred and seventy five thousand or two hundred thousand. Their habits and customs differ little from the Pesseys or Barlings, which has been stated.

I see no idol-worshipping among them. Some of them are followers of the false prophet; and they, with the Barling[s and] Pesseys are imposed on by their Mandingo brethren—priests—who sell them a scrip, or prayer or charm on a piece of paper, put in a leather bag, and carried round their necks or arms.

August 12th [Thursday].—I went to the mountains west of Quanger, passing through many a rice farm, all of which looked well. In some farms I saw females hard at work weeding rice. The birds are very troublesome, but they drive them away with a long lash of platted bark, which makes a sharp sound like a coachman's whip. After several obstacles, among high grass, and cane and briers, I came out on a rice farm, where I passed the night in a kitchen with nobody in it. After washing in the mountain stream which was near, and commending myself to my Heavenly Father, I lay down to rest on some green thatch, and a piece of mat, chewing a colar-nut and bark for my supper.

August 13th [Friday].—At dawn of day, after I had got all things right, the owner of the kitchen came, and wondered at seeing me there, but treated me very kindly, giving me some cassava, which I soon roasted, and for which I gave him a gun flint. The cassava I ate, with thanks to God. After some time, I concluded to go up the mountains; the path was most delightful. I went about two miles, and found the mountains to be a compact set of peaks rising one behind the other, those back much higher than those in front. There are no vales between these mountains, but a deep cut, terminating in a mountain stream. Upon some of the mountains are heavy forests, while others are covered with cane grass and low bushes, with here and there a rock projecting from the heavy grass. I saw a few huts on the farthest mountain. The people had their usual conveniences of pots, bowls, etc.; with their large mortars, some of which will hold nearly a peck of rice. There, these hardy mountaineers live through the rice season, sometimes going down to the city in the plain, seven miles, with fire-wood, and a few grains of pepper and okra leaves, for which they get some colar nuts, and oil.

After looking round some time, I commenced my return to the city. On my way, I attempted to go to the summit of a mountain, to have a view of the plain below; but such was the stubbornness of the cane-grass, I gave it up, and arrived in the city about three o'clock, much jaded by my ramble. There are a large number of palm-trees in the plain near the mountains, which yield great quantities of oil for the inhabitants. It was pleasing to notice the interest with which people inquired how I got along and fared among the mountains.

The blacksmith business is regularly attended to at Quanger, to supply the market with knives, etc. In some shops are dozens of men working at a time—one forging, one giving a finish by cold hammering, another making handles, another polishing them on a rock. They have good smiths tongs, but only a hard stone for an anvil. These smiths get their pay on the ground in colars, rice, ground-peas, corn etc.

August 14th [Saturday].—Regular market day, the [stir] was great, and exchange and barter going on at a brisk rate.[58] We purchased some colars, bananas, and salt, and three sorts of beans. There was about the same number of cattle as the Saturday before. For one flint we get ten colars; for one colar, five good ears of green corn. Three colars would buy rice enough for one person. The Mandingoes use sandals made of wood, and new hide. The wood sandals are like a small stool on four legs. There appears to be a disease which affects the people in the neck and throat, having the appearance of a wen.[59] It seems to be confined to the plains.

August 15th [Sunday].—We took a walk out of the south gate, and passed over a bridge about four hundred feet long. The path on the other side is very good, and winds around in the grass field in a serpentine course. We came to a ground-pea lot, in which we saw the hoof prints of wild cattle, which live in these grass fields not far from the city.

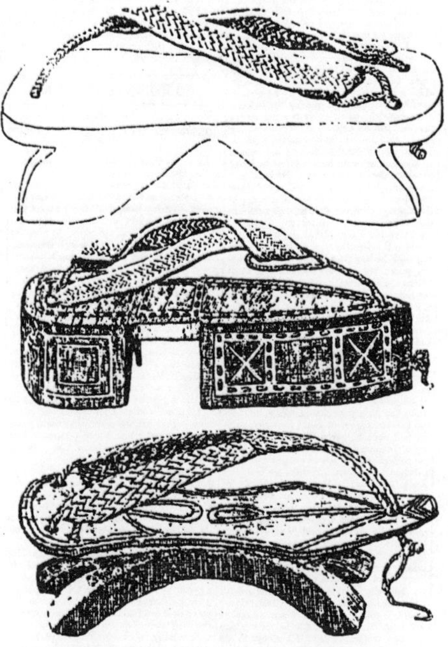

Figure 10. Four-footed Mandingo sandals worn in the interior. *Source: J. Büttikofer,* Reisebilder aus Liberia *(Leiden: Brill, 1890).*

August 16th [Monday].[60] We started from the city of Quanger, for the present temporary residence of King Carmer, and traveled on about five miles and arrived at the foot of the first chain of mountains, and after we had passed the chain through a low gap, we came to a small plain in which a new town was situated, and in it four or five looms as is customary in this part of the country. In this plain we passed a large quantity of water which of course came down from the mountains above us; in these plains is a good lot of black mud which makes it very unpleasant traveling in many places, and the high house grass whose long blades hang over into the narrow path adds no little to the annoyance of the traveller. In the plain we passed some rice farms which had been cut for some time, and others more recently, while others were ripening fast and so on in different stages of progress; we halted at the said small town and rested a while, where they had a little market, and from it we passed on through the other part of the country a tolerable good path except the water which was plentiful in this part of the plain. The com-

L. H. VII, No. 22 Jan 4, 1860

Poetry.

FOR THE LIBERIA HERALD.

A Voice to Liberia.

[*An Original Poem.*]

BY REV. M. B. BIRD.

Ah is it so? hot raging wars, blown up
By him, who science and religion vaunts;
Savage on savage by him fiercely turn'd,
For such foul purposes as all our nature wring;
O dreadful food by avarice thus sought!
O dreaded sword! thou fiery scourge, thou rod
Of human make, and bent by man to hell!
But for thy threats, and frowns, thy with'ring looks,
And slaught'ring power, reason had reign'd in peace,
And brought her laws to light, but thou hast dash'd
Her sceptre to the earth, thou hast compell'd
Men to believe, that white was black, that wrong
Was right, and brightest truth was false. Ah true,
Thy reign is fierce and dark! fain would we fling
Into the sea of deep forgetfulness,
All thy foul deeds, but e'en humanity
Demands, that all be brought into full day.
Yet how the history of the world unfold?
Who shall its catalogue of crimes unroll?
Sad thought, to this hard task, not one on earth
Was ever equal, or shall ever be.
Suffice it then to know, that yonder Isles
Of Western India, receiv'd their throngs,
From sources driven open by the sword,
Which true religion, could not look into
And live.
All systems their own centre have,
Serving as main-spring, to spread life and pow'r,
Hence, chains and slav'ry their centre had,
That hellish centre was the sending lash,
That drove out from the body wealth, and strength,
And soul itself, to pamper and to feed
A race, whose souls liv'd on sheer woe, whose mirth,
And whirling dances yet more wild, receiv'd
Their hellish zest from streaming tears, and blood,
Till the deep dreadful cup of sin and death,
Up to the brim was fill'd with wrath Divine,
And more than ov'rflow'd. O dreadful scene!
When on yon Queenly Isle, the fiery surge
At last o'erwhelm'd, all raging tyranny.
True liberty thus crush'd her daring foe,
And boldly trod him down into the dust,
Yea true, the Haytian bands triumphed ov'r all,
But in this trumph, deep, corruption lurk'd.
The tyrant at his ease had liv'd and roll'd,
And hence the unhappy lesson of his life,
By his triumphant scholars had been learnt,
Who in the element of liberty,
Had but been taught to see the love of care,
Where too for honest marriage, nought was seen,
But the low vices of concubinage,
Thus from this dread invested order sprang,
A nation yet long doom'd, to groan beneath
A load, of crushing ignorance and vice,
The wretched legacy of years gone by.
O fearful price of dear bought liberty!
Yet who would say, that all we had of life
Or wealth, were aught too much, or dear, to give,
To be a man, and not a bi-ped beast,
To bear the grinding burdens of sheer pride?
The price then is now paid, the prize is won!
But now the mighty question starts, from hearts
Yet bleeding from a thousand rending woes,
How keep the priceless prize so boldly won?
How? justly ask'd the Haytian conquerors,
How ward off from our now triumphant shores,
The vultures that still hover o'er our prize?
No, justify we cannot deeds of blood,
But Jesus o'er a bloody city wept
Here then, for one brief moment let us pause,
And like our peaceful Master drop a tear,
Yea let it be the language of our hearts;
For those who n'er were taught to trust in God,
Sieze eagerly on arms when danger threats,
How trust in Him who never yet they knew?

To be continued.

GEORGE L. SEYMOUR'S JOURNAL.

[CONTINUED.]

August 16th. We started from the city of Quanger, for the present temporary residence of King Carmer, and traveled on about five miles and arrived at the foot of the first chain of mountains, and after we had passed the chain through a low gap, we came to a small plain in which a new town was situated, and in it four or five looms as is customary in this part of the country. In this plain we passed a large quantity of water which of course came down from the mountains above us; in these plains is a good lot of black mud which makes it very unpleasant traveling in many places, and the high house grass whose long blades hang over into the narrow path adds no little to the annoyance of the traveller. In the plain we passed some rice farms which had been cut for some time, and others more recently, while others were ripening fast and so on in different stages of progress; we halted at the said small town and rested a while, where they had a little market, and from it we passed on through the other part of the country a tolerable good path except the water which was plentiful in this part of the plain. The common growth of the plains and mountains is grass, with here and there a clump of forest trees and their left slanting apparantly for fear their species will become extinct there were more on the mountain sides and near the streams on the mountain than on the plains. After we had passed the aforesaid plains we came to the foot of a mountain which we began to assend and up we went to elevation after elevation passing through the lowest gaps with peaks above us of four or five hundred feet in highth; in our assent we passed near a mountain stream the most delightful imaginable, for after we had climed up about six or seven hundred feet we found water sufficient to float a good size boat, in it the mandingo ladies bathed, and cooled their heated bodies (their were a good company of them along.) From their we still went into the mountain and attained the highth of more than two thousand feet above the plain in which the city of Quanger is located, which city could be seen from Payn's view on Johnson peak; the city was a distance of about fourteen miles from us, and this view was the last we had of it. From their we went up still and arrived at point lookout which afforded a tolerable view E. N E., S E. of plains mountains &c, at this point we halted to rest and on a large tree, I cut our names with date of month and year on which day I was thirty nine years of age, and for the last few years I have passed through many a change and interesting scenes and circumstance of which to-day must be recorded as one in which the variety of changes are so misterious in a short space of time; from that point we still went higher until we attained the top of Johnson's peak from which we could see peak after peak below us, and many elevated ones above us, and these are evidently Kong mountains if those near the city of Solong are not, we began to assend and wind around the mountain on its very sides where the path has appearantly been dug in places and a mistep would have pitched us head long down a steep mountain side to the bottom, a distance of several hundred feet, we passed, however without accident to a gap below which lay between Johnson's peak and the adjoining mountain, we wound around a little further and down a difficult zigzag mountain path and arrived at a small mountain town, which we found to be one to which we were recommended: this of course we were made to understand by signs; for we were without an interpreter, here as in many other cases before, we found a small market in active business style, but as usual their attention was drawn from their business to us. For a few moments, and some began to get ready for a run, and others to eye us with more satisfaction as they saw we did not disturb them. I soon had out some colars and pounded parched corn, it being the only food in the market ready cooked and we were hungry and wished something to eat immediately; but to the credit of the mountainers, I must say no one will be compeled to go a great distance hungry for between the towns you meet with females by the way side pedling their rice, corn &c, setting in groups of five or six for the purpose of accommodating the travellers, and getting a colar or two, and with the greatest kindness present the many travellers with what they may have in exchange as an evidence of mutual favor, we were presented with some clean rice at this town and furnished with a house for the night, and we had a good supper of rice and dried beef cured by us at the city Quangers. This little mountain town, which is elevated above the large plain from which we came several hundred feet, is a neat snug town indeed, surrounded with Plantain and Benanna trees, with corn and cassada patches near; and rice farms a few hundred rods distant on the mountain slopes, and on the path near the town and scatteringly around the town were some forest trees around the outskirts of the town very large. The condition of the place was an evidence that the people live well, and are industrious, and the variety of scenery makes the place look delightful, and must be regarded as one of the cheerfulest locations in the Kong mountains, elsewhere on the mountains are to be seen low scattering scruble looking trees, in connection with dark naked rocks, projecting from among the grass, which stood the storm and sun of ages, and ages more will pass and still they will be the shure land marks to the weary traveller in the grassy mountains of Kong. Traveller in these mountains must be very fatiguing in the dry season as there are no shades from the hot sun, and that fact has given the Mandingoes the idea of the umbrella hats mentioned in another place, thus of course the habits and customs of the people change or are conformable to the condition of the country in which they reside, I need not repeat, that the people are kind, for we found them disposed to do all in reason to make us feel welcome, and it need not be asked whether we felt ourselves among friends and whether we acted open and free, which we did, and I made it a point to conduct so that they would see that we felt the kindness shown us.

COMMUNICATIONS.

FOR THE LIBERIA HERALD.

ORIGIN OF WRITING AMONG THE VEYS.

Possibly, there is not to be found recorded in the annals of the world an invention of what kind soever, which had its origin in a circumstance so trivial as that to which the Art of Writing lately introduced among the Veys is attributed; and we seize upon the opportunity the times afford us, to give the simple facts of this ingenious and inestimable invention and the exhibition of mental power displayed therein, as we have them given to us.

Most discoveries made in either ancient or modern times are, for the most part, the result of the expenditure of immense sums of money, the sacrifice of health and, in very many cases, life itself.

But the idea, conceived by the Vey man, of inventing some means by which he might communicate his thoughts to his fellow in some other way than that of articulate sounds, was not suggested and brought to succeed by nights of toil and studious application of the mind. It is not the result of scores of years of experiment,; but it was prompted by a selfishness found, as a general thing, among the illiberal and narrow minded.

I would not be understood to say that the more illiberal and narrow minded men are, the more good results from them,—for this would be saying that "it is folly to be wise;" but that the selfishness which prompted the idea of the invention intended that the invention should benefit the selfish only.

During the time of the year when the Bassas and Veys are clearing off their lands for the coming "seed time," they make and use a great quantity of Palm Wine, especially when provisions are scarce. While this beverage does not impart any real nutriment to the body above the proportion of one to thirty, probably, of the quantity taken into the stomach, still, like the juice of the poppy, it stimulates the system, and, in the absence of food, keeps it, for a few days, from relaxing to a point beyond recovery.

At the time which we have mentioned, those of the younger men who had the art of getting the Palm Wine, or the sap of the Palm tree, (two persons generally being the owners of one or more trees,) in order that they might have the exclusive benefit of their wine, found it necessary to observe profound secrecy whenever they wished to "go to the palm wine tree," and therefore they agreed, that, whenever either of them made a certain character on the ground, or on the side of his mud hut, it was to be regarded by the other as a sign for them to go to their wine drinking.

Succeeding so well in this new mode of expressing their desires to each other in this particular, they invented signs for expressing other things which they did not wish to be known publicly. But the thing soon took shape, and became a subject of some thought with a view of making it subservient to the tribe generally. They concluded, that, if they could communicate their thoughts to each other respecting Palm Wine, and signify when they should retire to some secluded spot to enjoy a scanty meal, by certain signs made on the ground, and on the side of their mud huts, they could also, by increasing the number of those signs, and varying them, make known their thoughts and wishes to each other on any subject that might concern them.

On one occasion, two persons were walking out together; after going a little distance from the town, one of them turned aside in the woods, and from thence brought a jug of wine. His companion, knowing that he had not had an opportunity of putting the wine there, asked him how he knew it was there; to which the other replied "my friend informed me of it by certain signs made on the ground as we were about to start away." This circumstance incited his companion, on the spot, to a resolution to acquaint himself with this new mode of communicating ideas. The art went on to spread, the more considerate reducing it to some certain system, until it became widely diffused; still, it is now only in its incipient stage.

Thus, I have given to you, Messrs. Editors, and to the public, a plain statement of the alleged facts of the origin of the art of writing as it now exists among the Veys; soliciting, at the same time, a refutation of any thing I have written on the subject, by those who are cotemporary with this new invention, so that future historians may not be compelled to pick their way through a globe of conjectures, in trying to search out the origin and the time of the invention of letters by the Veys, as they have had to do respecting many other subjects, the origin of which is as wholly unknown to us as is the spot where man was made.

Yours respectfully,
D. B. WARNER.

Monrovia, Dec. 28, 1859.

We take no pleasure in Heralding every little aberration from right and consistency manifested by our people: we are as willing as any one to cover their frailties, whenever it can be done with consistency to our duty as devotees to the public good.

There are, notwithstanding, many little faults which will particularly insinuate themselves in the formation of the character of a new people. Habits of extravagancy, of prodigality; examples fatal, and pernicious will often steal in, unperceivable at first, but in time they will grow with our growth and strengthen with our strength, and when we will, we may not be able to eradicate them.

Mr. Blyden but slightly touched on some of these in his last Popular Lecture:—Rummaging, a few days ago, a file of old papers we crossed the following, which we extract, sincerely believing it merits the reading and consideration of some among us.—EDS.

THE WAY TO SPOIL GIRLS.

If any parent wishes a recipe how to spoil daughters, it can be easily and readily given, can be proved by the experience of hundreds to be certain and effacious.

1. Be always telling her, from earliest childhood, what a beautiful creature she is. It is a capital way of inflating the vanity of a little girl, to be constantly exclaiming "How pretty!" Children understand such flattery, even when in the nurse's arms, and the evil is done the character in its earliest formation.

2. Begin, as soon as she can toddle around, to rig her up in fashionable clothes and rich dresses. Put a hoop upon her at once, with all the artificial adornments of flounces, and feathers, and flowers, and curls; Fondness for dress will thus become a prominent characteristic and will usurp the whole attention of the young immortal, and be a long step toward spoiling her.

3. Let her visit so much that she finds no happiness at home, and therefore will not be apt to stay there and learn home duties. It is a capital thing for a spoiled daughter to seek all her happiness in visiting and change of place and associates. She will thus grow as useless as modern fashionable parents delight that their daughters should be.

4. Let her reading consist of novels of the nauseatingly sentimental kind. She will be spoiled sooner than if she perused history or science. Her heart will be occupied by fictitious scenes and feelings; her mind filled with unrealities, and her aims placed on fashion and dress, and romantic attachments.

5. Be careful that her education gives her a smattering of all the accomplishments, without the slightest knowledge of the things really useful in life. Your daughter won't be spoiled so long as she has a real desire to be useful in the world, and aims at its accomplishment. If her mind and time are occupied in modern accomplishments, there will be no thought of the necessity and virtue of being of some real use to somebody pervading her heart, and she will soon be ready as spoiled daughter.

6. As a consequence, keep her in profound ignorance of all the useful arts of house-keeping, impressing upon her mind that it is vulgar to do anything for yourself, or to learn how anything is done in the house. A spoiled daughter should never be taught the mysteries of the kitchen—such things a lady always leaves to the servants. It would be "vulgar" for her to know how to dress trout or shad, to bake, to wash, to iron, to sweep, to wring the neck of a live chicken, pluck it and prepare it for breakfast, or to do anything that servants are hired to do. As a mistress of a house, it is her duty to sit on a velvet sofa all day, in the midst of a pyramid of silks and flounces, reading the last flash novel, while her domestics are performing the labors of the house.

To complete the happiness of your *spoiled daughter*, marry her to a bearded youth with soft hands, who knows as little how to earn money as she does to save it. Her happiness will be *finished*, for her lifetime.—*Hartford Courant.*

Figure 11. A page from the *Liberia Herald* (4 January 1860) containing George L. Seymour's account.

mon growth of the plains and mountains is grass, with here and there a clump of forest trees and their left slanting [standing] apparantly for fear their species will become extinct[;] there were more on the mountain sides and near the streams on the mountain than on the plains. After we had passed the aforesaid plains we came to the foot of a mountain which we began to assend and up we went to elevation after elevation passing through the lowest gaps with peaks above us of four or five hundred feet in highth; in our assent we passed near a mountain stream the most delightful imaginable, for after we had climed up about six or seven hundred feet we found water sufficient to float a good size boat, in it the mandingo ladies bathed, and cooled their heated bodies (their were a good company of them along.) From their we still went into the mountain and attained the highth of more than two thousand feet above the plain in which the city of Quanger is located, which city could be seen from Payn's view on Johnson peak; the city was a distance of about fourteen miles from us, and this view was the last we had of it.[61] From their we went up still and arrived at point lookout which afforded a tolerable view E.N.E, S.E. of plains mountains &c, at this point we halted to rest and on a large tree, I cut our names with date of month and year on which day I was thirty nine years of age, and for the last few years I have passed through many a change and interesting scenes and circumstance of which to-day must be recorded as one in which the variety of changes are so misterious in a short space of time; from that point we still went higher until we attained the top of Johnson's peak from which we could see peak after peak below us, and many elevated ones above us, and these are evidently [the] Kong mountains if those near the city of Solong are not, we began to assend and wind around the mountain on its very sides where the path has apparently been dug in places and a mistep would have pitched us head long down a steep mountain side to the bottom, a distance of several hundred feet, we passed, however without accident to a gap below which lay between Johnson's peak and the adjoining mountain, we wound around a little further and down a difficult zigzag mountain path and arrived at a small mountain town, which we found to be one to which we were recommended: this of course we were made to understand by signs; for we were without an interpreter, here as in many other cases before, we found a small market in active business style, but as usual their attention was drawn from their business to us.[62] For a few moments, and some began to get ready for a run, and others to eye us with more satisfaction as they saw we did not disturb them. I soon had out some colars and pounded parched corn, it being the only food in the market ready cooked and we were hungry and wished something to eat immediately; but to the credit of the mountainers, I must say no one will be compeled to go a great distance hungry[,] for between the towns you meet with females by the way side peddling their rice, corn &c, setting in groups of five or six for the purpose of accommodating the travellers, and getting a colar or two, and with the greatest kindness present the many travellers with what they may have in exchange as an evidence of mutual favor, we were presented with some clean rice at this town and furnished with a house for the night, we had a good supper of rice and dried beef cured by us at the city Quangers. This little mountain town, which is elevated above the large plain from which we came several hundred feet, is a neat snug town indeed, surrounded with Plantain and Benanna trees, with corn and cassada patches near; and rice farms a few hundred rods distant on the mountain slopes, and on the path near the town were some forest trees around the outskirts of the town very large.[63] The condition of the place was an evidence that the people live well, and are industrious, and the variety of scenery makes the place look delightful, and must be regarded as one of the cheerfulest locations in the Kong mountains, elsewhere on the mountains are to be seen low scattering scruble looking trees, in connection with dark naked rocks, projecting from among the grass, which stood the storm and sun of ages, and ages more will pass and still they will be the shure land marks to the weary traveller in the grassy mountains of Kong. Traveller [Travel] in these mountains must be very fatiguing in the dry season as there are no shades from the hot sun, and that fact has given the Mandingoes the idea of the umbrella hats mentioned in another place, thus of course the habits and customs of the people change or are conformable to the condition of the country in which they reside, I need not repeat that the people are kind, for we found them disposed to do all in reason to make us feel welcome, and it nead not be asked whether we felt ourselves among friends and whether we acted open and free, which we did, and I made it a point of conduct so that they would see that we felt the kindness shown us.

August 17th [Tuesday].[64]—After breakfast, we finished the repairs of our sandals, and left the little town, and wound our way down the mountain, and crossed a beautiful stream of water, running at a rapid rate, and tolerably full. It rained in the night, and the path was quite slippery in some places; but our sandals were well spiked, and we could stand where our boys could not do so well. It was up and down mountain, same as yesterday, and every summit opened to our view other mountains, with grass rocks, and shrubby trees, some of which looked like apple-trees, with now and then a clump of forest-trees to enliven the picture. In about three miles, we came to a small town, about twenty three miles from Quanger. The headman of the town gave us a fowl, and I made him some little return. We then passed on to another small town, and received and returned presents. We then came to a small town presided over by the mother of King Carmer [?Sabouedou, 8°39'N, 9°9'W]. Here the mountains began to flatten down considerably. The old lady had many rice and *firney* farms, and appeared to live in good order.[65]

In these farms the boys were actively engaged in keeping out birds, which are very troublesome. We concluded to stop for the night; and, after a good wash in cold water, I sat down to my journal. This town is about twelve miles from where we stopped the night before. The rain here, and about the large plain, has been as if the heavy rains were about setting in. The rain in this section of country is not so heavy as near the coast; yet, when it falls, it swells the mountain streams rapidly, and in a few hours, in some places, they become impassable.

August 18th [Wednesday].—We left King Carmer's mother, and travelled ten miles up and down mountain, as yesterday, and arrived at the town of Wosodo, King Camer's present residence, where he was disposed to go, from his inclination for war, while many of his headmen were against him.[66] His Majesty was absent to the town of Jallerder, thus, we were compelled to wait his return. The people informed us he would be back in three or four days, two or three times, until thirteen days had expired; but we were not idle, for we went in search of game, and to look at the country. We looked for the wild ox, but saw none, yet frequently fell in with his hoof prints, and his paths in the grass, which covers hill and dale, as in other places, and, as it is high, makes it difficult to pass, and cuts the face, hands, and feet badly. On our return to the town, we shot several pigeons, of which, with rice, we made a hearty supper. We saw a Guinea fowl. They are quite plenty in this mountain district, with many birds, among which are the common rice-bird, so troublesome to farmers. In our rambles after game, we passed through several small towns, round each of which are fine gardens, containing cassava and sweet potatoes in large beds; also, egg-plants, pepper, plantains, and bananas.

In these Kong mountains, palm-trees are scarce, and oil is less plentiful than in the plains; yet I think they would thrive, if cultivated, as the soil is good for everything planted. The market is conducted mostly by females. In the one near Wosodo, colars and iron were the medium of exchange.

In the town of Wosodo were two fine mares, used by the Mandingoes, curbed and backed with bit and saddle of their own manufactory. There were also cows, bullocks, sheep, and goats. The people treated us with great kindness; and King Camer sent us eight bars of iron to purchase food until his return, and the women were very kind, and attended to the purchase of rice and oil for us, at the market. Thus thirteen days passed, in which we several times signified our wish to continue our journey.

August 30th [Monday].—We offered to pay boys to take our luggage, but all, with one consent, refused, as they wished us to remain till the king should return, and which we should have done; but we were deaf to their solicitations, and shouldered our knapsacks, gun, and ammunition—a work for four men. We were followed by some who entreated us to return back; but on we went, and passed through three towns, and up a mountain, giving our guns to the hands of a young man to carry for us; but by this time they all appeared willing and kind. But there was a man that followed us from Wosodo, up the mountain, to a town. We stopped there for a heavy shower of rain to pass, and then pushed on, and passed through the grass, which was wet and cold, the young man still with our guns; and when we had gone two or three miles, the young man being ahead, and out of sight, I was cut in the left shoulder and left hand, by some one secreted in the grass.[67] Brother Ash was close behind me, and as the man struck me with his cutlass the last time, Ash struck him with his walking-stick several blows; and the man ran, and gave the alarm, and they all fled back towards the town we had left—of course, our guns went with them; and we were left unarmed, except a hatchet, a cutlass, and a knife. Brother Ash followed them a little, and then returned, and bound up my hand, which was cut in a shocking manner, the back of the hand being entirely laid open. Of course, it was disabled. After it was bound up, we continued our walk without arms, with a firm trust in God that he would deliver; yet we had our fears, that as they had drawn blood, they would pursue us, and make a final dispatch of us both. We traveled on, however, my hand bleeding profusely, till we came to a small town, and procured some soot from over the fire, and applied to it. From there we walked a few miles, and came to a very rocky creek, and found it too deep to wade. We did not wish to swim, if we could avoid it, as it would wet every thing in our knapsacks; but while we were arranging for Brother Ash to swim over, and unite the vines which had been severed, several persons made their appearance in the path near us, and immediately set up a hideous yell, and brandished their weapons. I had but one course, and plunged into the creek, knapsack and all, and swam across, expecting every moment to feel the knife again. I got safe across, and struggled up the hill, but found my strength failing, and detached my knapsack, and turned into a path in the grass, and on my hands crawled back towards the creek, hoping to escape notice, as I made no mark by which they would be likely to follow me. In my haste to escape, I lost my hatchet, tin bookcase, and cap.[68] Finding no one was following, I crawled to the water side, and secreted myself in the grass. I began to think of my condition. It was an awful moment of horrid suspense. If I am murdered, how shall my family and government know of my end? I had to blame myself for leaving the town of Wosodo before seeing King Carmer. Thus I sat reflecting, until two hours after dark. I concluded to return to Wosodo, and throw myself on the mercy of the people. So I crept from my hiding place, regained the path, and swam the creek again, bare headed. I whistled in a low tone for Brother Ash, but receiving no answer, with a heavy heart I left the creek, and proceeded back to Wosodo.

August 31st [Tuesday].—I reached the town about the first cock-crowing, and went to the head woman's house, and found an entrance. I received good treatment, took off my wet clothes, washed in warm water, put on a dry country cloth, and laid down in the house occupied by us the day before, with sad reflections upon my change of circumstances. I consoled myself with the thought that it was a chastisement from the hand of God, that deals in mercy. My advice to travelers is, do not go without a guide, from the headman through whose country you may pass. The time spent in waiting is not lost, if you amuse yourselves in looking about.

I remained here several days, and heard nothing of Brother Ash, until a friendly Mandingo told me he was at the town of Wisermado, which gave me great joy, hoping to see him again soon, to dress my wounds properly. I was treated with kindness by all, particularly by a female, who dropped a sympathetic tear, and was as attentive as a mother, until King Carmer returned in a few days, with a large number of attendants. He received me with kindness, but informed me I should have remained till he came home, and all would have been right. He presented me with colars, as tokens of friendship, and informed me he should carry war to the dominions of King Barbenier, for cutting my hand; but we think the credit of the whole thing belongs to King Carmer. He is of tall, manly appearance, copper-color, with the Boosey mark in the face, crowned with a large Mandingo cloth cap, thickly set with trinkets, covered with red flannel and a leopard skin, with two claws of a mountain eagle, which he informed me would often carry away sheep or goats.

Brother Ash was absent twenty-three days; and, when he returned, he was an object of pity.[69] I had myself fallen away in flesh, from being dreadfully scratched with grass. Brother Ash was bare headed, and looked very wild. After he got a little rested, he informed me that, when we were attacked, he put down his knapsack, and gave the native sign of battle, by flourishing his walking stick. They followed his motion by a charge of arrows, which came so plentifully, that he soon took to the water, dove like a duck, and but one arrow hit him, which was in the shoulder blade. It stuck in his flesh, and it was some time before he got it out, in the water. In the creek he lost his cap. He gained an elevation, and saw his pursuers returning from the chase, with his knapsack. He supposed me dead. He continued his journey up the mountain, and stopped at a small town for the night. He continued his journey from day to day, till he was arrested, stripped naked, and a large stick fastened to his leg by an iron strap. He was kept in this condition ten days. He was then taken as a slave, with one hand tied to his neck, and driven to the large towns to be sold for a gun; but they could make no sale of him, and took him back to the town where he was captured; and after being without his clothes fifteen days, they were restored to him. He then met with two or more persons who spoke Sierra Leone English, and after that he was better treated.[70] He heard of my being at Wosodo, and taking a favorable opportunity, he ran away, and in two days he arrived at Wosodo, looking wild and much exhausted, having suffered very much.

Our suffering and ruin were nearly equal, but different in kind. It was, however, brought on ourselves, by being a little too fast in the prosecution of our journey. We should have waited for the king, and given him a good present, but we did neither; therefore, let it be a caution to future tourists to improve by our sufferings and experience. We lost everything, even our journal; but Carmer had the kindness to return some of my clothes, and most of my journal.

We left the town of Wosodo for the city of Quanger, where we remained a month; and from there we began our homeward march.[71] We were well treated in Quanger, and when we left it appeared to create regret among the people; for it appeared as if we were universal favorites of all. At the first town from Quanger, we were not allowed to pass through it, but around its walls, inside of the barricade, and out of the gate; and one young man ran and shut the outer gate before we arrived at it, but we, though manifesting no fear, giving a token of submission, another young man opened the gate, and permitted us to depart.

Arriving at the city of Boa, we were received with kindness in the evening by all; but in the morning [Sunday, 7 November] some young men were disposed to have some sport, threw some pepper into the fire, and others seemed disposed to create an excitement. We therefore left Boa, although it was the Sabbath, and got along very well to the city of Solong, where we were received with kindness.

We stopped at Solong ten days, and then left, in harmony with all, and arrived at the river, where the people were disposed to take advantage of us; for after we had paid on one side of the river, they compelled us to pay or dash on the other side.[72] From there we arrived at the lively, flourishing interior settlement of Carysburg, on the 8th Dec., 1858 [Wednesday], where we remained a few days, much pleased to see with what energy and activity business was prosecuted, and especially from the fact that most of the timber sawed is done by the natives of the country (who are so erroneously generally represented as indolent).

The new emigrants have a real missionary spirit. They take pains to instruct the natives in sawing, and thus Americo and native Liberians work side by side for the great cause of Colonization. Carysburg is and will be the morning star of Liberia; and it is my hope that star after star may arise in the east, until our political sky shall be all luminous with future glory. Interior settlements are the hope of Liberia. It must be understood the native population are in heathen ignorance and moral darkness.

I have done and said all I could in my journey, and hope to be charitably dealt with by the public. If favored with another outfit as a tourist, I hope more fully to meet the expectations of my fellow-citizens.[73] The great business of my life will be the good of Africa; for here I expect to spend the remainder of my days. I shall ever bear in mind that the Christian Church in Liberia should be foremost in this great work of moral and mental reform. Past, present, and future give evidence beyond cavil, that Colonization will not be able to sustain our institution fully, without the combined aid of our native citizens. We Americo-Liberians must identify ourselves with the interests of our race in general; and to that end the soothing emotions of Christianity are to be put in a position to act fully and effectually on the nation; and it is my belief the Church in Liberia is charged with that important duty. But if omitted in a point where she might accomplish much good, that omission will be the cause of great evil in the future.

With these remarks, I submit this journal to your Excellency's charitable inspection, and feel honored to subscribe myself,

Your humble and obedient servant,

George L. Seymour[74]

....

NARRATIVE

OF A

JOURNEY TO MUSARDU,

THE

CAPITAL OF THE WESTERN MANDINGOES.

BY

BENJAMIN ANDERSON.

New-York:
S. W. GREEN, PRINTER, 16 AND 18 JACOB STREET.

1870.

Figure 12. Original front page of Anderson's *Narrative of a Journey to Musardu*, 1870.

5

Benjamin J. K. Anderson, 1868–69

NARRATIVE OF A JOURNEY TO MUSARDU, THE CAPITAL OF THE WESTERN MANDINGOES.
BY BENJAMIN ANDERSON. NEW YORK: S. W. GREEN, PRINTER, 16 AND 18 JACOB STREET. 1870

INTRODUCTION

SMITHSONIAN INSTITUTION, JANUARY, 1870.

It had long been considered important by the friends of Liberia that an exploration should be made of the country east of the Republic. The only difficulty in the way was to find the proper man for the enterprise. President Warner had for a number of years been seeking for such a one, when the author of the accompanying narrative volunteered to undertake the exploration. He is a young man, educated in Liberia, of pure negro blood, and had previously served as Secretary of the Treasury under President Warner.[1] The narrative is printed without correction from the original manuscript, and the principal portion of the edition has been presented to the Smithsonian Institution by Mr. Maunsell Schieffelin, for distribution.

JOSEPH HENRY,
Secretary Smithsonian Institution

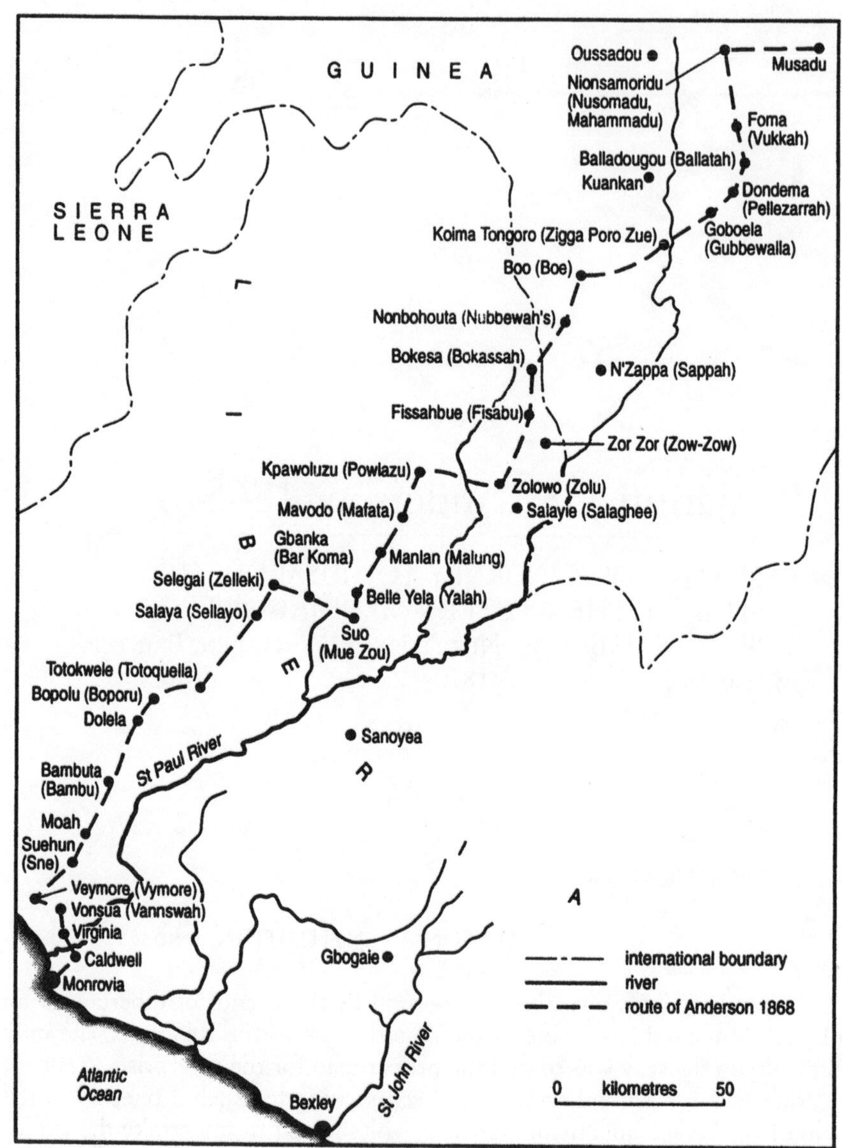

Map 9. Benjamin Anderson's journey, 1868–69.

A JOURNEY TO MUSARDU.

This account of a journey to Musardu, the capital of the Western Mandingoes, is the result of a proposal made by Mr. Henry M. Schieffelin, of New-York, through President D. B. Warner, of Liberia, who for six or eight years had been endeavoring, till now without success, to induce the inauguration of an expedition from Liberia, to explore the interior as far as possible. Mr. Schieffelin and Caleb Swan, Esq., of New-York, furnished the means necessary to carry on the exploration.[2]

No especial point was indicated by the promoters of this exploration; only the general direction was given, east and north-east. The especial point, however, agreed upon by my friends in Monrovia, was Musardu, the capital of the Western Mandingoes. This is the portion of the country of Manding which our citizens Seymore and Ash attempted to visit; but their travels were unfortunately interrupted in a manner that nearly cost them their lives.[3]

The Mandingoes have always excited the liveliest interest on account of their superior physical appearance, their natural intelligence, their activity, and their [p. 6] enterprise. No one has passed unnoticed these tall black men from the eastern interior, in whose countenances spirit and intellect are strongly featured.

Their diligent journeys from Tallakondah have allowed no sea-coast town north-west of the St. Paul's to remain unvisited. Their avidity for trade has drawn them from their treeless plains to the Atlantic ocean. Their zeal for Islam has caused the name of Mohammed to be pronounced in this part of Africa, where it otherwise would never have been mentioned.

Musardu can, by easy journeys, be reached from Monrovia in twenty-five to thirty days.[4] I was obliged, however, from the delays and inconveniences incident to interior traveling in Africa, to occupy thirteen months.

Sometimes I was compelled to spend considerable lengths of time in one place. I have not on that account burdened this report with insipid recitals of what, every day, nearly repeated itself. Whatever struck me as descriptive of the country, or illustrative of the manners of the people, that I have recorded.

I am sensible that the regions through which I have traveled are capable of yielding vaster stores of information, in a scientific point of view, than what I have afforded; but I shall be satisfied if this humble beginning succeeds in encouraging others in the same direction, and on a more extensive scale. I shall now proceed to narrate the journey from Monrovia to Musardu; but especially from Boporu [Bopolu, 7°4'N, 10°29'W] to Musardu.[5]

I shall rapidly march through the two grand divisions of the Boozie country. I shall first make the reader acquainted with the Domar Boozie; introduce [p. 7] him at once to the populous and thriving towns of Zolu [Zolowo, 7°39'N, 9°33'W], Zow-Zow, Salaghee, Fissahbue, and Bokkasaw.[6] Leaving

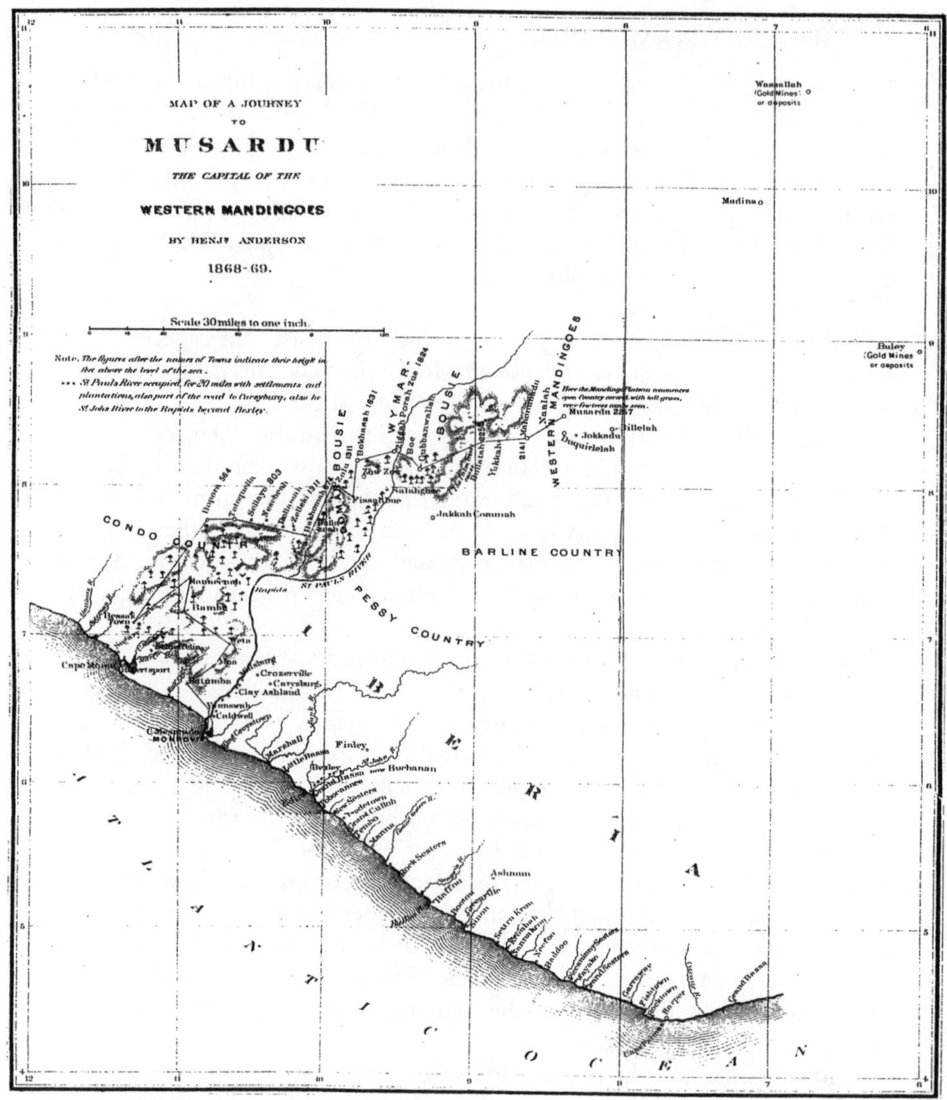

Figure 13. Map from *A Journey to Musardu, the Capital of the Western Mandingoes,* by Benjamin Anderson, 1868–69.

the Domar country, we shall enter the Wymar country, give time to rest at Ziggah Porrah Zue, in latitude 8° 14' 45", its capital, the vast and noisy market of which takes place every Sunday, upon the banks of the same river on which Clay Ashland, Louisiana, Virginia, and Caldwell are seated—the St. Paul's.[7] We shall then cross that river upon a suspension bridge of wicker-work, elevated twenty-five feet from its surface, and come into the territory of one of the most warlike kings in the Wymar country, the bloody Donilnyah.[8] We shall not tarry long in his presence; but, hastening away, nothing shall stop our progress—not even the Vukkah mountains, a boundary acknowledged to divide fertile hills of Wymar from the almost treeless plains of Manding.[9] Crossing these with the tramp and speed of a soldier, we shall quickly descend into the country of the Western Mandingoes; visit their principal cities;[10] and, finally, take up our abode in their very capital—Musardu.

The instruments with which observations were made were: One sextant, by E. & G. W. Blunt, New-York; one aneroid barometer; two thermometers-1st, 133°; 2d, 140°, by B. Pike, New-York; two small night and day compasses, by H. W. Hunter, New-York; one tolerably good watch; one artificial horizon.[11]

As for the accuracy of these calculations of latitude and longitude, whatever painstaking and the instruments enumerated above could do, has not been neglected.[12]

I have not been able to calculate the profile of the [p. 8] route according to the usual methods, because it was impossible to procure the proper instruments, with which a contemporaneous register ought to have been kept at Monrovia, during my absence.

Even the barometer with which I was furnished was an aneroid, an instrument that has to be referred from time to time to the mercurial barometer for adjustment. I can not say that the indications of the instrument were material departures from the truth. It certainly indicated the rise and fall of land in a satisfactory and unmistakable manner, both in going to and returning from Musardu.

At Totoquella, in latitude 7° 45' 24", and Boporu, June 9th and 13th, it ranged 29.36, 29.34.[13] Upon my return in March it ranged from 29.14 to 29.24. This difference may be ascribed, partly to difference of seasons of rains and dries, and partly to want of accuracy in the instrument itself.

I was not even able to ascertain directly the several heights of land by means of the boiling point of water, because my thermometers ranged only from 133° to 140° Fahrenheit. The highest rise of land was indicated by the aneroid at 27.61 inches; the boiling point of which would have been 208° Fahrenheit. See Davies & Peck's Mathematical Dictionary, page 338, "Table of barometric heights corresponding to difference of temperature of boiling water."[14] It is from these tables that I have made appropriate estimates of the elevations of land.

Taking the indications of the aneroid at the several places, and ascertaining from the tables the boiling [p. 9] points at each place, (which always rated higher than my two thermometers of 133° and 144° Fahrenheit,) I then made the calculation as if I had ascertained the boiling point directly from the thermometer. For example, the barometer and thermometer at Ziggah Porrah Zue stood 28.08 and 86°.[15]

The boiling point of 28.06 (see Tables) is	208° Fah.
From Table I. for 208° height, . .	2049 feet.
Proportional part for 0° 8', deduct.	408
	1641
Multiplier from Table II. for 86°, . . .	1112
Approximate height required, . .	1824 feet.

The number of longitudes would have been greater, had it not been for the difficulty of reading off the limb of the sextant at night.

On the 14th of February, 1868, I embarked the effects of the expedition in a large canoe, loaned me by Dr. C. B. Dunbar for the purpose.[16] We reached Virginia, on the St. Paul's, at six o'clock P.M. The next morning we started for Vannswah, a Dey village, four and a half miles in the rear of Virginia.[17] This village was once occupied wholly by the Deys, but their power is fast waning, and more than half the village is now in the hands of Mandingo traders from Boporu.

Here it was that I had made a previous arrangement for the conduct of the expedition, with a learned Mandingo, Kaifal-Kanda, who had lately arrived from his native town Billelah, a place near to, and scarcely second in importance to Musardu itself [p. 10].[18]

I was detained here three weeks waiting for him to arrange our departure.[19] In the mean time all my carriers, who were Kroomen, deserted me, with the exception of their head-man, Ben; being frightened by what the Dey people told them of the dangers of the road. Kaifal at first proposed to send me direct to Boporu; but my friends at Monrovia were so apprehensive that I should not be able to pass through that country, that I refused to go to Boporu. Subsequently events proved that their apprehensions were not entirely unfounded.

Boporu, though the most direct route, or the route most usually traveled, is also the place where the strongest opposition is offered to any one wishing to pass through. It is the place where the policy of non-intercourse originated. Its power and policy dominate over the surrounding regions.

Figure 14. Ashmun Street, Monrovia.
Source: The Philadelphia Colonization Herald, *1858*.

It was upon my refusal to go to Boporu that Kaifal sent me to Bessa's town, which is situated forty miles west of Boporu. And though it is somewhat independent of the authority of Momoru Son, the king of Boporu, the same practice prevails with respect to prohibiting all penetration into the interior.[20]

Before setting out on this expedition, I made very effort to join another civilized person with me; but the undertaking was considered of too dangerous a character.[21] I tried to prevail on some of the young men, who had but little else to do at the time; but was so entirely unsuccessful, that I fear their reputation for enterprise and hardihood must suffer when I related how they preferred the safe, soft, grassy streets of Monrovia to an expedition into the heart of their [p. 11] country, simply because it was said to be perilous. I thereafter received other discouragements, from such a quarter and of such a character that I must forbear to mention them.

Many stories were rife of the unsettled state of the country: that the roads between us and the interior tribes were infested by banditti, and that war was raging between interior tribes themselves; that between all these jarring forces, it was impossible for the expedition to survive forty miles. And this was the opinion of those who were in a condition to be the best informed. But as the expedition was pushed on in the very localities where these difficulties were said to exist, it was found that there were disturbances, but not of a character to entirely prohibit our progress.

The practice of exaggerating every petty affair into the proportions of a universal war, is used for a purpose; being often an artifice to produce general consternation, out of which the more knowing may cull every advantage for themselves.

Besides, it is the policy of our intervening tribes to get up scare-crow reports, to prevent intercourse between the interior and Liberia. Nothing is more dreaded, and especially by the Boporu Mandingoes, than the penetration of the interior by the Liberians. There is, therefore, a complete line of obstruction, extending east and west, in the rear of Montserrado country, which hinders or inconveniences trade. It deserves the immediate action of government, in order that the interior trade may be completely unfettered from such annoyances.

It is along this line that the Boporu Mandingoes [p. 12] and others are determined to be the "go-betweens" to the inland trade and Liberian enterprise. They it is who are chiefly engaged in making beef scarce, and country cloths small; who trammel and clog the Boozie and Barline trade.

On the 6th of March, having hired eighteen Congoes, to supply the place of the Kroomen who had deserted me, we started from Vannswah for Bessa's town, under the conduct of two of Kaifal's young men.[22] Bessa's town was the place pitched upon as our starting-point for Musardu, since I had refused to go to Boporu.

Passing, as rapidly as our burdens would permit, the towns of Vyrmore, Sne [?Suehun, 6°35'N, 10°40'W], Moah, Weta, and Bambu [Bambuta, 6°57'N, 10°33'W], we reached Mannèenah on Thursday, the 12th of March. We had been traveling in a north-eastern direction; halting here, we saw a large mountain, north-east by east, behind which Boporu is said to lie. We had now to change our course to westward, in order to go to Bessa's town.[23] All the towns and villages through which we had passed, except Weta, Bambu, and Mannèenah, belonged to the Deys. This tribe was once numerous and powerful, but is now scatteringly sprinkled in small and unimportant villages over the face of the country. They have a relic of their old antipathy against the Liberians. Slave-trade, war, and their absorption into other tribes have nearly obliterated every thing that distinguished them as a tribe. Old Gatumba's town, both in appearance and hospitality, is the only redeeming feature in this part of the country.[24]

In this region leopards are numerous, and sometimes [p. 13] dangerous. The female leopard is particularly dangerous when she has the care of her young. It is said that leopards never attack first, and will always shun you whenever they can do so. This rule, like many others, has some exceptions, and sometimes some very fatal ones. A female leopard having her cub with her met a man in a sudden turn of the road; she flew at him, and came nigh breaking the rule entirely as to him, but for the strength of his lungs and the speed of his legs, all of which had to be brought into desperate requisition.

At Weta's town an enormous leopard was shot by an old man. As soon as he saw the mammoth cat, he was taken with the trembles; but, remembering that it was only the matter of a few moments which should have the first chance for life, he leveled his piece at the head of the crouching animal, and in an instant had the satisfaction to see that the object of his fears was stretched helpless on the earth.

This trophy of the old man's prowess was borne home in triumph, and divided into many parcels. The chine-bone is considered the bone of contention; and, as soon as it is severed from the rest, it is thrown high in the air, in order that when it comes to the ground—

"Those may take who have the power,
And those may keep who can."

A general scramble ensues, in which it is clearly proved that a part is greater than the whole; for the chine-bone can produce a greater row, and a bigger fight, than if the whole animal, instinct with its living [p. 14] ferocity, had jumped plump into the middle of the crowd.

The physical features of the country are roughened by hills, valleys, and small plains; and similar inequalities of surface prevail to what may be seen in the rear of Clay Ashland; indeed, the Clay Ashland hills are a part of them, and must have been produced by the same physical causes.

These hills grow bolder and more conspicuous in outline as we advance in the interior. Sometimes linked together by gentle depressions, and sometimes entirely detached from each other, they form no definite range; rising and running toward every point of the compass, they present all the varieties of figure and direction that hills can assume.

Their composition, so far as could be discerned from their surface, was the ordinary vegetable mould, with boulders of iron ore, granite, white quartz, and a mixed detritus from these various rocks, charged in many places with thin-leaved mica, similar to that which is seen in the Clay Ashland hills.

Before we reached the margin of the Boporu, or Boatswain country, we passed through long and almost unbroken strips of forests, upon a road partaking of the uneven character of the country, and strewn for miles with sharp pebbles and vitreous quartz, rendering travel painful enough to the unshoden pedestrian. Hugh boulders of granite were dispersed here and there, relieving the gloom and monotony of large, shady forest trees. This region is intersected with numerous streams flowing over sandy bottoms or [p. 15] granite beds, with a temperature of 58°, 60°, and 62° Fahrenheit.

On Saturday, the 13th of March, we left Mannèenah, and after traveling forty miles westward, we reached Bessa's town, at six o'clock P.M.[25]

Bessa's town is in latitude 7° 3' 19", in the western portion of the Golah country. It is elevated about four hundred and eighty feet above the level of the sea.[26] This town is located in a small, irregular plain, studded with palm-trees, and hedged in by hills in nearly every direction. It is strongly fortified with a double barricade of large wooden stakes; in the space between each barricade sharp-pointed stakes, four feet long, are set obliquely in the ground, crossing each other; this is to prevent the defenses from being scaled. The town is of an oval form; the north and south points resting on the edge of swamps; the east and west points, which are the points of access, are flanked with a strong quadrilateral stockade, with four intervening gates between the outside gate and the town itself. There are guard-houses to each of these gates, and people constantly in them night and day. To a force without artillery this town would give some trouble. It contains about three hundred and fifty clay dwellings, of various sizes, and between eight hundred and one thousand inhabitants, who may be regarded as the permanent population. Of the transient traders and visitors it would be difficult to form any estimate. The houses are huddled together in a close and most uncomfortable proximity; in some parts of the town scarcely two persons can walk abreast. In matters of cleanliness and health, King Bessa can not [p. 16] be said to have seriously consulted the interests of his people.[27]

Bessa himself is a personage well known to one of our best citizens, Mr. Gabriel Moore.[28] He is of Mandingo extraction. I regret, however, to say that he is deplorably wanting in that sedateness and religious cast of feeling which usually forms the distinguishing characteristic of that tribe.

I was informed that he had purchased a dispensation from the rigid observances of that creed from some of the Mandingo priests, by paying a large amount of money. This license to do evil so affected our journey to Musardu, that it came nearly breaking up the expedition altogether.

It was on a Friday we arrived in this town—a day said to be always inauspicious. We introduced ourselves as being sent to him by one of his own countrymen, Kaifal Kanda, a Mandingo, living at Vannswah, with whom we were going to Musardu.

He affected to listen with great attention; spoke of the commotions of the interior, which, as he said, was a great obstacle and hinderance to all travelling just at that time. He also informed me that he would have to consult the other kings behind him before allowing me to pass; and he kept on creating difficulty after difficulty, all reasonable and fair enough in argument, but point-lank [point-blank] lies in fact. He had no consulting to do; for he was at that time at variance with the principal neighboring chiefs.

I was not pleased with my first audience, yet I was induced to make Bessa the following presents: three bars of tobacco, one double barreled pistol, one large brass [p. 17] kettle, one piece of fancy handkerchiefs, and one keg of powder. This gift was received with satisfaction, but it was hinted that the king was anxious to trade with me for the rest of my money. I had, therefore, to distinctly state that I did not wish to trade, as that would prevent me from accomplishing the object for which I had come, namely, to go to Musardu.

Bessa now began to show how much he disrelished the idea of my passing through his country, and carrying so much money "behind him," as he expressed it. He offered me his fat bullocks, country cloths, palm-oil, ivory, etc.; but I steadily refused to trade. Finding me inexorable in that respect, he began to grumble about the "dash," or gifts, I had made him. Some mischievous persons had told him that the gifts were insignificant to what it was the custom of Liberians to "dash," or present, kings; and Jollah, my interpreter, had some difficulty to persuade the king to the contrary; besides, he had his own reasons for remaining so incredulous.

I had struck the line of obstruction at this point. It was upon my refusal to go to Boporu that Kaifal had sent me to Bessa's town. Bessa, in carrying out this policy of non-intercourse with the interior, which is a standing, well-known, and agreed-upon thing throughout the whole country, now commenced a series of annoyances, his people acting in concert with him. He began with my Congoes. Every means that language and signs could produce was used to frighten and discourage them. They were told of the wars in the path. He also showed some Boozies whom he had in his town, whose faces were disfigured with [p. 18] hideous tattoo-marks, and whose front teeth were filed sharp and pointed, for the purpose of eating people; their long bows and poisoned arrows; their broad knives and crooked iron hooks, with which they caught and hewed to pieces those whom they pursued. But what more alarmed my Congoes than any thing else, was the prospect of being eaten by the Boozies. Bessa, to make this part more vividly horrible, had brought into our presence several of his man-eaters, who were said to delight in that business. He then brought in his war-drums, the heads of which were the skins of human beings, well tanned and corded down, while a dozen grinning human jaw-bones were dangling and rattling against each other with a noise that reminded my Congoes that their jaw-bones too might perform a similar office on some country war-drum. It was by such means that Bessa entirely succeeded in disorganizing the whole expedition. He gave the Congoes plainly to understand that they had better not hazard their lives in attempting to follow me to Musardu.

My carriers, who had hitherto shown willingness and obedience, now began openly to disobey my orders; and my difficulty was greatly increased from the fact that I had not been able to get a single civilized person to accompany me. I had no one, in consequence, to confer with, or to assist me in watching the movements of my mutinous Congoes. It soon became evident that there was an understanding between my Congoes and Bessa, and that all hands were conspiring together against me. Several times I had detected Bessa and the Congoes in secret consultation. I guessed at once the villainy hatching. I tried every means to induce [p. 19] the Congoes to disregard the idle tales that were told them by Bessa and his people; but neither advice, persuasion, nor the offer of donations above their pay could overcome the impression that had been made upon their minds respecting the dangers of the route. Big Ben, the Krooman, kept himself aloof from the plots of the Congoes, yet he was in favor of returning to Monrovia; and he made my ears ring with, "'Spose we no find good path; we go back now." The Congoes began to hold secret meetings by themselves, and to talk in a low, muttering tone. Matters were now brewing to some mischievous point; but what their resolves were, I could never learn. With my Congoes in open rupture, Bessa himself drunk, avaricious, and conspiring, I had now to exercise the greatest vigilance.

One night, exasperated at their mutinous language and conduct, we came to a collision, in which all of us had recourse to our arms, and but for the immediate interference of the town people, things would have certainly ended seriously. I should have been riddled with their balls, there being fifteen of them. King Bessa, attended by some of his people, came to allay the disturbance. He could not have been furnished a better opportunity of seemingly protecting me from the very mischiefs he had secretly instigated. He reproved the Congoes, and imposed a fine for breaking the peace—a gun and a piece of handkerchief being the cost of court. He never used his authority to enforce obedience on the part of the Congoes, which he could have easily done. No; he affected a neutral course, which had many by-paths to his own interest, [p. 20] and through which he managed to transfer many a bar of my tobacco into his own hands.

Much of Bessa's conduct arose from the defiant and refractory behavior of Prince Manna toward the government.[29] The moral effect of this man's conduct has been any thing but beneficial for Liberia. Bessa was continually referring, with pride, to a man who could defy the government with impunity. Unless the government shows energy and control, it will always be difficult to visit these parts—almost within the territorial limits of Liberia—for any purpose whatever. The fact was but too plainly humiliating, that we had lost *prestige* and respect. The policy of too much moderation and forbearance is often abused or misunderstood by warlike barbarians, whose swords are an appendage of their daily apparel.

Bessa now, in an advisory manner, repeated over and over again the difficulties of the route, adding to it the determination of my Congo carriers themselves not to go any further. To this he joined a series of petty annoyances—sometimes coming himself, and sometimes sending for me, to talk palavers. Then he would complain that the Congoes endangered the lives of his people by their hunting; that they would likely set his town on fire by their smoking-pipe, though his own people indulged in this thing not only to a greater degree, but solely through my liberality. But what exasperated me most was his practice of eavesdropping; his boys and people were continually lurking to hear what was said in my house. I was always expected to conclude his royal visits—which were frequent [p. 21], and which he gave me to understand were condescensions on his part—with large bars of my tobacco.

Bessa is naturally avaricious. This vice was unfortunately worked up to its worst resource; he drank night and day, until he had sufficiently steamed himself up to the courage for downright robbery. Drunk he gets every day; and after the first two or three hours of excess are over, he finally sobers down to that degree at which his avarice is greatest, and his regard for other people's rights least. There he remains.

His couch, upon which he reclines, and which is at once his bed and his chair of state, he never quits, but for a drunken carousal in the midst of his women. This bed is stacked head and foot with loaded muskets, huge horse-pistols, rusty swords and spears, while sundry daggers, with their points stuck in the ground, are ready at hand "for the occasion sudden." He seems to live in perpetual dread of assassination. His people never come in his presence but in an obsequious stoop, and they never recover an erect posture until they are out of his presence. But when the women came, then you might expect to see humanity go on all fours. It was difficult to know the height of some of the women on account of this servility.

Bessa is engaged in the slave-trade. Passing one morning through his town, I saw a slave with his right hand tied up to his neck, and fifty sticks of salt fastened to his back, about to be sent into the interior to be exchanged for a bullock. Six slaves, chained together, worked on his farms. He has numerous other slaves, but they were better treated.

I will not relate all the circumstances of his lashing [p. 22] an old slave until his cries drew the tears of all who stood by, nor his stamping in the breast of one of his slaves until death ensued, on account of some slight offense. His enormities are too many to recount them all, and would only weary the reader with what they know must be his habits, from what I have already said of him. He regretted to me the interference of the Liberians with the foreign slave-trade.

It was now the beginning of April, and I had not been able to proceed upon my journey. My Congo carriers refused to go any further. Kaifal, the Mandingo, still remained at Vannswah. I therefore tried to induce Bessa to hire me some of his people. I offered to pay him liberally if he would honestly engage in sending me forward. He accepted the offer, and received an amount of $66.40 in goods. He gave me four persons, to act as interpreters and guides; but I had no one to carry my luggage, and he took good care that no one should be hired for that purpose. He was continually telling me that my money "no got feet this time."

If I could have relied on my Congoes, I would have gone on, despite Bessa's attempts to prevent me; but their defection paralyzed all movement forward. I could bethink myself of no other resource than to return to Vannswah in quest of Kaifal. Not having any one in whom I could repose confidence enough to place my effects in their care until I returned from Vannswah, I had to run the risk of placing them in the hands of the king. On the 5th of

April, 1868, taking two of my Congoes with me, I came to Boporu.[30] There I met Seymoru Syyo, Kaifal's relation, a tall, fine-looking [p. 23] Mandingo, but whose very black countenance wore a still blacker cloud of displeasure because I had not come to him direct, instead of going to Bessa.[31] He scarcely deigned to look at me, especially as I was in no decent plight, having undertaken the journey barefoot, in order to cross the streams more readily. He at length gave me to understand that, so far as Kaifal's going to Musardu was concerned, it depended entirely upon his (Seymoru Syyo's) pleasure; muttered something about the war at Musardu; counted his beads, and then strode off toward the mosque, where they had just been summoned to prayer.[32]

On the 6th of April, 1868, I started from Boporu, and arrived at Vannswah on the 9th.[33] Kaifal affected regret at having cause me so much delay, telling me that it was owing to his preparation to get ready that he was detained so long. He now promised to march immediately. This he made a show of doing by sending his women and scholars forward, telling me to go on with them, while he should remain behind to pray for our success.[34] I consented; but he managed to lag behind so long, that I never saw him again until May 8th, and after I had left Bessa's and come to Boporu.

I now went back to Bessa's town, persuaded that Kaifal would soon follow.[35] As soon as I arrived at Bessa's, Ben, the Krooman, informed me that the Congoes had tried to induce the king to send them home, telling him that he might keep all my goods if he would only permit them to go home. I went straight to the king, and requested him to deliver to me my boxes; he at once hesitated, and I could scarcely get him to consent to let me have the box containing my [p. 24] clothes. After much contention and wrangling, he delivered up all the boxes, retaining the powder and guns. He then declared that I must pay him for all the Congoes I had placed in his hands; that I must pay him a piece of cloth and a gun for each one of them, as well as for feeding them while I was gone to Vannswah. He then made some other frivolous demands, which he deemed necessary to justify the robbery he was about to commit.

To make matters worse, the Congoes themselves now began to gather round me like little children, begging me to sacrifice all my goods, if it were necessary, to save them. "Daddy, no lose we this country, no lose we," was their continual whine. All spirit for a manly resistance had fled; nothing but the most abject cowardice prevailed. Before I started on the journey, I had thoroughly armed these Congoes; but the only use they had made of their arms was to resist my authority. Now a peculiar danger stared them in the face—they had not even courage enough to save themselves from slavery.

I refused to comply with the demands of the king to pay the boys. I became exasperated; but I was jammed between the power of the king and the cowardice and unfaithfulness of the Congoes. The king's Boozies, who walked the town with their broad knives to fight, and their teeth filed sharp to eat their enemies, confirmed the poltroonery of the Congoes as a standing and immutable fact.[36]

The king advised the Congoes to talk to me, telling them, "Your daddy has got the heart of an elephant; you had better talk to him." They attempted to talk [p. 25] to me; but I was too much angered at their cowardice and his robbery to listen to any thing. The king extorted $130; Ben, the Krooman, and Louis, a Congo, negotiating the business. I refused to have any thing to do with it. After he had taken this amount, Ben and Louis begged him to be satisfied. He told them that he would refer the matter to his women; if they consented, he would rest satisfied.[37] This female assembly was consulted, and from the subsequent conduct of the king, they must have resolved that I should pay doubly. The extortions were renewed to an amount of $25. This occurred on Friday and Saturday, the 23d and 24th of April.[38]

The next day [Saturday, 25 April] I was somewhat able to command my feelings. I resolved to go to Boporu. Nothing was more contrary to Bessa's wishes. He now tried his best to induce me to go on my journey through his country. He declared that unless the Congoes wanted to lose their heads, they should go along with me. He was willing to furnish guides and interpreters. But my resolution was taken; I was determined to go to Boporu; no blandishments nor hollow professions of friendship could lead me to trust him after what I had just experienced at his hands. As he had been visited by some suspicious persons, who even counted the number of my Congo warriors, it might have been agreed on to finish with murder what had been begun by robbery. We were allowed to depart without further annoyance. The Congoes were overjoyed; for they were sure that I was returning home. Bessa even sent six stalwart slaves to carry me, in order that my feelings might be soothed into some kind of forbearance [p. 26] toward him;[39] for he now began to fear that I might bring him to account, though it seemed he was willing to run the risk rather than restore the goods. I availed myself of the service of his carriers; but I left the king with the bitter intention to do him all the injury I could as soon as opportunity presented itself.

I arrived at Boporu on the 25th of April, 1868. Kaifal had not yet come, and did not arrive until three days afterward [Tuesday, 28 April]. He now appeared indignant at Bessa's conduct, and affected the greatest diligence for our setting out immediately for Musardu. But first, he would go to Bessa and influence him to restore what he had unjustly taken from me. He induced me to make considerable presents to his friend and relation, Seymoru Syyo, helping himself also in a manner which nothing but my great anxiety for him to hasten our journey would have allowed me to permit.

Before he went to Bessa's, the principal Mandingoes in the town, Kaifal, and myself, held a council, in which they strove to induce me to return to Bessa's with Kaifal; but I utterly refused. I would talk of nothing but soldiers, cannon, the burning of Bessa's town, and other furious things; which so alarmed the Mandingoes, that they begged me not to write to Monrovia about the matter until Kaifal had gone and tried to get the money. In this council, the Mandingoes reminded me that, as the Liberians and Mandingoes were one and the same people, I ought not to act with too great a severity; but I was not inclined to make common stock of my goods on account of that identity, and in a very impatient and unreasonable manner I gave them to understand that all their relationship to [p. 27] me depended solely on the restoration of my goods. If they failed in that, I was prepared to ignore all ties. I was in no humor for cant about kindred; I wanted my money; my feelings were sore at my disappointments and losses.

The expedition was deemed to have fallen in pieces. My interpreter, Jollah, also commenced to show signs of desertion and treachery. I had always suspected him with being implicated in Bessa's villainy; I was soon to discover that he had not been entirely ignorant nor innocent with respect to Bessa's designs. His connivance, or rather the assistance he gave Bessa, was so glaring, that the Mandingoes at Boporu did not fail to upbraid him with it. In his conversation, he plainly showed that he had gone over to Bessa's interest, though he still continued to follow my boxes. The Mandingoes contemptuously asked him in whose service he was, whether mine or Bessa's? Bessa, it seemed, had promised him largely if he (Jollah) assisted him successfully in his villainy. Jollah's crooked ways were such that I could no longer retain his services. Interpreters began to prove a dangerous attachment to the expedition. Owing to Jollah's double-dealing, I was obliged to have recourse to a Veyman to act as interpreter; and right in the middle of an important conversation which I was holding with Seymoru Syyo, this man suffered himself to be taken so ill as to become speechless, and he could only be induced to recover by the promise of a large (dash) present.[40]

Kaifal, it seemed, had greatly offended Seymoru Syoo by sending me to Bessa's instead of sending me direct to Boporu; but, as I have before shown, it was [p. 28] not Kaifal's fault that I did not go directly to Boporu. However, the fault was imputed to him, and as he could only regain the favor of Seymoru by gifts, it was thought no more than right that I should bestow them, as it was through my persistence in refusing to go to Boporu that he had got into the difficulty with Seymoru. As soon as my boxes arrived at Boporu, Seymoru altered his demeanor toward me. His dark and grumbling countenance immediately changed into a smiling intimacy and friendship. He would fain have posted me on wings to Musardu.

Though Boporu is the capital of the Boatswain or Condo country, and the usual residence of the king, Momoru Son, the king was at this time residing at a large town called Totoquella [Totokwele, 7°3'N, 10°24'W], eight miles north-east of Boporu.

As soon as Kaifal started for Bessa's town, I resolved to pay my respects to King Momoru. I arrived at Totoquella on May 7th, 1868 [Thursday]. I was kindly received, and at once stated to the king that I would have been to see him much sooner, but that I was a stranger in his country, and had supposed he resided at his reputed capital, Boporu; that when I came to that town, I was informed that he had gone elsewhere.[41] He replied that he was accustomed to divide his time between the two towns; sometimes residing at Boporu and sometimes staying at Totoquella. I then informed him of the object of my visit; and had to frame such an account of my former proceedings as to show that it had always been my intention to come to his country, but that I had been thwarted by many untoward circumstances. And true it was that I would have [p. 29] preferred, at the first, going direct to Boporu, had it not been for the reasons already stated.

Circumstances now forced me in that direction, and I addressed myself to the task of repairing the failures or misfortunes into which the expedition had fallen. The king was intelligent and communicative. He was, however, chagrined that the government—the new administration of which had just come into power—had not taken any notice of him, and sent him a (book) paper, expressive of its good feelings toward him, as had been the custom of all incoming administrations.[42] He was always referring to a treaty that had been made between him and President Benson, during the incumbency of the latter.[43] I had, therefore, to console him with the notion that, as soon as the administration had got fairly into operation, it would not fail to draw up an instrument similar to what President Benson had given him; as well as to make such other arrangement as would satisfy his utmost wishes. The king informed me that he was at the moment trying to stop a war between the Boozies and Barlines, two interior tribes;[44] that he had, in order to promote that purpose, sent five hundred sticks of salt into the Barline country, and the same amount to the Boozies; that he had instructed his messengers to use every argument to incline the parties to peace; that the war was not only hurtful to themselves, but that it damaged him by interrupting all intercourse between his country and theirs, and even with the natives whose country lay behind them. He had sent, therefore, to beg both parties to desist; but if neither would listen, he intended to indemnify himself for such losses as he sustained [p. 29] by their feuds, by seizing persons and property belonging to them in his country. If only one party was willing to comply with his requests, he intended to assist that side with his own military forces.

Thus I had to endure the spectacle of a barbarian king practicing a policy which all intelligent and enterprising persons must think ought to be practiced by the republic itself.[45] No one suspects that we leave to an untutored barbarian the quieting and settling of interior difficulties, while we remain ignorant of their very existence.

Every one would suppose that, to a source to which we look for a great part of our interior trade, such as country cloths, and bullocks, and ivory, a rational solicitude, at least, would be shown that it be not interrupted or broken off. Yet it is a fact that this royal barbarian, without revenue, and without any of the resources to which we pretend, by following the policy of interfering in all interior concerns, is better known and has greater influence from Boporu to Musardu, and even beyond, than the civilized Republic of Liberia; and this is done by sending a few sticks of salt, accompanied by a friendly request or a threatening mandate.

Salt, in the settling of difficulties, has a peculiar propriety—it is a sign of peace as well as a commodity of value for traffic. If it was the policy of the government to interfere in these concerns, a hogshead of salt might pacify the whole country from Boporu to Barline. The king had also interfered in a matter between the Boozies themselves; in which it seemed that one of their chiefs, faithless to the common interest, had [p. 31] clandestinely given assistance to the Barlines against his own country men. This treachery being discovered, he had been seized and confined—or put in stick, as they call it. This mode of confinement consists in having the ankle of the right foot bound securely to a heavy log, four or five feet long, by means of an iron band driven deep into the wood.[46]

The father of this recreant chief, before his death, had placed his children under King Momoru's protection. The king was therefore solicitous that this indiscretion should not cost the young prince his liberty, and perhaps his head; of the former of which he had already been deprived, and the latter was being seriously discussed among the Boozie chiefs. In this affair the king desired that, as I would have to pass through that country, he wished me to assist in pleading for the young man. I pledged my best efforts.

There was also a difficulty between the king and the Boondee people, who live north-west of Boporu.[47] These people hold a nominal fealty to King Momoru, and even this they are slack or remiss in acknowledging.[48]

The king now chose to remove his court from Totoquella to Boporu.[49] None was more eager for this change than myself; for it carried his person and influence just where I wished to make use of them. He left the town May 10th, 1868, accompanied by his courtiers, warriors, women, servants, and musicians of the last of which there were two kinds: those who performed on horns and drums, and those who sang the praises of the king, timing their music with a sort of iron cymbal, one part being fitted to the thumb of the left hand, and beaten with a piece of iron by the right.[50] When the king and his retinue had passed the outer gates of the barricade, a Mandingo priest came out and pronounced a benediction on the royal departure. As soon as this was over, we started; the king walking all the way: he had but to say the word, and they would have carried him. We were preceded by the singing men, who, with the clang of their iron cymbals and their vociferous vocalisms, nearly deafened me. After two or three hours spent in traveling, halting, singing, firing muskets, and all sorts of noisy demonstrations, we came to Boporu. The king entered the town and went directly to his own residence.

Every body came to do homage and welcome his arrival. But nothing appeared more respectful than the Mandingo priests, who came in a body, habited in their white and scarlet robes; tall, dignified black men, with countenances solemn and intelligent. It is remarkable how orderly and sociable these gatherings upon such occasions conduct themselves. Nothing of the rowdyism and clamor for which communities highly civilized are sometimes notorious. The day was concluded with dancing, feasting, and warlike exercises. The next day [Monday, 11 May] beheld every thing settled down into its usual routine. I was now to discover the character of Kaifal in its true light. He had always affected piety and uprightness; nothing very material had occurred to alter my opinion. To be sure, he had lately shown intense craving for my large silver spoon, yet I was inclined to be charitable to this human weakness. He went to Bessa's, solemnly assuring me that he would be gone but two or three days; he staid three weeks, which caused my patience [p. 33], and confidence too, to grow less.[51] I dispatched two of my boys after him. Upon the return of my messengers, I was informed that he had been generously entertained by Bessa, that a sheep had been slain, and other good offices done for him. I became alarmed lest such friendly cheer would lessen his zeal to recover my goods. But when I was further informed that Kaifal had been engaged in practicing certain rites, such as the interment of beef-bones bound round with transcripts from the Koran, which was to be efficacious for Bessa in peace or war, I immediately understood this last act to be directed against myself. I therefore lost no time in ingratiating myself with the king. And there was scarcely any thing I had to propose that was not favorably entertained and facilitated. I had strengthened my influence by gifts, as well as by the great amusement my stereoscope afforded him I had thoroughly instructed him in the purposes of my mission; and showed him how discreditable it would be to his name and his honor if any thing should befall me and my effects within the precincts of his dominions, so that I should not be able to carry out the wishes of the promoters of the expedition. In this part of my affairs I was particularly blessed by Providence in getting in my interest a near relation of the king's. He was a Golah man by the civilized name of Chancelor.[52] He had long resided both at Monrovia and Cape Palmas with one of the best citizens, Dr. S. F. McGill, and could speak English fluently, besides several native tongues.[53] He adhered with unflagging zeal to my interest, and never ceased importuning his royal kinsman night and day respecting my affairs [p. 34]. He was of mild disposition, full of encouragement and sympathy; having nothing to contradict the universal benevolence of his person and character except a huge, antiquated horse-pistol, without which he was never seen, and which became a subject of merriment, as being a burden without a benefit, perfectly innocent in all things except its weight. I had now determined to use all my influence against Kaifal and Bessa. I had been robbed of one part of my goods by the one, and inveigled out of another part by the other. The purposes of the expedition had been baffled, though I had striven to the utmost to accomplish them.

Momoru might be avaricious, but his avarice was a virtue to Bessa's rapacity and Kaifal's unprincipled dealings. If the king wished me to give him any thing, his requests were always accompanied with politeness and desert, arising from the prospect of his facilitating my journey to Musardu. I made a formal complaint against Kaifal and Bessa; presenting the king a written list of all the goods they had unfairly gotten from me. He convened the leading Mandingoes of the town and the principal chiefs. The king himself opened this grand palaver, declaring "that owing to the acts of some of the Mandingoes, many things had been said by the Liberians tending to lessen his character. Whenever the Liberians lost their money by trade or otherwise, he had always to bear the brunt of their dishonest actions and to suffer all kinds of disparagement of character." Nor did he neglect to cite the instances; mentioning as a particular case that of John B. Jordan, who had traded in that country and lost considerable amounts; and then he [p. 35] went on to detail, until he became angered.[54] The Mandingoes found it necessary to appease him by all sorts of condescension; even the singing men were called in.[55] It was necessary to adjourn, that the royal displeasure might cool off.

The next day the business was resumed. It is the custom for every body taking part in a (palaver) discussion, to deliver his argument or opinion walking up and down in the presence of his audience with a spear in his hands.

This mode was observed by all the chiefs who spoke on this occasion. Many of them delivered themselves with such spirit and sense as to draw the frequent acclamations of their hearers. They declared that they not only ought to be careful about provoking the Americans against them; but, as the money was for the purpose of (dashing) presenting the chiefs through whose country I might pass, I ought to be allowed to give it to whom I wished; and that none ought to accept it unless they were willing to accept the conditions of the gift also.

For the conduct of Bessa and Kaifal, the Mandingoes at Boporu seemed to have been held as sureties; certainly not by their own will or consent, but by virtue of their being most conveniently at hand for any purpose of indemnification that might arise. Kaifal, who was still at Bessa's town, was summoned to appear. Bessa was ordered to refund every article according to the list.

The messenger charged with this business went to Bessa's in the most formal manner, being in complete war-dress. It was, therefore, understood that there was to be no trifling [p. 35].

Things began now to conspire in my favor.

Just about this time a young man by the name of Sanders Washington, from the settlement of Virginia, went to Bessa's town for the purpose of trading.[56] Here he learned what had happened between Bessa and myself. He at once advised Bessa to restore the money before the consequences became serious. Bessa, becoming more sober than was usual with him, commenced to apprehend a severe chastising from the government, and right upon the heels of what was to be feared from the Americans came Momoru's no less dreaded demands.

Bessa quickly gave up the things to Mr. Sanders Washington, and consoled himself in a drunken spree. Mr. Washington immediately sent the things to Boporu.

Kaifal now made his appearance. It was the 28th of May, 1868. He came before the king and council dressed in a dark-blue tobe [robe]; a red cap bordered with a white band, the badge of his sacredotal order, on his head; sandals on his feet; his prayer-beads in his hands; his face and faculties prepared for the worst.[57] He was ordered to account for the manner he had conducted my affairs. He commenced defending himself by declaring that what had happened to me was the result of my own obstinacy; for when he wished to send me directly to Boporu, I had insisted on going elsewhere. He further said that if I could have passed through the country anywhere else, they would have never seen my face at Boporu; which was indeed true. He caused disagreeable questions to be put to me respecting that matter: this was his only advantage, and [p. 37] he clung to it. He declared that I had absolutely refused to go to Boporu, and that I had maligned the king, and that I had gone to Bessa's, where my indiscretion had got me into trouble and made me lose my money; that Bessa had acted in all things honestly.

His argument was partly true and partly false. All he averred respecting Boporu was indeed true; but borrowing the courage which the truth about Boporu gave him, his assertions about Bessa's conduct were bold and barefaced lies. I replied that it was solely upon his advice that I had gone to Bessa's; that as to my coming to Boporu, he plainly saw I was there, and that without consulting him.

He dwelt incessantly on my refusal to go to Boporu, and more than once it was convenient for me to rid myself of his vexing questions by placing the whole blame upon his interpreter.

We now came to that part in which he had taken my money and gone off to Bessa's, where he had staid so long that it became necessary to send for him. Being questioned why he had done so, his self-possession entirely forsook him, and though he referred the matter to a rapid manipulation of his beads, it brought him no relief. He told them over and over, but they failed to enlighten his mind so as to furnish prompt replies and ready answers. He finally stammered out something about his waiting for the new moon. He had not regarded that luminary when he was getting the goods.

He was made to restore according to the list.

I was now in possession of all my goods again, with the prospect of being able to prosecute the exploration with success [p. 38].

I was also in a better state of mind to attend to my affairs in that respect, though, as I had all along apprehended, the season for comfortable traveling, and especially for making astronomical observations, had nearly passed; indeed, upon every attempt at an observation, clouds and vapor made it a difficult and uncertain matter.[58]

Boporu, the capital of the Boatswain country, is in latitude 7°45[']08".[59] Its elevation above the level of the sea is about 560 feet.[60] The barometer, in the month of May and June, stands from 29.18 to 29.40; the thermometer ranges from 78 to 80 Fahrenheit. It is situated in a small plain near the foot of some high hills E.N.E. of it. Very high hills rise on every side, with an elevation from 300 to 650 feet, coursing along in every direction, some continuing three or four miles in length before their spurs come down into the valleys or plains.[61] The soil of the plains is chiefly white and yellow clay; but near the base of the hills, it is generally mixed with the detritus of granite and other rocks washed down in the rainy season from their sides. Granite boulders of various sizes are found on the sides and tops of these hills, and, unlike the granite of our cape, which is of a fine, dark flinty appearance, present many grades of tint and texture.[62] A large piece of granitic gneiss forms a part of the grave of King Boatswain, the present king's father, broken in such a way as to show the red, white, and gray in beautiful contrast.[63] A little art might have rendered it more worthy to mark so mighty a grave. Every tree, flower, and shrub of our cape repeats itself here, not excepting the water-lilies seen in the creeks as you go to Junk, though not in the same profusion [p. 39].[64]

At Totoquella, north-east of Boporu, and four hours' walk south-east from the former, the St. Paul's River presents rugged and impassable falls.[65] North-west of Totoquella are beds of specular iron-ore, which the natives break into fragments and use for shot.

The population of Boporu is of a mixed character, such as war, commerce, and the domestic slave-trade are calculated to produce; in consequence of which there are as many different languages spoken as there are tribes: Vey, Gola, Mambomah, Mandingo, Pessy, Boozie, Boondee, and the Hurrah languages.[66] The Vey language is used for general communication. The extent and population of these tribes are very variable elements. The population living in the town may be set down at three thousand; but then there are many outlying villages and hamlets; and considering these as the suburbs of Bopolu, they undoubtedly raise the population to ten thousand. Many of the Mandingoes themselves, though they reside in the town with their families, have villages of slaves and servants scattered in every direction, wherever the purposes of agriculture invite or encourage.

The Mandingoes possess strong moral influence.[67] Scarcely any thing is undertaken without consulting their priests, whose prayers, blessings, and other rites are supposed to give a propitious turn to all the affairs of peace and war. They are Mohammedans; but as the ruder tribes do not addict themselves to the intellectual habits of the Mandingoes, it has been found necessary to adjust that faith to the necessities of the case; and to temper some of the mummeries of fetichism with the teachings of Islam. Yet are there to [p. 40] be found individuals who do not prostitute their faith, and who are more scrupulous and sincere. It is believed by many persons that the Arabic learning of our Mandingoes, in reading and writing from the Koran, is merely mechanical, or a mere matter of memory.

Kaifal took a small Arabic grammar given to me by Professor Blyden, and showed himself thoroughly versed in all the distinctions of person, gender, and number, etc., in the conjugation of a verb. However, all are not equally proficient in this respect.

They have a mosque at Bopolu, where nothing enjoined by their religion is omitted. It is attended solely by the Mandingoes, none of the other tribes visiting it; not because they are prohibited, for the Mandingoes would make proselytes of them all if they could. It is sufficient for the "Kaffirs," (unbelievers,) as they are denominated by the Mandingoes, to buy the amulets, necklaces, and belts containing transcripts from the Koran sewed up in them, to be worn around the neck, arms, or waist as preservatives from the casualties of war, sickness, or ill luck in trade or love.

The Mandingoes are scrupulously attentive to their worship. They regularly attend their services three times a day: five o'clock in the morning; three o'clock in the afternoon, and seven o'clock in the evening.

In these services I was particularly attracted by the manner in which they chanted the cardinal article of their creed; and many a morning have I been reminded of my own duty, by their solemn musical voices reciting [p. 41]:

Figure 15. This is the *shahāda* or fundamental creed of Islam, translated from Arabic to English as 'There is no god but God. Muhammad is the messenger of God." *In Anderson, 1870.*

The Mandingoes living in the Boatswain country have many slaves.[68] The slave population is supposed to treble the number of free persons.[69] They are purchased chiefly from the Pessy, Boozie, and other tribes. Many are reduced to the condition of slaves, by being captured in war. Their chief labor is to perform the service of carriers for their masters in the trade of salt and country cloths carried between Boporu and Vannswah.

Inconveniences and troubles frequently arise from this kind of relationship. Sensible of their numbers and strength, the slaves sometimes make a struggle for their liberty. In the latter part of 1866, at the death of Torsu, King Momoru's uncle, it became necessary to settle some debts pertaining to Torsu's estate. His relatives, in order to pay off the claims, attempted to sell some of his slaves. These slaves were staying at a town called Musadalla's town, south-west of Boporu.[70] The attempt was resisted; some blood was shed; and a general revolt took place, in which all the slaves in the town determined to defend each other to the last extremity. They took full possession of the town, renewed the barricades, seized upon whatever arms were at hand, and made such other preparations as greatly alarmed their masters. This rebellion had been long proposed on; the death of Torsu and the attempt to sell some of their number, served as a favorable opportunity to achieve their freedom.

On the first outbreak, King Momoru sent them word [p. 42] to return to their former obedience, assuring them that he would overlook all past offenses. But while they were deliberating as to what answer they should return, one of their women publicly harangued them against listening to any proposals for reconciliation; that King Momoru only wished to induce them to submit, that he might the more easily punish them; that if their hearts began to quail, they had better give their spears into the hands of the women.[71]

This speech instantly determined them to stand fast in their first resolutions. Refusing all accommodation, they sought to strengthen their cause by purchasing the assistance of the Boondee people, who were at that time at variance with the people of Boporu. But the Boporu people had also managed, despite their difference with the Boondee people, to engage their services against the slaves. The Boondee war chief received the gifts of both parties; and in two weeks' time repaid the poor slaves with treachery enough to chop off their heads.

Arming himself and his people, he set out for Musadalla's town, and was admitted by his unsuspecting victims. After he had rested from his journey, and refreshed himself and his followers on their generosity, he proposed to review their numbers and their arms. Pretending to be earnestly enlisted in their affairs, he bade them lay their arms on the ground, or, as we term it, "ground arms," that he might the better judge of their efficiency.[72] The poor, credulous fools, by no means suspecting any perfidy, readily did as they were bid. At a given signal from the Boondee chief, his own people instantly drew their swords and bestrode [p. 43] the weapons of the poor slaves as they lay on the ground.

Thus disarmed they were thus again enslaved, seized, bound, and led out of the gates to the town of their betrayer, who at once sent word to Momoru that he had caught the "slave dogs."[73] He was rewarded, or rather he rewarded himself, by keeping all the women and children, sending to Momoru only the men and our heroine who, by her speech, had so greatly encouraged the matter. It was determined in council that the slaves should suffer the penalty of death.

On the morning of the execution they were demanded to say who were the chief instigators of the revolt; the poor creatures had but little to say. They were led out of the eastern gate, two hundred yards from which, and in the same direction, stands a high cotton-tree (bombax)—the place of execution.[74] They came down the path naked, and in single file, with their hands bound behind them. As the first person came on, the executioner with his broad and gleaming knife ran to meet him, and with dexterous cruelty emasculated him; after allowing him to bleed and beg awhile, he was snatched down to the foot of the tree, his head hacked off and tossed into a ditch on one side of the road; while the yet quivering trunk was thrown into a cat-fish pond hard by.

The woman was executed with circumstances shocking to humanity and decency. All the women in Boporu were compelled to go out and witness her fate.

But to the chief of this revolt it was reserved to be buried alive, heels up and head down, and a sharp stake, eight feet long, driven through his body level [p. 44] with the ground, and a tree planted over him. Their skulls now form a ghastly adornment to the eastern gate; and I have seen many persons go up to them and recognize an acquaintance.

It seems to be the practice in every town where the water favors it to have cat-fish pools. The fish are not allowed to be disturbed; they are not only the consumers of the offal of the town, but from their shark-like and snappish manner, a more fearful office can well be suspected. They are from one to three feet long, and will lie with patience and expectation in one spot all day long, their backs raw with scars, which their own ferocity inflicts on each other in the fierce struggle for food.

Boporu has a small market, held in the north-east suburbs of the town. The bartering is carried on solely by women. There is no established currency; the exchange takes place of one commodity for another, according to their mutual necessities. It is generally attended by one hundred and seventy-five to two hundred persons. The articles are palm-oil, rice, kaffee-seed, shallots—a small species of onion—meat, cotton stripes, tobacco, kola, earthen pots, etc.[75] A great many country cloths are made at Boporu, every family having a small loom. They would economize both time and labor if they would employ our large loom, instead of the narrow six-inch loom they use. I have no doubt they would do so, if any civilized person would interest himself to show them.

These people are very sensible of the superiority of every thing that comes from (Dru-kau) Monrovia, and they attempt to practice our civilization of themselves [p. 45].

The king has a frame house at Totoquella, with a piazza surrounding it, all of native construction. He also uses chairs, tables, beds, bedsteads, looking-glasses, scented soaps, colognes, etc.[76] He took great interest in examining my sextant, and even the pictures in my books; but that which afforded him the greatest pleasure was the stereoscope. He entreated me so earnestly to leave it with him, that I felt myself bound to gratify his wishes in that respect, though I had specially intended it for Musardu.

He was no less satisfied when I flattered him with the prospect of a school for children being established at Boporu, telling me that when John B. Jordan traded there, he was accustomed to get Jordan to teach him.[77]

The king spells a little, and is somewhat acquainted with numbers. This is the place for the missionary to be of service; but it seems that, though Mohammed has a small mosque and school at Vannswah, almost in the Virginia settlement, the Christians have neither church nor school at Boporu.[78]

The king's authority seems to be of a mixed character. In some things he acts absolutely; while in others, such as war, he takes the counsel of the subordinate chiefs. He is judge or arbiter of all important differences between his subjects. He is a most patient hearer of all matters brought before him. I have known him to remain in his hammock for whole days, listening to what was to be said by either side, and his decisions seemed to be generally satisfactory.

A very peculiar but advantageous method obtains in the administration of justice. In order to obviate all [p. 46] further trouble after the decision is given, both plaintiff and defendant have to advance the cost and expenses before the suit begins; the very articles in which these charges are to be paid are placed in conspicuous manner in the sight of every body. The presence of the money thereby becomes an incentive and stimulation to strenuous effort. As soon as the case is decided, nothing remains but for the victor to sweep the stakes. These cases between his subjects are frequently taxing and vexatious, yet the king is said to always preside with patience and a well-balanced impartiality.

But the king sometimes takes recreation from the severe affairs of life, at which time he is apt to enliven the hours of vacation from business with a glass of gin or whisky, and then he goes playfully around the town attended by his people.[79] It happens that his caprice is as innocent then as his gentle disposition is in his sober hours; for he hurts no one; only going from house to house, joking with and receiving little presents from his friends. Sometimes he attempts to dance, or to act some warlike feat; but want of youth and a rather fat body mar the practice. One day he insisted on the performance, to his no small discomfiture. He mounted himself upon an earthen hill, with a spear in each hand, in order to charge down in war-like style; starting in full tilt, he came sprawling to the ground with such violence as to scarify the royal bosom in a most unseemly manner.

Before I left Boporu for the interior, the king informed me that the distance, danger, and hazard were so great, that he must consult the sand-doctor as to [p. 47] the final issues of such a journey.[80] He declared that, upon all such important matters, he trusted not to human prudence alone.

This individual, the sand-doctor, by giving his fingers certain motions in a small pile of sand, is supposed to read the events of the future. We were carried into a thatch hut. Our diviner, spreading out a small pile of sand with his right hand, began to invoke the demon of the pile. The whole thing was conducted without thunder, lightening, or any thing else, except the rapid, voluble utterances of our diviner himself. Again and again it was demanded of the flinty wisdoms whether or not the expedition should be successful; the responses indicated by these sandy hieroglyphics bid us begone and prosper. Thus it was that superstition at this time seconded the purposes of a rational inquiry. The king not infrequently chided me because I was indifferent and incredulous about such matters.

Every effort was made by the Boporu Mandingoes to prevent my going. It was told to Momoru that if any thing befell me, he alone would be held responsible to the government. Even old Gatumba sent word to Momoru not to allow me, under any circumstances whatever, to pass and "go behind them"; for he declared that I was going for no other purpose but to ruin their trade.[81] It was the first time, I was informed, that the king had set himself in opposition to the advice and counsel of his chiefs, many of whom were greatly opposed to my passing through their country to go in the interior.[82] I therefore exerted the greatest industry in purchasing their silence or assistance. But to the Boporu Mandingoes I held threatening language, in [p. 48] which I informed them that if I did not succeed in going to their country, I would return and break up all their trade at Vannswah.

Mr. Schieffelin's money, however, was the most powerful argument. It prevailed over every obstacle; it reconciled me to prejudices and persons the most difficult to deal with; invoked the blessings of Mohammed on my head; caused even the sands to become things of sense in my favor; singularly enlightened minds that before could not see why I wished to go in the interior, and finally reduced the prospect of my going in the interior to the most undoubted moral certainty.

On the 14th of June [Sunday], I left Boporu for Totoquella;[83] and on June 16th, we left Totoquella for the interior, our company consisting of three Congoes—Jim, Alex, and Pickaninny—as carriers;[84] Chancellor, the Golah, as interpreter, and Beah, the Mandingo, as guide. The rest of my Congoes, numbering fifteen, had returned to Monrovia, giving all kinds of false accounts of our proceedings.

I had now again to experience the effects of the jealousy of the Mandingoes. They had determined that I should not reach Musardu. They therefore gave secret instructions to the Mandingo guide, Beah, who was to accompany me, to delay and shuffle all along the route, so as to exhaust my means and discourage my perseverance, and thus to finally thwart the expedition. It was through this man's tricks that I was compelled to spend six months in going to Musardu, when only one was necessary.

On Tuesday, the 16th of June, we left Totoquella for the interior, the direction being, with very little [p. 49] deviation, east. The hilly features of the country became more striking; large granite boulders were scattered here and there; small creeks, flowing over beds of sand and gravel, drained the country from every direction into the St. Paul's River. About half-past four o'clock P.M., we reached the north-western edge of the Pessy country, and halted at a small hamlet for the night.[85] Here the barometer stood 29.19; thermometer, 84°.

Wednesday, the 17th of June, six A.M., barometer, 29.20; thermometer, 78° Fahrenheit. We pushed on, and passed through another Pessy village. The Pessys seem to have an abundance of poultry, sheep, and rice; here we halted.

Thursday, the 18th of June, we started on our journey, the country bearing the same hilly appearance. We halted at a considerable village, called Sellayo [Salaya, 7°15'N, 10°18'W] about twelve o'clock. The chief was swinging in his hammock in a half-finished shed; he was sullen, and scarcely spoke; he, however, deigned to give us a little palm-wine. We made him a small (dash) present, at which he was quite displeased; but we cut short all grumbling by starting off soon in the morning.

Friday, the 19th, we passed through Nesebeah (red hill) and Pollamah [Kpoloma], Pessy villages, and halted at Zelleki's town at half-past three P.M.[86] This village contained 250 houses, built in the usual style; the body being of clay and of a circular shape, with thatched conical coverings. This village wore an indifferent appearance, showing scarcely any activity in any species of industry. On account of its sameness, we were [p. 50] glad enough to leave it. Outside of its barricade was a large creek containing cat-fish, as at Boporu.

The only thing that rendered the idle hours tolerable was King Momoru's daughter, who had married a Mandingo residing in the village. She very much resembled her father and was of the same jovial disposition; and when I left the village, she marched out before me, with my musket at shoulder-arms, at a military pace, imitating what she had seen at Monrovia the last time she was down there with her father.

Saturday, June 20th, 1868, we reached Barkomah [?Gbanka, 7°17'N, 10°8'W], the largest Pessy town in this direction. King Pato is not stamped by nature for a king, and his town is neither commendable for cleanliness nor industry. It contains 300 dilapidated houses, half a dozen cows, some large Mandingo dogs, about 800 inhabitants, and is surrounded on all sides by impenetrable jungle, which is considered a sufficient barrier from all attacks. It is difficult to conceive whether this plan of defense was suggested by cowardice or laziness. We were lodged in a miserable little hut, about twelve feet long by eight feet wide, and five feet high. We had to endure this bamboo cage for ten days, because our guide had friends, who made him as comfortable as we were wretched. We were delayed under various pretexts, the chief of which was that, as my boys had almost given out, assistance had to be procured for carrying our luggage.

On the 1st of July [Wednesday], we started from Barkomah, and crossed a considerable tributary of the St. Paul's River, seventy-five feet wide, running in the direction of south-west between banks of clay, eight feet on one [p. 51] side and fifteen feet on the other, with a velocity of forty feet in fifteen seconds.[87] The stream is ten feet deep in this place, and is known to overflow its banks on the eight-foot side in the depths of the rains. It is crossed on slender poles tied together.[88] Only one person can cross at a time; and just as the burdened traveler reaches the middle, he is arrested by a ticklish swaying that threatens to unbalance him into the waters below; here he dares not move until the restive poles regain their quiet. It has blighted many a prospect, or rather melted many a basket of salt. In days gone by, it was crossed by a suspension-bridge of wicker work, elevated fifteen feet above the surface, as appeared by the remains of longs and withes. This stream separates the Pessy country at this point from the Deh country.

The Deh people are a small tribe intervening between the Pessy and Bonsie people.[89] They seem to be a distinct people, and speak a strong, rough, guttural language, similar to our Kroo tribe on the coast, whom they resemble in many other particulars.[90] They have more fire in their eyes than the Pessy people, and are said to eat their enemies in war. After a half-hour's walk, we passed through the Dey [*sic,* Deh] villages of Mue Zue [?Suo, 7°18'N, 9°59'W] and Yalah [Belle Yela, 7°22'N, 10°0'W], and halted at Dallazeah. The Deh people, in proffering their hospitalities, offered us dog for dinner, which was politely declined.

On Thursday, the 2d of July, we started from Dallazeah. Farms of rice, corn, cotton, and tobacco succeeded each other in an order truly pleasing to look at. The people are very industrious. The women, on seeing me, began to tremble with fear; and though [p. 52] some of my people, with whom they were well acquainted, tried to assure them, they could not be persuaded to approach me. Keeping the direction east, we passed another Deh village—Malung, (water).[91] From here we came to the site of a large Deh town—Gellabonda, (lightening)—which had been completely destroyed by a civil war. It was so elevated that we had but to look E.S.E. to see a large part of the Barline country, and the very parts in which war was then raging. Indeed, we had hitherto followed the Barline route; but at two o'clock P.M. our guide,

Beah, changed the direction, remarking, as he did so, powder and ball were in the path he had left.[92] We halted at Mahfatah [Mavodo, 7°37'N, 9°46'W], a small Deh village.[93] At night, one of their houses caught on fire, and but for the activity of our people the whole of their frail bamboo dwellings would have been consumed. These people travel very little, and are consequently ruder, and, as I then supposed, less hospitable than the other tribes. We passed the 4th of July [Saturday] here, the barometer standing at 28.89, thermometer 80°; ten o'clock A.M., weather cloudy.

Friday, the 5th of July, we started on our journey, passing through several Deh villages.[94] We also crossed a small falls called Gawboah, with water rushing over granite beds colored red and gray, with seams of white quartz and red feldspar ramifying the bed in many directions. We halted at Zolaghee, the largest and last town of the Deh people.[95] This town contained 300 houses, more or less in a state of dilapidation. Nothing is more disagreeable than to be obliged to take quarters in these decaying clay-built towns, especially in the rainy season, when mud, trash, and [p. 53] all the soil, frogs, and vermin of the town dissolve, crumble, and creep too near not to annoy sensibilities accustomed to cleanliness. We managed to tolerate this town one day, in order to rest ourselves.

On the 7th, we reached the Bonsie country, or the Domar division of the Bonsies.[96] We passed through Powlazue [?Kpawoluzu, 7°35'N, 9°42'W], Unzugahzeah, Kaulibodah, and halted at Yahwahzue. These towns are large and densely peopled, surrounded with high and massive walls of clay and earth. It was here that the Barline people had been lately making reprisals, capturing the women and slaves on the farms. It was therefore necessary that our Bonsie friends should exercise constant vigilance, and be ready to sally forth from their walls at a moment's warning to repel these incursions.

You no sooner arrive in the Bonsie country, than a contrast of cleanliness, order, and industry strikes you. That tribe, continually represented to us as savage, fierce, and intractable, at once invites you into its large walled towns with all the hospitalities and courtesy that the minds of this simple, untutored people can think of.

I arrived at Zolu's town [Zolowo] on the 8th of July [Wednesday], 1868, at four o'clock P.M. The walls of this town are from eighteen to twenty feet high, consisting of clay, and very thick.[97] A regular salvo of musketry announced my entrance, and quickly a band of music made its appearance, consisting of twelve large and small ivory horns, and a half-dozen drums of various sizes and sounds.[98] I was conducted to the market space, in the centre of the town, and there welcomed amidst the [p. 54] blast and flourish of Bonsie music and the firing of muskets.

They were astonished and overjoyed that (a Weegee) an American should come so far to visit them in their own country.[99] A thousand strange faces, whom I had never before seen, were gazing at me. After their curiosity and wonder had been satisfied, they gave me spacious and comfortable lodgings, and commenced a series of hospitalities which, from mere quantity alone, became oppressive.

The next day [Thursday, 9 July], my friends would have me put on American cloth; to please them, I did so. I had not shaved for three months, and when I made my appearance in the 'Merican cloth, together with an unshaven face, the women and children fled in every direction from the frightfully-bearded Weegee. Many a Bonsie child was hushed to silence or sleep by being threatened with the Weegee. I annoyed the women and children at such a rate, that I soon deemed it necessary to take off the American cloth and the beard also.

This part of Africa likes a clean face, and especially a full-flowing gown, which is not only a more graceful attire, but more comfortable and healthy than the tight-fitting pieces which we call civilized clothing. This town, like Boporu, has its small daily market; but the large weekly market, which is held every Thursday, and to which the neighboring towns usually resort, is held at Zow-Zow [Zorzor, 7°47'N, 9°26'W], a very large town fifteen miles E.N.E. of Zolu.[100] I visited this market. The hum of voices could be heard in the distance like the noise of a waterfall. It is attended by five or six thousand people. The bargaining is generally conducted [p. 55] by the women, except the country cloth trade, which is carried on by the men. The exchange is generally a barter—one article is exchanged for an other, according to the mutual wants of the buyer and seller. Salt and kola, however, have the character of a currency, and large bargains are generally valued in these articles. They are the expression of prices in all important bargains. Kola usually performs the same service our coppers do in small bargains.[101] These markets also have the character of holiday or pleasure-days. Every one appears in his or her best attire. The women wear blue and colored country cloths girded tastefully around their waists, their heads bound round with a large three-cornered handkerchief of the same material. Blue beads, intermixed with their favorite "pateriki," (blue buttons) encircle their necks, their faces ornamented with blue pigment and smiles.[102]

In going around the market, and even on the road as you go to the market, you are sure to be loaded with ground-nuts, bananas, and rice-bread. Rice forms the chief breadstuff; cassavas and potatoes next.[103] Potatoes grow to an enormous size, and will weigh from six to eight pounds. My Congo carriers were greatly elated when they bought a bushel of white rice for four brass buttons and a few needles. Considering the large farms and the quantities of old rice from the previous crop which must remain unconsumed, rice can never be a source of profit to these people until they have a road and conveyance to cart it down to some civilized settlement.

The two great farming staples in the Boozie country are rice and cotton. Sometimes the rice and cotton are [p. 56] planted together, but most of the cotton-farms succeed the rice-farms. The cotton farms bear no proportion in size to the rice-farms, yet they are large; for they have to clothe a country densely populated, where men, women, and children all go clothed, and no foreign manufactures scarcely reach them. Cotton-gins would be a blessing to these people; for the manner in which they are obliged to prepare cotton for spinning is painful and tedious to the last degree of labor. This part of the labor is done by the women; the men do the weaving. The spindle is in the hands of every woman, from the princess to the slave. The dyeing of cloth is also done by the women, at which the Mandingoes are the most expert; and they know how to impart various shades of blue in a permanent and beautiful manner. Though they have abundance of camwood, I have never seen them use it for the purposes of dyeing. The chief colors used are blue and yellow; the latter color is extracted from bark. Taking into account that these people not only clothe themselves, but furnish the vast number of cloths that are brought to the coast to be used in the leeward trade, it shows what the cotton-producing power of the country would become if this primitive, barbarian industry were only assisted by some labor-saving machinery.

On the second day after my arrival [Friday, 10 July], I had a musical compliment paid to me. A dozen young ladies, from ten to eighteen years of age, serenaded me in the following manner: A large mat being spread on the ground before my door, the young ladies seated themselves and commenced singing one of the songs of their country, marking the time, as well as accompanying [p. 57] the music, by means of hollow wooden pipes four and a half inches long, through which the wind is forced by beating one end with the palm of the hand. When this compliment is paid to a friend, one of the young ladies who has tact and talent improvises a solo as to his good qualities, his bravery, his good looks, his generosity, etc., at the conclusion of which all join the chorus, repeating the words, "Emmamow," "Emmamow"—Thank you, thank you.[104] It is also a very delicate way of insinuation, when your liberality does not always satisfy their expectations. My liberality in some cases "becoming small by degrees and beautifully less," a young lady revenged herself on me by singing that I had a "giving face but a stingy heart," at which they all responded, "Kella? Kella?"—Is it so? Is it so?[105] Well, thank you; thank you. This is indeed a very delicate way of insinuation; but the ungenerous little rogue ought to have remembered that it was through my liberality that they were enabled to have all the fine brass buttons which they sported around their necks at the Zow Zow market. However, I hope it will be considered that I have done the state some service, when I announce that I have labeled nearly all the pretty women in the Boozie country as the property of the Republic of Liberia, with its military brass buttons, (pateriki).

The Boozies are a very polite people; the slightest favor is repaid with an "Emmamow"—Thank you. Do you dance or afford any amusement whatever, you receive the "Emmamow." Are you engaged in any labor or business for yourself or others, you are as heartily "thanked" by those whom it does not in the [p. 58] least concern as if it were for themselves. If you are carrying a heavy burden on the road, and happened to meet a friend, he thanks you as if you were doing it for him.[106] My Congo carriers, who were nearly fagged out with the weight of their burdens, used to be annoyed with this kind of civility, that contained all thanks and no assistance, and the Bonsie "Emmamow" was often exchanged for the Congo "Konapembo," (Go to the devil), an exhortation not unreasonable where misery is prolonged by politeness, and where one having his back bent, burdened, and almost broke, has to be stopped to be thanked and to snap fingers half a dozen times.

The soil of Zolu is chiefly a red sandstone, and the eastern road, worn down three feet by constant traveling and the successive washings of the rains, exhibits to this depth its internal peculiarities—red sandstone, consolidated in proportion as the depth increases, but of crude and crumbling consistence at the surface, with ramifications of clear and distinct veins of white quartz from one to two and a half inches wide. On some of the hills there are large boulders of granite, some of them have markings crossing each other nearly in parallels, in a direction from N.W. to S.E. and N.E. to S.W. The markings seem deeply ingrained, and are not so much sensible to the touch as visible to the eye. There is also in this country a stone of a very beautiful green color, capable of receiving a high polish, a large piece of which was placed at the eastern gate of the town for a stepping-stone, and which, in that position, from the frequent treadings it receives, had a finely polished surface. The character of the soil of [p. 59] the plains is principally clay and sand. The red sandstone at Zolu begins in the south-western portion of the Pessy country, at the town called Nessebeah, (red hill;) and it is in this vicinity that the soil, changing from a mixture of clay and sand and granite pebbles, forms a red clayey and sandy composition.[107] Nessebeah is located upon a very elevated hill of red clay and sand, which presents every grade of condensation from a loose soil to solid rock. In the town were huge granite rocks resting upon elevated beds of this red soil, as if they had been purposely placed there by human effort; but they owe their position to some former power of nature and the subsequent washings of the rains. The elevation and position of these rocks serve to show what vast quantities of soil have been washed down in the plains and valleys below. Very extensive views are had from this site. The sides of the hills being rather steep, the soil, on this account, is inclined to shelve down, and to lay bare entirely its color and composition from the top to the bottom. These red slopes form a curious contrast to the abundant green vegetation with which their summits and the plains below are clothed.

I arrived at Zolu on the 8th July [Wednesday]. Here it was that the Mandingo guide, Beah, according to the instructions that had been given to him by King Momoru, was to spend a couple of weeks in trying to reconcile the differences between the Bonsies and the Barline people. Zolu was also the town belonging to the young chief who had covertly assisted the Barline people, and who was now suffering the penalty of his perfidy. He was confined at Salaghee [Salayie or Salaye, 7°37'N, 9°30'W], a large [p. 59] town fifteen miles east of Zolu, by a chief called Daffahborrah.[108]

Three days after our arrival [Saturday, 11 July], Beah went to Salaghee, in order to open negotiations, both for the release of the young prince, Cavvea, and to stop the war between the Bonsies and Barlines.[109] King Momoru had already sent the same proposals for reconciliation to the Barline people by some Mandingoes, who were to act in concert with Beah in bringing about peace. Nor was Daffahborrah disinclined to entertain these proposals for peace. His town being on the confines of the Boozie and Barline territory, was more subject, on this account, to the incursions of the latter, and indeed on his town had fallen most of the brunt of the war.

Beah, after two days' absence at Salaghee, returned. He informed me that Daffahborrah had requested him not to bring me to his town, as he was afraid of the great war-medicine which his people told him I had in my possession. This war-medicine was a bottle of nitric acid, given me by Dr. Dunbar for the purpose of trying gold.[110] My Congoes having witnessed some of its effects on cloth, metal, etc., had given it a fearful reputation: A table-spoonful scattered in a crowd would kill a hundred men; the least bit on a thatch house would burn up a whole town; I had but to stand outside the walls and throw it in the air to cause destruction to any town. This bottle of "medicine" began to give me great inconvenience; every body refused to carry it. A big bandage of rags and thatch housed the fiery spirit; great was the ceremony in assigning its place wherever I happened to stop. Daffahborrah [p. 61] could not be blamed for refusing to see me. Beah returned to Salaghee, and remained three weeks.[111]

It was now about the beginning of August, and the depth of the rains; I therefore determined to shun all exposure from the weather. What I particularly dreaded was the losing or damaging my instruments in crossing the creeks, with which a country rugged with every feature of hill and dale is everywhere intersected. In the dries, many of them scarcely contain water enough to cover the foot; but in the rains, they become torrents, eight and ten feet deep, with a swift and destructive current, being, in fact, drains or gullies tilted toward the main reservoirs, the St. Paul's and Little Cape Mount rivers.[112] The rains had fairly set in; yet the quantity of water is much less than what I have been accustomed to experience on the seaboard at Monrovia.[113]

The country is every variety of hill, plain, and valley. Standing upon an elevation, it seemed to me that the people had attempted to cover the whole country with their rice-fields.[114] Toward the west could be seen the rice-hills enveloped in showers; succeeding that, whole mountain-sides of rice partly buried in vapor; next to that could be seen a brilliant sunlight, spread over the brown and ripening plains of rice below.

It would be difficult to describe into how many scenes sunshine, showers, clouds, and vapor can vary a locality, itself an expression of every variety of change. Only here and there could be seen patches of large forest-trees. So completely had this section of the country been farmed over and over, that only saplings of three or four years' growth covered the [p. 62] uncultivated parts. Nor will they be allowed to attain a greater age or size before the requirements of agriculture will clear them for rice and cotton-fields.

This is the chief reason why all the barricades, or walls of towns, in this section of the country, are formed of earth and clay, instead of the large stakes that are used by the natives living in the vicinity of Liberia.[115]

The Bonsie people have very tractable dispositions, and are wedded to no particular species of error. Fetichism has no stronghold on them.[116] They believe in that thing most that manifests the greatest visible superiority or power. They are greatly duped by the fraud and chicanery of the Mohammedan Mandingo priests.

In general physical appearance the Boozies are well built, generally from five and a half to six feet high in stature, with stoutly developed bodies, of sufficient muscular strength to hold a United States musket, bayonet fixed, at full arm's length in one hand. They are an exceedingly healthy people, and of very clean habits. They bathe regularly twice a day, night and morning, in warm water, besides the intermediate cold water baths they are sure to take at whatever creek they happen to cross in their daily walking. For cleaning the teeth, they use a brush made of rattan, admirably adapted to the purpose.

Paring the finger and toe-nails is carried to excess. And the women at Zolu are foolish enough to pluck away part of their eyebrows and eyelashes, things which nature had not too lavishly furnished them from the first.

Many of the women are very pretty; and for the [p. 63] many faces with which I am acquainted at Monrovia resemblances, and close resemblances, are to be found among the Boozies. Most of our people at Monrovia are fond of deriving themselves from the Mandingoes.[117] I am sorry to say that this Boozie type of resemblance does not confirm an origin so noble and consoling. We must therefore rest satisfied with humbler antecedents.

As soon as the weather permitted travelling, I insisted on Beah resuming the journey. But he framed many excuses, and finally, to rid himself of my importunities, ran off to Bokkasah [Bokesa, 7°54'N, 9°28'W] where his family resided. Thither I dispatched one of my boys, demanding his return; but he refused to come. Beah was trying to carry out the secret instructions he had received from the Boporu Mandingoes. To trammel and obstruct my going still more, he sent word to the Boozies at Zolu that they were not to allow me to go anywhere; for if any thing befell Momoru's American man, they alone would be held responsible for it. Three times I endeavored to leave this town; but the people, by entreaties, presents, and every means of persuasion they could think of, compelled me to relinquish my intentions.

Beah had duped them as to the real reasons of delay. Finally, it was appointed that if Beah should not return in two weeks, I was to go anywhere I chose. The time expired without Beah's making his appearance.

On Monday, September 21st, 1868, I left Zolu, and went to Fissahbue, a town in latitude 7°56'9"N., and longitude 9°50'43"W [Fissabu, 7°49'N, 9°28'W].[118] I was now entirely [p. 64] abandoned by my Mandingo guide, to grope my way to Musardu by inquiry or instinct.

Fissahbue is a double town, or a town partitioned into two parts; occupied in one by the Mandingoes, and in the other by the Boozies. It is well built and clean in appearance, with a population of three thousand inhabitants. The king, Mullebar, is a fine-looking old gentleman of fifty years, very generous-hearted; and who was the more interesting to me because he had an equal dislike to Beah.[119]

On Saturday, September 26th, we left Fissahbue for Bokkasah. The rough features of the country moderated into extensive plains of long fields of grass, ferns, and tall palms; the hills were at a short distance, trending along in a direction west and north-west. They had also changed the character of their formation from red sandstone to granite, and I was struck to see these round and bossy masses, with their water-courses shining and trickling down their slopes.[120] Some of their tops were thickly wooded, while small tufts or patches of grass were thinly scattered on their sides; but its brownish appearance showed that the sun had parched it in its stony bed at the first approach of the dries. West of Bokkasah, granite hills rose one above another, crowned with a dense forest. Whenever it rained, a noise resembling distant thunder was always heard. In the months of July and August, these hills are the site of a roaring cascade.

On the road, we fell in with people from all the neighboring towns, going to market. Sitting on the road-side were numbers of young women, with baskets of ground-nuts already shelled, offering them for sale [p. 65]. Our pockets and every other available place were immediately filled, gratis. Such is their custom to strangers; and their gift was particularly enhanced by the repeated liberality with which both hands went down into the basket, and came up piling full, to be emptied with a gracious smile into the capacious pockets of our country coats. Then followed an exchange of compliments; and the three languages—Boozie, Mandingo, and English—got into a confusion from which smiles and brass buttons alone could deliver us.

On we went, munching ground-nuts and receiving ground-nuts, snapping fingers and making friends, and occasionally consigning Beah to evil destinies. At last the road suddenly widened, broad and clean; and the din of human voices assured us that we had come upon the market and the town.

Bokkasah is in latitude 8°10'02 [Bokesa]. It is a double town, similar to Fissahbue, one part of which is Boozie, and the other Mandingo. The walls that contain the Boozie portion of the inhabitants make a circuit completely oval. That which comprises the Mandingoes butts up against and flanks the eastern side of the Boozie walls, and is also half oval in shape.

On entering the town, we were shown Beah's residence. Astonished at our arrival, he forthwith tried to make some slight atonement for his former shortcomings by the diligence with which he procured us comfortable lodgings. We were soon domesticated in the town, kindling up friendships on all sides. The Mandingoes made it a point to be foremost in all these alliances. Since I was going to their country, they took me in their special charge. Among the many attentions [p. 66] paid me, I was invited by a young Mandingo lady to go with her to see her mother. We had no sooner arrived at the house, than she commenced calling out, "Ma, ma!" I waited to hear what would follow; but the next words were in musical Mandingo, informing her mother that she had brought the Tibbabue (American man) to see her.[121] The Mandingoes use the same words in calling mother that we do. This interview ended satisfactorily in a large bowl of rice, with fried chicken, palm-wine, etc., together with a standing invitation to come to her house every day while I remained in Bokkasah.

The young lady was married to a young Mandingo by the name of Fatomah, whose father, Phillakahmah, resided at Boporu, but was then in the Barline country.[122] The kindness and good office of this family were untiring. I also had many friends in the eastern part of the town, who were constant in their attention to me.

Bokkasah contains about fifteen hundred houses, and about seven thousand inhabitants. It is very perplexing on the first entrance of a stranger to find his way in these towns; for the houses seem to be dropped by accident into their places, rather than placed after any organized method. Chancellor, my interpreter, though well accustomed to these kind of towns, was not at all times assured of his own whereabouts. A woman gave him water to bathe; after he had performed his ablutions, he found himself naked, lost, and ashamed to ask were he was. He wandered over the town with the vessel in his hand, until some one, guessing the truth, brought him home. One does not lose his way on account of the size of these towns, but on account [p. 67] of the manner in which the houses are sprinkled about. You can march up to your house without knowing it, so completely does similarity and confusion repeat itself.

The market at Bokkasah, which is held every Saturday, is one of the principal markets in the Domar country. It is attended by six or seven thousand people. The articles of exchange are numerous. It is also a great country cloth market. In all these markets throughout the Boozie and Barline countries, the small country cloth is not to be seen. It is owning to the mischievous industry of our friends at Boporu and its vicinity that these country cloths are reduced to so small a size. It is the business of these interlopers in trade to take large country cloths to pieces, and make them smaller. Similar is their dealing with every species of trade, to its great diminution and discouragement. If the interior trade amounted to millions of dollars in value to the republic, it could never reach our seaport towns while the border of our influence has been removed by tribal interference and war, and confined to the very seacoast settlements themselves. These obstructions can only be removed by the energetic action of government.

Bokkasah is a town very convenient and cheap for living. Abundance of vegetables, rice, beans, potatoes, plantains, bananas, ground-nuts, etc., are to be had at all times at the daily market.

While I was staying here, I dispatched one of my Congoes to Begby, a Mandingo chief, living at a town called Bokkadu [?Bakedu, 8°17'N, 9°42'W], near the Boondee country, in a westward [p. 68] direction.[123] As he was anxious to see some one who had come from an American town, and in American dress, I tried to gratify him in that respect. This Congo, before he reached Bokkadu, crossed the St. Paul's River on a bridge of wicker-work, and the Cape Mount River, which was much wider, on a corkwood float.[124] This journey occupied three days. Both of these rivers flow from the north-east.

Among some of the singular institutions that prevail in this country, is a kind of convent for women, in the mysteries of which every woman has to be instructed.[125] What these mysteries are I have never been fully informed. They consist in the main of a peculiar kind of circumcision and of certain other practices necessary for health. Attached to the outer wall of the town are the houses, fenced in on all sides from the gaze of passers-by, and especially excluded against the entrance of men. It is death to any man to be caught within the precincts, which is instantly inflicted without reprieve by the women themselves.

There are, however, holidays in which the rigid rules of the institution are relaxed, and every body is permitted to go in and see their friends without distinction of sex. During my stay here, one of these holidays occurred, and I was invited to visit the sacred grounds of this female mysticism. It consisted of rows of long huts built low to the ground, the lodgings of the devotees. Each complement belonging to a hut were seated in a line, in front of their dwellings, on a mat. Their heads were wound round with enormous turbans, and their bodies decked out in all the finery their friends in town could afford. They kept [p. 69] their heads hanging down in a solemn manner. Even children, six or seven years of age, were included in this moping, surly observance. Their friends from town crowded around, delighted at the sight, and with unfeigned pleasure asked me if it was not fine. I should have been more pleased to have heard these women and children laughing and singing in their rice and cotton-farms, than to have seen them tormenting themselves with a senseless, morose custom.[126] I was carried into one of their establishments, and made to shake hands with my moody sisters.[127]

As I have before related, this was the town in which my Mandingo guide, Beah, and all his family resided. Three days after my arrival, he disappeared, pretending he had immediate business at Salaghee [Salaye], leaving word with the town-people not to allow me to go anywhere until he returned. I was determined to free myself from his tricks, and I exposed to his friends his dealings with me when I was at Zolu. His friends, and especially his mothers and sisters, besought me to wait for him. After a week had expired, I grew impatient to start; but the whole family of women came, crossing their hands, and placing themselves in the most suppliant attitudes, crying, "Ejung, Ejung"-I beg you! I beg you![128] These poor women were honest, and knew nothing of their relation's crooked dealings. They made use of various ways to reconcile me to further delay. I had now been at Bokkasah three weeks, and had been foiled in every attempt to get away. The sort of hindrances through which I had now to struggle were not downright tyrannical opposition [p. 70]; they were of a more powerful and moral kind; supplications based upon kindness and generosity.

About this time an old Mandingo priest whom I had met at Bessa's town arrived. After he had been in town two days, he sent for me, and appeared glad to see me. I related to him the difficulties I experienced from Beah's actions. He advised me to be careful, and not to force my way through the country, as there had been a plot made to hurt me; and he went on to make many dark and pregnant insinuations. He exhorted me to patience and prayer, the contraries of which I had been provoked to by the artifices of Beah, and the consequent delays he had occasioned me. The next day the Mandingo priest told me that I had better make a "Sallikah," which is an offering to good luck.[129] This offering was dictated by the priest himself. It was to be a sheep, a penknife, a white country cloth, and ten white kola. Not knowing what divinity was to be appeased, I refused to make the sacrifice or oblation; for this priest was subsisting on a dry vegetable diet, the hospitality of his stingy brethren, and he was poor, very poor. The sacrifice or offering was to be delivered to him to be buried in the ground. But who could not see the crafty old priest and his hungry students in a congratulatory chuckle over a fat sheep, a penknife, a country cloth, and a fool of a Tibbabue?

This sort of priest is numerous, needy, cunning, and mischievous; they distribute themselves in all the towns between Musardu and Boporu; and they did not fail to present themselves to me throughout the journey as "god-men." But I gave them plainly to [p. 71] understand that I was not to be gulled by their practices.

I now dissembled my anxiety to depart, putting on a semblance of cheerfulness to abide where I was, and a perfect indifference about going anywhere. Every afternoon I would dress myself in my Mandingo toga, and go in the eastern part of the town to visit my friends. Here we would fritter away the time in talking and singing, and I musically entertained several of my Mandingo friends with the beauties of "Dixie."[130] We would then clap into our prayers, they repeating the Fatiha, and I reciting the Lord's Prayer.[131] A young lady begged that I would write off this prayer for her, in order that she might have it to wear around her neck, as well as to have fillets made of it to bind around her temples, as she was sometimes troubled with the headache.[132] I wrote it off for her; but I made her to understand, at the same time, that its efficacy consisted in healing the ailments of the soul, and not of the body. While we were thus handsomely enjoying ourselves, the terrible Dowilnyah sent his messengers for me to come and see him.[133]

Dowilnyah is the king of the Wymar Boozies.[134] His messengers were tall black men, with red and restless eyes, tattooed faces, filed teeth, hugh spears, and six feet bows.[135] They also had a reputation which remarkably corresponded with their appearance.

A discussion arose as to the safety of my going, and it caused a disagreement that ended in the return of the messengers without me. In a week's time the messengers returned again.[136] I had resolved to go with them. But my friends did all they could to dissuade [p. 72] me. Many of Dowilnyah's atrocities were repeated to me; how, when he had suspected the fidelity of one of his wives, he compelled her to pound the child of her supposed illicit connection in a mortar; how he had wantonly shot one of his wives, remarking, as he did so, that he had only shot a dog; his terrible cruelty to his prisoners whom he captured in war; and even his cruelty to his own children, one of whom he threw among the drivers, (*termites bellicosi,*) and which was so mutilated by these voracious insects that the child lost one of its arms.[137] He had no peer in cruelty and wickedness except Comma, who was now dead, but who, when living, went hand in hand with him in evil deeds.[138] Comma's town, it must be remembered, was the place where Seymore had his right hand nearly slashed off.[139]

I, however, left Bokkasah for Dowilnyah's on Monday, 2d of November, 1868, and arrived at Ukbaw-Wavolo, a village at which he was residing, on Thursday, the 5th of November 1868.[140]

Before reaching this village, we halted in our journey at Nubbewah's town [Nonbohouta, 8°3'N, 9°18'W]. It was well built, clean, and strongly fortified. We were brought into the presence of Nubbewah, the chief. He was an old man; tall, or rather long—as he was lying down—thin, and looked to be much emaciated by sickness. It was difficult to arouse him from the lethargic insensibility into which he had fallen. His attendants, however, succeeded in awakening him to the fact of our presence; but, as we still seemed to be regarded as a dream, I thought proper to quicken his consciousness by blazing away with my revolver against his earthen walls. This act perfectly [p. 73] startled him into a proper regard for our dignity and welfare, and thereupon we were well fed, comfortably lodged, and liberally presented with mats and country cloths, etc.

On Wednesday [4 November], we traveled until we reached Boe [Boo, 8°12'N, 9°13'W], a very large town belonging to the Wymar Boozies. This town, with some outlying villages, is the beginning of the Wymar country, which is separated from the Domar by a narrow creek, acknowledged as a boundary.[141] The village where the king was staying is E.N.E. of Boe, and about two and a half hours' walk from that town.

A temporary misunderstanding between the king and some of his chiefs had caused him to reside in this secluded hamlet.

It appears that Boe had been threatened with an attack from the Domar Boozies. Succor was immediately requested from Dowilnyah, who quickly marched from his capital, Gubbewallah, to the defense of Boe. He succeeded in defeating the Domars. But during his residence at Boe, so overshadowing was his influence and power, that the subordinate chiefs found themselves nearly stripped of the authority they were accustomed to exercise. A general dissatisfaction ensued, on which the king became so indignant that he withdrew from Boe, drawing in his train every thing that rendered that town attractive and important. He remained deaf to every solicitation to return. And here, at this village, he held his court, giving audience to the messengers of interior chiefs, granting favors, adjusting disputes. The village was alive with [p. 74] the chiefs of other towns, messengers going and coming, fine-looking women, warriors, etc.

When we drew near the village, we were requested by our guides to discharge our pieces, in order to inform the king of our arrival. This being done, we entered. The king, seated on a mat, was dressed in a gaudy-figured country robe; on his head was a large blue and red cloth cap, stuck all over with the talons of large birds. At his side was seated his chief counselor, whose name was Jebbue, a man of very large proportions, but of a mild and gentle countenance.[142] The king was surrounded by his people, all variously dressed in white, blue, striped, and yellow country coats.

His countenance assured us that he had not been misrepresented, notwithstanding his effort to compose it in a peaceful manner. It was one of the most threatening and the blackest visages I had seen for some time. He bade me welcome. A mat was then spread, upon which we seated ourselves.[143] Suddenly his iron horns and drums sounded, his warriors rushed forth from their concealed places, performing all the evolutions of a savage and barbarous warfare. The thundering plaudits of the people themselves increased the din. After this tremendous flourish had subsided, the king arose, and stepping forward, he waved his right hand in all directions, announcing by that gesture the uncontrolled authority with which he reigned in his dominions. Being welcomed again and again to his country, we were shown to our lodgings, which, though just temporarily erected, were comfortable.

Figure 16. Bolokolo Zaoro Bilivogui, born c. 1800 at Goboèla (or Gubbewallah), died c. 1870 at N'Zappa, in the wars. *Portrait by C. Jaloh, painted on a building in Boo, Guinea. Photograph by Melissa Leach, 1993.*

Figure 17. Residents of Boo pose on the remains of the town wall in 1993. *Photograph by Melissa Leach, 1993.*

Friday, 6th of November, 1868, I visited the [p. 75] king. Stating that we had come to see his country, and to make ourselves well acquainted with him and all his people, we then delivered our presents, which consisted of a piece of calico; a music-box, with which he was especially pleased; two pocket handkerchiefs, one pair epaulets, two bottles cologne, one clasped knife, three papers needles, one large brass kettle. He was delighted; he told me that I should not regret my visit to his country; and come who would after me, I should always hold the first place in his estimation; that he had been informed of all that had been said against him to prevent my coming to see him; but as I had disregarded these reports, he would show me that my confidence had not been misplaced.

He was anxious to see my revolvers, the fearful reputation of which preceded me everywhere I went. They were shown; their use explained, and their effect exaggerated. When he had also seen the astronomical instruments, his courage entirely forsook him. He requested me to give him some medicine to prevent his enemies from poisoning him. I replied that I had no such medicine; that by exercising the proper precaution in eating and drinking, he might be able to escape the evil intention of his enemies.

He next requested me to fire my muskets, that he might see the mysteries of a cap-gun; and he caused all the broken pieces of the exploded caps to be

Figure 18. Chief Diagbo (Diagba Ouro), warrior chief of N'Zappa (center, in robe with sword with his head turned away from the camera). Chief Nzebela Togba, of N'Zebela, is behind to the left, along with Magnan Formo, his colleague. The others are in their army. This photograph was taken at the moment of their submission to French forces in (1907). Chief Diagbo is Benjamin Anderson's "Jebbue." *Source: Inserted in F. Bouet,* Les Tomas *(Paris: Comité de l'Afrique Française, 1912). Courtesy of the Musée d'Histoire de Berne.*

gathered and preserved. I had to take some pains to dismiss his apprehensions that I would hurt him in any way.

He celebrated my visit to his country by a war-dance. He commenced it with some of his old habits, [p. 76] in which, however, palm-wine flowed instead of blood. After he had supped off about a quart of that beverage, he retired to his residence, and in the lapse of fifteen minutes, the clamor of his people and his war-drums signified his reappearance. He came forth with wild and prodigious leaps; a war-cap of leopard-skin, plumed with horse-hair, covered his head; he was naked to the waist, but wore a pair of Turkish-shaped trowsers. He had a large spear in his right hand. His dress and enthusiasm had completely metamorphosed him. His black and lowering countenance had undergone a terrible change, which was heightened by the savage grin which his white teeth imparted to it. The most frantic gestures now took place, amid the stunning plaudits of the whole town.

This being ended, the king called upon his women to give the finishing stroke to this happy business.

The ladies of Wymar are fond of dancing, and they spend much of their time in this amusement: they are not acquainted with the polite and delicate paces of their sisters in Monrovia; but for downright solid-footed dancing, they can not be surpassed. They are all fine, large, robust women, and have the happiest-looking countenances in the world.

African rulers in these parts travel very leisurely from one point to another, and at every intermediate place where they may halt, are sure to spend as much time as would be necessary to carry them to their final destination.[144] This careless, lounging habit of wasting time is an incurable one; arguments or persuasion strengthened by gifts can not overcome it.[145] The king had informed me of his intention to leave [p. 77] this village for his own town; the very day was appointed[.] He did not leave, however, until two days afterward. On Tuesday, 10th November, the king requested me to fire my muskets in order to announce to the neighboring towns and villages his departure.

He preferred my guns, because their report was louder than the cracking of his little English fusees, many of which I was assured had come to him by the way of Musardu through the Mandingoes.

At ten o'clock we started, the king being attended by his friends, bodyguard, musicians, and women. Happily the town to which we were going lay on the road direct to Musardu. About three o'clock we came to Ziggah Porrah Zue [Koiama Tongoro, 8°16'N, 9°6'W], the largest town and the capital of the Wymar country.[146] The king before entering the town made a halt to put on his robes. Every body dressed themselves. I was even requested to put on my uniform, which I did. After much firing and music, we entered, amid the applause and gaze of the whole town. After we had passed the gate and traversed the town some distance, we found ourselves encountered by another gate and wall; this contained the middle town. We passed on, and soon arrived at the gate and wall of the central town. Thus there are three towns, with their walls concentrically arranged. The inner walls were, however, much dilapidated, and served only to show in what manner the whole town had been successively enlarged; for as soon as an outside wall had been built around the new outside town, the inner wall was suffered to decay. The exterior or outside wall, though of great extent, was in good repair.[147] We were conducted to the market-space in the [p. 78] central town, which was spacious and convenient for holding large crowds. Some arrangements and order being introduced, a speech of welcome was delivered by the old chief of the town, Dowilnyah's uncle. At the conclusion, every trumpet, consisting of forty pieces, sounded. The band of ivory and wood belonged to the town; and it must be confessed that though the execution was simple, in effect it was really fine. Many speeches were made, the end of which was always concluded with music from the bands. These three bands did not all play at the same time, but successively, one after another, the king's band being allowed the precedence.

After speech-making came the war-dances of the principal chiefs, the women cheering them on. Each chief, as soon as he had performed his part, was immediately saluted by the king's body-guard, who, marching forward to meet him, acknowledged by that act his valor and achievements. Dowilnyah closed the festivities by exhibiting his own warlike prowess. We were assigned our lodgings. Every day we passed in this town was given to festivity and enjoyment.

One of their chief amusements was a "jack upon stilts," a fellow fantastically dressed, wearing a false face, and mounted upon stilts ten feet high fitted to the soles of his feet—with which he danced, leaped, and even climbed upon the houses.[148] He was full of clownish tricks and sayings, and made much sport for the crowds; he belonged to the king's train, a sort of king's fool. The women are really the industrious part of the population; for while their lords are wholly devoted to pleasure, palavers, and wars, the women are [p. 79] engaged in numerous domestic duties, and especially in spinning cotton. Here, also, as in the Domar country, the spindle is in the hands of every woman, from the princess to the slave. The women, however, enjoy themselves, particularly on market-days, which at this town takes place every Sunday.[149]

This market is seated on the banks of the St. Paul's River, and is carried on under the shade of large cotton (Bombax) and acacia-trees. The commodities of exchange are country cloths, cotton stripes, raw cotton, iron, soap, palm-oil, palm-butter, ground-nuts, rice, plantains, bananas, dried fish, dried meat, peas, beans, sweet potatoes, onions (chalots), snuff, tobacco, pipes, salt, earthen pots or vessels for holding water and for cooking purposes, large quantities of Kola[,] slaves, and bullocks. The bullocks are generally brought by the Mandingoes to the market. Palm-wine is not allowed to be sold in the market. Peace and order are secured by persons especially appointed for that purpose. After every body has assembled on the ground, these preservers of the peace with long staves in their hands go through the market, ordering every body to sit down; they then admonish the people to carry on their bargains peacefully and without contention. This preliminary being gone through with, the market is opened. It is generally attended by six or seven thousand people. There are several large markets held in the Wymar country; the one at Comma's town [Kuankan, 9°27'N, 9°8'W] is larger than this.[150] The daily market held in the central town is very convenient for making small purchases.

On Saturdays, sitting under the shade of large [p. 80] acacia-trees, I have watched the almost uninterrupted stream of people with their bundles and packs coming from every neighboring town and village to market. The bridge crossing the St. Paul's River would be laden or occupied from one end to the other, for hours, but it proved equal to the purpose for which it was built.

When the Mandingoes would arrive with their cattle, they would swim them across, but always experience difficulty in getting them up this side of the bank, on account of its steepness. No one seemed to think of remedying this inconvenience by sloping a pathway for the animals.

The bridge is a simple structure of wicker-work. From each side of the river the ends of the bridge depend from a stout branch of an acacia-tree. The roadway is of plaited ratan, two feet wide, and worked up on both sides about four and a half feet, to prevent falling over. It is further steadied and supported by a great number of strong and flexible twigs, which connect the bottom and the sides to every available limb of the trees growing on each bank. It is ascended by latters; its elevation is from twenty-three to twenty-five feet from the surface of the river, and spans a length of eighty-five feet.[151]

Ziggah Porrah Zue, the capital of the Wymar country, is in latitude 8°14' 45"; longitude 9°31'. Its elevation is about 1650 feet above the level of the sea. The barometer standing from 28.08 to 28.12. Thermometer ranging from 67° to 92° from November 14th to November 30th. It is seated on the St. Paul's River. The large market is held between the river and the wall of the town. I am informed that this river runs [p. 81] N.E. by E. into the Mandingo country, and that it takes it rise at the foot of some hills in that country. The Little Cape Mount River takes a similar direction; but in point of size, and in the number of its tributary creeks, it is superior to the St. Paul's.

The highest point of the slope or declivity of land from Monrovia to Ziggah Porrah Zue is from 1600 to 1700 feet above the level of the sea for a distance of latitude 116 miles. It is impossible that rivers thus situated should be any thing else but the drains of a country, and their course a series of cataracts and falls.

Every afternoon the king's body-guard performed their military evolutions. They had three war-drums, one of which was bound around with three tiers of human jaw-bones. A double-quick was beaten, to which they kept time for about half an hour, without tiring. They would then enter upon more violent motions, which were more of an athletic than a military kind. They were armed with English fusees, and heavy iron cutlasses of native manufacture. Their war-dress consisted of leopard-skins.

The Bonsie country is densely populated. The difference between the Domar and Wymar Boozie, is, that the latter marks his face from his temple to his chin with an indelible blue stain, while the former does not practice tattooing of any kind.[152] This tribe extends from the south-west portion of the Pessy country to the western border of the Mandingo country.

Dowilnyah now proposed to forward me on to Musardu under his protection—and a more powerful protection could not be obtained.[153] His own nephew [p. 82] was to accompany me. We left Ziggah Porrah Zue [Monday] November 30th, 1868, taking a direction E.N.E.[154] The country was open

Figure 19. Liana bridge across the Saint Paul River at Ziggah Porrah Zue (Koiama Tongoro) in 1993. *Photograph by James Fairhead.*

and covered with tall grass, cane-brake, and wild rice.[155] In an hour's walk we came to the town where the king formerly resided, Gubbewallah [Goboèla, 8°19'N, 9°2'W], meaning Sassa-wood tree, referring to a large old tree that grew in the middle of the town.[156]

We passed on, and halted at Pellezarrah [Dondema or Dondeno, 8°24'N, 8°55'W]—meaning several paths, because several paths crossed each other near the town.

Several large cotton-trees grew at the junction of these roads. The features of the country are hilly, but the slopes are longer and more gentle. One large hill had a gradual slope of nearly two miles, while its opposite side came down in a perpendicular line. Trees now indeed began to be scarce, the country being covered with cane-brake, wild rice, and very tall palm-trees. Some trees of that short, stunted species which grow on our beach at the Cape, were seen sparsely scattered here and there. We traveled over a hard soil of red clay, pebbles, and iron ore. The tall grass and treeless slopes, plains, and hills led my Congoes to declare that I had missed the route, and walked into the Congo country; and they commenced to thank me for returning them into their country Mesumbe.[157] We halted at Pezarrah [Pellezarrah] at six o'clock P.M. This town had suffered from fire in one part, and was being rebuilt. The whole direction traveled was E.N.E. Tuesday, 1st December, 1868, we started from Pellazarrah. After a walk of a quarter of an hour, the

Figure 20. "The elephants take possession of the cotton fields of Ballatah." Drawing in Anderson, 1870.

road led through a district which was a solid mass of iron ore. A short reddish grass struggled for existence on this extensive plain of metal [p. 83]. The iron was so pure that the road leading through it was a polished metal pathway, smoothed over by the constant treading of travelers.[158] It is said to be hardly treadable in the dries, it becomes so thoroughly heated.

We occupied three and a half hours in passing over these hills and plains of metal. We afterward came to high grass, through which some elephants had just passed. The palm-trees entirely cease. We halted at Ballatah [Baladougou, 8°26'N, 8°52'W] at three o'clock P.M.[159]

Wednesday, 2d December, 1868, at Ballatah. This is one of the most pleasantly situated of all the Boozie towns we had visited. The people insisted on our spending a day with them, that they might have some time to look at us. They killed a sheep, and furnished rice and other things in abundance. They then tried to prevail on me to undertake an elephant-hunt with them. Elephants are plentiful and large in this portion of the country, and every night they could be heard making a noise, while regaling themselves on the tender cotton-plants growing in the farms of the Ballatah people.

Artemus Ward declares that "Every man has his fort [*sic*]."[160] It is not mine to hunt elephants—especially to hunt elephants going in herds of ten or twelve, and that in an open country like Ballatah. I therefore declined the invitation to go on an elephant-hunt, telling my friends that I would postpone the pleasure to be derived from such amusements until I returned from Musardu.

Ballatah is in latitude 8°17'51". Its approximate elevation is about two thousand feet above the level of the sea; barometer standing 27.172.[161] It is not so large [p. 84] as the other Boozie towns, but far better laid out. The houses are not crammed so closely together. It contains about twenty-five hundred people; it is seated in a plain, and is commanded by very high and abrupt hills on its western side, while the land rolls off in gentle undulations toward the east. We were carried to some outlying villages north-west of Ballatah, situated at the foot of the same high hills that overlook that town. Here they were busy smelting iron. The furnaces were built of clay, and of a conical shape, from five and a half to six feet high, having clay pipes or vents so close to the bottom, arranged in groups of two and three, for the purpose of draught. The charcoal and iron ore are put in at the top. At the bottom is an opening through which the slag and other impurities are withdrawn.

Thursday, December 3d, 1868, we started from Ballatah. The direction was N.E., and parallel to a range of very high hills, called the Vukkah hills. These hills are from seven hundred to one thousand feet high, and are variously composed of granite, iron ore, and a reddish clay which, from the steep slopes near the top, had shelved down in many places.[162] The whole country, hill and plain, was covered with long grass and canebrake, interspersed with a short, dwarfish tree. The bark of this tree is rough and corrugated, the trunk is a foot in circumference, eight or ten feet high; and has an excessive branching top. The leaves small, and of an oval shape. Clumps of large trees occupied the sides and knolls of the hills.

These hills are of all sizes, and run in every direction. Toward the N. and N.E., a line of hills towers [p. 85] above the rest, the ridge of which makes a variety of outlines against the sky. These hills are not so ruggedly disposed as those in the Domar country. The slopes are gentler; only near the summit they sometimes change feature, taper off to a point, or go right up perpendicularly. To these hills and fastnesses the natives resort in time of war, carrying all their effects, their wives and children, to the most inaccessible parts. Judging from a hill which was shown me as being used for that purpose, some of them must be very safe retreats.

Agriculture in this country must be a very simple and easy process. No "cutting farm," as we call it, by felling trees and cutting undergrowth. The soil, though covered with tall grass and canebrake, is one of the highest fertility. When the sun has sufficiently parched the tall grass, it is sometimes burnt off, sometimes cut down and hoed in for manure. Farms of hundreds of acres can be prepared in a very short time; and the natives, with their small hoes, can well afford to have the large plantations of rice, cotton, and millet, which we saw.

Friday, 4th December, 1868, we reached Vukkah [Foma, 8°29'N, 8°50'W]. This town stands at the foot of a range of high hills of the same name. It is the last Boozie town, and the nearest to the Mandingo country.

These hills, called "Vukkah" by the Boozies, and "Fomah" by the Mandingoes, take a definite direction N.E.[163] They are the highest range, and form a marked and acknowledged boundary between the Boozie and Mandingo territories.[164] At the foot of this range are seated a number of towns, Boozie and Mandingo [p. 86].

The town of Vukkah was overgrown with wild cane and plantain-trees. The houses were dilapidated, presenting a disagreeable contrast to the usual neatness of the Boozie towns. The inhabitants are the most ill-favored of all the Boozies. This town is also notorious for the mischief and trouble it gives thoroughfarers; and but for our coming under the protection of Dowilnyah, it soon fell out what would have happened. We had not been in the town an hour before we had a row with one of the principal men of the place. He requested me to fire my musket, which I did a number of times, sufficient, as I thought, to please every body; but he insisted on several more rounds. I refused; he then told me to go on to Musardu, but when I returned I would find that my way home would not lie through that town. I was, however, under too powerful a protection to be disturbed. Dowilnyah was not to be trifled with. To take a head from a shoulder was mere pastime with him.

Much allowance, however, must be made for these African rulers. Tyrannical and bloodthirsty they sometimes appear; but this character is artificial, and practiced in many instances to inspire terror and respect, without which they could not hold their authority a single hour.

Beset by rivalships and conspiracies, they are forced, from the boisterous circumstances of their situation, to employ every means conservative of their authority and their lives.

Saturday, 5th of December, we started from Vukkah.[165] We had now crossed the Vukkah hills, and were fairly in the Mandingo country.[166] Many of the plains of this [p. 87] section of the country are terraced, one above another. Amends is made for a simple vegetation, by the ever-varying forms of relief the country presents, the farther you advance into it.

At three o'clock P.M., we were met on the road by several Mandingoes, who accompanied us to their town, Nu-Somadu, or Mahommadu [Nionsamoridu, 8°43'N, 8°50'W].[167] The walls of this town are quadrilateral in shape, each side being a series of bastions, which at a distance looks like some old fortified front [fort]. The walls, however, are so thin, that a four-pounder could demolish them in a very little time.[168]

We entered the town, and were entertained in a very hospitable manner. A house was given to us, small indeed in its dimensions to what we had been accustomed to in the Boozie country, but convenient and comfortable. Being wearied with the journey, I threw myself into a hammock, and commenced surveying alterations and arrangements which a change in the character of the country had introduced. The house was a circular structure of clay, with a conical roof made entirely of large canebrake and long grass. In looking

Figure 21. "Mahommadu." Drawing in Anderson, 1870.

around the walls, our eyes rested on a saddle, stirrups, bridle, with leather leggings, and a tremendous tower gun.

Sunday, the 6th of December, we attempted to pursue our journey; but the chief refused to allow us to depart before he had demonstrated his good-will and hospitality. He killed a heifer, and cooked it with onions. We satisfied our appetites, and made him an appropriate present. We then departed; arrived at Naalah [Nyela; 8°44'N, 8°40'W] late in the afternoon.[169] In the morning [Monday, 7 December], a trooper was at once dispatched to Musardu, to inform [p. 88] them that the Tibbabue (American) had come. In two hours he returned, telling me that the Musardu people requested that I would remain at Naalah until they had made preparations for my reception. I immediately sent them word that I had been so long coming to see their country that I would rather forego any public demonstration than be delayed any further. I was then answered to come on; they would gladly receive me.

Accompanied by several Mandingoes from Naalah and Mahommadu, we started for Musardu. Our interest in the journey was enlivened by the novel features of the country. In passing through the Boozie country, extensive views were frequently obstructed by a dense vegetation that hemmed in the sight on each side of a narrow foot-path. Here the peculiar features of the country are visible for miles. The towns and villages seated in the plains, people on foot and people on horseback can be seen at a great distance, and have more the air of light, life, and activity, than many parts of the Boozie country, where the somber gloom of immense forests conceals all such things. The large town of Du Quirlelah lay on our right; but from our elevated

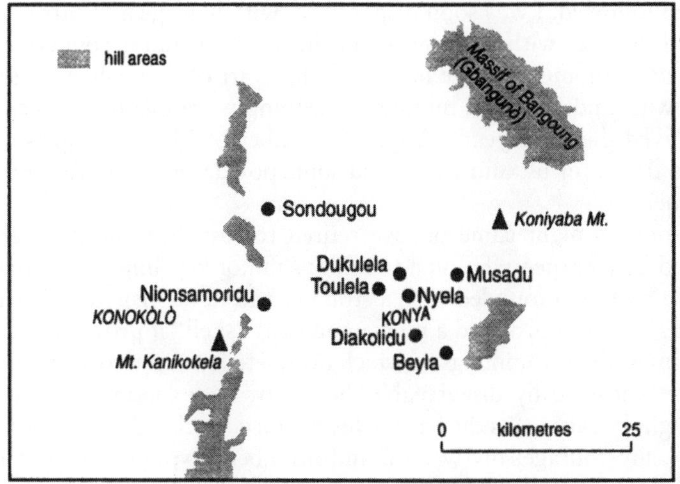

Map 10. Konya.

position, it might well be said to lie under us.[170] Going on, we descried a long, whitish border, raised a little above the height of a gentle slope. On drawing nearer, it proved to be the top of the south-western wall of Musardu.[171] We fired our muskets, and entered the town. We were led up a street, or narrow lane, that brought us into the square in which the mosque was situated. Here were gathered the king, Vomfeedolla [p. 89], and the principal men of the town, to receive us.[172] My Mandingo friends from Mahommadu opened the civilities of introduction with an elaborate speech; stating where I had come from, and for what I had come; the power, learning, and wealth of the Tibbabues. One of my friends, Barki, from Mahommadu, then engaged to swear for me, that I had come for no ill purpose whatever, but that I was moved entirely by an intelligent curiosity and friendly intercourse.[173] Dowilnyah's messengers then spoke in flattering terms of my demeanor and liberality in their country, and the wishes of the king, in consequence, that I should be treated in every way befitting an illustrious stranger and his particular guest. I had never before been so complimented, and I became uneasy at the high importance attached to the Tibbabue visit, fearing that great expectations in the way of dashes or presents might be disappointed.[174] For my bundles, bulky and pretentious in appearance, contained books, instruments, and clothes, more than the means upon which many hopes were then founding and growing. After the speeches were over, the king and his people gave me repeated welcomes, with the peculiar privilege of doing at Musardu whatever I was accustomed to do at Monrovia, a large liberty, granted only to distinguished strangers. An infinite number of salaams and snapping of fingers then followed. I was soon disposed of, with luggage and carriers, in the king's court-yard, with a house similar in structure and accommodation to the one at Mahommadu. We had learned the art of domiciling ourselves in these towns, and in fifteen minutes everything wore the appearance of our having lived there for years. A [p. 90] number of Mandingo girls came to sing and dance for us, and we wasted some powder by way of returning the compliment.

As soon as night came on, we retired to rest; but our slumbers were disturbed by a harper, who, in a tremulous minor key, improvised that since Musardu had been founded such a stranger had never visited it.[175] The harp itself was a huge gourd, and a most unmusical "shell" it proved to be. It had three strings, the thrummings of which disquieted me on two accounts. First, the noise, intrinsically disagreeable. Secondly, the expectations which that noise might be raising, as the bard in his *nocturne* declared my many gracious qualities, my courage, my wealth, and my liberality; upon the last two he dwelt with loud and repeated effort.

King Vomfeedolla in appearance has a mild, gentle countenance. His features would please those who are fond of a straight nose, broad forehead, thin lips, large and intelligent eyes, and a oval chin.[176] Like all the Mandingoes, his skin is a smooth, glossy black. In stature he is rather below the general towering height of this tribe. He does not possess the fiery energy of his royal Boozie brother, Dowilnyah, who, though many years his senior, far excels him in that respect.

In all councils Vomfeedolla seems to be entirely a listener, and to be directed and influenced by the older members of the royal family. He is said to be a great warrior; but the evidences around Musardu prove that if he is, he must belong to the unfortunate class of that profession.

The usual apparel or dress of the Mandingoes consists of four pieces—two pieces as a shirt and vest, an [and] [p. 91] one large coat or toga worn over all; a pair of Turkish-shaped trowsers coming a little below the knees: sandals for the feet, which are sometimes beautifully worked; and a three-cornered cap for the head.[177] These articles, made and worn as a Mandingo *only* can make and wear them, leave nothing to be desired, either as to taste and utility. This is said so far as the men are concerned. But I must deplore a fashion observed by the women, in wrapping up their faces and bodies in a manner truly ungraceful, and unhealthy, too.

Musardu is an exceedingly healthy place; there was not one prostrate, sickly person in the town. There is, however, a disease which sometimes attacks individuals in a peculiar way; it is an affection of the throat, causing a protuberance almost similar to what is called the "king's evil."[178] I inquired the cause, and they imputed it to something that impregnates the water during the height of the dry season, being the time when it mostly seizes persons.

The atmosphere of Musardu is very dry, and had a very favorable effect

Figure 22. Musadu from the air, 1993.
Photograph by Dave Partridge.

upon my watches, which were declared at Monrovia to be out of order; but as soon as I reached Musardu, every one of them began to tick away in a clear and ringing manner.

Musardu, the capital of the Western Mandingoes, is in latitude 8°27'11"N., longitude 8°24'80"W.; it is elevated two thousand feet above the level of the sea, and is situated amid gentle hills and slopes.[179] North and north-east two very high hills tower above the rest several hundred feet.[180] The population is between seven and eight thousand, but the many villages and hamlets [p. 92] increase it to a greater proportion. In the days of its prosperity, and before it had suffered from the damaging effects of war; it had occupied a larger space, and was not surrounded by any wall.[181] Though it has lost its former importance, Musardu is still considered as the capital of the Western Mandingoes, and its name is never mentioned but in terms of patriotism and respect. I often heard the old men of the town regret its past power and wealth. They told me that what I then saw of Musardu was only the ruins of a former prosperity. The town is laid off irregularly, with very narrow and sometimes winding lanes or streets. These lanes or streets cross each other in such a way as to give access to any part of the town. The houses are built facing the lanes, and the rear space is used as a yard for horses and

Figure 23. The main mosque of Musadu in 1986.
Photograph by Tim Geysbeek.

cattle.[182] In the south-western part of the town is the mosque. The walls having been injured by the weather, they had commenced to repair it. It is a quadrilateral building, surrounded by an oval-shaped wall, which is carried up eight feet, and upon which rest the rafters of a large conical thatch-roof.[183] The interior space is thirty-two feet long and twenty-two feet wide, and nine feet high. It is laid off in four compartments, by three intermediate walls running the length of the building. These separate spaces communicate with each other by three doors or openings in each intermediate wall. I do not know the purpose of the divisions, unless it is to grade the faithful.[184] It can scarcely accommodate more than one hundred and twenty persons, and must therefore be devoted to the most pious, or the leaders or teachers of Islam.[185]

On Monday, the 14th of December, 1868, the King [p. 92] Vomfeedolla held a military demonstration. He had summoned his infantry and cavalry from the nearest towns of Billelah [Beyla, 8°41'N, 8°38'W], Yockkadu [Diakolidou, 8°42'N, 8°39'W], Naalah, and Mahommadu.[186] The exercises commenced about two o'clock P.M., in the large square of the town.[187] The spectators and musicians had already assembled. All at once a trooper dashed past at full speed, as if he was reconnoitring the enemy. Several others followed, dispersing in different directions. The position of the enemy seeming to be determined, they soon returned. The trumpet then sounded, and a grand cavalry charge took place.[188] Riding up in line, with musket in hand, they would deliver their fire, and canter off to the right and left, in order to allow the rear lines to do the same. As soon as the firing was over, they slung their muskets, and, rising in the saddle, drew their long knives in one hand and their crooked swords in the other; the horse, now urged to a headlong gallop by the voice, carries his rider, standing in the stirrups, with furious velocity into the heat of the battle.[189] Such are the evolutions of the Mandingo cavalry. Their equipment is quite complete. They use saddles and bridles, and a peculiar and powerful bit; short stirrups; leather leggings, to which iron spurs are attached.[190] The cavalry from all the towns, according to various reports, ought to amount to fifteen hundred.[191]

In their open country, where the action of cavalry is greatly facilitated by the long, gentle slops, and wide, treeless plains, they would be no mean enemy. They often dismount, in order to act on foot. Each horse has a boy attendant to take care of him while his master is thus engaged. In real action, I have [p. 94] been informed, the little boys of the defeated party often suffer the penalty of their participation. Yet these dangers do not deter the little fellows from going; for they are frequently able to ride off the field as soon as any symptoms of defeat are perceived.

The king seems to act for the most part with the infantry, for he rode in front and led them on. They came in deep array, and with great clamor, but without organization, being directed solely by a flag or ensign of blue cloth. I was sorry that I had no flag of ours to present them.

After their exercises were over, they requested us to fire our muskets; upon which we delivered regular volleys with bayonets fixed, both to their astonishment and delight, caused by the quickness with which we loaded our pieces, our certainty of fire—unlike their fusees, which were continually snapping—and the deeper report of our guns.[192] As soon as all the exercises were finished, the king then distributed the presents I had given him to the chiefs of the several military divisions.[193]

Tuesday, the 15th of December, 1868.[194] My Mandingo friends began to press me to trade with them. I informed them that I had nothing to trade with; that my gifts to the king and the principal men of the town had exhausted my means so closely as to scarcely leave me sufficient to enable me to return home. Nothing could convince them that I had not pieces of handkerchiefs and calicoes concealed in my bundles. They tried every method to induce me to trade; they carried me to their houses and would get out their small leathern bags; these bags contained from ten to [p. 95] fifteen large twisted gold rings ("sannue.")[195] They then offered me horses, and finally concluded by offering to sell me some pretty female slaves. I informed them that the Tibbabues did not keep slaves; that I had not come to trade, but merely to visit their country; that upon my return home I would persuade my people to come and trade with them. At the prospect of a number of Tibbabues coming to their country to trade, they were exceedingly satisfied.

From trade we passed to war and politics, and having satisfied all their inquiries in these two particular points with respect to the Tibbabues, they made me acquainted with some of their wars and feuds. They had a special cause of grievance against a certain Mandingo chief whose name was Ibrahima, or Blamer Sissa, and who lived north-east, and three days' walk from Musardu, at a large town called Madina [Medina, 9°31'N, 8°12'W].[196]

It appears that Blamer Sissa came from Madina to visit his uncle, Amalah, who was then residing at Musardu, and that he was treated with great civility and distinction by the Musardu people; that being a powerful young prince, they solicited his aid against some Kaffres, or unbelievers, living over the eastern hills; that in compliance with their solicitation he went back to Madina, and soon returned to Musardu, bringing with him his cavalry and infantry, a numerous and formidable mass, who, in the end, came nigh doing their friends at Musardu as much evil as they had done the Kaffres, whom they had mutually agreed to plunder.[197]

Blamer Sissa stripped Musardu of every thing valuable [p. 96], and even carried off nearly all the pretty young women of that town.

On Thursday, the 16th of December, 1868, at seven o'clock P.M., Chancellor came running to my house to inform me that several suspicious persons, with their horses or jackasses, were lurking about the north-western side of the town; that they had sought admittance, but it had been refused them; that they had reported themselves traders, but the town people were on the alert, believing them to be Blamer Sissa's spies, who were only skulking around in order to gain all the intelligence they could, and carry it to their friends, who were supposed to be in strong force behind the north-eastern hills. Next morning, Friday, the 17th of December, the strange people were indeed seen on a hill north-west of the town, and cold must have been the sleep they had of it the previous night, for the thermometer stood at 52° at four A.M.[198] A council was held to decide how to act. Some proposed to send the young men out to kill them. Afterward it was more wisely determined to go out and order them to take their traffic and depart with it at once.

We accordingly went out, and after the usual salutations, they were given plainly to understand that neither they nor their trade could enter Musardu, and that they must depart without delay. But our strange merchants were not to be frightened off in that manner. They insisted that they had come for no evil purpose whatever, but simply to prosecute their trade. The conferences were prolonged until midday. While the conversation was going on, I had an opportunity to survey the suspicious group of new-comers. It consisted [p. 97] of two sturdy little jackasses, with enormous packs, containing what looked like, and after proved to be French blue baft, and five men. The one who acted as guide and interpreter was one of Blamer Sissa's people, and he alone served to confirm our suspicions. The other four were tall, black, good-featured people. One of them had his face and head bound up with a piece of white cotton, after the peculiar manner of some of the Arabs of the desert. They were all Mohammedans. I learned that they had come from the Senegal, had been to Futtah, passed through Kanghkah [Kankan, 10°23'N, 9°18'W], and had obtained this guide from Madina, to show them to Musardu.[199] I began to be interested in them. The Musardu people, however, remained deaf to every argument, and the Senegal merchants were compelled to pack their bundles on their asses, and go. Nay, the town people, to assure themselves of their going, followed them some distance. But the sight of such large bundles in such a time of need and self-interest, had sown the seeds of discord; and there was much contention now among the Musardu people themselves. Some were for allowing the merchants to enter the town. Others opposed it, alleging that such were always the artifices of Blamer Sissa when he wished to take a strong town; that he always sent some of his people ahead, who, under pretext of wishing to trade, introduced themselves into the town in order to open the gates at night to his forces. The contention grew so warm that they even came to blows.

On Saturday, the 19th of December, about nine o'clock A.M., news came to the town that the merchants [p. 98] had returned. We went out and found it really so; and when the order was repeated to them to go away, they absolutely refused, declaring that they had come to trade; that having left neither mother nor wife behind, the Musardu people might kill them if they wished to do so. Their firmness overcame the first determination of the Musardu people, who, after nearly having another quarrel among themselves, gave the merchants leave to trade outside of the town—a permission with which our Senegal friends seemed to be quite satisfied. It was difficult at the first to make out who our merchants were. No one could understand their language except the Mandingo interpreter from Madina, and it was this man who caused them to be seriously suspected, for he was one of Blamer Sissa's soldiers. These poor merchants, therefore, might have been subserving Blamer Sissa's purposes, without the least knowledge of it themselves. It was solely their interpreter that marked them as suspected persons.

On Monday, the 21st of December, our Musardu friends, after all their blustering determination against the merchants, admitted them into the town. Interest and avarice overcame all their patriotism and caution. The two jackass-loads of goods, not unlike the Trojan horse, were dragged into the town, and if Blamer Sissa had any designs on Musardu, they were accomplished.

Both in policy and energy Blamer Sissa seemed superior to the Musardu people; for in addition to the trouble he had already given them, and even the recent threats he had made, he knew how to introduce his own people in the town, who could give any intelligence with respect to Musardu he might desire [p. 99]. He is not the first prince who has taken a city by means of a jackass-load of merchandise. The Musardu people sent a thundering message of defiance and insult to Blamer Sissa, making the largest use of me to back it up. They sent him word that they were not at all dependent on him for trade or any thing else; that the Tibbabues were about to open trade with them, and would be their friends in peace and war; that even then a Tibbabue was negotiating that particular business in Musardu. They then took pains to exhibit the arms and means with which the destruction of Madina might sooner or later be accomplished. My muskets with their bayonets, my revolvers, and my person, were severally shown as designed for that especial object.

I was purposely questioned aloud as to the military resources of the Tibbabues: the little guns that fired any number of times without loading, and the big guns that burnt up cities at the distance of miles.[200] I gave such answers as I hope will make Blamer Sissa less troublesome to Musardu for the future.

It might be thought impolitic that I did not refrain from expressing myself as being in either party's favor. In this part of Africa, if hostilities are lukewarm, neutrality is possible; but where it burns with the flame of recent and bitter injuries, you are absorbed by either one side or the other, or torn in pieces by both.

The Musardu people are unfortunately situated. On the north they expect war with Blamer Sissa, and on the east hostilities have never ceased; the west and south-west are still open to them. It is the latter direction that opens itself to our enterprise, and promises [p. 100] much to our commercial prosperity. The chief articles of trade are gold, bullocks, hides, horses, and country cloths of every variety of dye and texture. Gold is worn extravagantly by the Mandingo ladies of Musardu. Their earrings are so large and weighty as to require a narrow piece of leather to brace them up to their head-bands, so that the part of the ring in the ear may not make an unseemly hole, as sometimes happens when this necessary support is neglected. Gold is certainly abundant, and would form a lucrative trade between Musardu and Liberia. I gave twelve sheets of writing-paper (kahtahsee) and four yards of calico for a large gold twist ring.[201] Had I come purposely to trade, and had gone through the usual practice of "jewing down," I could have purchased it for less.[202] These rings are perfectly pure, the natives never mixing any kind of alloy in the manufacturing of them. Many of my friends wondered at my making presents of watches, music-boxes, and calicoes when the articles might have been exchanged for gold or slaves; but as I was determined that the money should be religiously appropriated to the purpose for which it was sent out, I steadily refused every proffer, excepting such few things as I could conveniently bring back as samples of the production and industry of the country.

To carry on trade safely, free from the risks and interruptions incident to a country people by barbarians and semi-barbarians, and divided into so many jarring interests, it would be necessary to establish four trading forts—two in the Boozie and Barline countries, which would purchase country cloths, raw cotton, camwood, rice, palm-oil, etc.; and two in the Mandingo country [p. 101], where gold, bullocks, country cloths, and horses could be purchased at such rates as would amply remunerate for all the trouble, expense, and consumption of time necessary in such traffic. The individuals living in the forts would be abundantly supplied with food, as rice is produced in surplus quantities in the Boozie and Barline countries. Even the expense of clothing would be trifling, if they would use the cloth of the country. The natives declared that they would be glad to have such establishments among them. These forts would also second and strengthen any missionary effort that might be made out there; indeed, the two establishments could be made to work admirably together. The support, protection, and moral and material influence which would be exerted in the respective operations of each, would insure permanence and success. We would do well to commence the use of jackasses; indeed, it would be indispensable for the portage or transportation of luggage.[203] The Senegal traders at Musardu carried very large packs of blue cotton on their two sturdy little animals. Horses and bullocks would form no unimportant part of the trade. Mahommadu is a regular beef-market.[204]

The auriferous or gold district of this part of Manding is said to be principally at Buley.[205] Upon my first inquiry, I was told that Buley was a week's journey eastward; but upon my continuing to prosecute my inquiries respecting that country, Buley was immediately removed one week's walk further, making it two weeks' walk, and through hostile and dangerous districts, the people of which, as my Musardu friends informed me, would exact toll from me for passing [p. 102] through their country. Every difficulty was conjured up that was conceived to be sufficient to extinguish all interest for further inquiry, or to intimidate my going in that direction.

However, my Mandingo cousins have no doubt misrepresented the whole matter; for gold not only exists at Buley, but right there in their own country—otherwise I do not think it could be so plentiful among themselves, since they have little or no communication with the east.

At Buley, it is found mixed in fine grains with the superficial deposit. No one is allowed to sweep or pick up any thing in another's yard. The gold is separated by fanning and washing; it is then smelted and twisted, and ready for sale or use. They show some skill and taste in the preparation of these rings, and they are really worth their weight in gold. Our friends are sometimes equally skillful in preparing counterfeits, as my nitric acid had several occasions to prove. Impositions of this kind are generally punished by heavy fines.

In going to Buley, you pass successively Bendalah—where a very fine species of country cloth is made, of striped figure, and usually worn by the women—Tangalah, Tutah, and Gehway.[206] Now, if these towns are situated from each other at the usual distance of Africans—namely, a day's walk—Buley is but four days' walk east from Musardu, which I take to be the fact, despite the industry of my friends to prove to the contrary.[207] Unlike Musardu, it is a wooded country. This fact may give us some idea of the extent of those treeless hills and plains eastward. They are said to extend [p. 103] further north than in any other direction, where, indeed, cow-dung is used for fuel. The population of Buley is Mandingo. Gold is also obtained north of Blamer Sissa's town, at Wasalah.[208]

My friends now tried again to provoke me to trade, offering the same articles they had offered before—gold, horses, and female slaves. Indeed, this is all the Mandingoes of Musardu had to offer by way of trade.[209] Not a bullock or a country cloth was to be seen, though these things are notoriously the articles of merchandise belonging to Musardu. Every thing liable to be seized in war, from its being too bulky to be quickly removed or concealed, sad experience has taught them to keep out of reach, in some friendly Boozie town in the rear of the Vukkah hills; while nothing but the war-horse, and articles easy to be hid or carried off, are kept at Musardu. At every house can be seen muskets, cutlasses, powder-horns, war-belts, and war-coats, a powerful large bow, and four or five large quivers filled with poisoned arrows. I have seen them prepare the poison with which the points of the arrows are smeared over. It is a vegetable poison, consisting of one bulbous root twice as large as an onion, and two different kinds of small vines. It is boiled in a pot to a thick or gummy consistence, the color of which is black. It is said to be so fatal that if it wounds as much as the tip end of the fingers, it is certain death. The preparers of this fearful means of savage warfare but too clearly explained to me its effects before death completely ensues: the bleeding at the nose and ears; its nauseous attack on the stomach, and consequent spitting; the final despair of the individual in lying down, with his [p. 104] eyes set in a vacant death-stare—all of which was imitated with a terrible fidelity to the truth, and as one of the most horrible means of barbarous warfare.

This part of Mandingo is the country of the horse. There are two sizes: the large horse used for show and parade, and the small horse, used for war.[210] The latter is a hardy, strong little animal, capable, in his country, of bearing great fatigue. In battle, I am informed, he kicks and bites in a furious manner, and that when his master makes a capture of a fine young lady, he willingly receives the additional burden, and gallops off faster than ever. These horses are certainly well treated and cared for; and if Musardu is not characteristic for cleanliness, it is because the horse and his master equally occupy and almost equally litter up that capital.

I tried my best to obtain some date by which an approximate notion might be formed of the age of the city; but in matters of chronology our friends have been sadly careless. None of them could give the least intelligent hint. They said that the grandfather of the oldest man in the town declared that the town was there when he was born, and that all the other towns sprang from this one.[211] Its antiquity is an undoubted matter among themselves. I was shown their large market-place outside of the town, a few hundred yards from the south-western gate.[212] From the space it occupied, it would easily have contained eight or ten thousand people. The respective places were each commodity was exhibited for sale was pointed out; country cloths, cattle, gold, (dust and manufactured,) slaves, grain, salt, of which there were two kinds—the slab or rock-salt, which came on camels from the north-east, [p. 105] and our fine salt, gotten from the coast; ostrich feathers; leather, in the beautiful and soft tanning of which the Mandingoes are particularly expert; ivory, cotton, tobacco, and an infinite variety of domestic articles were all named, and the different places where they were sold designated.[213]

But war has abolished every sight of this commercial activity and life, and has introduced in its stead a barren space filled with weeds, grass, and the broken skulls and skeletons of enemies—desperate battle having been fought there between the Musardu people, aided by Blamer Sissa, and the eastern Mandingoes.[214]

The soil of the hills of Musardu is composed of reddish clay and sand, with boulders of iron ore intermixed. On the north-eastern side of the town are some large masses of black and gray granite. The plains are a whitish clay, and the very soil for a plow, being free from almost every obstruction.[215] The light tillage of the natives never goes more than four or five inches, with their little short-handled hoes.

About February or March, and sometimes sooner, the high grass and wild cane are cut down, to rot and manure the soil. Near the planting season, these vegetable fertilizers are turned in with the hoe; and from the crops of rice, of which there are three kinds; potatoes, ground-nuts, onions, peas and beans, large gourds, corn, pumpkins, etc., it must answer abundantly the purposes of agriculture. Tobacco is grown in plots, wherever a stream of water offers itself for frequent irrigation.[216] The rubbish and ashes of the town form excellent beds for this plant. They are generally laid out with great care, and watered three times a day [p. 106]. The Mandingoes are the great tobacco-raisers and snuff-makers of the country. They supply both themselves and the Boozies.

Musardu is singularly free from grasshoppers, rats, and mice, owing to the number of hawks that crowd the limbs of a solitary tree that may be standing here and there. Want of trees compels them to perch themselves on rocks, and when these are all occupied, they may be seen to cover the ground in dark patches. There are also large birds that particularly belong to the grassy plains of Musardu. They go in flocks of eight or twelve. In size, they

Figure 24. Beyla and Diakolidugu, with the Fon-Going Mountains to the west, in 1993. *Photograph by Dave Partridge.*

are as large as American geese, and, on account of their weight, do not fly very high, nor do they make long passages at a time. When they alight on the ground, they are enabled, by the length of their necks, to discover you before you can get within gunshot of them. Their hearing, however, is not very acute; for we have often crept up the brow of the hill, and come upon them suddenly. They are a very sagacious and shy bird; and though I and my Congoes tried our marksmanship many times, we were entirely unable to procure one of them. The Mandingoes are scarcely ever able to kill them. Their color is white, with a black band across their back and wings; and when flying, their leader never ceases to make a cawing noise. They are very gawky in their movements when walking on the ground, caused by their long necks, giving their heads a deliberative nod with every step they take.[217]

The Mandingoes are very attentive to their farming interests. They are, however, more given to trade then to manual labor. The leading vice of a Mandingo [p. 107] is avarice, which, by however much it is stimulated, the present state of the country affords him but little means to gratify. Nothing can be accumulated among themselves that war does not instantly dissipate. Nevertheless, they are quick and intelligent, easy to be managed by persuasion, and they offer to Liberia a more speedy prospect of assimilation and union than any other tribe with which I am acquainted. A strong moral advantage is already gained, from their being a reading and writing people, practicing a communication of ideas and an interchange of thought by means of the Arabic. They have a natural reverence for learning and mental superiority, and they never fail to respect it, whether it accords with their belief or not. No rudeness, no indecent and wrangling intolerance, was ever shown me during my stay among them. No difference of religion ever made them diminish the respect, attention, and hospitality which they conceived were due me. One of my Congo carriers is of the Baptist persuasion, and he used to make himself heard every morning, even to my own annoyance, by loud orisons. Still, our Mohammedan Mandingoes said nothing. It was respected as a prayer, and it was known to be a Christian prayer.

On the 19th of December [Saturday], I visited Billelah[,] Kaifal Kandah's native town.[218] In size it is nearly as large as Musardu. The houses are in a better condition; but in all other respects it resembles the parent city—the narrow lanes, horse stables, gardens, etc. The town seemed densely populated, at least with children.[219]

The next day [Sunday, 20 December] we started from Billelah for our home, Musardu, visiting on our way another town, Yockkadu [p. 108]. This town is about a quarter of a the size of Musardu, and similar in its arrangements, customs, and habits.[220] The chief of this town, Vawfulla, proved to be very hospitable.[221]

On Sunday [*sic,* Monday], the 21st of December, my Boozie attendants grew impatient to return home, and even prepared to leave me. I gave them full liberty to go if they wished, since I did not intend to make the least move until I had finished my business. The sky had been so hazy as to prevent my taking any observations. The fine dust of the Harmattans, together with the vast volumes of smoke and cinders from the grassy hills and plains that were burning, rendered it a difficult matter to take observations.[222] This was the cause of my delaying to return, and the consequent dissatisfaction of my Boozies, a people who are not willing to be kept from their homes any length of time. Chancellor, however, was enabled to appease their impatience by three yards of calico.

Having now exhausted the time, as well as almost all the means which had been assigned to carry out this expedition, I began to think of returning home; yet I must confess there was nothing more contrary to my wishes. Had it not been that family responsibilities demanded my return home, I should have still, with or without means, prosecuted my journey eastward—a direction which I have always had the presentiment contains the prosperity and welfare of Liberia.

On Friday, the 25th of December, at eight A.M., we bade farewell to

Musardu, and arrived at Mahommadu at six P.M.[223] Here we passed several days, in order to take [p. 109] observations and to see the market. This market is held every Wednesday, outside of the eastern wall.

On Wednesday, the 30th, this market took place. It contained three hundred head of cattle, which were offered at three or four dollars a head in our money. The usual articles of rice, onions, palm-oil, cotton, country cloths, tobacco, and iron were present. There were a number of slaves for sale, especially children. A pretty little Mandingo girl, about nine years of age, was sent to my house with one of my boys, in order that I might purchase her. She cost 9000 kolu, or about $15 in our money.[224] I was curious to know how she became a slave, as Mandingoes are seldom ever enslaved. I declined to buy her, on the ground that Tibbabues never held slaves. The child herself seemed to be disappointed; for she showed that she preferred falling into my hands in preference to her own people. The Mandingoes are harsher with their slaves than the Boozies. Among the Boozies it is difficult to distinguish the slaves by any mark of dress or usage; but the Mandingoes, though not excessively cruel, have drawn the lines of difference in so strong a manner that you can not fail to perceive them.[225]

A great many cattle remained unsold. The season of the dries is very severe on them, and they sometimes die from overdriving. Several died the next day after the market was over. They are the large, reddish, long-horned cattle, which we usually buy from the interior.[226] The highlands, from which they come, explains why they do not thrive so well as the black, short-horned, and sturdy cattle of the coast, known among us as the "leeward cattle [p. 110].

It was at this town that I first experienced the hospitality of these people in their own country. Our Mandingoes are Mohammedans; but they have an invincible partiality for Tibbabues, who are known to be Christians and the people of the book.[227] It is also well known that there is some difference in the creeds or beliefs; yet the unbelieving Tibbabue is sure to be housed, fed, and befriended in a manner that is not always practiced among the faithful themselves.

While they were repairing the wall of Mahommadu, I was requested to carry some of the mortar and place it in the wall, that it might be said that "a Tibbabue helped to build these walls." I contributed all I could to make them impregnable.[228]

During our stay there, we were also taken to their foundry, where they were busily engaged in preparing iron for the market. The pieces of pure iron taken from the furnaces are again heated; they are then reduced to a large triangular shape by pounding them with large, heavy stones—a process simple and laborious enough, and a work which is entirely left for the slaves.

Blacksmithing, such as the making of stirrups, bits, spurs, etc., is done by the Mandingoes themselves, as being a mechanical art too noble to be performed by slaves.

On Thursday, the 31st of December, we left Mahommadu, and reached Vukkah at half-past four o'clock P.M. We were now among the Boozies again. The Vukka hills run N.E. and S.W. The towns of Mahommadu and Vukkah stand at the very foot of the south-eastern slope. I am informed that many other Mandingo and Boozie towns are situated on the same [p. 111] side of this range. At Mahommadu, the plain, in a south-east direction, is only interrupted by swells and rolling hills, rising and running in every direction, and marked by no particular feature, except the reddish color of the soil, and their summits ridged with the dwarfish prairie tree before mentioned. The plains are white clay, mixed with beds of iron ore. At Mahommadu, the south-east slope strikes the plain at a great angle; but at Vukkah, it rests upon a series of small table-lands that extend out a half-mile before they finally come down into the plains. The vast spaces of grass and reddish soil are relieved by patches of dense vegetations, marking the gullies and ravines. Heavy blocks of granite are set in the sides of the Vukkah hills, awaiting only to be loosened by the rains to roll from their places to the bottom. At night, the whole country seems on fire, from the burning of the grass.

On January 1st, 1869, we left Vukkah, and reached Ballatah at two P.M. On the road, we passed several streams of water, flowing over granite beds, with a temperature of 58° to 60°, Fahrenheit. We had also passed over three plains, rising one above another, in which lines of trees traced off curious plots and divisions, as if they were purposely laid out for farming.[229] The spaces were filled in with green grass and scattering clumps of trees.

January 2d. From Ballatah, we traveled to the village of Gazzahbue.[230] January 3d, 1869. From Gassabue [*sic*], we reached Gubbewallah, Dowilnyah's residence.[231] The king was still at Ziggah Porrah Zue; but in three days he returned to his own town. Here, though anxious to [p. 112] hasten home, I was obliged to spend some time; since it is contrary to politeness to hurry away from the town of a great chief without having resided with him two or three weeks.[232] All my friends who had arrived from Ziggah Porrah Zue were delighted to see me, and they began to grow solicitous about my returning to their country again. Promises of all kinds were made if I would return; promises of a very peculiar kind were made by the king if I would only return.

The ladies of Wymar seemed no less anxious respecting me; and they frequently asked me why, since I possessed the means of making so many presents, I did not have a number of women to sing and clap hands and proclaim my importance, after the fashion of their great men. To which I replied that such was not the custom of "Weegees," or Americans. They were, however, unwilling that I should go through their country "unhonored and unsung"; they therefore proposed to compliment me with this custom, and merrily fell to clapping and singing; then rising their right hands to the sky, rent the air with their acclamations of praise and flattery.

On Monday, the 25th of January, we took leave of King Dowilnyah. The king presented us with several large country cloths, and a very large and heavy ivory. He had also sent for a horse; but we declined receiving the presents, as we had no one to carry them. He would have furnished us carriers, had it not been that they would have to pass through the Domars, with whom they were not on friendly terms.

About four o'clock P.M., we reached Boe. Here we spent a day to rest. On Wednesday, the 27th of January [p. 113], at four o'clock P.M., we came to Nubbewah's town. King Nubbewah was not at home when we arrived; but late in the afternoon this sick and feeble old man came stalking into the town, followed by his head warrior, and a number of young men, all armed.

In the evening they held a council, and Nubbewah himself delivered a speech with a violence of gesture and voice that little corresponded with the languid, sickly frame from which it came. Mischief was brewing; but where or on whom it would first light, no one of our party could conjecture. We only hoped that it would keep to its first purposes, and not fall on us.

It was a very clear moonlight. About twelve o'clock, Chancellor, who was generally very vigilant whenever there happened to be an unusual stir among the natives, detected one of the young men, with his cutlass gleaming in the moonlight, stealthily lifting up our door-mat. He was suddenly questioned as to what he wanted, which threw him into such confusion that he was only able to stammer out something about fire, and quickly withdrew. Several persons were then seen passing and repassing in the king's court-yard. We immediately concluded that such movements boded no good to us. We aroused our party, and prepared for a general onslaught, which we every moment expected; such being the usual method of these people's attacks. Nubbewah's town contains three thousand people, men, women, and children. The houses are crowded together. The king's own department is shut off from the rest of the town by high fences, and strongly guarded with a number of large Mandingo dogs. It is every way so situated that a petty wickedness can be [p. 114] committed covertly and conveniently enough, and nobody be the wiser.

All the houses are bamboo, and would burn like tinder. I therefore instructed my people that, should Nubbewah attack us, we must immediately set fire to the house we were in, and discharge our muskets into those who came at us first; that amid the hubbub of fire, smoke, and fighting, our chances for escape would be good as any one else's; that we must make for the gate nearest to our house, and march all night for Bokkasah. Our knapsacks were strapped on, our muskets in hand, and the torches blazing in the fire. There was more passing and repassing and distinct whisperings. Success with these people depends upon surprise; our bustling preparation placed a surprise entirely out of the question. In fifteen minutes all was quiet. Every one instinctively felt that the dangerous moment had passed; yet we kept on our guard.

The next morning [Thursday, 28th January 1869] we went to the king, who put on a most intelligent innocence. We made him a small present and immediately left his town. We arrived at Bokkasah at four o'clock P.M.

So far as the manner of carrying arms is concerned, it is always better to observe the usage of the natives. Arms always form a part of the dress of barbarians. The more formidable you can make yourself appear, the better for your peace and safety on these highways of African travel. To seem harmless does not always invoke forbearance; it sometimes suggests plots and attempts on life and property. It was that too much reliance on the simple-heartedness and good feelings of untutored barbarians that got Seymore's right hand [p. 115] nearly slashed off. It is preferable to try every way to induce their good-will, and at the same time to appear to be ready to resist their ill-will. Every person I met on the road was girded with a heavy iron sword, a quiver thrown over the shoulders full of poisoned arrows, and a powerful bow.[233] Adopting this example, I became a moving arsenal. I walked through the whole Boozie country with my bayonet fixed to my musket, my revolvers belted so as to be seen and feared at the same time, my sword swinging and clanging at my side; and when, to prove my *prestige* in arms, I was asked to fire my revolvers, I would draw and blaze away, several barrels going off almost at the same time—a serious defect, to be sure, but regarded in a very different light by my friends. The bulging fullness of my country costume was attributed to the concealment of similar arms, ready to go off at all points. This swaggering style was not without effect; for it was said that I had money to give my friends and arms to fight my enemies. I had almost forgotten to mention that I was informed by Dowilnyah that five principal chiefs were concerned in the assault on Seymore; that not one of them was now living; that their death was accounted as the punishment of God for this act of wickedness.

Seymore, relaxing all caution on account of the uniform good treatment he had received from the natives, thought them incapable of a different conduct. He was seriously convinced to the contrary. When villainy of this kind is to be perpetrated, the greatest secrecy among those who are privy to it is preserved. It is always the act of a few; for the feelings of the mass [p. 116] seem to be averse to such doings. Seymore's affair was mentioned in terms of reprobation by all who conversed with me about the matter. Comma's own son strenuously denied to me that his father had any part in the matter; though it is a fact notorious throughout the country that his father was a principal actor, and that the whole plot was concocted at the town of Boe.[234]

From Bokkasah we came to Fissahbue, on Monday, the 8th of February, 1869. On Tuesday, the 9th, we arrived at Zolu. King Momoru had not, up to this time, been able to effect a reconciliation between the parties. Every day they made reprisals on each other. While I was there, the Boozies succeeded in capturing several persons belonging to the Barline people. The wars of these people are, however, not attended with any sanguinary results. They consist mostly in surprising a few individuals where they can be suddenly come upon. Sometimes the roads are waylaid wherever their respective traders are supposed to pass. These, together with some other petty annoyances, constitute their principal mode of warfare. The large walled towns are seldom taken. Pitched battles are seldom fought; and even when these people may be said to take the open field, most is done by some war chief by way of displaying his individual prowess. If they were to indulge too much in war, they could never have the numerous and large markets with which their country is everywhere dotted.[235]

Tuesday, the 16th of February, 1869, we started from Zolu, passed the Boozie towns of Yahwuzue, Kaulitodah, Wuzugahzeah. On the road we met Beah, [p. 117] our Mandingo guide, with some Bokkasah traders, who informed that the Americans had carried war against Manna.[236] We halted at Powlazue. Wednesday, the 17th of February, we passed Zolaghee and its large creek, running over a bed of red feldspar granite. Thousands of fish, known among us as "bonies," were swimming close to shore, not at all annoyed by the people who were bathing in the same water.

We halted at Moffotah.[237] Thursday, the 18th of February, we passed Malang, Ballah, and Dahtazue, and halted at a small village.[238] On Friday, the 19th of February, we reached Barkomah. Saturday, the 20th, leaving Barkomah, we passed through several villages and the town of Nessahbeah. We halted at Sellayo, at six o'clock P.M.

Sunday, the 21st [February] starting from Sellayo, we passed Barpellum, where we saw a man who had been wounded in four places with a cutlass. He had been beset in the road by some unknown persons; showing, after all, the danger and insecurity of the roads, as well as the folly of traveling unarmed. After four P.M., we reached Totoquella, the residence of King Momoru, where we were received with every demonstration of joy and hospitality. Here we spent some time, in order to avail ourselves of the opportunity of completing calculations of longitude, which, when we were at Boporu, we had been unable to do on account of the weather.[239]

While we were staying at Totoquella, some of the king's people killed an elephant; and instead of beef we had elephant for dinner. The part regarded as a delicacy, and upon which we dined heartily, was the proboscis. He had not yielded his life in a tame, unbecoming [p. 118] manner; his death was attended with the flight of his enemies, the smashing up of gun-stocks, the stamping and rending of saplings. One musket had its barrel literally bent to an angle of ninety degrees. The narrow escape of the hunters themselves suggested to me what might have happened, had I attacked the herd of elephants feeding in the cotton-fields of Ballatah. There the country is open and exposed; here the friendly woods and jungle offer the hunter immediate concealment and protection. The elephants upon the highlands pertinaciously go in herds, and scarcely ever allow themselves to be separated. Intrepid elephant-hunters, accustomed to display firmness and certainty within six paces of a furious charge, are invited to try their prowess with the Ballatah elephants.

[The following texts by Edward Wilmot Blyden and Winwood Reade were inserted between pages 44 and 45 of the original publication. They were printed on paper that was slightly darker than the journal, and the paper was 1 millimeter smaller. The *African Repository* also published these texts in April 1870 (vol. 46, pp. 125–126)].

Just after the journey to Musardu was printed in January, the following letter was received from Rev. E. W. Blyden, Professor in Liberia College:

MONROVIA, FEBRUARY 5, 1870

Rev. J. B. Pinney:

Dear Sir: I have just returned from a brief visit to the Boporo regions.[240] Mr. W. Winwood Reade, an English traveler, author of *Savage Africa*, accompanied me. Rev. G. W. Gibson, of the Episcopal Church, anxious to respond to the urgent calls which are so loudly made for teachers from that quarter, sent out with me one of his candidates for orders to open a school in that country.[241] The King, Momoru was not at Boporo when we reached that town, but at Toto-Coreh, a fortified town ten miles on the east.[242] We proceeded thither, where the king received us in fine style, and especially welcomed the teacher. Two days after we arrived, on Friday, January 21st, he called his principal men together in a large open building in the town, and presented in their presence his own and his brother's children to form the nucleus of a school.

He exhorted the people on the importance of such establishments among them. He said that he himself having lived a little while at Monrovia when a boy—sent thither by King Boatswain, his father—had gained some insight into civilization, which had proved of so much advantage to him, and he only regretted that his knowledge was so exceedingly limited. He now felt grateful for the opportunity afforded him of introducing among the children of the country the advantage of book-learning.

I then read a chapter from the Bible and prayed, after which I took down the names of the boys presented, and gave them primers. They seemed delighted. After introducing to them the teacher—who made a few remarks—and entreating them to be kind to him, I dismissed the assembly by permission of the king. That was a day long to be remembered by all who were present. To me it was a great and solemn privilege. Mr. Winwood Reade, who proclaims himself a free-thinker, and who has not much faith in missions as religious agencies, could not resist the influence of the occasion. He drew up a paper giving his impressions of the [new page] country, etc., which he left with the king. I send you a copy herewith.

Mr. Gibson has assumed a great responsibility in opening a school at Toto-Coreh. I hope he will be sustained by his board. The Episcopalians are thus first in the field; but the field is large and needy.

Copy of a written statement made by Mr. W. Winwood Reade, and left with Momoru, King of the Condo country:

TOTO-KORIE, JANUARY 22, 1870.

I desire to state that having paid a visit to Momoru, King of Boporo, resident in this town, he received me hospitably, and made me a handsome present when I left him.

Momoru is evidently the most powerful king in the regions interior of Monrovia. He possesses the road from Musardu and other inland states to the sea; the whole of their trade is therefore in his hands.

It is my opinion that the favor of this king should be cultivated, not only by the Liberian government, but also by missionaries, travelers, and foreign merchants.

Momoru having received some education in Liberia, has much larger views than most native chiefs. On the present occasion a school having been established under the auspices of Professor Blyden, of Liberia College, he has shown a most laudable desire to further the education of the children of his town; he is also desirous that missionaries, and indeed settlers generally, should take up their abode with him.

Toto-Korie, situated about ten miles east of Boporo, appears to me to be well adapted for a settlement; as a trading station, it offers remarkable advantages, receiving as it does all the produce from the interior; the soil is suitable for all the requirements of a plantation, the situation seems healthy; stores, etc., can be brought up from the settlements in three days; and it is naturally of advantage to those who attempt to exercise a moral and educational influence over these people that their ruler should be well disposed towards projects of that kind, and apparently so well acquainted with the value of knowledge.

(Signed) W. Winwood Reade

Appendix to Benj. Anderson's Journey to Musadu, 1868

Introduction and Historiography

Edward W. Blyden translated the letter that the chief of Musadu, Vafin Dole, sent to the "king" of Liberia by way of Benjamin Anderson, and this was published as a separate appendix.[243] Vafin Dole's scribe, Mohammad Barta, wrote this letter in December 1868.[244] Anderson delivered the letter to President James S. Payne when he returned to Monrovia three months later. Vafin explained how Ibrahmia Sissi, the chief of Medina, ravaged Musadu during the 1860s. Vafin also assured the Liberian leader that he would receive all he " 'desired from our town,' " if God was willing. Liberia was seeking a direct trade route into the interior, and Musadu desired arms—" 'sword and iron.' " The people of Musadu expected the Liberian government to answer the letter, but this never happened. The government's failure to respond was a source of great embarrassment to Anderson when he returned to Musadu in 1874.

The Arabic original and Blyden's translation were sent to Henry M. Schieffelin later in 1869, and he sent the Arabic text and translation to the Smithsonian Institution to be published. The Smithsonian published the original text and English translation as a pamphlet later that year.[245] Some of the pamphlets were sold separately, and others were bound with the version of Anderson's 1869–69 journey, *Narrative of a Journey to Musadu* (1870), reproduced in the preceding chapter. In 1871, H. M. Schieffelin republished the "Appendix" in his *People of Africa* (Schieffelin [1871] 1974, 129–136). The 1868 letter regained significance during the d'Ollone-Anderson controversy of 1903 (see chap. 2).

Historical Contribution of the "Appendix"

Anderson explained how Ibrahima Sissi visited his uncle Amala (Amara) in Musadu, helped Musadu fight the "unbelievers" who lived in the "eastern hills," returned and "plundered" Musadu of "everything valuable," and again went back to threaten Musadu.[246] Anderson wrote:

> From trade we passed to war and politics, and having satisfied all their inquiries in these two particular points with respect to the Tibbabues, they made me acquainted with some of their wars and feuds. They had a special cause of grievance against a certain Mandingo chief whose name was Ibrahima, or Blamer Sissa, and who lived north-east, and three days' walk from Musardu, at a large town called Madina.
>
> It appears that Blamer Sissa came from Madina to visit his uncle, Amalah, who was then residing at Musardu, and that he was treated with great civility and distinction by the Musardu people; that being a powerful young prince, they solicited his aid against some Kaffres, or unbelievers, living over the eastern hills; that in compliance with their solicitation he went back to Ma-

> dina, and soon returned to Musardu, bringing with him his cavalry and infantry, a numerous and formidable mass, who, in the end, came nigh doing their friends at Musardu as much evil as they had done the Kaffres, whom they had mutually agreed to plunder.
>
> Blamer Sissa stripped Musardu of every thing valuable [p. 96], and even carried off nearly all the pretty young women of that town (this chap., 214).

The 1868 letter provided much more detail. According to the letter, Ibrahima came to Musadu at least seven years earlier—in approximately 1861, when he received Vafin Dole's daughter as a wife, and offered a "daughter" as a wife (and some money) to his uncle Amala to establish political alliance with the people of Musadu. Ibrahima agreed to protect Musadu and fight the non-Muslims who lived nearby (but, it would appear later, not the Kamara). Ibrahima fought the unbelievers in the region of Baghna, some 12 miles (20 kilometers) or so east of Musadu.[247] Ibrahima eventually returned to Musadu with his army, although he ordered his slave warriors to continue fighting while he stayed in Musadu with his entourage and troops. Conditions in Musadu became very desperate because Ibrahima's people took all of the food, domestic animals, and women as they deemed fit. People became hungry, the wealthy lost most of their possessions, and the number of poor rapidly increased. Ibrahima then returned to Medina when Musadu could no longer sustain his presence, but returned to Musadu at least one farming season later, after Musadu's economy started to revive. Back in Musadu, Ibrahima "'assaulted'" Salihu Shereef, "'the holy priest of the town,'" and took dozens of slaves, including sixty from Vafin Dole. Working from Musadu as a base, Ibrahima attacked Nionsamoridu, Khulila, and Jilila. Benjamin Anderson arrived in Musadu shortly afterward, and the people of Musadu used his arrival and the military aid that they hoped to secure from Liberia to taunt Ibrahima.

Anderson presented his history in a mode that is similar to the way oral traditions develop over time by compressing Ibrahima's three trips to Musadu into one and giving the impression that this could have happened during a much shorter time span. While the Musadu letter provides many more details than Anderson or Yves Person, it shows that Anderson was generally correct in the information that he gave about "Blamer Sissa," at least from the Musadu perspective.

The letter also supports the dating of the French historian, Person, and attests to the quality of his work, which provides further context. According to Person, Ibrahima Sissi's father, Mori-Ule Sissi, was the first person to initiate a *jihad* or "holy war" from Medina in 1835. Medina was the center for the Islamic state of Moriuledugu, named after the founder Mori-Ule. Medina was located nearly 62 miles (100 kilometers) northeast of Musadu in today's Guinea, near the Côte d'Ivoire border. Mori-Ule conquered the "animists" in Toron to the west and farther south, but was killed in 1845 while fighting the animist stronghold of Kurukoro.[248] Mori-Ule Sissi's son, Sere-Burlay, succeeded his father and led the Sissi from 1848 to 1859. Burlay moved his troops west and defeated the powerful Berete (Bility) in the Gundo region, roughly located about 50 miles (80 kilometers) northwest of Musadu, and tried to force everyone in his domain to convert to Islam.[249] The writer of this appendix identified Burlay as Abdullah, and Ibrahima as Brema.

The Konya-Manding, however, except for the inhabitants of the town of Musadu, revolted and killed Burlay in 1859 in Kurukoro, the same town where his father had been killed. When Burlay's brother, Ibrahima Sissi, became the leader of the Sissi army and prepared to attack the people of Konya in retaliation, Sugba Dole, the chief of Musadu, sent his son Vafin Dole to negotiate the Konya people's submission to Sissi. Sissi agreed not to fight them, but forced them to pay him tribute in return. As a goodwill gesture to gain the support of the Muslims of Musadu, Ibrahima Sissi married Vafin Dole's daughter, Madiya (Person 1968, 1:184–185; 1970, 84–88; Massing 1978–79, 52–53; Geysbeek research). Vafin Dole replaced his father as chief sometime between these events, from 1861 to 1868, when Anderson went to Musadu.

An Exact Fac-Simile of a Letter from the King of Musadu to the President of Liberia, Written by a Young Mandingo at Musadu, in Arabic, in the Latter Part of 1868.

Printed from Photographic Relief Plates, with a translation by the Rev. Edward W. Blyden, Professor in Liberia College. New York: Lithographic, Engraving & Printing Co., 1870.

Translation of an Arabic manuscript written by a young Mandingo at Misadu, the capital of the Western Mandingoes, two hundred miles northeast of Monrovia, for Mr. Benj. Anderson, who visited that town in the latter part of 1868.[250] By E. W. Blyden.

The original is in the possession of H. M. Schieffelin, New York.

Published for distribution, chiefly through the Smithsonian Institution.

In the name of God, the merciful, the compassionate.[251] O God! bless our lord Mohammad and save him. This letter from towns unto a town—from our town to your town; the name of our town is Masādu* (accent on the second syllable) that you may see what misfortunes have happened to our country, and carnage and slavery and hunger and poverty, and every injury, on account of the army.[252]

The king came forth from his town to our town; his name is Ibrahima Sisi, and his mother's name Shiri Sisi, and his father's name Mulul Sisi, and the name of his town and place of residence is Medina.†[253] His father [p. 6]

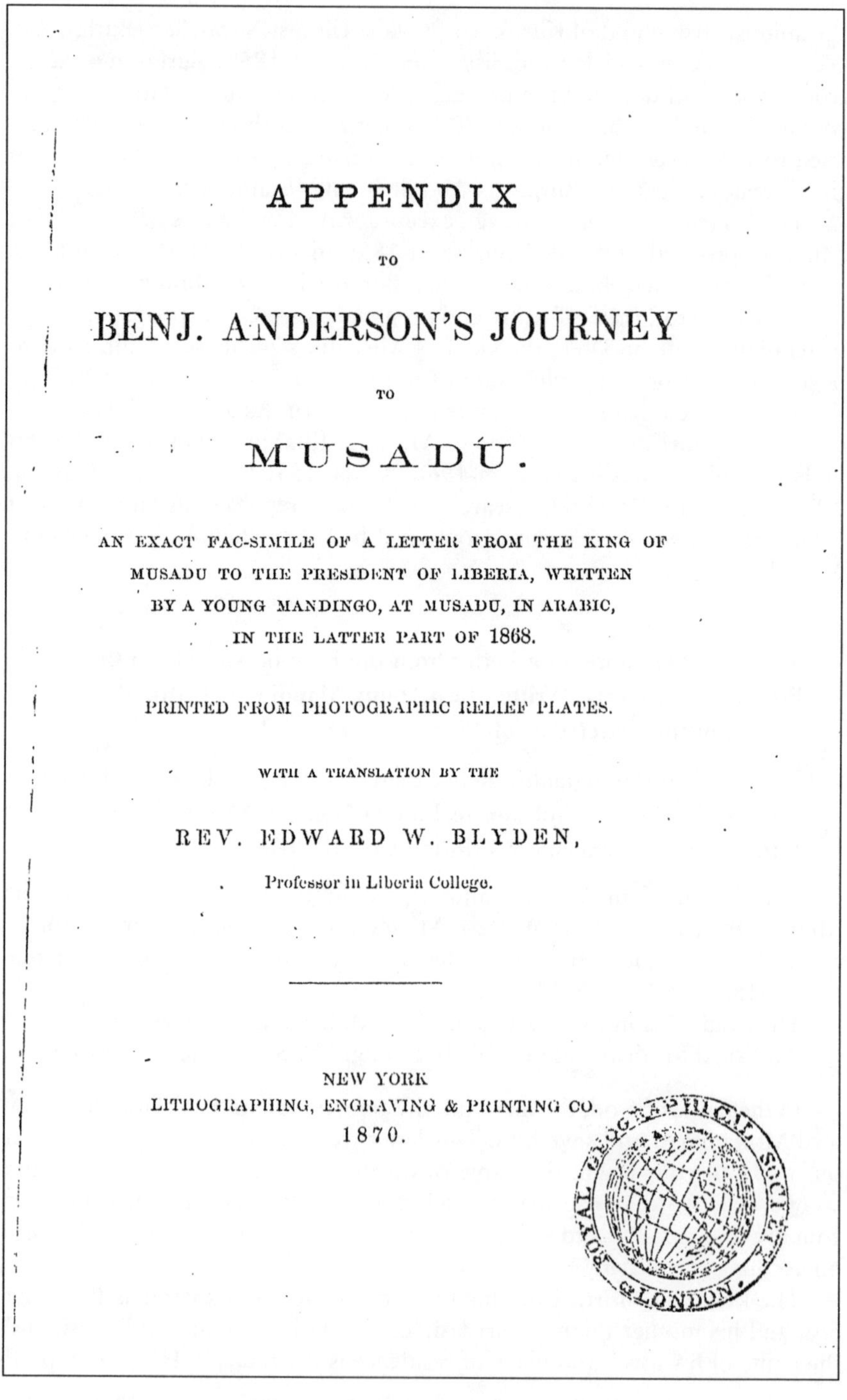

APPENDIX

TO

BENJ. ANDERSON'S JOURNEY

TO

MUSADÚ.

AN EXACT FAC-SIMILE OF A LETTER FROM THE KING OF MUSADU TO THE PRESIDENT OF LIBERIA, WRITTEN BY A YOUNG MANDINGO, AT MUSADU, IN ARABIC, IN THE LATTER PART OF 1868.

PRINTED FROM PHOTOGRAPHIC RELIEF PLATES.

WITH A TRANSLATION BY THE

REV. EDWARD W. BLYDEN,

Professor in Liberia College.

NEW YORK
LITHOGRAPHING, ENGRAVING & PRINTING CO.
1870.

Figure 25. Original front cover of Anderson's "Appendix," 1870.

travelled to your country (i.e. Mesurado). At that time there was a king in your country; his name was Amara. He gave to this king a wife, and gave to all the people of the country plenty of money; then he returned to his town and to his residence Medina (God knows all things). God gave him many children and a large kingdom called Moriuledugu, and he fought for God, and God killed him and he died in war.[254] He left nine male children. The name of the eldest was Abdallah.[255] He fought against the infidels (Kafirs) for God, and the enemy slew him, and he left his brother Ibrahima Sissi above mentioned.[256] Now Ibrahima is king after them. He entered our town on a certain Tuesday.[257] On that day he came to us with horses and a numerous, overwhelming and imprudent army, and entered upon an agreement with us and said, "O ye people of the town of Masādu, I have come with my army to fight against all those around you who are infidels or pagans." And we said, "Very well." And the king said, "I see that the pagans have injured you, and I have seen my father, Mulul Sisi, and my brother, Abdullah, that they fought for God and the Muslims, and I said I will humble them in battle, and there shall be no honor that a child should have his origin from the town of his parents."[258] And the people of the town [p. 7] said, "Preserve thou our honor, do not cause defilement or injury in our town." He said, "Very well; for this army will not injure anything except what I command it." And the people said, "Do what pleases thee, for this town is thine." And the king said, "I am going forth from our town that I may fight their towns who troubled you, and fight the Kafirs around you. Have you not heard the saying of the prophet (God bless him), I command that you fight men until they say there is no God but God."[259] And they said, "Yes, we have heard it, and we know it." And they said, "Do what thou hast said." And when he perceived that the people of the town were pleased with his speech, he went with his numerous and arrogant army and fought against the people of a town called Baghna, and returned to us and entered our walled town and our houses.[260] When he [Sissi] perceived that the believers had cut off relations between themselves and the pagans, and had destroyed all marriage connections between them, and had destroyed friendship, he [Ibrahim Sissi] said to the leaders of the slaves (the number of the leaders of the slaves was nine), "Fight, do not let (the enemy) gather one with another until they become numerous.[261] Gather yourselves together, and go around them and attack them on all sides. Every one who [p. 8] attempts to escape, capture for us, keep him or kill him. I will sit in the capital of the country, Masādu, with numerous boys and the large army."

And when he (the king) [Sissi] saw fowls in the town (Masādu) he took them, or goats or sheep or women, he took them for himself. And when he saw cows in the possession of any one he said, "Give them to me for the sake of the religion; I will give you slaves." When he said, "companion of the faith" he struck them and captured them, and he said, "These are the enemies of my father." And the people of the town said to him, "Desist, there is not in our town any money or food. Hunger has taken possession of us, and many of our children and slaves have either died or fled to our enemies on account of hunger; and all our rich men have become poor, and the poor have become numerous. Slaves have taken our female children to themselves without compensation." And when the king perceived the poverty of the people of the town, that they had neither money nor food nor power, he returned with his army to his town (Medina).

The chief [Vafin Dole] of the town (Masādu) then said, "O ye people of the town, plant, plant." And when the people of the town planted, they found food and money and calves from [p. 9] the pasture, and cows and sheep and goats and fowls and an abundance of food. And when he (Ibrahima) heard that God had produced for the people of the town [Musadu] whom he had abandoned, a greater abundance of everything, he returned to us with the army, and broke the agreement between us and our neighbors, both Muslims and Pagans. And when they [Ibrahima Sissi and his army] desired the journey to their home and to their country, they took from us the best in our town and our houses, our goods and our children and our wives and our neighbors and our slaves; and they said, "When we have removed their slaves and their children and their wives, they shall sweat with us."

And when we [the people of Musardu] heard this saying from them, the chief and king of the town, Fanfi Doreh, with his companions said, "O ye people of the town, do ye see the king and his army, how all that he has said he does not do it, and he does not desire it, except the destruction of the town." When he came he said, "I will fight for the Muslims," but he has had no one to fight against except Muslims, and there are no slaves except Muslims, and there are no poor except Muslims. The Kafirs have escaped from the calamities of the army. And say the Kafirs to us, "O ye Muslim people, help came to you to assist you against [p. 10] us." And this was a taunt from the Pagans to the Muslims. This was the king's weakness before the Kafirs. And we were in this condition for seven years. The king [Ibrahima Sissi] was a Muslim and all the people of his army were Kafirs except a few. And there was not one of the people of the town [Musadu] but feared when it was said, "The army is on the road." Men fled from their misfortunes. And all the wealthy people in our town had not anything left in their hands except one or two or three slaves; all were poor on account of the army, and we spurned them (the army); and the people of the town lost many things, and none but God can number them; and our king, whose name is Fanfi Doreh, lost sixty slaves.

On a certain day we [the people of Musadu] saw the people of the army, and they entered a town below us toward the west, and the name of the town was Yusumudu.[262] They attacked it until they spoiled the houses and broke down the walls and made the farms to suffer; and they wasted another town below us on the west; the name of this town is Khulila.[263] And when they returned to their town [Medina], some came to our town (Jilila) and they killed in it one hundred and eighty sheep and goats, and the people of that town were Muslims.[264] For this reason the people of our town [Musadu] refused their friendship [p. 11], reproached them, and did not say "Peace" to them. We thought that they were helpers of the religion of Mohammad, but they were not helpers of Islam, but they destroyed the religion of Islam. They were disobedient to God and followed Satan; and therefore I take refuge in God* from their punishment and their wickedness.[265] May God preserve us from them and from the evil of many visits from them. They [Ibrahima and his army] reviled the holy priest of the town [Musadu], and assaulted him, taking his garment from his loins and even his cap from his head, and they outraged him and dragged him over the ground, and they greatly damaged him with their feet; his name was Salihu Shereef.[266] They laid waste and destroyed all the treasures of the country. And no one knows the number of their evil deeds, and how to describe them, but God.

When they [Ibrahima and his army] entered the town [Musadu] they made the greater portion of the inhabitants of the town poor and destitute and vile, even the learned men became poor. If it had been known to us what they would to do us before it took place, we should certainly have driven them away, and they would not have entered. Says Hariri, in the Makamot, "We said they are weak and we are weak; they are men [p. 12] and we are men". . .*[267] They will not ever enter into our town. Verily God is mighty, and verily there is a refuge in God, and every man should seek to serve God in everything.

And, during this state of things, we learned on a certain day that there was a messenger [Benjamin Anderson] on the path from Durukoro to us, from a place on the west and its environs, and we [the people of Musadu] said, "Praise be to God for that. This is our wish and our ardent desire."[268] The army took from our town seven men, and selected the best of them, and some of their slaves, fifty belonging to some and under [*sic,* another] fifty belonging to others. Seven children of our town and the Imam saved themselves by flight. We said to the messenger, Ben Anderson, say to the king who sent thee to us as follows: "We have seen thy messenger.[269] Our town is not in its former condition. The king (Ibrahima) has troubled us. The army entered into our town and threw us into confusion. Assist us with iron and sword, and with everything. Thou knowest that he [Benjamin Anderson] has been a help. Thou lovest us and we love thee, and our refuge is in God and in thee, and in thy assistance and thy companionship. Give us whatever is in thy kingdom. Thy messenger has seen [p. 13] us in affliction on account of the war which has come to us. O my friend, when thou desirest to travel to us do not doubt or be troubled on account of our affairs. Come without doubt on account of the love between us and thee.

"There is Mohammed, called in our language, 'Sabsu,'* when thy messenger reaches him he reaches to us, and when our messenger reaches to him he reaches to thee; and likewise presents from thee to me may come through Mohammed, and presents from me to thee by the same means.[270]

"Oh, Mohammad Sabsu,† I visit thee, but thou dost not visit me, for my two children are with thee (in thy hand), viz., Nafaribu Mohammad and Maliki, thou keepest them for me.[271]

"Oh, Christians and Jews,‡ when ye desire to send to us, send to Mohammad Sabsu, and when your messages reach him, his servant Kuhi will forward them, for he loves us; and all that you desire from our town you will find, if it please God, according to your letter.[272] I am king of the army in our town, the protector of this large town. This town is the mother of the country—the name is Masādu.[273] Success is from God, if it pleases God. There is no strength or power but in God, the exalted, the mighty. The word is finished which I wished in this letter, and I pray for thee, O friend, that God may keep thee from the army and all its mischiefs. Peace upon Mohammed and the family of Mohammad.["]

The name of the writer of this book is Mohammad Barta. I have no learning—I seek learning. I am but a boy, but I think that there are learned men among us. The name of his father is Ibrahima, and of his mother Ayesha.[274] Success is from God.

Figure 26. Facsimile of the original letter sent with Anderson to the President of Liberia from the people of Musadu. *From Anderson's "Appendix," 1870.*

بسم الله الرحمن الرحيم صلى الله على سيدنا محمد هذه رسالة من بلاد الى بلد من بلدنا
الى بلدكم واسم بلدنا مساده وان انكر كم ما كان في الارض ضنا من المصيبة والقتل والعبيد
والجوع والبغر وكان فقر بسبب الجيش وكان الملك خارج من بلدنا [illegible] الى بلدنا اسمه
ابراهيم سسو واسم امه شرسسو واسم ابيه ملول سسو واسم بلده وداده مدين
وابنه سفر الى بلدكم حينئذ كان ملك في بلدكم هو عمر وعطاه المال واعطى
اهل البلد كلهم اجمعين المال كثيرا ورجع الى داره الى بلده مدين وعلم الله علما
كثيرا اعطى الله ولدا كثيرا وملكا عظيما وقتل الله ثم مات في الجهد وترك ولده عدده
تسع ذكرا واسم كبيرهم عبد الله وقتل كفار الله ثم قتل عدوه وترك اخونه
ابراهيم المذكور في اول الكلام ابراهيم سسو كان ملك بعدهما ودخل في
بلدنا ذات يوم يقال قلت لها اسم اليوم دخل فيه علينا كثير سوء لان ذاب مع
الجيش العرمرم عامر ودخل في المصلحات علينا وقال يا اهل البلد مساده ان
قد جاني مع الجيش ليقتلوا كل من كان حولكم من الكفار وقلنا نعم قال [illegible]
الملك اني ان الكفار قد ضركم وقال رايت ابي ملول سسو واخواني هو
عبد الله سسو قد قتلوا الله والمسلمين وقال انا فتح عليهم في القتل ولا يجد
او بحثة الولد عن موضع والده وقال اهل البلد انت حفظت حرمتنا لا تجعل الفساد
في بلدنا قال نعم لا وهذا الجيش لا يفسد كل شيء الا ما امرت الا ما امرتهم وقال
اهل البلد افعل ما شئت لان هذا البلد لك وقال الملك اني خارج من بلدنا ان يقتل
البلد اهم قد ضركم وقتل من حولكم من الكفار اما سمعتم قول النبي صلى الله
امرت ان اقاتل الناس حتى يقولوا لا اله الا الله وقالوا نعم سمعته وعلمه قالوا افعل
ما تقول به فلما علم الملك رضي اهل البلد على ما قاله ذهب مع الجيش الكثير
عاوم وقتلوا الكفار ان البلد اسمه بغز اسم بلد ورجعوا الينا ودخل علينا في بلدنا
ان في ذاوتنا ودورقا اسو فلما علم ان المومنين قد قطع الرحام بينه والكفرين وفساد
النكاح بينهم وفساد الحب قال الجلجهفاه لعبدهم وعدد ملك العبد تسع وقلهم
ملك كل واحد منهم قتال لا يجمع بعضهم على بعض لكثيرة جمعتهم قال لهم
اجمعوا ونجوا عليهم واتفقوا حولهم كل من يهرب منه اخذه الينا او
استره او قتلوا انا جلست في ام القرى او هي مساده واسم البلد مع غلام كثير

عدد عبيدهم تحت خمسون وبعضهم سواء وكلهم صار وغيرو بعضهم اشتروا انفسه وهولاء سبعة
والذ بلد ثاو صاحب البلد وقلنا الرسول بير بن انسن قل الملك الذي اوسلك الينا هو خمري يمر ذيبه
ورايت وسالكا وو الملك ليس بلدنا على حال فد يمر قد ضرتا الملك ذهب في بلدنا ابنتريا وكثير
ومنزلنا في حركة الجيش اسم مرد يمر ذيبه زاجمع عنا وانصرقا بالحديد سيف ومليع يه فج وانصر
نا بكل شيء انت تعلم انه معوو وانت تحب الينا وانا فحبك وملاذ بالله وبك وعونك وتبعك واعطاني
مرو واعطاني كلما في ملكك وسولك ويتني في ضيق القتل بسبب اقبل الينا يا حبيبي اذا اراد ترسل
علينا لا شك ولا تحيير في امرنا اني بعدد قبلك جاني بلا شك وبسبب الحب بيني وبينك هو محمد في
كلمنا سابس محمد اذ بلغ وسلك عليه بلغ علي واذ ابلغ وسولي عليه بلغ عليك وكذالك العطى اذا
عطاني بمال ابلغ الى محمد واذا اعطاك بمال ابلغ علي محمد يا محمد سابس محمد اقي او وو ك ولا ازووق لاو
ولد في يدك اثنين هما فعرب محمد مالك انت كلتهما الي يا النصارى يا يهود يا اذا اود وا ويرسل
الينا بلغ علي سابس محمد واو بلغ رسلكم عليه فد عيد ك هو تكه فيلهم وهو احب علي ذيمر ذيبه وكلما
احب مر بلد فا يجد اوشاء الله مسبب وسلك وانا ملك الجيش في بلد ثاو وحرمة هذ البلد عظيم انت
تطلبه بفضل الله علي تميرك بسبب ذالك الى بلد ثاو هذه البلد ام القرى واسمه مساد وي بالله التوفيق
اوشاء الله لا حول ولا قوة الا بالله العلي العظيم تمت الكلام في اواده في هذ الخط وانا نطلب
منك يا حبيبي مر كلما حفظنا الله به في الجيش وغيرها وامر كلهم اجمعين صل علي محمد وعلي ال محمد

واسم هذا الخط محمد برتي ليس لنا علم وانا [illegible] طالب العلم وصبي ولكن كثر العلماء لنا واسم
ابيه ابراهيم واسم امه عايشة سسر في كلمنا مع سنس يا الله التوفيق

انا كتبته [illegible] عبد الكريم لسبب المال اسم كتبه
فلميا سيع وابيه سه مر سبع وامه مسيكر

6

Benjamin J. K. Anderson, 1874

NARRATIVE OF THE EXPEDITION DESPATCHED TO MUSAHDU BY THE LIBERIAN GOVERNMENT UNDER BENJAMIN J. K. ANDERSON, SENIOR, ESQUIRE IN 1874.

Edited by Frederick Starr, Monrovia, Liberia: College of West Africa Press, 1912.

Introduction

"The interior of Liberia is still the least known part of Africa."[1] Liberians themselves have contributed little to our knowledge of their hinterland. In 1858, President Benson sent two Liberians, Seymour and Ash, into the interior and a description of their journey appeared in England in the Proceedings of the Royal Geographical Society in 1860. In 1868, Benjamin J. K. Anderson, a Liberian, was supplied with funds by American friends, chiefly Henry M. Schieffelin, for making a journey toward the Liberian frontier. The report of his expedition was printed in book form in New York in 1870, under the title *Narrative of a journey to Musahdu, the Capital of the Western Mandingoes.* This book has now become rare and it was reprinted, in whole or part, in W. H. Heard's *The Bright Side of African Life,* which appeared at Philadelphia in 1898.[2] In 1874, Mr. Anderson was authorized by the Liberian government to make a second expedition into the same region and on his return made a report to the authorities. This report should have been promptly printed by the Liberian government, for several reasons. The expedition was sent out by the government; it was a contribution to knowledge of Liberia made by a Liberian; it had possible political bearings.[3] It was not, however, printed at all until several years later and then privately, in installments in *The Observer,* a newspaper printed at Monrovia.[4] This paper had but a limited circulation and is today inaccessible to students. The report of Anderson's journey of 1874 is as good as unpublished. Various writers, especially French writers, have claimed that Anderson's works are unreliable and have even raised the question whether he ever went to Musahdu.[5] Now that Liberia's hinterland is really being penetrated and examined, it should be an easy matter to test his veracity. It seems to be to the interest of geographical science to have Anderson's report available. Whatever the merits or demerits of his work, they can only be known if the document itself is accessible. If Anderson's journeys are substantiated and his reports verified, he deserves great credit as having been practically the only Liberian, who has made a direct contribution to geographical literature.

I have believed it worth while to place this report before the public. The present edition of 500 copies has been printed by the generous aid of Dr. O. L. Schmidt of Chicago, whose interest in history and science is known and appreciated by a large circle of friends.

Frederick Starr

Monrovia, October 15, 1912.

NARRATIVE OF THE EXPEDITION DESPATCHED TO MUSAHDU, BY THE LIBERIAN GOVERNMENT IN 1874 UNDER BENJAMIN ANDERSON, ESQR.

The expedition consisted at first, of Peter P. Capehart, Assistant Commissioner and six carriers namely: Jos [*sic,* James] Lawrence, W[illiam] N. Yates, Robert Johnson, Joshua Simms, Henry Harrison, and Jno. [*sic,* John] Thomas.[6]

Having been furnished by the Government with the necessary means, I left Monrovia: Wednesday, May 6th. A. D. 1871 [*sic,* 1874] at 7½ o'clock a.m. and proceeding up the St. Paul's River touched at Virginia and took in Assistant Commissioner Capehart.[7] We reached Mr. Washington's wharf at 7½ o'clock p.m. and were till 8½ o'clock unloading, owing to a heavy storm of rain, and wind, the banks of the wharf being steep and slippery.[8] The next day [Thursday, 7 May] we proceeded to Careysburg and arranged to have the goods transferred thither, Mr. Washington having very kindly housed our

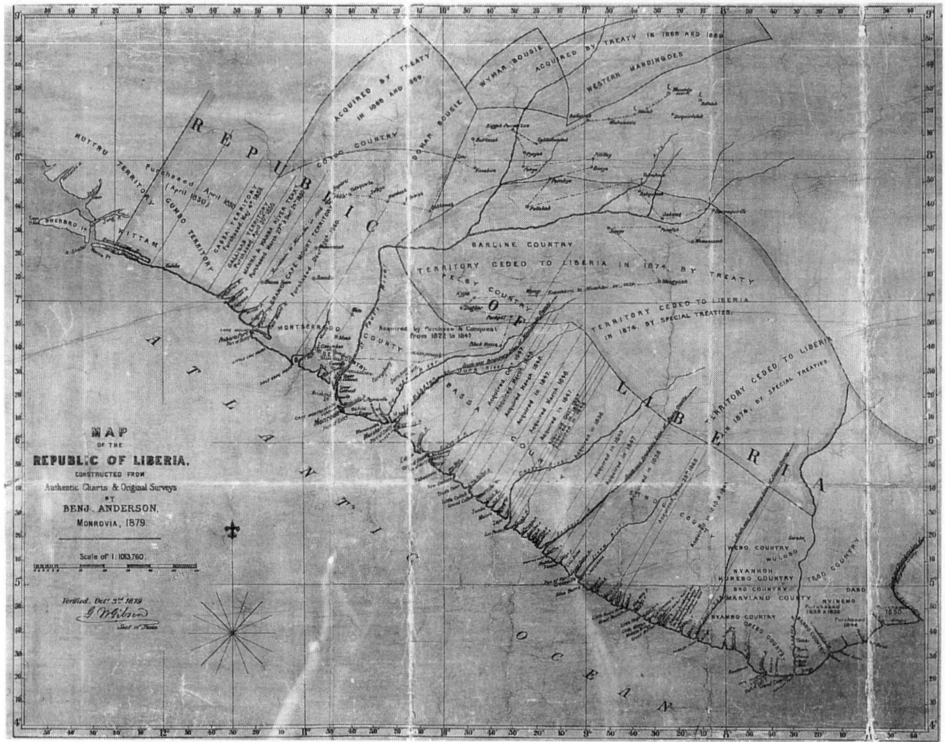

Figure 27. "Map of the Republic of Liberia Constructed from Authentic Charts and Original Surveys by Benjamin Anderson, Monrovia, 1879." *Courtesy of Public Records Office, London.*

effects until we could make such arrangement, free of charge.[9] Having succeeded in this, our next effort was to prepare for our journey in the interior, and having arranged the goods, etc. in convenient parcels for conveyance, it turned out that our baggage carriers were not sufficient by eight or nine men. Considerable time was spent in procuring hands, as very few persons could be found who were willing to venture even so far as the Pessey country on account of the wars and it was solely owing to the indefatigable efforts of Mr. James B. Dennis of Careysburg who did all he could to induce people to go with us that we were able to get off as soon as we did.[10] Every body dreading both the wars and the weather. On Monday 18th of May, we started from Careysburg; the road was all mud, creeks and marshes; one of the carriers, Johnson, fell into a creek and made an ugly cut under his left eye, besides wetting his kingjar of goods.[11] We spent two days at a small village called Gaystown in drying our goods and re-arranging our travelling-

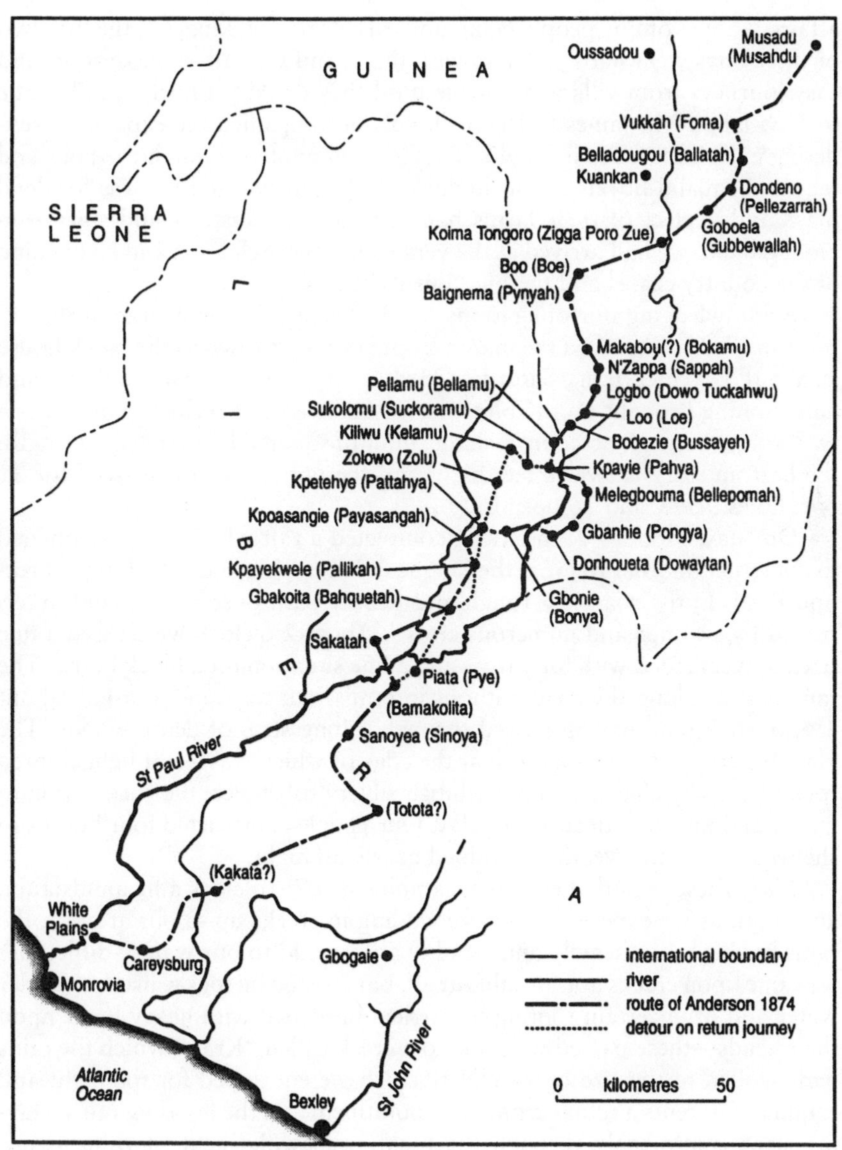

Map 11. Benjamin Anderson's journey, 1874.

affairs.[12] Some of our people being unused to carrying kingjars, the first two or three days went hard and sore with them, and we had to make short and easy journeys from village to village until they could get fairly [p. 6] broke to such labor. Mr. James B. Dennis kindly accompanied the expedition rendering every assistance he could. Having been piloted through the bogs and fens and squalid hovels of our idolatrous Queahs whose fondness for devil plays and neglect of their farms had caused much distress and starvation among them, we had arrived at the very edge, where clearing and an opening of the country ceases and the big "bush" begins.[13]

Acknowledging our obligations to Mr. Dennis, I took charge of the expedition and commenced the march from Simpson's town to the block house at about 1 o'clock p.m., Saturday 23rd of May, and by hard walking and half running brought up the block house between 6–7 o'clock p.m.[14] It is a two story structure, octagon in shape, built of squared logs ten feet in length; the bottom story is twelve feet high, and the upper six feet; pierced for 32 port holes below and 16 upstairs.[15]

On May, Monday 25th having completed a raft which we were obliged to construct in order to cross the Duqueah River—we started taking a direction E. N. E; the road is a rough and pebbly path over rolling land, interrupted by swamps and numerous creeks. About 2 o'clock we crossed a fine stream overshaded with lofty trees and a fine situation for a block house. The rain beat us along the road without intermission; we came to a halt about 4½, o'clock p.m. having passed through a long strip of dense woods. The place we stopped at was a creek at the edge of which was a soft light colored rock plentifully charged with a whitish silvery substance; the rock was laminated and mixed with seams of clay. Our people constructed four booths to shelter us from the weather. It rained nearly all night.

May, Tuesday 26th. Left this encampment at 7½ o'clock a.m. amidst rain, and soon, as we expected, we were wading in creeks up to our armpits, the rains having set in heavily and steadily and to add to our watery difficulties we came upon creeks not fordable at all, but crossed on logs waist deep under water and of uncertain footing to carriers burdened with heavy loads upon their heads—these passed we came to a creek called "Krah" which the rains had swollen to the size of a small river, so we encamped for the night and found in our tents a refuge from disappointment and the flooding rains. Having slept comfortably through the night, we awoke next morning (May, Wednesday 27th.) to belabor the tall trees standing on both sides of the river, with [p. 7] our hatchets, and succeeded in securing a dry and sure footing across this creek after a whole day's hard work. Our rice food in the mean time having given out, we had to subsist on palm cabbage and the tender buds of rattan, vegetable substances that the elephants had made rather scarce in that neighborhood, it being the region where these enormous quadrupeds usually roam and feed.[16]

At night it poured from the heavens and tested the capabilities of our tents to resist the weather, but these cloth shelters proved equal to the occasion. Our beds being elevated two feet from the ground, and our kingjars placed under our beds on poles laid lengthwise, were effectually protected from the weather. But for tents, both men and goods would have been drenched. Not over two hundred yards from our tents, our people in walking around discovered where several elephants had been feeding and perhaps eyeing our fires and tents.[17]

Thursday, May 28th. The creek had fallen 8 feet; but this would not have permitted us to ford it, for it was still from 10 to 12 feet deep and we did well to throw the large trees across it the day before. The rains had rendered the whole country a quagmire interrupted by long strips of dense woods. Such weather is entirely unfit for travelling. To a dense, damp and dreary wilderness succeeds the boggy quagmire and the swampy quagmire succeed creeks now swollen to small rivers; and the whole weary day is spent in walking, wading and swimming, pelted all along as we go by an intensely cold and pitiles[s] rain. We crossed three very large creeks, two of which had considerable falls; in the third we lost a gun but succeeded in recovering it—one of my people diving for it. Arrived at Pockpar's town at about 4½ o'clock p.m.[18]

May, Friday 29th. At Pockpar's town. This is a Pessey town situated on the South-Eastern edge of the Pessey country on a tributary of the Junk river.[19] The king was absent when we arrived, but he came to his town on Saturday [30 May]. Some of my people became greatly dissatisfied because I do not ration them with rice, fowls and goats.

June, Monday 1st. We had an interview with the king and read the law to him, making him to understand it in his own language, section by section. We then stated to him in familiar conversation the purpose of the government with reference to opening and keeping open, the road; and stopping the wars.[20] The King in his turn made us acquainted with the causes of the present troubles and disturbances in [p. 8] the country; the details of which though it was taken down at the time, it would be useless to give in this report. We made the king a suitable Present, and on Saturday June 6th. at 8 o'clock a.m.[21] we left this town taking a direction E and N E, and reached Kypah's at 2½ o'clock p.m.[22] This is a small village of sixty or seventy thatch and clay houses with nothing very important either in character of the people or in the features of the country. Kypah is an old chief of very pacific disposition and spends much of his time in reconciling differences between his neighbors. While there he got us to adjust a difficulty between himself and another chief named Dogbar, living N. West from him. Kypa [Kypah] accused Dogbar, of kidnapping his daughter; both parties having appeared before us and made their statement, Dogbar at once simplified the matter by simply demanding the money he had paid on the girl, which enabled us to give judgment quickly and equitably by remanding the girl to her father and ordering the money to be returned to Dogbar.[23]

On Friday, 12th of June, we went from Kypa's town to Dogbar's.[24] Dogbar informed us that Pockpar and Kypa had acted without consulting the other heads of the country; namely Seaway, Dogbar[,] Fuella and Darpella.[25] He said that Pockpar and Kypa had done the same when W. S. Anderson had visited them; that was the reason we were not on the great Barline road, but were carried in roundabout paths [to the south of the Barline road] so that some persons might get money out of us. He proposes to call [on] the Kings living on Barline road near him, that they might consult about the road.[26]

Saturday 13th of June. News came to town that Waugi, a powerful chief living east of Kypa's town had sent war upon Pockpar, burnt his town, captured his people and killed the King himself, and that they would soon attack Dogbar's town, where we were then: we made preparation at once to defend the place and kept guard regularly. The whole country was in a state of alarm. The people of Dogbar were so cowardly that they were afraid to stay and defend their own town, but as soon as night came on would go out to conceal themselves in the huts of old farms leaving their town to be defended by us. One evening when they were about to exercise this cowardly precaution, our men stacked their arms across the path leading to the gate itself.[27] The poltroons thus confined found various excuses and expedients to sneak out of the town [p. 9].[28]

My own people soon commenced to show signs of uneasiness and apprehension and openly expressed a wish to return home, declaring that it was impossible to go through a country so filled with war. I tried to allay their fears as well as I could. One night just before they were ordered on guard they came in a body to persuade me to return; they had before been holding frequent conferences among themselves. They declared their fears to me, to proceed any further on account of the wars, they wished to get me to agree with them to return. I told them I was determined not to return unless there were stronger reasons than those they alleged. I further told them that in order to get me to return home they would have to write and sign a paper stating that they of their own will refused to proceed any further and that they took the government property as they were responsible for its conveyance and protection and had compelled me to return home with it; that by giving me such a paper they might perhaps force me to return. They afterward grew ashamed and returned to their duty.

Dogbar requested that we would stay with him a little while, as the war was reported to be raging all around the country; we consented. He also instructed us to send for Darpella who was in friendship with Waugi in order that he might be sent to Waugi's to propose a conference of all the chiefs, together with the Commissioners, that all difficulties might be talked over and settled. Darpella was sent for, came and readily accepted—went to

Waugi's and informed him of what we proposed and prepared the way for our visiting that Chief without causing any fears on his part.

June Thursday 18th.[29] Left Dogbar's and came again to Kypa's [town] where we had called all the kings of the country; here we made an attempt to settle all differences and to combine them together; the Chiefs consisted of Kypa, Dogbar, Dogfella, Seefray and Darpella.[30] They agreed to open and clean the road and to have no more feuds among themselves. We showed the folly of allowing Golah people to come into their Country, plunder and devastate every thing and then return to their own home loaded with spoils—they all condemned it and declared they would not encourage such a thing again.[31]

On Friday 19th of June we started from Kypa's and went to Waugi's. After four hours walk over a tremendous hill mean Eastward direction we came to Waugi's town situated on a considerable elevation.[32] The town was filled with armed men, a mixed crowd of Golahs, Veys, Pesseys [p. 10] and Haumths armed to the teeth.[33] The king himself was not seen as he was said to be in consultation with the chiefs of the war band. He afterwards came forth and received us. The war play afterward began, all of them dancing around in a circle. Zodoponga, Golah chief and one of Waugi's allies in this war called myself, Capehart and one of the men in the ring and commenced a series of impertinent questions which in the end made me angry.[34] Such as "where did you all come from? Who sent you? To what chiefs were you sent?" To which he received answers equally insolent and very unsatisfactory. Waugi immediately interfered and put a stop to proceedings that were fast engendering a row.

But the Golah and Vey people recognized in us their friends and acquaintances, and gave themselves very little trouble about who ever might be displeased with us. They jocularfly [jocularly] told us how they had followed us, dogged and watched our movements; how we had kept them from taking Pockpar's town before they did—spoke with eontempt [contempt] of the Pessey people; and wanted to know why we had not passed through their Country as they knew better how to treat Americans than any other tribes.[35] When they conversed with each other they would do so in English.[36] The smallest piece of leaf tobacco or pinch of salt was received with thankfulness. Whenever they went out foraging they would come and get our people to carry along with them that we might get our share. Waugi had purchased this war from Fahquaqua for the special purpose of destroying Pockpar's town.[37]

On Saturday 21st [*sic,* 20th] of June we had interview with king Waugi; he gave us a sheep for our breakfast. We read and explained to him the act of the Legislature and thoroughly informed him of the object of our mission to his country, to all of which he readily agreed.[38] He then explained the causes of the present war and brought witnesses to prove that Pockpar had stopped the path and had made his people conceal themselves in the bush and had shot several of his (Waugi's) people and taken his cattle: this Pockpar had done several times; and that he, Waugi, could not send a bullock or a boy but what Pockpar was sure to stop them, shooting the boys and taking the bullocks.[39] Even the war which he, Waugi, now had, Pockpar had first purchased it from Fahquaqua to fight the Gibbee people—and nearly all the Golahs got killed by the Gibbee people.[40] So after they were whipped, they went to Pockpar for compensation for their losses but he failed to give them any satisfaction, [p. 11] and the Golahs considered the war as being still in Pockpar's country at the beck and call of any one who chose to purchase their services.

He, Waugi, had therefore taken advantage of this state of things and had purchased them to make war against the very people they came to fight for. The complete overthrow of Pockpar was the result. The king further informed us that since this end was accomplished he would send the war home; and that the country should be not further disturbed by it.

We tried to induce the king to compose all differences between himself and the surrounding chiefs; and a council was at that time being held in the town for that purpose as we had accordingly arranged it through Darpella.

Being wearied with the squabbles and petty broils of the Pessey people, I was determined to tarry no longer in this section of the country; but to push on to Barline.[41] The king engaged to furnish me with the same guides that had conducted W. S. Anderson to that country in 1871 [*sic*, 1870]; there were however the usual delays that always attend any arrangement made with our country people.

Provisions were scarce, but there was no day that we did not obtain something to eat, and we could not expect regular supplies of food in a country desolated and disorganized by war.[42] My people, who before, at Dogbar's, where they were supplied with abundance of food—had discovered a childish disposition to return home, now grew outrageous in their clamors. It was simply amusing to see men showing fears about wars that had not even dared threaten, much less attack them. It will now be shown, that this very war respecting which there was so much dread, was chiefly instrumental in carrying out the intentions of the Government.

Between the hours of nine and eleven o'clock, Assistant Commissioner Capehart came to me and said he was going home: this announcement seemed to me rather simple and sudden, for there had been no misunderstanding, no altercation, no difference of opinion between us as to conducting of the Expedition; and it was known to Capehart, that we were to go, as soon as we got our guide to Barline. True I had remarked that there was not hearty co-operation on the part of Capehart in assisting me to quiet the fears of the men—but yet I expected his adherence in this business of the Government.

I replied to Capehart that if he abandoned his post in that manner [p. 12], it would be an act of desertion and so accounted by the Government. He said that he was able to satisfy the Government as to the propriety and reason of his act; and he persuaded the men to the same effect. They were however not altogether sure of his ability to do so; and there was a hesitancy in two or three to join those who wished to abandon the Expedition and return home, but being severely scolded by their companions for not being all of one mind they reluctantly consented to join in returning. They now began to invent, in my hearing sufficient reasons for going back, that they could get nothing to eat. They were however stinted in nothing that could procure them food, and beside we all shared alike and ate at the same time. It was nothing but the simple desire to go home, that animated them. It was the result of a conspiracy to return, begun at Dogbar's where they had abundance. Their movement was now entirely under the management of Capehart, and towards the close of the day they would get together and sing:—

"Far way from home, Far way from home
"Far way from home Capt'n Capehart, far way from home.
"I don't want to go up there, go up there, go up there.
"I don't want to go up there, too far away from home."

Meaning that they did not wish to go to the Mandingo Country through the Barline Country where war was then rampart [rampant] from one end of that region to the other.

About 11 o'clock Thursday, June 25th, the following individuals headed by Capehart, abandoned the Expedition carrying their arms with them, namely, James Lawrence, Congo, William Yates, Congo, Joshua Sims, American, Henry Harrison, Congo, John Thomas, Congo, Andrew Givens, American, Richard Lambright, American, Thos. White, American, Thos. Wadworth, Golah, Robert Johnson, American—Six Americans, Four Congos, and one Golah, leaving but these men remaining with me, Geo. Wadsworth, American, Daniel Coleman, American, and Robert Smith, Congo.[43] Every influence was brought to bear upon those three men to make them desert; but they faithfully adhered to their duty. Six of these people abandoning Government property, tents, ammunition, merchandise, books, instruments, etc., had been regularly hired according to law; had drawn up a contract and taken an oath to perform their duty, and had also received an advance from the Government. The act elicited the sympathy of all the natives of the town and they visited my house in numbers to assure me [p. 13] of my perfect safety. The king [Waugi] declared that he would send me on to Barline without them; and he could not understand how people in government service, were at liberty to abandon it whenever they pleased, and go back home. Thus it was that the Government business was shamefully abandoned, and had our barbarians acted as atrociously as our people had acted dastardly and devoid of all sense of honor, and of duty, the few of us who remained would have assuredly had our throats cut, and all of the Government goods would have been plundered.

I expected my full share of vexation and perplexity when Providence gave a turn to my affairs but little expected by myself.

Early on Tuesday morning, June 30, Zodopanga came and offered me as many of his people as I should need for the compensation of 3 ps. of hdkf. to carry me a day's journey to Boway's town, in a more peaceful and plentiful region, and on the direct road to Barline.[44] I accepted his offer and beheld myself in one hour's time travelling on the very road which recent occurrences had indicated, I should not be able to go on for sometime.

One hour's brisk walk carried me out of the limits of Waugi's territory, and instead of farms plucked of the last cassada stalk—were to be seen mountain sides of corn and rice, and soon succeeded, neat villages, whose clean clay cottages and spacious kitchens, lowing cows and bleating sheep, I gladly exchanged for the wretched squalor and dirty hovels of Waugi's warlike town.[45] I reached Boway 5 o'clock p.m.[46]

Though I had succeeded in getting away from Waugi's, yet I did not have the power of locomotion for all my luggage, when I pleased, and whenever I pleased. I had fifteen kingjars with only five carriers—having procured two hands at Waugi's to go the whole route in addition to the three I already had. I now commenced to feel all the inconveniences, consequent upon Capehart's desertion. I had now to resort to the practice of getting whatever chief I should visit, to send me on to the next chief, a most dependent and inconvenient plan, as you are in this case left at the will and caprice of any barbarian chief to send you on if he choose, or raise any obstacle to your going that may suit his interest or prejudice. I therefore always had it understood before I made any presents to a chief that my being sent on to the next king was one of [the] conditions upon which he received his present, and it si [*sic,* is] this system, together with my strictly refusing to trade that enable[d] me to go on at all [p. 14].

Wednesday, July 1st, at Boway's or Bowauh's, I stated to this chief my business, and gave him his present, 4 ps. hdkfs. with the understanding of his furnishing carriers for my extra kingjars; every thing agreeably acceded to and as punctually carried out.

Thursday, July 2nd. Left Bowauh's town, Wangynah;[47] at 10 o'clock a.m. and reached Sinoya [Sanoyea, 6°58'N, 9°58'W] at 12:20 o'clock.[48] On Friday 3rd, July, we had an interview with the rulers of this town which seemed to be under the authority of two headmen or chiefs, Seeway and Bahtah, they gave their consent to every thing, and said, the Americans could come at any

Figure 28. "King of Sanojii." This is Siwi Wockpaling, of Sanoyea, taken four years before he died in 1911. Anderson spelled his name "Seeway" or "Seaway." This photograph is part of an album of photographs taken during a seven-month tour of Liberia by S. M. Owen in 1907. *Courtesy of the Royal Anthropological Institute, London.*

time and share the whole country—that they would be glad to have them come.[49]

When I spoke to them of the wars, they replied that wars there were, but that there was not a war throughout the whole Pessey country that would interfere with us. I gave them their present, they asked for rum, but I told them that the Government had purposely excluded this article, as it wished every one to be in full possession of his senses when they made agreements with the Government; that they made such havoc among themselves by the use of gun and powder, that they need not be surprised if the Government for a long while excluded these three articles altogether, rum, guns and powder.

Tuesday 7th, of July.[50] Left Sinoya at 7 o'clock a.m. and came to Ponafah's town at 9 o'clock a.m., direction N. East.[51] I now saw that I was traversing a portion of country cut up into small independent communities, not over one or two hours walk from each other-hostile, jealous, weak and poor; and that the Expedition would have to be bothered with every village kingdom of a dozen huts, that we should happen to fall upon.[52] Had I had my own carrie[r]s they would have been treated with the unimportance that their insignificance deserved, instead of having to regard them with the same consideration and to make them as large a present as the greatest king in the country. But it was in their power to consume our means by exactions or theft and to lengthen out time and distance of the journey by going round about paths to serve their own, or the interests of their friends. They were also in possession of the knowledge that they were carrying my kingjars in consequence of my own people having run away from that service. The only wonder is that they did not abuse their opportunity sooner and to a greater extent than what they did.

We now repeated the same duties of delivering our message and [p. 15] making presents as usual and on Wednesday, 8th of July, took our leave of this town and came to Wawantah.[53] The face of the country was wrapt in a vegetation rank and vigorous from the daily rains; the roads were deeply cut into narrow gullies. The feature of the land generally is of that up and down hill and dale character that repeats itself everywhere 15 or 20 miles in the rear of the seaboard of Liberia.

Left Wawantah Thursday, July 9th, and traveled in a level plain direction N.E.—came to Barmaquirlla's town [Bamokolita, 7°11'N, 9°50'W].[54]

Left Barmaquirlla's town Saturday, 11th of July—the level plain continuing. Crossed St. Paul's River upon a raft, the river being 100 yds. wide at this point; came to Sakatah [7°13'N, 9°49'W];[55] the largest and best town I had seen in the Pessey country, situated on a hill which by barometrical measurement is 150 feet high from the general level of the plain.

The St. Paul River was joined by a considerable tributary at this point where we crossed it—coming from the east;[56] but the river is said to be uninterrupted for a good distance before you reach the next rapid; the general direction from which the river flows itself is North East by East[;] indeed the river has a great bend in this section of the country to the Eastward; it then seems to turn up and go N. E. and North by East. The king of Sakatah, Popowa Keang, was a venerable fine-looking old man certainly different in his manners and appearance from any I had hitherto seen in the Pessey Country.[57] I had almost forgot to mention that I had the good fortune to meet him at Barmaquirlla's town and he showed the civility to leave off his business and to accompany me to his place; and it was chiefly owing to his presence that I met no trouble in being ferried over the river without toll. I had indeed got out of a region of Pessy country which bears a name strikingly descriptive of the filth and poverty of the people who inhabit it, and which though it does strict justice to those whom it is meant to designate cannot for want of decency be inserted here.[58]

On Saturday [*sic,* Sunday] night, July 12th, report was brought to the town, that war was approaching: it coming, it seems, from a king who formerly resided in the town, but who from some cause had moved away and

The Observer vol II, #11 11 Sept 1879

THE MUSAHDU RAILWAY.

Report of meeting called by Mr R. A. Burnell, and headed "Trade with Africa," held at 9 Gracechurch St. Thursday July 24th.

Thornton, was asked to take the chair. Addressing Mr Criswick he stated to the meeting that the concessionaries, Mr Burnell and Mr Criswick, he understood were anxious to sell the concession granted them by the Liberian Government for a railway 200 miles in length. Some very imperfect maps were exhibited for which Mr Criswick apologised. Mr. Criswick explained the terminal station would be on the wharf he lately occupied and his plan was to follow the line of the river for about 30 miles. Although the Liberians claim the right of the land for about 80 miles in the interior they really have but a small part. He described the land and elevations and that the line would cross the mountains which were 200 feet high, between Monrovia and Musahdu. 35 miles from the Coast he found a very thick population but so dear was transport that it cost £8 a ton to carry goods 20 miles. Once across the mountains a very high class of Africans were met with, far superior to any to be found near the Coast.

These natives now draw their supplies from caravans which come from the Nile, and the shores of the Mediterranean. The price of salt by 80 sticks equal to one bushel was 15 dollars, equal £3. This came to £ 80 a ton, a Bullock cost 80 sticks of salt. At these remarks some of the gentlemen expressed great surprise particularly merchants trading with the East Coast.

Iron was so easily obtained by smelting that the natives attached very little value to it.

England is entirely excluded for the present from trade with the interior solely owing to their being no means of transport. The Mahomedan natives interest is identical with the Liberian Govt. to further the railway, but there is no doubt the natives *en route* would not like it. The Liberian Govt. would have to protect it while building, by force. One of the kings asked the Liberian Govt. some time since to send an Ambassador but they did not comply. When asked by the chairman, Mr. Criswick admitted that he had not been on the East side of the hills so the information was from hearsay. It was suggested that the Concession should be read. The Chairman after reading it considered the Concession one of the most meagre he had ever read. He asked Mr. Criswick what his wishes were again. After speaking to Mr. Burnell, they replied that their wish was to sell the Concession. The Chairman thought it might be advisable to form a committee to co-operate with Messrs. Burnell and Criswick to look into the terms of the Concession.

T. Christy, addressing the Chairman asked if it was generally known that the Liberian Govt. did not permit European merchants to trade direct with the Natives or to travel into the interior with the object of trading, and the clause in the Concession for the Railway distinctly stated that no trading establishments shall be opened. The Chairman and the whole of the meeting expressed great surprise and appealed to Mr. Criswick to know if he was aware that such was the case. Mr. Criswick admitted such was the law at present; but he had every hope that this law would be changed as the feeling amongst all the merchants was that all Countries should have liberty of trading in the republic of Liberia.

Mr Talbot asked what price they asked for the Concession. Mr. Criswick said they had not quite fixed it.

T. Christy then asked the Chairman if he had considered the gauge proposed named by Mr. Criswick via 3 feet, and if it be did not consider that the 18 in. guage was amply large enough for all the requirements of such a railway.

Mr. Gabib Then placed on the table a book with drawings and particulars of the Railway indicated by T. Christy. (Plans of which you have in your office and which have been seen at work by many Liberians. The same Railway worked admirably during the agricultural show at Kilburn and tickets of invitation have been issued by the Duke of Sutherland for gentlemen who are interested to come to his garden in London and see the Railway at work on the 30 and 31st of July. He has ordered miles of this Railway for his estates in Scotland)

The meeting were unanimous in considering that this railway was the one that should be proposed to the Liberian Government. One gentleman remarked that it could be laid down at one tenth of the expense and supposing after a few years so much work offered that it would not suit, it would be easy then to lay down a broader gauge.

Mr. Talbot, wished it to be distinctly understood that he would not buy shares or take shares or subscribe to a railway undertaking for the sake of holding shares in a Railway, but that he would only participate in such an undertaking providing he could erect trading establishments wherever he wished. In these remarks every gentleman in the room agreed It was moved by Mr. Talbot and seconded that a syndicate should be formed.

THE BOUNDARY QUESTION.

THE EDITOR OF THE OBSERVER.

Sir.

After the return of our North-West Boundary Commission from Sulymah, it was reported by the government that a copy of the proceedings of the joint commission had been sent from the Department of State to the British Foreign Office, and endeavours would be made as the Commission had failed, to close this vexed question by direct negotiations between the two governments.

We have since been credibly informed that no copy of the proceedings of the Commission has been sent from this Office of State to the British Foreign Office, only a communication relative to the disagreement of the Commission, and referring the noble lord, (the head of that department) to a copy of the proceedings said to have been or which would be furnished him, by his own (or the British) Commissioners, as if we knew any thing about that, or had any thing to do with what he was furnished with by his own people. No, Mr. Editor, in our humble opinion we think that the State Department should have furnished a true and correct copy of all the proceedings under the seal of the department, and then made all the necessary references to this copy, and not have bound itself down to a document, that the honorable Secretary of State has never seen and which has not the seal of his office on its face. Have we not yet as a nation, gotten sufficient experience in regards to rash and hastily entered into engagements? Have we so soon forgotten the famous "Protocol" on this same question by which we helplessly bound ourselves and from which we only escaped by adhering to it to the very letter, although at heavy pecuniary loss to ourselves which we could but ill afford. We are sure that if the honorable Secretary of State has forgotten the people have not, and are crying out against his gross neglect of so important a duty.

It was also reported, emanating from the Department of State that copies of the proceedings of the Commission would be printed for circulation among the people, Has that been done? No. Our eminent and distinguished Secretary of State has been too busy preparing "A New and Beautiful Edition of the Constitution and Statute laws of the Republic," for which he will receive $... to think of attending to these arduous though legitimate duties of his department. And so he goes on as a prayer somewhere between the lids of his own church book reads, doing those things which he ought not to do and leaving undone those things which he ought to do.

Truly the sovereign people of this Republic has much to demand at the hands of those whom they have "for a time" appointed to rule over them.

I am, yours respectfully,

OCCASIONAL.

NARRATIVE

OF THE EXPEDITION DESPATCHED TO MUSAHDU,

By the Liberian Government In 1874,

UNDER BENJ. ANDERSON ESQR,

The St Paul River was joined by a considerable tributary at the point where we crossed it—coming from the east; but the river is said to be uninterrupted for a good distance before you reach the next rapid; the general direction from which the river flows itself is North East by East indeed the river has a great bend in this section of the country to the Eastward; it then seems to turn up and go N. E. and North by East. The king of Sakatah, Popowa Keang, was a venerable fine looking old man certainly different in his manners and appearance from any I had hitherto seen in the Pessy Country. I had almost forgot to mention that I had the good fortune to meet him at Barmaquilla's town and he showed the civility to leave off his business and to accompany me to his place; and it was chiefly owing to his presence that I met no trouble in being ferried over the river without toll. I had indeed got out of a region of Pessy Country which bears a name strikingly descriptive of the filth and poverty of the people who inhabit it, and which though it does strict justice to those whom it is meant to designate cannot for want of decency be inserted here.

On Saturday night, July 12th, report was brought to the town, that war was approaching it: coming, it seems, from a king who formerly resided in the town, but who from some cause had moved away and became thereafter hostile to his friends: the people of the town kept watch all night, nothing appeared.

Monday July 13th. We had an interview with the king; he begged us to interpose and use our offices in stopping a war between himself and the king who had formerly lived in the town and was now threatening him with war. We promised to do all we could as we had it particularly given in charge to us to stop wars. We therefore sent to our warlike neighbor, a messenger, (a disinterested party who did not live in the town with us) in order to sound the king as to measures of peace: and without waiting for his return I despatched on Tuesday 14th, July two of my people with the flag to another party whom I learned was aiding and abetting his war. He became so frightened that he sent me a goat a white country cloth and two of his people to assure me, that he was not a party to any war whatever, but that the king of Phansfuro had called together a large war and was about to send it somewhere, but where he did not know. We sent to the king of Phansfuro who had war raging unbridled in his town, even beyond his own control: he declined to come where I was or to dismiss his war. The whole truth was that it was out of his power to do either. The war had been assembled, and go somewhere it must—or it would have turned its injury upon the one who bought it and devoured him.

I have been informed that these bought wars often do their purchasers more damage that the enemy against whom it is intended they are to fight.

On Saturday July 18th, about 3, O'clock p. m. I beheld a large town towards the South west on fire: it was afterwards found that the war had fallen upon the town and had taken it at a great loss to themselves.

I now began to grow anxious about the internal affairs of the Expedition, and became solicitous to know what amount of goods I had on hand, how much had been used in presents and other miscellaneous expenses, and whether I had sustained any losses by my stranger-carriers, whom I had been obliged to employ, and whose conduct had given me some uneasiness owing to the undue and hasty speed with which they always outran and distanced my own people—and myself—who though anything else but slow pedestrians, were always left far behind whatever might be our efforts or remonstrances.

Upon my first setting out, it had been my endeavour to give system and organisation to our party, as respected the particular duty assigned to each person. Those who were carriers were especially so by appointment. Only one person who was thought to be the most responsible and honest for the purpose was selected to get articles that might be called for, out of the kingjars:—and the whole business was so arranged that the Chief of the Expedition might be able to give his attention purely to those affairs and higher duties which it was known to be impossible for the others to discharge.

After the defection and following desertion of Capehart and the men, the whole plan became deranged, and alterations had to be made in accordance with the diminution we had suffered in our numbers.

At Wangi's I took stock in order to see if what I had on hand would enable me to carry though the expedition as I had projected it in my own mind. It stood as follows:

A: Wangi's, Saturday 27th June, A. D. 1874. 78 Ps. of Hdkfs, 16 Ps. of Calico, 9 Ps. Brillant. A mixed quantity of Beads, 4 Brass kettles, 4 kegs of Powder, 6 Baltic Shirts books, instruments and Bibles. Besides the Chief Commissioner's own goods which he had credited from Sherman and Dimery for the purpose of speculation at Musahdu.

It had been reported just the day before the men left that 40 heads of tobacco was on hand—but not a leaf was to be found after they had gone and 1 doz small round looking glasses were also missed according to the list—also more than one half of the gun caps were carried off and we only had in all 2 boxes containing 250 caps in each—500 caps—the expedition had 3 guns left to defend itself with, and one of them was obtained by making after one of the deserters and seizing it from him.

At Sakatah, stock was again taken together with an account of what had been expended as presents and in other miscellaneous Expenses. At the intervening places no one would be so foolhardy as to count his money: unless he did so for the special purpose of losing all.

At Sakatah Saturday July 18th. A. D. 1874. Amount of goods on hand 22 Ps. Hdkfs, 6 Ps. Calico, 6 Ps. Brilliant 6 Small Looking glasses, 4 kegs of Powder, 4 Brass kettles, 6 Baltic Shirts.

Monday 20th. of July.

Travelled from Sakatah to Bahquetah, king Seekokibo, direction East. Crossed a northern branch of the St. Paul's River, called "Ya." Went from Bahquetah to Yahtendah, king Yahseeah. Saturday 25th. July left Yahtandah and came to Pallikah the most important town of the middle Pessy Country.

The present aspect of this town but ill accorded with its former reputation. Kalminyah the king had lately died and it had been visited by a war which had burnt one half of it, The people were at the point of starvation when we arrived. They had planted extensively but some time must elapse before the crops would be ripe.

There was a war going on between these people and another Pessy tribe called the Pelle or Belle people which had harassed the Country for two years, without any advantage being gained by either party. I offered to mediate between them, but the Pallikah people behaved with so much insincerity that nothing definite or satisfactory could be arrived at.

It was at this town or while coming from Yahtandah to Pallikah, that the expedition suffered serious losses in its stock of goods. This robbery came from a source which it was difficult to provide against or prevent, since it was perpetuated by one of my own carriers: a Pessy man by the name of Miller whom I had hired in my great need, at Wangi's. He could speak English well, and his conduct was such as to gain greatly upon my confidence. The articles taken consisted chiefly of a dozen pieces of Madras Hdkfs. and several pieces of Calico. This man and his boy had charge of a kingjar containing goods which I had designed for Musahdu. As soon as he got to Pallikah he gave it out that he did not intend to go any farther; and as he had considerable influence over the others, he succeeded in shaking their determation also to go with me: and great confusion and indecision prevailed among them, The road between Yahtandah and Pallikah is the worst possible: and I had scarcely met so many ditches, holes, stobs gutters and creeks in any one day's travel since I had been walking. My own people begged to be relieved from their kingjars as they were entirely fagged out with carrying them. I consented to do so, telling them that they must be sure to keep up with the people who were carrying their kingjars. When I was scolding them about what had happened, they told me it was impossible for them to keep up with all the Country people as they walked or ran with different gaits and in separate parties.

Thus robbed and thus again deserted and conspired against, my prospect of getting to Musahdu was very poor indeed. In the mean time I was taken seriously ill in consequence of the exposure I had been subject to, and the anxiety of mind I had undergone. For two days I was unconscious of what was going on around me. The expedition was now considered as ended or broken up: It had suffered discomfiture at all points: robbed of its means, deserted by its carriers, and its Chief conductor half crazed, was lying prostrate and helplessly ill. All now with one or two exceptions began to behave in an indifferent or reckless manner: the ammunition was stolen and sold: bottles containing medicine and writing ink disappeared: stolen solely for the purpose of getting the bottles: insolence and petty theft was the order of the day. I recovered but slowly; and my staggering motion in attempting to walk convinced all, that if I had any power of locomotion it had better be expended in a journey towards home, instead of persisting in going to Musahdu. My ailing left me with a swimming in my head from which to this day, I have not recovered: and I neither get up or lie down, but what the sensation is painfully present. The town was not only destitute of the commonest necessaries of life, but hunger was so severe that several children died from the effects of it: all of us were scantily fed and I had been compelled to pay, at one time, 3 yds of calico for a quart of rice. Hunger had to be borne with in the day, and war had to be watched for at night.

As soon as I regained my strength, my first care was to get away from Pallikah, I gave my attendants to understand that goods or no goods, whether they had ammunition to protect themselves with or not I intended to march them to Musahdu, they protested; but it was no use; I was sufficiently peevish from my late sickness to insist on having my own will and mulishly, obstinate enough to go just where anybody else did not wish to go, a frame of mind certainly not the most amiable, but good enough for those upon whom I was just then exerting it.

Pallikah is beautifully located, and was no doubt justly entitled to all the praise that has been bestowed upon it. But upon my arrival its glory had departed and no vestige remained of what I have heard about it Its wall consists of clay and flat rocks firmly put together: There is a camwood forest about 2 or 3 hours walk north-west of the town—there were some large ivory in the town for sale. If peace and order could be established Pallikah would be among the first towns in the Pessy Country. Having made its Chief, Quiilebah, a suitable present. I took my leave of this town. August, Wednesday 19th—passed a town called Payasangah and came to Pattahya a town seated on very high hill. The country is level all around with moderate sized hills rising here and there.

The Observer.

MONROVIA. SEPTEMBER 11th. 1879

BLACK ENGLISHMEN.

There is a delusion very common among the black and coloured inhabitants of English Colonies that they are Englishmen. Because they do not suffer such open oppression, and meet such unconcealed hatred and contempt on account of their dusky skins as do their American(?) brethren; because the law does not make any marked distinction; because schools are open to them, and churches are for all alike, these people lose sight of the impalpable and almost unappreciable barrier, which is nevertheless as strong as the bands of Death, and which sets them bounds beyond which they may not pass. Perhaps occasionally some event awakes them from their delusive dreams and they learn that there is a wide difference made between them and their fairer brethren; but it is to the interest of their rulers to lull them back into their lethargy, and a well-timed promotion of some black man, or more frequently empty promises, removes their temporary discontent, and leads them to believe that class prejudice rather than color antipathy is the power they have to combat, and that by elevating themselves and being useful to the Colony they must sooner or later reach the desired goal—Equality. This dream like the pleasant delusions of the lotus eater renders these men oblivious of the thousand petty slights and annoyances which they meet at every turn and disguises the bitter fact of their subjection, for a subject race they are and ever must be while Englishmen rule. Unlike her ancient prototype, whose citizenship knew no distinctions of creed, class, or color; but who guaranteed benefits to every individual, no

Figure 29. Edition of the *Observer,* 11 September 1879, containing the account of Anderson's 1874 journey to Musadu.

became thereafter hostile to his friends: the people of the town kept watch all night nothing appeared.

Monday July 13th. We had an interview with the king;[59] he begged us to interpose and use our offices in stopping a war between himself and the king who had formerly lived in the town and was now threatening him with war.[60] We promised to do all we could as we had it particularly given in charge to us to stop wars. We therefore sent to our warlike neighbor, a messenger, (a disinterested party who did not live in the town with us) in order to sound the king as to measures of peace: and without waiting for his return I despatched on Tuesday 14th, July two of my people with the flag to another party whom I learned was aiding and abetting his war. He became so frightened that he sent me a goat[,] a white country cloth and two of his people to assure me that he was not a party to any war whatever, but that the king of Phanefuro had called together a large war and was about to send it somewhere, but where he did not know.[61] We sent to the king of Phanefuro who had war raging unbridled in his town, even beyond his own control: he declined to come where I was or to dismiss his war. The whole truth was that it was out of his power to do either. The war had been assembled, and go somewhere it must—or it would have turned its injury upon the one who bought it and devoured him.[62]

I have been informed that these bought wars often do their purchasers more damage that [*sic,* than] the enemy against whom it is intended they are to fight.

On Saturday July 18th, about 3, o'clock p.m.[63] I beheld a large town towards the South west on fire: it was afterwards found that the war had fallen upon the town and taken it at a great loss to themselves.[64]

I now began to grow anxious about the internal affairs of the Expedition, and became solicitous to know what amount of goods I had on hand, how much had been used in presents and other miscellaneous expenses, and whether I had sustained any losses by my stranger-carriers. [*sic*] whom I had been obliged to employ, and whose conduct had given me some uneasiness owing to the undue and hasty speed with which they always ontran [outran] and distanced my own people—and myself—who though anything else but slow pedestrians, were always far behind whatever might be our efforts or remonstrances.

Upon my first setting out, it had been my endeavor to give system and organization to our party, as respected the particular duty assigned to each person. Those who were carriers were specially so by appointment. Only one person who was thought to be the most responsible and honest for the purpose was selected to get articles that might be called for, out of the kingjars:—and the whole business was so arranged that the Chief of the Expedition might be able to give his attention purely to those affairs and higher duties which it was known to be impossible for the others to discharge.

After the defection and following desertion of Capehart and the men, the whole plan became deranged, and alterations had to be made in accordance with the diminution we had suffered in our numbers.

At Waugi's I took stock in order to see if what I had on hand would enable me to carry through the expedition as I had projected it in my own mind. It stood as follows:

At Waugi's, Saturday 27th June, A.D. 1874, 78 Ps. of Hdkfs, 16 Ps. of Calico, 9 Ps. Brilliant.[65] A mixed quantity of Beads, 4 Brass Kettles, 4 Kegs of Powder, 6 Baltic Shirts[,] books, instruments and Bibles. Besides the Chief Commissioner's own goods which he had credited from Sherman and Dimery for the purpose of speculation at Musahdu.[66]

It had been reported just the day before the men left that 40 heads of tobacco was on hand—but not a leaf was to be found after they had gone and 1 doz. small round looking glasses were also missed according to the list—also more than one half of the gun caps were carried off and we only had in all 2 boxes containing 250 caps in each—500 caps—the expedition had 3 guns left to defend itself with, and one of them was obtained by making after one of the deserters and seizing it from him.

At Sakatah, stock was again taken together with an account of what had been expended as presents and in other miscellaneous Expenses. At the intervening places no one would be so foolhardy as to count his money: unless he did so for the special purpose of losing all.

At Sakatah Saturday July 18th, A.D. 1874. Amount of goods on hand 22 Ps. Hdkfs, 6 Ps. Calico, 6 Ps. Brilliant[,] 6 Small Looking glasses.[,] 4 kegs of Powder, 4 Brass kettles, 6 Baltic Shirts.

Monday 20th of July. Travelled from Sakatah to Bahquetah [Gbakoita, 7°16'N, 9°44'W], king Seekokibo, direction East. Crossed a northern branch of the St. Paul's River, called "Ya."[67] Went from Bahquetah to Yahtandah [?Gbakwele, 7°24'N, 9°51'W], king Yahseeah. Saturday 25th, July[,] left Yahtandah and came to Pallikah [Kpayekwele, 7°28'N, 9°37'W] the most important town of the middle Pessey Coantry [*sic*].[68]

The present aspect of this town but ill accorded with its former reputation. Kalminyah the king had lately died and it had been visited by a war which had burnt one half of it, [*sic*] The people were at the point of starvation when we arrived. They had planted extensively but some time must elapse before the crops would be ripe.

There was a war going on between these people and another Pessey tribe called the Pelle or Belle people which had harassed the Country for two years, without any advantage being gained by either party.[69] I offered to mediate between them, but the Pallikah people behaved with so much insincerity that nothing definite or satisfactory could be arrived at.

It was at this town or while coming from Yahtandah to Pallikah, that the expedition suffered serious losses in its stock of goods. This robbery came from a source which it was difficult to provide against or prevent, since it was perpetuated by one of my own carriers: a Pessy man by the name of Miller whom I had hired in my great need, at Waugi's. He could speak English well, and his conduct was such as to gain greatly upon my confidence. The articles taken consisted chiefly of a dozen pieces of Madras Hdkfs. and several pieces of Calico. This man and his boy had charge of a kingjar containing goods which I had designed for Musahdu. As soon as he got to Pallikah he gave it out that he did not intend to go any farther: and as he had considerable influence over the others, he succeeded in shaking their determination also to go with me: and confusion and indecision prevailed among them, [*sic*] The road between Yahtandah and Pallikah is the worst possible: and I had scarcely met so many ditches, holes, stobs, gutters and creeks in any one day's travel since I had been walking.[70] My own people begged to be relieved from their kingjars as they were entirely out fagged with carrying them. I consented to do so, telling them that they must be sure to keep up with the people who were carrying their kingjars. When I was scolding them about what had happened, they told me it was impossible for them to keep up with all the Country people as they walked or ran with different gaits and in separate parties.

Thus robbed and thus again deserted and conspired against, my prospect of getting to Musahdu was very poor indeed. In the meantime I was taken seriously ill in consequence of the exposure I had been subjected to, and anxiety of mind I had undergone. For two days I was unconscious of what was going on around me. The expedition was now considered as ended or broken up: It had suffered discomfiture at all points: robbed of its means, deserted by its carriers, and its Chief conductor half crazed, was lying prostrate and helplessly ill[.] All now with one or two exceptions began to behave in an indifferent or reckless manner: the ammunition was stolen and sold: bottles containing medicine and writing ink disappeared, stolen and sold for the purpose of getting the bottles: insolence and petty theft was the order of the day. I recovered but slowly; and my staggering motion in attempting to walk convinced all, that if I had any power of locomotion it had better be expended in a journey towards home, instead of persisting in going to Musahdu. My ailing left me with a swimming in my head from which to this day, I have not recovered: and I neither get up or lie down, but what the sensation is painfully present. The town was not only destitute of commonest necessaries of life, but hunger was so severe that several children died from the effects of it: all of us were scantily fed and I had been compelled to pay, at one time, 3 yds of calico for a quart of rice. Hunger had to be borne with in the day, and war had to be watched for at night.

As soon as I regained my strength, my first care was to get away from Pallikah, I gave my attendants to understand that goods or no goods, whether they had ammunition to protect themselves with our [or?] not I intended to march them to Musahdu, they protested: but it was no use; I was sufficiently peevish from my late sickness to insist on having my own will and mulishly obstinate enough to go just where anybody else did not wish to go, a frame of mind certainly not the most amiable, but good enough for those upon whom I was just then exerting it.

Pallikah is beautifully located, and was no doubt justly entitled to all the praise that has been bestowed upon it. But upon my arrival its glory had departed and no vestige remained of what I have heard about it[.] Its wall consists of clay and flat rocks firmly put together: There is a camwood forest about 2 or 3 hours walk north-west of the town—there were some large ivories in the town for sale. If peace and order could be established[,] Pallikah would be among the first towns in the Pessey Country. Having made its Chief, Quirlebah, a suitable present. I took my leave of this town.[71] August, Wednesday 19th—passed a town called Payasangah [Kposangie, 7°29'N, 9°38'W] and came to Pattahya [Kpetehye, 7°30'N, 9°37'W] a town seated on a very high hill.[72] The country is level all around with moderate sized hills rising here and there.

On Friday August 21st, started from Pattahya and reached Bonya [Gbonie, 7°30'N, 9°38'W] about 1. o'clock p.m.[73]

Saturday 22nd of August we had an interview with the king of Bonya, king Fillingi. He had been at war and was still at war with a chief named Daffaborah.[74] They had fought each other for ten years. It was proposed that I should attempt a mediation as both parties were heartily tired; but, out of pride, continued to carry on a languishing war with each other still.

While I was in the act of interfering to put an end to this feud, on Sunday morning [23 August] [a] crowd of women and children came rushing into the town crying, and a general lamentation took place all over the town, Daffaborah had made a raid upon one of king Fillingi's town called Pillillay, had captured two hundred women, killed a half a dozen men, and these who had first come into the town were a part of those who had escaped. The king at once grew wroth and refused to let me carry out my intentions to negotiate a peace between him and Daffaborah.

Finding that nothing could be done in this respect, we consulted with the king about our own departure; but he was loath to have us leave him so soon: whether he wished to detain us for the sake of our assistance, should he be attacked, or to keep off an attack by the report of our being at his town we are not able to say, but he alleged that he feared something might happen to us, as the war bands were roaming all over the country, and the thick bush was filled with armed men watching the paths. He said that God had truly made some men different from others and that the American people did not seen [seem] to fear anything: that we had come to Pockpar and found war, come to Sakatah and found war, come to Seehokbo's [Seekokibo's] and found war and had come to his town and found war and still we wish to go on.

On Thursday, 27th August, we accompanied the king [King Filling] to Pillillay. More than one half of the town was burnt and we walked over ground charred with cinders and burnt timber and covered with blood and lots of flies, we were detained at this town until Monday, 7th of September, owing to the inclemency of the weather.[75] Having travelled in a direction East and N. East we came to the St. Paul river about noon which had become a rapid torrent in consequence of the rains.[76] Here we were detained until 5½ o'clock p.m. in trying to cross the river, and a dangerous time we had of it. There was a raft made out of five logs about 14 feet long. The first load in crossing consisted of six individuals and 4 kingjars, which being paddled into the center of the stream became unmanageable and was driving rapidly to the falls below. The excitement of our people on shore, and the cries of the poor fellows on the raft who inplored [*sic*] us to help them were truly heartrending, fortunately they were enabled to grasp a limb of a tree that extended unusually far out in the river, at the risk of capsizing. As soon as they were safely landed on the other side, they refused to return unless I paid them right down, for their services, for they were not of my party, but had only volunteered to assist me in crossing. I called out to them that unless they wished me to commence a regular fusil[l]ade from my side of the river they had better not meddle with my king jars.

Jackque, a young friend of mine, managed afterwards to persuade two of them to return with the raft and after much tugging and pulling to get ourselves up stream, we were embarked to take our share of being likely precipitated over the falls. Bravely we contended with the stream and were nearly across, when grasping a bush, it gave away under the force of the current and away we went, drifting down to the roaring falls. I urged my people to every exertion and nearing the shore and getting hold of a strong vine held on, to the submerging of the raft, and the knocking overboard of two of my people; they however held to the raft. Had not the king jars been tied on these logs we should have lost every thing, but Providence helped us. Three of my people, strong and expert swimmers, trusted themselves to this stream and, after they got out, they promised themselves not to try the experiment again, they were carried nearly to the falls. The river at this point is 150 feet wide. The fall, from its noise and roaring would have been sufficient to have bumped anyone's brains out had he been swept down there.

About 5½ o'clock having got all across we started to come up with the nearest town, but night overtook us. A worse road, full of ditches, holes, streams and logs; a darker or more rainy night never caught an unfortunate traveller. One of my carriers was completely knocked up and concluded to sleep in the woods all night, we however pushed on without knowing whither we were going: After stumbling over every rock and falling into every ditch that crossed the path and groping along as best we could, we at last discovered a light nearing us and knowing it was some of our people who had already reached the town and were now returning to search us up,—we soon called out to each other, and were guided for the rest of the road by torch light[.] We arrived at the town, where we were comfortably housed and were enabled to dry and warm ourselves and take some sleep.[77]

The Country being in a disturbed condition, we were not only annoyed by the discomfort of the road but by the dread of being mistaken for some sneaking war party and fired into by the watchers and guards of the path: and even should we escape these, we should likely not obtain admittance into the town at that time of night, for our own people might not be able to persuade the town people to open their gates. So many stratagems have been practiced among themselves to capture towns, that every thing is suspected. we [*sic*] arrived at this town about 11 o'clock at night [Monday, 7 September].

The next morning we pushed on Eastward to Dowaytan [Donhoueta, 7°31'N, 9°21'W], the king of which town treated us with so much hospitality that we felt ourselves somewhat compensated for all the troubles of the day and night before. All along the road could be seen large and extensive rice farms, there seemed to be no limit to the number.

I was now informed that after I crossed the St. Paul River I had left Barline Country, and had entered a different region of the Pessy Country, certain it was their towns were larger and the population dense: their farming was on an enormous scale.[78] The Barline people, and especially the people of Pallikah se[e]med to have obtained a bette[r] reputation than they deserved: they were meaner and less hospita[b]le, or they may have appeared so owing to the universal disturbances going on in their Country.

Wednesday 9th of September.[79] Started from Dowaytan to go to Pahya [Kpaiye, 7°43'N, 9°23'W], king Kryneseh.[80] This king is considered the greatest and most powerful king in this section of Country. Taking a direction North and North East we walked hard all day until 5 o'clock p.m.

When we had walked half of the day we changed the direction of our course and went directly west and South west, passing the walled towns of Pongya [Gbanhie, 7°33'N, 9°21'W] and Bellepomah [Melegbouma, 7°34'N, 9°19'W]: we came through several farming villages at one of which we halted at 5½ o'clock p.m. and passed the night.[81] Started for Pahya next morning [Thursday, 10 September], at which we arrived about 10 o'clock a.m.[82] The king was absent: in coming to this town we crossed two rivers running parallel to each other; one a branch of the St Pauls and the other the St Pauls River itself, the first a hundred feet and the second a hundred and fifty feet wide:—both were spanned by bridges of wicker work in excellent order.[83] In crossing the second bridge two men demanded toll of us. I refused on the ground that I was not a trader, but sent by my government to see their king: they remained inexorable and I continued stubborn and walked off refusing to pay anything for which they stopped one of my king jars, the last that crossed over; and for their pains had to bring it themselves to the town, and got a severe chiding together with risk of paying for anything, I might say, was lost out of the kingjar.

The king, as we before mentioned, was absent but we were most kindly received by the town people. On Sunday 11th. of October while we were waiting for the king to return, Capehart the assistant Commissioner, accompanied by two Congoes, came.[84] As soon as he arrived, he set to work to learn by secret inquiring among my people, what had become of all the goods, which he said, he had left with me—and received from my Pessy boy John, the answer, that he ought to have stayed with the expedition instead of running away and he then would have seen what had become of the goods,. [*sic*] He affected great sympathy with the Americans [Daniel Coleman and G. W. Wardsworth] on account of their scantiness of clothes and began to make presents with the hope and purpose of extracting some mischievous information out of them. He came back deeply embittered against me; and to gratify his spleen did the expedition evil service on more than one occasion.

Capehart's appearance certainly perplexed the good understanding we had with the people of the town, for seeking some one who could talk Vey he gave all kings [*sic,* kinds of] accounts of the Expedition—what large presents the government had sent them: that I had ever so much money when he was with me; that he could not tell what had become of all the money: that no one had stopped me on the path, and no one had taken my money; what could I have done with so much money.[85] This is the kind of service he rendered the Expedition from Pahya to Musahdu.

These statements so exasperated my people who knew the whole truth, that they took the pains to inform the people of the town, that it was owing to Capehart's conduct alone that the Expedition sustained the heavy losses which disabled it from making the usual present. The business had suffered irreparable injury from his hands. He had now returned to finish up his evil task; and to completely cross purpose the further progress of an Expedition he had already crippled by his former desertion.

On Thursday, 15th, October, the king arrived and justified both in his noble appearance and by his attention and hospitality all that I had heard of him.[86]

I had now to undergo another humiliating annoyance: the goods in the Government kingjars had given out and I was now using my own goods as presents or to purchase food. One of my carriers, an American, seemed to act as thief by appointment to the Expedition and in performance of that duty stole the very last present I had reserved for king [p. 24] Kryneseh: in vain he was remonstrated with when openly caught in former smaller thefts. He was determined that nothing should be wanting to make him the worst and the last thief. But he was faithful to the Expedition, followed it through its fortunes and misfortunes, for a good many of the latter of which the Expedition is deeply indebted to him.[87]

The king had a philosophy of temper that enabled him to smile at his own disappointment and to sympathize with mine, but as for me, I became furious.

Thus it was that the time of the Commissioner instead of being occupied in observing the features of the country through which he passed, its resources of wealth and commerce, the manners and customs of its people was chiefly absorbed in dealing with the crimes and misdemeanors of a criminal court: theft, desertion, robbery, treachery principally committed by his own people. Started from Pahya on Wednesday, 21st October, passed the towns of Pellamu, Wayi and came to Bussayeh [Bodezie, 7°49'N, 9°19'W] where we slept. It is a large densely populated town: direction E. North E.

Left here on Thursday, 22nd October, and passed through Loe [Loo, 7°51'N, 9°17'W] a town of considerable size and the clay walls of which were in good condition; passed Dowo Tuckahwu, came to Sappah [N'Zappa, 7°57'N, 9°16'W], a very large town.[88] It is a border town half Boozie and half Pessey. We had now passed the limits of the Pessey country.[89] all [*sic*] the other towns after Sappah being fairly Wymar Boozie.[90] Leaving Sappah we came to Bockamu [?Makobou, 8°1'N, 9°18'W], king Gavahsee's town halting there a few moments to gratify the curiosity of the people.[91] We pushed on and came to Pynyah [Baignema, 8°8'N, 9°16'W] where we halted for a couple of days to rest ourselves.[92] This large portion of the Pessey country from where we had crossed the St. Paul's River at Pahya to the borders of the Boozie country was in a peaceful condition, the towns were large and provisions in abundance.

Pynyah is a large Boozie town ruled by my old friend Dowilnyah.[93] Left Pynyah on Sunday 25th, and in company with a man whom Dowilnyah had sent from Gubbewallah [Goboèla, 8°19'N, 9°2'W] to attend me on the route came to Boe [Boo, 8°12'N, 9°13'W] and reached Ziggah-Porrahzue [Koiama Tongoro, 8°16'N, 9°6'W] where the great market was going on about 10 o'clock a.m.[94] Several Mandingoes mounted on their horses attend. We reached Gubbewallah on Sunday 25th, of October A.D. 1874, about 6 o'clock p.m.[95] I was now in a town which I had visited in 1868, about six years ago.[96]

The king Dowilnyah, looked as hearty as ever, and was very glad to [p. 25] see me. Again we had to protect ourselves against the insinuations of Capehart: and truths had to be told on him which the king would have never known had it not been for his officiousness to do evil. We made the king a present of a tent, a flag, a fine sword and several other minor articles: and on Monday November 2nd, 8:30 o'clock a.m. went from Gubbewallah in a direction N. and E. passed through one of Dowilnyah's half towns; and came to Pellezarrah [Dondema or Dondano, 8°24'N, 8°55'W], where a large market was going on, and where Jebbue or Eboe, Dowilnyah's former Counsellor now presided as Chief;[97] at 2 o'clock p.m. The road all along led through long grass and canebrake: the trees as usual begin[n]ing to disappear.

Tuesday, 3rd. of November. Left Pellezarrah direction E. E. N. E. crossed the Vukkah hills and came to Ballatah [Baladougou, 8°26'N, 8°52'W] at noon.[98] We were bid to wait some time before the gates; that the town people might collect in the square for to receive us: this practice seems to prevail throughout this section of the country where the strangers visit their towns. No one will assume the res[p]onsiblity of admitting strangers in the town until the town people have been assembled in the square to see and interrogate them. Precaution for their safety is the reason why they resort to this particularity. We were admitted, and as it was partly known who we were[,] Dowilnyah having sent his attendants along with us—we were most cordially received and welcomed again and again. The people began to bring their gold rings for trade but I could spare nothing to make purchases as I had to make small presents even to these subordinate rulers of Dowilnyah's country. I gave the Chief of this town a present of a brass kettle, and had made a similar present to the chief of Pallezarrah.[99]

Left Ballatah on Wednesday 14th [*sic,* 4th], taking a direction North and North East, the Yukkah range being on our left and parallel to our route.[100] The whole Country on each side of our path was covered with farms of rice, corn and sweet potatoes. After two hour[s] farther walking we came upon a region certainly delightful to look on, spread all over as far as the eye could reach with farming hamlets,—flocks of sheep—herds of cattle, the herd close to our path must have contained at least fifteen hundred,—and every hillock seemed to have its herd. But the motion of the yellow black herds one or two miles away, grazing in the green plains below—was a peculiar sight. This is the farming and grazing district of the town of Vukkah [Foma, 8°29'N, 8°50'W] once an insignificant dirty little Boozie village, but now grown to a flourishing and important Mandingo [p. 26] town.[101] We reached Vukkah 12 o'clock noon, where after the usual halting at the gate to await the gathering of the town people, we were introduced and found it filled with Mandingoes, to whom the numerous herds of cattle belong; these people having been forced out of their own country by war, a region north east of Musahdu and a day's walk from thence.

Thursday, November 5th, we remained all day at this town to give ourselves some rest, and to survey a neighborhood that made such substantial progress since our last visit in 1868.

We were struck with the fact, that the Mandingoes of this town were not Mahommedans, and we were soon informed of the circumstances, that had caused them to be here. The Chief of these Mandingoes whose name is Nyammah, was reigning in prosperity and peace in [a] country which is a day's walk North east of Musahdu as we have above mentioned.[102]

His nephew Sargee who lives and holds independent sway over the region, bordering westward on his uncle's territory, is represented as a turbulent and warlike prince, sparing the dominions neither of his friends or relations.[103] He made a demand upon his uncle Nyammah for troops to assist him in his raids over the country, for he wanted to walk about, as he expressed it; whereupon his royal kinsman did not exactly flatly refuse him but excused himself from contributing to Sargee's forces on the ground that most of his people were occupied with their farms.[104]

This answer so displeased Sargee, that he formed the design of driving his uncle from the country; and of having no one close to him that did not either cooperate with him or become subject to his authority. He has acted up to his policy, for he has either subdued all his neighbors and brought them into submission or violently expelled them from the country,—chasing his uncle to the very foot of the Vukkah hills and still threatening to force him over these mountains into the Boozie country.[105] In these operations he did not even scruple to include Musahdu and its subordinate towns, some account of which shall be given in our narration further on, when we come to describe our stay in Musahdu. Vukkah is in daily expectation of further attacks during this dry season.

We visited the market of Vukkah and found it plentifully supplied with a variety of articles such as earthen pots of many sizes and designs [p. 27]—cooking wood—rice, palm butter, craw-fish, catfish, soap, tobacco, potatoes, pepper, corn, iron, kola, ground-nuts, onions, snuff—cow's milk butter at which my own, people were astonished for no one dreamt of seeing nice fresh butter at 8 and 10 cents per lb. at Vukkah when it was selling at Monrovia for seventy five cents or a dollar per pound—yet there was no room for a doubt for the facts were before our eyes and there were half a dozen of us to see it, taste and purchase it.

There are many fine horses at Vukkah; but I was particularly struck with the art and perfection with which these people renew their gunstocks. Vukkah may be said to be famous for its manufacture of butter and gunstocks as Ballatah is famous for its manufacture of iron; a description of which I had to give in an account of my former visit to Musahdu in 1868 and 69.[106] Several villages belonging to Ballatah are devoted to this special business.

On Friday November 6th.[107] We left Vaukah [Vukkah] for Musahdu after having made the king a present of my best military Coat which by the avaricious maneuvering of another of his nephews, Tobah by name, fell into his possession; but it was a mantle destined not to fall on Tobah's shoulders not indeed because they were too broad but because the stature of this scheming nephew was full seven feet high which not only made the coat too short but made it go by chance as well as by fit to its rightful owne[r] Nyammah, a moderate sized man like myself.

On our way to Musahdu the road was so hemmed in on each side by tall grass, that we could scarcely get a look at the Country.[108] Direction E. north East: we turned southward and came to a Village about 3, o'clock where we halted for the night.

On Saturday November 7th, we started at 7, o'clock and regained the main road—passed through Vokkadu and a little village where we ate some potatoes, and came to Musahdu [Musadu, 8°46'N, 8°37'W] itself about 3 o'clock p.m.[109]

Making the usual halt that the people might gather in the town, we were introduced and received with demonstrations of welcome.

Tuesday, November 9th. we had an interview with the king Vomfeedolla, stating to him the particular object of our visit.[110] But now a serious difficulty arose which I had all along foreseen and expected. In 1868 in the month of December, when I was at Musahdu the king and the principal men of the town wrote a long and important letter to the President or we may say the Government, to which no reply during five or six years had been made.[111] It was natural enough to suppose [p. 28] that before we could open or begin any fresh matter, some explanation would be given as to what disposition had been made of this letter or whether there was any reply to it. Nothing properly had been done that might be considered an answer to what had been written to us, and it was awkward enough to come with new propositions when the first or old ones received no attention whatever. The king therefore wished to know whether I had any reply to what he and the Chiefs had written, and if it took us six years to answer one letter, and if I was sure that I had delivered his letter to the government. I replied that my coming back again to his country together with what I was sent to read and say to him, was considered and intended by the government as an answer to his letter. That true five or six years had elapsed, but what was merely an experiment or trial then had been now organized into a law; and communication would be more frequent and regular.[112] I had been compelled as I have before related to arrive in this country without any goods, owing to the conduct of my people in deserting. The consequences of their behavior were the more grievously felt when I began to come among these large communities where it was eminently necessary for the sake of the character of the government to be able to make respectable presents. I was only enabled to present the king of Musahdu with a pair of boots, one of our flags and some writing paper. When I started on the Expedition Hon. H. W. Dennis, gave me half dozen large Arabic bibles, finely printed and well bound.[113] Reserving one of them for myself I gave four of them to the king to be distributed among his men of learning and one I sent through him to Medina to Blamer Sissy, with his name written in it and the day, date and place of it[s] bestowal together with the names of the Commissioners presenting it.[114] I wrote similarly in the others.[115]

These Books were a wonder in Musahdu, for no one had seen such enormous and at the same time such fine specimens of Arabic printing; besides the books were excellently bound[.][116]

One afternoon I had the pleasure of hearing one of the learned men whom I had seen attend the Imaum at the Mohammedan service reading the *Altakween,* the "Beginning[.]"[117] He was sitting on the ground and had the book spread out before him: he would read two or three lines in Arabic and then tell its meaning in Mandingo to those standing around. I must therefore be allowed some credit, and I hope the honor will not be grudged me, when I say that I am the first Missionary that ever carried our Scriptures into that portion of Soudan, and this I have done to some purpose I am persuaded; since then, they will be read and understood: While my brethren of various denominations have confined their labors for a half hundred years to the wooden-headed tribes of our coast.[118] When I was at Vukkah, Capehart took a notion to amuse himself with one of Mr. Morris's papers, the Liberia Advocate;[119] many copies of which had been given to me by his Agent, Mr. Good for distribution.[120] That number furnished a piece in Arabic characters with a full translation in English. It began well—inviting the Chief to come and see us &c., but midway it contained an unsavoury revelation about our once being slaves. Now the Mandingoes have a hard hearted and unalterable opinion respecting the freest man if he has once been a slave.[121] Capehart called my attention to this imprudent disclosure, which so alarmed me for my future standing in Musahdu that I cut out the offending passage, both the English and the Arabic, leaving the Mandingoes to conjecture what they pleased as to what caused those two uneven gaps in that paper. Remembering that Prof. Blyden once complained to me how hurtful in its influence a similar writing contained in the prefatory remark of some Bible brought from Beirut,—might prove, I wondered how the present mischievous confession could have ever crept into a piece meant to be a general invitation to the noblest Africans in the land, as well, as also, to show our own dignity and importance.[122]

Since my visit to Musahdu in 1868 that ancient town has been troubled by a warlike Expedition as scourging as Blamer Sissy['s] incursion, and account of which I have given in my Narrative of journey to Musahdu in 1868 and 69. In the beginning of the dries in 1873, Sargee's war bands having scoured the whole Country, at length marched against Musahdu itself and held that capital in siege for seventy five days: the people were in such straits that they were compelled to dig wells in the town to supply themselves with water and to use the material out of which their houses and horse stables were built, for fuel to cook with.[123] Sargee all the while, accompanied by his horse men rode around the walls taunting and insulting the inhabitants. One day the besieged people called out to him asking what had they ever done to him that he should bring war against them; to which it was answered what had the chickens done to the hawks that the hawks were always seizing and devouring them: an answer equally true and equally cruel, Sargee had no better reason than the hawks.

These unrelenting Cavaliers are said to put a very simple alternative to a poor foot soldier who can neither further fight nor fly: they hail him to "Stand and you are a slave; run and you are a corpse."

Things were now growing desperate in Musahdu: soon all food of every kind would be exhausted: the besiegers were in possession, and consuming the farms outside. It was therefore resolved by the Musahdu people, that messengers would have to be sent to Blamer Sissy for aid,—with whom it seems they were now, not only upon good terms, but in close relationship,— In order to get their messengers clear of Sargee's army who had surrounded the town and was narrowly watching every movement, a battle would have to be fought. Three messengers were selected so that if one or two fell the third at least might escape to perform the service. The messengers were made ready; the day was appointed: the people of the town issued forth and desperately engaged Sargee's force; in the general melee, the messengers escaped.[124] The people withdraw [*sic*] again into the town having sustained some loss, but effected their purpose[.] Two weeks thereafter Blamer Sissy came with his famous cavalry of a thousand horse[s] and an arrangement was made between him and Sargee that the latter should in none of his enterprises in that section of the Country disturb any Mohammedan town: and Musahdu in particular was to be considered inviolable: on the other hand Sargee was to be at liberty to wage war against any caffre (pagan) town Mandingo or Boozie, that he choosed.[125] Pleased with this settlement of an affair in which he would have been inevitably worsted had they come to blows, Sargee confirmed his understanding with Blamer Sissy by an oath; presented the king with two hundred captives which he had taken in his wars: and took his departure for his own capital Barqunah [Gban Kundu or Gbangunò 9°0'N, 8°35'W].[126] His war-bands are still preying upon such Mandingo towns as are not able to withstand their attacks. Sargee can muster a cavalry of five hundred horses.

The Mandingoes of Musahdu were anxious to know our military resources, and whether we could bring our forces into their Country: why we did not come in numbers and trade, since a few of us were not afraid to venture a journey to their Country. They suggested the idea that we should make an establishment. They were animated no doubt with the idea, that this would give protection, permanence and safety to their own home, in addition to the advantages of trade; they assured us that they were willing to travel backward and forwards in our company with their cattle and trade, but that the Pessy Country was too unsettled for them to attempt traffic by themselves through it.

I had made the king an insignificant present, but he had so delicate a sense of hospitality that he seemed studious to show that his regard for our comfort was not abated in any respect on that account: and he would often come himself with the people who brought our food in order to see it properly delivered to us.[127]

He became an attentive and patient listener to all I had to say for the government. He earnestly represented to me his difficulties; solemnly assured me, that even my visit to Musahdu would be construed into all kinds of purposes and engagements with the government, that even his own friends became jealous, suspicious and envious. His friends would suspect he had received large gifts and would demand their share—his enemies would likely pounce upon him as soon as I was gone hoping to wrest from him by violence and war, what they supposed I had given him. He regretted much that I had not brought him a good quantity of powder. He brought up the letter business again: wanted to know in what light I had represented him to the government; and he so agitated my feelings and sympathies, that I endeavored to reconcile his mind and to assure him that the government would certainly be more mindful of his Country and his affairs hereafter; and that he might always be sure of at least one visit a year; and that he should send some of his men of learning to Monrovia to represent in full the state and condition of his Country, whereupon I was given to understand, that had the letter been answered it would have established confidence and assured them of a proper reception and treatment.

Not answering the letter was looked upon by the Chief men of Musahdu as little less than an insulting indifference; and I hope that this will be the last instance in which in our dealing with the powerful and intelligent communities of Soudan we will show a carelessness, that would be culpable negligence, if it was practiced towards the rudest savages to be found on the continent.

One day we had an interview in which several Mandingoes from Bopora, took part: and the assistant Commissioner [Capehart] (talking in Vey) according to his custom did the expedition as much ill service as it was in his power.[128] Stating the great amount of money I had started with, a great portion of which was destined for Musahdu: his entire ignorance of what had became of it, that he had lately joined the expedition by a different route and found that the money was gone: that he would have the whole matter looked into when he got home. The Mandingoes at Musahdu are not easily carried away by every wind and doctrine: and my friends not only informed me of what was said to my detriment but advised me not to bring my assistant again with me to Musahdu as he had been laboring to injure me.[129] Then was the truth as to his conduct and the consequent loss of the goods fully set forth; and the Mandingoes were brought to know that about the expedition, which they otherwise would never have learned.

After I had been in Musahdu several days I was introduced to Blamer Sissy's general, Dah Cidee: he was a young man about 28 or 30 years of age.[130]

Blamer Sissy in order to insure the safety of Musahdu and its neighboring town, had placed detachments of troops in all of them: the whole being under the command of this young general. We became fast friends and were wont to exchange visits. He was inclined to be communicative, but he was certainly surly. I never saw him smile or laugh once during my whole stay in Musahdu. He came to my house often and I suspected him of prying into my affairs in order to report to his master Blamer Sissy at Medina, all he could learn respecting me. When we had become very intimate he [was] continually pressing upon me to go to Medina—spoke contemptuously of the Musahdu people, declared that what they had was nothing to what Blamer Sissy's kingdom could show: that his master had gold by the measure, the great size of Medina, its large population—its wealth in comparison to all I had seen in Musahdu: and outside reports confirmed that what he said was true,[.] He wished me to go and spend a year there. One morning on visiting his house he offered me a heavy gold ring for paper. I proposed to give him eight sheets of writing paper for it: he charged ten. I did not haggle, but paid it down and also gave him a sheet as a present. The next day a Bopora Mandingo informed him, that I had not given him enough by twice the amount and representing the matter to the king, had the bargain re-opened. I grew angry, and stood upon my pride and refused to give a single sheet more, though I had abundance of paper. I resented the interference of the Bopora Mandingo: and with more pride than profit demanded a return of the paper and the bargain to be cancelled; and I was heartless enough to return even a gift of rice which the young man had made me in consequence of our bargain and our friendship: a piece of foolishness of which I have often since repented. Dah Cidee commenced to take it to heart and I could see that the young man's feelings were deeply wounded in the business, but his Musahdu friends or more strictly the Bopora Mandingoes who were at the bottom of the whole of it—would not let him exercise the wishes of his own heart: so he came the next morning and openly confessed that he was in the wrong, but that in all his actions he was closely watched; and that he was not free to do as he pleased outside of the especial business on which he had been sent. I thereupon tried to make amends for my own harshness and gave him three sheets of paper: telling him at the same time, that a bargain was a bargain with a Tibbabu (an American) and that we never receded from the terms of a bargain, when once it had been agreed upon and the article exchanged. He said that what he really wanted was powder. I told him I had none for sale.

On Thursday 12th of November, the king [Vafin Dole] went to the Mohammedan service full dress and on horseback accompanied by his relations similarly mounted. The service was held outside the mosque on the eastern side: all the principal men of the town came on horseback. The Imaum dressed in a Scarlet Cloak mounted a stool covered with a white cloth while six attendants held a large white covering over his head during the time he was reading the service.[131] Dah Cidee finely mounted and in full war dress, and accompanied by a detachment of his soldiers came to service and received a special blessing from the Imaum.

The service occnpied [occupied] two hours; they sat in regular rows upon their knees: as soon as their worship was over they mounted their horses and rode around the mosque several times. In this exercise a young lad of sixteen was carried by his steed under the eaves of a house and swept off: the vicious animal accompanying the act with a kick with both hind feet, which fortunately missed the boy, but would have certainly killed him if the blow had reached him.

Many of these animals are fiery and vicious and have a knack of biting and kicking and running up against obstacles to bruise your limbs or brush you off.[132] One of my friends, who seemed to be desirous of seeing his horse play his wanton tricks on a Tibbabue, saddled and bridled him for me to ride, but I called one of my carriers, Coleman, a tall Kentuckian and a tyrant and a terror to rude and evil horses.[133] The Mandingo refused to let Coleman mount him for Coleman came at him as if he would throw the horse instead of the horse throwing him.

In the afternoon the king sent word that I must accompany him to the great square where the Mahommedan services were still going on: this time out of condescension to me he went on foot, and I dressed myself somewhat after their fashion and went with the king and took my place beside him on his carpet. The military exercise commenced and many speeches were made in which the Liberians were complimented upon their regard for Musahdu in having sent messengers twice to see the town and the king, which had not been done to any other Mandingo Community in their country. This I know disturbed the jealousy of Dah Cidee whose growing dislike to the Musahdu people showed itself daily for he was in constant palavers with them about his soldiers; and he was always underrating them to me and exalting the importance of his own Sovereign, Blamer Sissy.

The military gathering was very large: it consisted of Archers who seemed to be a body particularly by themselves, Fusileers, whose muskets made out in firing, always snapping two or three times before they would fire. The cavalry was a strong and very effective body. Seeing that I was pleased at the way they managed their horses: my friend hinted to me that I must stop coming to Musahdu on foot, that I must ride, that every gentleman in Musahdu had a horse, that I was well able to buy one, that I had obliged their King to come on foot to the great play because I did not know how to ride.

Figure 30. Manding warrior by Mohammed Chejan Kromah in Macenta, Guinea, 1992.

That if I bought a horse they would soon learn me, and that we could then go easily to any of the neighboring towns together. This was a very good admonition in this part of Africa.

Many little incidents interesting in themselves and illustrative of the character and manners of these people occurred, during the nine days of my abode in that town.

Once I went to pay Dah Cidee a visit and seeing a number of fine looking young men standing around him, I inquired who they were, individually, and received the invariable answer "Blamer Sissy Siafah," ie Blamer Sissy's soldiers.[134] They were the finest looking young men both in feature and in stature that I had ever seen. We quickly became intimate friends. One morning going out the southern gate leading to the market hill, several of them were on the hill playing with their arms and as soon as they saw me made a semblance of attacking. I immediately charged them sword in hand—apparently killing the first and wounding two of his comrads and they were exceedingly amused at seeing the Tibbabue jumping around in big boots and doing deeds of valor. Coming out of this same gate another morning I met a number of Blamer's young soldiers who ranged themselves in a line and extended their muskets slanting to the ground, which is a military salute of respect with them. They little knew the feelings that act provoked in my breast. It is hard to say which, is in most need of the other: the Liberians of the Mandingoes or the Mandingoes of Liberians. One thing is certain, that it will not be wisdom for Liberia to remain another year out of Soudan commercially or politically.

As the weather promised fair I attempted on Friday 13th, of November, to take an observation; my artificial horizon of quicksilver was giving me no little trouble and exhibiting a surface scarcely as large as a twenty five cent piece, and that covered with scum. While I was standing near waiting for a favorable opportunity, with my sextant in hand there being white flying clouds,—a woman with that meddling ruinous curiosity belonging to her kind, put her hand on the vessel containing the quicksilver and tilted it: in a moment it was in a thousand spangles on the sandy ground beyond the possibility of collection or recovery. I was exasperated enough to have struck her to the ground, but the poor creature was sufficiently stricken with fright, and I strove to practice that even temper of mind, of which king Krymeseh in the Pessy Country had given me an example: to be moved, excited or provoked at nothing; especially as so many misfortunes were happening to me and to the expedition under my conduct. I afterwards substituted palm-butter well strained, which being gradually warmed by the rays of the sun gave me a wide clear, and unobscured horizon superior in every respect to the darkened limited one I had just been deprived of.

It is the ambition of the Mushadu Mandingoes to speak English: this is particularly so with the women—One of my Congoes carried away by an undue feeling of affection or politeness was accustomed to address all the women he met in Musahdu, by the name of My Dear. Going out one morning through the eastern gate to take an airing, I was accosted by a Mandingo girl "My Dear Tibbabue ekoonah," i.e. My Dear American good morning:'—on she passed triumphing in her own mind that she had effected something in English, not knowing that she had really said more than perhaps, she intended.[135] The term was afterward universally applied to us by the women: and I could not but anathematize the Congo for his foolish sentimentalism. But the stranger that may now enter the gates of Musahdu will be assuredly greeted with it by the women if he is an American.

I now began to think of taking my leave of Musahdu and signified my intention to the king: he requested me to sit down.[136] He then held his two hands together and caused his people to fill them up with gold rings, saying that he had intended what I saw, for me with the expectation that I would have returned quickly and brought him some trade; that he had even persuaded his people to get together their cattle and gold so as to have a lot of trade on hand ready when I should have returned. But I had gone and stayed away so long and had even made him so ashamed among his own people: that he scarcely knew how to depend on me. I told him that all he said was true, yet it was not my fault; but that I would labor hereafter to prevent a recurrence of a similar neglect and would farther try and bring along with me some American traders and establish them in his country. He gave me another letter to the government, with the intimation that he hoped we would not take six years more to answer that.[137]

On Monday 16th November we took our final leave of Musahdu and coming to the same village we had quartered at when we were on our way to this town, we found it so occupied as not to be able to afford us lodgings. We had therefore no other resource but to push on to Vukkah quite a long stretch from Musahdu and which we attained only by hard and rapid walking: the elevated hills of Vukkah seemed to be at our feet but it took us from 7 o'clock a.m. to 6 o'clock p.m. to reach town itself.[138]

Tuesday 17th November rested at Vukkah. Between Vukkah and Musahdu, are the great plains of iron, of which I had occasion to speak of in my travels of 1868 and 69. Owing to the distance and the great haste we were in, to gain the town before night, we could give but little attention to the appearance of objects around us, but seeing a black substance obtruding itself, in patches and peices [*sic*], through the soil, iron ore and stunted reddish grass, I stepped out of the road and took small piece[s], and which has since proved to be[,] by persons capable of judging—what I suspected it was—stone or anthracite coal.[139] It is really needed where it was found if any use is to be made of those plains of metal from whose bosom it was taken. But Vukkah and its neighborhood, is a mineral district, and will prove valuable in more respect, than one whenever it comes to be examined.[140] Our friends at Vukkah showed us all kinds of hospitality upon our return. These

Mandingoes exhibit an ingenuity and talent in every thing they attempt. On the night of our arrival, with an instrument the sounds of which resembled the tones of a piano, they came and serenaded us. The instrument is a curious construction of 8 keys of a hard and sonorous wood attached to a double number of gourds sized to regulate the sound.[141] They are certainly, by nature skilful musicians and ahead of our Veys who are not to be lightly held in that respect.

About 5 o'clock p.m. Tuesday 17th. of November—a tornado came up; the country is situated, that in these exertions of nature, you may be standing in a region wholly undisturbed, while it is raging in another plainly visible to you. So it was at Vukkah: a tremendous clap from the east, and thereafter black and grayish clouds muttering with thunder and every now and then quickening with lightning, came billowing along the sides of the Vukkah hills while their summits were at the same time lit up with the glory of a setting sun; presenting a scene of grandeur never seen and impossible with us down this way because of the absences of great physical developments of land.

We started from Vukkah 7, o'clock a.m. [Wednesday, 18 November] and passed through the same flourishing district along the base, of the Vukkah hills we had passed through before on coming to Musahdu. The cattle had not been turned out, and the women were busy milking. The animals seemed to be very tame, for they were confined in no way during the process of milking, the women milking one ten or fifteen minutes and then going to another. The pens or yards made of the crooked brushwood of the country stretch along the path on each side, and are also scattered in all directions over the face of this fruitful plain. My own people had a happy time of it and I could scarcely get them away from the place owing to the Mandingo girls interfering with corn and potatoes and invitations to help and wait until they cooked rice, &c. We travelled on with the Vukkah hill[s] on our right and reached Ballatah about 10½ o'clock a.m.

Some of my people who lagged behind reported to me that a Mandingo Chief accompanied by 25 warriors—having been driven from his home by Sargee, was on his way to Dowilnyah's to seek protection and [p. 38] a place to reside within the Boozie territory.[142] Had we been established there, this man would have resorted to us. A travelling fort in that country would be the nucleus of a Liberian-Mandingo settlement numbering many towns as large as Vukkah or Musahdu itself, and that before 2 years had elapsed.

This chief had to pass through Ballatah but the king, Pownla, on account of some old feud refused to allow the distressed man a passage; we ourselves strove to prevail on the king, but he remained obstinate.

Pushing on from Ballatah we came to Pellezarrah [at] 4 o'clock p.m. On Thursday 18th.[143] November, we left Pellezarrah 8 o'clock and passed the towns of Vasser Assahghi [,] came to Gubbewallah [at] 2½ o'clock p.m. That afternoon about 5 o'clock, we had a very hard shower of rain accompanied with hail.[144] Left Gubbewallah Saturday 21st November and came to Ziggah Porrah-Zue about 10 o'clock having crossed the St. Paul's River: travelling briskly we passed Boe and came to Pynyah.[145]

Left Pynyah Monday 23rd [November], passed Yuckubori and Yabu the road all along being remarkably level, we halted at Yokabu, king Gavasee's town and accepted his hospitality of fowl and rice, firing my revolver for his gratification; we passed on to Sappah and came to Formu a new town being built by the Sappah people.[146] All these people showed us uniform kindness and I endeavored to requite them as well as I was able[,] not hesitating to part with my wearing apparel piece by piece. We left Formu on Tuesday 24th November the last Boozie town, and began to traverse the Pessey region: we passed Bassyahwaney a Pessey town and crossed a branch of St. Pauls river on a floating bridge made to rise and fall with the swelling of the stream[,] its course at this point is E. E. S. E. We arrived at Pahya 1½ o'clock p.m.[147]

On Monday November 30th started from Pahya direction west: passed one of Krymeseh's towns Suckoramu [Sukramu or Sukolomu, 7°43'N, 9°29'W], and came to a town called Kelamu [Kilimu] the people of which refused at first to let us pass as they seemed to be hatching up some mischief among themselves, after wrangling and parleying for some time they at last consented to let us pass aronnd [around] the inside barricade so that we might regain the main road: this was the only town during our whole journey that was unkindly disposed towards us: about 4 o'clock we were unexpectedly introduced into Zolu [Zolowo, 7°39'N, 9°33'W] [,] a town I had spent sometime in on my first visit to Musahdu in 1868.[148] We had edged our way Westward on [to] the Boozie Country again. My friends were delighted at seeing me again. Leaving Zolu Tuesday December 1st and passing through one of its villages we arrived at Pattahya at 3 o'clock p.m.[;] the road was a private path made to avoid war parties.[149] a [*sic*] rougher road for holes, ditches, and every other obstruction we had not met. From Pattahya we reached Pallakah about 10 o'clock.[150] On Thursday [3 December], we started from Pallakah and came to Jowah, on Friday [4 December] we passed Bellamu, Yangwelli[,] Pallingah and came to Bockquetah Seetroeebo's town 3 o'clock p.m. Staurday [*sic*], 5th of December having crossed the St. Pauls river we came to a town called Pye.[151] December Monday 7th journeying from Pye and passing a village we came to Barmaquirlla's town where we met the king of Sakatah[,] Popowskearg who had changed his place of abode in consequence of the treacherous conduct of some of the people of Sakatah.[152]

Tuesday 8th of December we started from Barmaquirlla's town, and passing through several small villages we came to king Baryta's town where we breakfasted.[153] Pushing on to Ponafah's town we reached Sinoya [Sanoyie]: the next day we came to Darpellas town.[154] On Thursday 10th we started from Darpellas—direction south and south west—passed through 8 villages and came to Dogbar Krapo—we halted at this town and rested several days.[155] On Monday 14th December we took our leave unaccompanied however by assistant Commissioner Capehart who choosed to remain at this town: for two successive days we had to take up our quarters in the woods there being no town for 2 or 3 days walk between the town we had left and the vicinity of Careysburg, we therefore had to "bush" it.[156] On Wednesday [16 December] during our travel the path was so obstructed by trees and vines pulled down by the Elephants, that we could scarcely make our way over them. This region plentifully abounds with them. We got in to George Simpson's town[,] a Pessey man[,] about 3 o'clock.[157]

He complained to me of the conduct of Capehart's people in passing through and seizing his fowls, after they had deserted and was [*sic*] returning home from Waugi's town. I made him all the amends I could, and tried to smooth his feeling in the matter.

Thursday 17th of December we started from Simpson, gained Careysburg, pushed on and arrived at Mr. A. Washington's on the St. Pauls River about 4½ o'clock p.m. and on Friday [18 December 1874] 1 o'clock we were walking in the streets of Monrovia.[158]

In Submitting this report to your Excellency [President James S. Payne], I have to say, that the [p. 40] Expedition was well furnished, so far as goods or merchandise was concerned: or the means which was [*sic*] necessary to secure the favor of those among whom it had to pass: and yet, no expedition was ever more cursed or rendered unfortunate through the disaffection and improper conduct of its own people. The expedition was, however, forced, in spite of all difficulties, to its destination, nor should it have seen Monrovia again, had it not done so.

THE PESSY COUNTRY.

It will be seen—may it please your Excellency that it would be of immense service and advantage, if we were to establish some show of power there, that is, if the government were to do so.

It is a district populous and fertile enough, but so distracted, not by real war, but petty feuds; that for want of order and quietude, it benefits us very little. It is however, beyond all doubt, the granary of this portion of Liberia; and the place from which is to be derived all our manual labor.

A system should be inaugurated in which any number of small or even large children, being procured, should be brought down and bound in our Courts under certain restriction and regulations (learning to read and write in addition to their trade or avocation) imposed by the government on those who are to be their guardians. This would be a great blessing to the Pessies in general who are a people of a mild and moldable disposition, and who from their docility and tractableness, bid fair to out travel all our surrounding tribes in manual and artizan labor. The distinction has not been sufficient by [*sic,* sufficiently] understood between laboring, and by civilizing and bookishly educating our natives: Since many have been bookishly educated without being really civilized, and have become the worst elements in the body politic: while it is a fact that the civilized native even if he is not so bookishly educated is the best member of society: though a just mean makes the best man.

The government can easily dominate the Country itself, by erecting 10 block houses which is sufficient to span within an easy day['s] march of each other to the Boozie section, close to Musahdu; or within four days walk of that place. It would introduce a settled order peace and encouragement to industry among them as they now stand. The Pessy Country is where we are to get our grain and manual labor from: they also manufacture a great number of Country cloths.

But they cannot, be said to be wealthy, that is, you cannot go to a single man and have a dealing of a thousand dollars with him.

He cannot offer you a hundred head of cattle: he cannot sell you a thousand weight of ivory or a thousand pieces of cloth: Yet from their collective industry, pretty much like it is in the Coastwise trade (where time and trust is also largely allowed)—the population being dense—you can by travelling from place to place secure a great deal. Introduce order and security, and that which is a great deal will become an immense quantity.

There are people there, that is, the kings of large sections of territory, who would be glad if the government would establish protection, along the roads, and assume rule where nobody rules and all is anarchy and confusion: —and as kings Keany and Krymeseh say, they would join the government in working or fighting to establish that end: they say they are willing to make the roads where the government wishes and as it wishes, but the government must keep them open: no one Pessy king, having power or authority enough to keep a road open beyond the extent of his own territory: These people are willing for anything the government chooses to propose and promise cooperation in every way.[159]

In improving a road already made[,] no better people could be employed for cheapness or whatever else.

In making regular civilized roads, where the wheel-barrow[,] spade and pickaxe are to be handed:—under proper direction and for a very small amount, the Pessy people would both please and surprise us.

So here is a Country extensive in territory and dense in population and easily manageable.

THE BOOZIE COUNTRY

may be said to be in a similar condition and stepping out of that section into the region of the

MANDINGO LAND

We came to a country and people somewhat different to deal with.[160] The Mandingo country is an elevated plateau 192 miles in a straight line from Monrovia direction North 47°45'30" East; and by an easy dry time journey can be reached in 12 or 15 days.[161] When you get there, you come among communities large, powerful and warlike; and not without intelligence, and in an open country.

From a single individual you can purchase 2 or 3 hundred head of cattle—gold in quantities can be bought: horses at $30, $40 and $50 apiece.

Civil commotions are quite frequent, troublesome and upon an extensive scale. Commerce being the forerunner of civilization, the Government would have to establish in this country a strong trading fort, with an armament of 2 guns and 50 men: this located at the base of the Vukkah hills could hold its own without difficulty—our merchants trading to and fro and acting in conjunction. All the trade in cattle, gold and horses would certainly be attracted to this point. In fact we would have command of the trade, and a prosperity with which we are entirely unacquainted and unused to, would soon visit this section of Liberia. Besides the Mandingoes themselves would come down with their substance in the same way that they now go to the Gambia and the Senegal: places much farther removed from their country by 5 or 6 hundred miles than what Liberia is. Both the governments and the merchants of the above named places take pains, to foster, encourage and protect such inter-communications, not acting as we do: alike indifferent, insensible and ignorant of the only sources from which we can derive prosperity and wealth.

The means of which we are capable, is adequate to the Enterprise because of our natural assimilation to the tribes: and the distance being so much shorter.

I must call your Excellency's special attention to one matter, and that is the time of travelling, or indeed of any practical operation in the interior: this must be always in the dries, or the season very near it. The rains permit nothing in the way of observation, comfort or facility of travelling, the whole country is covered with an excessive, rank vegetation; the rains flood and deluge the very sections that deserve investigation. It is a complete obstruction to everything in the way of seeing and examining: to say nothing of the exposure and damage to the health of the people engaged, and the ruining of goods, instruments and books necessary to carry on operations with.

Pertaining To Our Interior Policy.

We must give the natives better examples of our steadiness of purpose, and the regularity of our engagements, than what our late dealings with them have shown. At Sinoya king Seeway gave me a paper made by our people in 1854, signed by D. J. Beams, then came the effort of Mr. Roye in 1870 by

Commissioner W. S. Anderson.[162] Ours followed four years after in 1874. The natives in the Pessy Country complain, that what we read to them in the Resolutions were very good, but then were we sure that we were coming back again: the Americans were in the habit of coming out there, and making promises, and they never saw them again for years afterwards. The same complaint fell upon us at Musahdu—of not keeping our word—and with greater force. The letter written by king Vomfudolla of Musahdu in 1869 [*sic,* 1868] to the government received no attention, and when I went back again to that Capital—no explanation I could give seemed to render satisfaction,—I have included a copy of it in this report, in order that it may receive attention.[163]

I must therefore recommend to your Excellency, that delinquencies of the kind by the government be not repeated, but immediate action and a satisfactory answer be made to the Musahdu Mandingoes, this dries. It concerns interest and purposes, that we cannot afford to be indifferent about if we are true to ourselves as a nation:—and it will look very ill on our part if the natives can show that they have exhibited a greater concern for us—all of which we have suffered to pass by unheeded—than what we have manifested with all our pretensions to civilization and religion[.]

The Resolution of the Legislature was thoroughly and extensively read and circulated among the natives: Particular pains was [*sic*] taken with that matter by the Chief Commissioner; and the natives throughout the Pessey country, and the Boozie Country,—and the Mandingo Country where the expedition went—have them now put away and kept to be shown at whatever time we may visit those Countries again; either as evidences of our promptness, and the honor with which we regard our engagements, or as an example of the manner, in which we triflingly and falsely give our word.[164]

In these matters our true interests are best consulted by a strict adherence, to our written word: it gives influence, some honor and respect: things not to be lightly estimated.

The calculations on which the Map of the expedition is founded, is the result of much pains-taking, and a great deal of mathematical labor, and yet not a tithe have been given to this business such as it deserves: for reasons of want of proper assistance: but more so from the want of proper instruments a list of which I have given below for your Excellency's recommendation to the Legislature[.][165] They are identically such as are used in similar operations, all over the world, and are really indispensable to a correct locating of places upon the earth's surface.

They are as follows:

1. Patent Circle, made by Pistor and Martins at Berlin 5 inch radius with 2 verniers reading to 10 sec. with lamp for night reading; cost 90 rix dollars, one rix dollar being 68 cents $72.1 [*sic*]. Patent Sextant by the same makers, called the Prismatic Sextant reading to 10 sec. cost 80 rix dollars—$52.40.[166]

7

The Journeys and the Interior

As the first descriptions of these regions of what are today Liberia and the Republic of Guinea, the diaries tell of populous and vibrant economies, thriving on the traffic between forest and savanna, coast and interior. The large fortified towns and their hamlets which are described; the peoples and their languages; their trade, farming, and industry; and their alliances and political relations will provide a foundation through which further reappraisal of Liberia's past can progress. Yet even as these accounts describe prosperity, they tell of warfare and the cultural transformations associated with it. They tell of slavery, depopulation, and economic decline, which continued on into the twentieth century.

In this chapter, we identify the languages, ethnonyms, and polities that the travelers described and contextualize the events they documented. Our intent is to clarify some of the comments and descriptions made in the texts in a more comprehensive way than notes permit and to indicate where the accounts themselves contribute to wider debates concerning this region and its political, social, and economic history. We begin by locating the languages that the travelers heard spoken and described. Sharing a common language, of course, does not imply having common political interests. We go on to describe the turbulent political mosaic of the region and the ways that the travelers' journeys and experiences were framed by it. In particular, the accounts describe a great deal of warfare. A casual reading of the texts can leave the reader with an image of an anarchic region, with villages fighting countless petty and pointless wars, an image which Anderson himself sometimes promoted in his 1874 account. The impression is of a culture of warfare and of a lack of order motivating the Liberian colonists to intervene for the common good.

Yet a closer reading of these accounts enables a series of regional political alliances to be discerned with a clarity and detail hitherto impossible (cf. Person 1968; Holsoe 1966; 1976–77). Internal tensions and conflicts between them were shaped by the need to trade, to access export markets for goods and slaves, and to import weaponry. When engaging with this, wittingly or not, the travelers' position as "aloof civilizer" was untenable. The way Liberians engaged with the populations they traded with and passed through played into the balance of power and the course of interior conflicts.

Languages

Descriptions of languages that travelers gave often fade into descriptions of peoples, assumed united through their common language. In making such ethno-linguistic associations, it is hard to discern the degree to which the travelers were reflecting their own perceptions about language and ethnicity, those of the peoples they encountered, or were rather reflecting some iterative relationship between the two. Undoubtedly making ethno-linguistic associations was common to political discourse in the interior at the time, but as we shall clarify, political alliances frequently crosscut any such ethno-linguistic boundaries. Certainly, all the travelers drew strong ethnic stereotypes, as was common for the time (e.g., see Johnston [1906] 1969, chaps. 27–29). Sims, for example, described the "Kpellays" or Guerzé as a "savage, barbarous tribe." Yet while drawing on such stereotypes, the accounts also frequently illustrate real political and historical differences between those speaking a common language: for instance, between the Waima and the Domar Loma, or between the Barlain and the Bokomu Kpelle. And when Sims finally reached the Guerzé, he described anything but savagery and barbarism.

The region is dominated by three major groups of languages: Mande languages, West Atlantic languages, and Kruan or Kru-type languages. The historical roots and interrelationships among the region's languages have been the subject of numerous studies, which there is no need to review here, but which assist in placing the ways the travelers depicted the dialects and peoples they encountered.

Mande Languages

Musadu, which Seymour and Anderson were struggling to reach, was considered a Manding capital. Anderson termed its people "Mandingo" and the place "Manding." At times, Sims used the term "Manni" to refer to the place and people. Anderson's use of the term "Manding" corresponds broadly to people who speak a cluster of Northern Mande languages that linguists now call Manding (comprising Bamanakan, Maninkakan, Mandinka, Dyulakan, Maraka-Dafinkan, and Manyakan), spoken across a large swathe of West Africa that includes present-day Mali, Guinea, Côte d'Ivoire, Sierra Leone, Liberia, and Gambia.[1] The Vai people call all Manding *Manimor/mòò,* or "Mani people." Manni (Mani) or Manding is also a variant of the name of the thirteenth-century empire that the legendary Sunjata founded—Mande, Manden, Mandin, or Mali (Jansen et al. 1995; Austin 1999; Conrad 1999b)—and the name of the peoples (Mane or Mani) who invaded the present-day Liberian–Sierra Leone coast in the sixteenth century (see, e.g., de Almada c. [1594] 1984, 24 ff.; see also Hair 1968a, 8). Yves Person has argued that the leaders of these Mani were descendants of Fongama Kamara, who came from Konya, just south of Musadu (Person 1971, 675–680). Sims made many references to these people from Manni, whose "capital" was Musadu.

Yet Sims also distinguished the Manni-Mohammedans from the "Mandingoes." He wrote that the "Mandingo" and the "Manni" were traders and migrants, and that they dressed the same and looked alike. But he associated the latter with a "kingdom," being more "civilized," speaking a different language, and being more "rigid" Muslims. He located the Manni-Mohammedans whom he met in the interior of Kpelle country as those who originated from Musadu and its environs. In this he seems to have been making cultural, linguistic, and religious distinctions between those who are today referred to as the Manding of Konya and the Manding who lived west of the Fon-Going Mountains; both speak Manyakan, one of the core Manding languages (Cutler, with Dwyer 1981, 4; Cutler, with Talawoley 1981, 4; Dwyer 1989, 50; see also Delafosse 1901, 218–219, 267–268, 305; Welmers 1958, 1974, 1–2; Hair 1968a, 53; Dalby 1971, 5–6; Vydrine 1999, 9). The Konya Manding speak Konyakan, or the "language of Konya," one of several Manyakan dialects. Busekan is one of the largest Manyakan dialects spoken west of the Fon-Going Mountains. It is odd that Sims suggests that these languages were "entirely different"; the linguistic difference was certainly not a matter of language but of dialect—Konyakan versus Busekan and other western Manyakan dialects.

The Konya-Manding still claim to be imperious over their western Manyakan kinspeople, who, they often say, speak *Maniya-tu* or "bush Mandingo." This distinction between what are essentially the Bopolu Manding and the Konya Manding of Musadu took on added meaning for Benjamin Anderson a decade later when he criticized the former for obstructing Liberian efforts to make contact with the "Western Mandingoes." D'Azevedo observed, in Anderson's case, that "The 'Mandingo' there [Bopolu] had become 'different' so that it was necessary to look further into the hinterland [to Musadu] for contact with the 'real' Mandingo" (1994, 221).

Sims noted that many of the languages of the region were related, a position now upheld in language classification, which considers Manding, Vai, Loma, and Kpelle as part of the broad family of Mande languages. But nowadays, linguists draw distinctions between Northern, Southwestern, and Eastern Mande groups (Dwyer 1989; Vydrine 1999).

The Vai language, variously referred to as Vey or Vy, has been the subject of much historical inquiry. Vai speakers inhabit the coastal region, but unlike other peoples there, their language is closely affiliated to the Konyakan language of Musadu. Linguists classify Vai as a Northern Mande language, but not as Manding. Thomas Bowen, as early as 1857, wrote that "The Vy people . . . belong to the same extensive ethnical family as the Mandingoes" (Bowen [1857] 1968, 40; see also Rambo 1849, 305). Historians have since reached consensus that the earliest Vai descend from the sources of the Niger, near the intersection of present-day Sierra Leone, Guinea, and Liberia, with some later groups migrating from Musadu to the coast.[2]

Sims spoke Vai and found that he could exchange greetings with Ibrihims, a Manding trader from farther north at Jenne in today's Mali. Nevertheless, Sims needed his interpreter's assistance to continue the conversation. Sims suggested that Vai was also related to Kpelle. Today, Kpelle is classified as a more distantly related Southwestern Mande language, along with Loma (or Toma or Boozie), Bandi, Mende, and Loko (Cutler, with Dwyer 1981, 4; Welmers 1949; Hair 1968a; Dwyer 1989, 50). Kpelle speakers are, in the texts and elsewhere, variously referred to as Pessi, Pessah, Pessies, Kpessi, Kpwessi, Gberese, and Guerzé, with the latter being the Guinea variant (see Welmers 1949, 209). At the time of these accounts, there were several major polities that spoke dialects of Kpelle. The Barlain (Gbalein) spoke this language, as did the Bokomu Kpelle with whom they persistently fought, according to Anderson, Sims, and Seymour. The Bokumu Kpelle were referred to by Anderson as Kpesseh and by Sims as Pessahs. According to Sims, the Barlain spoke the same language as the Pessahs, though they denied all relationship with them. Sims also suggested that the Barlain were at war with a different people called the Kpellays, who are probably located in the Kpelle of present-day Guinea (Guerzé), which he later apparently visited.

Historians now accept that Kpelle speakers once lived as far north as Musadu and Konya, and that they had close social, political, and economic ties with the Manding-speaking Konyaka, who eventually came to dominate this area. The Konyaka began to sever their ties with the Kpelle as they forced the Kpelle to migrate into the forest, perhaps during the fifteenth and sixteenth centuries (Person 1984, 312, 317). The Boozie peoples are today referred to as the Loma in Liberia and the Toma in Guinea. Again, however, those who spoke this language inhabited distinct polities at the times when Seymour and Anderson passed through their territory. Anderson used the term "Boozie" or "Boosey" to refer to several groups, including the Wymar Boozie and the Domar Boozie. Today, they are known in Guinea as the Waima Toma and the Ziama Toma—and in Liberia, the Ziama Loma were centered in the Zorzor district. The origins of the term "Boozie" to refer to people who call themselves "Loma" remains obscure. It predates the arrival of Americo-Liberians.[3] Jeanette Ellen Carter cites a popular story from a Loma newspaper: "Those living in Guinea are known as the Toma. In Liberia, they are also known as the Buzi. The latter term is apparently derived from the name of an important Loma chief, Buse, from Fisebu living possibly in the late eighteenth century, who sent men to the coast. When querried as to whom they were, these men replied 'We are the Buse's men' and hence the appellation Buzi.[4] The Boondee people, who live northwest of Bopolu are the people today called Bunde, who form a clan within the Voinjama chiefdom of Liberia and are considered to be Loma speakers" (*Loma Weekly,* 28 June 1963, in Carter 1970; see also Holsoe, d'Azevedo, and Gay 1969; Holsoe 1979b).

Other Southwest Mande speakers mentioned in Anderson's 1868–69 account include the Hurrah and the Mambomah. Hurrah are known today as the Mende, who mainly live in Sierra Leone, although some do live in the Vahun chiefdom of the Kolahun District of Liberia (Holsoe files).[5] "Mambomah" was the generic term then for the people who today are called the "Bandi" (Holsoe 1979b, 11).

West Atlantic Languages and Kruan Languages

The accounts also refer to peoples who speak languages unrelated to the Mande groups. In particular, the Gola language is now classified as part of the West Atlantic group, along with the Kissi. In the coastal region, however, the languages spoken are mainly classified as Kruan, including the Dei (or Dey), Deh (or Kuwaa, or Belle), Kru, Wee (or Krahn), Bassa, and Grebo (see chap. 5; Holsoe 1979b, 8, 13, 18, 22–23; Duitsman 1982–83, 28, 31; d'Azevedo 1995, 93 n. 95).

The Dei or Dey speakers whom Benjamin Anderson met had their former power base north of the Saint Paul River in and behind Vannswa (Vonsua), extending along the coast, north of the Mano River and into Sierra Leone. They resisted the settler colonization of Cape Mesurado throughout the 1820s. Over the next three decades, Dei power weakened considerably as the settlers gradually moved up the Saint Paul River, as the Gola in the interior expanded southward, and as Manding traders became more influential. Under this onslaught, the Dei were overwhelmed and pressed to a small coastal strip while the Gola overran the Dei's interior towns. The Gola even crossed the Saint Paul River to form what came to be known as the Todi and Deng Gola areas (Holsoe 1971b; 1976–77, 3; d'Azevedo 1994, 198–216).

These Dei or Dey are not to be mistaken for the Deh who appear later in Anderson's first trip, inhabiting what today is known as the Belle- or Kuwaa-speaking area. These are the most northern and western remnants of what was once probably a larger Kruan-speaking region from here to the coast. Though it is best to avoid using the term "Belle" because it refers to cannibals, these people are still widely called "Belle." At some point, perhaps during the sixteenth-century Mani invasions, the territories between the coastal Dei and these Kuwaa were separated by the influx of Kpelle speakers from the east and Gola speakers from the north and west (Person 1971, 681; Jones 1981). Paynesville, where Seymour established his interior mission, appears to mark the southern boundary of the intrusion of the Kpelle speakers into the Kruan (Bassa) region, which separated the Kuwaa (Belle) from their Bassa, Gbi-Doru, and Wee (Kruan) cousins.

The Bassa people, whom Seymour referred to a great deal, inhabited land between the coast and his interior home of Paynesville and also spoke a Kruan language. Anderson wrote about the "Gibbee" who lived around Mount Gibi. At least today, they are Bassa speakers.

The "Basees" referred to by Sims, who frequented the Barlain markets, were probably Bassa, but they were certainly at some distance from their home territory. Yet Seymour journeyed from the Bassa borders to Barlain Kpelle in under six days, and presumably traders knowing the route and people could cover the 60 to 80 miles much faster. And it is not inconceivable that enclave villages of Bassa speakers persisted farther north. Anderson's "Mamba-Bassa," one of the groups that comprised the "Condo confederation" in Bopolu, were Bassa.

Linguists would now question Sims's interpretation that the Bassa and Kpelle were related. In classification, both languages belong to the Niger-Congo family, but Bassa is a Kruan language and Kpelle is a Mande language. Any similarities that Sims noted were probably based on loan words rather than on structural similarities. Kroomen, who comprised Anderson's carriers, were Kru (Krao) speakers, whose home territory was down the coast in what today is Sinoe and Grand Kru counties.

In some cases, it is difficult to identify with certainty the meaning of some names that the travelers used. We have been unable to identify Anderson's "Haumths," who lived among the Gola, Vai, and Kpelle. The "Bandas" in the Bopolu area might have been a Bandi or Kpelle clan (Holsoe files). Anderson's "Queahs" were a Kruan-speaking people no longer recognized as a separate ethnic group who resided to the immediate interior of Monrovia.

English

Several of those whom the travelers met spoke different forms of English. Today, linguists identify four types of English in Liberia (Hancock 1970–71; Singler 1981, 17–24). Liberian Pidgin English and Interior English are respectively spoken along the coast and in the interior by those who have little or no Western schooling. Sims's guide, Gotorah, for example, spoke Liberian Pidgin English. Characteristically, "th" shifts to "d" when it comes at the beginning of a word, so that "them," "this," "these," and "that" are respectively pronounced "dem," "dis," "dese," and "dat." Liberians who attend Western schools learn to speak Vernacular Liberian English. Settlers who trace their descent from the United States or the West Indies speak Settler English. That Sims, Seymour, and Anderson also used British English terms such as "row," "His Majesty," "half-shire," and "beck and call" reflected the influence that Great Britain and its literature had on Liberia up to the early twentieth century (Crummell [1862] 1969, 12–13; Singler 1981, 10). These terms have largely dropped out of usage in Liberia, though some of these features may still exist among the older Americo-Liberians who live up the Saint Paul River. Portuguese loan words also appeared in Liberian English, such as "*sarvy*" (as used by Sims) from the Portuguese *sabe* or *saber:* "to understand" or "to know," as do words such as "*kwenda*" and "*ampemba*" from other African languages, such as Ki-Congo, which mean "to go" and "devil." These are examples of words from several African and European languages that have been incorporated into the different forms of Liberian English (Brown 1999, 32, 39).

Peoples and Politics

The travelers made many observations which suggest that linguistic groupings did not map neatly onto political unities. By combining observations from the different accounts, it is possible to construct a picture of the shifting mosaic of political interests, alliances, and even large-scale federations during this period. Understanding this mosaic is also important for understanding the routes that the travelers took, the problems they encountered in certain locations, and the impact of these journeys on regional politics. We begin tracing these political dynamics with the political confederation focused on the town of Bopolu, which is a key to understanding the politics in the other regions discussed: Barlain Kpelle, Southern Kpelle, Loma, and Musadu.

Bopolu

Sometime before 1800, fighters from the Loma, Bandi, Manding, and Kpelle region defeated Dei forces in the region of Bopolu and established the town of Bopolu to serve as a halfway station for traders between the distant interior and the coast. By funneling trade through this town, its leaders could profit from its trade. In this way, the "Condo confederation," as it came to be known, became large and important. A mixture of groups living in close proximity around Bopolu had existed for some time. Condo included Loma, Bandi, Manding, Kpelle, Fula, Mamba-Bassa, Gola, Vai, "Brandahs," "Wrahs," and "Bandas." The rulers of these groups comprised a council, and most decisions were made on a unanimous basis. Each group lived in its own quarters, and many outlying towns were ethnically defined, so that one particular group lived there. For instance, Saplema was Loma. Totokwele, the chief's town, was mainly Bandi. Groups often fought on independent terms but shared their booty with the other members of the confederation ("The Kondahs" 1840, 334–335; Holsoe 1966, 1976–77, 2; d'Azevedo 1994). Whereas Anderson wrote that the Vai language was used for general communication, perhaps indicating the importance of the Manding (both Manding and Vai are Northern Mande languages), Sims, in contradiction, observed the use of an especially developed Creole as the common language of Bopolu.

It is possible that a confederation of this nature had existed in the region at least since the 1700s, described by Dapper's sources as the Hondo (Dapper [1688] 1670, 381; [1668] 1686, 165). The importance of the Condo confederation was, however, associated with the rise of King Boatswain. A leader of this Condo confederation, Sao Boso, or King Boatswain, emerged as the chief sometime before 1820. It was he who came to the assistance of the Americo-Liberian settlers and "saved the colony" when it was on the verge of annihilation from hostile neighbors in 1822. Presumably, he was aware of the importance of such settlements for regional trade, from the example of Sierra Leone that had been founded some decades earlier, and saw advantage in nurturing and holding the key to the new colony. He gained control over trade from Bopolu to Monrovia by exerting authority over the intervening Gola chiefdoms. Although backed by the force of his "standing army," he seems to have secured further control through a marriage alliance, in marrying a Gola wife.

Good relations with the Americans and control over this trade route were achieved in part through the assistance of Gatumba (Getumbe), whose father was Vai and whose mother was Gola and who was a chief of the Dei-speaking village of Suehn, which Anderson visited in 1868. He was a loyal supporter of Sao Boso and the confederacy and was related to Sao Boso's Gola wife, whose marriage he may well have arranged. It was the same Gatumba who had been at Cape Mesurado in 1822 (selling a group of slaves) when Americans (Lt. R. F. Stockton and Dr. Eli Ayers) landed to negotiate land for the new colony with the local Chiefs. Gatumba subsequently worked in the interests of the confederation.

The confederation became powerful under Sao Boso, and when he died in 1836, he claimed to control thirty-two barricaded and innumerable half-towns. Whether this was his personal domain or that of the political confederation known as Condo, over which he exerted some control, remains unclear. The issue of his successor led to ruptures in the confederation, in its good relations with the coast, and in its capacity to facilitate, control, and profit from interior trade. War spread as factions from Sao Boso's once unified confederation started to vie for control of trade routes.

It appears that Gola factions in the confederacy deliberately caused ruptures in trade with Monrovia to exert authority. Gola interests had been eclipsed early on in the succession issue, and one can speculate that Gatumba thus chose to demonstrate the importance of Gola to the confederation by disrupting the Bopolu-Monrovia trade paths. He supported Gola factions hostile to the American settlement and was even behind some attacks on American settler towns along the Saint Paul River in 1840. Liberians responded to this, sending Governor Buchannan to destroy Gatumba's village of Suehn. But gradually, both by controlling trade between Bopolu and the coast and through military strength, Gola forces emerged as the most powerful element to the confederation. The Gola defeated Dei, Kpelle, and Bassa elements in war and resisted both Manding attempts to trade with the coast and Americo-Liberian efforts to extend trade into the far interior (Holsoe 1976–77, 2–3; d'Azevedo 1994, 198–221; see also "Following the Trail of Benjamin Anderson" 1973).

During Sao Boso's life, several Americo-Liberians visited Bopolu. Relations were cordial, and Liberians judiciously overlooked the confederation's lucrative export of slaves from ports farther west (Gahlinas). After Sao Boso died in 1836, the ensuing wars over succession disrupted Liberian missions to Bopolu.

It was not until the 1850s that political relations within the confederacy were normalized again and its dealings with the Americo-Liberians improved. Improved relations were sealed when one of the sons of Sao Boso and his Gola wife, Momolu Sao (Sims's Memmoru Sowe and Anderson's Momoru Son), who had been living in Monrovia with the McGill family, was invited back to Bopolu to head the confederacy. By then, Gola interests in the confederation had gained ascendancy. Gatumba had gained influence throughout the confederation, and he was able to act as "kingmaker," ensuring that Momolu Sao—related to him on his mother's side—became the leader of the Condo confederation (Holsoe 1971b, 350–351; d'Azevedo 1994, 220, 225–226).

That Momolu Sao inherited his position despite being a younger brother may have been because of his good connections with the increasingly powerful Liberian republic. Yet younger brothers often became militarily more powerful than their older brothers in the Manding world, where brother rivalry is notorious (Jansen and Zobel 1996). Rather than live in Bopolu,

Momolu Sao moved to neighboring Totokwele on the Musadu road, a village founded by his father with the help of Bandi supporters (Holsoe 1976–77, 3–6). Both Sims and Anderson on his first journey passed through Bopolu when Momolu was alive, but after he died in 1871, political relations in the confederacy deteriorated once more.

Barlain Kpelle

Although those in the Barlain kingdom spoke the Kpelle language, Sims noted how the Barlain people claimed to be distinct from other Kpelle more to the east and to have vanquished the original Kpelle inhabitants of the province. In 1858, Barlain was certainly a populous and vibrant economic center, with Sims reporting the cycle of daily markets and the multitudes visiting them from neighboring territories and beyond. In 1858, most of its towns had substantial populations of Manni-Mahametan (Manding) traders who "settled in Barlain for the purpose of trafficking with King Boatswain's people." According to Sims, they accounted for half of the population of Pallaker (Kpayakwele) and a third of the population of Bamaquorli (Gbakwele).

Yet at the time of the visits in 1858, indigenous leaders of Barlain appeared to resent the control over regional trade that the Condo confederacy exerted and the Manding trader elements in their society which this confederacy favored. It appears that only the Manding elements in Barlain could profit from trade with the coast, which had to be channeled through Bopolu plying the "Great Barlain road" that Anderson spoke of in 1874. In Bopolu, non-Manding traders were discouraged, penalized by high taxes and the threat of enslavement.

Sims provided an invaluable account of the way that the interior peoples from Barlain mounted opposition to the Condo trading monopoly. In the 1850s this could not take the form of open revolt, as the Condo confederacy and its allied Gola and Southern Kpelle forces had, "after a hard fighting, succeeded in shutting their enemies up in their own country." Opposition had to be more subtle, drawing on a second source of indigenous power, one of its "secret fraternities" known as "Mama" ("Mamma"). Sims wrote that the cult of the Mama spirit was a powerful force in the region, and "all the kings, princes and headmen were his agents" (chap. 3, 106).

According to Sims, Mama originated in Bousa (Loma). He actually suggested that "Mama" was the spirit of a Loma prince who had who had supposedly decamped to Barlain, died there in 1856, but "remained living in splendor somewhere in or near Pallaka, a report to that effect having been promulgated by his followers" (chap. 3, 113). All interior peoples were encouraged to be initiated and to swear an eternal alliance against peoples who were not members of the league. Members vowed not to fight each other, to support each other "unto death," not to prevent anyone from joining, and not to enslave members. Crucially, they also vowed to open trade routes between the coast and the interior. The fraternity became powerful, and "people came hundreds of miles to take the Mama gree-gree." Tactically, the leaders welcomed the chief of Bopolu, Momolu Sao, to be initiated in 1857, who, "to his astonishment," found that, without breaking faith with Mama, he could no longer prevent the interior natives from coming to the beach and trafficking with the Liberians. He could not have known the vows until he became a member. Momolu Sao felt tricked and was almost deposed by others in the confederacy, who resented the threat to their trading monopoly. It was not surprising that Sims took the "talk of war" between Barlain and its neighbors seriously.

And war soon came. By the time of Anderson's first visit, armed conflict superseded the more subtle anti-Manding trader techniques using Mama. Anderson noted that Barlain, presumably in alliance with Waima Loma and its leader, Dowilnyah, through the Mama cult, was at war with the Domar Loma and the Condo axis to which it belonged.

The Waima Loma had deposed the Manding faction of Jaka Kaman Kamara that Seymour had encountered before Benjamin Anderson's visit there. The Manding fared badly in Barlain too. By the time of W. S. Anderson's visit to Barlain's capital city of Kpayekwele in 1870, there had been a complete "cleansing" of the Manding from Barlain. He "did not see a single Mussulman, not even a priest, in any of the large towns" (Blyden 1870, 283). Anderson also described the towns' impressive (and newly rebuilt) defenses.

In this alliance, the Barlain were the enemies of the Domar Loma leaders who still retained their allegiance to the Condo axis—albeit perhaps with internal opposition. In 1868, Anderson recounted how Barlain Kpelle had been at war with the Domar Loma. Moreover, he also indicated that within the Domar Loma there were strong factions sympathetic with the Waima Loma–Barlain cause. Indeed, the chief of Zolowo, the Domar Loma town which Anderson visited, had covertly assisted the Barlain Kpelle in this war but had been found out and so had fled to Salaghee or Salayie, east of Zolowo.[6] Although Salaghee was allied to the confederacy, it had suffered much in the war as it bordered on Barlain Kpelle. The Condo leader, King Momoru, sought to negotiate an end to these wars. Indeed, Anderson's Mandingo guide, Beah, was far more than a guide, having been instructed by King Momoru to reconcile the differences between the Domar Loma and the Barlain Kpelle.

The Barlain Kpelle–Domar Loma war continued. In 1874, when Benjamin Anderson actually passed through Barlain Kpelle, he noted how Barlain Kpelle forces in Bonya continued to fight the Domar Loma–Condo alliance in Salaghee, and had been fighting for ten years. Other towns in Barlain Kpelle did not fare well in these wars. When Benjamin Anderson visited Kpayekwele four years later, it "had been visited by a war which had burnt one half of it." The people "were at the point of starvation." They had been attacked not by Domar Loma forces, but by "another Pessey tribe called the Pelle or Belle people," which had harassed the country for two years, without any advantage being gained by either party (chap. 6, 255). These were the Kpelle, who lived in the Bokomu area that borders the Barlain to the southwest and the Kpelle-speaking area south of the Saint Paul River. They were, according to Sims, allied with Gola and Condo interests and were at odds with Barlain Kpelle during the war.

In 1874, Anderson, who approached Musadu via Barlain and who counted the Waima Loma among his friends, did not attempt to cross the front line into Domar Loma country. He took a more easterly route via N'Zappa which—we can presume—also formed part of the anti-Condo warring alliance. When he returned, though, he strayed into Zolowo, in Domar Loma country, in a hurry to return. Zolowo, which although within Domar Loma had many sympathizers in Barlain, had a secret path across into Barlain and sent Anderson along this path to "avoid war parties" (chap. 6, 274).

Southern Kpelle

There is ample evidence from the accounts of Anderson and Sims that the Condo alliance had considerable sway within Southern Kpelle country, limiting the capacity of interior peoples such as Barlain Kpelle to trade through Southern Kpelle to the coast. Sims noted that Condo, Gola, and Southern Kpelle forces had, by 1858, shut up interior peoples in their own countries (chap. 3, 112). Although Condo control of Southern Kpelle was probably achieved in part through alliance for mutual advantage, it would appear that Condo had a strong upper hand in this relationship. This was most notable in trade patterns: interior regions such as the Barlain Kpelle could trade through Southern Kpelle in the 1850s along "the great Barline road," which ran through their country on the south side of the Saint Paul River (chap. 6, 246). Yet as we have seen, this trade route was open only to Manding traders, presumably operating in accordance with Condo policy, a control which Liberians sought to evade.

The influence of Condo on Southern Kpelle became clear when Benjamin Anderson passed through Southern Kpelle country in 1874. On entering, he became embroiled in conflict. The first towns which Benjamin Anderson visited as he journeyed inland were Pockpar's and Kyapar's. It appears that these towns were not "on the Great Barline road" (chap. 6, 246), but several other towns with which they were federated were, among them Dogbar's town, Seaway's town (Saneyie), Fuella's town, and Darpella's town. Anderson heard later (from the Southern Kpelle chief Dogbar) that W. S. Anderson had traveled to Barlain via these same villages four years earlier. Whether W. S. Anderson's route was accidental or at the behest of the leaders of these villages is unclear, but using this route certainly seems to have angered other neighboring towns. That the Liberians had even begun to institute this route through the establishment of blockhouses would have worried these other towns further. So when Benjamin Anderson journeyed into Southern Kpelle (i.e., south of the Saint Paul River) via the very same villages, neighboring Southern Kpelle chiefs in this federation failed to treat this as coincidence and accused Pockpar and Kyapar of acting "without the consent of other chiefs in the country."

It would appear that these other Southern Kpelle chiefs saw in the activities of these renegade villages a threat to their own trading interests, being on the Great Barlain road, and seeing their monopoly undercut. They accused the other chiefs of taking Benjamin Anderson by "roundabout paths so that some persons might get money out of [them]" (chap. 6, 246). But it would appear as well that these other chiefs also saw a greater danger. The main Barlain Kpelle road passed through these villages, but Condo interests regulated its trade. In encouraging passage along other routes, the renegade Southern Kpelle chiefs appeared also to be operating against Condo interests. Was Condo to be suspicious that this reflected broader dissent among allied Southern Kpelle chiefs (in an era in which dissent against Condo was likely)? If so, then presumably the activities of the renegade chiefs would bring war to the country more generally. Inviting the wrath of Condo forces was to be avoided.

The latter concern would have been very real. From the moment Benjamin Anderson set foot in Southern Kpelle country, he was being followed, "dogged and watched" by Condo forces (chap. 6, 247). They followed him to Pockpar's village. After he left, they destroyed the village, enslaved the people, and killed Pockpar—a stark warning to other Southern Kpelle chiefs to keep in line. The Condo forces were, at that time, garrisoned in Waugi's town. Dogbar, who hosted Anderson, also grew afraid that the Condo forces would soon attack him and implored Anderson to send for Darpella, a known ally of Waugi. Dogbar also publicly distanced himself from the other renegade chief, Kypah, when Anderson arrived by kidnapping the daughter of Kypah.

Although Benjamin Anderson suggested that Waugi had "purchased" this war party for the special purpose of destroying Pockpar's town, it would appear that there was more to it. As Anderson noted, the war party was watching Anderson's movements, and not just seeking to attack Pockpar. Second, the Condo had their own forces resident in this region of Southern Kpelle, "a mixed crowd of Golahs, Veys, Pesseys and Haumths armed to the teeth" (chap. 6, 247). Third, the Condo forces were led by a Gola chief (Zodopanga) who had been sent by Fahn Kwekwe (Fahquaqua), the ruler of the area known today as the Lofa-Gola chiefdom, north of the Saint Paul. Fahn Kwekwe was a key figure in the Condo confederacy, as a first cousin of Momolu Sao of Bopolu; their Gola mothers were sisters (Holsoe 1976–77, 3–6). Although Momolu Sao had died by this time, the Gola-Condo alliance still sought to prevent unregulated trade between the Liberian settlement and the Barlain Kpelle–Waima Loma alliance, with whom Condo allies were then at war. And here was Anderson, carrying ammunition and heading for Barlain.

Benjamin Anderson said that he managed to arrange a meeting of Southern Kpelle chiefs in the region who lived on the Barlain road, and that they agreed "to open and clean the road." Rather grandly, Anderson claimed to have shown them "the folly of allowing Golah people to come to their Country, plunder and devastate everything, and then return to their own home loaded with spoils" (chap. 6, 247). Wittingly or unwittingly, Anderson was inciting Southern Kpelle to work against Condo interests. The very next day, he encountered the Condo army, learned that he had been tracked, and faced a barrage of hostile questions, asking why he was passing through Pessay and not Gola country, where "they knew better how to treat Americans" (chap. 6, 247).

Eventually, the leader of the Condo army led Anderson back to "the Barlain road." But, before going, most of Anderson's co-travelers decided to opt out and return home, surely worried about the road ahead. The main problem for them would not be in traveling through the rest of Southern Kpelle, but in crossing the front line from Condo-influenced Southern Kpelle to independent Barlain Kpelle (chap. 6, 255). Here again, Anderson encountered war and the unruly, freelance behavior of army forces. Anderson first traversed the Saint Paul River to the village of Sakatah in what is now the Bokomu Kpelle region, and then crossed the Yea tributary to enter Barlain Kpelle. War parties, presumably Condo, were stationed in the Bokomu Kpelle area, fighting the Barlain Kpelle. On entering Sakatah, one war party (we can presume Condo in makeup) was immediately rumored to be making for the town. Perhaps through Anderson's intervention this was avoided, and the war was "deflected" onto another village. In what must have been against the interests of the Condo forces, the king of Sakatah then facilitated Anderson's journey across the front line to Barlain Kpelle. One is not surprised to find that by the time of Anderson's return, the Sakatah king had been deposed. On his return, Anderson did not attempt to cross from Barlain via Bokomu Kpelle, but instead crossed the Saint Paul River directly into Southern Kpelle country.

Anderson interpreted the wars he encountered in Southern Kpelle as squabbles and petty broils. Given the broader picture, however, it appears that the squabbles were linked with a broader political matrix, and especially the Gola people's concern that the trade to the interior was going to bypass them by moving to the south side of the Saint Paul. Exactly whether or why it was Pockpar who had first "invited the Gola war party" to the region, as Waugi told Anderson, may never be known (chap. 6, 248). The image Anderson had was that such forces were mere mercenaries. Although they surely operated at times in such a "freelance" fashion, the forces would appear to have had other strategic roles. That Pockpar had sent the warring party into its virtual annihilation in a fight with the Gibi people may have been a trick—certainly the residual army took its revenge.

In short, in promoting the Southern Kpelle–Barlain Kpelle road to Musadu, W. S. Anderson and Benjamin Anderson in 1870 and 1874 were taking sides in a longstanding war; they were acting against the interests of the Gola-Condo alliance and in favor of the more interior peoples, the Barlain Kpelle and the Waima Loma.

The Waima Loma and Kuankan

In 1858, Seymour made observations which suggest that the Condo conferederation extended its influence as far north as the Loma-dominated country around Solong (Zolowo) and Kuankan. He referred to the "Suloang Busa" as "part of the Condo country," and to "King Carmers," or Jaka Kaman Kamara, based at "Quanger" (Kuankan), as the "King of Upper Condo country" (chap. 4, 143). This influence is reflected on the 1879 map that Anderson published, showing how Upper Condo regions which had not yet been visited had been annexed to Liberia (fig. 27). However, it is unclear from the accounts to what extent, and in what ways, these territories operated independently from the confederation's nucleus at Bopolu.

While Bopolu is known to modern scholars as the capital of the Condo country, Seymour described Jaka Kaman as "King of Upper Condo country" and the rightful King of upper Buzi country (chap. 4, 143, 144). Thus, although the Waima were Loma speakers, they were at Seymour's time integrated within the wider political confederation within which much regional trade was conducted.

That Jaka Kaman was a patrilineal descendant of the legendary Manding warrior-chief of Musadu, Foningama, indicates the extent to which the Condo confederacy had its origins in the earlier deft state building of the Manding Kamara of Musadu. The Kamara and its allies from Musadu and other areas used Kuankan as a base throughout the second half of the nineteenth century to increase their influence over Loma-speaking regions. Yet this expansion depended upon alliance as well as warfare (see Massing 1978–79, 52–56). It is quite possible that Jaka Kaman's mother, whom Seymour visited west of Oussadou, was a Loma speaker. Certainly Jaka Kaman, like his "brother" King Seiyea of Forsormer (Fassangouni), bore what the writers referred to as the "Weamo" (Waima) mark and so was an initiate of the Loma institution empowered to scarify in such ways.

Although Seymour wrote that Jaka Kaman was Manding, and the French reports in the 1890s stated that his son Kaman Kekula was "Malinke" (see, e.g., Murdza 1979, 424), both applied models of ethnicity that transcended any ethnic affinities, which did not so easily map onto the political realities at that time.

The political map of the Waima Loma altered between Seymour's visit in 1858 and Anderson's in 1868. The balance had moved against the Kamara and Manding, and perhaps created a reason for the Waima Loma to create ties with the Barlain Kpelle. Jaka Kaman had died a year before, in 1867 and was succeeded by his son Kaman Kekula. But within a year, the capital of the region had switched to the more ancient and thoroughly Loma town of Koiama Tongoro, the regional center of the Loma "Poro" secret society that King Dowilnyah controlled. It appears that with the waning of the political influence of Musadu, Waima factions reclaimed power independent of the Condo confederation. The tensions in this transfer of power do not appear to have been resolved when Anderson passed through in 1868. First, the Domar Loma (or today's Gbunde Loma) south of Waima appear to have remained loyal to the Condo confederation and had just attacked the Waima Loma at Boo, whom Dowilnyah successfully defended. By then, however, the southern villages of Waima Loma (including that of Forsormer (Fassangouni), headed by Jaka Kaman's brother in 1858) appear to have either seceded from Waima authority to Domar, opting for the Kamara-led confederation, or to have been defeated by the Domar. The Waimar-Domar border shifted from south of Forsormer when Seymour described it in 1858 to just south of Boo when Anderson described it ten years later. Crossing this border proved rather difficult for Anderson both on the way out and on his return. The difficulties that Dowilnyah had with other chiefs in Boo when Anderson was there presumably related to the tension between the advantages of maintaining good trade relations within the Kamara confederacy—and hence loyalties to the Kamara of Kuankan—and with the more independent-minded Loma, wary of political subordination to the Manding.

This political tension and transformation helps us understand several other elements in the text. First, we see why Seymour took the northern route from Boo to Musadu via Kuankan and Oussadou, whereas Anderson traveled from Boo to Koiama Tongoro and then east, avoiding Kuankan, and crossed into Manding across the Vukkah Mountains.[7] These mountains were an acknowledged border but were notorious for the hostilities that they presented travelers. It also accounts for the hostility that Anderson—associated as he was to Dowilnyah—met at the border town of Vukkah. In this vein, we also can see why Anderson met with hostility at Nonbohouta immediately after he crossed out of Waima to Domar country on his return journey.

In 1874, the "Condo route" that Seymour had taken was even further compromised, as Momolu Sao of Bopolu had died, leading to further problems of succession there. On this journey, Anderson completely avoided the Bopolu–Domar Loma route, taking instead the southern route via Barlain

Kpelle and then a roundabout, more southerly route to Boo which completely avoided Domar Loma. Finally, we see why Dowilnyah placed the blame for Seymour's attack firmly on Jaka Kaman and five other chiefs (who had all since died by "divine retribution"). Presumably, they had been the Waima chiefs loyal to the now-ousted Jaka Kaman. It is probable that when Anderson met Jaka Kaman's son Kaman Kekula, who protested his father's innocence, this was not in Waima country, where he would have been in danger, but perhaps in Musadu.

During the next several years, Kaman Kekula formed alliances with Musadu's chief Vafin Dole and other Manding to unseat dissident Loma factions such as those led by Dowilnyah. While in 1884 the Loma nearly repulsed Kekula and destroyed Kuankan, in the early 1890s the shoe was on the other foot, when Samori helped Kaman Kekula try to forge a route to Liberia's coast to get more arms. Kaman Kekula's advance into Liberia is known as the Sofa War. Kaman Kekula went to Bopolu, where his forces used this opportunity to strike against the Gola, who had sealed off routes to the coast and on the coast through the Vai "Tewo" region that borders modern-day Liberia and Sierra Leone (Holsoe 1974). Kekula later sided with the French against Samori when the French captured Samori's stronghold of Kerouane. The Loma took Kuankan in 1902 and drove Kekula's son and successor, Macé Bigné, to Beyla. The Manding regained possession of Kuankan with French help five years later (Blyden to Coppinger, 13 August 1891, in Lynch 1978, 425–431; Holsoe 1976–77, 4–5, 7; Massing 1978–79; Murdza 1979, 122–127; Fairhead and Leach 1994, 495–496).

Musadu

Benjamin Anderson referred to Musadu as the capital of the Western Mandingoes. The Americo-Liberians thought of Musadu as a capital in economic and political terms, viewing Musadu as the main trading depot between the savanna and the coast. But even at the time of Anderson's first visit it was in decline. According to oral traditions, Musadu was an early economic and political stronghold in the subregion. It was good for fishing, hunting, and farming and was a transit point between forest and savanna for traders. The town was allegedly founded by Musa Kromah and increased in stature as a military power when Foningama Kamara arrived, perhaps by the early sixteenth century, and made his headquarters there (Geysbeek 2002, chaps. 5, 7). When Anderson arrived, Musadu was therefore probably more than three hundred years old and would have been known as a "capital" for generations (Person 1972, 5–10; Brooks 1993, 71–74, 287–290).

Musadu is known as the foremost of the five towns of Konya (*Konya soluulu*), along with Diakolidu, Beyla, Dukulela, and Nyela. Anderson implied that these towns constituted a confederation under Musadu (chap. 5, 219). Oral traditions elaborately support Vafin Dole's contention that Musadu was "the mother of the country" (see chap. 5, 236) and explain how the Kromah (lead by Diakoli), the Bility (Beete), the Dukule, and the Nyen clans left Musadu and respectively founded these federated towns: Diakolidu, Beyla, Dukulela, and Nyela (Geysbeek and Kamara 1991, 67–69). Anderson spoke of this process in 1868 when he recorded claims that "all the other towns sprang from this one" (chap. 5, 219).

Although it was still known as "the old Kamara town," by the time of these accounts, the Kamara had been completely expelled from Musadu and were prohibited from having a permanent house there because they had abused their power at one stage (Geysbeek 2002, chap. 8). The town nevertheless remained strong after the Kamara were forced to leave, being controlled by the Kromah, the Bility, and the Dole, and retaining its status as a key northern trading center for the Condo confederation (Person 1987, 259).

It was from Musadu that the Kamara and other Manding under the Kamara's leadership extended their influence southwest into the Loma forest region and down the Lofa River toward the Macenta region, Bakedu, Bopolu, and the coast. In this way, the town was foundational to the Condo confederation, "the sacred capital of the Kamara" (Person 1968, 1:242, 288; 1987, 259). Oral accounts from Kuankan indicate that the Kamara acquired power in Waima Loma territory under Jaka Kaman Kamara of Kuankan in alliance with Musadu. The relationships between Musadu and Waima Loma areas often remained cordial, not least when the Kamara influence in Waima was strong, as in Seymour's time. Yet this relationship was surely as fragile as Kamara authority in Waima Loma. Between the visits of Seymour and Anderson, Musadu's power had waned. Ibrahima Sissi had looted Musadu twice in the previous seven years and was threatening for a third time when Anderson arrived in Musadu in 1868 (see chap. 5, 231). At the same time, the fortunes of the powerful Kamara of Upper Condo (chap. 4, 143), as Seymour described, had fallen. Linked in power, Kamara and Musadu were also linked in decline.

Both Ibrahmia Sissi and Saji Kamara put considerable pressure on Musadu and its region during the 1860s and 1870s, respectively. In the early 1880s, Musadu's confederation fell apart when Samori Touré defeated Ibrahma Sissi and executed the leaders of the Musadu confederation who had supported Sissi: Vafin Dole of Musadu, Mani Bakari Kromah of Diakolidu, Abudu Sware of Nionsamoridu, and Gbégbédu Kamara of Kuankan (Person 1968, 1:340–344; 1970, 84–88). After Samori crushed his opposition in Konya in 1881, he installed Kabine Kromah as Konya's leader, but in Diakolidu. This significantly lowered Musadu's status. Diakolidu and its sister town, Beyla, became the political capitals of the region (Person 1968, 1: 452 n. 68). The French made Diakolidu their administrative capital. Diakolidu subsequently became the most important trading town in the region (Chevalier 1909, 25–26; Duboc 1938, 225; Person 1975, 1483–1485; Ford 1990, chap. 3).

These cases of Condo, Southern Kpelle, Bokomu Kpelle, Barlain Kpelle, Domar Loma, Waima Loma, and Musadu repeatedly illustrate how people allied themselves closely to the narrow units of clan, chief, or region, but not necessarily to the "tribal" level which the Liberian government formalized during the next century (d'Azevedo 1989; Wylie 1989). These narrower units came to form what today the Liberian government calls "clans," territorial areas which have had some political cohesiveness. As the travelers' accounts serve to emphasize, not all of the clans are necessarily related by kinship. This local focus in politics, however, was compatible with broader alliances, again not necessarily tribal in character, through which regional political interests were fought. And this broader political field interplayed with differing interests between factions in the smaller "clan" units.

The accounts also illustrate how the populations of many towns now in Liberia were mixed, not least in including Manding settlers. The latter were frequently housed in separate town sections. The accounts suggest that relationships between the Manding and the other local residents were characterized by a mixture of alliance and separation and were variable and dynamic, as they are to the present. In Barlain, for instance, Seymour inferred that the Manding were farmers and were relatively settled, and were not simply present in the region as traders and clerics. The extent to which the Manding maintain distinctiveness remains an issue in the region. It is said that many do not allow their daughters to marry local men, but equally, many Manding men marry local women (in Kissi, Gola, and Mende villages, for example) and over only a generation can become culturally, politically, and economically incorporated into local society (Weisswange 1976; Ford 1989; Leach 1994; Fairhead and Leach 1996).

To take one example, Anderson observed relations between Loma and Manding in Bokesa, both of whom claim that their ancestors came from Musadu. A century later, by the mid-1960s, they still lived in different parts of Bokesa; they worked together but had separate secret societies, wedding ceremonies, and death rituals. The Loma could speak only a few words in Manding, but the Manding were fluent in both languages. This pattern was changing in the 1960s, as some Manding were growing up learning less Manding and "becoming Loma" (Weisswange 1974). Underlying tensions surfaced during Liberia's civil war and again started to split the two peoples (Højbjerg 2002).

Population and Towns

Many of the main towns described from Barlain northward were larger than Monrovia, or indeed than the entire Americo-Liberian population on the coast at that time. Moreover, in several locations, large towns were noted in high concentrations. Remarks by Sims about large-scale depopulation related to slave trading also suggest that many of the areas uninhabited at the time of his visit had previously been occupied. "Neighbouring peoples of the Pessah," Sims wrote, "armed and equipped by the slavers, carried death and desolation into the very heart of the Pessah country. Thousands and thousands were slain; thousands and thousands were carried into slavery; whole districts were depopulated" (chap. 3, 113).

In one of his earlier reports, Seymour gave similar testimony farther east, near the Saint John River, where encountering many deserted towns, he attributed low population density to "the effect of the slave trade and the continual wars." Both these cases refer to Kpelle or Kpelle borderland regions and to people there whom Sims characterized as less warlike than neighbors and as having suffered disproportionately from the effects of the slave trade.

Nearer the coast, Sims and Anderson noted the sparse populations and the related difficulties in travel because of this. Yet whether this area had never been inhabited or had been depopulated somewhat earlier is unclear. Dapper's account from around 1630 and the scanty evidence of other sixteenth- and seventeenth-century visitors to the coast suggest the latter, indicating that this coastal region was populous and prosperous in the mid-seventeenth century (see Jones 1983b, 25–27; Fairhead and Leach 1998, chap. 3). It has been suggested that depopulation in the vicinity of Monrovia could have been linked to American colonization and its impacts on the local economy ("Trade in Montserrado County" 1881). It is quite possible that such depopulation was an intentional strategy of the Condo confederacy to limit the capacity of Monrovia to pursue alternative trade routes.

The accounts do not give sufficient information for anything like a full reconstruction of the region's population at the time. They do, however, enable estimates of occupancy in certain towns, through relating numbers of houses, numbers of people, or both. Seymour and Anderson estimated the number of houses and occupants in twelve towns that they visited. Sims made estimates for one or the other, but not both. Seymour's general average ratio of houses to persons was 1 to 3.95, very close to Anderson's of 1 to 4.05.[8] Thus a 1 to 4 household-to-occupant ratio can thus serve as rough approximation to make estimates where numbers were not provided (see also Porter 1956, 61–65).[9]

Populations are also hard to assess given the potential mobility of people between these major towns and their dependent settlements. The travelers frequently made a distinction common in the region between "towns," which were usually fortified, and "half-towns." Half-towns were small villages that were settled from—and depended politically on—a larger town. They sometimes grew out of farming encampments occupied during the wet season. Half-towns would become quarters of the parent town, or could become separate towns if they were originally built far enough away. Whitehurst, for example, wrote that King Boatswain's half-towns were temporary residences for his slaves and for dependants of his headmen (Whitehurst 1836, 276),

Relative Ratio of Dwellings to Population

TOWN	HOUSES	PEOPLE	KNOWN RATIO	SOURCE
		James L. Sims		
Tawn	100	+ *400*		Sims, p. 94
Daydee	= size of Tawn	= size of Tawn		Sims, p. 95
Zama	+ *150 to 170*	600 to 700		Sims, p. 95
Ding	= size of Zama	= size of Zama		Sims, p. 95
Passilla	200	+ *800*		Sims, p. 95
Tuma	200	+ *800*		Sims, p. 100
Pallaquorly	− 500	2000		Sims, p. 101
Bata-ta	larger than Pall.	larger than Pall.		Sims, p. 101
Kelling		few people		Sims, p. 103
Pallaka	*−1000*	4000		Sims, p. 106
Gorlu	*−1000*	4000		Sims, p. 109
Kamo	− *500*	2000		Sims, p. 114
		George L. Seymour		
Paynesville	20	100	1:5	Seymour, 1856
Jourporpar's	85 (80)	425 (400)	1:5	Seymour, p. 125
Partargea	+ *60 to 70*	300 to 400	1:5/5.7	Seymour, p. 127
Pallarkar	+ *75*	300		Seymour, p. 128
Zanga	156	600	1:3.8	Seymour, p. 130
Wiruentar	+ *225*	900		Seymour, p. 132
Solong	− *550*	2200		Seymour, p. 133
Kiemer	180	900	1:5	Seymour, p. 136
Kleemoo	+ *238*	950		Seymour, p. 136
Vogermer	+ *300*	1200		Seymour, p. 136
Devarnee	300 to 400	1800	1:4.5/6	Seymour, p. 137
Quanyer	400	1900	1:475	Seymour, p. 139
Blackabelley	+ *425*	1700		Seymour, p. 140
Forsormer	700	3000	1:4.3	Seymour, p. 140
Boo	900	3600	1.4	Seymour, p. 141
Quanger	1500	4000 to 5000	1:2.7/3.3	Seymour, p. 143
		Benjamin J.K. Anderson		
Bessa's town	350	800 to 1000	1:2.3/2.85	B.A. 1868, p. 166
Zelleki's town	250	+ *1000*		B.A. 1868, p. 184
Barkomah	300	800	1:2.7	B.A. 1868, p. 184
Zolaghee	300	− *1200*		B.A. 1868, p. 186
Bokkasah	1500	7000	1:4.6	B.A. 1868, p. 193
Ballatah	*625*	2500		B.A. 1868, p. 206
Musardu	*−1750 to 2000*	7000 to 8000		B.A. 1868, p. 211
Yockkadu	*−438 to 500*	1750 to 2000		B.A. 1868, p. 221
Nubbewah's T.	*−750*	3000		B.A. 1868, p. 224

but that did not apply everywhere. Half-towns were usually not fortified, and inhabitants would seek security in the principal town during attacks. Others, however, were founded explicitly as "hiding" villages, associated with defenses in dense forests and rocky caves. In other cases, smaller villages would coalesce into larger settlements. For example, Jeanette Carter wrote that Zolowo, one of the towns that the three travelers visited in the Barlain region, was founded when five small towns came together to form "one large community." This happened as a defensive measure during a time—perhaps at the turn of the nineteenth century—when "continuing wars" started to disrupt life among people who lived in smaller villages that did not have walls (Carter 1970, 28–29, 43–44).

It is also common in the hinterland for towns to be partitioned between autochthonous populations and "strangers," be they captured slaves or trading communities such as the Manding. Several towns mentioned in these texts were "double" in this sense, including Fissabu, Kpayekwele, and Bokesa. The town referred to as Zear by Seymour and as Nyar by Sims was probably a separate settlement. This town was close to or adjacent to the main town of Kpayekwele and served as a base for Manding traders. The towns were separated a little distance from each other. The inhabitants thus benefited from the arms, proficiency in warfare, medicines, and trade the Manding brought while retaining some distance from strangers, whose conformity to local norms could not be assured. The separation also ensured that religious practices would not conflict. It is interesting to note, for instance, the location of women's Sande Society activities in houses attached to town walls. In the absence of such walls, Sande houses may be in town, but many activities take place in the concealment of a specially designed patch of forest next to or outside the bounds of the town.

Most towns had defenses around them in times of strife, although it appears that they were sometimes allowed to fall apart when times were peaceful. In the north, barricades generally took the form of mud walls. The farthest south that a mud fortification wall is mentioned here is in the Barlain region.

Mud town walls were typical from this region to the savanna, as it was possible for them to withstand the rains as they were thatched on top. W. S. Anderson gave a detailed description of the impressive walls surrounding Kpayekwele (Blyden 1870, 283). Yet twelve years earlier, Sims noted that the walls were not in satisfactory condition, suggesting that some rebuilding had gone on in the interim (chap. 3, 115). French occupying forces forcibly dismantled most walls in what became Guinea. The walls in Liberia have gradually decayed. Nevertheless, the ruins of walls can still be discerned today in many settlements and serve as a monument through which older villagers relate their history.

Farther toward the coast, the rainfall was too great for mud walls and

Figure 31. Graves of Kings, Boporo. From S. M. Owen's 1907 album. *Courtesy of the Royal Anthropological Institute, London.*

timber was plentiful. Fortifications consisted of wooden palisades. Sims, for example, referred to the barricaded town of "Daydee" (chap. 3, 95). However as Smith (1989, 99–119), who discusses barricades in West Africa, makes clear, they took many forms. They could refer to an entire wooden stockade encircling the town or merely to a stockade across the town entrances. Whitehurst published an unusually thorough description of the sophisticated defensive devices which could be incorporated into wood barricades in Pahboolah in 1836, similar perhaps to some of the barricades that the travelers saw:

> The barricade is composed of split timber about five inches through and twelve feet high, which being pointed, are first placed in the ground, consisting the outer circumference of the wall: the inner wall is composed of sticks of the same thickness, but about nine feet in length, and placed about three feet from the first. This being effected, with the doorway contiguous to water, and generally two others, the vacant space is filled up by sticks of wood placed in a longitudinal direction, compact and close, so that a body of solid wood, three feet thick, is formed. This, of course, is impervious to any of the light arms with which the native is furnished; and to guard against the effect of an *escalade,* the top of the wall is furnished with long sticks, about two inches at the base, terminating at a point, and twelve feet in length, which are laid

Figure 32. Photograph of the old wall of Zorzor. From George Schwab, *Tribes of the Liberian Hinterland* (Cambridge: Harvard University Press, 1947). *Courtesy of the Peabody Museum, Harvard University.*

> in fascines of three to four on the uprights, at an angle of 45°, and which are thus continued until the whole barricade is surmounted with this network. From the pliability of the rods used, together with their being laid in a direction which points them outward of the barricade, it would be impossible for them to support the weight of a man who should venture on them, as he must inevitably be thrown back from their elastic tendency, and should this not occur, expose him to the fire of those within. (Whitehurst 1836, 107–108)

Sometimes the wooden stakes took root, growing again into the forest trees from which they had been cut. This gave the borders of some villages the character of "impenetrable jungle," rendered more impenetrable still as lianas, thorn bushes, and other vegetative fortifications were encouraged to grow. In 1868, Anderson encountered one such village, Barkomah, in Bokomu Kpelle country, with dilapidated houses, "surrounded on all sides by impenetrable jungle, which is considered a sufficient barrier from all attacks" (chap. 5, 185). He attributed this to cowardice or laziness, perhaps misunderstanding the deliberate, effective, and labor-saving nature of vegetation fortification.

Figure 33. Boussédou (Boussémai) after French troops took the village, 2 April 1907. *Source: Inserted in the copy of F. Bouet,* Les Tomas. *Courtesy of Musée d'Histoire de Berne.*

Figure 34. The defensive wall of Boussédou, as it was being destroyed. *Source: Inserted in the copy of F. Bouet,* Les Tomas. *Courtesy of Musée d'Histoire de Berne.*

Figure 35. The gate of Boussédou, as it was being destroyed. *Source: Inserted in the copy of F. Bouet,* Les Tomas. *Courtesy of Musée d'Histoire de Berne.*

Figure 36. "Fortifications of the village of N'Zébela, circular fence, ditch, and wall. Group in the ditch." 1907. *Source: Inserted in the copy of F. Bouet,* Les Tomas. *Courtesy of Musée d'Histoire de Berne.*

Figure 37. "Here, one sees how a fortified village is organized inside." Soldiers demonstrate the firing platform. There is a pile of stones close by for the defendants to shower over their assailants. *Source: Inserted in the copy of F. Bouet,* Les Tomas. *Courtesy of Musée d'Histoire de Berne.*

Gates represented the only openings to a fortress or stockade and had to be carefully constructed and protected (e.g., see figs. 32, 35, 37, 38). Frequently, one had to enter a town through the gates of successive fortification palisades or walls, as Seymour described in entering Solong (Zolowo). Defensive strategies extended to layouts within villages. Houses were at times clustered close together, allowing residents who knew the village's layout an advantage in negotiating its passage ways and deciding whether to hide, escape, or attack. The Mende, for instance, described this strategy to T. J. Alldridge in the late nineteenth century (Alldridge 1901; see also Siddle 1969, 34; Abraham 1978, 15–18).

Houses, at least north of Bopolu, were generally circular with clay walls and thatched conical roofs, even now typical of the region. In Kpelle country, Seymour described very low, thatched, mud-walled huts with a mushroom-like appearance, similar to house styles farther south, more commonly associated with the Vai in the coast area to the west and with the Dan to the east (see Schulze 1973, 92–93). Farm huts, kitchens, and the like were frequently not built to last, using wooden or bamboo uprights as walls. Royalty occasionally had more impressive dwelling structures, such as Momolu Sao's frame house at Totoquella with a piazza surrounding it. They were probably modeled after those of the settlers on the coast, who brought American conceptions of architecture with them from the United States (Belcher, Holsoe, Herman, and Kingston 1988).

Towns themselves were kept clear of vegetation, except for one or more special trees such as the silk cotton tree, *Ceiba pentandra,* the sasswood tree, *Erythrophleum guineensis,* or one of the numerous fig species, *Ficus spp.* These trees, and sometimes others, are often associated with stories telling of the town's foundation and encapsulated powers important to founders and their descendants, as seen in stories told about the founding of Kuankan. They are sometimes said to be planted over special protective "medicines" or sacrificial objects, and their continued presence and upkeep is important for the safety and prosperity of inhabitants (see, e.g., Gottlieb 1992; Fairhead and Leach 1996, 76–79, 89).

Warfare

Warfare appears pervasive in these accounts, although one might recall how Seymour suggested that "war is not a common thing." But while frequently violent in the extreme, war was no indication of uncontrolled barbarism. Rather, there was a political economy of warfare, driven by both internal and external conditions, in which war gained its own momentum.

Internally, it seems that minor disputes between polities—such as the kidnap of a daughter—could sometimes erupt into war. There were few mechanisms to adjudicate disputes peaceably between groups other than turning to a third party, such as an outsider who could be deemed neutral to serve as an intermediary, although some of the literature for the area assumes that special initiation societies—discussed later in this chapter—played that role. This was certainly not to suggest that the societies of the region had no law and order. In contrast, the accounts describe the important role of judge that chiefs played (see Gibbs 1965) and a number of incidents where punishments—which would be deemed harsh by modern European and American standards—were meted out for offences ranging from rape to theft. All the travelers observed executions. Another common punishment that Sims and Anderson described was confinement by means of a heavy log fastened to the leg by a chain, a practice continuing to the present in parts of the region (David C. Conrad, personal communication, 1995). Other analysts have similarly documented people being placed "in stick" (Schwab 1947, 99; see also Whitehurst 1836, 274, 309).

The business of warfare and the insecurity it generated also created its own self-sustaining momentum. Citizens required the protection of effective warlords. The very existence of towns could depend on the status of a leader;

if a leader died, the town would often "go down" and the population disperse, as Seymour described for the towns he visited. Part of successful warfare was the ability to attract additional fighters by forging alliances with neighboring chiefs or by "purchasing a war," that is, assembling a war party by paying mercenaries and promising booty. Once a war party was assembled, however, it was difficult for a chief to sue for peace, as the army had its own momentum and needed the rewards of plunder. Anderson amply described this during his second journey. The role of war chiefs and mercenary soldiers seems to have been important in shifting balances of power. Mercenaries fought for those who purchased their services so long as they were well paid. The existence of freelance fighting forces need not, of course, rule out broader orchestration or regulation of mercenary fighters. Indeed, it appears to have suited the Condo confederacy to unleash units to destabilize regions of Southern and Bokomu Kpelle while maintaining a military presence there. This is a military strategy that so-called weak African states still use to the present (Schatzberg 1988; Reno 1997).

The texts give some detailed descriptions of the techniques of war and the use of a variety of weapons, including guns, swords and knives, iron claws, and bows and arrows, by war chiefs and their soldiers. Techniques in the forest region are graphically described for neighboring Mende regions by Malcolm (1939). Certainly, the accounts document the prevalence of wars in the dry season, when the weather permitted mobility and the demands on male farm labor were low.

In the north, warfare techniques were somewhat different, relying as they did partly on cavalry, as Anderson documented at Musadu on his first trip. Cavalries were most effective in the open savannah, where they could mount surprise raids on their enemies and withdraw quickly. Horses were less useful in attacking fortified towns and were of almost no use in the forest (Law 1976, 121). In the forest-savanna transition zone, the thick bush that was often established around villages was extremely effective in removing the advantage of cavalry in warfare. Nevertheless, as Musadu exemplifies, the infantry represented the bulk of the army, consisting of many slaves whose chief weapons were bows and arrows. In 1868 and 1874, respectively, Anderson wrote of the "poor foot soldier" and the boys who attended to the infantrymen, both of whom could have been slaves (chap. 5, 213; chap. 6, 266). In his 1868 letter, Vafin Dole spoke of Ibrahima Sissi's nine commanders who were the "leaders of the slaves" or infantrymen (chap. 5, 233). The cavalry followed the infantry and only became engaged in battle after the infantry used their arrows to disorient enemy lines (Legassick 1966, 96; Law 1976, 120; 1980, 133–146).

Anderson's descriptions of war around Musadu suggest that the cavalrymen fired but did not reload muskets from horseback; they instead fought with their swords and knives either on horseback or on the ground if fighting at close quarters. Not until the early 1890s, when Samori started to purchase rifles, could cavalrymen in this part of West Africa shoot repeatedly while remaining on their horses (Law 1980, 146; fig. 31). Shooting was also facilitated by the adoption of the stirrup from the Arabs (Law 1980, 107; Webb 1993, 226).

Cavalries in the savannah were generally divided into two categories: heavy and light. A heavy cavalry consisted of large, imported horses from the north, whose fighters used spears, swords, and muskets. The light cavalry that Anderson witnessed in Musadu in 1868 was marked by smaller, locally bred horses, whose warriors used lighter javelins, swords, cutlasses, bows and arrows, and muskets (see Smith 1989, 48–50). Anderson noted that the "large horse" was "used for show and parade," and that the "small horse" was "used for war" (chap. 5, 218).

Women usually did not fight directly but did play other significant roles in war, whether in guarding medicines which were thought to assist success or in acting as intermediaries and message carriers.[10] Among the Manding and many of their neighbors, powerful women—usually mothers, sisters, or wives—guided their sons, brothers, or husbands and directed the occult power that they needed to became great political and military leaders. They could also have a political impact by forming alliances through marriage, mediating between major rulers, providing critical food supplies, and seizing leadership opportunities—even military ones—during critical moments (Conrad 1999a).

All of the texts provide instances where women held leading positions of political authority over men. Sometimes, it seems, women took on such roles temporarily when their husbands or brothers were absent or indisposed. Seymour was hosted by the sister of the "king" of Solong (Zolowo), "who appears to be the third in the kingdom" (chap. 4, 133). In other cases, seniority accrued to women by virtue of age, co-wife status, or other ranks. Seymour, for example, referred to important decisions being made by the king's sister (chap. 4, 133). Certainly, the texts add much supporting evidence to arguments in the literature that women have long been able to acquire positions of leadership and authority in this region.

Political Culture

Political and social life in the hinterland can be closely connected to the activities of what the regional literature often refer to "secret societies," fraternities which are pervasive in this region, existing in many locally and historically specific variants into which members must be initiated.[11] Sims and Seymour give a relatively detailed discussion of the "Marmar" Society, but apart from this and a few comments in Anderson's texts, reference to these societies are scanty. Perhaps the travelers took them for granted or ignored them because this activity was so much apart of the "paganism" which they believed was detrimental to African society (d'Azevedo 1995, 76, 93–94 n. 100). Perhaps also the societies may not have been very manifest to the travelers.

Anderson referred to the women's society, generally known today as Sande, and to the location of its activities in houses attached to town walls. In the absence of such walls, Sande houses may be in town, but many activities take place in the concealment of a specially designated patch of forest next to or outside the bounds of the town. While the Sande structures women's political affairs, a key role is to regulate women's fertility and childbirth. Poro is a key men's society in much of the region, providing one dimension of men's political interaction and regulating aspects of men's fertility. All men and women would probably have been initiated into their respective societies during extended periods in the "bush school" of their natal towns. This, and subsequent society activities, is strictly out-of-bounds to members of the opposite sex. The knowledge and medicines controlled by the men's and women's societies—each respected by the other—creates some balance in gender relations in the region. Sims refers to the "Zo," seemingly a generic term given to the senior officials of many societies or holders of important medicines that entailed secret knowledge passed down through particular families (see Harley 1941, 8–11).

Through membership in these societies, men and women are linked to regional political networks. The particularly detailed account of the "Mama" society that Sims provided and summarized above exemplifies how these "secret societies" could originate and be transformed around regional political and economic alliances, and how the historical conditions of trade or warfare may have shaped their specific forms and popularity. Sims's description of Mama, in particular his refutation of opinions current in Monrovia," seems to have been prompted by the following article that appeared in the *Liberia Herald* on 4 February 1857, and which exemplified the unease which these societies stirred among Liberians:

INCENDIARY MOVEMENTS.

From authentic intelligence, we learn that *Bombo* the notorious Vey Chief captured and imprisoned for a time in this city in 1853, since his escape, has taken up his abode in the *Barlain* country and has established an order ot *Gree gree* worship called *Mamma,* (honor of the ancestor) by which means he is endeavoring to consolidate the interest of every tribe, making common cause of every matter. We are sorry to say, that up to the present date of our information, he has already succeeded too well. This coalition in our opinion, has a specific object, and it is well for us to be on the lookout. The character

> of this gree gree is taking pretty rapidly with the several tribes in this country; natives estranged to the Barlain dialect, are going out consistently to be initiated into the secrecies of this mysterious god of Bombo's creation. The superstition of the natives is very easily awakened, and any thing calculated to excite their cupidity, set on foot by such a known character as Bombo, cannot fail to take well, especially, when pains are taken to get up a foolish pageant ceremony at which a bull or two are slaughtered, or a human victim offered to establish its character. Thousands on thousands will be proselyted to the creed of this defender of ancestral rights, who will be implacable in their enmity to every opposing principle. We cannot say positively, what object Bombo has in view; but we fear his purpose is to attack some of our settlements, and it is well in case our suspicions be properly founded, to be prepared to give him a warm reception. The natives of Sinoe country still assume a hostile attitude; but the interdict which has been ordered to be continued to the coast, if rigidly enforced, will no doubt, work a better result than arms.

Sims's reinterpretation of Mama would have calmed Liberians down. These societies regulated the moral order and adjudicated disputes. Seymour described an execution which seemingly took place under Mama auspices. It seems from Seymour's discussion that these rituals and codes related to Mama are far older than this article—and Sims—suggest them to be. Either Mama must have been synonymous with Poro, or alternatively Mama is a type or local transformation of Poro. If so, it is probably related to the Belly-Poro that Dapper described as early as the seventeenth century (Dapper [1668] 1670, 402 ff.; [1668] 1686, 179 ff.; see also Jones 1983b, 30–34). To our knowledge, no specific mention has been made of the term "Mama" in the twentieth century. However, among the Gola in the early twentieth century, a similar organization, the Kanga Society, occurred and served as a basis to rally Gola to oppose the central Liberian government's occupation of their territory. An oath was taken and a certain ritual occurred which determined the loyalty of its followers on pain of death for assisting the enemies of Gola (d'Azevedo 1969).

Important to regulating alliances, trade, reproduction, and the moral order, these societies were also important in warfare, instructing in the arts of defense, village defenses, armament, and attack, and in the secret forms of communication achieved through whistling or by drums. Linked to this role, men's society was also important to the construction of bridges, which was as key to the mounting of war as it was to trade. The construction of bridges was carried out in absolute privacy under the auspices of a "devil" (in Sims's description called "*silo sale*") from which women and non-initiates, such as resident traders, were strictly excluded (see Welmers 1949). Manding Muslims, particularly, largely held themselves outside the secret societies by this time, and this was another reason why they lived in separate sections of towns.

The background and motivations of Sims and Seymour appear to have made them particularly interested in other aspects of "religious" practices, although they often interpreted them in terms which reflected their own positions. Sims discussed beliefs concerning the "Supreme Being" (chap. 3, 111). This attention appears somewhat exaggerated, reflecting Sims's bias. Most of the peoples in the region do have names for a God or supreme being (e.g., see Schwab 1947, 315–319; Zahan 1974, 1; Taryor 1989, 3–7; Konneh 1996b). However, few ritual practices in the region address a supreme being directly; rather, they employ the mediation of other agencies, spirits known as djinni, earth and water forces, or ancestors. For example, the Bassa have an indigenous notion of a "high god," but "ancestral spirits, nature spirits, witches and 'water people'" seem to be more important to them on a day-to-day basis (Siegmann 1969, 38–39).

Djinni, or "spirits," such as the "white rooster" that Sims mentioned, can take many guises. Many are associated, as in this case, with water and are important to the regulation and maintenance of proper water flow. Political leadership is often associated with claiming the capacity to mediate with spirits. Such mediation can be the claimed prerogative of certain chiefs and families and an important source of power (Gibbal 1984; Brett-Smith 1994). Phenomena and objects of various kinds—such as certain rocks, trees, and animals—can be considered the manifestations or homes of djinni or ancestral spirits and may be carefully protected for this reason. An example that Anderson described in detail were the "sacred" catfish at Bopolu, described later by other authors (e.g., Johnston [1906] 1969, 825; Sibley and Westermann 1928, 76). Blyden, for example, wrote that these catfish were in Marvo Creek, which ran about one hundred and fifty yards east of town. He also said that Momoru cared for them as well as he did his chickens (Blyden 1871c, 241). A Methodist missionary named Rev. C. A. Pitman visited Bopolu and described what he saw at the catfish pools:

> Here, at Bopora, may be seen Mor-mor-ro's famous tame catfish. These live in a creek which runs below the town. I am told that the late king was accustomed to feed them regularly. They were regarded [as] his gods, the protectors of his kingdom, givers of his wealth and popularity. There is a law exempting them from sharing the common fate of fishes. No one is allowed to interfere with them whatsoever. . . . Since Mor-mor-ro's death little or no attention is given to the taking care of them, though I think that much care and attention is given to see that they (the fish) contribute largely to the caretaking of others, especially the unbelieving Mohammedans and less scrupulous pagans. The consequence of all this is that the fish have largely disappeared, and those that remain have become very wary. (Pitman 1877, 15–16; see also Camphor 1909, 325–326)

Treating catfish and their pools as sacred is common in the region (see Paulme 1954; Conrad 1990, 44). Living to an old age, they are frequently associated with ancestral spirits and have a guardian who uses them for divination. Protected catfish were usually fed regularly and abundantly and could even—as Anderson observed—be thrown the bodies of dead slaves.

The travelers described many other objects giving access to or symbolizing power. For example Sims observed clay "idols" in Barlain, similar to the personal face masks that the Mã (Mano) people used (see, e.g., Harley 1941, plate 4; Zetterström 1980, 56), except that these are made of wood or occasionally brass. Cowry shells, used on "idols" and imported from the Indian Ocean, were associated with occult power and used as a form of money (Johnson 1970a–b).

Cowrie shells, linked with the occult, were used in divination and were put on such things as whisks, masks, guns, and the "little idols" that Sims described (see Welmers 1949, 213; Sundström [1965] 1974, 94–110; McNaughton 1988, 53–54, plates 74–75; Prussin 1986, 82; Alpern 1995, 24). Divination was also carried out using earth and sand; Anderson described a sand doctor, sometimes called a "sand-cutter" or diviner, who drew marks in the sand to evaluate a person's situation and to give advice. In reading the signs drawn in the sand, the diviner is said to be able to note good fortune or danger (McNaughton 1988, 54, 55, plates 34–37; Brett-Smith 1996, 53–54).

War leaders and chiefs often had elaborate and powerful hats. The most notable instance is given by Seymour's 1858 journal, which supports oral traditions showing that the Chiefs who rule Kuankan possess a cap that has been reportedly handed down from one Kamara chief to the next for generations.[12] A person from the Kuankan area, Wata Mammadi Kamara, explained how it was made and what it looked like:

> The hat is sewn. It has some very small thread on it, and some big thread on it, and some designs on it. That is how it was made. Many *lisimu* are also on it. Nobody can look inside of it. When a person is going to put it on their head, they can't look on the inside. Even the people who surround that person can't look inside the hat. The *moli*—The *moli* are the ones who made the hat. (Kamara n.d., lines 1205–1217)[13]

Seymour's information complements Wata Kamara's description. According to Seymour, some of the thread that the *moli,* or "cleric," used to make the cap was red. Some of its *lisimu,* or "talismans," consisted of trinkets, two eagle claws, and leopard skin. Seymour's statement that the cap was "large" suggests that it was a symmetrically styled hat that warriors, hunters, and sorcerers wore. Shorter Muslim caps fit more closely to a person's head. The "trinkets" or amulets may have been iron or valuable metals, such as gold, silver, copper, or brass, which are associated with sorcery, healing, secrecy, ascetics, and protection. Red is associated with power and sacrifice in Manding culture. The interior of the cap may have had Arabic script and magic squares written on the inside, having reportedly been made by a cleric. Wata Mammadi Kamara stated that no one is allowed to look into the interior of the cap; this is consistent with the idea that the spirits of the hat and the wearer become joined when the person dons the hat. The hat represents a source of protection and power when honored and signals danger when abused (Cashion 1984, 159–163; Prussin 1986, 80–85; McNaughton 1988, 125; Conrad 1990, 132; Brett-Smith 1996, 42).

The writers described body parts of elephants and leopards that people used as symbols of power. The Temne of Sierra Leone associate leopards with authority, conquest, and protection and elephants with legitimate authority (Lamp 1983, 227). Manding images of these animals are very similar to those of the Temne. Sims noted that a key symbol of Mama was an elephant hair whisk, an insignia which remains common in society affairs to date. On several occasions in the diaries, kings were observed to sit on leopard skins, while leopard teeth, both real and made of brass, were often an accompaniment to a leader's regalia and to masked figures. Leopards, common in the region at the time, also carry a wider range of associations, such as being the totem of the Kamara from Musadu to the coast (Weisswange 1976, 8; Geysbeek 2002, chap. 7). The real fear of leopards taking people is compounded by fears of shape shifting, a belief that certain people can transform themselves into leopards in order to harm others (Jackson 1990). Apart from the obvious fact that leopard jaws can tear flesh, leopard bile is a particularly powerful poison. This potential is elaborated in sacred "leopard societies" in some parts of the region where leopards are reputed to prey on human flesh (see, e.g., Strong 1930, 100–102). These possibilities, in turn, make the hunting of leopards problematic.

Certain trees are significant to the spirit world, among them the silk cotton tree (*Ceiba pentandra* or *Bombax buonopozense*), which is particularly important throughout the region. One of the executions that Sims described, for example, took place at the foot of a silk cotton tree. These trees are generally thought to be the abode of spirits, particularly "witches," at night. Cotton tree roots commonly provide shrines to particular or generic ancestors or to particular sacrificial events made to ensure the prosperity of the village.

Sorcery, common to beliefs among many people in the hinterland, is not discussed in any great detail in the accounts. However, Sims did make an oblique reference to a "witch" trial-by-endurance. Usually the suspect drinks a decoction of Sasswood (*Erythrophleum guineensis*), characteristically red, a tradition germane to most pre-colonial accounts of the West African coast. Sims linked this tree to the fictitious Upas tree of Java, which westerners from the late eighteenth to the mid-nineteenth century believed produced a very "violent," "poisonous," "evil," and "deadly juice" that should be avoided at all costs (*Oxford English Dictionary,* 2d ed., s.v. "Upas").

Islam

The travelers, like Blyden and many of his contemporaries, saw Islam as a higher form of religion than the local religious practices: they believed that Muslims had achieved a more advanced level of "civilization" and that the spread of Islam could help the "native peoples." The settlers also acknowledged that there were many similarities between Christianity and Islam. Nineteenth-century relations between the two religious groups were largely marked by tolerance, with hopes that some Muslims would convert to Christianity (Walls 1999). Thus, Benjamin Anderson distributed Bibles in Musadu in 1874, proclaiming that he was "the first missionary that carried our scriptures in that portion of the Soudan" (chap. 6, 265). Occasionally, however, some Christians charged Muslims with worshiping the "false prophet," Muhammad, as Sims did on occasion (see Marsh 1856, 14–15; Bowen [1857] 1968, 42; "Beautiful Manuscripts from Negroes in Africa" 1863, 19–20; Prost 1869, 129; Wilson 1869, 3320; Pitman 1878, 17).

It was the reputation of Musadu, a leading center of Islam in the southern savannah, that partly drew the travelers to it. African scholars confirmed this reputation. A Muslim cleric, Karfal Nejl, wrote—in the late 1860s—that Musadu was the greatest center of Islamic learning south of Kankan, having eighteen "learned men," five whose "intellect is world-embracing" (Tracy 1869, 240–241).[14] Several other important Muslim towns provided training: Vonsua (three scholars), Bopolu (five scholars), Bakedu (two scholars), Kulil (two scholars), and Nionsamoridu (two scholars) (Tracy 1869, 240–241; see also Hopewell 1958, 45–48, 84–90; Person 1979, 273). A scholar from Kankan, Ibrahima Kabawee, wrote similarly in 1871 of Musadu's central position:

> We are all under one rule, and we belong to the sect of the Malikees. Our religion and the religion of the Arabs is one religion. The extent of our country is from Boporo to Soudan, and from Musardu, and Medina, and Kankan, and Futah, and Hamd-Allahi, and Jenne, and Timbuctu—all these cities have one religion. . . . The King of Kankan (Mahmud-a-Shafee) is a Shafee by sect. The King of Musardu is partly Muslim and partly pagan. The King of Boporo is a great pagan. ("African Literature" 1871)

Musadu's mosque seems to have been built prior to the mosque in Bopolu, and to mosques in other towns. When Blyden went to Bopolu in 1870, he noted that the people sent some of their Ramadan offerings to Musadu (1871c, 326; see Person 1968, 2:136). In 1877, C. A. Pitman observed that Musadu sent missionaries to Vonsua every year (Pitman 1877, 4).

While the accounts support the association of Islam with the Manding populations of the hinterland, they also acknowledge—as did Sims, quoting Bowen—that not all Mandingoes were "Mahometans" ([1857] 1968, 41–

42). Islamic practices were clearly spreading rapidly in the region among non-Manding populations, although to be understood cross-culturally, adjustments and syncretisms were necessary. Again, the travelers' own positions colored their observations in this respect. Anderson, for example, described the Loma as "greatly duped by the fraud and chicanery of the Mohammedan Mandingo priests"—perhaps an opinion with which he felt his readership would sympathize (chap. 5, 191). It is more likely that the Loma-Manding relationship involved Loma in employing certain Islamic techniques for manipulating the forces of local religion. Others seem to have adopted Islam's tenets without full adherence to its practices and sanctions; for instance, Chief Bessa, whom Anderson met, probably did not keep a strict fast during Ramadan or pray five times a day, while "Mandingo priests" might have also lifted the sanction of drinking alcoholic beverages, one of Bessa's favorite pastimes (chap. 5, 169).

Traders have usually been seen as the initial "carriers of Islam" in West Africa prior to the era of the nineteenth-century holy wars (*jihads*). Clerics were the "agents of islamicization" who propagated Islam. While many clerics doubled as traders when their clerical work could not fully support them, leading clerics were not traders (Levtzion 2000, 6). Anderson's accounts, it has been argued, reverse this argument, supporting the notion that the cleric was the key pioneer of Islam, and that the role of the trader was secondary (Fisher 1971, xv–xvii; see also Hopewell 1958, 33–35). In any case, it seems that their roles were complementary and that, as Anderson noted, traders frequently introduced Islam to new areas as they developed commercial routes.

Several Islamic sects seem to have existed in the region at the time. A French writer wrote that the Qadiriya brotherhood was present in Musadu and Bopolu during the late nineteenth century. Anderson's mention of prayer beads when he met Seymoru Syyo—more commonly known as Sayon or Saganogo—at Bopolu suggests that he was affiliated with the Qadiriya (Fisher 1971, xviii). The Qadiriya may have become present in Kankan as early as the sixteenth century, and it remained the dominant brotherhood until the Tijaniyya came to rival it in the mid-nineteenth century (Hopewell 1958, 41–45; Kaba 1973; Person 1979, 261–263). Furthermore, inferences that Anderson made which suggested that Syyo was a leader in Bopolu further establish a sustained tradition of learning in the region, led by Syyo clerics, who started a "major renewal of learning" in the subregion in the late eighteenth century (Wilks 2000, 102).

Like most nineteenth-century Liberians, the travelers usually referred to all Islamic leaders and teachers as "priests," but one can distinguish between imams and clerics. The main responsibility of an imam is to lead prayer and to officiate at different ceremonies, as Anderson emphasized during his 1874 journey. Communal leaders then, as today, select one or more persons to be the imam for a mosque. The imam should, when possible, be a scholar, be physically able to perform his duties, and be a man of moral integrity (Ivanow 1953, 165; Kaba 1973, 336). In Musadu, the position may be hereditary. Vafin Dole wrote that the imam of Musadu was Salihu Shereef, or Sherif (see chap. 5, 235). In 1993, the first of Musadu's three imams was a Sherif. The importance of the Sherif in this case may go back to stories of how a cleric named Talata Sherif helped Foningama gain power in Musadu and beyond (see Fisher 1971, ix–x; Geysbeek 2002, chap. 5).

The primary obligation of a cleric, like the "old Mahometan priest" Ibrihims whom Sims met (chap. 3, 96), is more directed toward teaching, foretelling the future, leading prayers during life-crisis rituals, and making talismans and sacrifices. "Clerics" who have little training in Islamic education and use Islamic writings for "magical qualities" are often called "*moli*" or "*mori*" in Manding and "*marabout*" in French. Clerics can be contrasted with *kalamòò* or *karamogo,* "scholars" or "teachers" (literally "book people"), who earn their position through studying the key writings of Islam as their primary basis for making decisions. The distinctions between *kalamòò* and *moli* are sometimes very fluid, however, and people can become clerics because of heredity (Wilks 1968, 167; Hopkins 1971, 108–109; Fisher 1971, xvi; Kaba 1973, 336; 1976, 410; Person 1979, 260–261; Levtzion 1985; Corby 1988, 47–49; Launay 1992, 150–151).

Islamic training passed through various stages. Ibrihims had probably advanced to the second of three levels of education that could be attained in the region. Primary education combined academic and physical work. Girls and boys learned the fundamentals of Arabic, practiced how to write Arabic on wooden slates, and memorized portions of the Qur'an. Boys who memorized large portions of the Qur'an and showed a special interest in learning moved on to study Qur'anic commentaries and legal works in the second stage. Musadu provided the highest quality of education at this level from this part of the southern savannah to the Liberian coast. Students went to the Fulbe capital of Timbu, the Jakhanke town of Tuba in the Futa Jallon, and further on to northern Mali or Mauritania for additional training in the third stage ("The African Coast" 1827, 245; Blyden 1871c, 331; 1871d, 138; 1872b, 293–294; 1873, 315; Kaba 1976, 410–411; Sanneh 1989).

Ibrihims had visited Jenne, Timbuktu, Timbu, Sierra Leone, and Monrovia before he met Sims in Passilla. Jenne and Timbuktu were important economic and religious centers during the rise of the Mali Empire in the early fourteenth century. Timbuktu became the leading Muslim town two centuries later during the Songhai period. While its intellectual activity began to decline after the Moroccans conquered it in the late sixteenth century, Timbuktu remained the key center of Muslim education and scholarship for the next two hundred years. Jenne maintained its independence after the Mali Empire declined and was also an important Muslim town (McIntosh 1998, 264–

267; Hunwick 1999). Ibrihims, who learned or taught as he traveled, may have been one of the thousands of Jakhanke clerics who spread Islam throughout much of West Africa by the nineteenth century. The Jakhanke were traders who specialized in teaching and spreading Islam through peaceful means (Sanneh 1989; Wilks 2000).

Much Islamic writing was in circulation in the hinterland. For instance, Anderson indicated that the Manding in Musadu possessed bound volumes of the Qur'an. Some of the Qur'ans in circulation were probably carefully inscribed by hand, as Whitehurst described twenty years earlier: "All of their books are the result of their own labor, being transcribed with a great deal of elegance, and of which the greatest care is taken. Some of the covers are very elegant specimens of their work in leather, generally in the form of a pocket book. The leaves are all separate, of the same size, and their marginal appearance is as accurate as though it were the work of a press" (Whitehurst 1836, 276; see also Bravmann 1983, 21).

Writing was also found on "talismans," or *lisimu* (Fisher 1971, ix). These are charms written on scraps of paper or leather and may be either worn in a leather neck, wrist, or waist pouch or hung to protect an object or place. Sometimes, the ink is dissolved in water (*nasi*) and drunk. Arabic writing was—and remains—a strong source of power and protection, even for non-Muslims. This is an example of the incorporation of Islamic powers—in this case the written word—into the same field of power play as local religion (see Bledsoe and Robey 1986; Bravmann 1983, 32–41; Frank 1998, 51–58). Benjamin Anderson described how Bessa, for instance, commanded the interment of beef bones bound with transcripts from the Qu'ran, to be efficacious in peace or war. Qur'anic verses frequently etched on talismans were sura 12:64 and sura 45:20 and the "chapters of refuge," suras 113 and 114. These were also often accompanied with the saying: "'In the name of God, the Merciful, the Compassionate, I take refuge in God from Satan, whom we hate'" (Blyden [1871d]). In some cases, such talismanic papers were traded over long distances. In 1871, Blyden translated one which a cleric wrote in the Futa Jallon. He suggested that copies were "sold to the credulous as a means of warding off evil from individuals and communities, to be employed especially during seasons of epidemics" (Blyden [1888] 1994, 207).

Benjamin Anderson noted the high demand and price of writing paper in the interior, which was indicative of literacy, largely in Arabic. According to recent scholarship, this is too early for the syllabic scripts in Mende, Loma, Kpelle, Bassa, and Gola, which were not recorded until the twentieth century, except for the Vai script, which was developed during the mid-nineteenth century (Dalby 1970; Hau 1973; Tuchscherer 1999).

Another trade implication of Islam concerned characteristic styles of dress associated with Muslim Manding in the interior. For instance, both Seymour and Anderson described their characteristic Turkish-style trousers, gathered at the ankles in Seymour's case and "coming a little below the knees" in Anderson's (chap. 4, 129; chap. 5, 210). Early Arabic writers observed that many Africans wore skins as their main form of clothing in the twelfth and thirteenth centuries. Chiefs and other elite were more disposed to wear wool and cotton clothing. By the early sixteenth century, European writers observed that most people wore clothes made out of cloth. Europe's travelers to West Africa during and after the sixteenth century described or illustrated "Turkish," "Moorish," or "Arab" dress (Hair, in Donelha [1625] 1977, 281; Sieber 1972, 23–29). When the development of the horizontal loom made cloth more available to the masses, cloth dress—the clothing of choice for the Muslims of the north—became more common as Islam spread. Muslim traders and clerics created a market for cotton products as they traveled from Ottoman and Muslim North Africa to Timbuktu and Jenne, the forest, and the coast (Hodder 1980, 203–205; Frank 1998, 46–48). Anderson described Manding women in Musadu as veiled; the rules have relaxed since Anderson's time, as nowadays most women in Musadu do not usually wear veils.

At Bopolu, Benjamin Anderson noted three of the five times that Muslims are supposed to pray each day. The five times of prayer are daybreak, noon, mid-afternoon, sunset, and evening, although Anderson omitted the noon prayer and one of the last two prayers. While many of the Manding probably prayed five times a day, some would have only prayed in the mosque two or three times a day, the rest of the prayers being conducted in the fields or at work. Nevertheless, Blyden, who visited Bopolu the same year, wrote: "Five times a day did we see devout men repairing to the house of prayer, to conform to the letter of the law" (Blyden 1871c, 324). Perhaps Blyden was only referring to the adults who remained in town and went to every prayer.

Anderson heard part of the creed, the *shahāda,* the first pillar of Islam, which is translated "There is no god but God. Muhammad is the messenger of God" (fig. 15). One must recite this phrase before becoming a Muslim (Khalîl [1916] 1980, 293–309; Esposito 1991, 89). Blyden recorded greetings that Muslims used at the time. According to Blyden, Muslims sometimes followed *Salaam aleikum,* "Peace be with you," with *Aleikum-e-Salaam, wa rahmatu 'llahi wa barakatuhu,* "With you be peace, and the mercy of God and His blessing." Muslims responded to a Christian's *Salaam aleikum* with *Salaam ala man taba el-huda,* "Peace to him who follows the right way" ([1988] 1994, 213). Anderson and Blyden also both noted the music that was typical of local Islam (see Monts 1990, 115; Charry 2000). Anderson was a musician, which explains his attentiveness to this aspect of Manding culture.

At one point, Anderson's first journey was delayed by his interpreter, Kaifal, who wanted to await the new moon. Muslims measure time by the lunar rather than the solar calendar. Each month is about twenty-nine and a half days long and begins with the rising of each new moon. The most important new moons are those that usher in the month of Ramadan and the feast of *Fitr* (Khalîl [1916] 1980, 55; Nawwab, Speers, and Hoye 1980, 167). Many Muslims also anticipate the rising of the other new moons of the year (Ali's translation of the Qur'an [1934] 1977, 75), so Kaifal may have told Anderson that he wanted to celebrate this event before leaving. Kaifal was not speaking of the new moon that marks the entry to Ramadan because Ramadan started later during the journey, on 3 December (Blyden 1871c, 325; "The Feast of Ramadan" 1871, 115).

While Islam represented to the travelers and to the Liberian settlers a higher form of religion than others practiced in the region, there is evidence that religious practices were rather more syncretic than these ideals would suggest. In seeking out Musadu, the Islamic educational center of the region, the travelers focused on Islamic purity as portrayed in West Africa, leading to a portrayal of impurity and negligence among many of those met along the way. This reinforced the ideals of the interior which they came with and took away.

Incessant warfare had deep ramifications in population and political culture. Yet to consider it as a cultural phenomenon typical of the region at this time would be to overlook both the structural features of the conflicts (trade, international trade, arms, slavery) and the historically specific motivations which drove them, rooted in regional memory and contemporary affairs. Warfare also became integral to many aspects of everyday life and left its mark in the landscape and vegetation, issues to which we now turn.

Trade and Markets

Since the fifteenth century, the region had been part of a global economy, linked to Atlantic trade routes by contact with European traders operating along the coast. Before then, it was linked with the trans-Saharan trade. Long-established local trade articulated with these international trade networks, particularly along routes which linked the coastal forests with the savanna kingdoms farther north (Massing 2000; Wilks 2000).

Of these routes, the best known to present-day scholars is the great "Misado path" linking Bopolu with Zolowo, then to Boo, and onward to Musadu. Yet between these towns, the exact location of the great "path" seems to have varied. To a great extent, "natural" features circumscribed these paths. Where possible they avoided large river crossings, often following convenient watersheds, and avoided high mountain passes, following convenient valleys. The accounts also indicate that there were other well-trodden trade routes. Anderson wrote explicitly that the Manding had several routes to Musadu, and that he took one of the two or three shortcuts. The texts also refer to wider trading links. Anderson, for example, met merchants from Senegal in 1874 who wanted to conduct trade at Musadu, suggesting that the latter was well-known as a trading entrepôt and aptly connected to the larger trade routes in West Africa that lead to the savanna.

Powerful leaders kept tight control over trade routes, and as the travelers found to their detriment, this sometimes created problems for an interior journey. While certain Americo-Liberian traders such as Sanders Washington were evidently able to slip in and out of the interior with little or no trouble as long as they were involved in petty trade, people tried to block Anderson in 1868 because he told everyone that he was going to Musadu. This, unlike trading done by Washington, was a threat to people in the middle such as the Gola and the "Boporo Mandingo," who felt that Anderson was trying to undercut their status as middlemen (d'Azevedo 1994, 241n.54). Bessa, for example, was a middleman between the coast and Bopolu who conducted a productive trade in slaves, salt, and other goods, and he did not want Anderson and the Liberians to threaten his position.

The Liberians and their government placed great emphasis on keeping good relations with the leaders of Bopolu, as it was through Bopolu that a considerable amount of trade flowed to Monrovia. Yet they were also keen to expand trade with the interior. Early settlers on the coast had hoped that the Saint Paul might provide river passage for trade farther into the interior. Seymour suggested that the Saint Paul was navigable far into the interior to Pallarker (Kpayekwele), although this optimism was contradicted by Sims's observation of a solid bed of rock across the river between Tawn and Daydee. In fact there is a falls at Millsburg which blocks farther travel on the river. In 1874, Anderson discussed Liberia's later plans to build trading forts, which would expand the ability of Liberians to trade in the interior and to conduct missionary work.

Most major towns in the interior had a market, and the travelers often visited these or found themselves in town on market day. Their record of the dates and days on which they occurred, as well as their descriptions, confirm that most localities had a cyclic pattern of periodic marketing that followed a seven-day week. Neighboring towns had markets on different days, so traders could move from one market to another in a cycle (see Handwerker 1980). In Barlain, Sims described how the markets occurred on a seven-day cycle. In certain parts of the Loma-Manding margins, such as around Boola, there was reportedly a five-day-week cycle of markets (Goerg 1986, 200).

Sims, Seymour, and Benjamin Anderson generally claimed that Kpelle and Manding women were the main local marketeers, in contrast to long-distance traders who were mainly men. Anderson described how, on market day in Ziggah-Porro-Zue (Koiama Tongoro), "peace and order are secured by persons especially appointed for that purpose"(chap. 5, 202), a pattern which continues into recent times. Sims found a similar "officer" in the Barlain town of Jangay (Kposangie) (chap. 3, 109). Each town was responsible for peace at the market, in return for which each market holder paid a small sum.

Special laws and officials which regulated activities in the market place were common throughout the region (Griaule 1977). This highlighted the central importance of the market in helping to ensure and economic stability. Secure markets and trade routes helped ensure the order and prosperity of a political unit.

Exchange took place through a wide variety of currencies. The main local currency that the travelers in this volume described were kola nuts, iron bars, cotton strips, powder, pipes, nails, copper and brass rods, strings of beads, gun flints, salt sticks, baskets of salt, and bars of tobacco (see Whitehurst 1836, 277). Also in circulation were Liberian bills and coins from the United States, Mexico, Britain, Holland, Germany, France, Spain, and Ceylon (Sundström [1965] 1974, 92–97; Akpan 1975, 16–17). The Liberian government circulated paper money in denominations of one, three, five, and ten dollar bills, and a fifty cent bill; it did not begin to issue dollar coins until 1961 (Chavers 1864, 9; Krause and Mishler 1982, 1197–1201).

The "bar trade" to which the travelers referred was an advanced form of barter in the interior in goods that went beyond immediate consumption needs. "Bars" were also called "rounds," "bundles," "heads," and "guns." A "bar" represented a relatively fixed unit of import-export goods, such as alcohol, rum, tobacco, iron, slaves, cowries, ivory, and European currency that had equivalent values. The value of "bars" tended to fluctuate with the market (Fyfe 1962, 9) and depreciated the nearer one was to the source of the said good. Kola bars, therefore, lessened in value as one approached kola-producing areas in the forest, while Seymour noted that the price of rice got cheaper as one got closer to the coast (see Sundström [1965] 1974, 73–83; Curtin 1975, 240–264). Mungo Park and Thomas Winterbottom wrote that twenty leaves of tobacco equaled one bar at the turn of the nineteenth century. A "gallon of spirits" was worth "a *bar* of rum," and one bar was equivalent to one gallon of rum (Park [1799] 1983, 19; Winterbottom [1803] 1969, 172–174). Three decades later in Monrovia, one bar was worth approximately one average country cloth, ten pounds of coffee, or about twenty-two to thirty cents (Ashmun 1827a, 272; "Coffee" 1827, 218; Devany 1830, 100; see also Carey 1825, 155). In 1858, Seymour documented the equivalents for "the native *bar* or *barr*" to cloth, gunpowder, tobacco, pipes, nails, beads, and copper and brass rods (1858b, 13).

A salt "stick" was a hollowed-out bamboo tube that was filled either with dried ocean salt from the coast or with the high quality rock salt that could be obtained from the north (Curtin 1975, 224–228; Lovejoy 1985, 660–662). The salt in the "stick" weighed about eleven pounds (five kilograms) (Sundström [1965] 1974, 130); a slave was worth one hundred sticks. In an early description of salt sticks in Liberia, D. W. Whitehurst wrote: "The *Salt Sticks* are strips of bamboo, of about three feet in length, formed into cylinders of three inches diameter. Into them the salt is closely packed, and an outward envelope of leaves very compactly arranged, enables it to be transported without danger from rain. An able bodied man will carry from sixteen to twenty of these sticks" (Whitehurst 1836, 148).

Years later, W. S. Anderson wrote that salt was hardened by tying one hundred fifty to two hundred sticks together with twine, wrapping them in leaves, and placing them over a fire for several days (Anderson 1866, 339). Benjamin Anderson wrote in 1874 that fifty sticks could be exchanged for a bullock, and that slaves could carry up to fifty sticks on their backs (chap. 5, 168). According to Thomas Winterbottom, up to two hundred pounds of salt could be placed in baskets measuring seven feet long and one and one-half to two feet wide (Winterbottom [1803] 1969, 171–172). Near the end of the century, Alfred King explained that one stick was worth twelve cents, and that ten sticks were once able to buy a slave in Bopolu (King 1882a). These slave prices may have been depressed due to the embargo on the Atlantic trade. Bowen ([1857] 1968, 72–73) and Camphor (1909, 114) provided similar information.

Exchanges could also be "tied" to other commodities as currency, using elaborate schema (Sundström [1965] 1974, 110). For example, Seymour wrote that one bushel of rice was worth four yards of cloth, or thirty leaves of tobacco, or one pound of gunpowder, or one-half pounds of beans, or two gallons of salt (Seymour 1857a, 198).

Trade Commodities

A large variety of products were imported into the hinterland through foreign trade and were subsequently used and traded there. Among those that the travelers referred to were guns of various kinds, which are discussed later in this chapter. The travelers observed the use of calicoes, popular printed cotton skirts from India that came in white and blue, and madras handkerchiefs which were made in India (Alpern 1995, 7). These were silk or cotton and came in several patterns, mainly in red, blue, and yellow. Handkerchiefs were principally used as loincloths, bandannas, and neck and head coverings (Alpern 1995, 10). Liberia maintained trade links throughout the nineteenth century for Indian madras (Voorhees 1834, 22; "West African Mails" 1873, 30; Syfert 1977a, 195). Blue beads were trade items that European traders brought to the coast, which were then traded inland (Alpern 1995, 22–23). By the seventeenth century at the latest, Europeans started to introduce hammocks from the Americas to Africa. They were primarily luxury items, serving as the "first taxis" for the local elite and foreigners (Alpern 1995, 30–31). Writing paper became a trade commodity in West Africa by the late seventeenth century. The smoking pipes to which Seymour, particularly, drew attention could have come from Europe or could have been made locally, many being made out of the same stone as the stone sculptures found in parts of the region. The Dutch, English, and French exported millions of pipes to West Africa during the pre-colonial period (Calvocoressi 1975; Hill 1976; Philips 1983; Alpern 1995, 26–27). Brass kettles were used for washing water, both by local people and by the travelers. These had long been an important trade item imported to the coast by slavers or traders in exchange for items such as ivory and camwood. By the 1850s, many were American made (see Sundström [1965] 1974, 228–232; Alpern 1995, 15–16). Although the accounts to do not make clear the extent to which the ivory trade was locally developed, it seems surprising that Ash told Harriette Brittan after his 1858 interior journey with Seymour that "the natives, up there, appear to be ignorant of the value of ivory, and yet that there is some there that would take seven or eight men to carry" (Brittan [1860] 1969, 316). If there was such ignorance, it certainly did not endure, as later in the century, the interior empire of Samori Touré traded ivory through Liberia and Sierra Leone in exchange for arms and ammunition (Person 1968, 2:906–910, 930–931).

Other products traded within the hinterland, or indeed exported from it, were of more local origin. In his 1878 inaugural address, President Gardner referred to "Musardu" as "the great mart of Cattle, Beni seed, Rice, Cotton, Country cloths, and gold" (1878, 8). Local products were not only those produced through agriculture and industry, discussed below, but also those collected and processed from the region's soils and vegetation. Anderson discussed the interior gold fields in 1868. Gold and golden jewelry were observed by the travelers adorning inhabitants and in local markets. Seymour, particularly, noted the impressive jewelry and gold worn that many women wore. Early in his 1858 journal he implied that such wealth in jewelry was confined to Manding ladies, but by the time he reached Toma country he described it as more general.

Salt was a sign of peace and a valuable trade commodity, given universal dependence on it for retention of body fluids in the tropical climate, as a preservative, and for taste. As Seymour and Anderson observed, for the near interior regions of Liberia, the main source of salt was from the ocean. Anderson wrote that salt was sent up from the coast in exchange for country cloths from the interior, presumably from Bandi and Loma areas. Some rock salt also came from the northern savanna trade routes, from the Sahara. Small amounts of potassium chloride were manufactured from local plant materials, but this was insufficient to support the whole population (see Sundström [1965] 1974, 122–126; Holsoe 1979a, 66).

Kola (khola, cola) was an important item of trade from the more southerly, forested areas of the hinterland into the savanna. Native to the region, the kola tree (*Cola nitida*) has long been actively multiplied by local populations to enrich forest patches (Chevalier and Perrot 1911; Lovejoy 1980; Ford 1992; 1995; Goerg 1986).[15] To the present, kola nuts are chewed as a stimulant and an appetite suppressant, sometimes being called "Mandingo man's alcohol," as Muslims substitute them for alcohol, which Islam prohibits. Kola also plays a central part in any symbolic gift or offering, with white kola especially used as gifts. Kola was often exchanged for iron, as kola producers in the forest traded hoes and other iron implements for their produce. Many blacksmiths also became kola traders (White 1974, 13; Lovejoy 1980, 112–114).

Certain forest products became part of the export trade from the coast. One was camwood (*Baphia nitida*), which Seymour observed as being especially abundant in the forests near Paynesville, and Sims described as covering a third of the forests of Barlain. Used in the manufacture of red dye, camwood was a very profitable European and American export item. Together with camwood, palm oil and kernels were one of the principal Liberian exports (Akpan 1975, 7–10) and indeed were of growing importance to West African exports generally at this time. The Manding made blue indigo dye from the wild and cultivated plants of *Lonocharpus cyanescens* and *Indigo fera tinctoria,* respectively (Schwab 1947, 127; Curtin 1975, 15).

Palm oil from this part of the forest fringe was also exported northward to the drier savannas, the regions where the oil palm does not grow. The oil palm (*Elaeis guineensis*) is indigenous to the West African forest region. The self-propagation of palms is frequently encouraged by farmers, who enrich used land and fallows with them (Fairhead and Leach 1996). As the travelers observed, oil palms can also be tapped for palm wine. But, as references in the texts to "saving palms" indicate, inhabitants had to take care not to reduce their oil production. Careful wine tapping does not kill oil palms, but does prevent their fruiting during the period of tapping. Most inhabitants then, as now, seem to prefer wine from the raffia palm (*Raphia vinifera*) when this is available.

The primary accounts in this book indicate that slaves continued to be important commodities for the Atlantic trade and internal use until the late nineteenth century. Slaves, minimally, worked for others involuntarily, were marginalized socially, and were controlled by others (Robertson and Klein 1983, 3). In Manding and Vai society, people were generally divided into three categories: freeborn royalty and commoners at the top; nearly casted specialists, or *nyamakalawu,* such as bards, smiths, leatherworkers, potters, and Islamic praise singers, in the middle; and slaves at the bottom (Holsoe 1977; Conrad and Frank 1995; Johnson 1999, 10–11). Although the Kpelle, Loma, Gola, and other peoples mentioned in the accounts did not have a middle tier of endogamous-casted persons, they did have individuals and groups who specialized in different professions.

As in other parts of West Africa, the writers gave ample evidence of how persons became enslaved through long-term wars, quick raids, robbery, and trade (Bazin 1974, 115). For instance, Sims wrote writes about the "piratical excursions" of the "Kpellays . . . against their neighbors" (chap. 3, 115), and

Seymour told how Jaka Kaman Kamara returned with "thousands of victims" after coming from some of his "military expeditions" (chap. 4, 144). Anderson wrote that many became slaves in the ten-year war that Fillingi and Daffaborah fought. While Anderson was in Bonya (Gbonie) in 1874, Daffaborah captured "two hundred women" and killed some men after he raided Pillillay. Seymour and Anderson, respectively, said that slaves were regularly sold in the markets of Solong (Zolowo) and Bopolu. According to Sims, slaves were then traded for guns, powder, and salt. Seymour said that Ash's captors tried to trade Ash for a gun, but that Ash was not valuable enough. Anderson wrote that Bessa traded some of his cattle for slaves.

People still sold slaves for the external Atlantic market and for the internal markets at midcentury. When Sims, Seymour, and Ash traveled into the interior in 1858, slaves were being driven to the coast to be sold to European slavers. There was no transatlantic demand for slaves when Anderson went to Musadu ten years later. Slaves were still being shipped to the Americas at midcentury to help meet the demand for more laborers. Although British and American naval vessels largely stopped the sale of slaves on the coast by 1850, the British, French, Cubans, and others still made sporadic attempts to acquire slaves from the Liberian coast until 1860. Sims mentioned the Cuban slave trader Pedro Blanco who operated in the Gallinas in the mid-1830s, and Sims personally freed twenty-one slaves who were being sold to the French slaver Captain Chevelier at Cape Mount. By the beginning of 1860s, the last of the export slave trade ceased from Liberia's shores, due to the efforts of the Liberian government and foreign navies, particularly the British and American. Warfare increased as chiefs fought over the distribution of remaining slaves. Male slaves were executed because they had mostly served, in the past, as trade items. Women and children were put to work on farms. Slaves were still exported from the forest to the savanna until the end of the century and were used for other reasons, such as for bridewealth and to pay off debts (Sundström [1965] 1974, 75–80; Holsoe 1977, 295–297; 1979, 69; Handwerker 1980, 10; Jones and Johnson 1980; Jones 1983a, chaps. 5–6).

Otherwise, French vessels claimed to employ volunteer immigrant laborers to take to their colonies in the Indian Ocean islands in the 1850s. The British needed workers in the West Indian islands. In fact, local chiefs made many of these laborers available. Chiefs acquired these workers through various forms of domestic slavery or prosecuted wars to capture them. By mid-April of 1858, the ship *Regina Coeli,* which Sims mentioned, at anchor off Manna, had two or three hundred emigrants on board. Many of them were manacled. Following a scuffle, the crew killed several emigrants; the other emigrants killed the crew in retaliation. A British vessel eventually towed the ship into the harbor (Blyden 1866, in Givens 1976, 147–148; Holsoe 1977, 296).

Sims, particularly, demonstrated how demands for the Atlantic slave trade generated violence and exacerbated the system of slavery that existed in many parts of Africa before the Europeans came:

> the Pessah people . . . were never a warlike people, until driven into it by the slave-hunters . . . the Veys, Goulahs, and Kroos . . . carried death and desolation into the very heart of the Pessah country. Thousands and thousands were slain; thousands and thousands were carried into slavery; whole districts were depopulated, and in fact, a regular war of extermination has been kept up against the Pessahs, ever since the days of Pedro Blanco. On the other hand, the Manni-Mohammedans, in the rear of the Pessahs, carried on a slave-hunting war as disastrous to these unfortunate people as the one so vigorously prosecuted against them by the Veys and others living near the coast. (chap. 3, 99).

Sims's note about depopulation helps reveal who enslaved whom. Here, he said that the Kpelle were victims of the Manding to the interior and their Vai, Gola, and Kru neighbors (chap. 3, 99). Benjamin Anderson wrote that the Manding in Bopolu purchased Kpelle and Loma slaves in the market, and that the Waima Loma sometimes captured their Barlain neighbors along the border. The writers noted several other instances where neighbors enslaved neighbors.

Slaveholders used their slaves for many reasons. Some were treated well and were given responsibility. Others were worked hard, and some were treated cruelly. Sims and Seymour implied that the slavery that they encountered in Africa was "modified" or "mild" compared to slavery in the U.S. Benjamin Anderson did not compare slavery in Africa and the U.S. but noted the different way that slaves treated each other in the areas where he traveled. "The Mandingoes," he wrote, "are harsher with their slaves than the Boozies" (chap. 5, 222). Sims claimed that the Kpelle treated their prisoners of war very cruelly (chap. 3, 115). Note here the distinction that Africans made between slaves captured in war and those who were purchased (Bazin 1974, 119). Slaves such as the women who, according to Sims, worked for the wife of Dagla's chief were probably treated better than many other slaves. Some slaves became warriors; a few accrued great privilege, but most risked their lives when they fought. The boy attendants of whom Benjamin Anderson wrote—who took care of their master's horses—might not fare so well in battle. These boys could have been young and relatively new captives who were being trained to become cavalryman (Legassick 1966, 96–97). Slaves also served as porters. Sims and Anderson observed slaves carrying salt, country cloth, and personal goods.

Many slaves farmed. In the regions were the travelers journeyed, labor was scarce; there were not nearly enough people to work the land that could potentially be farmed (d'Azevedo 1969a, 8; Holsoe 1979a, 69). The Condo confederation not only controlled most of the slave trade that flowed between the Mano and Saint Paul Rivers, but also had numerous slave villages. Anderson noted in 1868 that the Manding of Bopolu had "villages of slaves and servants scattered in every direction, wherever the purposes of agriculture invite or encourage," and that there were three times more slaves than free people. Anderson saw Bessa's slaves, who "worked on his farms" in chains, and wrote of slaves farther in the interior who farmed in Barlain Kpelle (chap. 5, 169). The 1868 letter from Chief Vafin Dole noted that the important men in Musadu owned many slaves; Dole himself owned sixty. Many of these slaves farmed the tobacco and other crops that grew in the region. No doubt, Anderson and the other writers did not record several other instances where they saw slaves engaged in farming and other activities.

Benjamin Anderson's statements that he was offered "some pretty female slaves" in Musadu, and that "a pretty little Mandingo girl" in Nionsamoridu cost "about $15 in our money" shows the high value of women slaves (chap. 5, 222). In many contexts villagers valued women more than men. Women could produce more children, assimilate into society easier than men, farm and fulfill other labor-intensive tasks, be pawned, and become influential and trusted confidants (Robertson and Klein 1983).

Agriculture

The accounts give a vivid impression of the great variety of crops produced in the region. In Seymour's early account of the Kpelle, for instance, he listed these as including rice, Indian corn (maize), pepper, kola,

> a kind of breadstuff having a stem like the corn stalk, with an ear on the top like puss-tail flag; and another kind much like the broom corn; sweet potatoes; yams; egg-plant, cucumbers, arbor beans, tomatoes, radishes, mustard, pineapple, plantain, banana, guava, papaw, grandadilla, orange, lime, lemon, cotton plant, indigo . . . peanuts, ____, blackeyed peas, coffee, cocoa for chocolate and a variety of pepper. (Seymour 1858a, 8)

Many of these plants were locally domesticated. The headwaters of the Niger River, which foreigners were curious to find, was part of the "West African cradle of agriculture," where Africans domesticated crops such as African rice (*Oryza glaberrima*), sorghum, fonio ("firney"), and different kinds of millet (Murdock 1959, 66–67; Fairhead and Leach 1996, 104). Other crops of local African origin include yams, palm nuts, gourds, and some types of bananas (Murdoch 1959, 64–71). Many crops, however, came from other parts of the world: melons, pomegranates ("pankana"), sugarcane, eggplants, onions, citrus fruits, and cucumbers from the Mediterranean, some overland from Asia; and rice (*Oryza sativa*), bananas, plantains, Asian yams, coconuts, mangoes, breadfruits, ginger, and other spices from Asia that

Europeans introduced; European shippers brought maize or corn, cassava ("cassadas"), sweet potatoes, kidney beans, lima beans, capsicum peppers, pumpkins, squash, tomatoes, pineapples, papaya ("pawpaw"), guavas, avocados, cashews, ground nuts, tobacco, and okra from the Americas (Alpern 1992).

Rice was at this time, and remains, the culturally preferred staple throughout the interior. As the travelers noted, rice was the dominant crop in local food production in both the forest and the savanna regions. Some historians have suggested that African rice cultivation was at this time relatively recent to the more southerly parts of the hinterland, where it was introduced by Mande speakers in the fifteenth century (see, e.g., d'Azevedo 1962, 522–523). This supposition was based partly on work concerning the incidence of malaria in certain Liberian populations (Livingstone 1958). However, these texts support other evidence from that period (see, e.g., Savage 1839; Hall 1836) that rice cultivation and trade in the Liberian coast and interior was long established by the nineteenth century and probably dates from far earlier times, long prior to Mande and European influences (see Massing 1980, 119; Jones 1983b, 26–27; Fairhead and Leach 1998, 48–53). The Portuguese probably introduced a more productive white Asian rice (*Oryza sativa*) to West Africa in the sixteenth century (Jones 1983b, 26; Alpern 1992, 20–21; see also Johnston [1906] 1969, 668). Sims made two references to white rice, while Benjamin Anderson distinguished between "wild rice" (presumably *Oryza glaberrima*) and two other types of rice. Anderson and Sims mentioned only a fraction of the rice varieties that farmers grew. Research has amply documented the selection, manipulation, and use of a large number of varieties by the region's farmers, both historically and presently, to meet variable ecological and social needs (Portèreres 1965; Richards 1986; Thomasson 1991).

Rice could be processed and cooked in various ways, and this varied by locality. Indeed, villagers' reservations to Sims that they did not "know how to cook for Americans" is an acknowledgment that different people's tastes vary (chap. 3, 101). Most of the region's inhabitants like their rice cooked soft. It is dehusked by pounding and winnowing and can be parboiled first to swell the grains. Early harvested rice can be pounded into flakes and roasted as a snack, and rice may also be pounded into flour for funerals and other special occasions. The "firney" that Seymour observed is fonio *(Digitaria exilis; foni* in Manding). Today this is sometimes known as hungry rice, a small grain which, when prepared, resembles couscous and would be harvested during the rainy "hunger" season to fill the food supply gap before the main upland rice harvest.

Tobacco is another crop that received much attention from the travelers and indeed was grown extensively, especially in the more northern areas traversed by their routes. It still is today. Europeans started to export tobacco from the Americas to West Africa by the early sixteenth century (Philips 1983, 317; Alpern 1992, 30–31; 1995, 26–27). The travelers said that tobacco was used as currency and for smoking, chewing, and sucking (see Schwab 1947, 104–105). Writers differ as to whether Africans used tobacco more for smoking, chewing, or snuffing (Whitehurst 1836, 177; Büttikofer 1897, 61; Johnston [1906] 1969, 994). Certainly there was opposition to smoking in the region, whether voiced in the terms of one repentant smoker, who claimed that smoking put some people in a state of "narcotic drunkenness" and that some of the chemicals in tobacco leaves were poisonous (C. 1882), or in terms of its contravention of Islamic tenets. Some nineteenth-century reports note that the Manding used tobacco, probably against the Maliki legal tradition to which they very broadly belonged (Khalîl [1916] 1980, 55). Others emphasized snuff taking: According to Etta Donner, "long ago the Mandingo brought the leaves of a dwarf species of tobacco into the country; these are powdered, mixed with salt and pepper, and chewed or used as snuff" (1939, 124). In 1868, Anderson wrote that the people of Musadu grew tobacco in town, and that the Manding were great snuff makers who supplied snuff to themselves and to the Loma (chap. 5, 219). Whitehurst conjectured that the Manding and Fula snuffed tobacco more than any other groups (1836, 177–178; see also Ashumn 1827a, 275).

Yet the main reason why the Manding probably harvested so much tobacco was because of its value as currency. Tobacco "bars" were dried black tobacco, tied up and wrapped in green leaves. The value of each bar was determined by its weight and size (Donner 1939, 124; Jones 1983a, 47). The U.S. Minister to Liberia, John Smyth, wrote: "Tobacco is the common currency and coin of the interior races of Liberia, even of the Mohammedan Negro, who does not use it, but trades with it. This is love of tobacco in civilized settlements, but invariably it is so in native towns, villages, and half-towns. . . . This article of import is always in demand" (Smyth 1885). As this quotation suggests, and as Seymour noted, tobacco was also imported from Cuba, and one of the many international ports with which Liberia traded was Havana (Todson 1840, 82). Tobacco was placed in containers such as goat horns, cane tubes, and silver boxes.

In a number of places, the texts give insight into the farming patterns and practices of the time and the ways that land and labor were used. Frequently, large contiguous areas were planted: in Kpelle country, Seymour claimed to have seen one hundred acres of rice. Such a large area probably represented the grouped fields of all the individual farm households of a whole village (see Kellemu 1971; Currens 1976; Gay 1989). Farming "households" (and hence fields) at this time would also have been large, comprising as they did the dependants and domestic slaves—including the women and children—of the more senior inhabitants. Most of the descriptions support a picture of the shifting cultivation type of horticultural technology still practiced in much of the region. After land clearance, the first year is used for rice and the second year for other crops; at the time of the accounts, this was frequently cotton, which had been intercropped with rice in the first year. Other crops could also be intercropped with rice or cultivated in smaller, separate fields or gardens. Seymour saw rice intercropped with cotton at Solong (Zolowo); oral histories from Toma regions confirm the prevalence of this pattern at the time (Fairhead and Leach 1994). After two years of use, the land is then allowed to become fallow for a number of years. Fallow lengths probably varied depending on ecological, demographic, and economic conditions. Anderson observed three-to-four-year fallow periods in Toma country, which would appear short from the perspective of many modern analysts, who consider seven years as a minimum if soil degradation is not to ensue. But as recent research confirms, the region's farmers have their own means of deeming a fallow "mature"—such as when it contains certain indicator plants—and would not necessarily consider fallows of three to four years as short (Fairhead and Leach, field notes). And short fallows are not necessarily unsustainable.

The travelers did not pay much attention to the differences in agricultural practice which would have existed along the forest-savanna ecotone. These would have included differences in crop varieties, fallowing patterns, soil preparation, and the use of fire. While essential in land preparation, fire in the south had to be set to burn carefully dried cut trees and undergrowth. At Musadu, Anderson discussed land preparation without mentioning fire setting. In this savanna region, the tall grasses would generally have been laid over in preparation for the passage of the usual dry season fires in March or April, after which the ash was turned into the soil and the grass root "stumps" removed with a hoe. Anderson's visits were in November and December.

Anderson seems to describe inland valley swamps and plains, which would have been used for rice production in the rainy season and carried important green pasture in the dry season. These would probably have been gradually leveled and broadened by managing silt deposition by floods and by irrigation, longstanding practices in the region (Fairhead and Leach 1996).

The division of labor for upland farming that Sims described in Kpelle country is typical of much of the Liberian region. Men clear or "brush" the mature fallow and fell the larger trees, while women clear the rest of the field's cut vegetation into piles. These would be burnt some weeks later in the dry season, when they have dried. Planting and harvesting were generally joint activities between women and men. Rice planting is staggered over a relatively long period, with different rice varieties used for different planting dates or soils. As Seymour noted near Kuankan, women weeded rice fields. Thus women held essential positions in farming (see Schwab 1947, 131–136). Sims observed women working in a typical large labor group, which would probably be working each member's field in turn. The Kpelle word for these work groups is "*kuu*" (Gibbs 1965, 223). Major farming tasks in parts of the interior were and remain accompanied by assorted music, whether gourd rattles for women's work or drums, as Sims heard, for men's. While drumming can be merely for rhythm and to accompany singing, it may also communicate instructions to the working men in a drum language known only by initiates of the men's secret society.

Industry

Metalwork was highly developed in the hinterland. As a smith himself, Seymour was particularly interested in iron and made several references about smiths, furnaces, and iron products in his writings. Seymour and Anderson gave descriptions of Kpelle, Loma, and Manding smithing processes, and the travelers listed numerous items that blacksmiths made, including knives, fire tongs, dog bells, spear and arrow heads, iron bars, hoes, swords, iron cutlasses, spurs, horse bits, iron spurs, stirrups, crooked hooks, and billhooks; the last was a cutlass-type tool with a hooked end. Cutlass is a general term "for a number of curved, broad-bladed cutting tools and weapons that included machetes, billhooks, and chopping knives" (Alpern 1995, 17; see also Sundström [1965] 1974, 193–194). Crooked iron hooks were probably attached to ropes for hunting purposes.

Iron smelting was also a well-developed regional tradition in Kpelle and Loma areas and those farther north. Anderson first mentioned smelting villages located near the plentiful supplies of wood found then—as today—on the slopes and summits of the Fon-Going Mountains. Contrary to the arguments of Goucher (1981), the wood growth in the vicinity would probably be sufficient to sustain such an industry (Fairhead and Leach 1998). Anderson's discussion attested to the ancient iron-working traditions among the Loma. Sims and Seymour spoke to the quantity and quality of Kpelle iron and to their skills in smelting (see Schulze 1970–71; White 1974; Thomasson 1987).

Seymour noted that smiths set up shops at the gates of Solong (Zolowo), Forsormer (Fassangouni), and Boo. Smiths, in part, probably constructed their shops near town gates to reduce the possibility of sparks blowing from their forges and setting fires to the thatch roofs of other buildings. Preserving the "sanctity" of the smith's forge was a deeper cultural reason why smith built their shops away from the center of town. Smiths needed to main good communication with the spirit world to harness the occult power that that they needed to fashion their objects and imbibe them with power. Non-smiths were not permitted to move into the central area where the smith worked, so they would not "pollute" or "contaminate" the "spiritual balance" that the smith needed to maintain with the spirits (David Conrad, personal com-

Figure 38. An intact village wall fortification, showing the blacksmith forge outside the gate. *Source: Inserted in the copy of F. Bouet,* Les Tomas. *Courtesy of Musée d'Histoire de Berne.*

munication, 24 February 2000; see also McNaughton 1988; Brett-Smith 1994; McIntosh 1998, 177).

The iron ore in the hinterland was considered of exceptional quality, as much of it was over 50 percent iron (Schulze 1973, 159). In 1882, Eli Whitney wrote to the U.S. Consul in Liberia, John Smyth, and asked about the quality of iron in Liberia. Whitney had inherited his famous father's business, which manufactured firearms (Green 1956, 194–196). Smyth responded by quoting from a conversation with Anderson and from Anderson's account: "He [Anderson] said he was not able to speak positively as to whether the ore contained phosphorous or not, nor could he speak as to the percentage of iron in the ore, but in conformation of his printed narrative, he insisted that the ore was nearly pure iron" (Smyth to Eli Whitney, Jr., 28 November 1882).

Seymour sent specimens of iron ore and iron utensils made from it back to America to be surveyed, via a Baptist minister and blacksmith named Rev. Aaron P. Davis. The result was a "Report—pure iron, 98.4%, made by A.A. Haynes, Assayer for the State of Massachusetts" (Richardson 1959, 315). Davis sent a sample of the ore to Mr. Coppinger in Philadelphia and wrote:

> I send you a piece of African ore, just as dug from its native bed, or broken from among rocks. I have seen and conversed with a number of natives, who

> affirm that it is actually the pure ore, or just as taken from its native bed. I obtained a piece through Mr. George L. Seymour, who had tried in vain to dissect it, and I being of that craft, he brought it to my shop for that purpose. When he brought it, it appeared like a craggy rock, of yellowish color on its surface, and, with a very small exception, it could not be separated but by heavy and hard pounding with my largest sledge-hammer and a chisel prepared for that purpose. I also send you a teaspoon which is made of some of the ore, which in its crude state is superior to the iron brought here for sale by English merchant vessels. . . . I am told by the natives that it is plentiful, and about 3 days' walk from our present place of residence; it is gotten by digging and breaking rocks. It is also said to be in large lumps. In these parts, the natives buy no iron, but dig it out of the ground, or break the rocks and get it, as the case may be. ("Pure Native Iron" 1855, 63)

Nionsamoridu was known as one of the centers of iron production in this region, and notably for the "Kissy penny" or "Guinze" (*gbèzèn*). These T-shaped iron pieces were used as currency in Loma, Kissi, and Mende regions, and their supply seems to have been regulated through the Poro Society. Beavogui suggests that the Manding had "a certain monopoly in the fabrication of Guinze," and that "It was under the control of the local chiefs"—categorized by ethno-linguistic federations (Beavogui 1973–74, 45). Thus Giziwolu Guinze came from the forges in the vicinity of Sibiribaro and Gizima and were commanded from Nionsamoridu. It was from these places that the volume of Guinze was controlled in the market and regulated according to consumption (see White 1974). In addition to iron, some blacksmithing used copper, either from coastal trade or from Nioro and other sites further inland (Sundström [1965] 1974, 217–243; Herbert 1984, 14, 17–18). The iron ore of the Fon-Going Mountains is of such high quality and quantity that a railway and deep port is now being prepared for its export via Conakry.

Leatherwork was another significant industry. Sims saw Gola and Kpelle leather workers, Seymour made a brief reference to Loma tanners, and Seymour and Anderson discussed Manding leather-making practices. The Manding tanned leather and made leather leggings, saddles, stirrups, bridles, and bags. The residents of Musadu also sold leather hides. Most of these items would have been produced by specialized leatherworkers, or *garanke,* in Manding society who were and continue to be members of the nearly casted *nyamakalawu* (Frank 1998).[16]

Locally grown cotton was woven into cotton stripes which could be used as money (Hodder 1980, 206). In 1836, Whitehurst reported that one fathom (about six feet) of white cotton cloth was equivalent to one-half bushel of rice (Whitehurst 1836, 150). They were also sewn together both into clothing and country cloths: that is, large blankets, frequently patterned, and colored with indigo dye and brown thread. Indeed locally grown and woven cotton was the source of most people's clothing, together with a little use of imported cloth. A characteristic garment for senior men was the "country coat"—a robe of local cotton cloth ("country cloth") with a large pocket in the center (Johnston [1906] 1969, 181, 302, 305). That even children were clothed is an indicator of the economic prosperity of the region. By the early twentieth century, elders remember, it was very difficult to clothe children, a stark reminder of the economic decline in the intervening period. Women throughout the region presumably went bare-topped, which was the common pattern until the recent past.

The reliance on locally grown cotton for clothing meant that cotton production at the time, and its dominant role in local agriculture, far exceeded that of the twentieth century, when imported cloth became more popular and widely available. The Toma in Guinea recognize two past types of cotton, one of which is the perennial woody bush variety (*Glossypium spp.*). Notably, this is not the kapok of the "cotton" trees *Ceiba pentrandra* and *Bombax buonopozense*.

Equally, the double-heddle looms used for weaving the narrow cotton strips typical of the region were a ubiquitous site in the towns and villagers that the travelers passed through. Seymour claimed to observe women weaving near Kuankan, an unusual sight given that in this region weaving is normally men's work. Later he observed what appears to be a more normal division of labor, with men weaving and women carding, spinning, and dyeing the cotton. In the present, cotton cloth production is frequently subject to a complex gender division of labor and product rights, with women owning the raw cotton which they might have planted as intercrops and retaining some rights to the finished cloth, even if woven by a man.

Sims wrote that the Kpelle women of Seewau-ta "produced earthen-ware beautifully ornamented" (chap. 3, 104). While the Manding introduced their own pottery traditions when they emigrated from the savannah, the ancestors of the Kpelle, Loma, Bassa, and others who preceded the Manding to the forest had long ago developed their own forms of pottery making (Atherton 1970–71; McEvoy 1970–71; Orr 1971–72; Gabel, Borden, and White 1972–74). The pottery industry also included the manufacture of the fine smoking pipes that the travelers observed in Pallaker (see Hill 1976; Philips 1983).[17]

Games and Music

The accounts also made many references to local African and American games and public entertainments—and to the ways the travelers were drawn into these. For example, Sims observed that the Gola were "addicted to gambling" (chap. 3, 95). Gambling remains a key feature of life in the region today, whether over board games or—in a more metaphorical sense—in the volatile political arena of village courts (see Leach 1994; Richards 1986). Gambling is often mentioned as a reason why children were pawned.[18]

Sims encountered what seems to have been traveling players, both men and women, telling *ndoma* (chap. 3, 120). "*Ndoma*" is the generic term for "story" in various Southwestern Mande languages, where such tales are distinguished from history (see, e.g., Cosentino 1982). Seymour confirmed the presence of traveling players visiting the Manding town of Pallarker, describing these as "musicians" (chap. 4, 129). Whether these were *jeli* or griots, whose roles in the Manding world are reserved for history telling, entertainment, and advising patrons, is unclear. Griots were the endogamous *nyamakala* in Manding society who specialized in singing and playing music. Benjamin Anderson, for instance, noted in 1874 that that Manding bards "are certainly, by nature skilful musicians and ahead of our Veys who are not to be lightly held in that respect" (chap. 6, 273). It was common for an important individual, when traveling, to be accompanied by musicians to herald his departures and arrivals in town. Anderson even described such an occasion, where "musicians" sang the praises of Chief Momolu Sao when he left Totoquella for Bopolu (chap. 5, 174; see Person 1964; Johnson 1986, chap. 2; Conrad and Frank 1995, 1–7).

Benjamin Anderson, a musician himself who sang and played the guitar and other stringed instruments (see chap. 2), provided the best descriptions of musical instruments. He made over one dozen references to musical instruments and performers in his two accounts and correctly recorded the three measures of music that represent the musical accompaniment to the Islamic creed. During his first trip, he mentioned the horns and drums and the iron cymbal that the musicians played as they led Momolu Sao out of Totoquella (chap. 5, 174). The latter, called "*kende*" in Kissi areas, is a hollow, split, banana-shaped iron bell, which is associated with men's initiation (see Schaeffner 1990, 39–43). In Manding areas, this would have been one of two kinds of iron instruments: *négé* or *naryinya* (David Conrad, personal communication, 19 December 1995). In 1868, Anderson wrote about a "bard," or griot, who played a "harp," a "huge gourd, . . . a most unmusical 'shell'" (chap. 5, 210). Six years later in Vukkah, he described an eight-keyed piano-type instrument with "a double number of gourds sized to regulate the sound" (chap. 6, 273). The Manding respectively call both instruments *kora* and *balafon*. When Sims left Monrovia, he wrote that the "natives" played their "rude wooden horns" (chap. 3, 93). These were "most likely wooden or ivory instruments with a conical bore. If they did not have a mouthpiece, they had an opening on the side or at the end that is blown like a trumpet so that the vibration of the lips could create sound waves" (Laura Arntson, personal communication, 14 April 1996). Vai horns are most prevalent in this part of western Liberia.

Firearms

Guns were part of the weaponry of warfare, were key trade items, and were important for hunting. The level of detail about firearms in the accounts and other writings of the period suggest their major significance to settlers. Sims, Seymour, and Anderson made several references to guns and muskets. They specifically mentioned Danish guns, English fusees, revolvers, pistols, a United States musket, a cap gun, a rifle, a tower gun, and a cannon. It is not possible to identify specifically any of these firearms because of the imprecise terminology used, the unclear descriptions, and the counterfeit manufacture of firearms. Nevertheless, some key distinctions can be drawn between them, while the accounts give some indication of the development of firearms technology at the time.

One way that firearms can be distinguished is by how they are loaded: through the muzzle (muzzle loaders) or through the rear (breech loaders). Some are loaded through the muzzle with a ramrod to drive the powder and shot through into the barrel, as Gotorah did in one scene that Anderson described. The most common muzzle loaders in West Africa during the nineteenth century were the newly developed percussion cap locks and older-styled flintlocks. Many kinds of flintlocks were available in Africa, including tower guns, musketoons, buccaneers, birding guns, or fusees. Gunflints became common import items as the flintlock replaced the earlier matchlock; these were chips from a flint or similar stone which were set in the hammer, where they helped produce the spark that ignited the gunpowder. Flints could only be used twenty to fifty times, so spares had to be purchased (Norte 1873, 104; Smith 1989, 86; Alpern 1995, 22). Flints were thus a principal means of exchange along with salt, powder, and tobacco (Whitehurst 1836, 277).

Tower guns were among the strongest of the common trade guns that circulated in West Africa. Their name derives from their supposed testing at the firing range at the Tower of London before they were sold (White 1971, 177; see also Whitehurst 1836, 209). Sims met a chief's son carrying a "Danish gun." Also known as a "Dane gun" or "long Dane," this five-to-seven-foot-long flintlock was first made at the Ernst von Schimmelmann factory at Hellebek, on the island of Sjælland (Zealand) in Denmark, and became the most popular firearm that West Africans imported from Europe from the mid-eighteenth to the early nineteenth centuries. Dane flintlocks sold so well that the British copied them and eventually produced more than the Danes. Dane firearms became popular in Africa because they were cheap, simply made, fairly accurate because of the long barrel, and could usually be repaired by local blacksmiths. Dane guns, however, often exploded and rarely worked when they got wet.

Fusees, which Benjamin Anderson observed among the Manding of Musadu, were also known as "fuzees" or "fusils." "Fusee" is an ambiguous term that usually referred to flintlock muskets. During the seventeenth century, other muskets, such as the snaphaunce, the carbine, and the birding gun, were also called fusees. Fusees measured three to four and a half feet long, being generally longer than carbines and shorter than Dane guns (Headrick

1981, 197–199). Where the Musadu Manding obtained their "English fusees" is not precisely clear but testifies to the scale of the West African trade routes of which they were a part, and to the importance of arms to this trade. They probably came from Freetown, Sierra Leone, which later became Samori Touré's principle source of modern firearms.

Anderson described a double-barreled pistol in 1868, which he called a "dragon pistol" or "horse pistol." This was probably one of several types of flintlock pistols which were popular during the late eighteenth and early nineteenth century. European pistols sold in West Africa were manufactured in England, Holland, and France (Carman 1955, 141–144; Wilkinson 1981, 62; Alpern 1995, 21). Anderson also had a revolver. Revolvers such as the Colt, the Smith and Wesson, the Adams, the Tranter, and the Webley became popular during and after the 1850s and were exported to Liberia (Rhodes 1978, 66–76; Wilkinson 1981, 15–16).

Many small cannon were also sold as peripheral items in the firearms trade. Cannons were primarily used to create fear from the noise that they generated, as Anderson threatened in 1868 (Smith 1989, 81; Alpern 1995, 20).

Americo-Liberians had better access to more modern arms than Africans in the interior. Breech loaders became the prototype for rifles that European and North American armies came to use by the mid-nineteenth century. As barrels and bullets improved, rifles became more accurate, efficient, and easier to use than muskets. Africans were able to purchase rifles by the 1860s as Europeans developed new models and sold their old stock. The timing, however, was such that most of the guns that Sims and Seymour mentioned were probably muzzle loaders. Prior to the twentieth century, the terms "musket" and "rifle" were used interchangeably.

When Anderson referred to a United States musket, he could have been speaking of the repeaters and single-shot breech-loading rifles that started to replace Danish muskets after the 1860s: the Smith and Wesson, the Spencer and Henry, or the U.S. Springfield (Peterson 1964, 105; Headrick 1981, 98). A decade earlier, when J. J. Roberts requested that the American Colonization Society send U.S. muskets to immigrants who were settling in the "frontier" (Roberts to W. McLain, 10 February 1845, 154), these probably referred to the older-style muskets. The firearms that Anderson's entourage exhibited in Musadu were certainly faster and more powerful than those which the people of Musadu possessed. Anderson probably used the percussion-cap musket, which could be reloaded more quickly and far out-performed the early-nineteenth-century flintlock with respect to range, consistency of fire, and durability during the rainy season. Developed in 1807, the percussion cap replaced the flintlock and was the firearm that led to the rifle (Headrick 1981, 85–86).

While an "arms race" ensued in West Africa, older-style Dane guns nevertheless continued to be popular in some parts of the interior until the end of the century. Apart from military purposes, guns were used as symbols of prestige, and their large size was an advantage. The "king's son" who carried the Danish musket on his shoulders clearly did this to show his rank (chap. 3, 96).[19]

Blacksmiths made most bullets from lead or iron. Polished stone, palm kernels, fragments of cowry shells, grain, goat droppings, and other items were also used. Europeans exported bullets to the coast, but they were too expensive to be widely purchased (Legassick 1966, 100; Headrick 1981, 107; Smith 1989, 86; Alpern 1995, 22). The "Pot legs" that Sims mentioned were balls made out of iron pots. Sometimes, the small iron balls that form the base of pots were used as shot; Whitehurst noted that families rarely had more than two or three iron pots because so many pots were melted down and made into bullets (Whitehurst 1836, 147; see also Büttikofer 1897, 60; Schwab 1947, 231; Harley 1996, 6–8).

Some gunpowder was locally manufactured (Tham 1972–74), although most Africans purchased their powder from Europeans via trade networks with the coast. African powder was poorer than imported powder because it absorbed too much moisture and did not work consistently. Imported powder stayed drier and burned more easily but was more expensive and less available. Gunpowder is comprised of saltpeter (niter or potassium nitrate, 75 percent), charcoal or carbon (15 percent), and sulfur (10 percent). The powder with the lowest saltpeter content was the best for African muskets because it reduced the explosion capacity and increased the longevity of gun barrels. Inhabitants often added charcoal or sawdust to their gunpowder to lower the level of saltpeter, making the charge less explosive and less apt to damage the gun barrels (Richards 1980, 56). Sulfur was not needed, but when used it doubled the force of locally made charges when added to saltpeter and charcoal. Africans imported sulfur.

Powder was shipped to Africa in five- to one-hundred-pound barrels, and sometimes measured up to one-fifth of Europe's total exports. In the mid-nineteenth century, Africans valued French powder more than Danish, Dutch, English, or American. In 1868, Musadu's chief regretted that Benjamin Anderson did not bring him a good quantity of powder, which Musadu particularly needed during this turbulent period (chap. 5). Gunpowder was also used at ceremonies and on special occasions, such as that which Sims described when he visited Du-gla-ta (see Park [1799 and 1805] 1983, 88; Donner 1939, 45–46).

Animals and Hunting

Animal products, from both domestic and hunted animals, also contributed to the life and economy of the interior. The travelers described the small herds of cattle that the villagers kept; these are generally of varieties resistant to the trypanosomiasis (sleeping sickness) endemic to the forest zone (Schulze 1973, 136; Church 1980, 125–131). The "large, reddish, long-horned cattle" that Anderson described during his 1868 journey are the N'dama cattle from the savannah (chap. 5, 222); these were less resistant to sleeping sickness during the nineteenth century than the "black, short-horned, and sturdy cattle of the coast" known as the Muturu (Johnston [1906] 1969, 907–909; Schulze 1973, 136). Some kinds of red "bush cow" or buffalo (*Bubalus nanus* or *Syncerus nanus*) seem to have been present but were becoming exterminated by the mid-twentieth century (Johnston [1906] 1969, 730–734; Strong 1930, 1:183–184). Curiously, in Kissi regions, oral tradition recalls that these interbred with livestock (Fairhead and Leach, field notes).

Trypanosomiasis also affected where horses could be kept. Sims and Anderson both observed horses in or near Manni or Konya. In the mid-nineteenth century, horses were also found in the Kissidougou-Guekedou region and farther west in Sierra Leone, where they were linked to warfare (particularly the "sofa" cavalry of Samori Touré) and became a symbol of chiefly authority. This is farther south than one would expect to find them today, as they are no longer evident even in the region of Musadu.

Anderson was especially interested in elephants, an interest perhaps sparked by his exposure to the animals in Ballatah in 1868. Several years later, in an effort to increase the number of animals to supplement human labor in Liberia, a "company" was reportedly formed with Vice President Warner to tame elephants and bring them to the coast. Anderson was apparently nominated to lead this venture, and someone wrote a letter to the *West African Reporter* supporting Anderson. While this anonymous writer did not know if Anderson was a good shot, having never heard if Anderson ever killed any big game, he wrote that Anderson had read so much about elephants that he probably knew how to trap and tame them. According to the writer, Anderson said: "the horse loses vigor the moment he descends from the elevated plains of Manding; a few years labor knocks up the ox; while the elephant, big and strong, long lived and tractable when trained, flourishes under the very same circumstances to which the other animals succumb." According to this writer, Anderson longed to see the day when the elephant would "grace . . . the streets of Monrovia with its presence" ("Elephant Taming in Liberia" 1880, 86).

At the other end of the animal spectrum, Sims encountered "driver" or "army" ants. Of the genus *Dorylus,* these have strong jaws that can rip flesh, travel in large numbers as Sims indicated, and have been known to eat animals and human beings that have become incapacitated. Two nineteenth-century writers said that driver ants could be prevented from crawling into beds by placing the legs of the beds in bowls of vinegar (Hölldobler and Wilson 1990, 511–512, 584–590). Another person explained that one could stop driver ants from climbing into one's bed by placing "hot ashes around the foot of each bedpost" (Rockwell 1842, 307). Sims lamented an unfortunate boa constrictor (python) that "drivers" caught, and Anderson explained in 1868 how Dowilnyah punished one of his children by casting the child among driver ants. These ants "mutilated" the child to such an extent that the child's arm was lost.[20]

Animals were hunted using a variety of methods: with guns, dogs, nets, and traps. It seems that hunting was, at the time, an important local "profession," with expertise linked to proficiency in warfare. Indeed, many of Sunjata's warriors in the days of the Mali Empire were probably hunters (Levtzion 1973). At one stage, Sims seemed to describe the activities of a hunters' society, which was a closed fraternity within which hunting practice and lore is organized, and which supplied the necessary skills and "medicines" through apprenticeship (see Cashion 1984; Johnson 1999, 14–15). In many parts of the interior, killing an elephant would be the apotheosis of "being a hunter." Indeed, it is such an event as to acquire symbolic importance as the marker or foundation of a territory or dynasty (Hill 1984). Hunting nets were probably tied from string made from strong "rattans" (climbing palms, e.g., *Eremospatha macrocarpa*), while animal traps used a wide variety of techniques (e.g., see Schwab 1947, 75–76). The "Mandingo dogs" remarked upon by Anderson in Chief Pato's town may well have been used in hunting, as well as acted as guards, served as a food source, and occasionally sacrificed. Crüwell spoke of "the lame dog of the Mandingo breed, a regular hound . . . who limped with one or on two or three legs" (Crüwell 1878, 38–39). Stigma is usually attached to dogs in areas were Islam has become an integral part of Manding life (Conrad 1990, 45 n. 32). Thus, to the present, most Manding do not keep dogs, although more Manding conceivably owned dogs during the mid-nineteenth century, as Islam did not become more important and widespread until Samori started to wage his own brand of *jihad* in the 1880s (Person 1979).

Landscape and Vegetation

From the coast to Musadu, the journeys crossed several vegetation zones. From the humid coastal strip they traversed the full width of the forest zone, crossed the "transition" zone where forest and grassy vegetation are found in a mosaic pattern, and—around Musadu—finished in grasslands almost devoid of trees. The accounts describe these changing vegetation patterns and the topography they overlaid as well as give insights into the ways people's activities were shaping the landscape.

In places, the travelers walked in high forest, relatively free of undergrowth, characteristic of mature, old-growth forest. A very old forest tends to have a more open understory beneath the canopy, through which one can travel relatively easily. Sims described this near Tawn and Kelling (Kele), and Seymour in parts of Barlain Kpelle (chap. 3, 94, chap. 4, 130). Unbroken strips of forest were described by Anderson just before Bopolu. Presumably, the population density of this area was thin, and much of the land remained covered with high forest. Yet even in the heart of the humid forest zone, most vegetation was heavily modified by people, with high forest having been converted extensively for farming into managed bush fallows. Interpretation of vegetation from these accounts, however, is difficult because strips of forest in these coastal regions were commonly maintained on either side of paths for military defense, so path-side vegetation need not accurately reflect the vegetation of a locality as a whole (see Thompson 1911; Maugham-Brown 1943).

In a number of places, the travelers described landscapes which were densely populated and farmed, and hence bore little forest cover. Today, many of these are heavily forested. One such area is the lower half of Barlain country. It would seem that most of the Barlain towns have not survived, and much of the lower half of the Barlain country is now in forest, which is part of the national system of forest reserves. Another densely forested area is in the Boo region in what is now Guinea, where descriptions of short fallows are congruent with the relatively high populations described in this area. Today this area is within the Ziama Forest Reserve (Fairhead and Leach 1994).

Despite the modified nature of the forest vegetation they passed through, however, the transition from the zone where dense vegetation dominated to the lighter, grassy vegetation farther north was a significant journey marker. In 1868, Anderson contrasted "the air of light, life, and activity" of the savannas with many parts of the Loma country, "where the somber gloom of immense forests conceals all such things" (chap. 5, 208). The texts help us identify where this boundary lay. It is generally assumed that forests are in recession, with savannas encroaching on declining forests. Yet in many cases, the texts describe a landscape very similar to that found today. Moreover, in some places, they suggest that to the contrary, grassland was found farther south than it is presently, with savannas observed by the travelers where today there is forest (Fairhead and Leach 1994).

Seymour started to see prairie fields as they approached Kuankan, and in the Kuankan market, wood was for sale, suggesting its local scarcity. He also noticed that palm trees started to thin out when they reached Oussadou, near where they were first attacked. In 1868, Anderson noted that trees started to become more sparse by the time he reached Gubbewallah (Goboèla), and that Pellezarrah (Dondano) was a grassland or savannah area with no palm trees. Vukkah (Foma) had much cane break (either *Andropogon gayanus* or

Pennisetum purpureum) and small trees. The landscape up to Musadu was the "almost treeless plains" of Manding (chap. 5, 159). These descriptions conform quite closely with what one would see today.

But farther south, near Beigna, Seymour also described ridges covered with cane grass and "scarcely any tree but the palm." From the top of the mountain now known as Koiribolegue, within the Ziama forest reserve, he observed that

> the prospect is beautiful; for on either side is a plain, and on each plain a large town is visible.[21] No part of the country can be called barren, except the naked rocks. The plain is covered with small bushes and grass, and it gives the country the appearance of an old farm, with palms standing scattered all over it. The grass is cut down and burnt, and the land planted in rice, corn, cassava, ground-peas, etc., all of which looks as thriving as if it was land from which heavy timber had been cut. (chap. 4, 143)

Today the mountain and the plains beneath it are covered with a dense, semideciduous forest which constitutes an international biodiversity reserve (Fairhead and Leach 1994).

Farther south still, in present-day Liberia, Sims noted that at Suloang (Zolowo), "the heavy forest and dense undergrowth begin to diminish, giving way to an open country, interspersed by little prairies; consequently, firewood is scarce and very dear" (chap. 3, 119). Anderson also noted the lack of forest here in 1868 but attributed this to it being farmed over. As he journeyed on through Fissabu for Bokesa, "the rough features of the country moderated into extensive plains of long fields of grass, ferns, and tall palms" still in Liberia (chap. 5, 192).

Palm trees ideally need about seventy-nine inches (two thousand millimeters) of rain spread over eight months of the year to grow, though they can survive with fifty-one inches (thirteen hundred millimeters) if it rains over the same period of time. The minimum rainfall needed for oil palms is thus much less than what is needed for lowland rainforest conditions that characterized the Loma territory west of Vukkah (Foma) and the Fon-Going Mountains (Church 1980, 62, 105). Therefore, palm trees can successfully exist in the rainforest and the southernmost portions of the savannah, such as that which Seymour described here, where trees and plants which need more rain cannot grow.

At the end of his journal, Sims wrote, "There are no trees in Manni, the whole country is prairie; for firewood the people have to substitute cow dung" (chap. 3, 123). Similarly, Yaya Dole, a grandson of Benjamin Anderson's Vafin Dole, said in 1986 that during the time of his father in the late nineteenth century, "There was no wood. . . . They only used to get wood that nobody wanted. Trees have only recently started [growing] there" (Dole 1986; see also Fairhead and Leach 1996, 63–85).

At several places in the accounts, clumps of distinctive high-forest vegetation are described, sometimes around towns. This was so in the forest and in the savannas. Groves of trees, enriched with kola, are commonly encouraged or maintained around villages to afford wind protection and possibly to assist in fortification. Whether maintained for economic crops or defensive purposes, these groves are also a very common sign of old settlements. Seymour's description of "islands of forest" surrounding villages northwest of Kuankan, of an inner ring of plantain and banana, itself surrounded by a ring of large forest trees, is particularly characteristic of the region. Such forest islands are often established or protected around village settlements and around some abandoned villages. Such forests provide various useful plant products, a suitable microclimate for tree crops, shelter from wind and dry season savanna fires, shelter for ritual and initiation activities, and, in some cases, the "homes" or "village" of djinni or "spirits" (Fairhead and Leach 1996).

The travel diaries were written to be internally coherent, not requiring the kinds of contextualization which we have provided in this chapter. Nevertheless, readerships then were less clouded by subsequent writings concerning the African interior, linked to the colonial scramble for Africa and European administrations from the 1890s onward. A wholly new genre of representation emerged at this time: anthropologies, histories, and ecologies, which portrayed life and landscape. Furthermore, these nascent disciplines took shape around descriptions of a region that had just suffered decades of war linked to colonization and nation-state building. Oral accounts relating to earlier periods were the only available record. The prosperity which they portrayed could be, and has been, easily dismissed today as romantic and self-aggrandizing exaggeration, yet this idea gains powerful support from these texts.

Notes

Introduction

1. All the terms which can be used to describe the settlers or colonists carry political overtones. We use the term "Americo-Liberians" to describe those who settled in Liberia from America and the Caribbean. We use "African American" to describe Americans who, because of their African ancestry, remained enslaved or subordinated in the U.S. Nineteenth-century Americo-Liberians were therefore a subset of African Americans. This book does not deal with second-generation settlers and issues surrounding their identity. Many settlers and their descendants often used the term "Americo-Liberian" to symbolize their beliefs that they were different from the "natives" and that Africa must be made over in the image of America. Only as the Tubman administration began its "unification" program in the 1950s did the government discourage the use of this term and those such as "mulatto" and "Congo" (Schmokel 1969, 157; Blamo 1971–72, 24, 29; Singler 1981, 182; Brown 1999, 38).

2. Since locating and publicizing the existence of these texts in the academic community, extracts have appeared in *The Pepper Bird* (Sims [1860] 1996), and they have been referred to, e.g., by Richards 1996.

3. For tabular itineraries that summarize the places and some of the key things that happened on each of the journeys, see our unpublished "Appendix to Americo-Liberian Exploration in West Africa." A hard copy has been deposited at the library of Michigan State University. An Internet version can be found at *http://www.studiomayhem.com/liberia/liberiaexplorers.htm* (accessed 13 February 2003).

1. The Liberia of the Journeys

1. Jefferson or one of his family members is now thought to have fathered the six children of Sally Hemings, one of his slaves (*Guardian*, 28 January 2000).

2. Blyden was born in the Virgin Islands in 1832 and migrated to Liberia in 1850. He lived most of his adult life in Liberia but resided in Sierra Leone for lengthy periods as well. He ran unsuccessfully for the presidency of Liberia, held the posts of Secretary of State and Secretary of the Interior, and served as Liberia's ambassador to London and Paris. He was the principal of Alexander High School, a professor and one-time President of Liberia College, and a newspaper editor in Monrovia. He held various positions in Sierra Leone and went on two expeditions into the interior for the British government. In 1888, he published his most famous book, *Christianity, Islam and the Negro Race*. Blyden retired in Freetown, Sierra Leone, and died in 1912 (Holden 1976; Lynch 1967; Benjamin 1979).

3. There are many accounts of the early years of Liberia from which we draw on here, from those written close to the time from the perspective (e.g., Wilkeson 1839) to the more recent works considering the new colony in its context (e.g., Shick 1980; Liberty [1977] 1999).

4. This was probably an exaggeration. Although it is not clear what Liberia considered its territory in 1858, the estimate for Liberia's population in the 1950s was about eight hundred thousand (Porter 1956).

5. See Sherman (1975) for Liberian intellectuals in general and, for example, Lynch (1967) on Blyden, Moses (1989) on Crummell, and Moses (1998a) on Washington.

6. See also Blyden to John C. Lowrie, 15 January 1875, in Lynch (1978, 178–184).

7. In this regard, Dunn (1992) describes in detail the changing policy of the Episcopal Church in Liberia.

8. Such hypotheses are questioned in Conteh (1988), among others. One reason for the high mortality may be that some slave owners freed their elderly and invalid slaves for Liberia to save having to support them. We thank Christopher Fyfe for this observation.

9. E. J. Roye is usually presented as the first nonmulatto president, but some reports suggest that Benson was "Perfectly Black" (Commons 1865, 5, question 3962, 33; see photographs in Shumard 1999, 13, 17; and see fig. 2 for Benson). Although representation of the Roye episode is still influenced by Blyden, who was an interested party, further research may generate less clear-cut narrations of these events. Our thanks to Christopher Fyfe for drawing our attention to the Parliamentary Papers reference.

10. See James Watt and Dr. Thomas Winterbotton in 1794 (Watt [1794] 1994; Winterbottom [1803] 1969), Gaspard-Théodore Mollien in 1818 (Mollien 1820), O'Beirne in 1821 (O'Beirne [1821] 1979; cf. Laing 1825), Réné Caillié in 1828 (1830), Rev. George Thompson in 1842 (1852), and Hyacinthe Hecquad in 1850 (1853), and Blyden to Alexander Bravo, 10 March 1873, in Lynch 1978, 117–139.

11. For example, Ashmun, Lewis, Dungey, Williams, Jacobs, Whitehurst, Bowen, Liberius, Sims, Blyden, Kister, Pitman, King, and Lyon, among others, traveled to Bopolu (see d'Azevedo 1994).

12. The letter from President Roberts, Monrovia, 18 August 1865, is found inside an edition of Anderson's 1868–69 journey (published in 1870), located in State University of New York at Binghamton's library. We thank Martin Ford for providing us with a photocopy of this material.

13. This was probably Daniel Beams, a freeborn Catholic from Norfolk, Virginia, who had immigrated to Liberia only two years earlier, at the age of twenty ("List of Emigrants [*Linda Stewart*]" 1853, 26–27).

14. John Kitton to R. Muchison, Archives of the Royal Geographic Society, London.

15. The notion of the superior intelligence of inland peoples was linked to ideas of "preparation" for receiving the gospel.

2. Journeys in the Interior

1. The 1830 U.S. census registered seven "heads of families" in Hartford who had the last name of Seymour, and a George Seymour was the father of one of these families (Jackson and Teeples 1977a, 109). This George was a "free colored person"

who, in 1830, was between the ages of thirty-six and fifty-four. His wife, whose name was not given, was also the same age. George and his wife had five sons and three daughters. Two of their sons were between the ages of ten and twenty-three, and two of their daughters were less than ten years old ("File Microcopies of Records in the National Archives" 1946). The George L. Seymour who went to Liberia was eleven years old in 1830. His sister Mary, who went to Liberia in 1852, was only five years old in 1830. Their ages thus fit the profile of the Hartford George Seymour family, so this may have been the same family in which George and Mary were raised.

2. Greenleaf might have only sent copies of other constitutions to Monrovia rather than help write the draft constitution as was once thought (Burrowes 1998, 1–7; see also Johnston [1906] 1969, 158; Henries 1954, 85).

3. In Seymour 1855, 1857a, 1858e.

4. Seymour's "Pessay" in this instance are the Southern Kpelle who live south of the Saint Paul River. The Southern Kpelle are known today as the Katata and Totota Kpelle. The Bokomu Kpelle lived west of the Saint Paul, and the Barlain Kpelle lived farther to the north (see maps 2–3, 5). None of the explorers reached the Kpelle who lived east of Barlain in the area that surrounds the modern Guinean town of N'Zerekore. The travelers also bypassed the Kpelle who live in central Liberia. These are the Jokwelle, Zotaa, Kpai, Panta, and Vavala Kpelle on today's maps that encompass towns such as Gbarnga and Ganta (Gay et. al. 1969; Schulze 1973, 103; see also chap. 7).

5. Also in *ATL* (1857; passed at sessions December 1856 and January 1857) and in *ATL* (April 1857), in *The Statute Laws of the Republic of Liberia.* Monrovia (1856).

6. There are several other sources for this information: Benson (1858b, 130); "Amounts Subscribed by Citizens of the City of Monrovia" (1858, 131–132); Seymour (1858c, 200–201); "Seymour's Travels in Western Africa" (1860, 302); Brittan ([1860] 1969, 315); *Forty-First ARACS* (1858, 21); see also d'Azevedo (1995, 92 n. 89).

7. Augustus Washington's life and work has written about and republished in Moses (1998a) and Shumard (1999; *http://www.npg.si.edu/exh/awash/index.htm* [accessed 13 February 2003]). Primary sources for this short biography are from Washington (1851, 259–265; 1854, 185–188; 1855a, 296–297; 1855b, 178; 1859, 331–333; 1864, 90–91); "List of Emigrants [*Isla de Cuba*]" (1854, 88–89); "Meeting of [the] Connecticut Colonization Society" (1855, 239); "Latest from Liberia" (1858, 131); Crummell ([1862] 1969, 141); Johnson (1867a, 172; 1867b, 215; 1868, 314); "Arrival of the Golconda" (1868, 308); "Hon. Augustus Washington" (1868, 376); "Inauguration Day at Monrovia" (1872, 271); "Latest from Liberia" (1858, 118); and Roberts (1875, 4) (see also Syfert 1977a, 109, 192).

8. Seymour's handwriting in his 1 April 1858 letter clearly indicates that Ash's first name was Levin. Yet the *NYCJ*'s publication of Seymour's 1 April letter reported that his first name was Lewis, as did an article in the *Home and Foreign Record* ("Seymour's Travels in Western Africa" 1860, 494). Another publication of one of Seymour's letters said that Ash's first name was Elim (Seymour 1860c, 278).

9. The U.S. census does not record a head of household named Levin Ash in Indiana in the census of 1850 or 1860 (Jackson and Teeples 1976a; Jackson et al.

1987, 17, 27; Kratz Indexing, comp., 1986, 31–32). The Pennsylvania and Philadelphia census records for 1850, 1860, and 1870 list dozens of William Taylors (Jackson, Teeples, and Schaefermeyer 1976a, 1569; Jackson et al. 1987, 976; Steuart 1989, 1962).

10. That is, the 40-mile interior boundary.

11. This account can be found in Seymour (1860b). This is an impoverished account, presumably abstracted from a longer version in the *LH* that we have been unable to obtain. It underscores the importance for Liberian history of locating editions of this newspaper.

12. The *Linda Stewart*'s manifest spelled his name "Simms."

13. He made reference to Daniel Defoe's *Robinson Crusoe* (1719) when reflecting on his surroundings, for instance, and quoted from act 1 of Shakespeare's *Henry IV* in commenting on sharp trading practices. He also used biblical quotes, largely from the King James Version.

14. When the transatlantic vessels docked offshore, "Kroomen" went to the ships in their canoes and transported the passengers and goods to shore (see, e.g., "Voyage to Liberia—Continued: The Emigrants" 1857, 85).

15. B. Castendyk to R. Murchison, August 1859, March 1860, Archives of the Royal Geographical Society.

16. The Internet reference for information on the Castendyk family is *http://www.bautz.de/bbkl/t/treviranus_g_g.shtml* (accessed 10 July 2002). Pastor Treviranus is also famous for having lodged Friedrich Engels during Engels's formative years in Bremen (Caver 1989, 12, 14, 16; Voigt 1997).

17. Delaney and Castendyk were traveling with the owners of the ship, Johnson, Turpin, and Dunbar ("African Exploring Expedition" 1859).

18. Notes from the Liberian legation in the U.S. to the Department of State, 1882–98, film 4400, roll 1 T-807, U.S. Consulate, Monrovia, Liberia (National Archives, Washington, D.C.).

19. John Kitton to R. Murchison, 18 April 1860, Archives of the Royal Geographical Society; see also Du Bois 1903, 215–227.

20. The 1850 Maryland census lists dozens of Andersons from Baltimore and nearly two hundred from the entire state, but does not have an "Israel" (Jackson and Teeples 1976b, 6; Jackson 1996, 4). It would be very interesting to research the life of Anderson and his family in Baltimore and the Americas before he sailed to Africa, as Shumard ([1999]) has done for Augustus Washington.

21. This "Brief Sketch" was found in the Department of Special Collections of the the Joseph Regenstein Library at the University of Chicago in the Frederick Starr Papers, box 9, folder 9.

22. In addition, a handwritten note in the State University of New York, Binghamton, copy of Benjamin Anderson's *Narrative of a Journey to Musardu* (1870) states that "Mr. Anderson went from Baltimore, Dec. 1851, there 16 years old—born free—1870, 35 years old."

23. See a short article titled "The *Liberia Packet*" (1846, 352–355) for a good description and drawing of the *Liberia Packet*. For an account of some of the things that the Andersons and other nineteenth-century emigrants might have experienced

as they crossed the ocean and landed in Monrovia, see Peterson ([1854] 1998, 38–51) and "Voyage to Liberia—Continued: The Emigrants" (1857).

24. A handwritten note in the State University of New York, Binghamton, copy of Anderson's 1870 book states that Anderson "sometimes" worked at "the Story of Mr. Johns."

25. After hearing about a friend's experiences on the battlefront in Cape Mount in 1900, Blyden wrote, "[the story] brought to my mind my own experiences in two of such campaigns—one in the same Cape Mount in 1853, and the other in Sinoe County in 1856. Very few survive who shared in either of those experiences. I can recall only three in Montserrado County—Ex-Judge Dennis, Hon. Benj. Anderson and Henry Cooper, Esq.; there may be others" (1900, 8; see also Lynch 1967, 15; Massing 1980, 91). Blyden did not name Anderson or anyone else when he published his "Expedition to Little Cape Mount" (1853).

26. For more information on this school and Mr. Horne, see "The Monrovia Academy" (1856, 120); "Notes: Mr. Benjamin Anderson" (1881); "Educational Work in Liberia" (1883, 90); Lynch (1967, 156; 1978, 242, 300).

27. President Roberts said that Anderson was a captain in 1875 (Roberts 1875, 72), and President Arthur Barclay stated that Anderson was a colonel when he died (1911, 31).

28. In his introduction to the publication of Anderson's first trip to Musadu, Joseph Henry, Secretary of the Smithsonian Institution, wrote that Anderson served President Warner as Secretary of the Treasury (see chap. 5, 157). Henry evidently was just referring to Anderson's final three weeks in office in January 1864 in the new Warner administration. The previous president's cabinet officials remained in office until the legislature ratified the candidates whom the new president nominated. Others have written that Anderson left this position in 1866 (Johnston [1906] 1969, 250; Fisher 1971; Schulze 1970–71, 3) or in 1868 (d'Azevedo 1995, 65; see Cassell 1970, 410).

29. "Friends in Monrovia" is an expression that Anderson used in his first journey.

30. We have not found an independent primary source which verifies Johnston's claim that Anderson returned to the U.S. for a visit.

31. According to handwriting in the title page in the State University of New York, Binghamton, 1870 *Narrative of a Journey to Musardu,* Schieffelin gave the book to C. Snown (Caleb Swan?). Appended to the cover is a three-paragraph letter that President J. J. Roberts sent to Swan on 18 August 1865, which told of Roberts's 1843 journey up the Saint Paul River (see Roberts 1845, referenced above). Swan was therefore interested in Liberia's interior before Anderson went to Musadu in 1868. In 1903, Anderson wrote that "the patrons of this expedition of 1868 and 9 were Mr. H. Schieffelin, Mr. Caleb Cushing and another prominent gentleman or [*sic*] New York, U.S.A." (Anderson, 1903b, 7). Did Anderson confuse the names Swan and Cushing, or was Swan, who happened to have the same first name as Cushing, the "other prominent gentleman?"

32. The original copy in Special Collections at Yale Divinity School in New Haven. was published in paperback (12.7 centimeters by 18.6 centimeters). Its title is *Journey to Musardu* on the cover and *Narrative of a Journey to Musardu, the Capital of the*

Western Mandingoes on the inside. Both titles were cited thereafter, with the latter being the most common. In the same year, a hardback book, a copy of which we examined from Brown University, was also published (11.7 centimeters by 19.4 centimeters). The name of this version was *Narrative of a Journey to Musardu;* it included both the paperback edition of Anderson's 1868–69 journey (see chap. 5) and Vafin Dole's 1868 letter, "Appendix to Benj. Anderson's Journey to Musadu" (chap. 5, 231). At the end of the century, the U.S. representative to Liberia, William H. Heard, republished Anderson's journey in his book *The Bright Side of African Life* (Heard [1898] 1969, 100–179). More recently, Humphrey J. Fisher published Anderson's two journeys in his book *Journeys to Musadu* (Fisher 1971).

33. For a history of the publication and use of this letter, see the introduction to the "Appendix" in chap. 5.

34. The Arabic document such as the one that Schieffelin published (Schieffelin [1871] 1974, 69–73) is one of just a few examples of documents written by Africans before the twentieth century that are known to exist. These and several others that were published in the *AR* and elsewhere were written in Monrovia or Kankan.

35. That is, Benjamin Anderson on his first trip to Musadu in 1868–69. The writer did not mention Sims, Seymour, or Ash, a clear indication of how these previous expeditions were vanishing from the memory for some in Monrovia.

36. Or Anderson's journal at least has not been located, this being one of many "missing" documents that researchers hope to find.

37. W. S. Anderson called this town Pallarker, which is now called Kpayakwele (also known as Kpaiyakwele and Kpayakole), at 7°28'N, 9°37'W; this city is also Sims's Pallaka, Seymour's Pallaker, and Benjamin Anderson's Pallikah. Sims lived in "Polaka" from 4 February to 1 March 1858. The town's ninety-year-old Chief, Bassee Darn, and the other people of the town treated W. S. Anderson well. In 1874, Benjamin Anderson wrote that Pallikah was the most important town in Barline country, and that the King's name now was Kalminyah.

38. That is, the people in Bopolu.

39. Queah is modern Kwea, whose people speak Kruan. The modern name and location of Karpestown is unknown, but it is Benjamin Anderson's Kypah's town (chap. 6, 245). The modern name and location of Wah Gie Place is unknown, but it is Benjamin Anderson's Waugi's town (chap. 6, 247) and is described in "Eastward Empire" (1873) as on the southeast boundary of the "Barline Pessa country." Actually, as Benjamin Anderson's trip suggests, the Waugi lived nearer the coast in what today is presumably either the Fuama or Sanoyea chiefdom.

40. The modern name and location of Pok-bah is unknown, but it is Benjamin Anderson's Pockpar (chap. 6, 245). For a discussion about the development of coffee production and trade during this time, see Ford (1995, 400–402). Allen Bennet Hooper was a very wealthy coffee grower and trader. In the eulogy that was written after Hooper died in 1879, it was noted that Hooper went to "Palaka, in the heart of the Pessy Country" and introduced cotton ("The Eulogy at Planter's Hall" 1879).

41. Here the "Pessa" refers to the Kpelle people living south of the Saint Paul River.

42. "Boson" is another name for Sao Boso or Boatswain of Bopolu ("The Attack

on Heddington" 1840, 194–195; Kistler 1865, 308; Holsoe 1966; d'Azevedo 1994, 204–205). The "Boson people" were the people of the Condo confederation around Bopolu.

43. These were commercial, not political treaties. Note that Benjamin Anderson did not say that the government occupied this land on the map that he published in 1879 (fig. 27).

44. Apparently, Roye found that while he had been away, Anderson had not kept quarterly accounts as the law required. Even when Roye finally applied to Anderson to have these accounts made up, Roye was unable to obtain them (Dennis 1870; "Annual Message of President Roye," *AR* 47 [1871]: 101).

45. Robert Arthington used his wealth in life and through his legacy to facilitate the growth of British Protestant missions in Africa. See *http://www.martynmission.cam.ac.uk/CArthington.htm* (accessed 13 February 2003).

46. Crüwell was not mistaking this "young Englishman" for Anderson, as Crüwell knew about Anderson and documented several aspects of Anderson's journeys in his book *Liberian Coffee in Ceylon* (1878, 43–45, 134–136). Nothing else, to our knowledge, is said about this alleged visit to Musadu. There are no "known" written records which state that a white "Englishman" from England traveled to Musadu at this time.

47. Josephine had migrated to Liberia with her husband Aaron W. Treadwell in 1863. Josephine planned to return to the U.S. after her husband died but instead married the newly famous explorer. Josephine had one son, Benjamin Jr., who later became a surveyor, musician, soldier, newspaper businessman, and politician ("Brief Sketch" [1910]; Brown 1980, 58).

48. Summaries of this act appeared in "The Regions Beyond" (1875, 14–15), "Interior Annexation" (1875, 72) and "Outlook for the New Republic" (1888, 112–113). The "1874 interior law" is our title, as the legislature did not title this act.

49. The "interior boundary" refers to the 40-mile boundary.

50. According to one report, the government sent several Commissioners out to "several counties." They did not leave until the rainy season and had not returned back when Anderson arrived from Musadu in December 1874. According to information in Monrovia at the time, "rumor places them a considerable distance in the interior" (see "Interior Annexation" 1875, 72). Who were these Commissioners? Did some of them go but never return? (See Whetstone 1955, 54.) Note the claim on Anderson's 1874 map in areas of upper Grand Bassa, Sinoe, and Grand Gedeh Counties: "Territory ceded to the Republic of Liberia in 1874 by particular treaties" (fig. 27). The Frederick Starr Collection has one of these treaties, which three Liberian Commissioners signed with the Chiefs of Krebbo (Krebo or Klebo) on 13 August 1874. Krebbo is a tract of Grebo land located to the interior of Cape Palmas ("Eastern Liberia," map, in Johnston [1906] 1969, 496; Schulze 1973, 103, no. 32; Kurtz 1985, 5, no. 13).

51. "The said Commissioners" refers to Benjamin Anderson and Peter Capehart (chap. 6, 241).

52. According to C. Abayomi Cassell, Anderson believed that this provision would have "an excellent effect upon the future relations of the two sections of the populations and the ultimate growth and prosperity of the country" (Cassell 1970, 346).

53. This change in route was an important shift, for it was through the central area of Liberia, from Monrovia, that the government directed its interior policy in the twentieth century.

54. The 1874 map and close reproductions have suffered the same fate. Only Anderson's 1868–69 map has been republished (see, e.g., Cassell 1970; Anderson 1971; d'Azevedo 1995).

55. For example, see McPherson (1891, 44), "The Cape Palmas Reporter" (1900), d'Ollone (1903, chap. 14), "Letters of an Itinerant" (1918, 7), "Educational Work among the Native People" (1928, 4), Davis (1953, 99–100), Richardson (1959, 104); Person (1975, 2125); Liebenow (1987, 26).

56. James Irvine was a British trader who had been involved in West African trade since 1866. He was known for his refusal to trade in alcohol (Davies 1976, 88 n. 17). Crüwell noted that Irvine was renowned for trade in Liberian coffee seed (1878, 134). He appears to have been a Methodist, as his 17 Water Street, Liverpool, trading address was noted as a Methodist "mission" (Zahniser 1957; *http://208.197.163.184/E_Books/FreeMeth/Earnest/Ec_10.htm* [accessed 13 February 2003]). It certainly welcomed many travelers from Liberia, including Blyden. Indeed, Blyden gave Anderson's 1874 manuscript to Irvine to read before the British Association (Blyden to John C. Lowrie, 4 September, in Lynch 1978, 228). Yet the only paper published was Irvine's own, which commented extensively on Anderson's 1874 journey (Irvine 1877, 378–388).

57. Anderson did not name Beahway and Nyawora in the published version of his 1874 trip. Anderson's placement of town coordinates for Beahway and Nyawora indicates that he made more estimates of longitude and latitude than what he released in the published account of his trip.

58. King Pockpar reportedly ceded his land to Liberia sometime between 28 May and 6 June 1874.

59. King Kryneseh reportedly ceded his land sometime in 1874 between 10 September and 19 October or between 25 and 29 November. This was when Anderson was either walking to or returning from Musadu.

60. "Nymar" is now known as Wymar, or Waima.

61. King Keang reportedly ceded his land to Liberia between 11 and 20 July 1874.

62. King Bamarquella reportedly ceded his land to Liberia sometime between 9 and 11 September 1874 or on 7 December of the same year while Anderson was respectively going to or returning from Musadu.

63. See, for instance, *Sixty-ninth ARACS* (1886, 12); Johnston ([1906] 1969, 254); Karnga (1909, 32; 1926, 44); "Discouraging Features" (1921); Seton (1926, xiv); Anderson (1952, 90); *A Brief History of Montserrado County* (1965, 51); Lynch (1967, 48); Cassell (1970, 261–262); Saha (1985, 222–223).

64. As in the case of Anderson's first wife, Mary Ware, Elizabeth Pointer is not listed as one of the persons who migrated to Liberia after 1842 (Murdza 1975; Brown 1980).

65. According to d'Azevedo, Anderson was the Secretary of the Treasury from 1876 to 1878 (1995, 65). Payne might have appointed Anderson to this position when he became president in January 1876. See also Seys (1870), Sabin (1974, 187), and Dunn and Holsoe (1985, 150).

66. All but one of the segments from 11 September to 25 December exist (Ander-

son 1879a–g). None of the parts that were probably published from 11 July to 29 August and 9 October exist, because those issues of the newspaper are apparently "lost." The *Observer* (Monrovia) published its segments of Anderson's trip in roughly equal lengths. Given the amount of text that the newspaper printed for each of the known parts from September to December, one can closely project that the *Observer* began publishing Anderson's journey five issues earlier on a fortnightly basis, beginning on about 11 July 1879.

67. Philip, Son and Nephew of Liverpool, published Anderson's map in color, sixty-four centimeters by forty-nine centimeters. A color copy of Anderson's map has not been found, but the black-and-white map that Anderson drew in Monrovia was recently located in the British Foreign Office (see Penfold 1982, 155, no. 1411) and is reproduced in fig. 27. A few months after Anderson produced this map, a "regular subscriber" of the *Observer* (Monrovia) wrote that he or she hoped to "soon see a suitable text book published to accompany the map" to help instruct the present and future generation about "the land they occupy" ("Our Common Schools" 1880). We are not aware that Anderson's 1879 map was ever published for wide distribution in any mission magazine, textbook, or similar medium during Anderson's lifetime. In 1883, the Consul General for Liberia in Paris, Leopold Carrance, wrote that "the map drawn up by the Hon. Benj. Anderson found his [France's Minister of Foreign Affairs] approval, and was taken as the basis of the work of these Gentlemen"—cartographers in France's "War Office," who had been commissioned to draw maps of Liberia and surrounding regions (Carrance 1883, 15; see also Gibson 1883, 16; Russell 1888). Indeed, several maps were published that directly used Anderson's map as a template. Regnauld de Lannoy de Bissy of France's war department drew a map of Liberia and part of today's Sierra Leone, Guinea, and Cote d'Ivôire, and published his map in 1883 (1883; *Notices* 1886; see also Klaus 1990, 351, no. 2521). Colonel Wauwermans and Pierre Bourzeix republished Lannoy de Bissy's map in 1885 and 1887, respectively; Wauwermans's map was in color (Wauwermans 1885; Bourzeix 1887; see also Rouire 1894, 494). The Germans included some of the territorial demarcations of Anderson's 1879 map in the early 1890s (Lüddecke [1890]; Büttikofer 1890). Finally, the Liberian government published a close approximation of Anderson's map in 1892 to help support its argument that France was illegally trying to occupy land that Liberia claimed ("Map of Liberia" 1892; see also Johnston [1906] 1969, 255). Also, a sketch map that someone, perhaps Anderson, drew in 1877, relating Musadu to Falaba in Sierra Leone, exists mysteriously in the Royal Geographical Society in London. It is unclear where this map was drawn.

68. Even at the dawn of the new century, G. W. Gibson, Liberia's former Secretary of State who had become President, proclaimed the government's need to build "Railways and Tramways" ("Liberian Minerals and Trading" 1902, 105–106). Gibson's plea would not be realized for another half-century, until Liberia's first railway—from Monrovia to Bomi Hills—was completed in 1951 (Schulze 1973, 190).

69. Box 1, folder 7 of the Frederick Starr Liberia Research Collection at the University of Chicago.

70. See also the *Sixty-ninth ARACS* (1886, 12); Akpan (1973, 224); Holsoe (1976–77, 6); Murdza (1979, 53, 57, 116–167); and Saha (1985, 222–223).

71. The legislature incorporated the Liberian Interior Association on 11 January

1883 ("The Liberia Interior Association" 1881; "The Liberia Interior Association, Limited" 1881; *ATL* [1882–83], 18; see also Sawyer 1992, 196–197).

72. "Stilts" is a reference to the older-style Americo-Liberian houses that rest on cement bricks, cement slabs, and logs (see Belcher, Holsoe, Herman, and Kingston 1988).

73. Benjamin John Knight Anderson Jr. later became the "Surveyor for Montserrado County" like his father (Stevens 1910, 8). He was a musician and a member of the militia and was a lay delegate to the Methodist Annual Meetings ("Notes on the Proceedings of the Liberia Annual Conference, 1920", 5; "Liberia Annual Conference" 1921, 3). Benjamin Jr. was involved in the newspaper business for three decades; he was an agent of the *Living Chronicle* ("Living Chronicle" 1902), the Business Manager of the *Liberia Recorder* ("The Liberia Recorder and Its New Editor" 1902; 1906, 5), the Associate Editor and Agent General of the *African League* ("African League" 1910; 1918), and the Assistant National Secretary of the *Liberian Citizen's League* ("Official Organ" 1932; Caranda 1932, 7). He also entered opposition politics, becoming Monrovia's local Chairman of the National True (or Union) Whig Party of Liberia (Anderson 1911) near the time of his father's death. Several years later, he was a leader in the People's Party ("That Celebrated Election Case" 1927, 8; *Manifesto Adopted at the Headquarters of the People's Party* 1933). Benjamin John Knight Anderson's son, another Benjamin J. K. Anderson, was born in 1906 and attended the College of West Africa in the mid-1920s. In 1928, the government sent him to the Colorado School of Mines in Golden, Colorado. Anderson attended Mines from September 1929 to February 1930, and then transferred to Evening Vocational School (Emily Griffith Opportunity Occupational School?) ("Government Scholarships" 1928; Colorado School of Mine's Registrar's Office, personal communication, 27–28 September 1995; Ruth Vander Maas, personal communication, September 1995). One of Benjamin Anderson Sr.'s "granddaughters or daughters" married Professor Ward, who taught at the University of Liberia ("Following the Trail of Benjamin Anderson" 1973, 1974).

74. On 2 September 1879, Secretary Gibson informed Leopold Carrance that the Liberian government had "created" the Order of African Redemption "at the recent session of our National Legislature," and that the legislature had conferred that order upon Carrance. The legislature could thus have presented the order to Anderson as early as 1879 (Gibson 1879).

75. See Murdza (1979, 339–351; 490–491) and Gershoni (1992a, 29–32; 1992b, 196–197, 202) for the text, maps, and discussions of the 1892 Franco-Liberia treaty.

76. The British Royal Geographical Society also recorded the transfer of Anderson's book ("Accessions to the Library" 1870, xciii, chap. 2, 57). The Smithsonian Institution showed its approval of Anderson's first journey by publishing his 1868–69 account at H. M. S. Schieffelin's behest. The Secretary of the Smithsonian Institution, Joseph Henry, wrote the introduction to this first book (see chap. 5, 157). Reade refers to Anderson's 1874 map, published in Liverpool in 1879.

77. Anderson references the 1868 letter from King Vomfeedolla (Vafin Dole), which was not a treaty and did not make any agreements (chap. 5, "Appendix"). The *Liberia Recorder* published the 1868 letter six months later on 26 March 1904 (vol. 6, no. 8).

78. The most likely explanation of what Anderson meant regarding his nickname derives from Delafosse's letter, where he stated that the people of Musadu called Anderson "*Musadu Eibabu Fima,*" or *Musadu Tubabu Fina,* which means "the black white man of Musadu" (Delafosse 1903, 805). Perhaps Anderson means here Daniel Coleman, George Wadsworth, or Peter Capehart, the "Americans" or "civilized" men who accompanied him on his second trip. The *Observer* (Monrovia) published Anderson's 1874 journey in 1879 (Anderson a–g).

79. Indeed, four years later, the French acquired much more land from Liberia in the Franco-Liberian Agreement of 1907 (Hertslet 1909, 1140–1142; Murdza 1979, 492–493; Gershoni 1992a, 32–40; 1992b, 200, 202).

80. The French geographer E. Réclus (1887) draws on Anderson's journey of 1860 [*sic*] and refers to his work simply as "Musardu." He also refers to "Letter from the King of Musadu to the President of Liberia, 1868." His map outlines the path of Anderson's two journeys and appears to be derived from Büttikofer (1884), not Anderson.

81. The editor of the *West African Mail* who published Delafosse's article, W. A. Morel, noted that Delafosse's support for Anderson "rendered a service to the cause of truth" by showing that the issue was not merely one of partisan politics ("Anderson and His Detractors" 1903, 6).

82. Heard [1898] 1969, 100–179. Delafosse was stationed in Monrovia at the time that Heard published Anderson's book, which explains how he knows that Anderson never gave Heard permission. Blyden also claimed that he (Blyden) was "well known" in Musadu (Blyden to Coppinger, 2 October 1885, in Lynch 1978, 347).

83. Delafosse evidently did not see Seymour's 1858 journal, but Seymour's trip with Ash remained significant enough in the minds of the Liberians to be mentioned alongside Anderson as one of Liberia's important explorers.

84. "Mechanic Street" is present-day Carey Street.

85. The "Condo" and the "Pessey" are the Southern Kpelle.

86. The "Domar-Boozie," that is, Buzye, Loma, or Toma.

87. The "Wymar Boozie," that is, Waima, Loma, or Toma.

88. The bridge is actually made of lianas.

89. Anderson is incorrect in this, as the Dion River at Musadu flows north. The Diani's (Saint Paul) source is near Oussadou, now ruined.

90. The "Farmington" is now called the Junk River near Marshall, which is also where the Duqueah River joins.

91. During or after the 1868–69 expedition, someone sketched drawings of Ballatah and Mahommadu (figs. 20 and 21). By 1903, photography was widespread.

92. This is true for Monrovia and Bereby, but Musadu is only 5 miles (8 kilometers) away from Beyla. By the time d'Ollone reached Beyla, much of Musadu lay in ruins, and many of the inhabitants would have scattered. When Captain Prost reached Konya in April 1893, he found that Diakolidu and Beyla had been burned, and that Musadu was in ruins (Person 1975, 1419). Colonel Combes made the same observation when he traveled through Konya three years later (Combes 1896, 42). The Dole started to rebuild Musadu in 1896 (Person 1975, 1522 n. 144).

93. See the youthful-looking picture of d'Ollone, standing with Hostains, on the

page facing the title page of d'Ollone's book *De la Côte d'Ivoire au Soudan et à la Guinée*. This was published in Paris in 1901 and is evidently the photograph to which Anderson was referring. This is the same photograph that appears in fig. 6.

94. Translation: "It would appear one would need to submit this original map to some modifications to make it less inaccurate."

95. "The Letter from the King of Musadu to the President of Liberia brought by Hon. B. J. K. Anderson" (1904, 5). The *Liberia Recorder* published the 1868 letter in its previous 26 March 1904 issue (vol. 6, no. 8).

96. Salifu 1965.

97. Apparently, "our grandfather" refers to Benjamin Anderson.

98. Anderson's men took tents on their journeys. Anderson specifically said that he was housed in "the king's courtyard" upon his arrival in Musadu during his first journey. He was not as specific about his accommodations during his second trip. What Yaya and others said cannot be completely discounted, but it seems most likely that Anderson probably stayed in town given his status as a celebrated guest. Perhaps some of Anderson's porters slept in some of the tents that they transported from Monrovia, and Anderson may have spent some time there. The fact that Yaya specifically mentioned the tent minimally suggests that Anderson's tents left some impression on the residents of Musadu, whatever the reason.

99. Is this a faint memory of Anderson or some of the French administrators writing in their journals?

100. It is difficult to tell whether Mammadi interpreted for the French or "the American."

3. James L. Sims, 1858

1. This section is from *MCJ*, n.s., 10, no. 4 (September 1859): 65–69, itself from the *Star of Liberia* (June 1859). See also edited text in *NYCJ* 9, no. 12 (December 1859). "Suloany" in the title should be "Suloang." Jehudi Ashmun, the first agent of the American Colonization Society (ACS), founded Caldwell in 1825. Ashmun named the settlement after the first secretary of the ACS, Elijah Caldwell (Shick 1980, 73–74).

2. "Mind" is Liberian Pidgin English for "pay attention" or "seriously consider." Sims either smoked a pipe, or Gotorah said this to remind Sims not to take people like Governor Tom too seriously.

3. This was probably a landlord-stranger relationship (see Fyfe 1962, 8; Launay 1979).

4. The numbers in brackets throughout represent original page numbers.

5. Seymour, by contrast, wrote that the Saint Paul could be navigated much farther into the interior. Earlier settlers hoped that the Saint Paul might provide river passage for trade into the interior. However, it was clear that the falls at Millsburg would hinder this (see chap. 2).

6. That is, Gola, the Deng area, now a chiefdom.

7. Americo-Liberians and other writers of the nineteenth and early twentieth century commonly made references about the physical features, intelligence, and industriousness of each group (see, e.g., Johnston [1906] 1969).

8. "Passah," or "Kpesseh," the Kpelle who live in the Bokomu area that borders the Barline Kpelle (Gbalein-Faala) to the southwest.

9. "Sarvy" is from Portuguese *sabe* or *saber* and means "to know" (Wilson 1947, 60).

10. Non-Muslim chiefs and clerics often found it mutually advantageous to work together. The latter usually assimilated into society quickly, filling many of the roles of "traditional priests" (Levtzion 2000, 68). Note below how this old cleric, Ibrihims (Abraham), was stationed under a shed writing amulets near the chief's residence. The chief, though probably not a Muslim, retained a Muslim cleric and wore Manding clothes. "*Allah Akbah*" means "God is most great" in Arabic.

11. White was a sign of purity and no ill will.

12. "Drukora" means "under" or "near the Du [River]" in Vai and Manding. Monrovia is located along the Du River. The lower part of the Du is today called the Mesurado River.

13. "Cassadas" are equivalent to the modern cassava (manioc).

14. The Vai writer Thomas Besolow remarked that this was a common phrase (Besolow 1891, 88).

15. The "Mandingo cloth" refers to a long garment, or "boubou," made from stripes of woven local cotton.

16. That is, "It is me, Dwarrow," today spelled Dwalu.

17. This section of the text is from *MCJ*, n.s., 10, no. 13 (June 1860): 207–215, itself taken from the *LH*. See edited versions in the *NYCJ* 9, no. 12 (December 1859), and *Philadelphia Colonization Herald*, n.s., no. 123 (September 1860).

18. They traveled from the Southern Kpelle to the Bokomu Kpelle area when they crossed the Saint Paul River.

19. A Spaniard from Cuba settled in the Gallinas (today's southern Sierra Leone) as a slave trader up until circa 1834 (Jones 1983a, 5–6).

20. One of the ironies of these comments is that the people in the central region of Liberia, the last group to hold out from Liberian central government control and actively fight, were the Kpelle of the Jorkwelle area, around the town of Gbanga (Akpan 1973, 233; Stakeman 1986, 112).

21. This statement echoes one argument made in justification of the colonization of Liberia by Americo-Liberians at the time: that colonization stopped slave trading in the interior and provided the conditions for peaceful trade. The conditions under which the Kpelle trade with the coast are explored in chap.7, which notes in particular the influence of the Condo confederacy, as well as the Liberians, on this. Seymour noted that many Kpelle were unable to trade directly to the coast (Seymour's letter, 2 July 1857).

22. This single line is from *NYCJ* 9, no. 12 (December 1859).

23. Major farming tasks were and remain accompanied by assorted music. The drums here were probably orchestrating the men's tree felling, as women's labor groups are more commonly accompanied by gourd rattles.

24. "Quee-ar-pie!" is Kpelle for "American or white man (*quee* or *kwii*) come (*pie or pa*)" (Thach, with Dwyer 1981, 109, 139).

25. This exemplifies the very common use of indirection in presenting a gift.

26. This segment to the end of the next paragraph is taken from *NYCJ* 9, no. 12 (December 1859). The *MCJ* did not publish Sims's description of the execution.

27. This is probably a euphemism for rape.

28. This section is from *MCJ,* n.s., 10, no. 13 (June 1860): 210–215. Portions are also in the *NYCJ* 9, no. 12 (December 1859).

29. "Nu-sjewa" is Kpelle for "man/person (*nuu*) meat (*sjewa/sua*)" (Thach, with Dwyer 1981, 118, 125).

30. These two lines are from *NYCJ* 9, no. 12 (December 1859).

31. This section is from *MCJ,* n.s., 10, no. 5 (October 1859): 84–87, which picks up from the same segment that omitted the two previous lines. Edited versions are also in the *NYCJ* 9, no. 12 (December 1859); *MCJ,* n.s., 10, no. 13 (June 1860): 210–213; and *Philadelphia Colonization Herald,* n.s., no. 123 (September 1860).

32. Known today as part of the Kpo mountain range.

33. That is, "djinn" ("genie," "*jina*") or "spirit." Such spirits are important in local religion throughout the region. Many are associated, as in this case, with the regulation and maintenance of proper water flow. Mediation with them can be the claimed prerogative of certain chiefs and families and an important source of power (Gibbal 1984; Brett-Smith 1994).

34. "Du-gla-ta" is a reference to the name of the large ruined town, described as above.

35. "Bamaquorli" is also spelled "Gbakole," "Bamakweli," "Barpaley" (Seymour), and possibly "Yahtandah" (Anderson, 1874). "Pallaka" is also spelled "Kpaiyakwele" and "Kpayakole" on modern maps. This is Seymour's "Pallaker" or "Pallakar," W. S. Anderson's "Polaka" (1868), and Benjamin Anderson's "Pallikah" or "Pallakah" (1874).

36. The phrase "vast multitude" is probably from Matthew 13:2, when it speaks of "great multitudes" (King James Version).

37. Blyden published part of this paragraph and cited the *MCJ* as his source (1872a, 291).

38. Benjamin Anderson's "Western Mandingoes," where Musadu is located.

39. The Tartars are Turkic speakers who are the historically dominant people of Crimea, north of the Black Sea. Europeans used ethnic names such as "Tatar," "Turk," and "Moor" to refer to the Muslims and Ottomans who lost most of their holdings in North Africa during the early 1880s; they viewed Tatars suspiciously as wanderers, thieves, beggars, savages, horsemen, and dishonest Muslims (*Century Dictionary and Cyclopedia,* s.v. "Turks," 1891; Bowen [1857] 1968, 224; Lewis 1982, 22; *Oxford English Dictionary,* s.v. "Tartars," 2d ed., 1989; Abun-Nasr 1987, 289). In describing the Tatars as "restless," Sims could have been referring to Muslims, the Tatars fleeing their homeland during the 1850s, or both. The Crimean War contributed to the decline of Liberian coastal trade during the mid-1850s (Syfert 1977a, 191; Fisher 1978). This may have affected Sims's grocery business and caused him to travel into the interior to examine new sources of income. Some Liberians transferred negative images about the Tatars to the Manding. This reflected the ambivalent attitude that Americo-Liberians began to develop of the Manding during the second half of the nineteenth century (d'Azevedo 1994, 197–202). The quotation is from Shakespeare's *Henry IV,* act 1, scene 1 (1854, 509).

40. This was Thomas Jefferson Bowen, the Southern Baptist missionary who stayed in Liberia for the first five months of 1850. He traveled to the town of Sama near "Bopolu" while he was in Liberia, and then went to Nigeria to work as a missionary among the Yoruba and ([1857] 1968).

41. Blyden published the next several lines, which end with "necessities for the market" (1872b, 291). Twelve years later, W. S. Anderson wrote that he did not find any Muslims when he went to "Palaka" ("Eastward Empire Points the Way!" 1873, 332). By contrast, in 1870, W. S. Anderson indicated that the people had done some rebuilding over the years. He wrote that the walls were in good condition, that they were six feet thick and eighteen feet high, and that they had gates and watchtowers ("Eastward Empire Points the Way!" 1873).

42. This section is from *MCJ*, n.s., 10, no. 13 (June 1860): 213–215. An edited version is in the *Philadelphia Colonization Herald*, n.s., no. 123 (September 1860).

43. From Reginald Heber's hymn "From Greenland's Icy Mountains," first published in 1827 (Moffatt and Patrick 1928, 124).

44. Lime is calcium oxide, which is used to make cement and to help neutralize acid in the soil. Lime is thus useful for builders and farmers (Church 1980, 143; Steve Cumings, personal communication, 1995). According the geographer Willi Schulze, there is no limestone in Liberia (Schulze 1973, 14). Perhaps there is some in Guinea.

45. "Wau-i-wu-ta" is Seymour's "Wiruentar."

46. "Jangay" is also spelled "Kpowasangye" or "Kposangie." It is Seymour's "Zanga" and Benjamin Anderson's "Payasangah" (1874).

47. "Saturday" is "*Sivili*" in Loma (Dwyer 1981, 196). "Monday" is "*Taana*" in Loma (Dwyer 1981, 183).

48. This section is from *MCJ*, n.s., 10, no. 14 (July 1860): 217–221, copied from the *LH* (April 1860).

49. In many parts of the region—including Loma and Kissi country to the north—the "devil" who builds bridges is the spirit associated with the men's power association or "secret society" (*silo* means "male," and *sale* means "medicine") but can refer to the society itself (Welmers 1949). See Gittins (1987) on this in relation to the Mende. It would not be only women, but any non-initiate in society, such as stranger-traders, who would be excluded.

50. This "American Traveller" was Thomas Bowen. Sims took this quote about the Egugun masked dancer from Bowen's book, which was published just one year earlier (Bowen [1857] 1968, 138).

51. These appear very like the "Ma" masks found among the Mã (Mano) and Dan peoples (Harley 1941).

52. Boombo was the ruler of a town called Bomboja, on the north side of the Lofa River in the Gawula section of the Vai country. He was Bandi by birth and came to the coast as a warrior. This is the same "Bombo" discussed in the *LH* article on the Mama (chap. 7) and is the chief whom Edward Blyden fought in 1853 (Lynch 1967, 15).

53. Memmoru, or Momolu Sao, was a son of Sao Boso, or "King Boatswain."

54. Perhaps from Shakespeare's play *Richard III,* act 1, scene 1, line 12, where the Duke of Gloucester says, "He capers nimbly in a lady's chamber to the lascivious pleasing of a lute."

55. This might be a cryptic reference to the Crimean War, 1854–56. Thanks to Christopher Fyfe for this observation.

56. That is, Guerze country, in today's Prefecture of Yomou, Republic of Guinea.

57. The Manding sometimes call elephants (*sama*) "*soba,*" or "big (*ba*) meat (*so*)" (Cutler, with Dwyer 1981, 118, 130).

58. For examples of how people hunted elephants elsewhere in Africa, see Arnoldi and Ezra (1992).

59. "Ngarella" is probably Seymour's "Zear."

60. This section is from *NYCJ* 10, no. 8 (August 1860), whole no. 116.

61. "*Sali pellimu*" is, literally, "medicine house" (Thach, with Dwyer 1981, 149, 154).

62. Montserrado is the county in which Monrovia is located.

63. The "Upas" is an oblique reference to a "witch" trial-by-endurance (see Strong 1930, 1:102–104).

64. As the deal was not witnessed, Kata could deny that it took place.

65. Nineteenth-century Liberians called heavy wind gusts "tornados." This derives from the Portuguese word *trovoadas* or "thunderstorms" (McDowell 1838, 264; Lugenbell 1850, 14; Brooks 1993, 15–16).

66. The text here seems to be broken, with the part dealing with the journal from Pallaka to Bananella missing. The modern name and location of Bananella is not known.

67. "Suloang" is Seymour's "Solong" and W. S. and Benjamin Anderson's "Zolu."

68. Seymour measured this wall at 12'6" high. This wall was not standing by the late-1960s, although the "older men" could "still indicate its location" (Carter 1970, 28–29, 43–44).

69. That is, George L. Seymour, Levin Ash, and William Taylor. Taylor was sick and stayed with Sims after Seymour and Ash headed farther into the interior (see chap. 4).

70. "Big Sissa" refers to his elder sister.

71. "Black but comely" is from the Song of Solomon 1:5(King James Version).

72. Sims took this quote from Bowen's book ([1857] 1968, 41–42).

73. *Arabian Nights* had been recently translated into English by Richard Burton, the explorer.

74. "Memmoru Sowe" was Momolu Sao, the son of Sao Boso and a Gola mother.

75. "Sowe Boatswain" is also identified as Sao Boso.

76. These "respectable citizens" are the members of the McGill family.

77. The edited version from this section to the end of the account is in *Philadelphia Colonization Herald* (November 1860).

78. According to Yves Person, Sugba Dole was the chief of Musadu at this time. Sugba's son was Vafin, or Anderson's Vomfeedolla (Person 1968, 1:184). The Manding of Musadu claim that Vafin Dole's father's name was Kosi (Geysbeek, field notes). Sims's Vai, or Vey-Mami, then, may be a corruption of *N'va* or "my father" (a term of respect, or to be taken literally) and his mother's name, Mami. If this is the case, the chief's full name was probably N'va Mami Kosi Dole.

4. George L. Seymour, 1858

1. This section is from *NYCJ* 9, no. 9 (September 1859), whole no. 105.

2. Earlier in April, Seymour helped settle a dispute that had led to a "war" between "king" Borwandow and a neighboring "head-man." Seymour returned to Paynesville or "Old Field" by 19 April (a Monday) and began his journey ten days later (Seymour 1858e).

3. This is a letter from Presbyterian *Home and Foreign Record,* which published an extensive summary of Seymour and Ash's trip in 1860. They based their article on Seymour's account "published in one of the Liberia papers"—the *LH.* Seymour sent the *Home and Foreign Record* a copy of the *LH* series and "incorporated in his journal a letter [that the *LH* did not publish] dictated by one of the chiefs he visited." This chief was Jourparpar, and the following is the letter from Jourparpar that the *Home and Foreign Record* published ("Seymour's Travels in Western Africa" 1860, 304).

4. The old town was on a hill, but the current town is in the valley.

5. "Liberia's Lone Star" refers to the Liberian flag, with one star and eleven stripes, modeled after the United States flag in 1847 (Henries 1954, 198).

6. Schulze (1970–71) saw and described these.

7. "Partargea" was later written "Portayea," Anderson's (1874) "Pye." Seymour first noticed that people covered clay pots here. He attributed this to Manding influence (see 30 July entry). Towns were on hills for defensive purposes, even if it made obtaining water difficult.

8. "They should have named it Mount Benson" is an editorial comment, not something that Seymour wrote. Seymour (and Ash) frequently named various locations to honor Liberians, disregarding what the local people called these places—reproducing the colonial mentality of the era.

9. "Barpaley" is also spelled "Gbakole," "Bamakweli," Sims's "Bamaquorli," and Benjamin Anderson's (1874) "Yahtandah." "Pallaker" is also spelled "Kpayekwele," "Kpaiyakwele," "Kpayakole," Sims's "Pallaka," W. S. Anderson's "Polaka," and Benjamin Anderson's "Pallikah" or "Pallakah." Sims called King Barsedon "Basse Darn."

10. In a summary of Seymour's journey from the *Home and Foreign Record* abstracted from the *LH,* there is more information given on suspension bridges: "Our travellers give an interesting account of several swinging bridges which they saw on the way. They were constructed by interweaving large forest vines or creepers, and attaching them to abutments on the opposite sides of the river. They were further sustained by single vines, fastened to the trucks of trees along the margin of the river, or to horizontal branches overhead. One of these bridges was found to be more than forty feet long, and could support as many men as could stand on it at one time. Mr. Seymour starts the question, whether the Americans did not borrow the idea of swinging bridges from Africa" ("Seymour's Travels in Western Africa" 1860, 203).

11. "Zear" is Sims's "Ngarella" ("waterside"). "Zear" may derive from the name's rendition in Manding, as "*nji-ya*" (*ji-ya*) ("water place") (Cutler, with Dwyer 1981, 134, 147).

12. The "young Liberian" is James Sims, who stayed with "King Bassee Darn" in "Palaka" for nearly one month in February (chap. 3).

13. Pallarkar is the same town that he visited on 22 May.

14. Vomba is the headman of the Manding part of town.

15. "On a field white [ripe] for the harvest" is a quote from John 4:35 (King James Version).

16. This contradicts James Sims's observations.

17. This segment is from *NYCJ* 9, no. 11 (November 1859).

18. "Zanga" is also spelled "Kpasangie," Sims's Jangay, and Benjamin Anderson's (1874) Payasangah.

19. Varsheardupar is also called Vase Dupa.

20. The "young man" refers to James Hines. "Mr. Hines" is probably John O. Hines, an "industrious mechanic and thriving farmer" who later gained a reputation for manufacturing cotton cloth (*LH* February 1863; "Liberian Cloth" 1867, 344; "Items from 'The African Republic: New Manufacture' " 1868, 45).

21. The Wamo people are also called the Waima.

22. This section is from *NYCJ* 9, no. 12 (December 1859).

23. "Wiruentar" is Sims's Wau-i-wu-ta. That is, the King of Sulong (modern name, Zolowo).

24. "Salad and greens" presumably refers to an assortment of local leaves, for cooking with palm oil, to make a sauce for rice.

25. "Sims Fork" is probably modern Kavo Creek.

26. That is, from the Kpelle-speaking Barlain country into the Loma-speaking "Busi" country.

27. "Solong" is Sims's "Suloang" and Benjamin Anderson's (1868, 1874) "Zolu."

28. "King Barmo" is Sims's "King Bahmo."

29. This remark is ironic given that women are the main cultivators in Loma rice farming, within the gendered division of labor in Loma country, although it is men who cut the forest (Kellemu 1971; Currens 1976).

30. A mill seat is a break or falls in the river that is an ideal place to construct a mill.

31. Seymour and Ash might have named Mount Joseph after the "founder" of Liberia, Joseph Jenkins Roberts. Roberts had just finished serving his second term in office in 1856, with Seymour as a member of the House of Representatives.

32. This section is from the *NYCJ* 10, no. 1 (January 1860), whole no. 109.

33. Cattle are a sign of wealth, and there are consequences for those without—see, for example, James Gibbs's film *Cows of Dolo Ken Paye*.

34. This is the gold which Benjamin Anderson associated with the Manding heartland.

35. "Carmer's town" is also known as "Kama Kekula's town," modern Kuankan. "Misardo" is modern Musadu or Moussadougou.

36. Sometime during this part of the trip, Seymour wrote to President Benson and told him that he (and Ash) were within a "three days travel of the capital of the Mandingo country" ("Explorations in Africa" 1859; *Forty-second ARACS* 1859, 26).

37. "Bamboo" is Liberian English for the Raffia palm (*Raphia vinifera*).

38. White Plains was a Methodist mission. We have not been able to positively identify this particular Hooper.

39. That is, Jaka Kaman Kamara, Kaman Kekula's father.

40. "Weamo" is also spelled "Waima Toma" or "Loma."

41. For a picture of a pole bridge, see Strong (1930, 145).

42. This section is from *NYCJ* 10, no. 3 (March 1860), whole no. 111.

43. "Parmer" is also spelled "Pama," "Baignema," and is Benjamin Anderson's "Pynyah." "Patebo" is not clearly readable in the original.

44. That is, the beginnings of the savanna.

45. Some words are not clear in the original. Those we supply would fit the empty spaces and seem to be correct.

46. Seymour also writes "Boa"; Anderson, "Boe."

47. For an example of artificial braids made of plastic hair, see Arnoldi (1995, 62–67).

48. About twenty-two letters of this sentence are illegible.

49. Mount Jane was perhaps named after J. J. Robert's wife, Jane Waring (Henries 1954, 217; Shick 1980, 47).

50. About twenty-one letters of this sentence are illegible.

51. The villages mentioned here are Boo to the east and Kotia—now abandoned—to the west.

52. Seymour is misinformed on this point. The stream is probably the Vere, a tributary of the Saint Paul, no parts of which are near Musadu. However, this crossing is near the main path to Musadu.

53. The next known westerner who reportedly traveled from Monrovia to Kuankan was Methodist missionary "Mr. Jackson." According to Alexander Camphor, the principal of the College of West Africa, Jackson went to Quanger in 1907. Jackson marveled at the townpeople's "twelve feet high, and four feet thick" mud wall and "their thrifty class of people" (1909, 35–38). It does not seem conceivable, however, that "Mr. Jackson" traveled to Kuankan in the early 1900s: the French had occupied the area by this time, and Kuankan had been ransacked a few times in the previous two decades in wars that involved Samori and the Loma who helped the French subjugate the Manding (the Liberian representative William Lomax supported the Loma in this effort). These wars severely disrupted the region's economy and population (Massing 1978–79; Murdza 1979, chaps. 7–8; Fairhead and Leach 1994). In addition, Camphor's description of "Mr. Jackson's" trip compares closely with some of the details that Seymour wrote when he went to Kuankan. "King Carmers" was Jaka Kaman Kamara; his son "Kagular" (next paragraph) was Kaman Kekula Kamara. Benjamin Anderson called "King Carmer" "Jakkah Commah."

54. This could be the Dyomandu (Jomandu) war that Samori had with the Berete (Bility) (Person 1968, 1:256). Dyomandu is a village just 3 miles (5 kilometers) north of Oussadou. Joladu could also be Diarradou (Jaladu or Dyaradu), located about 12 miles (20 kilometers) northwest of Kuankan (Person 1968, 1:257), or even Dumadu, noted in the same war (Person 1968, 1:268 n. 99). Kuankan would be implicated in each of these cases.

55. Kuankan is actually about 190 miles (306 kilometers) away from Monrovia

and 160 miles (257 kilometers) from Grand Bassa (near Edina). Seymour estimated that he walked about 15 miles (24 kilometers) per day ("Seymour's Travels in Western Africa" 1860, 302).

56. This is probably Dyagbo or Jabo, the chief of Sondu near Tibe Mountain (Person 1968, 1:429). Jabo might have been a Kamara, as the Kamara had, much earlier, established themselves as the chiefs of Sondu (Geysbeek and Camara 1994, 75).

57. "Lewis's mountains" may perhaps be named after one of the sponsors of their trip—John N. Lewis ("Amounts Subscribed by Citizens of the City of Monrovia" 1858, 131). Lewis was an ex-Virginian who was part of the constitutional convention, was a four-time Secretary of State, and was spared execution with W. S. Anderson and others after helping to arrange the disastrous 1871 loan with Britain (Burrowes 1989, 73–74).

58. "Stir" is only partially legible and could be incorrect.

59. "Wen" is a name for a sebaceous cyst (Smith 1995).

60. This section is from *LH* 12, no. 22 (January 1860). This is the "original" text (fig. 11). An edited version may be found in the *NYCJ* 10, no. 4 (April 1860).

61. "Payn's view" was named after Paynesville, Seymour's point of origin.

62. "Johnson's Peak" is presumably today's Boron Sal. Seymour was following the nineteenth-century belief, which Mungo Park introduced, that a vast mountain range named the Kong was located in the distant interior of West Africa (Park [1799 and 1805] 1983). Explorers, merchants, and cartographers said that the Kong Mountains were gold laden, snow covered, and a "barrier to the interior." In many striking maps of the time, the Kong was shown to extend in an east-westerly direction and to divide the southern rivers from northern flowing ones. In the late 1890s, the French proved that the Kong Mountains did not exist (Bassett and Porter 1991). Seymour's portrayal of the Kong Mountains indicated what was believed to be the potential opportunity and profit that lay beyond the Kong. James Sims may have been thinking of the Kong Mountains when he wrote about "the 'cloud capped' mountains of Pessah. . . . As far as the eye could reach, east and west, was a chain of mountains" (102). For a discussion of the "Kong Mountains" on H-Africa, see *http://www2.h-net.msu.edu/~africa/threads/index.html#Maps* (accessed 13 February 2003). *Kong* translates as "mountains" in Manding. *Condo* or *Kondo* more than likely is *Kbng-ndb,* "in the mountains." The mountain town mentioned is probably Sokebaladougou (8°39'N, 9°9'W), or possibly Bonkoguadu (8°33'N, 9°11'W).

63. One rod equals 16.5 feet or 5.03 meters (Davies and Peck 1867, 505).

64. This section is from *NYCJ* 10, no. 4 (April 1860).

65. *"Firney"* is "fonio," or "accha" (*Digitaria exilis*), a cereal grain that is smaller than rice (Murdock 1959, 68).

66. Wosodo is also called Oussadu (e.g., in Bouet 1912), 8°45'N, 9°8'W, and is now ruined. This shows the persistent tensions that existed between supposedly allied villages, and hence the tendency for such alliances to shift over time. The tensions between Jaka Kaman's Kamara family and the southern Boozie developed into warfare in the 1890s (Fairhead and Leach 1994, 495–498).

67. Some of Samori's followers might have attacked Seymour and Ash (see chap. 4, 152).

68. Perhaps Seymour carried his journal in his "tin bookcase."

69. Ash was gone until 22 September.

70. This again attests to the importance of commercial links that extended between this area and Freetown.

71. Seymour and Ash remained in Quanger until about the end of October.

72. That is, Seymour and Ash were in Solong until about Monday, 22 November.

73. Perhaps Seymour and Ash disappointed some of their contributors and well-wishers by not reaching Musadu and not making agreements to direct more trade to the coast.

74. "Your Excellency" is a reference to the President of Liberia at the time, Stephen A. Benson.

5. Benjamin J. K. Anderson, 1868–69

1. Anderson served under President Warner for the last three weeks of January 1864, until Warner replaced Anderson with Chavers on 28 January (see chap. 2).

2. This section is from the original publication of Anderson's book (Anderson 1870g). The *AR* published a serial account of Anderson's 1868–69 journey; their first section begins here (Anderson 1870a, 132–145). Portions of the original that the *AR* omitted are noted in the endnotes.

3. This seems to be the first time that the term "Manding" is used to identify the Manding in Liberian literature (d'Azevedo 1994, 238 n. 48). Sims used "Manni" to refer to the place and the people. Anderson called the people "Mandingo" and the place "Manding." We thank Joseph Lauer for this last observation.

4. Anderson correctly calculated Monrovia's coordinates to be 6°18'30"N, 10°48'30" W. Europeans knew Monrovia's longitude by the mid-seventeenth century (Roggeveen and Robijn [1687] 1971) and had close estimates of Monrovia's latitude one century later (Norwich 1983, 413–414). Monrovia's exact position was known by the early to mid-nineteenth century (Ashmun 1830; Sherman 1830, 112; "Colony of Liberia" [map] 1833; Coyle [1845] 1947). Similarly, in 1879, Ibrahima Sissi's envoy to Monrovia told President Gardner that his caravans could travel from Medina to Monrovia in twenty-four days if the roads were open (see chap. 2). Medina (9°31'N, 8°12'W) was actually 55 miles (87 kilometers) northeast of Musadu.

5. Although Anderson devoted more than one-third of his book to recounting the events that transpired before he left Bopolu, he was cueing his readers that the most important part of his book dealt with his journey after he left Bopolu (d'Azevedo 1995, 73).

6. "Zolu" is Sims's "Suloang" and Seymour's "Solong."

7. Ziggah Porrah Zue's (Koiama Tongoro's) actual coordinates are 8°16'N, 9°6'W. Later, Anderson estimated that its longitude was 9°31'W. Anderson was off by 14 miles (23 kilometers) north and 29 miles (47 kilometers) to the west. Diagonally, he was off by about 32 miles (51 kilometers).

8. "Donilnyah" is Dowilnyah, who resided in Gubbewallah (Goboèla).

9. The Vukkah Mountains are also called "Foma" to the Manding. "Vukkah" is the Loma term.

10. This is a reference to the main towns near Musadu that Anderson visited: Beyla, Diakolidu, Nyela, and Nionsamoridu.

11. Blunt, Pike, and Hunter purchased these instruments for five hundred dollars, and Schieffelin shipped them to Liberia ("H. M. Schieffelin, Esq." 1867, 268; Richardson 1959, 94).

12. Anderson began his journey from Monrovia with correct longitudes and latitudes, but his calculations became more then forty minutes off by the time he reached Bopolu. Throughout the trip, Anderson's positions varied 13 miles (21 kilometers) and 43 miles (69 kilometers) from their actual location. Anderson's troubles with his watches, sextants, and instruments, the weather, and his use of Paris rather than Greenwich to estimate his position partly explains his inaccuracies and variations (see chap. 2; Murdza 1979, 407 n. 301). For excellent works on the historical geography and cartography of West Africa, see Bassett and Porter (1991) and Stone (1995).

13. Totoquella's (the modern-day Totokwele's) north latitude is 7°4'N (*Liberia Gazetteer* 1968, 52). Anderson was off by 41°N, or nearly 38 miles (60 kilometers).

14. Charles Davies and William G. Peck published this book less than one year before Anderson began his trip (Davies and Peck 1867). This may have been one of the items that Schieffelin sent to Anderson, along with the various navigational instruments.

15. The highest altitude around Ziggah Porrah Zue is 570 meters (1870') (Guekedou 1960, map, NC-29–14), so Anderson's estimate was very close. Davies and Peck prepared a table that they claimed gave "pretty good approximate results" that estimated the "altitude above sea level" after determining the boiling point of water (1867, 338). They devised another table that provided corresponding numbers to be multiplied against the temperature of the air. Later in this account, Anderson wrote that Ziggah Porrah Zue's elevation was 1650 feet (503 meters).

16. This is Charles Burgess Dunbar, Sr., who was born in about 1831 and died on 2 October 1878. He was a medical doctor, a plantation owner, and a merchant, and a member of the Baptist Church. Dunbar was one of the joint founders of the Independent Restoration Grand Lodge and the Free and Accepted Masons of Liberia in 1851 and 1867, respectively. He became the Grand Master of both lodges. Dunbar was also a member of the three-man executive committee that replaced E. J. Roye as the President of Liberia for one week at the end of 1871. The committee relinquished its position to Vice President James S. Smith when Smith returned to Monrovia from Grand Bassa County ("Liberian Affairs: Trade and Agriculture" 1873, 156; Johnson 1878; Cassell 1970, 251; Shick 1980, 57, 162; Dunn and Holsoe 1985, 76, 249). Anderson walked from his house on Mechanic Street (present-day Carey Street) to Waterside (see chap 2; B. 1878; "The Improvements of Monrovia" 1914, 1).

17. "Vannswah" is the modern Vonsua, near Brewersville.

18. Kaifal, or Kalifa, was an Arabic scholar from Beyla who lived in Vonsua. This is the same "Mandingo priest" from "Vonzwah" whom Blyden knew, though this does not necessarily imply that Blyden recommended Kaifal to Anderson (see Blyden [1871b] 1874, 70–71; d'Azevedo 1995, 86–87 n. 64). We are not certain about the identity of Kaifal's last name. Kanda could be equivalent to the Manding clan (*jamu*) name Kane, it could be a clan name with which we are unfamiliar, or it could be a praise name that is a contraction of a phrase, such as "Kaifal, one of the great *mori*

kandaw." *Mori* means "cleric" in Manding; the *mori kandaw* were one of the five Soninke *mori* clans who came from Wagadu. These clans were the Sissi, the Bility, the Toure, the Silla, and the Sherif or Diane (Conrad 1999b, 37 n. 214; David Conrad, personal communication, 23 February 2000). Not surprisingly, men from each of these clans except for the Silla and the Diane appear as clerics—Mohammed Barta (Bility), Ibrahima Sissi, and Samori Touré. Clans of Soninke heritage who live in today's eastern Guinea and Liberia now speak Manding languages, have largely adopted Manding culture, and are considered by many to be Manding. Yet they retain their Soninke names and trace their roots back to the Soninke state of Wagadu or one of the Wagadu successor states that emerged before Sunjata Keita founded the Mali Empire in the early to mid-thirteenth century (Frank 1998, 9). "Billelah" is Beyla, about 5 miles (8 kilometers) southeast of Musadu.

19. Anderson was detained from 15 February to 6 March 1868.

20. "Momoru Son" is Momolu Sao, the son of Bopolu's former ruler Sao Boso (see chap. 7).

21. A "civilized person" was the Liberian settler term for an individual who was a Christian and presumably of American origin.

22. A few weeks later, on 10 April 1868, Blyden wrote this letter to someone in New York:

> Since I last wrote you, Mr. Benjamin Anderson, Ex-Secretary of the Treasury, has set out on his exploring journey. He was a few days ago between Boporah and Musadu, northerly from Monrovia. He is travelling under the care of the Mandingo priest [Kaifal-Kanda] of whom I wrote you. This priest wrote me a few days ago, in Arabic, that he had sent some of his people to assist Anderson in carrying his baggage to a distant town, and when they returned he would himself join Anderson. It will be pleasing to you to learn that such a correspondence has commenced between Liberia and the interior. (1868, 220)

Kaifal may have written to Blyden when he sent Anderson to Bessa's town with eighteen hired Congo carriers and "two of Kaifal's young men" (chap. 5, 163). The only other time Kanda could have written this letter was on 6 April or shortly thereafter when he sent Anderson back to Bessa's town for the second time with "his women and scholars." Kanda's letter shows the potential that the people in Monrovia had for keeping somewhat informed of Anderson's travels and the effectiveness of interior-coastal communication in general. Kaifal wrote in this instance, and Anderson wrote to Monrovia a few weeks later. Blyden's statement from Kaifal that Anderson was between Bopolu and Musadu by 10 April is not consistent with Anderson's record that he did not leave Bopolu for Musadu until 7 May.

23. "Vyrmore" may refer to Veymore, or perhaps Vai Morlu. The area around Vyrmore was considered Dei territory. By 1885, "Veymora" was "a Mandingo trading town in the settlement of Clay-Ashland" near the coast (Petition to H. R. W. Johnson, Clay-Ashland, 15 October 1885, LGA, Ex. Corr. 1885–88; Johnston [1906] 1969, 434, facing map). Moah is a Dei town, possibly named after the river (6°43'N, 10°39'W). "Mannèenah" is the modern Medina, just west of Bopolu. The modern name and location of Bessa's town is unknown. It is probable that it is just to the west of the Bopolu area, somewhere along the Lofa River, sitting astride a trade route

there. This would help explain Bessa's acquaintance with the Vai area and with Manna's behavior in the Gallinas.

24. The chief of Suehn was the Dei Chief Gatumba or Getumbe (chap. 7).

25. Actually, 13 March 1868 was a Friday. One cannot easily walk that far in a day; there appears to be a misjudgment here on the part of Anderson.

26. See Bowen [1857] 1968 for a comment about Bessa's town. "Golah" is also spelled "Gola." For a discussion, see d'Azevedo (1994, 240–41 n. 51).

27. The title of "King" is not an indigenous one but Anderson's.

28. The Moore family was very involved with the local peoples in the region north of the Saint Paul River. Gabriel Moore was one of the leading merchants in Monrovia from the late 1860s to his death on 6 August 1885. He was born in the United States in about 1815 and migrated to Liberia when he was twenty-one years old. He started his first successful business venture in Bopolu, where he reportedly learned Manding, Gola, Kpelle, Dei, Bassa, and Kru ("Monrovia in 1866" 1866, 328; "Inauguration Day at Monrovia" 1872; *Fifty-sixth ARACS* 1873, 18; Haven 1878, 8; "Our Liberia Letter" 1881b, 132; "Death of Gabriel Moore, Esq." 1886, 43). In 1843, Moore accompanied J. J. Roberts on a government exploration up the Saint Paul River to visit Gola chiefs and sign treaties (see chap. 2; Roberts 1845; see also "Interior Roads" 1873, 334). Being multilingual, Moore sometimes worked for the government as a translator to resolve problems that arose in the interior region of Montserrado County ("Death of Gabriel Moore, Esq." 1886, 43; Huberich 1947, 2:1233). Moore had a farm in Caldwell and established the commercial enterprise of Messrs. G. Moore and Son ("A Day on the St. Paul's River" 1865, 138; *Sixty-fifth ARACS*" 1882, 39). In 1867, Moore helped found the Ancient, Free, and Accepted Masons with C. B. Dunbar Sr. and William S. Anderson (Cassell 1970, 251). Shortly before Moore died, the U.S. Minister to Liberia, John Smyth, wrote that Moore was "the oldest and most respected and most successful merchant in the Republic" (Smyth 1880, 23–24).

29. Prince Manna was the ruler of the Gallinas, a mainly Vai-speaking area in what is now Sierra Leone. Prince Manna challenged the Liberian government, which had signed treaties of sale with local rulers in the Gallinas in the late 1840s and early 1850 (Jones 1983a, 81–114; d'Azevedo 1994, 240 n. 51).

30. If the distance from Bessa's town to Boporu took only a day to cover, it was probably about 25 miles away.

31. "Sey" may have been his (Morlu's) mother's first name, and "Morlu" his first name. The Manding add their mother's name to their own to distinguish themselves from their half-brothers and others with like names. "Syyo" is a form of the Soninke clan name Saio, Saiyon, Sayon, Sano, Sanyo, or Saghanughu (see chap. 7). Seymoru Syyo was a leader in Bopolu and a leader in the Manding quarter. Momolu Sao, living at Totokwele, was the overall ruler of the area (see d'Azevedo 1994, 214). When Alfred King traveled to Bopolu fourteen years later, he noted that Seymoru or "Simoro Syyo" was an "elderly gentleman" and a respected elder (King 1882b).

32. This may be a reference to the intermittent fighting between Musadu and the non-Muslims in the east that the Anderson later mentioned in this account.

33. Namely, a Thursday, thus a three-day walk for about 50 miles (80 kilometers). Anderson apparently took the direct route from Bopolu to Vannswah through Gola

territory that he purposely avoided when he began his trip and went to Bessa's town (see d'Azevedo 1994, 223). He would have gone to Bambuta and then back the way he came.

34. The scholars were presumably, Kaifal's Muslim students.

35. The sentence refers to the time Anderson left Vonsua, sometime after 9 April and before 8 May, when he reached Bopolu. He was definitely there on 23 and 24 April, see p. 170.

36. The "king's Boozies" sound very much like mercenaries, just as Bandi men served Momolu Sao in "Boatswain's Country" during the same period (Holsoe 1976–77, 6). The Loma had an area of its own in the Vai country.

37. Presumably, the women are being consulted for their work in preparing food for the Congoes.

38. This was actually Thursday and Friday.

39. "Carry me" can be taken two ways: either Bessa's carriers carried Anderson in a hammock, or they escorted or accompanied Anderson (and, in this case, helped transport his loads), as this phrase suggests in any form of Liberian English.

40. A "Veyman" or a Vai man, that is, a man from the Cape Mount region who spoke Vai or considered himself to be Vai.

41. Anderson wrote a letter to Monrovia before he left Bopolu, sometime between 7 May and 12 June. After reporting about the difficulties that he had encountered, he wrote, "I am completely surprised at the favorable manner that Momora entertains such expeditions. I am determined, by the help of God, to go through with this matter" ("Liberian Exploration" 1868, 286).

42. James Spriggs Payne, the fourth President of Liberia, took office in January 1868.

43. Stephen Allen Benson, the second President of Liberia, served from January 1856 to January 1864. There is no information, to our knowledge, about this treaty.

44. The Boozies were Loma speakers and the Barlines, Kpelle speakers; see the discussion in earlier accounts, concerning this conflict.

45. Momolu Sao was hardly "a barbarian." The McGill family raised him in Monrovia, and Momolu understood something of their ways. It would seem that Anderson was here writing to his American audience, and maybe an uninformed audience in Monrovia. It is impossible that Anderson did not know of Momolu Sao's earlier life among the settlers.

46. This occurred to Ash during his trip with Seymour.

47. "Boondee people" refers to the Bunde, the most western Loma-speaking people in Liberia.

48. As part of the Condo confederation, the Bunde were settled around the town of Saplima.

49. As in the case of the Mali Empire, the Condo confederation's authority center was not so much at a specific place, but where the chief lived and where the ceremonial and ritual affairs of the polity were performed (see Conrad 1994, 365).

50. This date, 10 May, was a Sunday; Anderson had thus spent two full days there. The musical procession befitted an important person, such as the ruler.

51. Kaifal stayed until Monday, 1 June.

52. Chancelor, Anderson's eventual 1868–69 guide, was Gola, like Momolu Sao's

mother, and had spent time with Samuel Ford McGill. When Alfred B. King traveled to Bopolu in 1882, he met Chancelor. King called him "the celebrated *Chancellor Walworth* of *Andersonian notoriety*" and described him as "brown skinned, intelligent, wide awake, active, though old" (1882b; 1882c; see also d'Azevedo 1995, 74).

53. Momolu Sao, like Chancelor, also spent time with one of the McGill families in Monrovia, indicating some effort on the part of the McGills to develop trade contacts with the interior. Samuel McGill was born in Baltimore in January 1815 and died on 26 June 1871. McGill moved to Liberia with his father and brother in 1826. As the McGills set out to become one of the leading commercial families in Liberia, Samuel sailed back to the U.S. to attend medical school at Dartmouth College. He returned to Liberia in 1838 and became Liberia's first doctor of African descent. The American Colonization Society appointed him as colonial doctor, and he trained many other Liberians. McGill served as the Acting Governor of the Maryland colony from 1848 to 1853. He started to direct his family business in Cape Palmas with his brother in 1856 ("The Late Dr. McGill" 1871, 287; Cassell 1970, 112, 156, 184; Wiley 1980, 314) and moved to Monrovia by the mid-1860s to invest in commercial shipping. He and his brothers exported palm oil and sugar from the Saint Paul River and had several warehouses and stores in Monrovia ("Monrovia in 1866" 1866, 328; *Fifty-sixth ARACS* 1873, 44).

54. John Bradberry Jordon was born as a slave in New Orleans in 1817. Jordon's freedom was granted upon his master's death, and he migrated to Liberia aboard the *Oriole* in 1852. Jordon's wife, Otilla Julien, grudgingly journeyed to Liberia with him but sailed back to the United States in 1853. The Liberian legislature granted John a divorce because his wife refused to return to Liberia. On their 1852 voyage, the Jordons journeyed to Liberia with George Seymour's sister, Mary Cisco, and her family. Jordon set up a sugarcane farm on both sides of the Saint Paul River in Virginia and Caldwell, purchased a steam mill in 1857, and became a prosperous sugarcane cultivator. Jordon served as the Secretary of the Treasury in President Benson's administration before he died in 1862 ("Departure of the *Brig Oriole*" 1852, 349; "List of Emigrants," 1852, 350; "An Act Divorcing John B. and Otilla Julien Jordan" 1859, 46–47; "Arrival of the General Pierce" 1865, 229; "A Day on the St. Paul River" 1865, 138; Wiley 1980, 328; Shick 1980, 112; Dunn and Holsoe 1985, 26, 255).

55. The phrase "the singing men" refers to the *jeli* or griot.

56. This is John Sanders Washington. The mention of Washington's and Jordon's presence in the interior indicates the nature of ongoing trade by settlers traveling to the interior for business. See Sims's earlier mention of the Liberians who visited Barlain in 1856 and a 1852 *NYCJ* account, presumably from a trader (Liberius 1852). Washington lived in Vonsua in 1872 (Blyden 1873, 318). On his later trip to Bopolu, Alfred King spoke of a preacher from Virginia named W. S. Washington whose nickname was "Sanner" (Sanders) (King 1882a). King's Washington may be the same as Sanders's Washington, who was the Superintendent of Zodakie Mission, which later became the Baptist Ricks Institute near Vonsua nine years later. According to Blyden, Washington lived among the "aborigines" when he was young and that he knew several languages (Blyden 1889, 27–28). In 1899, the Ricks Institute issued a "circular" which stated that Rev. John S. Washington was the General Superintendent of the school, having given the land ("Progress in Liberia" 1889, 115–117). In 1903,

"Rev. J. S. Washington" spoke and prayed during the weeklong meetings that took place in Monrovia when President Arthur Barclay and other Liberian government officials helped settle some age-old disputes between the Gola, Vai, Manding, Kpelle, and Dei ("Settlement of Interior Difficulties" 1904). This was also the J. S. Washington who was one of Liberia's leading coffee exporters in 1892 (Cassell 1970, 357).

57. This description of the special cap and robe indicates that Kaifal was a "scholar" or "teacher" (*kaamoo*). Throughout much of West Africa, students who memorized the Qur'an and attained advanced schooling in Islamic studies were formally awarded turbans, staffs, and decorative gowns (Wilks 1968, 169; Launay 1992, 150).

58. The annual rains begin by late May and early June.

59. Bopolu's actual coordinates are 7°4'N, 10°29'W (*Liberia Gazetteer* 1976, 22). Anderson's north latitude was off by nearly 38 miles (61 kilometers). Yves Person (1968, 1:308–309 n. 61) started to trace Anderson's 1868 trip from Bopolu, sometimes giving alternative names for towns and providing coordinates from Schwab (1947). Schwab's coordinates are not always correct, so we rely on modern gazetteers and maps when possible. Even the gazetteers and modern maps sometimes vary by one or two degrees. The more recent maps are, presumably, more accurate than the older gazetteers.

60. Modern maps indicate that the elevations of the mountains in and around Bopolu are about half of what Anderson postulated (Behrendt and Wotorson 1974, map of Bopolu).

61. In traveling from Monrovia to Bopolu, Karl Hasselman noted that the "flat plains had changed to soft undulating country and then to the hilly region differentiated into high mountains with plateaus at different levels between hills." Bopolu "is located in a small depression surrounded by hills" ("Following the Trail of Benjamin Anderson" 1973, 1974, 5).

62. The "granite" Anderson refers to here is actually basalt.

63. When Blyden went to Bopolu a few months later, Anderson said that King Boatswain's grave was located where a new building was being built for Boatswain's son Momoru. The grave and house were opposite the market and town square (Blyden 1871c, 241). This rock is about three feet high and is still situated in an open area in the center of Bopolu (see fig. 31).

64. "Junk" refers to the Farmington River, also called the Du River, to the east and southeast of Monrovia (see p. 355, n. 90).

65. The original site of Totokwele is situated on the eastern side of the town where there are graves and an old orange tree ("Following the Trail of Benjamin Anderson" 1973, 1974, 8).

66. The second section of the *AR*'s publication of Anderson's trip starts with this paragraph (Anderson 1870b, 162–174).

67. Anderson focused almost exclusively on the Manding segment of Bopolu's population and incorrectly assumed that Momolu Sao was under the authority of the Manding (d'Azevedo 1994, 214–215, 224).

68. The *AR* excluded the story about this slave rebellion in the next ten paragraphs (Anderson 1870b, 162–174). Blyden also wrote about this slave revolt (1871c, 259–260; see also d'Azevedo 1995, 61).

69. Similarly, three-quarters of the population in Vai areas are estimated to have been slaves during the early nineteenth century (Holsoe 1977, 294).

70. "Musadalla's town" is Musa Dorle's town, or Dolela, south of Bopolu on the main road to the coast. The Dorle or Dole are a Soninke family who were part of the same clan as Musadu's chief Vafin Dole (see Fisher 1971, xi–xii).

71. For a similar story of how a woman near Macenta twenty years later boldly threatened to fight when her husband negotiated with the enemy, see Conrad (1999a, 218–220).

72. Anderson's military background comes out here.

73. The Manding consider dogs to be unclean and rank them lower than most other animals (la Rue 1930, 173; see also Conrad 1990, 45). Momoru, then, cursed the slaves and reminded them of their position in life by calling them "slave dogs."

74. Reports of similar activities at this place occurred in the 1830s (Whitehurst 1836, 307, 309, 313).

75. "Kaffee-seed" is presumably the form of coffee (*Coffea liberica*) found indigenously in Liberia (Schulze 1973, 125–126).

76. These are tastes the chief acquired from his residence in Monrovia with the McGill family.

77. Blyden instigated the establishment of this school in 1871, eventually located at Totokwele (Lynch 1967, 52).

78. Eleven years later, C. A. Pitman similarly lamented: "I am informed that the Mohammedans send from Musahdu missionaries yearly to Vonzuah, a distance of two hundred miles or more. Here this, Church of Christ in Liberia, Europe, and America—a missionary from Musahdu to within twelve and a half miles of Monrovia!" (Pitman 1877, 4). Anthony D. Williams of the Methodist Episcopal Church established the first school at Bopolu in 1835. The school was closed three years later when the teacher who followed Williams was recalled to Monrovia as conditions in Bopolu became unsettled after Sao Boso died (Holsoe 1966, 16–17).

79. The King's indulgence in alcohol is one reason why Ibrahima Kabawee said that Momolu Sao was "a great pagan" ("African Literature" 1871, 114). Blyden considered Momolu to be "half Mohammedan and half pagan in his genealogy": half-Manding and half-Gola (Blyden 1871c, 261).

80. "Sand-doctors" are also sometimes called "sand-cutters" or diviners, and they draw marks in the sand to evaluate a person's situation and give advice (see McNaughton 1988, 54, 55, figs. 35–38; Brett-Smith 1994, 60–62).

81. Gatumba was the Dei chief in Suehn, on the road to the coast, who was involved in the attack on the settlers in 1840.

82. This is a rare but useful comment that Anderson made about the decision-making process in the Condo confederation.

83. Anderson had been in Bopolu since the 25 April, fifty days, waiting to advance to the interior.

84. Or "pikin," a name from Portuguese which means "small child," although the term is often restricted to boys. Here, the name carried on as an adult's name. The "ny" or "ni" added at the end of "Pikin," as in "Pickaninny" here, may be pejorative if "ni" derives from Manding, as it means "small."

85. The "Pessy country" is the modern-day Bokomu Kpelle area.

86. It is possible that "Zelleki" is "Siliki" or "Sidiki," a common Manding name. There is, however, a town in this region called Zelegai (Selegai), which may be the same town mentioned, located at 9°19'N, 10°4'W.

87. By this time, the rainy season was well underway. This is probably the Tuma Creek, which flows into the Saint Paul River.

88. The cross-tied poles are typical of this kind of crossing (see Strong 1930, 1: 145, fig. 101).

89. The Deh are the modern Kuwaa, also known as the Belle, who live in the interior of today's western Liberia. The Dei, or Dey, are a completely different people who live along the coast (Dunn and Holsoe 1985, 56). "Bonsie" should be "Bousie" (Loma). This is the first of many places where the typesetter apparently replaced "u" for "n."

90. Anderson was absolutely correct—the Kuwaa speak a language which is part of the Krao language group.

91. Malung was probably named after the Malang creek, about 7°31'N, 9°53'W.

92. Anderson seems to be suggesting that there were two particular routes, the Barline route, probably through Kpayekwele and on into Boozie country, and the one which ran north of Barline through Zolowo that Anderson eventually followed.

93. It is interesting that the name ends with "tah," which is Kpelle for "town," while in Kuwaa it would be "ghee," "ge," or "gi."

94. "Friday," 5 July, is actually a Sunday.

95. "Zolaghee" is possibly the modern Zolagii.

96. Today these Bonsies are known in Guinea as the Ziama Toma.

97. According to oral tradition, Zolowo was a "sanctuary" to which refugees fled during times of unrest because Zolowo's walls were impregnable and Zolowo's soldiers were fearless ("Following the Trail of Benjamin Anderson" 1973, 1974, 39–40).

98. These would be the side-blown horns typical of this area. Music for the entrance and departure of leaders and honor guests was common in the region, as in the previous case of Momolu Sao leaving Totokwele.

99. "*Wee*" (or "*wui,*" "*wuigii,*" "*wuitaa,*" or "*wigi*") means "Western," "English," "American," or "white" in Loma. A variant of "*wee*" joined with "*zunui*" ("man" or "person"), as in "*wuitaazuni,*" means "Western man" (Dwyer 1981, 161, 202; Vydrine 1987, 114).

100. Zorzor is the district headquarters and is located in the Gizima clan, Loma chiefdom. As of the mid-1980s, the weekly market was still held on Thursday. For a discussion about the migration movements of the Loma and Manding into Zorzor district and environs, see Weisswange (1976).

101. Coppers were one half , one , and two cent pieces ("An Act Supplementary to an Act, Entitled an Act Authorizing the Circulation of Copper Coin" 1857, 194; Krause and Mishler 1982, 1197–1198).

102. "Pateriki" were military buttons.

103. The potatoes are sweet potatoes (*Ipomoea batata*).

104. "Thank you" in Loma is *è màmà* (Sadler 1951, 10).

105. This is the correct translation from Loma (Vydrine 1987, 89).

106. This is a custom that continued in the whole region until at least the mid-1980s.

107. "Nessebeah" is a Kuwaa (Belle) town which Anderson passed on 19 June.

108. "Salaghee" is Seymour's "Sarway." It is located in the modern-day Palama clan and Kpelle chiefdom, in Lofa County. Gbalein is now a clan within this chiefdom. One informant in Salayea said that Daffahborrah, also known as Dawollah or Dahborrah, probably ruled until the late 1890s. This elder claimed that Daffahborrah was very powerful because of an alliance he had formed with the Buluyiema Loma, who live west of Zorzor ("Following the Trail of Benjamin Anderson" 1973, 1974, 52–53).

109. Elders in Zolowo said that the correct spelling of Cavvea's name was "Covea," and that Covea was the nephew of the chief of Zolowo, Zakama ("Following the Trail of Benjamin Anderson" 1973, 1974, 40).

110. That is, Dr. Charles Dunbar. One can pour nitric acid on a mineral to determine if it is gold. Brass and copper will bubble up, and a mixture of gold, brass, and copper will turn black. A gold-silver mixture will not immediately turn black, so persons sometimes sold this alloy to escape detection (Garrard 1980, 87–89).

111. Until about 4 August.

112. The Little Cape Mount is known today as the Lofa River.

113. Whereas Monrovia can have as much as two hundred fifty inches of rain a year, in this part of the interior it is about seventy inches of rain (Schulze 1973, 25).

114. Anderson was describing what Seymour termed "Benson's View."

115. This may be so, but it may also be part of a cultural tradition out of the savanna, where admittedly there would also have been limited wood and the walls could stand because there was less rain.

116. Anderson apparently saw little of the secret societies and their masqueraders.

117. Anderson seems to have been directing this barb against the Monrovia elite—the "mulatto" element (d'Azevedo 1995, 77, 82).

118. The third part of the *AR* account begins with this paragraph (Anderson 1870c, 195–204). Anderson leaves on 21 September, after having been at Zolowo since 8 July, or seventy-five days. Anderson was off in calculating the location of Fissabu by 8 miles (13 kilometers) to the north, 25 miles (40 kilometers) to the west, and 43 miles (69 kilometers) diagonally.

119. Elders in Fissabu said that one of their chiefs, Bodu, controlled twelve towns sometime before the Liberian government colonized the area in the early twentieth century ("Following the Trail of Benjamin Anderson" 1973, 1974).

120. "Round and bossy masses" is an apt phrase for the inselbergs which are found in the area, the remnants of the cores of volcanoes.

121. The etymology of *tibbabue* or *tubabu,* translated as some form of "white man," is a matter of debate. Some argue that *tubabu* comes from the Arabic *tabîb,* which means "doctor," while others disagree (see Bazin [1906] 1965, 629; Jaschke 1955, 189; Delafosse 1955, 779; Webb 1995, xxvi).

122. "Phillakahmah" can be written Fila Kama (Kamara?).

123. "Bokkadu" might be Bakedu (Bakiedu, Bakiemai), located in the Kwadu-Boni chiefdom, Voinjama District. Bakedu was an old town and an important com-

mercial center along the Lofa River that linked coastal trading areas such as Cape Mesurado (Monrovia) and Cape Mount with Beyla and Kankan (Person 1968, 1: 107, 109, 309 n. 61; 1990, map 2; Fisher 1971, xiv; Weisswange 1976, 4; Geysbeek and Camara 1994, 77). In 1867, Karfal Nejl wrote that "Balikad" was one of a half-dozen towns between Bopolu and Musadu where Muslim scholars lived (Prost 1869, 129; Tracy 1869, 240). Bessa's town may have lain along this route. Boondee is now called Bunde clan in the Voinjama chiefdom, Lofa County.

124. Anderson was wrong, but only in that this river, the Via, is a tributary to the Saint Paul River. Cape Mount River was usually called the Little Cape Mount River at this time, but is known today as the Lofa River. Corkwood (*Musanga Smithii*) is a very lightweight wood when dry, but becomes very strong when it gets wet (see Holsoe 1954, 7).

125. Anderson was clearly referring to what is today called the Sande Society.

126. He apparently did not see the subsequent days of celebration (see, e.g., Holsoe 1980).

127. Anderson obviously did not want to shake the hands of these girls. Not only did he believe they were being wrongly treated, but this scene conflicted with his otherwise high praise of Loma women (d'Azevedo 1995, 77).

128. *Ejung* or *Ijã* is Manding for "I beg [you]"—"I (*e/i*) beg (*jung/jõ*)" (Cutler, with Dwyer 1981, 85).

129. *Sallikah,* or *Sillaka, salaka,* or *saraka,* is from the Arabic word *sadaqa* (*sadaka*). As Anderson correctly stated later in the paragraph, this means "sacrifice" or "offering." This kind of sacrifice can usually be made freely and is not obligatory (Weir 1953, 483–484; McNaughton 1988, 59; Launay 1992, 196–219).

130. "Dixie" was a tune written by Daniel Emmett from Ohio for a minstrel singing group nine years earlier. "Dixie Land" represented the South, and the song portrayed Northern beliefs that blacks were inferior and that slavery benefited slaves. The highly formal singing style of the song contrasts with the use of the black American dialect of the times (Lloyd 1968, 144–145; Fred Mayer, personal communication, January 1996). While it may seem ironic that Anderson played this song that glorified slavery, Anderson stated here that he used "Dixie" for its musical component rather than its lyrics. Anderson was, according to an unpublished obituary, a talented musician: "He developed early a taste for music and was a favorite among his comrades because of his ability in handling the stringed instruments, particularly the guitar. He was at a time leader of the Methodist Church Choir [of Monrovia, and] also of the National Choir on several important occasions. As a guitarist he was easily first among his peers. He possessed a sweet and charming voice, which was never heard to better advantage than when accompanined by the guitar"("Brief Sketch" [1910]).

131. The Fatiha is sura 1 of the Qur'an "In the name of God, Most Gracious, Most Merciful. Praise be to God, the Cherisher and Sustainer of the Worlds; Most Gracious, Most Merciful; Master of the Day of Judgement. Thee do we worship, And Thine aid we seek. Show us the straight way, The way of those on whom Thou hast bestowed Thy Grace, Those whose (portion) is not wrath, And who go not astray" (Ali's translation of the Qur'an [1934] 1977). The Lord's Prayer is found in Luke 11: 2–4 and Matthew 6:9–13.

132. Thus using it in a similar manner to the Muslim *lisimu,* or talisman.

133. Dowilnyah, or Daoronyan, was a Beavogui (Person 1968, 1:434, 446 n. 11; 1975, 2125). The Manding equivalent of Beavogui is Kamara (Adam 1951, 95). One century later, the people of Zigida still remembered Dowilnyah's legendary power and ability "to carry war" ("Following the Trail of Benjamin Anderson" 1973, 1974).

134. The "Wymar Boozies" are the Waima, also called the Koiama (Koymay).

135. Their faces were more likely scarified. The Waima had a distinctive facial scarification remarked upon by most travelers.

136. Three weeks after the "old Mandingo priest" arrived from Bessa's town on about 17 October, Dowilnyah's messengers went to Bokesa to get Anderson. They returned without him, going to Ukbaw-Wavolo, where Dowilnyah was staying (next paragraph). They walked back to Bokesa one week later to get Anderson. Anderson and his entourage went with Dowilnyah's escorts the second time.

137. The Latin name for the "driver" that Anderson described is *Dorylus. Termites bellicosi* is a term that nineteenth-century writers used for termites or "white ants" (Winterbottom [1803] 1969, 292–334; Rockwell 1842, 306; Welmers 1949, 228).

138. Anderson placed "Jakka Commah" on his 1868–69 map just below Gubbewallah (fig. 13).

139. Seymour and Ash were actually attacked some distance northeast of Kuankan. Seymour's left hand was badly cut, not his right hand (chap. 4, 152).

140. Anderson had been at Bokesa since 26 September, thirty-seven days. Ukbaw-Wavolo may no longer exist. It was probably a satellite village of Boo, two and one-half hours northeast of Boo. Elders in Boo said that Anderson passed back through this town when he returned to Monrovia. Ukbaw-Wavolo seems to have been one of Dowilnyah's temporary residences (see "Following the Trail of Benjamin Anderson" 1973, 1974).

141. As was common throughout many parts of Africa before colonial rule, jurisdictions over "boundaries" were run by small local polities, not by large "ethnic" or "multi-ethnic" states. See the discussion at H-Africa's "Boundaries" web page, particularly John Thornton's entry of 21 January 1999 (*http://www2.h-net.msu.edu/~africa/threads/index.html#Boundaries* [accessed 14 February 2003]).

142. Jebbue was an official who would be later called by the Liberian government a "chief's speaker." When Anderson returned in 1874, he learned that "Jebbue or Eboe, Dowilnyah's former Counsellor now presided as Chief" in the town of Pellezarrah (see chap. 6). One hundred years later, elders in Zigida said that a man named Yabo succeeded Dowilnyah and was probably his spokesman. Dowilnyah Willeh succeeded Yabo ("Following the Trail of Benjamin Anderson" 1973, 1974). Note that the name of the senior chief in fig. 18—holding the sword and looking aside in disgust—is Diagbo or Diagba. This Diagbo is the Yabo of the Zigida oral history and is probably Anderson's Jebbue. Yabo was the chief who oversaw the division of the lands as the Liberia-Guinea frontier was drawn up and directed the moving of the royal house from Goboèla on the Guinea side to Zigida in Liberia. He is said to have died in 1916 ("Following the Trail of Benjamin Anderson" 1973, 1974).

143. Note that they were not seated on chairs, which were reserved for chiefs. In this case, though, the chief was also sitting on a mat.

144. Cementing relations was one purpose in travel, in addition to reaching a set destination.

145. This is the conflict between Western "clock" time, and African "social" time.

146. A Guerze informant said that the name of Ziggah Porrah Zue is associated with termite mounds. The Loma name is properly transcribed as *Sigi polo zu*. "*Sigi*" refers to the "tala" termite mound, "*polo*" to "earth," and "*zu*" to "village." Toupou (1989) argues that the name properly means "the village from which other villages obtain the termite earth." Though Ziggah Porrah Zue replaced Gubbewallah as the "capital," Dowilnyah did not live here permanently. Dowilnyah seems to have had one main residence, in Gubbewallah it seems, but moved from town to town.

147. The ruins of Ziggah Porrah Zue's walls are visible in the village today.

148. The "jack upon stilts" is the well-known stilt-dancing masked figure. For a photograph in a Loma setting, see Højbjerg (1993, 94).

149. Elders recall Sunday as the date of the market, but this has now changed to Thursday. The market is still crowded on market day.

150. Kuankan is the same town that Seymour and Ash visited before they were attacked.

151. In 1903, Anderson wrote that "This bridge is made of strong twigs and grass rope very skillfully plaited together," and that it was "about 100 ft. long" (chap. 2, 85). See the photograph of this bridge today (fig. 19).

152. The "Domar" are the modern Loma of Zorzor District in Liberia and the Ziama Toma of Guinea.

153. The fourth part of the *AR* segment starts with this paragraph (Anderson 1870d, 226–233).

154. Anderson had been there for twenty days.

155. "Cane-brake" is the two-to-three-meter-tall grass characteristic of the humid savannas, probably either *Andropogon gayanus* or *Pennisetum puerperum* (elephant grass).

156. The sasswood tree is *Erythrophleum guineensis,* which is often planted as a tree to mark a town and its foundation.

157. The "Congoes" had been taken as slaves from savanna areas.

158. Anderson is here walking over an "iron mountain," a major iron ore deposit, containing some of the highest-grade iron ore ever found. By 2001, the multinational corporation Rio Tinto Zinc (RTZ) had a concession over this and was planning to exploit the ore over the next thirty years by building a railway line to Conakry.

159. The name "Ballatah" indicates a shift from Loma or Toma to Manding, with Anderson using the Loma spelling: "town" is *ta* in Loma or Toma, and *du* or *dougou* in Manding.

160. Artemus Ward was also known as Charles Farrar Browne, a U.S. humorist who lived from 1834 to 1867 (Austin 1964).

161. According to modern maps, the highest point of elevation near Ballatah or Baladougou is 1984 feet (six hundred five meters).

162. This part of the mountain measures from 3,821 feet (1,165 meters) to 5,432 feet (1,656 meters). While Anderson's estimations of altitude were fairly accurate, he might have underestimated the height of this range because he did not climb to the top to make his calculations. Today, the Vukkah hills are known as the Fon Range.

163. In 1903, Anderson gave an idyllic image of Vukkah (see chap. 2, 86).

164. This mountain range still marks a linguistic and cultural boundary between the Loma and the Manding. In addition to the Loma being more prevalent on the western side of the range, the Konyaka-Manding from the Beyla area call the Manding who live on the western side "Toma-Maniya" ("Loma Manding") or "Tukolo-Maniya" ("Maniya in the forest").

165. In 1903, Anderson wrote that Musadu's Chief "Vomfeedolla sent an escort to bring us into the capital" when he reached Vukkah (see chap. 2, 86). This suggests that Vukkah represented the farthest extent of Musadu's influence. The Musadu chief also knew of Anderson's approach, as did Dowilnyah when Anderson was delayed in Bokkesah (see d'Azevedo 1995, 80).

166. As Anderson left Vukkah and headed for Nionsamoridu, he later wrote:

> We now descend into the Mandingo country proper, passing through the outlying villages and farms until we come to one of the large towns Mahammedu, where the great market of the country is held every Wednesday. The roads on each side is hemmed in where they are taken up in farming by cane-brake and long grass. In the dries this is a source of trouble and danger for if this stubble once takes fire, the conflagration spreads far and wide. (chap. 2, 85)

167. "Nionsamoridu" is also spelled "Nionsomoridu." The Manding more frequently say "Yusumodu." Yves Person wrote "Nyonsomoridugu." Anderson also wrote "Mahammedu" or "town of Mahammed" (see chap. 2, 85). The name of this town in the 1892 Liberian-French treaty is "Mahomondon." The 1892 treaty placed Nionsamoridu in Liberia, and the neighboring towns of Nyela (Anderson's Naala) and Musadu in Guinea (Hertslet 1909, 1135). Hunters reportedly founded Nionsamoridu, and Jakhanke-Sware clerics from Nionsamoridu are said to have supported Foningama and Samori (Person 1968, 1:428, 432, 445; 1979, 265; Geysbeek and Kamara 1991, 68; Geysbeek 2002). Anderson was so impressed with Nionsamoridu and its environs that he or someone else sketched a picture of "Mahommadu" (fig. 22). In 1903, Anderson wrote that "Nothing but the pencil or photographic art can do justice to these magnificent efforts of nature" (chap. 2, 86).

168. A wall no longer surrounds this town. The French colonial forces ordered the dismantling of all such fortifications.

169. According to the oral traditions, a person from the Nyei (Nye, Nyen, Naa) clan left Musadu and founded Nyela (Geysbeek and Kamara 1991, 67). "Naala," or "Nyela," means "Naa" or "Nye town." "La" is added to a name in Manding, as in *Naala,* to denote a settlement when the name in question is a clan name. "Du" is appended, as in *Musadu* ("Musa's town"), when the town's name is based on an individual's first name.

170. Anderson is mistaken here, as Du Quirlelah (Dukulela) was to his left; 8°46'N, 8°40'W (at least it is today). On his way to Musadu, Diakolidu would have been to his right. According to most oral sources, the Bility people of Beyla gave the Dukule of Musadu permission to found Dukulela ("Dukule's town"). Some disagree, saying that the Sefu (Sherif) were the ones who gave the Dukule permission to settle

on the land that later became Dukulela. The Manding say that these Dukule are Soninke clerics who emigrated from the Soninke state of Jafunu (Zafunu), in northwest Mali. The Soninke founded Jafunu before Sunjata formed the Mali Empire (Lewicki 1971, 518; Levtzion 1973, 47–48; Geysbeek and Kamara 1991, 67).

171. One now sees the top of Musadu's white mosque far off in the horizon, the thin wall probably having been destroyed when the French conquered the area in the 1890s (see chap. 2).

172. Vomfeedolla's name in present-day oral traditions is Vafin Dole. This Vafin Dole is the author of the 1868 letter, Fanfi Doreh (chap. 5, 231). Samori executed Vafin Dole and other chiefs from the Konyan at Worokolo in 1881 after Vafin and others failed to defend the Sissi (Person 1968, 1:340–344). After Samori's successful seige of Kankan in 1881, he marched south to fight Ibrahima Sissi (see chap. 2). Sissi had taken Solimana and Sankaran from Samori in the late 1870s when Samori was focusing on more northerly areas. In 1881, Samori confronted Sissi at Worokolo. Vafin Dole of Musadu, Mani Bakari Kromah of Diakolidu, Abudu Sware of Nionsamoridu, and Gbegbe Kamara of Kuankan went to Worokolo to assist Sissi. Samori won and executed Vafin and these other chiefs from Konya (see Massing 1978–79, 52–56).

173. "Barki" is also "Bakari," "Balaki," or "Boakai," from one of Muhammad's first converts: Abu Bakr.

174. Anderson did not seem to appreciate that the people of Musadu accepted him as a representative of another government with whom they might be able to forge a military alliance and establish commercial ties (d'Azevedo 1995, 80).

175. Anderson was describing a bard (a griot or *jeli*) who played a *kora*.

176. This may be another place where Anderson was mocking his fellow Americo-Liberians in Monrovia who tried to claim descent from the Manding (d'Azevedo 1995, 77).

177. This appears to be styled after a hunter's hat.

178. The"king's evil" is probably a goiter, caused by a lack of iodine or because iodine is blocked by food eaten, such as cassava leaves. It may also say something about the kind of salt that is available.

179. Musadu is actually at 8°37'W, 8°46'N (*Guinea Gazetteer* 1965, 115). Anderson's coordinates placed Musadu 22 miles (35 kilometers) too far to the south, 13 miles (21 kilometers) too far to the east, and 25 miles (40 kilometers) off diagonally.

180. Anderson was probably referring to the Konidiaba (Konidyaba or Koniyaba) and the Koundiani Mountains. The highest point on the former is 3,960 feet (1207 meters). The Koundiani is slightly northeast of Musadu and west of Konidiaba, and is 3,232 feet (985 meters) tall (Beyla map, NC-29–11).

181. This is a reference, at least in part, to Ibrahima Sissi's treatment of Musadu earlier that decade.

182. If the Manding stabled their horses rather than allowed them to freely graze outside their town walls, they were probably fed by slaves who carried food in from the fields. The people may have kept their horses in stables to protect them from tsetse flies and raiders and to prevent them from trampling small gardens within the town walls and on farms outside (Law 1976, 131). The Musadu area was so good for

horses that Samori Touré sent a Fula man to pasture a few dozen of his horses in Musadu until the people of the region revolted against Samori in 1888 (Person 1968, 2:913). Konya was also good for cattle. Samori's troops took all of the cattle from Konya when they retreated in 1888 (Chevalier 1909, 26).

183. This might be the same mosque that a Catholic missionary, Père Bouyssou, visited in 1913 (Le Long 1949, 24). Vafin Dole's grandson Yaya said that this was a "male mosque," in contrast to a "female mosque," which is round (in Geysbeek 2002; see Marty 1922, 129–130; Person 1979, 261; Prussin 1995, 22–24, 51–53). The residents of Musadu started to build a new mosque on this site in 1962; the mosque was formally completed in 1994.

184. The women would have prayed together in at least one of the compartments, separating them from the men.

185. Musadu was the leading center of Islam from its location in the southern savannah to the coast (chap. 7).

186. These are the "principle towns" that Anderson referred to at the beginning of this account. This sentence implies that these towns comprised some type of confederation under Musadu.

187. This would have taken place after the early afternoon prayer during the fasting month. The people of Konya, therefore, made a special effort to impress Anderson.

188. This trumpet could have been ivory, iron, or wood (see Johnston [1906] 1969, 1023, 1026).

189. For a picture of a crooked sword, see Bravmann (1983, 52).

190. Adopted from the Arabs, the stirrup allowed riders to use their legs more effectively to control their horses and to use their upper bodies to shoot (Law 1980, 107; Webb 1993, 226).

191. This was a considerable cavalry or *sofa,* if Anderson was correct, for this is the largest that Samori Touré's cavalry ever got (Legassick 1966, 97, 107; see also Webb 1993, 232–239). Musadu's ability to muster this many horses shows Musadu's influence and substantial resource base. The letter that Vafin Dole sent to the Liberian government with Anderson in 1868 indicates that the residents of Musadu owned at least a few hundred slaves. As was common in other parts of West African, one reason why slaves were valuable was because they were exchanged for horses (Law 1976, 124, 131; Webb 1993).

192. Anderson's firearms were faster and more powerful than those which the people of Musadu possessed. Anderson probably used the percussion-cap musket, which could be reloaded more quickly than flintlocks. The contrast between the "deeper sound of [his] guns" with the "snapping" of his hosts suggests that Anderson was using a larger caliber bullet (James Harbeck, personal communication, April 1996).

193. Some of these chiefs were leaders of contingents who came from the outlying towns. Each town might have contributed footmen and cavalry (Legassick 1966, 96–97). One oral tradition states that Musadu's army was divided into nine sections during Samori's time. Six of the divisions mainly consisted of Dole, Sissi, Beete, Kromah, Sayon, and Dukule, and *nyamakala,* or people from semicasted occupational groups (Geysbeek 2002).

194. The fifth section of the *AR*'s publication begins with this paragraph (Anderson 1870e, 258–266).

195. *Sannue* or *sani* is Manding for "gold" (Cutler, with Dwyer 1981, 99). In 1880, the U.S. Minister to Liberia, John Smyth, reported that "Mandingo gold" was to be found in this part of the interior (Smyth 1880).

196. Medina was located 5 miles (8 kilometers) west of Gbeleba-Kobala in Guinea, near today's Côte d'Ivoire border, 55 miles (88 kilometers) northeast of Musadu. In 1879, after speaking with Ibrahima Sissi's envoy who visited Monrovia, President Gardner said that "Medina is represented as abounding in cattle, Hides, Goats, Sheep, Horses, Asses, Rice, Peas, Corn, Ground-nuts, Cotton, Country cloths, Butter, Rock-salt and Gold in great abundance" (Gardner, 1879). Samori destroyed Medina in 1881, but the town's ruins were still present when Yves Person conducted his research in the late 1950s (Person 1968, 1:13; 1990, map 3).

197. The 1868 Musadu letter, published as an appendix at the end of this chapter, said that the area "over the eastern hills" was the eastern region of Gbana. The Musadu letter provides a more complete description of what Anderson briefly summarized here about Blamer, or Ibrahima, Sissi's poor treatment of Musadu.

198. Mid-December is at the height of the cold season, when the dry harmattan winds cool the atmosphere considerably.

199. The "Futtah" is the Futa Jallon region in eastern Guinea. Labe, one of the Futa Jallon's key towns, is about 110 miles (177 kilometers) from the modern Senegal-Guinea boarder and another 220 miles (354 kilometers) to Kankan. The distance from Kankan to Medina's ruins is 94 miles (151 kilometers). The Kankan-Musadu route is 112 miles (180 kilometers) apart, and the journey from the old Medina to Musadu is 55 miles (88 kilometers). These represent the shortest distances between each location. In short, traders from Senegal traveled a minimum of 442 miles (712 kilometers) if they went directly from Kankan to Musadu, and 479 miles (771 kilometers) if they went by way of Medina. That they needed interpreters suggests that they might have been Wolof rather than Manding-Dyula, since Senegambian Mandinka is at least 80 percent mutually intelligible with the Manding of Guinea (Dwyer 1989, 50–51; Long 1972, 9).

200. Here, Anderson exaggerated the potential of the cannon to make Sissi more fearful.

201. "*Kahtahsee*" is from the Arabic *kayt, ktâb, kitâb*—"book" (Jaschke 1955, 165). Similarly, the Manding say "*kayidi*" or "*kàfá*" (Maninka-English Dictionary n.d.; Vydrine 1999, 257), the Fulbe say "*kaytaaji*" (de Wolf 1995), and the Wolof say "*kayit*" ("bi," "wi") or "*keyit*" ("bi," "wi") (Nussbaum, Gage, and Varre 1970).

202. This seems to be the first time in writing where Liberians associated the Manding with the Jews (d'Azevedo 1994, 197, 229; see also Konneh 1992, 177). For later references, see A. (1879), la Rue (1930, 87), Freeman (1952, 54), and "The Tribes of the Western Province and the Denwoin People" (1955, 32). See Sayers (1927, 76) for a Sierra Leone example.

203. Although used extensively for pack carrying in the savannas, jackasses or donkeys do not survive long in the forest for reasons of disease (Curtin 1975, 222).

204. Nionsamoridu is strategically located along a pass between the Fon-Going

Mountains that links Konya with Kankan and has been was an important gateway for trafficking goods between the forest and savannah for centuries (Person 1968, 1: 251).

205. "Buley" is Bure, a large region that encompasses the modern town of Siguiri in northeast Guinea, identified as having been the ancient gold fields of the Mali Empire (Levtzion 1973, chap. 12; McIntosh 1998, 30–33, 267–281).

206. We are unable to identify these three towns.

207. The modern town of Siguiri (in Bure) is 186 miles (299 kilometers) north of Musadu. Thus, at a good pace of 30 miles (48 kilometers) per day, this would have been about a six-day journey.

208. "Wasalah" is Wasulu or the Wasolon region. These reports of gold might have been enough cause for some to form the Mining Company of Liberia after Anderson returned in 1869 (Schulze 1973, 146). Some stated that Anderson's main reason for going to Musadu in 1874 was to find this gold (Johnston [1906] 1969, 490; Karnga 1909, 32; Cassell 1970, 286). Someone even claimed that "the Colonization Society" had planned to "build a city" at "Bila," or Beyla ("Discouraging Features" 1921).

209. Note Anderson's surprise at the few number of goods that were available. This must have been in contrast to the many stories that he and other interested settlers on the coast had heard about this "capital of the western Mandingoes" (see d'Azevedo 1995, 85).

210. The large horse refers to the Arabian horse, while the small horse refers to the indigenous West African horse. For a discussion of horses, see chap. 7.

211. If the oldest man in Musadu was born around 1780 (making him eighty-eight years old), then Musadu existed by the early eighteenth century at the very latest—allowing for approximately thirty years per generation (Person 1972, 5–10). With reference to the "other towns," they could have been speaking narrowly about Beyla, Diakolidu, Dukulela, and Nyela, which "sprang" from Musadu (see chap. 7).

212. The Manding in Musadu today call this marketplace the *lòòfèlò* or "old market."

213. Ostriches can still be found in the desert and in open thorn scrub from southern Mauritania and Senegal east through Mali and Niger to northeastern Nigeria and Chad (Serle, Morel, and Hartwig 1977). Whether they used to be found in these more humid savannas is not known. Their feathers may have been a trade item.

214. Yves Person believed that the "eastern Mandingo" was a reference to Saji Kamara and his followers (1968, 1:289).

215. These plains did indeed come to be the focus of efforts to introduce ox ploughs from the early colonial period onward.

216. The people still grow tobacco in plots in Musadu.

217. This bird is possibly a wood ibis (*Ibis ibis*).

218. The original has a misplaced comma and reads: "I visited Billelah Kaifal, Kandah's native town."

More than a half-century later, someone wrote that Anderson returned to Monrovia on his second journey with "a great variety of mineral specimen from both Musardu and Bila [Beyla]" (untitled article 1921, 4). Anderson did not indicate that he went to Beyla on his second mission. He either evidently picked up some minerals from Musadu and Beyla on his first trip or did this on his second trip, but not in Beyla.

219. This supports traditions which say that the Bility left Musadu and founded Beyla (Geysbeek and Kamara 1991, 67).

220. Diakolidu, or Yockkadu, may thus have had from 438 to 500 homes, and perhaps 1,750 to 2,000 people (see chap. 7, 299). Diakolidu is now much larger than Musadu, as the French made Diakolidu the administrative capital of Beyla province (Chevalier 1909, 25–26; Duboc 1938, 225; Person 1968, 1:452 n. 68; 1975, 1483–1485). According to oral tradition, Jakolo (Diakolo) Kromah migrated from Musadu and founded "Diakolidugu," "town of Diakolo" (Geysbeek and Kamara 1991, 67).

221. "*Vawfulla*" could be *va* ("Father"), *Fula* (*Fulbe).*

222. The harmattans are cold, dry winds that blow from the Sahara during the dry season.

223. The sixth part of the *AR*'s publication of Anderson's trip begins here (Anderson 1870f, 297–301). The next day, Edward Blyden and W. Winwood Reade departed for a journey to Bopolu that lasted into the next month (Blyden 1871c). Blyden originally thought about going to Musadu and Kankan on this trip ("Tour among West-African Mahommedans" 1869, 127). Anderson took nearly the identical route home that he used to reach Musadu.

224. This may be kola. Today, fifteen dollars would purchase between seventy-five hundred and fifteen thousand kola nuts, depending on the season. Anderson was there early in the kola season when prices would have been quite low. Susan White, alternatively, wrote that "kolu" is the Loma term for "iron bar" and suggested that Anderson was speaking of iron money in this instance (White 1974, 11).

225. Evident here is the contrast between the stratified society of the Manding (and Vai) with their castes and the southeastern Mande (among them the Loma), who did not have these social divisions (see chap. 7).

226. These are perhaps the cattle known today as "Senegal" cattle.

227. The Qur'an describes Jews and Christians as "the people of the book" in sura 3, verses 64–80, and in other places (see Blyden 1871c, 240).

228. Ibrahima Sissi had "broken down" these walls earlier in the 1860s (see chap. 5, 234).

229. Anderson may have been describing inland valley swamps and plains, which would have been used for rice production in the rainy season and carried important green pasture in the dry season.

230. Anderson either bypassed Pellezarrah and went directly to Gubbewallah, or forgot to mention that he had visited this town when going to Musadu.

231. Anderson earlier said that Gubbewallah was Dowilnyah's capital.

232. Anderson only stayed with Dowilnyah for one day when he passed through six years later.

233. Here Anderson was clearly overlooking the large number of women who would travel to markets unarmed. Also, mindful of his own position as a soldier, Anderson here offered a good description of the arms that his African counterparts bore (see Frank 1998, 50).

234. "Comma's son" is Seymour's "Kagular."

235. Anderson's analysis of warfare underplays the extent of periodic major wars in which war towns were destroyed. For example, see Sims's descriptions of the Barlain-Kpelle wars. Much of the Loma area was depopulated in wars between 1870 and the late 1890s (Fairhead and Leach 1994, 495–498). Equally, the relationship between warfare and trade was sometimes less relevant to trade, in that people used war to attempt to control trade location, direction, and profits.

236. That is, Prince Manna of Gallinas, during President James Spriggs Payne's incumbency.

237. "Moffotah" was earlier written as "Mahfaftah," and is probably Mavodo in the modern Bokomu chiefdom.

238. "Dahtazue" is probably the earlier-mentioned Dallazeah.

239. Anderson stayed in the Bopolu area for just over one month before he returned to Monrovia on 26 March 1869 ("Interior Exploration" 1869, 277).

240. Actually, this journey was a year prior.

241. "G. W. Gibson" refers to Garretson Wilmot Gibson, who was later the president of Liberia from 1900 to 1904. This candidate was J. W. Tucker (G. W. Gibson to S. D. Denison, 20 June 1870, Domestic and Foreign Mission Society Papers, Episcopal Church Archives, Austin, Texas, B-box 17).

242. "Momoru" is Momolu Sao. "Toto-Coreh" is Totokwele.

243. This title and the title on p. 232 appeared in the published version in 1870. Vafin Dole is Fanfi Doreh in this letter, Vomfeedolla in Benjamin Anderson's account, and Vafin Dole with Yves Person (1968, 1:184) and today's informants.

244. Years later, Anderson wrote that Mohammad Barta was Vafin Dole's private secretary (see chap. 2, 58). Barta is an alternative spelling for Berete, Bility, or Biliti, the clan that founded neighboring Beyla (Billelah) (David Conrad, personal communication, 23 February 2000).

245. In 1903, Anderson wrote that "numbers of the translated copies [were] distributed in pamphlet form" (see Anderson, 1903a, 11).

246. Ibrahima Sissi is Anderson's Blamer Sissa and Yves Person's Sere Brema (Person 1970, 85).

247. This may be a reference to the region of Gbana, situated northeast of Musadu at roughly 8°45'N, 8°25'W.

248. The Toron is the major region that is mainly located in today's Côte d'Ivoire. The Ivorian city of Odienne is in the center of the Toron. Odienne's coordinates are 9°31'N, 7°36'W. Kurukoro's coordinates are 9°13'N, 7°57'W. It is situated about 29 miles (47 kilometers) southeast of Medina and 54 miles (87 kilometers) northeast of Musadu.

249. The center of the Gundo region is the Manding town of Linko, 9°23'N, 8°49'W.

250. The scribe is Mohammad Barta (Berete, Biliti), who identified himself as such in the last paragraph of this letter.

251. This is the *basmala,* the line that introduces all of the suras or chapters of the Qur'an except for sura 9. By praising God, this phrase sums up man's subordinate relationship to God (Ali's translation of the Qur'an [1934] 1977, 14 n. 18).

252. This letter is from the towns in Konya which were at least nominally under

Musadu's direction: Beyla, Diakolidu, Nyela, Dukulela, and possibly Nionsamoridu. * Thus spelled in the MS.; sometimes it is written Misādu and sometimes Musādu [EB]. [Edward Blyden's footnotes in the original appendix are marked by stars (*), crosses (†), and double crosses (‡). Schieffelin used numbers rather than symbols that started over for each new page].

253. Mulul Sissi: this is Yves Person's Mori-Ulé Sisé, who led the Sissi of Medina from the 1830s to 1845 (Person 1970, 82). "*Ule*" is a contraction of "*wulèn.*" "*Wulèn*" means "red" but can be translated "light skinned" in this context (Cutler, with Dwyer 1981, 136). †This is a very extensive Muslim city, surrounded with mud walls, about two days journey east of Misādu. Ibrahima, who presides over it, is an enterprising and powerful young Mussulman Chief, having a large army, consisting of an infantry and a cavalry of a thousand horses. He is not a very scrupulous Muslim, however, as appears from the MS [EB]. [Blyden took the information in this note from Anderson's 1870 book (see chap. 5, 233)].

254. Ibrahima Sissi died in 1845, fighting in Kurukoro.

255. "Abdullah" (Abd Allah) is Arabic for "servant/slave of God" (Humblot 1919, 397). This is Yves Person's Burlay (Sèré-Burlay), who succeeded Mori-Ulé Sissi and was killed in 1859 (1970, 83).

256. "The infidels" refers to the animist Manding of Kurukoro, c.1859.

257. "Our town" is Musadu.

258. "The king" is Ibrahima Sissi. Sissi means here that all the population will be enslaved.

259. The Sissi declared *jihad* on everyone who did not say the *shahada,* or creed—"There is no god but God, and Muhammad is the messenger of God." The closest that the Qur'an comes to this line of justification is sura 9, verse 5, which states that Muslims should fight "Pagans" until they "repent," pray, and give regularly (see Peters 1995, 370–371). The Sissi and other like-minded groups along the Niger were influenced by the Fulbe leader Usman dan Fodio of today's northern Nigeria, who declared *jihad* against the lax Hausa and Fulbe during the early nineteenth century. Uthman wrote that a Muslim must make war upon the heathen King who will not say "There is no God but Allah'" (dan Fodio [1804–1805] 1979, 138).

260. "Baghna" may be Gbana, located east of Musadu. Gbana has the reputation in the oral traditions of being the stronghold of non-Muslims (Geysbeek 2002). "Baghna" might also refer to Seymour's "Barbenier" people, who seem to have been located in the hills to the east of Musadu. Sims called them the "Bababeeias." Benjamin Anderson wrote of "King Barbenier." Samori Touré could have led these people from the late-1850s to the early-1860s (Person 1970, 85, see chap. 2, 46).

261. Part of Ibrahima's army was comprised of slaves. The letter does not indicate if their leaders were also slaves (see Legassick 1966, 96–97; Bazin 1974, 114).

262. "Yusumudu" is Nionsamoridu, Benjamin Anderson's Nu-Somadu or Mahommadu.

263. Anderson helped the townspeople repair this wall when he passed through "Mahommadu" on his way back to Monrovia in 1868. Anderson did not say why the wall was in a state of disrepair. The whole area was the scene of sporadic warfare

throughout the 1860s. As walls were critical to the protection of a town, every effort would have been made to rebuild walls as quickly as possible after they were damaged (Smith 1989, 99). Ibrahima stripped the farms around Nionsamoridu as he laid siege and prepared to attack. Khulila is not identified.

264. "Jilila" is not Musadu but is near today's Jilila, or Guirila. Lansedougou (8°50'N, 8°30'W) is one of the towns in Jilila. This can also be translated in Manding as "the water." The sources of three rivers mark the borders of Jilila: the Kourani and Monsoro to the north, and the Dion (which flows past Musadu) to the south. That the writer, Mohammed Barta, referred to Jilila as "our town" may either say something about where he was from or imply that Jilila was somehow part of the Musadu confederation.

265. *Koranic form for introducing deprecatory invocations.—*Trans* [EB]. [This is probably from the "refuge verses" in the Qur'an which are the first verses of suras 113 and 114. They begin with, "I seek refuge with the Lord."]

266. Salihu Shereef, or Salifu Sherif, was probably a descendant of the famous Talata who, according to many oral accounts, helped Foningama, the legendary founder of the Kamara dynasty in Musadu, or Foningama's descendants gain power in Musadu and Konya (see, e.g., Fisher 1971, ix). The Sherif were a Soninke clan who followed the Maliki school of law like most other Muslims in West Africa (Massing 2000, 286). In 1993, the three leading imams in Musadu in order of importance were a Sherif, a Kane, and a Bility (Geysbeek 2002).

267. This is Muhammad al-Qasim ibn Ali al-Hariri, an Iraqi from Basra who was born in 1054 and died in 1122 A.D. This quote comes from al-Hariri's classic fifty-chapter book called the *Makamat,* or "Assembly." Thomas Chenery published an English translation of the first twenty-six chapters or "assemblies" with notes in 1867 (Chenery [1867] 1969). F. Steingass did the same for the last twenty-four chapters in 1898 (Steingass [1898] 1969; see also Grabar 1984). Muslims in Sierra Leone also used al-Hariri's *Makamat* (Maculay 1871, 243). * MS. not intelligible here [EB].

268. Vafin Dole sent troops to escort Anderson to Musadu once Anderson reached Vukkah on 4 December 1868. This means that the people of Musadu were well aware of Anderson's intended visit. They could have learned of his visit as early as April when Anderson first reached Bopolu or even earlier. † Monrovia [EB].

269. "The king" is the President of Liberia, James S. Payne.

270. *Momoru Sau, King of Boporo [EB]. [That is, Momolu Sao (Sims's Memmoru Sowe, and Anderson's Momoru Son), son of Sao Boso and ruler of Bopolu, who headed the Condo confederacy.]

271. †The King of Masādu here addresses the King of Boporo, as Mr. Anderson had to pass through this town going and coming [EB].

272. ‡The Mandingoes regard the Liberians as composed of Christians and Jews [EB].

273. Benjamin Anderson similarly wrote that "all the other towns sprang from this one" (chap. 5, 219). This refers to stories which claim that Musadu was the original Manding town in the Konyan, and that people left Musadu to found Beyla, Diakolidu, Dukulela, and Nyela (see chap. 7).

274. Mohammad Barta's father and mother.

6. Benjamin J. K. Anderson, 1874

1. Frederick Starr (1858–1933) republished Anderson's 1874 journey in 1912 (Anderson 1912). Frederick Starr was a controversial but popular anthropology professor who taught at the University of Chicago from 1892 to 1923. He traveled throughout Asia, Africa, and Latin America and went to Liberia from September to November 1912 (Cash 1976). His father, Frederick Starr Sr., was a Presbyterian minister from New York who championed the cause of abolition and advocated sending freed slaves and their descendants back to Africa (Starr 1862). While in Liberia, Starr arranged for the College of West Africa to publish Anderson's journey in book form in Monrovia. While none of the material in the Frederick Starr Liberia Research Collection or the Frederick Starr Papers that are housed in the Special Collections department at the University of Chicago's Regenstein Library indicates the source that Starr used, Starr probably had access to old copies of the *Observer* (Monrovia), the newspaper that published Anderson's trip more than fifty years earlier. He might have even seen Anderson's handwritten journal, the old explorer having died just two years earlier. As Starr self-financed his trip to Liberia (Starr 1913a), he might have also paid to publish the book. Starr further advanced the cause of Liberia by publishing a book on Liberia (Starr 1913a) and by holding exhibits of artifacts from Liberia in Chicago and other places in the late 1910s.

The selections from the *Observer* serve as the basis of the text here. Starr's version is used where the *Observer* issues are missing. In 1903, Anderson wrote that he still had his 1868–69 and 1874 journals. Anderson also published part of his "astronomical calculations," "itinerary," and "meteorological observations" in 1903 (figs. 7–8). The government failed to publish Anderson's second account when the legislature was petitioned to do so the same year that French Captain Henri d'Ollone accused Anderson of never having traveled to Musadu. This section begins from Anderson (1912, 3), which Starr published. Starr evidently published Anderson's account in honor and commemoration of Anderson, who died two years earlier.

2. In Heard ([1898] 1969, 100–179). According to Maurice Delafosse, Heard republished Anderson's first account "without Anderson's authorization" (1903).

3. This refers to the reported annexation of parts of the hinterland by Liberia, as a result of the treaties which various chiefs signed on Anderson's second expedition (see chap. 2; Murdza 1979, chaps. 6–8).

4. See Anderson (1879a–g). Not all of the *Observer* (Monrovia) issues of Anderson's account have survived, to our knowledge, so the missing portions have been supplemented from the complete account that Frederick Starr published in 1912. (For a history of the text, see chap. 2). One week after the *Observer* finished publishing Anderson's account, the editors added this notice: "The Narrative of the Expedition despatched to Mushadu, by the Liberian Government under Benj. Anderson, Esqr. in 1871 [*sic*, 1874], was concluded in our last number except the itinerary, meteoriogical [*sic*] and mathematical tables—no facilities to print those. Suppose we collect the entire matter and attempt to publish it in book form[.] Who will assist us by subscription? Send in your names and subscriptions to '*The Observer*' " ("The Narrative of the Expedition" 1880).

5. Starr is referring to the controversy which surrounded Captain d'Ollone's charge in 1903 that Benjamin Anderson never went to Musadu (see chap. 2).

6. The text of the expedition starting at this point is taken from Starr's 1912 published version, starting with p. 5. We cannot locate an issue of the *Observer* (Monrovia) that published this section.

Peter Capehart left Murfeesboro, North Carolina, when he was six years old, along with forty-seven other Capeharts. They were all born as slaves and were emancipated by T. Capehart. The men were farmers, and the women were "washers," "cooks," and "seamstresses" ("List of Emigrants [*Liberia Packet*]" 1852, 104). Capehart grew up north of the Saint Paul River and learned Vai as a youth.

Later in this account, Anderson wrote that Lawrence, Yates, Harrison, and Thomas were "Congo," and Johnson and Simms were "American." It is tempting to think that Simms was related to J. L. Sims of chap. 3, but no evidence of this has emerged.

7. Anderson might have left Carey (Mechanic) Street where he lived and boarded a canoe at Waterside, as he did in 1868.

8. This is Augustus Washington, who was born in Trenton, New Jersey, in 1821 and died in Monrovia on 7 June 1875 (see chap. 2). He was living on the south side of the Saint Paul. Anderson and his companions probably stayed at Augustus Washington's house for the evening. A missionary named Mary B. Merriam visited Washington's house six years earlier, and the following is her romantic description of what she saw. Anderson and his men might have experienced some of the same things, except that it was raining when they arrived:

> The signs of cultivation gradually increased as we sailed [up the Saint Paul River]. On the opposite side was a plantation of sugarcane waiving gently in a slight breeze, and looking not unlike wheat. There were patches of it in the woods, which were seen more frequently. At last we reached the place of Mr. W. The boats stopped at the foot of a broad path, or avenue, leading to a house on a rising ground. There was quite a crowd of natives before the door, with their merchandise; for Mr. W. is an important man, and had much to do with them. Unfortunately, he had gone farther up the river that day; but his wife, dressed in the usual pretty white muslin, received us pleasantly. She kindly led us to a parlor in the second story. A servant brought us water from a "cooler." Two or three other women, as neat and gentle as Mrs. W., were here. They said little, but tried to make us comfortable; for we were very warm and tired. Mrs. W. took us to a room adjoining, where, with water and basins, we were much refreshed. . . . I will note that the furniture in the room was neat and pretty, that the counterpane and pillows on the bed were snowy white, and no dust to be seen anywhere. We staid a little while in the parlor, and the ladies showed some daguerreotypes [taken by Washington, himself]. . . . After resting a little while, we took our departure. ("Home Life in Africa" 1868, 327)

9. In 1872, the Liberian legislature authorized the construction of a twenty-foot-wide road to connect Careysburg with Monrovia ("An Act to Open a Public Road from Careysburg to the City of Monrovia" 1872, 10–11). Was the road completed by the time Anderson and his company set out for Musadu?

10. Dennis was a black American settler who was the Superintendent of the community at this time (Holsoe files).

11. A "Kingjar" was a wicker container with a "hamper attached to a stout frame of sticks" that one carried on one's back with a thump around the forehead (see Johnston [1906] 1969, 1028 [photo], 1031). Anderson took eighteen kingjars. One was destined for Musadu.

12. The party stayed in Gaystown Tuesday and Wednesday, 19–20 May 1874.

13. The Queahs were Kruan-speaking people living between the Bassa to the south and the Dei to the north. The "devil plays" were local religious activities most likely accompanied by music and dancing, where the "devil" was a masked figure. The "big bush" was the high forest, which had not been cut for farms. This section of land is presumably the end of the Careysburg District, over which Dennis was Superintendent.

14. "Brought up" in this context means "arrived at."

15. Another person suggested that the government built the "blockhouse" or "stockade" of wood rather than stone (W. 1870, 371). This blockhouse was the building that the government built along the Duqueah River to house and facilitate government mission caravans (e.g., see fig. 5). The "port holes" were places from which one could shoot.

16. Palm "cabbage" grows at the top of palm and coconut trees and is the heart of the newly forming fronds. After the cabbage is taken out of the tree, it is cooked and served on rice, cassava, or whatever is available. Liberians usually only eat palm cabbage when little other food is available because its extraction involves cutting down the tree. Anderson's men did this in the situation described here. Palm cabbage has become a more common food item during the Liberian civil war.

17. As this was a government expedition, these could have been army tents (*ATL* 1870, 11).

18. The location of Pockpar's town is unknown. Anderson later estimated that it was 81 miles (130 kilometers) from Monrovia. W. S. Anderson had visited this town, calling it Pok-bah, in 1870, and his companion Allen Hooper settled there (see chap. 2).

19. It is interesting that Anderson made no mention of Gola people, who supposedly occupied the south side of the Saint Paul River in Deng and Todee. Presumably their excursions toward Gibi were the precursors of their final settlement in Deng and Todee—all part of an attempt to become middlemen in the interior trade toward the coast, as they had done in the area to the north of the Saint Paul in the area between that river and the Lofa River. In addition, it is clear that the Pessay or Kpelle at this time were much farther to the interior than they are today, and as far south as the Du River.

20. Anderson read part of the 1874 interior law to Pockpar. According to section 2, "the said Chiefs or Chieftains may have the privilege of executing deeds of cession, ceding their territory to the Republic of Liberia." The law instructed Chief Commissioners to draw up documents for the local leaders to sign, as the Commissioners and Chiefs did in Klebo in August 1874 (see chap. 2, n. 50). Anderson signed the first of many treaties with Pockpar, although he did not mention these treaties in his account. In this treaty, Pockpar reportedly ceded his land to Liberia here or between 24–30 November on his return trip (see chap. 2, 70).

21. After a week there.

22. The location of Kypah is unknown. The old man, Kypah, probably founded Kypah. W. S. Anderson visited this town four years earlier and called it Karpestown.

23. This money refers to the expenditures which Dogbar had made to support the woman or were part of a bride price.

24. The party stayed in Kypah for six days. This location is unknown. Dogbar reportedly ceded his land to Liberia under the provisions of the 1874 interior law at this time or when Anderson returned from Musadu in December between the 11th and the 14th. The towns of Beahway and Nyawora were also under his domain (see chap. 2).

25. This was an inter-Kpelle conflict, with persons from the outside (such as Zodoponga, a Gola, helping Darpella) contributing to the war.

26. This route was probably more direct, probably more closely parallel to the Saint Paul River.

27. The men are now in areas of walled towns.

28. "Poltroon" was a common word of the times that meant, among other things, "spiritless coward" (*Oxford English Dictionary,* s.v. "Poltroon," 2d ed., 1989).

29. The 18th was six days after their arrival.

30. Dogfella is listed as Fuella on p. 246. Seefray is listed as "Seaway" on p. 246 and as "Seeway" on p. 250. All of these are probably chiefs living in the area that is today called Salala chiefdom.

31. That is, the Gola came as mercenaries, having been recruited by certain chiefs in their fights against others.

32. The location of Waugi's town is unknown. This is W. S. Anderson's "Wah Gie."

33. The Haumths were probably Mende (Holsoe 1979b).

34. Zodopanga was possibly from the Gola area north of the Saint Paul River, today part of the Lofa-Gola chiefdom.

35. That is, on the north side of the Saint Paul River.

36. This seems a bit surprising, but Gola and Vai are not members of the same language family.

37. Waugi had probably purchased the war with slaves. Fahquaqua, or Fahn Kwekwe, was the ruler of the area today known as the Lofa-Gola chiefdom, north of the Saint Paul River, and was also a first cousin of Momolu Sao. Their mothers were Gola and sisters (Holsoe 1976–77, 3–6).

38. The "act of the Legislature" refers to the 1874 interior law (see chap. 2).

39. In order to trade to the coast, Waugi had to send goods through Pockpar's area.

40. The "Gibbee people" were the Bassa-speaking people living in and around Mount Gibi.

41. Anderson did not fully appreciate the desire of the Kpelle for free-trade access to the coast. Note that the Pessey and the Barline, both Kpelle speakers, were very divided at the time.

42. This contrasts with Anderson's 1868 earlier description of the almost negligible effects of war on trade and marketing when he was north of the Saint Paul River, which was a very different trade situation.

43. In 1860, two freeborn George Wadsworths (or Wardsworth) migrated to Car-

eysburg from Newberry District, North Carolina, aboard the *Mary Caroline Stevens*. One, twenty-eight years old, left Baltimore on 21 April and arrived in Monrovia on 30 June ("List of Emigrants [*M. C. Stevens*]" 1860, 140–142). The second George Wadsworth, four years younger, sailed from Baltimore on 1 November and probably landed in Monrovia during mid-December ("List of Emigrants by the *M. C. Stevens*, Nov. 1, 1860" 1860, 363–365). Dr. James Hall, the Commissioner of the American Colonization Society, was a cabin passenger on the November voyage. Another traveler on the second voyage was twenty-six-year-old Rev. T. E. Dillon from Toledo, Ohio, who closely followed the trail of the just deceased George L. Seymour to the hinterland behind Bexley twelve years later. G. W. Wardsworth was the sheriff of Careysburg in 1878 ("A Few Days at Careysburg" 1878). This G. W. was probably one of the Georges who immigrated to Careysburg in 1860 or George Jr., the son of the second George. The first George also had a son named George, but this son's middle name was Presly. Some of G. W. Wardsworth's descendants lived in Careysburg until the late 1980s. Benjamin Anderson's George Wadsworth might be the same G. W. Wardsworth. Daniel Coleman, from Kentucky, is the same man discussed in chap. 6, n. 133.

44. That is, pieces of handkerchiefs. Boway (now spelled Boweh) was the name of the chief, and Wangynah [Wanggina or Wehnita?] was the name of the town. Wangynah was probably in the area which today is part of the Sanoyea chiefdom, where Sanoyea is one of the major towns. The "direct road" is nearer to the Saint Paul River.

45. The party had traveled into a new "chiefdom."

46. Anderson reached Boway on the same day, Tuesday, 30 June.

47. Wangynah may no longer exist.

48. "Sinoya" is also spelled "Sanoyie" and "Sanoghie." Up until at least the mid-1980s, Sanoyea was the headquarters of the Sanoyea chiefdom, a Kpelle-speaking area. They covered this 9-to-10-mile (14–16 kilometers) walk in two hours and twenty minutes.

49. Seeway (earlier spelled "Seaway") was Siwi Wockpaling, the grandson of a Kpelle trader who migrated from Guinea during the late eighteenth or early nineteenth century (fig. 28). Sanoyea had shifted from a safe haven and lightly populated area in earlier times to a growing area characterized by small-scale wars by the time Anderson passed through in 1874. Sometime during the mid-nineteenth century, Seeway emerged as a powerful leader who helped bring some order and stability. He formed an alliance with other chiefs and established a confederation. Seeway became more powerful as he acquired more slaves, which he sold to the Vai along the coast. He also forced neighboring chiefdoms to pay tribute to him. He died in 1911 (Stakeman 1986, 70–77). Randolph Stakeman gives an account of Siwi's rise to authority:

> Siwi was at first simply the head of his lineage and the leader of a small area his family inhabited. Sometime after the middle of the 19th century Siwi and two other nearby lineage heads formed a mutual defense pact [probably Anderson's "Dogbar," "Fuella," and "Darpella"]. Siwi took command as war leader whenever they were threatened by attack and he directed the military operations of all three areas. He instituted a conscription program which

> made death the penalty for young men and their fathers who refused to go to war. . . . The other areas of the confederation had at first only delegated military powers to Siwi. Informants from these areas insisted that their ancestors had been Siwi's allies not his subjects. Siwi had expanded his position as a lineage leader by becoming the war leader. He used his position as a war leader to attract clients and to participate in the slave trade. He traded war captives to Vai traders from the coast who would use them as domestic slaves or sell them to neighbouring African groups. People who had heard about Siwi came to Sanoyea to become Siwi's clients. (1986, 76–77)

50. Anderson had been there five days.

51. The location of Ponafah's town is unknown; perhaps it is Fanyapolu, 7°19'N, 9°55'W.

52. These "small independent communities" came to form what today the government calls "clans," territorial areas which have had some political cohesiveness. Not all of the clans are necessarily related by kinship as in the classic anthropological definition of the term (see Fulton 1968; d'Azevedo 1989; Wylie 1989).

53. The "message" was the 1874 interior law (see chap. 2).

54. Barmaquirlla reportedly ceded his land to Liberia at this time or between 7–8 December, when Anderson was returning to Monrovia (see chap. 2). Barmaquirlla was in Nyarly country, and the chief town in Barmaquirlla was Pye ("Official Notice" 1879, in chap. 2, 70), which Anderson visited on his return.

55. Sakatah does not feature on current maps, but was in what today is the Bokomu chiefdom, a Kpelle area west of the Vai River. According to the treaty signed during Anderson's visit (see chap. 2, 70), Sakatah was the chief town in Ya Poroh country.

56. Beginning here, the account is taken from the original publication in the *Observer* (Monrovia) 2, no. 11 (11 September 1879; see also fig. 30). This tributary was the Vai River. The Saint Paul and Vai Rivers merge at 7°12'N, 9°49'W (Liberia map, Zorzor Quadrangle, I-773–A). Yves Person began to trace Anderson's journey at this point (1975, 2125–2126).

57. In the treaty signed by Popowa Keang (see chap. 2), his name is spelled Bopowa Keang.

58. Anderson was traveling from one section of Pessey country (Barmaquirlla's town) to another section of Pessey country (Ya Poroh or Sakatah), that is, from the Southern Kpelle area south of the Saint Paul River, which was considered politically different from the Bokomu Kpelle area north of the river.

59. At this time or in a situation similar to this, Anderson read the 1874 interior law to Popowa Keang. Popowa Keang reportedly ceded his land to Liberia (see chap. 2).

60. Here is an example of the use of a third party to mediate a dispute.

61. White is a sign of peace and a pure heart.

62. The King of Phanefuro purchased mercenaries to fight for him. If they did not fight for him, they would turn on the chief himself.

63. A week after arriving at Sakatah.

64. This is presumably in the Bokomu Kpelle area. According to oral traditions collected in the mid-twentieth century, the chief and soldiers were often killed in

situations like this. The women and children would be taken into slavery (Bledsoe 1980, 17).

65. "Brilliant" refers to the shiny fabric for dresses with a patterned weave in relief, which was imported into Liberia from Europe and North America.

66. Sherman and Dimery was a merchant company in Monrovia that engaged in transatlantic shipping (Cassell 1970, 262–263). According to Syfert (1977b, 230 n. 61), Reginald A. Sherman was Liberia's Secretary of War: "Sherman and Dimery owned at least six vessels which it operated from its office at Monrovia, maintained several coastal factories, and had commercial ties to the New York firm Yates and Porterfield." Akpan (1975) and Brown (1941, 135) add that Sherman and Dimery traded with firms in England, France, and Germany. J. T. Dimery was on Liberia's Board of Trade, appointed to that position by President J. J. Roberts ("Presidential Appointments" 1873, 185). This is an interesting revelation, especially since Anderson was on a government-sponsored expedition.

67. "Bahquetah" was later spelled "Bockquetah." The party crossed what today is known as the Vai River; thus it was moving from the Bokomu Kpelle area into the Barlain Kpelle area.

68. Yahtandah is later spelled Yahtanday. This is possibly Sims's "Bamaquorli" and Seymour's "Barpaley." "Pallikah" is also spelled "Kpaiyakwele" and "Kpayakole." Anderson spells this "Pallakah" as well; Sims, "Pallaka"; Seymour, "Pallaker"; and W. S. Anderson, "Polaka." "Pessey Coantry" is the Barlain Kpelle country.

69. "The Pelle or Belle" are probably the people known today as the Kpelle (Pelle) and who were also called the Pessay. If this is the correct identification, then they are definitely not Belle or Deh speakers.

70. "Stobs" are posts, stumps, or stakes.

71. Anderson had been there approximately twenty-six days.

72. "Payasangah" is also spelled "Kpowasangye." This is Sims's "Jangay" and Seymour's "Zanga."

73. This section comes from the *Observer* (Monrovia) 2, no. 12 (25 September 1879).

74. Anderson spelled this "Daffahborrah" in his first account. Daffahborrah was the chief of Salaye, 7°37'N, 9°30'W. Salaye is a Kpelle-speaking town and is today part of the Kpelle chiefdom of Lofa County. Gbonie is a Barline town, Kpelle speaking, and now also part of the Kpelle chiefdom of Lofa County.

75. Anderson had been at Gbonie six days. Anderson had been detained at Pillillay for eleven days.

76. The Saint Paul is today known in this region as the Niandi River on the Liberian maps and as the Diani (Yano) River on Guinea maps. This river also represents part of the Liberia-Guinea border. It marked the border from Barline to another part of Kpelle, called "Guerze" in today's modern prefecture of Yomou (Guinea).

77. This may be at or near the modern village of Foloionié, in Yomou, Guinea, 7°29'N, 9°23'W.

78. These are Kpelle of the Boo chiefdom (see Germain 1984, 109–110).

79. That same day, in Monrovia, Edward Blyden wrote: "Yesterday a number of men from Musardu, just in from Boporu, informed me that there are now assembled at Bopolo—which has been completely rebuilt—ten powerful Chiefs—four Moham-

medan and six Pagan—engaged in negotiations for the settling of the country, which has for a long time been disturbed" (Blyden to William Coppinger, 7 September 1874, in Lynch 1978, 172–173).

80. Anderson later spelled this "Pahya" and "Pah-ye" in the treaty (see chap. 2).

81. They actually walked north and then northwest.

82. For pictures of the "remains" of Kpaiye's "mud fortifications," see Atherton (1970–71, 109–110). In a later letter, referring to his journal, Anderson also wrote in 1903: "Pahya, Weimor Country. Pahya is a large town surrounded by 3 concentric thick walls made of a dobe and flat granite rocks mixed, the walls being 26 feet high, 8 and 9 feet at the bottom and tapering off towards the top. Here the prairie lands begin and the trees are disappearing" (see chap. 2, 84). On his return trip, Anderson said that Pahya was in Pessey (Kpelle) country. The latter seems to be the correct designation.

83. This branch is probably the Bolo-Va, at 7°26'N, 9°7'W (*Guinea: Official Standard Names* 1965, 19). Anderson had thus recrossed the Saint Paul River and was now on the north side of it.

84. They waited in Pahya for six weeks.

85. The *Observer* (Monrovia) 2 no. 13 (9 October 1879) issue has not been located by us, so this section is taken from Starr's 1912 edition, pages 23–27.

86. This was King Kryneseh, who reportedly ceded Pahye and his "district" to Liberia during his meeting with Anderson (see chap. 2).

87. Unlike Anderson's naming of Capehart, who treated Anderson poorly, Anderson did not identify the "American" thief in this case because of the good service that he later rendered to the expedition.

88. N'Zappa was the capital of Gizima (Person 1975, 2125).

89. This region is called Kpelle or Guerzé today.

90. The Waima Loma.

91. Bockamu was probably revisited by Anderson on his return when he called it Yokabou.

92. "Pynyah" is Seymour's "Parmer."

93. From Anderson's 1868–69 trip.

94. Anderson estimated that Gubbewallah was 135 miles (216 kilometers) from Monrovia. The actual distance is about 180 miles (290 kilometers). Boe was visited by Seymour (called "Boo" or "Boa") and by Anderson in 1868. Ziggah-Porrahzue controlled a crossing of the Saint Paul or Diani.

95. Gubbewallah is another large walled town on the Saint Paul River itself—this river is about twenty feet wide, with a suspension bridge on wickerwork swinging over it. The last of Anderson's thermometers apparently broke in Gubbewallah. On 31 October, the weekend before Anderson left Gubbewallah, a "tornado" from the east hit the area (see chap. 2, fig. 7).

96. Anderson had, in fact, visited not just Goboèla, but also Koiama Tongoro and Boo.

97. Anderson stayed in Gubbewallah for eight days. See chap. 5 for Anderson's earlier meeting with Jebbue. See fig. 18 for the photograph of a defiant Jebbue.

98. The "Vukkah hills" are the Simandugu range, or the Fon-Going hills.

99. "Pallezarrah" was spelled earlier as "Pellazarrah."

100. "Yukkah" was earlier spelled "Vukkah."

101. Note that between 1868–69 and 1874, Vukkah, or Foma, once on the northern borders of Loma country, had evidently become predominantly Manding.

102. "Nyammah" is Person's "Nyama Kamara," the Manding chief of Simandugu related to the Loma chiefs (1968, 1:270–283, 433–444; 1975, 2126).

103. Person called this "the war of the Kamara," where many Kamara, such as Nyammah, resisted Sargee's, or Saji Kamara's, ambitions of empire (1968, 1:431).

104. Nyammah's "royal kinsmen" were the Kamara, descendants of Musadu's ancient Chief Foningama. Nyammah, Saji, and Kaman Kekula of Kuankan also descended from Foningama. According to Yves Person, young Saji forced Nyammah Kamara, the chief of Simandu, to flee from the Pic de Tibe to Foma as Saji was trying to establish his supremacy among the Kamara (Person 1968, 1:270–283, 285, 433–444; 1975, 2126).

105. The "Boozie country" is the modern Loma or Toma country.

106. See the 1868 letter reproduced at the end of chap. 5.

107. This section comes from the *Observer* (Monrovia) 2, no. 14 (23 October 1879).

108. This is in contrast to Anderson's statement that he could see a long way when he passed through this area in December of 1868.

109. We have not been able to identify "Vokkadu" in this area. "Vokkadu" may be a misprint of "Yockkadu," modern Diakolidu, which is just west of Beyla (see Person 1975, 2125).

110. Actually, 9 November was a Monday. "Vomfeedolla" is Vafin Dole.

111. This is the 1868 letter reproduced in chap. 5.

112. This is the 1874 interior law summarized in chap. 2.

113. Anderson is referring to Henry Wesley Dennis, an Americo-Liberian born in the U.S. state of Maryland, who was the Agent for the American Colonization Society in Monrovia at the time (Dunn and Holsoe 1985, 57).

114. "Blamer Sissy" is Ibrahim Sissi.

115. Three years later, Mr. James Irvine informed the Society of Arts of Liverpool that "The traveller . . . [Anderson] had in his bag a dozen Arabic Testaments: these, by intimation posted on the townhall he proposed to distribute, and in less than hafl [half] an hour they were all off his hands" (Crüwell 1878, 135).

116. This was one of five editions of the complete Arabic Bible that the American Bible Society and the British Foreign Bible Society published between 1867 and 1872 in New York and London. The 1867 New York edition, which Indiana University library holds, is 24.8 centimeters by 17 centimeters by 7.2 centimeters (Maculay 1871, 243; Jessup 1869; Darlow and Moule 1963, 72–75; see also Makdissi 1997).

117. The "Beginning," Genesis, chronicles the account of creation and stories of persons such as Adam, Noah, and Abraham, whom Muslims regard as prophets (e.g., see Launay 1992, 172–173; Conrad 1999b, 69–70, 99–100). There are similarities between the biblical and qur'anic accounts, so this section of the Bible would have been familiar to the people in Musadu.

118. "Soudan" is from *Bilad al-Sudan* (Arabic), "the land of the black people." Anderson spelled it the French way. Early Arab geographers called the land south of the Sahara where the blacks lived "Sudan."

119. Edward S. Morris was a Philadelphian who was a midcentury backer of agricultural development in Liberia. This newspaper was printed in the United States and was widely circulated in Liberia ("A Liberian Newspaper" 1873, 121). The issues of the *Liberia Advocate* which published this story could not be located.

120. This is probably John W. Good of Washington, D.C., who sailed to Monrovia from New York aboard the barque *Mendi* on 23 May 1859 when he was twenty-six years old. Accompanying John was his twenty-two-year-old wife, Isabella, and his one-and-one-half-year-old daughter, E. L. Jane. John and Isabella were born free and belonged to the Episcopal Church. John was a "carpenter" and had a "poor education" like his wife ("List of Emigrants from New York to Liberia" 1859, 301).

121. This is not unique to the interior. See Holsoe (1977) for the Vai.

122. Blyden lived in Beirut for three months in 1866 to learn more Arabic (Lynch 1967, 47–48).

123. The "beginning of the dries" probably occurred between mid-October and late December 1873. Recent oral testimony of Saji's siege provides the essential information that Anderson recorded in 1874. A grandson and great-grandson of Vafin Dole said that Saji advanced on Musadu from the east, encircled the walls of Musadu, and attacked the market on market day (Geysbeek 2002). Also, the people used horse and cow dung to cook with.

124. Yves Person was told that the messengers who escaped were Suleimani Dole and Suleimani Dukule (1968, 1:288). Recent testimony is similar, saying that the escapees were a Dole, a Dukule, and a Sissi (Geysbeek field notes).

125. In 1879, Ibrahima Sissi's envoy who went to Monrovia boasted that Ibrahima could muster a cavalry of ten thousand and many more infantry (see chap. 2, 75). Samori Touré began his military career in the Sissi army during the 1850s, so he probably patterned his cavalry after Sissi's (Law 1980, 12, 33).

126. Today, people often call him Gbangunò Saji.

127. This section is from the *Observer* (Monrovia) 2, no. 15 (13 November 1879).

128. "Bopora" is modern-day Bopolu.

129. Anderson quotes from Ephesians 4:14 here—"[not] carried about with every wind of doctrine" (King James Version).

130. Could "Cidee" be "Sidibe," a Fulbe name? Some of the Manding and Fulbe in northeast Guinea have strong ties through intermarriage, the latter being called the "Fula-Mandingo" by the Manding. So, it is not inconceivable that Sissi could have sent a trusted Fulbe commander to represent him. If Dah Cidee was not in Musadu when Anderson first arrived, he was probably in one of the surrounding towns and returned shortly after Anderson's arrival. Yves Person could not identify him (Person 1975, 2126).

131. The "Imaum" was perhaps Salihu Shereef (see chap. 5, "Appendix").

132. This section is from the *Observer* (Monrovia) 2, no. 16 (27 November 1879).

133. This is Daniel Coleman. Slaves and freed blacks in Kentucky used horses on farms. Some also raised, trained, and rode horses on horse plantations (Alvey 1992, 146–148). Coleman would have learned how to break "rude and evil horses" in the United States if he had worked with horses in Kentucky. Coleman boarded the *Mary Caroline Stevens* on 12 November 1857 at the age of nineteen and settled in Careysburg. Coleman was among eight other people of the same last name whom Thomas

Coleman emancipated ("List of Emigrants by the *Mary Caroline Stevens,* 3d voyage" 1857, 355–356). Benjamin Anderson later said in this account that Coleman was from Kentucky. The 1850 U.S. census does not list a Thomas Coleman in Christian County, Kentucky (Jackson 1990, 193). The 1840 census lists two "free white persons" under the name Thomas Coleman in Christian County who owned male slaves of Daniel Coleman's age involved in agriculture (Population Schedules 1840).

134. Mounted horsemen like this were later known in Liberia later in relation to Samory as "*siafa*" or "*sofa,*" with the meaning in Manding probably "horse father" or cavalry member (see Conrad 1999b, 200).

135. "Ekoonah" ("E-koonah") is *Ni sooma,* or "good (*ni*) morning (*sooma*)," in Konyakan (Cutler, with Dwyer 1981a, 45). In Vai, this would be *Ya kune,* which would seem to come closer to the text.

136. That is, to wait.

137. We suppose that this letter is no longer extant. This seems to be another letter like the 1868 letter that Vafin Dole wrote rather than a treaty.

138. In 1903, Anderson published "An Itinerary Table of the Exploration of [the] Journey from Musahdu to Monrovia, made in 1874" (see fig. 8, chap. 2, 83) to help substantiate the fact that he went to Musadu. Much of the additional information about Anderson's return journey to Monrovia that follows in the notes comes from fig. 8. According to the chart, Anderson left Musadu at seven o'clock on the morning of 17 November (not 16) and arrived at Vukkah at six o'clock that evening. Anderson estimated that they walked 30 miles (48 kilometers) that day. The shortest actual distance is 27 miles (43 kilometers). The party stayed at this village the night of Friday, 6 November, through Saturday, 7 November.

139. Concerning iron ore: Anderson was not wrong about this, but it is uncertain whether coal is indeed found here. It has not been knowingly exploited, and relatively little coal has been found in West Africa (Church 1980, 143–144). Anderson described iron smelting with charcoal, not coal (see chap. 5).

140. As it has been. See chap. 5, 204 n. 158.

141. It would seem that this was a simple form of a balafon, a kind of xylophone.

142. This section comes from the *Observer* (Monrovia) 2, no. 17 (11 December 1879). This "Mandingo Chief" could have been a Kamara who was fleeing from Saji during the Kamara war. This incident suggests the extent to which ethnic boundaries were often irrelevant to local politics. Here we have the splitting off of a faction within a Manding region, and one part—as armed capable warriors—seeking asylum in Loma country, presumably as warriors. There are many instances in Kissi regions where the arrival of such warrior strangers was important to the villages.

143. According to Anderson, they walked 25 miles (40 kilometers) that day, from Vukkah to Pellezarrah. Actually, the party left Pellezarrah on the 19th.

144. Dowilnyah signed "an agreement" with Liberia on 20 November 1874. According to the summary of the treaty, the Liberians and the Waima Boozie [Loma] were to "live in peace with each other and Dowilnyah would not hinder trade through his country" (see chap. 2, 70; Holsoe 1976–77, 5).

145. The Saint Paul is called the "Diani" here.

146. The party stopped at Yokabu, or Bockamu, on the way to Musadu. In his 1903 itinerary, Anderson wrote that he left Pynyah at six o'clock in the morning and

arrived at Tornu, or Tormu, at four o'clock in the afternoon (see chap. 2). Tornu, or Tormu, is apparently the same as Yokabu. It is probably modern Makobou, 8°1'N, 9°18'W. Sappah is also called "N'Zappa" here.

147. They traversed from Loma to Kpelle territory at this point in their journey. The area around N'Zappa by the beginning of the twentieth century would be considered Kpelle or Guerze speaking. As for the name "Bassyahwasey," Anderson earlier wrote "Bussayeh," which is probably the modern Bodezie. The branch of the Saint Paul River that is near Bodezie is the Wunia or Moume River, now known as the Oule River.

148. "Krymeseh" is earlier spelled "Kryneseh."

149. Anderson also spelled "Pattahya" "Arranya."

150. "Pallakah" is probably modern-day Kpayekwele, Anderson's earlier "Pallika."

151. Earlier, "Bockquetah" was called "Bahquetah," modern Gbakoita. Anderson, in his itinerary, estimated that they covered 20 miles (32 kilometers) that day, from Jowah to Bockquetah. "Seetroeebo" was written earlier by Anderson as "Seekokibo." Possibly, "Pye" is the modern-day Piata (7°13'N, 9°46'W), which is probably Seymour's "Partargea."

152. Pye was Barmaquirlla's main town (see chap. 2). On his first encounter on their way "up," Anderson wrote "Popowa Keang."

153. "Baryta's town" possibly refers to Wawantah, as in Anderson's upward journey.

154. They also passed Ponafah's town. The location of Darpella's town is unknown. Anderson did not visit this town on the way to Musadu.

155. Anderson stayed at Dogbar's town on the way up from 12 to 18 June, but he had also stayed at Kypa's town—is this a joining of the two names?

156. Capehart and some of his men had stolen some "fowls" from George Simpson, who lived just a three-day walk from Monrovia, so they chose to stop here. Capehart probably wanted to avoid Simpson. It was at Waugi's town that they had initially abandoned the expedition.

They left Dogbar at six o'clock in the morning and stopped at their first encampment at three o'clock in the afternoon. They had crossed this "bush" area from 25 to 28 May. This was after an estimated walk of 30 miles (48 kilometers) that day. They left at five o'clock the next morning and reached Hind's Creek twelve hours later.

157. They left Hind's Creek at five o'clock the next morning and arrived at Simpson's town, for an estimated 25-mile (40-kilometer) journey that day. They had last left there on 23 May.

158. Anderson and his entourage left Simpson's town at six o'clock in the morning and reached Augustus Washington's home at White Plains at five o'clock in the afternoon. Anderson wrote that this was a 48-mile (77-kilometer) journey. It is hard to believe that they did this in a day. Anderson said that they walked 25 miles (40 kilometers) the next day, the journey being from 6 May to 17 December 1874, or 227 days in length, and mentioning 61 days of actual travel (forty-one days outward and twenty-one days on the return).

159. "Krymeseh" is Kryneseh of Pahya.

160. This section is from the *Observer* (Monrovia) 2, no. 18 (25 December 1879).

161. The direct route from Monrovia to Musadu is actually about 230 miles (370 kilometers). Anderson also estimated that Musadu was "430 zig-zag miles" (691 kilometers) from Monrovia, based on the route that he took.

162. Daniel Beams left Norfolk, Virginia, aboard the *Linda Stewart,* on 27 November 1852. Beams was twenty years old at the time, and he traveled with his father, Francis. Both men were Catholics and were born free ("List of Emigrants [*Linda Stewart*]" 1853, 26–27). William Spencer Anderson was also on this voyage. Beams was President Payne's Secretary of the Treasury when Benjamin Anderson went on his first voyage to Musadu (Dunn and Holsoe 1985, 137). This "paper" was presumably a treaty that Seeway signed with the Liberian government. "W. S. Anderson" is William Spencer Anderson (see chap. 2), who went on his journey into the interior during the tenure of President Edward James Roye, 1870–71.

163. Vomfudolla is Vafin Dole.

164. The "Resolution of the Legislature" is the 1874 interior law (see chap. 2).

165. The map Anderson refers to is his 1879 map (fig. 27). Anderson supplied some of the calculations that he used in 1903 when he partially showed how he derived the longitude of Musadu and Bonya (Gbonie) (see chap. 2, fig. 7).

166. This may be a reference to one of several denominations of Rix dollars from Ceylon (now Sri Lanka) that filtered into the Liberian economy during the nineteenth century (Krause and Mishler 1982, 1062–1062; see Parsons 1950, 14). Rix dollars were also used in the Gambia and in Senegal (Curtin 1975, 258).

7. The Journeys and the Interior

1. "Mandingo" and "Manding" are respectively the English and French forms of the same word. Scholars generally accept Manding as the cover term for these three people groups. The term "Mandingo" is more problematic because Liberians and others often call all Muslims or persons from the savannah "Mandingo," even many who are not Northern Mande–speaking Manding peoples. The type of Manding whom Benjamin Anderson encountered from Monrovia to Musadu were the Maniyaka. The subset of Maniyaka who lived in and around Musadu were the Konyaka (Dalby 1971, 2; d'Azevedo 1994, 199–201; Vydrine 1999, 9; Geysbeek 2002).

2. For debates concerning Vai history, see Hair 1968a; Holsoe 1967, 1974; Dapper [1668] 1670, 379 ff.; [1668] 1686, 252 ff.; Jones 1983b; Person 1971, 675–676; Jones 1981; Lamp 1983; Massing 1985.

3. According to a man called Harrison, who claimed to have traveled inland from Cape Mount in c. 1780, and who related his story to the to the Governor of Sierra Leone, Ludlum, in 1808, he (Harrison) walked through Gurah (Gola), Candoh (Condo), Beysee, Plai (Kpelle), Boosee (Boozie), Gissee (Kissi), etc. (Hair 1962, 220). According to Hair, "The Gbunde and the Loma are today also known as the 'Kimbuzi' and the 'Buzi.'" The term "Buzi" was thus presumably current among traders and Vai people on the coast, whom Harrison was living among.

4. This echoes accounts given to Schwab (1947, 19) and Germann (1933, 12). Many thanks to Christian Højbjerg for providing references.

5. "*He-ahu*" is the Bandi word for "Mende," and "*Hulo*" is the Gola and Vai term for "Mende" (Holsoe 1979b, 21).

6. Salayie is located in the modern-day Palama clan and Kpelle chiefdom, in Lofa County.

7. The Vukkah Mountains were also called the Foma to the Manding (see chap. 5). "Vukkah" is the Loma term.

8. Seymour's low and high ratios were 1 to 27 and 1 to 6; Anderson's were 1 to 2.3 and 1 to 4.6. Seymour and Anderson's combined average total was 7,613 houses to 28,013 occupants—1 to 3.68, with the lower and higher total estimates ranging from 3.87 to 4.11.

9. Slightly varied ratios such as 1 to 3.5 and 1 to 5 could have been used to calculate the numbers of people and houses that Sims, Seymour, and Anderson did not provide. These represent more accurate numbers than the across-the-board 1 to 4 ratio that is used, but these writers did not provide enough information to apply staggered ratios for the towns missing one of the categories of numbers. However, because the three explorer's numbers, like Porter's, generally reflect the trend that the occupant-household ratio probably differed in areas that had a greater or lesser number of homes, these differences are noted in the table with less than (−) or more than (+) symbols in front of each of the numbers. All of the estimated figures on this table which are placed in italics could differ by as much as 20 percent or more. Ratios are only listed where the writers provided complete numbers for the population and number of homes.

10. For significant contributions of women to warfare and political action, see Bledsoe (1980) on the Kpelle, Day (1994) on the Mende, and Conrad (1999a) on the Manding.

11. For instance, see Fulton (1972), Bellman (1984), and Bledsoe (1984) on the Kpelle, Holsoe (1980) and Monts (1984) on the Vai, d'Azevedo (1980) on the Gola, McNaughton (1988) on the Manding, Leopold (1991, chap. 5) and Højbjerg (1999) on the Loma, and Little (1965, 1966), Jones (1983b), Kalous (1995), and Ellis (1999) in general.

12. Djobba Kamara interviewed Kewulen and Jala Kamara in Kuankan in December 1985. During the interview, Jala Kamara, the chief of Kuankan, showed Djobba the chief's hat. Jala said that Jaka Kaman had worn the hat, and that it had been passed down to the succeeding chiefs. This was allegedly the same hat that was passed down to Foningama Kamara, the chief of Musadu, much earlier (Geysbeek 2002).

13. Wata Mammadi Kamara's testimony comes in a cassette tape recording that Geysbeek purchased from Amara Sissi in Monrovia in 1992.

14. For more information about the important role that Musadu and many of these other towns had in teaching and disseminating Islam, see Morrison (1897, 90), Marchard (1897, 105), Chatelier (1899, 128–129, 162), Arcin (1911, 90), Le Long (1949, 24–25, 108), Hopewell (1958, 45–48, 84–90), Person (1968, 2:136; 1979, 263), and Rivière (1969, 321–323).

15. Torkel Holsoe, a forestry advisor to the Liberian government in the 1950s, planted kola trees along the boundaries of the national forest reserves, thinking that they might be a way to keep the boundaries brushed.

16. For early-nineteenth-century descriptions of Manding leatherworkers in Li-

beria, see Winterbottom ([1803] 1969, 91–92), Ashmun (1827b, 82–83), and Todson (1840, 82–83). See Frank (1998) for an overview and illustrations.

17. For discussions about the historical role of Mande-speaking women in pottery making and farming, see La Violette (1995) and Frank (1998).

18. For examples of gambling in Liberia, which included spinning ivory, playing the popular game of *warri,* and throwing cowry shells, see Whitehurst (1836, 109–110), Harris (1865–66, 30), and Schwab (1947, 159–160, fig. 100).

19. In addition to the sources cited in the above paragraphs, we have also drawn from the following pages to provide information about firearms and projectiles: Legassick (1966, 100, 104), Kea (1971, 197–205), White (1971, 174–176), Inikori (1977, 355–357), Richards (1980, 48, 53), Headrick (1981, 85–107), Müller (1981, 86–87, 118–120), McNaughton (1988, 35, plates 28–30), Smith (1989, 80–85), Conrad (1990, 62–63), and Alpern (1995, 20–22). We thank John Wood (personal communication, November 1995) and James Harbeck (personal communication, April 1996) for giving practical descriptions about the production and use of firearms.

20. See also Johnston ([1906] 1969, 672–673; 655–659) and Strong (1930, 194–196).

21. The villages mentioned here are Boo, to the east, and Kotia—now abandoned—to the west.

Bibliography

Unless otherwise indicated, most of the Liberian newspapers cited herein can be found in the C. Abayomi Cassell Collection and the Albert Porte Papers at the Center for Research Libraries in Chicago and the Maryland State Colonization Society Papers at Michigan State University.

Several other primary sources come from the *Observer* (Monrovia), the dispatches from the United States consuls in Monrovia, the notes from the Liberian delegation in the United States to the Department of State, and the records of the Department of State relating to the internal affairs of Liberia. The dispatches, notes, and records are from the National Archives (National Archives and Records Service, General Services Administration) in Washington, D.C. These sources are housed at several institutions, including Michigan State University.

Abbreviations

AR	*African Repository (and Colonial Journal)*
ARACS	*Annual Report of the American Colonization Society*
ATL	*Acts of the Legislature of the Republic of Liberia*
JAH	*Journal of African History*
LH	*Liberia Herald*
LSJ	*Liberian Studies Journal*
MCJ	*Maryland Colonization Journal*
MSCSP	Maryland State Colonization Society Papers
NYCJ	*New-York Colonization Journal*

A. 1789. "Clayashland." *Observer* (Monrovia) 2, no. 12 (25 September).

Abraham, Arthur. 1969. "Some Suggestions on the Origins of Mende Chiefdoms." *Sierra Leone Studies* 25:30–36.

———. 1978. *Mende Government and Politics under Colonial Rule: A Historical Study of Political Change in Sierra Leone.* Freetown: Sierra Leone University Press.

Abun-Nasr, Jamil M. 1987. *A History of the Maghrib in the Islamic Period.* Cambridge: Cambridge University Press.

"Accessions to the Library." 1870. *The Journal of the Royal Geographical Society* 40: xciii.

"According to the Official Returns." 1853. *LH* 3, no. 20 (24 May): 79. Also in *ATL* (April 1857), in *The Statute Laws of the Republic of Liberia.* Monrovia, Liberia: G. Killian, Printer.

Act Authorizing the Appropriation of $3000.00 for Exploring and Opening Roads into the Interior of the Several Counties. 1857. *ATL* (December 1856, January 1857, April 1857), in the MSCSP, reel 31, 195–196.

Act Divorcing John B. and Otillia Julien Jordan. 1859. *ATL* (December 1857–58), 46–47. Monrovia, Liberia: G. Killian, Printer, Liberia Herald Office.

Act Supplementary to an Act, Entitled an Act Authorizing the Circulation of Copper Coin, and Making the Same a Circulating Tender in This Republic. 1857. *ATL* (December 1856, January 1857, April 1857), in the MSCSP, reel 31.

Act to Amend an Act Authorizing the Establishment of a Uniform Currency. 1857. *ATL* (December 1856, January 1857, April 1857), in the MSCSP, reel 31.

Act to Open a Public Road from Careysburg to the City of Monrovia. 1872. *ATL* (1871–72), 10–11. Monrovia, Liberia: L. R. Leone, Printer, Republican Office.

Adam, J. 1951. "Noms de clan en pays Toma (Guinée Française)." *Première Conférence Internationale des Africanistes de l'Ouest* 2:95.

"Adventures in Life—Exploration Tour." 1856, 1857. *LH* (no. 1) 6, no. 18 (3 December 1856): 15; (no. 3) 7, no. 1 (7 January 1857): 3.

"Affairs in Liberia." 1871. *AR* 47, no. 8:252–253.

"Affairs in Liberia." 1872. *AR* 48, no. 10:309–311.

"Affairs in Liberia." 1873. *AR* 49, no. 1:21–23.

"Africa." 1861. *Home and Foreign Record* 12, no. 2:45.

"The African Coast to the Windward of Liberia." 1827. *AR* 3, no. 8:241–248.

"African Exploring Expedition." 1859. *NYCJ* 9, no. 10.

"African League." 1910. *African League* 6, no. 1 (July): 6.

"African League." 1918. *African League* 20, no. 6 (December): 4.

"African Literature." 1871. *AR* 47, no. 4:113–115. Also in *Liberia Register* (24 December 1870) and reprinted in Scheiffelin [1871] 1974, 69–73, with the full text of a letter in Arabic by Ibrahima Kabawee.

Akpan, M. B. 1973. "Black Imperialism: Americo-Liberian Rule over the African Peoples of Liberia, 1841–1964." *The Canadian Journal of African Studies* 7, no. 2:217–236.

———. 1975. "The Liberian Economy in the Nineteenth Century: The State of Agriculture and Commerce." *LSJ* 6, no. 1:1–24.

Ali, A. Yusuf, translation and commentary. [1934] 1977. *The Holy Qur'an.* United States: Muslim Student Association.

Alldridge, T. J. 1901. *The Sherbro and Its Hinterland.* London: Macmillan and Co., Limited; New York: Macmillan Co.

Allen, William H. 1878. "The Elevation of a Race and the Redemption of a Continent." *AR* 46, no. 3:65–71.

de Almada, André Alvares. [c. 1594] 1984. *Brief Treatise on the Rivers of Guinea.* Translated and annotated by P. E. Hair. Liverpool: University of Liverpool.

Alpern, Stanley B. 1992. "The European Introduction of Crops into West Africa in Precolonial Times." *History in Africa* 19:13–43.

———. 1995. "What Africans Got for Their Slaves: A Master List of European Trade Goods." *History in Africa* 22:5–43.

Alvey, R. Gerald. 1992. *Kentucky Blue Grass*. Jackson: University Press of Mississippi.

"Amounts Subscribed by Citizens of the City of Monrovia to the Exploring Expedition for 1858, under the Conduct of George L. Seymour, of Grand Bassa County." 1858. *AR* 34, no. 5:131–132.

"Anderson and His Detractors." 1903. *West African Mail* 1, no. 31 (30 October): 804. Republished in the *Liberia Recorder* 6, no. 2 (28 November 1903): 6.

Anderson, Benjamin J. K. 1870a–f. "The Country East of Liberia." *AR* 46, no. 5 (1870a, 132–145); 46, no. 6 (1870b, 162–174); 46, no. 7 (1870c, 195–204); 46, no. 8 (1870d, 226–233); 46, no. 9 (1870e, 258–266); 46, no. 10 (1870f, 297–301).

———. 1870g. *Narrative of a Journey to Musardu, the Capital of the Western Mandingoes,* with "Appendix to Benj. Anderson's Journal to Musardu." New York: S. W. Green, Printer.

———. 1879a–g. "Narrative of the Expedition Despatched to Musahdu, by the Liberian Government in 1874, under Benj. Anderson Esqr." *Observer* (Monrovia) 2, no. 11 (11 September 1879a); 2, no. 12 (25 September 1879b); 2, no. 14 (23 October 1879c); 2, no. 15 (13 November 1879d); 2, no. 16 (27 November 1879e); 2, no. 17 (11 December 1879f); 2, no. 18 (25 December 1879g).

———. 1885. "Letter from Hon. Benjamin Anderson (9 July 1884)." *AR* 61, no. 1:29–30.

———. 1899. "Reminiscences of Liberia's National Anthem." *The New Africa* (August).

———. 1903a. "Anderson Did Go to Musahdu." *LR* 5, no. 22–23 (29 August): 10–12.

———. 1903b. "Mr. Anderson's Second Reply." *LR* 6, no. 2 (28 November): 7–8.

———. 1903c. "Prof. Anderson's Reply to Captain d'Ollone: THE OBJECTIVE POINT." *LR* 6, no. 3 (19 December): 6–7.

———. 1912. *Narrative of the Expedition Despatched to Musahdu by the Liberian Government under Benjamin J. K. Anderson, Sr. Esquire in 1874*. Edited by Frederick Starr. Monrovia, Liberia: College of West Africa Press.

———. 1971. *Narrative of a Journey to Musardu, the Capital of the Western Mandingoes [1870], Together with Narrative of the Expedition Despatched to Musahdu . . . in 1874*. Edited by Humphrey J. Fisher. London: Frank Cass and Company.

Anderson, Benjamin J. K, and Son [Benjamin J. K Anderson, Jr.]. 1892. Anderson and Anderson Jr. to Ezekiel E. Smith, 17 June. *Liberia* 1 (November): 25–30.

Anderson, Captain B. J. K. [Jr.]. 1911. "Speeches That Notified Dossen and Dennis." *African League* 12, no. 9 (March): 1.

Anderson, Earle. 1952. *Liberia: America's African Friend.* Chapel Hill: University of North Carolina Press.

Anderson, W. S. 1866. "A Liberian's Visit to Bopora." *AR* 47, no. 11:338–340.

"Annexation of Medina." 1880. *AR* 56, no. 4:55–56.

"The Annexation of the Interior of the Kingdom of Medina." 1879. *Observer* (Monrovia) 2, no. 12 (25 September).

"Anniversary of Liberian Independence." 1881. *AR* 57, no. 10:135–136.

"Annual Meeting of the Massachusetts Colonization Society." 1846. *AR* 22, no. 7:225–227.

"Annual Message of President Roye." 1871. *AR* 47:98–103.

Arcin, André. 1911. *Histoire de la Guinée Française.* Paris: Challamel.

Arnoldi, Mary Jo. 1995. "Crowning Glories: The Head and Hair." In *Crowning Achievements: African Arts of Dressing the Head,* edited by Mary Jo Arnoldi and Christine Mullen Kreamer, 53–68. Los Angeles: Fowler Museum of Cultural History, University of California.

Arnoldi, Mary Jo, and Kate Ezra. 1992. "Sama Ba: The Elephant in Bamana Art." In *Elephants: The Animal and Its Ivory in African Culture,* edited by Doran H. Ross, 99–111. Los Angeles: Fowler Museum of Cultural History, University of California.

"Arrival of the General Pierce." 1856. *AR* 32, no. 8:228–229.

"Arrival of the Golconda." 1868. *AR* 44, no. 10:308–309.

Arthington, Robert. 1873. "Liberia to the Niger." *AR* 49, no. 8:255.

Ashmun, J. 1827a. "Curiosities from Liberia." *AR* 3, no. 9:272–275.

———. 1827b. "Leather Dressing." *AR* 3, no. 3:82–84.

———. 1830. "Map of the West Coast of Africa from Sierra Leone to Cape Palmas: Including the Colony of Liberia." *AR* 5, no. 2.

Atherton, John H. 1970–71. "Liberian Prehistory." *LSJ* 3, no. 2:83–110.

ATL (1857–58). 1858. Monrovia, Liberia: G. Killian, Printer, Liberia Herald Office.

ATL (1857–61). 1862. Monrovia, Liberia: G. Killian, Printer, Liberia Herald Office.

ATL (1869–70). 1870. Monrovia, Liberia: G. Killian, Printer, Liberia Herald Office.

ATL (1870–71). 1871. Monrovia, Liberia: L. R. Leone, Printer, Republican Office.

ATL (1871–72). 1872. Monrovia, Liberia: L. R. Leone, Printer, Republican Office.

ATL (1873–74). 1874. Monrovia, Liberia: T. W. Howard, Printer, Government Printing Office.

ATL (1875–76). 1876. Monrovia, Liberia: T. W. Howard, Printer, Government Printing Office.

ATL (1878–79). 1879. Monrovia, Liberia: T. W. Howard, Printer, Government Printing Office.

ATL (1882–83). 1883. Monrovia, Liberia: T. W. Howard, Printer, Government Printing Office.

"The Attack on Heddington." 1840. *AR* 16, no. 13:194–197. Originally published in the *New York Journal of Commerce.*

Austin, James C. 1964. *Artemus Ward.* New York: Twayne Publishers.

Austin, Ralph, ed. 1999. *In Search of Sunjata: The Mande Oral Epic as History, Literature, and Performance.* Bloomington: Indiana University Press.

B., H. D. 1878. "The Streets of Monrovia." *Observer* (Monrovia) 1, no. 6 (26 September).

Bailleul, Père Charles. 1981. *Petit dictionnaire: Bambara-Français, Français-Bambara.* England: Avebury Publishing Company.

Barclay, Arthur. 1911. *Message of the President of the Republic of Liberia, Nineteen Hundred and Ten,* 1–32. Monrovia, Liberia: Government Printing Office. Found in the Svend E. Holsoe Collection, Indiana University.

"The Bark *Mendi* and Her Emigrants." 1859. *AR* 35, no. 10:300–301.

"The Barline Country." 1870. *AR* 46, no. 10:315–317.

[Barta, Mohammad]. 1870. "Appendix to Benj. Anderson's Journey to Musadu . . . 1868." Translated by E. W. Blyden (with Arabic text). New York: Lithographic, Engraving, and Printing Company. Also in Schieffelin [1871] 1974, 129–134 (with Arabic text and English translation); and in the *Liberia Recorder* 6, no. 8 (26 March 1904): 9–10.

Bassett, Thomas J., and Philip W. Porter. 1991. " 'From the Best Authorities': The Mountains of Kong in the Cartography of West Africa." *JAH* 32, no. 3: 367–413.

Bazin, H. [1906] 1965. *Dictionnaire Bambara-Français.* Ridgewood, N.J.: Gregg Press.

Bazin, Jean. 1974. "War and Servitude in Segou." *Economy and Society* 3, no. 2:107–143.

"Beautiful Manuscripts from Negroes in Africa." 1863. *AR* 39, no. 1:19–21.

Beavogui, Siafa. 1973–74. "Les relations historiques entre le pays Manding et le pays Loma, des origines à l'implantation coloniale." [Guinea]: D.E.S. IPGAN.

Becker-Donner, E. 1940. *Hinterland Liberia.* New York: A.M.S. Press.

Beete, Alhaji Ibrahim. 1993. Interviewed by Baba Dole and Tim Geysbeek in Musadu on 9 December. Transcribed and translated by Faliku Sanoe in Monrovia in 1994.

Behrendt, John C., and Cletus S. Wotorson. 1974. "Total-Count Gamma Radiation Map of the Bopolu Quadrangle, Liberia." Washington, D.C.: U.S. Government Printing Office.

Belcher, Max (photographer), Svend E. Holsoe, and Bernard L. Herman (texts), Rodger P. Kingston (afterword). 1988. *Land and Life Remembered: Americo-Liberian Folk Architecture.* Athens and London: University of Georgia Press.

Belcher, Stephen. 1999. *Epic Traditions of Africa.* Bloomington: Indiana University Press.

Bellman, Beryl L. 1984. *The Language of Secrecy: Symbols and Metaphors in Poro Ritual.* New Brunswick, N.J.: Rutgers University Press.

Benjamin, George J. 1979. *Edward W. Blyden: Messiah of Black Revolution.* New York: Vantage Press.

Bennedict, S. 1843. Bennedict to Mr. Phelps, 4 March. *AR* 19, no. 8: 233–234.

Benson, Stephen A. 1852. Benson to the editor. *LH* 3, no. 9:34.

———. 1858a. Benson to the Citizens of Liberia, 11 January. *AR* 34, no. 5:131.

———. 1858b. Benson to R. Gurley, 6 February, in "Latest from Liberia." *AR* 34, no. 5:130–131.

Bentley, W. Holman. 1887. *Dictionary and Grammar of the Kongo Language.* London: Baptist Missionary Society and Trübner and Company.

Besolow, Thomas E. 1891. *From the Darkness of Africa to the Light of America: The Story of an African Prince.* Boston: Frank Wood, Printer.

"Bexley." 1841. *Forty-fourth ARACS,* 37.

Beyan, A. 1989. "The American Colonization Society and the Origin of Undemocratic Institutions in Liberia in Historical Perspective." *LSJ* 14, no. 2:140–151.

———. 1991. *The American Colonization Society and the Creation of the Liberian State: A Historical Perspective.* New York: University Press of America.

Binger, Captain. 1890. "Voyage du Captaine Binger, 1887–1889." *Supplement au Journal le Temps* (March).

———. 1892. *Du Niger au Golfe de Guinée par le pays de Long at le Mossi (1887–1889).* Vols. 1 and 2. Paris: Librairie Hachette et Cie.

Bird, Charles. 1970. "The Development of Mandekan (Manding): A Study of the Role of Extra-linguistic Factors in Linguistic Change." In *Language and History in Africa,* edited by David Dalby, 146–159. London: Frank Cass and Company.

Bissy, Regnaule de Lannoy de. 1883. "Liberia. Sur les renseignements fournis par Benjamin Anderson." *Bulletin de la Societe Royale de Geographie d'Anvers* 8, no. 1. Reprinted in Klaus 1990, 351, map no. 2521.

———. 1885. *La carte d'Afrique au 1/2,000,000.* Paris: Association française pour l'advancement des sciences, Congrès de Grenoble.

———. 1886. *Service geographique de l'armée: Notices sur la carte d'Afrique au 1/2,000,000.* 2d ed. Paris: Impr. Nationale.

Blamo, J. Bernard. 1971–72. "Nation-Building in Liberia: The Use of Symbols in National Integration." *LSJ* 4, no. 1:21–30.

Bledsoe, Caroline H. 1980. *Women and Marriage in Kpelle Society*. Stanford, Calif.: Stanford University Press.

———. 1984. "The Political Use of Sande Ideology and Symbolism." *American Ethnologist* 11: 455–472.

Bledsoe, Caroline, and K. M. Robey. 1986. "Arabic Literacy and Secrecy among the Mende of Sierra Leone." *Man*, n.s., 21:202–226.

Blondiaux, P. 1897. "Du Soudan à la Côte d'Ivoire." *Renseignements Coloniaux et Documents: Supplément au Bulletin du Comité de l'Afrique* 7, no. 11:367–376.

Blyden, Edward W. 1853. "Expedition to Little Cape Mount (March Letter)." *LH* 3, no. 7 (6 April).

———. 1857. "Liberia as She Is; and the Present Duty of Her Citizens." *AR* 33, no. 11:326–336.

———. 1868. "Work among the Mohammedans." *AR* 44, no. 6:219–220.

———. 1870. "Barline Country." *AR* 46, no. 9:282–283.

———. 1871a. "The Arabic Language at Sierra Leone and Bathurst." *AR* 47, no. 8:242–244.

———. [1871b] 1874. "Arabic Manuscript in Western Africa." In *The People of Africa,* edited by H. M. Schieffelin, 69–73. Ibadan: Ibadan University Press.

———. 1871c. "The Boporo Country." *AR* 47, no. 8:236–242; 47, no. 9:258–262; 47, no. 11:321–337.

———. 1871d. "Mohammedanism in West Africa." *AR* 47, no. 5:133–148. From the *Methodist Quarterly Review* (1871). Also in Schieffelin [1871] 1974, 74–98; Blyden [1888] 1994, 199–216; and Givens 1976, 128–138.

———. 1871e. "Visit to Sierra Leone." *AR* 47, no. 6:168–171. From the *New York Evangelist.* Also in Schieffelin [1871] 1974, 62–65.

———. 1872a. "Letter from Professor Blyden." *AR* 48, no. 5:145–147.

———. 1872b. "Liberia, Its Status and Its Field." *AR* 48, no. 10:289–297. From *The Methodist Quarterly* (July).

———. 1873. "Travels in Liberia." *AR* (no. 1) 49, no. 10:313–319; (no. 2) 49, no. 12:373–376.

———. 1874a. "The Mission Field in and around Liberia." *AR* 50, no. 6:185–188.

———. 1874b. "Onward to the Interior." *AR* 50, no. 12:357–361.

———. 1881a. "Letter from Rev. Dr. Blyden," 18 January. *AR* 57, no. 5:56–58.

———. 1881b. Blyden to William Coppinger, 18 January. Papers of the American Colonization Society, 20/1, no. 6549-56, reel 164.

———. 1881c. "Liberian Affairs: Letter from Rev. Dr. Blyden." *AR* 51, no. 5: 56–58.

———. 1882a. "Egypt and the Slave-Trade of Africa." *AR* 58, no. 10:115–119.

———. 1882b. "Report of President Blyden." *AR* 58, no. 10:117–119.

———. 1884. "Letter from Rev. Dr. Blyden." *AR* 60, no. 7:93–94.

———. 1886. "A New World." *AR* 62:15–40.

———. [1888] 1994. *Christianity, Islam and the Negro Race.* Baltimore: Black Classic Press.

———. 1889. "The Zodakie Mission and Vonswah." *AR* 65, no. 1:25–30.

———. 1890. "The Koran in Africa." *AR* 66, no. 1:101–107.

———. 1891. "The Late Henry M. Schieffelin, Esq." *AR* 67, no. 1:5.

———. 1900. "An Interesting Letter from Dr. Blyden," 7 November 1899, to Dr. Camphor. *The New Africa* 2, no. 1:8–10.

———. 1915. "A Vision of the Interior." *The Liberian Times* 2, no. 12 (31 July): 1–2. Reprinted in Givens 1976, 318.

Bouet, F. 1911. "Les Tomas." *Renseignements Coloniaux et Documents: Supplément à Afrique Française* 8:185–200; 9:220–227; 10:233–246.

———. 1912. *Les Tomas.* Paris: Comité de l'Afrique Française.

"Boundary between French and Liberian Possessions" 1892. In *The Map of Africa by Treaty,* 3d ed., edited by E. Hertslet, 1130–1136. London: Frank Cass and Company.

Bourzeix, P. R. Pierre. 1887. *La république de Liberia.* Paris: Alcan Lévy.

Bowen, Thomas J. [1857] 1968. *Adventures and Missionary Labours in Several Countries in the Interior of Africa from 1849 to 1856.* London: Frank Cass and Company.

Bravmann, René A. 1983. *African Islam.* Washington, D.C.: Smithsonian Institution Press.

Breitborde, Lawrence B. 1979. "Structural Continuity in the Development of an Urban Kru Community." *Urban Anthropology* 8, no. 2:111–130.

Brett-Smith, Sarah C. 1994. *The Making of Bamana Sculpture: Creativity and Gender.* New York: Cambridge University Press.

———. 1996. *The Artfulness of M'Fa Jigi: An Interview with Nyamaton Diarra.* Madison: University of Wisconsin, Madison, African Studies Program.

A Brief History of Montserrado County. 1965. Monrovia, Liberia.

"Brief Sketch of the Life and Character of the Late Hon. Benj. J. K. Anderson, M.A., Ph.D., K.C." N.d. [1910]. Typescript manuscript. Frederick Starr Research Collection at the Department of Special Collections, Joseph Regenstein Library, University of Chicago, box 9, folder 9.

British Museum General Catalogue of Printed Books: Photolithographic Edition to 1955. 1963. Vol. 166. London: Trustees of the British Museum.

British Museum General Catalogue of Printed Books: Photolithographic Edition to 1955. 1965. Vol. 4. London: Trustees of the British Museum.

Brittan, Harriette G. [1860] 1969. *Scenes and Incidents of Every-day Life in Africa.* New York: Negro Universities Press.

Brockman, Norman C. 1994. *An African Biographical Dictionary.* Denver: ABC-CLIO.

Brooks, George E. 1993. *Landlord and Strangers: Ecology, Society, and Trade in Western Africa, 1000–1630.* Boulder, Colo., San Francisco, and Oxford: Westview Press.

Brown, George W. 1941. *The Economic History of Liberia.* Washington, D.C.: Associated Publishers.

Browne, Charles Farrar [Artemus Ward, pseud.]. 1898. *The Complete Works of Artemus Ward.* New York: A. L. Burt Company.

Brown, I. 1857. *Biography of Robert Finley.* Philadelphia: J. W. Moore.

Brown, Robert H. 1999. "Approaches to the Development and Implementation of a Bilingual Educational Programme in Liberia." *LSJ* 24, no. 2:30–52.

Brown, Robert T. 1980. *Immigrants to Liberia, 1843–1865: Alphabetical Listings.* Philadelphia: Institute for Liberian Studies.

Brownell, T. C. 1869. "Missionary Exploration by a Native." *AR* 45, no. 10: 308–313.

Bulman, Stephen P. D. 1999. "*Sunjata* as Written Literature: The Role of the Literary Mediator in the Dissemination of the *Sunjata* Epic." In *In Search of Sunjata,* edited by Ralph Austin, 231–251. Bloomington: Indiana University Press.

Burrowes, Carl P. 1989. "Black Christian Republicans: Delegates to the 1847 Liberian Constitutional Convention." *LSJ* 14, no. 2:64–87.

———. 1993. "Some Structures of Everyday Life in Pre-Liberian Coastal Societies, 1660–1747." *LSJ* 18, no. 2:231–244.

———. 1998. "Textual Sources of the 1847 Liberian Constitution." *LSJ* 23, no. 1:1–41.

Burton, Richard. 1863. *Wanderings in West Africa.* New York: Dover Publications.

Büttikofer, J. 1884. *Bijbladen Tijdschrift van het Aardrijks.* Amsterdam: Genootsch.

———. 1890. *Reisebilder aus Liberia.* Leiden: E. J. Brill.

———. 1897. "A Few Observations on the Native Tribes of Liberia." *Liberia* 10:57–66.

Buxton, Thomas Foxwell. [1839] 1968. *The African Slave Trade and Its Remedy.* London: Dawsons of Pall Mall.

C., M. H. 1882. "Tobacco!" *Observer* (Monrovia) 5, no. 18 (October 12).

Caillié, René. 1830. *Travels through Central Africa to Timbuctoo; and Across the Great Desert, to Morocco, Performed in the Years 1824–1828.* Vols. 1 and 2. London: Henry Colburn and Richard Bentley.

Calvocoressi, David. 1975. "European Trade Pipes in Ghana." *West African Journal of Archeology* 5:195–200.

Camphor, Alexander Priestly. 1909. *Missionary Story Sketches: Folklore from Africa.* Cincinnati and New York: Jennings and Graham, and Eaton and Mains.

"The Cape Palmas Reporter." 1900. *LH* 3, no. 16 (19 July).

Caranda, D. C. 1932. "A Citizen's Mass Meeting." *Liberian Sentinel* 1, no. 1 (August): 7–8.

Carey, Lot. 1825. "Conversion of a Native African." *AR* 1, no. 5:154–155.

Carman, W. Y. 1955. *A History of Firearms: From Earliest Times to 1914.* New York: St. Martin's Press.

Carrance, Leopold. 1883. Carrance to G. W. Gibson, 8 June. In *Certain Papers from the Department of State,* 15–16). In U.S. Consulate Despatches 1863–1906, no. 170, microfilm 4391, roll 8.

Carter, Jeanette Ellen. 1970. "Household Organization and the Money Economy in a Loma Community, Liberia." Ph.D. diss., University of Oregon.

Cash, John M. 1976. "Guide to the Frederick D. Starr Papers." Unpublished manuscript. Joseph Regenstein Library, University of Chicago Library, Special Collections.

Cashion, Gerald A. 1984. "Hunters of the Mande: A Behavioral Code and Worldview Derived from a Study of Their Folklore." Ph.D. diss., Indiana University.

Cassell, C. Abayomi. 1970. *Liberia: History of the First African Republic.* New York: Fountainhead Publishers.

Caver, T. 1989. *Friedrich Engels: His Life and Thought.* London: Macmillan Press.

Chamberlin, William J. 1991. *Catalogue of English Bible Translations.* New York: Greenwood Press.

Charry, Eric. 2000. *Mande Music: Traditional and Modern Music of the Maninka and Mandinka of Western Africa.* Chicago: University of Chicago Press.

Le Chatelier, A. 1899. Islam dans l'Afrique Occidentale. Paris: G. Steinheil.

Chavers, J. H. 1864. "Report of the Secretary of Treasury," 7 December, 1–18. Monrovia, Liberia: T. W. Howard, Printer, Liberia Herald Office. Also in U.S. Consulate Despatches 1863–1906, no. 170, microfilm 4391, roll 1.

Chenery, Thomas. [1867] 1969. *The Assemblies of Al Hariri, Translated from the Arabic, with an Introduction and Historical and Grammatical Notes.* Vol. 1. Westmead, Farnborough, Hants, England: Gregg International Publishers.

Chevalier, Auguste. 1909. "Dans le nord de la Côte d'Ivoire (mission scientifique de l'Afrique occidentale française)." *La Geographie* 20:25–29.

Chevalier, Auguste, and M. Perrot. 1911. *Les kolatiers et les noix de kola.* Paris: Challamel.

"Christian Missions." 1889. *AR* 65, no. 1:21–25.

Church, R. J. Harrison. 1980. *West Africa: A Study of the Environment and Man's Use of It.* London and New York: Longman.

"Coffee." 1827. *AR* 3, no. 7:218–219.

Cole, Henry B. 1971–72. "The Press in Liberia." *LSJ* 4, no. 2:147–155.

"Colonization." 1886. *Sixty-ninth ARACS,* 11–13.

"A Colored Colonists Views." 1845. *AR* 21, no. 11:342.

Combe, George. [1819] 1845. *A System of Phrenology.* New York.

Combes, Colonel. 1896. "A la poursuite de Samori." *Renseignements Coloniaux et Documents: Supplément au Bulletin du Comité de l'Afrique Francaise*: 41–44.

Conrad, David C. 1992. "Searching for History in the Sunjata Epic: The Case of Fakoli." *History in Africa* 19:147–200.

———. 1994. "A Town Called Dakalajan: The Sunjata Tradition and the Question of Ancient Mali's Capital." *JAH* 35, no. 3:355–378.

———. 1999a. "Mooning Armies and Mothering Heroes: Female Power in Mande Epic Traditions." In *In Search of Sunjata: The Mande Oral Epic as History, Literature, and Performance,* edited by Ralph Austin, 189–225. Bloomington: Indiana University Press.

———, ed. 1990. *A State of Intrigue: The Epic of Bamana Segu According to Tayiru Banbera.* Oxford, New York, and Toronto: Oxford University Press.

———. 1999b. *Epic Ancestors of the Sunjata Era: Oral Tradition from the Maninka of Guinea.* Madison: University of Wisconsin, Madison, African Studies Program.

———. Forthcoming. *Almami Samori and Laye Umaru: Nineteenth-Century Muslim Heroes of Mande Epic Tradition.* Madison: University of Wisconsin, Madison, African Studies Program.

Conrad, David C., and Barbara E. Frank. 1995. "*Nyamakalaya:* Contradiction and Ambiguity in Mande Society." In *Status and Identity in West Africa: Nyamakalaw of Mande,* edited by David C. Conrad and Barbara E. Frank, 1–26. Bloomington: Indiana University Press.

Conrad, David C., ed., and Sory Fina Camara, narrator. 1997. "The Epic of Almami Samori Touré." In *Oral Epics from Africa: Vibrant Voices from a Vast Continent,* edited by John William Johnson, Thomas A. Hale, and Stephen Belcher, 68–79. Bloomington: Indiana University Press.

Conteh, Al-H. 1988. "Accounting for Liberia's Population through Her Censuses." *LSJ* 13, no. 1:104–132.

Conteh, Isatou, Miguel Gomes, Bakari K. Sidibe, David E. Skinner, and Nicholas Wood, eds. 1987. *A History of the Migration and the Settlement of the Baayo Family from Timbuktu to Bijini in Guinea Bissau.* Banjul, Gambia: Diaspora Press.

Corby, Richard A. 1988. "Manding Traders and Clerics: The Development of Islam in Liberia to the 1870s." *LSJ* 13, no. 1:42–66.

A Correspondent. 1852. "Tour into the Interior." *NYCJ* 2, no. 3 (March). From *LH.*

Cosentino, Donald J. 1982. *Defiant Maids and Stubborn Farmers: Tradition and Invention in Mende Story Performance.* Cambridge: Cambridge University Press.

"The Country Adjacent to Liberia." 1851. *NYCJ* 2, 10 (October).

Coyle, R. [1845] 1947. "Map of Liberia." In *The Political and Legislative History of Liberia,* by Charles H. Huberich. New York: Central Book Company.

Crummell, Alexander. [1862] 1969. *The Future of Africa.* New York: Scribner; Detroit: Negro History Press.

———. 1871. "Letter from Rev. Alexander Crummell." *AR* 1, no. 47:14–15.

Crüwell, G. A. 1878. *Liberian Coffee in Ceylon.* Colombo: A. M. and J. Ferguson.

Currens, Gerald. 1976. "Women, Men, and Rice: Agricultural Innovation in Northwestern Liberia." *Human Organization* 35, no. 4:355–365.

Curtin, Philip D. [1964] 1973. *The Image of Africa: British Ideas and Action, 1780–1850.* Vols. 1 and 2. Madison: University of Wisconsin Press.

———. 1972. "African Reactions in Perspective." In *Africa and the West,* edited by Philip D. Curtin, 231–244. Madison: University of Wisconsin Press.

———. 1975. *Economic Change in Precolonial Africa: Senegambia in the Era of the Slave Trade.* Madison: University of Wisconsin Press.

Cutler, Sue, with David J. Dwyer. 1981. *A Reference Handbook of Maniyakan [Koniyakan].* East Lansing: Michigan State University African Studies Center.

Cutler, Sue, with Abu Varflai Talawoley. 1981. *A Learner Directed Approach to Maniyakan.* East Lansing: Michigan State University African Studies Center.

Dalby, David. 1970. "The Historical Problem of Indigenous Scripts of West Africa and Surinam." In *Language and History in Africa,* edited by David Dalby, 109–119. London: Frank Cass and Company.

———. 1971. "Distribution and Nomenclature of the Manding People and Their Language." In *Papers on the Manding,* edited by Carleton T. Hodge, 1–13. Bloomington: Indiana University, Research Center for the Language Sciences.

Dapper, D'Olfert. [1668] 1670. *Africa: Being an Accurate Description and Complete History of Africa.* Translated by John Ogilby. London, 1670.

———. [1668] 1686. *Description de l'Afrique.* Amsterdam: Waesberg, Boom and van Someran.

Darlow, T. H., and H. F. Moule, compilers. 1963. *Historical Catalogue of the Printed Editions of Holy Scripture in the Library of the British and Foreign Bible Society.* New York: Kraus Reprint Corporation.

Dauvillier, Captain. c. 1905. "History of the Cercle of Beyla: Part 1—The Manian Malinkes." From Papers of Dauvillier, APC 105, carton 5, dossier 14. Archives d'Outre-Mer de France, Aix-en-Provence.

Davies, Charles, and William G. Peck. 1867. *Mathematical Dictionary and Cyclopedia of Mathematical Science.* New York: A. S. Barnes and Company.

Davies, P. N. 1976. *Trading in West Africa.* London: Croom Helm.

Davis, L. G. 1975. "Black American Images of Liberia." *LSJ* 6, no. 1:53–72.

Davis, Stanley A. 1953. *This Is Liberia: A Brief History of This Land of Contradictions with Biographies of Its Founders.* New York: William-Frederick Press.

Davis, W. M. 1890. Davis to Honorable James G. Blaine, 28 November. In Notes from the Liberian Legation in the United States to the Department of State. T-807, film 4400, roll 1.

Day, Lynda. 1994. “The Evolution of Female Chieftainship during the Late Nineteenth-Century Wars of the Mende.” *International Journal of African Historical Studies* 27, no. 3:481–503.

“A Day on the St. Paul’s River.” 1865. *AR* 46, no. 5:137–140. From the *LH.*

d’Azevedo, Warren. 1962. “Some Historical Problems in the Delineation of a Central West Atlantic Region.” *Annals of the New York Academy of Sciences* 96, no. 2:512–538.

———. 1969a. “A Tribal Reaction to Nationalism (Part 1).” *LSJ* 1, no. 2:1–21.

———. 1969b. “A Tribal Reaction to Nationalism (Part 2): The Era of Stabilizing Sectionalism.” *LSJ* 2, no. 1:43–63.

———. 1980. “Gola Poro and Sande: Primal Tasks in Social Custodianship.” *Ethnologische Zeitschrift Zurich* 1:13–23.

———. 1989. “Tribe and Chiefdom on the Windward Coast.” *LSJ* 14, no. 2: 90–116. Abridged version published in *Rural Africana* 15 (1971): 10–29.

———. 1994. “Phantoms of the Hinterland: The ‘Mandingo’ Presence in Early Liberian Accounts.” Part 1. *LSJ* 19, no. 2:197–242.

———.1995. “Phantoms of the Hinterland: The ‘Mandingo’ Presence in Early Liberian Accounts.” Part 2. *LSJ* 20, no. 1:59–97.

de Grey, Earl, and Ripon. 1860. “Address to the Royal Geographical Society of London.” *The Journal of the Royal Geographical Society* 30:c–cxcii.

———. 1861. “Address, at the Anniversary Meeting of the Royal Geographical Society, May 28, 1860.” *The Journal of the Royal Geographical Society* 6: 172–175.

De Wolf, Paul P. 1995. *English-Fula Dictionary (Fulfulde, Pulaar, Fulani): A Multidialectical Approach.* Berlin: Reimer.

“Death of Gabriel Moore, Esq.” 1886. *AR* 62, no. 1:43.

“Death of Henry M. Schieffelin, Esq.” 1890. *AR* 61, no. 10:126.

Delafosse, Maurice. 1900. “Un état negre: La République de Liberia.” *Renseignements Coloniaux et Documents: Supplément au Bulletin du Comité de l’Afrique Française* 9:165–194.

———. 1901. *Essai de manuel pratique de la langue Mande ou Mandingue.* Paris: Ernest Leroux.

———. 1903. “The Franco-Liberian Controversy.” *West African Mail* 1, no. 31 (30 October): 805. Also in *Liberia Recorder* 6, no. 2 (28 November 1903): 6–7.

———. 1955. *La langue Mandingue et ses dialectes (Malinké, Bambara, Dioula).* Vol. 2. Paris: Imprimerie Nationale, Librairie Paul Geuthner.

Delany, M. R., and R. Campbell. [1860] 1971. *Search for a Place: Black Separatism and Africa.* Ann Arbor: University of Michigan Press.

Delany, Martin Robison. 1861. *Official Report of the Niger Valley Exploring Party.* New York: T. Hamilton.

Dennis, Henry W. 1852. Dennis to Rev'd. Wm. McLain, April. In the American Colonization Society Papers, Miscellaneous Correspondence, microfilm no. 177B, Frame 0629. Svend E. Holsoe Collection, Indiana University.

———. 1870. Dennis to Coppinger, 10 December. In the American Colonization Society Papers, Letters Received, Foreign, 5, 15/1 1869–1870, reel 164, nos. 04558–59.

———. 1873. "Arabic Letter from a Native African." *AR* 46, no. 11:347–349.

Denny, Frederick M. 1985. *An Introduction to Islam.* New York: Macmillan Publishing Company; London: Collier Macmillan Publishers.

"Departure of the *Brig Oriole.*" 1852. *AR* 28, no. 11:349–350. From the *NYCJ.*

Devany, Francis. 1830. "Examination." *AR* 6, no. 4:97–105.

Dillon, Thomas E. 1871. "A Voice from Africa." *AR* 47, no. 10:291–295.

"Discouraging Features." 1921. *Liberian Patriot* (21 August).

"Discoveries in Africa." 1859. *Philadelphia Colonization Herald* (June).

Dole, Yaya. 1986. Interviewed by Tim Geysbeek, Muhammed Kromah, and Mustafa Kromah in Musadu on 23 March.

Donelha, André. [1625] 1977. *An Account of Sierra Leone and the Rivers of Guinea of Cape Verde.* Edited and translated into English by P. E. Hair. Lisbon: Junta de Investigaçoes Científicas do Ultramar.

Donner, Etta. 1939. *Hinterland Liberia.* Translated by Winifred M. Deans. London and Glasgow: Blackie and Son.

Doreh, Fanfi [Vafin Dole] (Chief), and Mohammad Barta (Scribe). 1870. "Appendix to Benj. Anderson's Journey to Musadu . . . in 1868." Translated by E. W. Blyden (with Arabic text). New York: Lithographing, Engraving and Printing Company. Also in Schieffelin [1871] 1974, 129–136 (with Arabic text and English translation), and *Liberia Recorder* 6, no. 8 (26 March 1904): 9–10.

Du Bois, W. E. B. 1905. *The Souls of Black Folk: Essays and Sketches.* London: Archibold Constable and Company.

Duboc, General. 1938. *L'épopée coloniale en Afrique occidentale français.* Paris: Editions Edgar Malfére.

Duignan, Peter, and L. H. Gann. 1984. *The United States and Africa: A History.* Cambridge: Cambridge University Press and Hoover Institution.

Duitsman, John. 1982–83. "Liberian Languages." *LSJ* 10, no. 1:27–36.

Dunn, E. Elwood. 1992. *A History of the Episcopal Church in Liberia, 1821–1980.* Metuchen, N.J.: Scarecrow Press.

———. 1995. *Liberia.* Oxford and Santa Barbara: Clio Press.

Dunn, D. Elwood, and Svend E. Holsoe. 1985. *Historical Dictionary of Liberia.* Metuchen, N.J., and London: Scarecrow Press.

Dwyer, David J. 1981. *Lorma: A Reference Handbook of Phonetics, Grammar, Lexicon, and Learning Procedures.* East Lansing: Michigan State University African Studies Center.

———. 1989. "Mande." In *Niger-Congo Languages,* edited by John Bendor-Samuel, 47–66. Lanham, Md., New York, and London: University Press of America.

"Eastward Empire Points the Way!" 1873. *AR* 49, no. 11:332–333. From *The (Liberia) New Era.*

"Educational Work among the Native People." 1928. *The Educational Outlook* 1, no. 4 (April): 4–6.

"Educational Work in Liberia." 1883. *AR* 59, no. 7:90–91.

"Eighteen Hundred and Eighty." 1880. *Observer* (Monrovia) 3, no. 1 (8 January).

Ejofodomi, L. E. 1974. "The Missionary Career of Alexander Crummell in Liberia, 1853–1873." Ph.D. diss., Boston University.

"Election." 1873. *AR* 49:22.

"Elephant Taming in Liberia." 1880. *AR* 56, no. 8:86. From the *West Africa Reporter.*

Ellis, Stephen. 1999. *The Mask of Anarchy: The Destruction of Liberia and the Religious Dimension of an African Civil War.* Washington Square: New York University Press.

"The English Loan." 1872. *AR* 53, no. 5:137–138.

Esposito, John L. 1991. *Islam: The Straight Path.* Oxford: Oxford University Press.

"The Eulogy at Planter's Hall in Memory of Hon. Allen Bennet Hooper, the Father of the Coffee Enterprise in Liberia." 1879. *Observer* (Monrovia) 2, no. 17 (11 December).

"Exploration." 1872. *AR* 48:46–47.

"Exploration in Africa." 1855. *NYCJ* 4, no. 12, whole no. 61.

"Exploration of Africa." 1860. *NYCJ* 10, no. 12, whole no. 108.

"Explorations." 1860. *Forty-third ARACS,* 17–19.

"Explorations." 1873. *Fifty-sixth ARACS,* 46.

"Explorations East of Liberia." 1858. *NYCJ* 8, no. 4, whole no. 88.

"Explorations in Africa." 1859. *NYCJ* 9, no. 3, whole no. 99.

Fairhead, James, and Melissa Leach. 1994. "Contested Forests: Modern Conservation and Historical Land Use in Guinea's Ziama Reserve." *African Affairs* 93:481–512.

———. 1996. *Misreading the African Landscape: Society and Ecology in a Forest-Savannah Mosaic.* Cambridge: Cambridge University Press.

———. 1998. *Reframing Deforestation—Global Analyses and Local Realities: Studies in West Africa.* London and New York: Routledge.

"The Feast of Ramadan." 1871. *AR* 47, no. 4:115–116.

"A Few Days at Careysburg, Jottings by the Way." 1878. *Observer* (Monrovia) 1, no. 6 (26 September).

Fifty-seventh ARACS. 1874. *AR* 50, no. 2.

Fifty-sixth ARACS. 1873. *ARACS,* 16–19. Also in the *AR* 49, no. 2 (1873): 42–45.

File Microcopies of Records in the National Archives. No. 19, roll 7, p. 13. Fifth census of the United States 1830, population schedules, Connecticut, vol. 2. Washington, D.C.: National Archives, 1946.

"The First August Demonstration at Clay-Ashland." 1870. *AR* 46, no. 11:339–342. From the *Baptist Missionary Magazine*. Also in the *Liberia Register*.

Fisher, Alan W. 1978. *The Crimean Tatars*. Stanford, Calif.: Hoover Institution Press.

Fisher, Allan G. B., and J. Humphrey Fisher. 1970. *Society and Muslim Society in Africa: The Institution in Saharan and Sudanic Africa and the Trans-Saharan Trade*. London: C. Hurst and Company.

Fisher, Humphrey. 1971. New introduction to *Narrative of a Journey to Musardu the Capital of the Western Mandingoes Together with Narrative of the Expedition Despatched to Musahdu by the Liberian Government*, by Benjamin J. K. Anderson, v–xxiii. London: Frank Cass and Company.

dan Fodio, Usman. [c. 1804–1805] 1979. "Despatch to the People of the Sudan." In *Sources of the African Past*, edited by David Robinson and Douglas Smith, 138–139. New York: Africana Publishing Company.

"Following the Trail of Benjamin Anderson." 1973, 1974. Typewritten manuscript, Monrovia, Liberia, in the Svend E. Holsoe Collection at Indiana University.

Foote, Andrew H. 1854. *Africa and the American Flag*. New York: D. Appleton and Company.

Ford, Martin. 1989. "Nimba's Conquest, Mandingo Trade and the Rashomon Effect." *Liberia-Forum* 5, no. 8:18–31.

———. 1990. "Ethnic Relations and the Transformation of Leadership among the Dan of Nimba, Liberia (ca. 1900–1945)." Ph.D. diss., State University of New York, Binghamton.

———. 1992. "Kola Production and Settlement Mobility among the Dan of Nimba, Liberia." *African Economic History* 20:51–63.

———. 1995. "The Political Economy of Taxation in Liberia, ca. 1830–1930." *Research in Economic Anthropology* 16:397–419.

"The Forerunner of Africa." 1858. *Philadelphia Colonization Herald* (March). From the *New York Commercial Advertiser*.

Forty-first ARACS. 1858. *AR* 34, no. 3:65–88. Also in the *Forty-first ARACS*, 6–28.

Forty-second ARACS. 1859. *Forty-second ARACS*, 5–29.

Fraenkel, Merran. 1964. *Tribe and Class in Monrovia*. London: Oxford University Press for the International African Institute.

"The Franco-Liberian Controversy." 1903a. *West African Mail* 1, no. 28 (9 October): 742. Also in the *Sierra Leone Weekly News* 2, no. 68 (31 October).

"The Franco-Liberian Controversy." 1903b. *Liberia Recorder* 6, no. 2 (28 November): 7.

"The Franco-Liberian Controversy." 1903c. *West African Mail* 1, no. 30 (23

October): 793–794. Also in *Liberia Recorder* 6, no. 2 (28 November 1903): 4.

"Franco-Liberian Relations." 1904. *West African Mail* 2, no. 57 (29 April): 98. Also in *Liberia Recorder* 6, no. 2 (4 June): 3.

Frank, Barbara. 1998. *Mande Potters and Leatherworkers: Art and Heritage in West Africa.* Washington, D.C., and London: Smithsonian Institution Press.

Franklin, J. H. 1901. "La question de Libéria." *Questions Diplomatiques et Coloniales: Revue de Politique Exterieure* 12:523–531.

Freeman, H. Boakai. 1952. "The Vai and Their Kinsfolk." *The Negro History Bulletin* 16, no. 3:51–62.

"The French Claims to the Liberian Hinterland." 1903. *West African Mail* 1, no. 20 (14 August): 55. Also in *LR* 5, no. 24 (12 September 1903): 9.

"From Liberia." 1859. *Daily National Intelligence* 27, no. 14,528 (25 February).

"From Liberia: Presbytery of Western Africa." 1860. *AR* 36, no. 9:275–276.

Fulton, Richard M. 1968. "The Kpelle Traditional Political System." *LSJ* 1, no. 1:1–19.

———. 1972. "Political Structures and Functions of Poro in Kpelle Society." *American Anthropologist* 75, no. 5:1218–1233.

Fyfe, Christopher. 1962. *A Short History of Sierra Leone.* Oxford: Oxford University Press.

Gabel, Creighton, Robert Borden, and Susan White. 1972–74. "Preliminary Report on an Archeological Survey of Liberia." *LSJ* 5, no. 2:87–105.

Gardner, Anthony W. 1878. *Inaugural Address of His Excellency President A. W. Gardner, Eighth President of Liberia, Delivered Jany 7th, 1878 before the Senate and the House of Representatives.* Monrovia, Liberia: T. W. Howard, Printer, Government Printing Office. In U.S. Consulate Despatches 1863–1906, no. 170, microfilm 4391, roll 7.

———. 1879. *Message of the President of the Republic of Liberia to the First Session of the Nineteenth Legislature* (10 December). Monrovia, Liberia: T. W. Howard, Printer, Government Printing Office. In U.S. Consulate Despatches 1863–1906, no. 170, microfilm 4391, roll 7.

Garrard, Timothy F. 1980. *Akan Weights and the Gold Trade.* London: Longman.

Garrett, G. H. 1892. "Sierra Leone and the Interior to the Upper Waters of the Niger." *Proceedings of the Royal Geographical Society* 7:446.

Gay, John H. 1989. "Cognitive Aspects of Agriculture among the Kpelle: Kpelle Farming through Kpelle Eyes." *LSJ* 14, no. 2:23–43.

Gay, John H., Warren d'Azeuedo, William E. Welmers. 1969. "Language Map of Central Liberia." LSJ 1, no. 2:41–43.

Germain, Jacques. 1984. *Peuples de la fôret de Guinée.* Paris: Academie des Sciences d'Outre-Mer.

Germann, P. 1933. *Die Völkerstämme im Norden von Liberia. Ergebnisse einer*

Forschungsreise im Auftrag des Staatlich-Sächsischen Forschungs-Instituts für Völkerkunde in Leipzig in den Jahren 1928/1929. Leipzig: R. Voigtländers Verlag.

Gershoni, Yekutiel. 1985. *Black Colonialism: The America-Liberia Scramble for the Hinterland.* Boulder, Colo., and London: Westview Press.

———. 1992a. "The Formation of Liberia's Boundaries, Part One: Agreements." *LSJ* 17, no. 1:25–45.

———. 1992b. "Formation of the Liberian Boundaries, Part Two: The Demarcation Process." *LSJ* 18, no. 2:177–202.

Geysbeek, Tim. 2002. "History from the Musadu Epic: The Formation of Manding Power on the Southern Frontier of the Mali Empire." Ph.D. diss., Michigan State University.

Geysbeek, Tim, and Jobba K. Kamara. 1991. "'Two Hippos Cannot Live in One River': Zo Musa, Foningama, and the Founding of Musadu in the Oral Traditions of the Konyaka." *LSJ* 16, no. 1: 27–78. Errata, *LSJ* 16, no. 2: 105–107.

Geysbeek, Tim, ed. 1999. "The Impeachments and Trials of President James S. Payne and Secretary Benjamin J. K. Anderson: The Documentary Evidence (Part I)." *LSJ* 24, no. 1:27–55.

Geysbeek, Tim, ed., and Vase Camara, narrator. 1994. "A Traditional History of the Konyan (Fifteenth–Sixteenth Century [Guinea]): Vase Camara's Epic of Musadu." *History in Africa* 21:49–85.

Gibbal, Jean-Marie. 1984. "Le signe des génies." *Cahiers d'Études Africaines* 94, no. 24: 193–203.

"The Gibbee Country, Liberia." 1872. *AR* 48, no. 6: 168–171. From the *Colonization Journal.* Also in Scheiffelin [1871] 1974, 139–143.

Gibbs, James L., Jr. 1965. "The Kpelle of Liberia. In *Peoples of Africa,* edited by James L. Gibbs, Jr., 197–240. New York: Holt, Rinehart and Winston.

Gibson, Rev. G. W. 1869. "Liberia and the Interior Tribes," *AR* 45, no. 5:135–136. Originally published in *The Spirit of Missions.*

———. 1870. Gibson to S. D. Denison, 20 June. Domestic and Foreign Missionary Society papers, Episcopal Church Archives, Austin, Tex., b-box 17.

———. 1879. Gibson to Leopold Carrance, 2 September. Frederick Starr Research Collection at the Department of Special Collections, Joseph Regenstein Library, University of Chicago, box 1, file 7.

———. 1883. Gibson to Hon. Leopold Carrance. In *Certain Papers from the Department of State,* 16–17). In U.S. Consulate Despatches 1863–1906, no. 170, microfilm 4391, roll 7.

Gittins, A. J. 1987. *Mende Religion: Aspects of Belief and Thought in Sierra Leone.* Nettetal, Germany: Steyler Verlag and Wort und Werk.

Givens, Willie A., ed. 1976. *Selected Works of Dr. Edward Wilmot Blyden.* Robertsport, Liberia: Tubman Center of African Culture.

Goerg, Odile. 1985. "Sur la route des noix de cola en 1897: Du moyen-Niger à

Boola, marché Kpelle," 75–97. In *The Workers of African Trade,* edited by Catherine Coquery-Vidrovitch and Paul E Lovejoy. Beverly Hills, Calif.: Sage Publications.

———. 1986. *Commerce et colonisation en Guinée, 1850–1913.* Paris: Editions L'Harmattan.

Gottlieb, A. 1992. *Under the Kapok Tree: Identity and Difference in Beng Thought.* Bloomington: Indiana University Press.

Goucher, C. L. 1981. "'Iron is iron 'til it is rust': Trade and Ecology in the Decline of West African Iron-Smelting." *JAH* 22, no. 2:179–189.

"Government Scholarships." 1928. *The Educational Outlook* 1, no. 5 (May).

Grabar, Oleg. 1984. *The Illustrations of the Maqamat.* Chicago and London: University of Chicago Press.

Gracey, Rev. J. T. 1877. "Mohammedanism in West Africa—First Paper." *The Christian Advocate* 51, no. 14 (5 April). In the Svend E. Holsoe Collection, Indiana University.

Gray, Major William. 1825. *Travels in Western Africa in the Years 1818, 1819, 1820 and 1821 from the River Gambia . . . to the River Niger.* London: J. Murray.

Green, Constance. 1956. *Eli Whitney and the Birth of American Technology.* Boston and Toronto: Little, Brown and Company.

Green, Kathryn L. 1987. "Dyula and Sonongui Roles in the Islamization of the Region of Kong." In *Rural and Urban Islam in West Africa,* edited by Nehamia Levtzion and Humphrey J. Fisher, 97–118. Boulder, Colo.: Lynne Rienner Publishers.

Griaule, M. [1965] 1977. *Conversations with Ogotemmeli: An Introduction to Dogon Religious Ideas.* Oxford: Oxford University Press.

Griffin, Farah J., and Cheryl J. Fish, eds. 1998. *A Stranger in the Village: Two Centuries of African-American Travel Writing.* Boston: Beacon Press.

Grimal, P. 1991. *Dictionary of Classical Mythology.* London: Penguin.

"A Gross Injustice." 1903. *Sierra Leone Weekly News* 19, no. 45:4–5 (11 July). Also in *LR* 5, no. 22–23 (29 August 1903): 7, and *Liberia* 28 (February 1906): 83–85.

Groves, C. P. 1948. *The Planting of Christianity in Africa.* Vol. 1. London: Lutterworth Press.

Guekedou. 1960. Map prepared by Army Map Service, NC 29-14. Washington, D.C.

Guinea: Official Standard Names, Gazetteer No. 90. 1965. Washington, D.C.: Office of Geography, Department of the Interior.

"H. M. Schieffelin, Esq." 1867. *AR* 43, no. 9:269.

Hair, P. E. 1962. "An Account of the Liberian Hinterland c. 1780." *Sierra Leone Studies* 16:218–226.

———. 1968a. "An Ethnolinguistic Inventory of the Lower Guinea Coast before 1700: Part I." *African Language Review* 7:47–73.

———. 1968b. Introduction to *Outlines of a Grammar of the Vai Language,* by S. W. Koelle, i–vi. Hants, England: Gregg International Publishers.

Hall, J. 1836. "Tour of Dr. Hall up the Cavally River." *Missionary Herald* (USA) August: 312–314.

Hancock, Ian. 1970–71. "Some Aspects of Liberian English." *LSJ* 3, no. 2:207–213.

Handwerker, W. Penn. 1980. "Market Places, Travelling Traders, and Shops: Commercial Structural Variation in the Liberian Interior Prior to 1940." *African Economic History* 9:3–26.

Harley, Eugene L. 1996. "Forest Ferneries: Memories of a Childhood in the Liberian Bush." *The Pepper Bird* 1:6–8, no. 10.

Harley, George W. 1941. "Notes on the Poro in Liberia." *Papers of the Peabody Museum of American Archeology and Ethnology, Harvard University* 19, no. 2:1–36.

Harris, J. M. 1865–66. "Some Remarks on the Origin, Manners, Customs, and Superstitions of the Gallinas People of Sierra Leone." *Memoirs Read before the Anthropological Society of London* 2:25–36.

Harrison, Christopher. 1988. *France and Islam in West Africa,* 1860–1960. Cambridge: Cambridge University Press.

Hau, Kathleen. 1973. "Pre-Islamic Writing in West Africa." *Bulletin de l'I.F.A.N., B,* 35, no. 1:1–45.

Haven, Gilbert. 1877. "Trip up the St. Paul's River." *AR* 54, no. 10:104–111.

———. 1878. "The Legislature and Supreme Court." *AR* 54, no. 1:6–10.

Haynes, J. B. 1900. "A History of Liberia Needed." *The New Africa* 2, no. 2 (February): 14.

Headrick, Daniel R. 1981. *Tools of Empire: Technology and European Imperialism in the Nineteenth Century.* New York and Oxford: Oxford University Press.

Heard, William H. [1898] 1969. *The Bright Side of African Life.* New York: Negro Universities Press.

Hecquard, M. 1853. *Voyage sur la côte et dans l'intérieur de l'Afrique occidentale.* Paris: Bénard.

Hening, Mrs. E. F. [1850] 1853. *History of the African Mission of the Protestant Episcopal Church in the United States with Memoirs of Deceased Missionaries, and Notices of Native Customs.* New York: Stanford and Swords.

Henries, A. Doris Banks. 1954. *The Liberian Nation: A Short History.* New York: Hermann Jaffe.

Henry, Joseph. 1870. Introduction to *A Journey to Musardu,* by Benjamin J. K. Anderson. New York: Frank Cass and Company.

"Henry M. Schieffelin." 1891. *Seventy-fourth ARACS,* 3.

Herbert, A. S. 1968. *Historical Catalogue of Printed Editions of the English Bible, 1525–1961.* London: British and Foreign Bible Society; New York: American Bible Society.

Herbert, Eugenia W. 1984. *Red Gold in Africa: Copper in Precolonial History and Cuture.* Madison: University of Wisconsin Press.

Hertslet, E., ed. 1909. *The Map of Africa by Treaty.* 3d ed. Vol. 3. London: Frank Cass and Company.

Hill, John H. 1987. "Peter the Hermit." In *Dictionary of the Middle Ages.* Vol. 9. New York: Charles Scribner's Sons.

Hill, Matthew H. 1976. "Archeological Smoking Pipes from Central Sierra Leone." *West African Journal of Archeology* 6:109–119.

———. 1984. "Where to Begin? The Place of the Hunter Founder in Mende Histories." *Anthropos* 79:653–656.

"L'hinterland du Liberia." 1903. *Bulletin du Comité de l'Afrique Française* 6: 193–194.

Hodder, B. W. 1980. "Indigenous Cloth Trade and Marketing in Africa." In *Textiles of Africa,* edited by Dale Idiens and K. G. Ponting, 203–210. Bath and Leeds: Pasold Research Fund and W. S. Maney and Son.

Hoffman, C. C. 1862. "A Missionary Journey up the Cavalha River, and the Report of a Large River Flowing near the Source of the Former." *Proceedings of the Royal Geographical Society* 6:66–67.

Højbjerg, Christian Kordt. 1993. "Fetish and Space among the Loma: An Examination of a West African Medicine." *Folk: The Journal of the Danish Ethnographic Society* 35:72–101.

———. 1998. "Tradition Invented or Inherited? The Construction of Loma Ritual and Cultural Knowledge." Paper presented at the fifth biennial EASA conference, Frankfurt, 4–7 September.

———. 1999. "Loma Political Culture: A Phenomenology of Structural Form." *Africa* 69, no. 4:535–554.

———. 2002. "Masked Violence: Ritual Action and the Perception of Violence in an Upper Guinea Ethnic Conflict." In *Religion and African Civil Wars,* edited by N. Kastfelt. London: Hurst and Company.

———. Forthcoming. "Recurrent Violence: Reflections on Loma and Mandingo Ethnic Enmity in Liberia and Guinea."

Holas, Bohumil. 1952. *Mission dans l'est Liberian.* Dakar: IFAN.

———. 1975. *Contes Kono: Traditions populaire de la forêt Guinée.* Paris: Larose.

Holden, Edith. 1976. *Blyden of Liberia: An Account of the Life and Labors of Edward Wilmot Blyden, LL.D. As Recorded in Letters and in Print.* New York, Washington, D.C., and Hollywood: Vantage Press.

Hölldobler, Bert, and Edward O. Wilson. 1990. *The Ants.* Cambridge: Belknap Press of Harvard University Press.

Holsoe, Svend E. 1966. "The Condo Confederation in Western Liberia." *Liberian Historical Review* 3, no. 1 (1966): 1–28.

———. 1967. "The Cassava Leaf People: An Ethnohistorical Study of the Vai People with Particular Emphasis on the Tewo Chiefdom." Ph.D. diss., Boston University.

———. 1971a. "A Case of Stimulus Diffusion? A Note on Possible Connections between the Vai and Cherokee Scripts." *Language Sciences* 15 (1971): 22–24. Also in *The Indian Historian* 4, no. 3 (1971): 56–57.

———. 1971b. "A Study of Relations between Settlers and Indigenous Peoples in Western Liberia, 1821–1847." *African Historical Studies (International Journal of African Historical Studies)* 4, no. 2:331–362.

———. 1974. "The First 'Vai' Migration." Paper presented at the Sixth Annual Liberian Studies Research Conference, Madison.

———. 1976–77. "The Manding in Western Liberia: An Overview." *LSJ* 7, no. 1:1–12.

———. 1977. "Slavery and Economic Response among the Vai (Liberia and Sierra Leone)." In *Slavery in Africa: Historical and Anthropological Perspectives,* edited by Suzanne Miers and Igor Kopytoff, 287–304. Madison: University of Wisconsin Press.

———. 1979a. "Economic Activities in the Liberian Area: The Pre-European Period to 1900." In *Essays on the Economic Anthropology of Liberia and Sierre Leone,* edited by Vernon R. Dorjahn and Barry L. Isaac, 63–78. Philadelphia: Institute for Liberian Studies.

———. 1979b. *A Standardization of Liberian Ethnic Nomenclature.* Philadelphia: Institute for Liberian Studies.

———. 1980. "Notes on the Vai Sande Society in Liberia." *Ethnologische Zeitschrift Zürich* 1:79–109.

Holsoe, Svend E., Warren L. d'Azevedo, and John H. Gay. 1969. "Chiefdom and Clan Maps of Western Liberia." *LSJ* 1, no. 2:23–39.

Holsoe, Svend E., and Tim Geysbeek, eds., and Alhaji Mohammed Dukule, narrator. 1998. "A Short History of Samori." *LSJ* 23, no. 2:61–77.

Holsoe, Torkel. 1954. *Forest Opportunities in the Republic of Liberia.* Washington, D.C.: Foreign Agricultural Service and Forest Service, United States Department of Agriculture.

"Home Life in Africa." 1868. *AR* 44, no. 11:326–328.

"Hon. Augustus Washington." 1868. *AR* 44, no. 12:376.

"Hon. W. S. Anderson's Address." 1870. *AR* 46, no. 11:339–341.

Hopewell, James Franklin. 1958. "Muslim Penetration into French Guinea, Sierra Leone, and Liberia before 1850." Ph.D. diss., Columbia University.

Hopkins, Anthony. 1973. *An Economic History of West Africa.* London: Longman Group.

Hopkins, Nicholas S. 1971. "Mandinka Social Organization." In *Papers on the Manding,* edited by Carleton T. Hodge, 99–128. Bloomington: Indiana University; The Hague: Mouton and Co.

Huberich, Charles Henry. 1947. *The Political and Legislative History of Africa.* Vols. 1–2. New York: Central Book Company.

Humblot, P[ierre]. 1918, 1919. "Du nom propre et des appellations chez les Malinké des vallées du Niandan et du Milo (Guinée française)." *Bulletin*

Comité d'Études Historiques et Scientifiques (1918): 519–540; (1919): 393–426.

———. 1921. "Kankan: Metropole de la haute Guinée." *Supplement à l'Afrique Française* 6:129–140, 153–164.

———. 1951. "Épisodes: De la legende de Soundiata." *Notes Africaines* 52:111–113.

Hunwick, John, ed. 1999. *Timbuktu and the Songhay Empire: Al-Sa'di's Tarikh al-Sudan Down to 1613 and Other Contemporary Documents.* Leiden, Boston, and Köln: Brill.

"Ibrahima Sissi." 1881. *Observer* (Monrovia) 4, no. 17 (22 September).

"Incendiary Movements." 1857. *LH* (4 February).

Iliffe, John. 1983. *The Emergence of African Capitalism.* Minneapolis: University of Minnesota Press.

Iloeje, N. P. 1980. *A New Geography of West Africa.* London: Longman.

"Impeachment of the Ex-Secretary of the Treasury." 1878. In Despatches from United States Ministers to Liberia 1863–1906, no. 170, microfilm 4391, roll 7, document no. 294. Republished in Geysbeek 1999, 39–42.

"Impeachment of Honorable B. J. K. Anderson (Suspended) Secretary of the Liberian Treasury." 1878. In Despatches from United States Ministers to Liberia 1863–1906, no. 170, microfilm 4391, roll 7, document no. 289. Republished in Geysbeek 1999, 35–36.

"The Improvements of Monrovia." 1914. *African League* 16, no. 1 (October): 1–2.

"Inauguration Day at Monrovia." 1872. *AR* 48, no. 9:269–273. From the *(Liberia) Lone Star.*

Inikori, J. D. 1977. "The Import of Firearms into West Africa, 1750–1807: A Quantitative Analysis." *JAH* 18, no. 3:339–368.

"The Interior." 1851. *NYCJ* 1, no. 15 (December). From the *LH* (1 October).

"Interior Annexation." 1875. *AR* 51:72.

"Interior Exploration." 1869. *AR* 45, no. 9:277–278. From the *True Whig of Liberia* (10 April 1869).

"Interior Roads." 1873. *AR* 49, no. 11:334–335. From *The Republican.*

"Internal Affairs Boss Taken to Task." 2000. *The News* (Monrovia). Distributed by allAfrica.com, from the Friends of Liberia e-mail news. Accessed 15 September 2000.

Iroko, A. F. 1982. "Le rôle des termitières dans l'histoire des peuples de la république populaire du Bénin des origines à nos jours," *Bulletin de l'I.F.A.N.* 44, no. 1–2:50–75.

Irvine, J. 1877. "Our Commercial Relations with West Africa and Their Effects upon Civilization." *Journal of the Society of Arts* (March 16): 378–388.

"Islamic Fundamentalism or Electoral Ploy?" 1995. *New Democratic Weekly Review* (17–24 November): 10.

"Items from the *African Republic*: New Manufacture." 1868. *AR* 45, no. 2:45.

"Items of Intelligence: Chiefs in Council." 1874. *AR* 50, no. 11:351.

Ivanov, Vladimir Alekseevich, ed. and trans. 1953. *The Truth-Worshippers of Kurdistan.* Leiden: E. J. Brill.

Jabateh, Aleo. 1995. "Who Told You That?" *New Democratic Weekly Review* (17–24 November): 12–13.

Jackson, Michael. 1990. "The Man Who Could Turn into an Elephant: Shape-Shifting among the Kuranko of Sierra Leone." In *Personhood and Agency: The Experience of Self and Other in African Cultures,* edited by Michael Jackson and Ivan Karp, 59–78. Uppsala, Sweden: Uppsala University; Washington, D.C.: Distributed for Smithsonian Institution Press.

Jackson, Ronald Vern, et al. 1976. *Kentucky 1850.* North Salt Lake, Utah: Accelerated Indexing Systems.

Jackson, Ronald Vern, W. David Samuelson, Shirley P. Jackson, Jo Ann Limb, Richard Saldana. 1987. *Indiana 1860 South, Indiana 1860 North.* Accelerated Indexing Systems.

———. 1988. *Virginia 1850 Slave Schedule Census Index.* Salt Lake City, Utah: Accelerated Indexing Systems.

———. 1990. *Kentucky 1850 Slave Schedule Census Index.* North Salt Lake, Utah: Accelerated Indexing Systems.

Jackson, Ronald Vern, ed. 1996. *Federal Census Index: Maryland 1850 Slave Schedules.* West Jordan, Utah: Genealogical Services.

Jackson, Ronald Vern, and Gary Ronald Teeples, eds. 1976a. *Indiana 1850 Census Index.* Bountiful, Utah: Accelerated Indexing Systems.

———. 1976b. *Maryland 1850 Census Index.* Bountiful, Utah: Accelerated Indexing Systems.

———. 1977a. *Connecticut 1830 Census Index.* Bountiful, Utah: Accelerated Indexing Systems.

———. 1977b. *Maryland 1840 Census Index.* Bountiful, Utah: Accelerated Indexing Systems.

———. 1978a. *Connecticut 1840 Census Index.* Bountiful, Utah: Accelerated Indexing Systems.

———. 1978b. *Kentucky 1840 Census Index.* Bountiful, Utah: Accelerated Indexing Systems.

Jackson, Ronald, Gary Ronald Teeples, and David Schaefermeyer, eds. 1976a. *Pennsylvania 1850 Census Index.* Vol. 2. Bountiful, Utah: Accelerated Indexing Systems [Accelerated Indexing Systems].

———. 1976b. *Virginia 1850 Census Index.* Bountiful, Utah: Accelerated Indexing Systems.

———. 1978. *Pennsylvania 1840 Census Index.* Bountiful, Utah: Accelerated Indexing Systems.

———. 1987. *Pennsylvania 1860 East.* North Salt Lake, Utah: Accelerated Indexing Systems.

Jansen, Jan, Esger Duintjer, and Boubacar Tamboura, eds., and Lansine Diabate, narrator. 1995. *L'epopée du Sunjata, d'après Lansine Diabate de Kela.* Université de Leyde, les Pays-Bas: Research School CNWS (CNWS Publications).

Jansen, Jan, and Clemens Zobel, eds. 1996. *The Younger Brother in Mande: Kinship and Politics in West Africa.* Leiden: Research School CNWS.

Jaschke, Richard. 1955. *English-Arabic Conversational Dictionary.* New York: Frederick Ungar Publishing Company.

Jessup, H. H. 1869. "Liberia and the Arabic Language." *AR* 42, no. 10:304–305.

Johnson, H. W., Jr. 1867a. "Letter from Liberia." *AR* 43, no. 6:171–173. From the *Ontario Messenger.*

———. 1867b. "[Letter] from Mr. H. W. Johnson, Jr." *AR* 43, no. 7:215–216.

———. 1868. "Letter from Mr. H. W. Johnson Jr." *AR* 44, no. 10:311–14.

Johnson, John William. 1986. *The Epic of Son-Jara: A West African Tradition.* Text by Fa-Digi Sisòkò. Analytical study and translation by John William Johnson. Transcribed and translated with the assistance of Charles S. Bird, Cheick Oumar Mara, Checkna Mohamed Singaré, Ibrahim Kalilou Tèra, and Bourama Soumaoro. Bloomington: Indiana University Press.

———. 1999. "The Dichotomy of Power and Authority in Mande Society in the Epic of *Sunjata.*" In *In Search of Sunjata: The Mande Oral Epic as History, Literature, and Performance,* edited by Ralph Austin, 9–23. Bloomington: Indiana University Press.

Johnson, Marion. 1970a–b. "The Cowrie Currencies of West Africa." Part 1 (1970a), *JAH* 11, no. 1:17–49; part 2 (1970b), *JAH* 11, no. 3:331–353.

Johnston, Harry. [1906] 1969. *Liberia.* New York: Negro Universities Press.

Jones, Adam. 1981. "Who Were the Vai?" *JAH* 22:159–178.

———. 1983a. *From Slaves to Palm Kernels: A History of the Galinhas Country (West Africa) 1730–1890.* Wiesbaden, Germany: Franz Steiner Verlag GMBH.

———. 1983b. "The Kquoja Kingdom: A Forest State in Seventeenth Century West Africa." *Paideuma* 29:23–43.

———. 1987. "A Critique of Editorial and Quasi-editorial Work on Pre-1885 European Sources for Sub-Saharan Africa, 1960–1986." *Paideuma* 33:95–106.

Jones, Adam, and Marion Johnson. 1980. "Slaves from the Windward Coast." *JAH* 21:17–34.

Jones, Hannah A. B. 1962. "The Struggle for Political and Cultural Unification in Liberia, 1847–1930." Ph.D. diss., Northwestern University.

Joucla, E. 1937. *Bibliographie de l'Afrique occidentale française.* Paris: Société d'éditions géographiques, maritimes et coloniales.

Kaba, Lansiné. 1973. "Islam, Society and Politics in Pre-colonial Baté, Guinea." *Bulletin de l'I.F.A.N.* 35, no. 2:323–344.

———. 1976. "The Politics of Qur'anic Education among Muslim Traders in the Western Sudan: The Subbanu Experience." *Canadian Journal of African Studies* 10, no. 3:409–421.

Kalous, Milan. 1995. "The Human Archetype of Male Circumcision and the Poro-Type Secret Society on the Upper Guinea Coast of West Africa." *Archív Orientální* 63:305–329.

Kamara, Wata Mammadi. n.d. Cassette history purchased for Tim Geysbeek by Amara Cissé in Monrovia on 18 September 1992.

Kante, Bala. 1971–72. "Monographie du pays Kuranko." In "Memoire de fin d'étude supérieures." Thesis, Kankan Institut Polytechnique Jules Nyerere de Kankan, République de Guinée.

Kaplan, R. D. 1994. "The Coming Anarchy: How Scarcity, Crime, Overpopulation, and Disease Are Rapidly Destroying the Social Fabric of Our Planet." *Atlantic Monthly* (February): 44–76.

Karnga, Abayomi. 1909. *The Negro Republic on West Africa.* Monrovia: College of West Africa Press.

———. 1926. *History of Liberia.* Liverpool: D. H. Tyte and Company.

Kastenholtz, Raimund. 1991–92. "Comparative Mande Studies: State of the Art." *Sprache und Geschichte in Afrika* 12–13: 107–158.

Kea, R. A. 1971. "Firearms and Warfare on the Gold and Slave Coasts from the Sixteenth to the Nineteenth Centuries." *JAH* 12, no. 2:185–213.

Kellemu, John. 1971. "Swamp Rice Cultivation among the Kpelle." *Liberian Research Association Journal* 3, no. 1:1–17.

Khalîl, M. [1916] 1980. *Maliki Law: Being a Summary from French Translations of Mukhtasar of Sidi Khalil (d. c. 1365).* Translated and edited by F. H. Ruxton. Westport, Conn.: Hyperion Press.

King, Alfred B. 1882a. "A Tour of Bopora." Part 2. *Observer* (Monrovia) 5, no. 6 (13 April).

——— 1882b. "A Trip to Bopora." Part 4. *Observer* (Monrovia) 5, no. 8 (11 May).

———. 1882c. "A Trip to Bopora: Homeward Bound." *Observer* (Monrovia) 5, no. 16 (15 September).

———. 1888. "Outlook for the New Republic." *AR* 64, no. 10:110–113.

Kister, J. 1865. "Tour to Bopora." *AR* 46:308–312.

Klaus, Wolfram. 1990. *Plane und Grundrisse Afrikanischer Stadte.* Berlin: Deutsche Staatsbibliothek, 1990.

"The Kondahs." 1840. *AR* 16, no. 11:334–335. Also in *MCJ* 1, no. 16 (15 September 1842): 248–249.

Konneh, Augustine. 1992. "Indigenous Enterprises and Capitalists: The Role of the Mandingo in the Economic Development of Modern-Day Liberia." Ph.D. diss., Indiana University.

———. 1996a. "Citizenship at the Margins: Status, Ambiguity, and the Mandingo of Liberia." *African Studies Review* 39, no. 2:141–154.

———. 1996b. *Religion, Commerce, and the Integration of the Mandingo in Liberia.* Lanham, Md.: University Press of America.

Kratz Indexing, comp. 1986. *Indiana 1860 Census Index.* Salt Lake City, Utah: Kratz Indexing.

Krause, Chester L., and Clifford Mishler, eds. 1982. *Standard Catalogue of World Coins.* Iola, Wis.: Krause Publications.

Kurtz, Ronald J. 1985. *Ethnographic Survey of Southeastern Liberia: The Grebo-Speaking Peoples.* Philadelphia: Institute for Liberian Studies, no. 7.

La Rue, Sidney. 1930. *The Land of the Pepper Bird.* New York and London: G. P. Putnam's Sons.

La Violette, Adria. 1995. "Women Craft Specialists in Jenne: The Manipulation of Mande Social Categories." In *Status and Identity in West Africa: Nyamakalaw of Mande,* edited by David C. Conrad and Barbara E. Frank, 170–181. Bloomington: Indiana University Press.

Labouret, H. [1931] 1968. Preface to *The Negroes of Africa: History and Culture,* by Maurice Delafosse, translated from the French by F. Fligelman. Port Washington, N.Y.: Kennikat Press.

Laing, Alexander Gordon. 1825. *Travels in Timmannee, Kooranko, and Soolima, Countries of West Africa.* London: John Murray.

Lambert, A. 1861. "Voyage dans le Fouta-Djallon." *Tour du Monde,* no. 3 (13 September).

Lamp, Frederick. 1983. "House of Stones: Memorial Art of Fifteenth-Century Sierra Leone." *The Art Bulletin* 65, no. 2 (June): 219–237. For an adaptation in French, see "Sculptures Anciennes en Pierre." In *La Guinée et ses héritages culturels,* by Frederick Lamp, translated by Sabine Mattson and Jacqueline Niemtzow, with Michèle-Berthe Fournel and Charles Djibi Camara, 14–25. Conakry: Service d'Information et de Relations Culturelles [USIS], Ambassade des Etats-Unis, 1992.

Lander, Richard. 1830. *Records of Captain Clapperton's Last Expedition to Africa.* 2 vols. London: H. Colburn and R. Bentley.

Lander, Richard, and John Lander. 1832. *Journal of an Expedition to Explore the Course and Termination of the Niger.* 3 vols. London: John Murray and William Clowes.

Last, Murray. 1987. "Reform in West Africa: The *Jihad* Movements of the Nineteenth Century." In *History in West Africa,* edited by J. F. A. Ajayi and Michael Crowder, 2:1–47. London: Longman.

"The Late Dr. McGill." 1871. *AR* 47, no. 9:287. From *The Republican* (10 July).

"The Late Expedition for Liberia [*Liberia Packet*]." 1850. *AR* 26, no. 4:103–106.

"Late from Liberia." 1875. *AR* 51, no. 10:117–120.

"Latest from Liberia." 1858. *AR* 34, no. 5:129–131.

Latourette, Kenneth Scott. 1975. *A History of Christianity: Reformation to the Present.* Vol. 2. Rev. ed. New York and London: Harper and Row.

Launay, Robert. 1979. "Landlords, Hosts, and Strangers among the Dyula." *Ethnology* 18:71–83.

———. 1992. *Beyond the Stream: Islam and Society in a West African Town.* Berkeley and Los Angeles: University of California Press.

Law, Robin. 1976. "Horses, Firearms, and Political Power in Pre-colonial West Africa." *Past and Present* 72:112–132.

———. 1980. *The Horse in West African History: The Role of the Horse in the Societies of Pre-colonial West Africa.* Oxford: Oxford University Press for the International African Institute.

Le Long, M. H. 1949. *N'Zerekore: L'evangile en fôret Guinée.* Paris: Librairie Missionnaire.

Leach, Melissa. 1994. *Rainforest Relations: Gender and Resource Use among the Mende of Gola, Sierra Leone.* Edinburgh: Edinburgh University Press for the International African Institute.

Legassick, Martin. 1966. "Firearms, Horses, and Samorian Army Organization, 1870–1898." *JAH* 7, no. 1:95–115.

Leopold, Robert S. 1991. "Prescriptive Alliance and Ritual Collaboration in Loma Society." Ph.D. diss., Indiana University.

"A Letter from the King of Musadu." [1870] 1871. In *The People of Africa,* edited by H. M. S[chieffelin], 129–136. New York: Anson D. F. Randolph and Company.

"The Letter from the King of Musadu to the President of Liberia Brought by Hon. B. J. K. Anderson." 1904. *Liberia Recorder* 6, no. 9 (9 April).

"Letter from Rev. George L. Seymour." 1860. *AR* 36, no. 2:60–62.

"Letters of an Itinerant." 1918. *Liberia and West Africa* 20, no. 3–4 (April–May): 7.

Levtzion, Nehemia. 1973. *Ancient Ghana and Mali.* London: Methuen and Company.

———. 1985. "Sociopolitical Roles of Muslim Clerics and Scholars in West Africa." In *Comparative Social Dynamics,* edited by Erik Cohen, Moshe Lissak, and Uri Almagor, 95–107. Boulder, Colo., and London: Westview Press.

———. 2000. "Islam in the Bilad al-Sudan to 1800." In *The History of Islam in Africa,* edited by Nehemia Levtzion and Randall L. Pouwells, 63–92. Athens, Oxford, and Cape Town: Ohio University Press and James Currey.

Lewicki, Tadeusz. 1971. "Un état Soudanais medieval inconnu: Le royaume de Zāfūn(u)." *Cahiers d'Études Africaines* 11:501–525.

Lewis, Bernard. 1982. *The Muslim Discovery of Europe.* New York and London: W. W. Norton and Company.

Lewis, Tayler. 1871. "The Koran: African Mohammedanism." *AR* 47, no. 6: 163–167.

Leynaud, Emile, and Youssouf Cisse. 1978. *Paysans Malinke du haute Niger: Tradition et développement rural en Afrique soudanaise.* [Bamako?]: Impr. Populaire du Mali.

"Liberia." 1873. *AR* 49, no. 2:42–45.
"Liberia." 1875. *Fifty-eighth ARACS,* 11–15.
"Liberia." 1880. *Sixty-third ARACS,* 40–41.
"Liberia." 1888. *Sixty-fourth,* no. 4:47–48.
"Liberia." 1903. *West Africa Mail* (16 October).
"Liberia Annual Conference." 1921. *The Liberia Methodist.* 1, no. 1 (March): 2–4.
"Liberia Explorations." 1861. *Philadelphia Colonization Herald* (October).
"Liberia Interior Association." 1881. *Observer* (Monrovia) 4, no. 17 (18 October).
"Liberia Interior Association, Ltd." 1882. *Observer* (Monrovia) 5, no. 18 (12 October).
"Liberia Interior Exploration." 1859. *NYCJ* 9, no. 9, whole no. 105.
"Liberia Methodist Mission." 1873. *AR* 49, no. 7:195–198.
Liberia: Official Standard Names. 1968. Washington, D.C.: Geographic Names Division, Army Map Services.
Liberia: Official Standard Names. 1976. Washington, D.C.: U.S. Board on Geographic Names.
"The *Liberia Packet.*" 1846. *AR* 23, no. 11 (November): 352–355.
"The Liberia Recorder." 1906. *Liberia Recorder* 7, no. 24 (2 June): 5.
"The Liberia Recorder and Its New Editor." 1902. *The New Africa* 4, no. 6 (June): 17, 167.
"Liberian Affairs: Trade and Agriculture." 1873. *AR* 49, no. 5:156.
"Liberian African Exploration." 1858. *Philadelphia Colonization Herald* (May).
"A Liberian Caravan." 1857. *MCJ* 8, no. 22 (March): 364.
"Liberian Cloth." 1867. *AR* 44, no. 11:344–345. From *The African Republic,* partly published in "Progress in Liberia," *AR* 45, no. 3 (1868): 75–76.
"Liberian Exploration." 1868. *AR* 44, no. 9:286.
"The Liberian Explorer." 1859. *NYCJ* 9, no. 3:99. From the *Pennsylvania Inquirer.*
"A Liberian Explorer." 1860. *Philadelphia Colonization Herald* (September).
"Liberian Intelligence: Musardu." 1871. *AR* 47, no. 1:17. From the *Liberia Register.*
"Liberian Methodism Under the World: Program of the Methodist Episcopal Church." 1921. *The Liberia Methodist* 1, no. 7 (September): 2–3.
"Liberian Minerals and Trading." 1902. *Gold Coast Globe and Ashanti Argus,* 105–106. In U.S. Consulate Despatches 1863–1906, no. 170, microfilm 4391, roll 13.
"Liberian Missions." 1859. *Philadelphia Colonization Herald* (October).
"A Liberian Newspaper." 1873. *AR* 49, no. 4:121.
"Liberia's Friends: 'Succumbed to Friendship?'" 1880. *Observer* (Monrovia) 3, no. 8 (22 April).
Liberius. 1852. "From Our Journal." *NYCJ* 2, no. 3 (March). From *LR.*

Liberty, C. E. Zamba. [1977] 1999. *The Growth of the Liberian State: An Analysis of Its Historiography*. N.p.: Obichere Research Center.

Liebenow, J. Gus. 1987. *Liberia: The Quest for Democracy*. Bloomington: Indiana University Press.

Lindroth, S. 1955. "Adam Afzelius: Swedish Botanist in Sierra Leone." *Sierra Leone Studies,* n.s., 4:194–207.

"List of Emigrants." 1852. *AR* 28, no. 6:181–184.

"List of Emigrants [*Brig Oriole*]." 1852. *AR* 28, no. 11:350.

"List of Emigrants [*Isla de Cuba*]." 1854. *AR* 30, no. 3:88–89. From the *NYCJ*.

"List of Emigrants [*Liberia Packet*]." 1852. *AR* 28, no. 4:118–119.

"List of Emigrants [*Linda Stewart*]." 1853. *AR* 29, no. 1:26–30.

"List of Emigrants [*Mary Caroline Stevens*]." 1860. *AR* 36, no. 5:140–145.

"List of Emigrants by the *Mary Caroline Stevens,* 3d voyage." 1857. *AR* 33, no. 12:355–358.

"List of Emigrants by the *M. C. Stevens,* Nov. 1, 1860." 1860. *AR* 36, no. 12: 363–365.

"List of Emigrants by the Ship *Elvira Owen.*" 1856. *AR* 32, no. 8:248–254.

"List of Emigrants [*Banshee*]." 1854. *AR* 30, no. 1:19–24.

Little, Kenneth. 1965. "The Political Function of the Poro (Part One)." *Africa* 30, no. 4:349–365.

———. 1966. "The Political Function of the Poro (Part Two)." *Africa* 36, no. 1: 62–72.

"The Living Chronicle." 1902. *Living Chronicle* 2, no. 5 (12 June).

Livingstone, Frank B. 1958. "Anthropological Implications of Sickle Cell Gene: Distribution in West Africa." *American Anthropologist* 60, no. 3:533–562.

Lloyd, Norman. 1968. *The Golden Encyclopedia of Music.* New York: Golden Press.

Long, Ronald W. 1972. "The Northern Mande Languages." Paper presented at the Conference on Manding Studies, London, School of Oriental and African Studies.

Lovejoy, Paul E. 1980. "Kola in the History of West Africa." *Cahiers d'Études Africaines* 20, no. 1–2: 97–134.

———. 1985. "The Internal Trade of West Africa before 1800." In *History of West Africa,* edited by J. F. A. Ajayi and Michael Crowden, 1:648–690. London: Longman.

Lüddecke, R. [1890]. *Afrika in Blattren IM Maasstab von 1: 10.000.000.* Gotha, Germany: Justus Perthes.

Lugenbell, J. W. 1850. *Sketches of Liberia: Comprising a Brief Account of the Geography, Climate, Productions, and Diseases, of the Republic of Liberia.* Washington, D.C.: C. Alexander, Printer.

Lynch, Hollis R. 1967. *Edward Wilmot Blyden: Pan Negro Patriot, 1833–1912.* London: Oxford University Press.

———, ed. 1978. *Selected Letters of Edward Wilmot Blyden.* Millwood, N.Y.: KTO Press.

M[orrell], E. D. 1905. "Liberia: Dr. Blyden's Mission to France." *LR* 7, no. 11 (15 July).

Macbriar, Robert Maxwell. 1839. *Sketches of a Missionary's Travels in Egypt, Syria, Western Africa . . . etc.* London: Simkin, Marshall and Company.

Maculay, G. I. 1871. "The Arabic Language at Sierra Leone and Bathurst." *AR* 47, no. 8:242–244.

Mahmud, K[halil]. 1974. Introduction to the 2d edition of *The People of Africa.* Edited by H. M. Schieffelin, v–xxiii. Ibadan: Ibadan University Press.

Makdissa, Ussama. 1997. "Reclaiming the Land of the Bible: Missionaries, Secularism, and Evangelical Modernity." *American Historical Review* 102, no. 3:680–713.

Malcolm, J. M. 1939. "Mende Warfare." *Sierra Leone Studies,* o.s., 21:47.

Malik, Imam. 1985. *Muwatta.* Translated, with notes, by Muhammad Rahimuddin. Lahore, Pakistan: Sh. Muhammad Ashraf Publishers, Booksellers and Exporters.

Manifesto Adopted at the Headquarters of the People's Party. 1933. Monrovia, Liberia. In the Albert Port Papers, roll 1.

Maninka-English Dictionary. n.d. Kankan, Guinea: Christian and Missionary Alliance.

Manning, Patrick. 1988. *Francophone Sub-Saharan Africa, 1880–1985.* Cambridge: Cambridge University Press.

"Map of Liberia." 1892. *Liberia* 3 (November 1893).

Marchard. 1897. "La religion Musulmane au Soudan français." *Renseignements Coloniaux et Documents, Supplément au Bulletin du Comité de l'Afrique Française* 4 (October): 91–111.

"Married." 1848. *LH* 16, no. 11 (25 August): 43.

Marsh, George P. 1856. "Address of Hon. George P. Marsh." *Thirty-ninth ARACS* (1856): 10–17.

Martin, Jane. 1969. "How to Build a Nation: Liberian Ideals about National Integration in the Late Nineteenth Century." *LSJ* 2, no. 1:15–42.

Marty, Paul. 1922. *Études sur l'Islam en Côte d'Ivoire.* Paris: E. Leroux.

Massing, Andreas. 1978–79. "Materials for a History of Western Liberia: Samori and the Malinke Frontier in the Toma Sector." *LSJ* 7, no. 1:49–67.

———. 1980. *The Economic Anthropology of the Kru (West Africa).* Wiesbaden, Germany: Franz Steiner Verlag GMBH.

———. 1985. "The Mande, the Decline of Mali, and the Mandinka Expansion towards the South Windward Coast." *Cahiers d'Études Africaines* 99, no. 26:21–55.

———. 2000. "The Wangara, an Old Soninke Diaspora in West Africa?" *Cahiers d'Études africaines* 40, no. 2:281–308.

Maugham-Brown, H. 1943. "Sei Bush Belts in Sierra Leone." *Farm and Forest* 4:8–9.

Mayer, K. 1951. "Forest Resources of Liberia." *Agricultural Information Bulletin,* no. 67. Washington, D.C.: Forest Service USDA.

McDowell, R. 1838. "African Sketches: Two, Climate, Soil, and Productions of Liberia." *AR* 14, no. 9:264–268.

McEvoy, Frederick D. 1970–71. "Some Proposals for Liberian Archeology." *LSJ* 3, no. 2:129–141.

McIntosh, Roderick J. 1998. *The Peoples of the Middle Niger: The Island of Gold.* Malden, Mass., and Oxford: Blackwell Publishers.

McNaughton, Patrick R. 1988. *The Mande Blacksmiths: Knowledge, Power, and Art in West Africa.* Bloomington: Indiana University Press.

McPherson, J. H. T. 1891. *History of Liberia.* Baltimore: Johns Hopkins University Press.

Mechlin, J. 1831. "From the Colony," Mechlin to Rev. R. R. Gurley, 15 June 1831. *AR* 7 (December): 301–310.

"Meeting of [the] Connecticut Colonization Society." 1855. *AR* 31, no. 8:237–241.

Mehlinger, L.R. 1916. "The Attitude of the Free Negro toward African Colonization." *Journal of Negro History* 1:276–301.

"Message of President Gardner." 1880. *AR* 56, no. 7:113–121.

Meyer, R. R. B. 1914. "List of Books on Liberia in the Library of Congress." [Washington, D.C.]: Library of Congress, Division of Bibliography, 1–11 (plus three additional pages).

Miller, Joseph C. 1980. "Introduction: Listening for the African Past." In *The African Past Speaks,* edited by Joseph C. Miller, 1–60. Kent: Wm. Dawson and Sons.

Miller, R. M. 1975. "Home as Found: Ex-Slaves and Liberia." *LSJ* 6, no. 2:92–108.

Moffatt, James, and Millar Patrick, eds. 1928. *Handbook to the Church Hymnary.* London: Oxford University Press.

Mollien, Gaspard-Théodore. 1820. *Voyage dans l'Intérieur de l'Afrique aux sources du Sénégal et de la Gambie, fait en 1818.* Paris: Imprimerie de Mme Ve Courcier.

Mondjannagni, A. C. 1975. "Vie rurale et rapports vill-campagne dans le Bas-Dahomey: Thèse pour le doctorat d'état es lettres." University of Paris, 2 vols.

"Monographique de la region administrative de Beyla." n.d. Typewritten manuscript, in the possession of Tim Geysbeek, 24 pages with two maps.

"The Monrovia Academy." 1856. *MCJ* 8, no. 8 (January): 120.

"Monrovia in 1866." 1866. *AR* 47, no. 10:327–329. From the *Cavalla Messenger.*

Monts, Lester. 1984. "Conflict, Accommodation, and Transformation: The Effect of Islam on the Music of Vai Secret Societies." *Cahiers d'Études Africaines* 24, no. 3:321–342.

———. 1990. "Social and Musical Responses to Islam among the Vai." *LSJ* 15, no. 2:108–124.

Morrison. 1897. "Les écoles au Soudan français." *Renseignements Coloniaux et Documents, Supplément au Bulletin du Comité de l'Afrique Française* 4 (October): 81–91.

Moses, Wilson Jeremiah. 1989. *Alexander Crummell: A Study of Civilization and Discontent.* New York: Oxford University Press.

———, ed. 1998a. "Five Letters on Liberian Colonization (1851–1863), Including an Original Biographical Sketch of Augustus Washington." In *Liberian Dreams: Back-to-Africa Narratives from the 1850s,* edited by Wilson Jeremiah Moses, 179–224. University Park: Pennsylvania State University Press.

———, ed. 1998b. *Liberian Dreams: Back-to-Africa Narratives from the 1850s.* Edited by Wilson Jeremiah Moses. University Park: Pennsylvania State University Press.

Mouser, Bruce. L., ed. 1979. "Brian O'Beirne: Journal, January to April 1821." In *Guinea Journals: Journeys into Guinea-Conakry during the Sierra Leone Phase, 1800–1821.* Washington, D.C.: University Press of America.

Müller, Heinrich. 1981. *Guns, Pistols, Revolvers: Hand-Firearms from the Fourteenth to the Nineteenth Centuries.* London: Orbis Publishing.

Murchison, Roderick I. 1870. "Sir Roderick I. Murchison's Address." *The Journal of the Royal Geographical Society* 40:cxxiv–clxxviii.

Murdock, George Peter. 1959. *Africa: Its Peoples and Their Culture History.* New York, Toronto, and London: McGraw-Hill Book Company.

Murdza, Peter John, Jr. 1975. *Immigrants to Liberia, 1865–1904: An Alphabetical Listing.* Newark: Liberian Studies Association in America.

———. 1979. "The Tricolor and the Lone Star: A History of Franco-Liberian Relations, 1847–1930." Ph.D. diss., University of Wisconsin–Madison.

"The Musahdu Railway." 1879. *AR* 2, no. 11 (11 September).

Naber, S. P. L'Hornoé, and J. J. Moret. 1910. *Op expeditie met de Franschen.* The Hague: Mouton and Company.

The National Union Catalogue: Pre-1956 Imprints. 1969. Vol. 62. London: Mansell.

The National Union Catalogue: Pre-1956 Imprints. 1977. Vol. 525. London: Mansell.

Nassau, R. H. 1873. "Address of Rev. R. H. Nassau, M.D." *Fifty-sixth ARACS,* 43–50. Also in *AR* 49, no. 3:78–84.

Nawwab, Ismail I., Peter C. Speers, and Paul F. Hoye, eds. 1980. *Aramco and Its World: Arabia and the Middle East.* Washington, D.C.: Arabian American Oil Company.

"Necrology." 1891. *Seventy-fourth ARACS,* 3.

Nesbit, William. [1855] 1998. "Four Months in Liberia, or African Colonization Exposed (1855)." In *Liberian Dreams: Back-to-Africa Narratives from the*

1850s, edited by Wilson Jeremiah Moses, 79–126. University Park: Pennsylvania State University Press.

"The New Franco-Liberian Frontier." 1908. *The Geographical Journal* 31:105–106.

"A New World: Explorations." 1886. *AR* 62, no. 1: 15–40.

"The New York State Colonization Society." 1846. *AR* 22, no. 6:188–196. Also in the *MCJ* (July 1845): 181–187.

Niane, D. T., ed., and Djeli Mamoudou Kouyaté, narrator. [1960] 1980. *Sundiata: An Epic of Old Mali.* London: Longman Group, 1980. First published in French in 1960, and in English in 1965.

Norte, George C., Jr. 1873. *Firearms Encyclopedia.* New York: Harper and Row.

"The North Western Boundary of Liberia." 1886. *AR* 62, no. 4:73–74.

"The North Western Boundary of Liberia." 1888. *AR* 64, no. 10:132.

Norwich, Oscar I. 1983. *Maps of Africa: An Illustrated and Annotated Carto-Bibliography.* Johannesburg and Cape Town: A. D. Donker.

"Notes: The First of December." 1900. *LR* 3, no. 21 (13 December).

"Notes: Foumba Sissy." 1880. *Observer* (Monrovia) 3, no. 2 (22 January).

"Notes: Hon Benj. Anderson." 1881. *Observer* (Monrovia) 14, no. 17 (18 October).

"Notes: Measures Are on Foot." 1879. *Observer* (Monrovia) 2, no. 12 (25 September). Also in *Sixty-third ARACS* (1880): 12–13.

"Notes: Mr. Benjamin Anderson." 1881. *Observer* (Monrovia) 4, no. 20 (10 November).

"Notes: The Narrative of the Expedition." 1880. *Observer* (Monrovia) 3, no. 1 (8 January).

"Notes: The Notable Foumba Sissy." 1880. *Observer* (Monrovia) 3, no. 1 (8 January).

"Notes on the Proceedings of the Liberia Annual Conference, 1920." 1920. *Liberia and West Africa* 21, no. 10–11 (March–April): 5.

"Notice." 1881. *Observer* (Monrovia) 4, no. 4 (24 February).

Nussbaum, Loren V., William W. Gage, and Daniel Varre. 1970. *Dakar Wolof: A Basic Course.* Washington, D.C.: U.S. Office of Education and the Center for Applied Linguistics.

O'Beirne, B. [1821] 1979. "Journal, January to April 1921." In *Guinea Journals: Journals into Guinea-Conakry during the Sierra Leone Phase, 1800–21,* edited by B. L. Mouser. Washington, D.C.: University Press of America.

"The Official Body." 1882. *Observer* (Monrovia) 5, no. 3 (9 February).

"Official Notice." 1879. *Observer (Monrovia)* 2, no. 11 (11 September).

"Official Organ of the Liberian Citizens' League: Official Directory for the Year 1932." 1932. *Liberian Sentinel* 1, no. 1 (August).

d'Ollone, [Henri Marie Gustave]. 1901. *De la Côte d'Ivoire au Soudan et à la Guinée.* Paris: Librairie Hachette.

———. 1903. "Côte d'Ivoire et Libéria: Variations cartographiques relatives a ces contrées et état actuel de nos connaissances." *Annales de Geographie* 12, no. 62:130–144.

Olson, James S. 1996. *The Peoples of Africa: An Ethnohistorical Dictionary.* Westwood, Conn., and London: Greenwood Press.

"The Opening up of Africa." 1882. *AR* 58, no. 7:81–84.

Orr, Kenneth G. 1971–72. "An Introduction to the Archeology of Liberia." *LSJ* 4, no. 1:55–79.

Osbeck, Kenneth W. 1982. *One Hundred Hymn Stories.* Grand Rapids, Mich.: Kregel Publications.

"Our Common Schools." 1880. *Observer* (Monrovia) 3, no. 3 (21 February).

"Our Liberia Letter." 1881a. *AR* 57, no. 7:78–79.

"Our Liberia Letter." 1881b. *AR* 57, no. 10:132–133.

"Our Paris Correspondent on the Dispute." 1903. *West African Mail* 1, no. 28 (9 October): 743. Also in the *Sierra Leone Weekly News* 20, no. 9 (31 October 1903): 2 (68), and *LR* 6, no. 1 (7 November 1903): 7.

"Outlook for the New Republic." 1888. *AR* 64:110–113.

"Papers in the Case of Impeachment against J. S. Payne, President of Liberia." 1877. In Despatches from United States Ministers to Liberia 1863–1906, no. 170, microfilm 4391, roll 7. Reproduced in Geysbeek 1999, 38.

Park, Mungo. [1799 and 1805] 1983. *Travels into the Interior of Africa.* London: Eland Books.

Parsons, H. Alexander. 1950. *The Colonial Coinages of British Africa with the Adjacent Islands.* London: Spink and Son.

Paulme, D. 1954. *Les gens du riz.* Paris: Plon.

Payne, James S. 1860. *Politial Economy as Adapted to the Republic of Africa.* Monrovia, Liberia: G. Killian, Printer, Liberia Herald Office.

———. 1877. *Message of the President of the Republic of Liberia to the First Session of the Sixteenth Legislature.* Monrovia, Liberia: T. Howard, Printer, Government Printing Office. In U.S. Consulate Despatches 1863–1906, no. 170, microfilm 4391, roll 7.

Penfold, P. A., ed. 1982. *Maps and Plans in the Public Record Office.* Vol. 3, *Africa.* London: Her Majesty's Stationery Office.

Pereira, Duarte Pacheco. [c. 1506–1508] 1937. *Esmeraldo de situ orbis.* Translated and edited by George H. T. Kimble. London: Hakluyt Society.

"Permanent Committees and Executive Council of the League." 1932. *Liberian Sentinel* 1, no. 1 (August).

Person, Yves. 1961. "Le Kissi et leur statuettes de pierre dans la cadre de l'historie Ouest-Africaine." *Bulletin de l'institut Français d'Afrique Noire* 23b:1–59.

———. 1962. "La jeunesse de Samori." *Revue d'Histoire d'Outre-Mer* 50:151–180.

———. 1964. "Chronology and Oral Tradition." Translated by Susan Sherwin. In *The Historian in Tropical Africa,* edited by J. Vansina, R. Maunay, and L. V. Thomas, 322–338. London: Oxford University Press. First published as "Tradition orale et chronologie," *Cahiers d'Études Africaines* 2, no. 7 (1962): 462–476.

———. 1968. *Samori: Une révolution dyula.* Vols. 1 and 2. Dakar: Memories de l'Institut Fondmental d'Afrique Noire.

———. 1970. "Samori and Resistance to the French." In *Protest and Power in Black Africa,* edited by Robert I. Rotberg and Ali A. Mazuri, 80–112. New York: Oxford University Press.

———. 1971. "Ethnic Movements and Acculturation in Upper Guinea since the Fifteenth Century." *International Journal of African Historical Studies* 4, no. 3:669–689.

———. 1972. "The Dyula and the Manding World." Paper presented at the Conference on Manding Studies, London, School of Oriental and African Studies.

———. 1975. *Samori: Une révolution dyula.* Vol. 3. Dakar: IFAN-Dakar.

———. 1979. "Samori and Islam." In *Studies in West African Islamic History,* vol. 1, edited by John Ralph Willis, 259–277. London: Frank Cass.

———. 1984. "The Coastal Peoples: From Casamance to the Ivory Coast." In *UNESCO General History of Africa,* vol. 4, edited by D. T. Niane, 301–323. Berkeley: Heinemann.

———. 1987. "The Atlantic Coast and the Southern Savannas, 1800–1880." In *History of West Africa,* vol. 2, edited by J. F. A. Ajayi and Michael Crowder, 250–300. London: Longman.

———. 1990. *Cartes historiques de l'Afrique Manding (fin du 19e siècle): Samori une revolution Dyula.* Paris: Centre de Recherches Africaines.

"Personal." 1872. *AR* 48, no. 10:311.

"Personal: Foumba Sissi." 1881. *Observer* (Monrovia) 4, no. 17 (22 September).

"Personal: Foumba Sissy." 1880. *Observer* (Monrovia) 3, no. 2 (22 January).

"Personal: Mr. Benjamin Anderson." 1882. *Observer* (Monrovia) 5, no. 4 (23 February).

Peters, Rudolph. 1995. *The Oxford Encyclopedia of the Modern Islamic World,* edited by John L. Esposito, s.v. "Jihad," 369–373. New York and Oxford: Oxford University Press.

Peterson, Daniel H. [1854] 1998. "The Looking-Glass: Being a True Report and Narrative of the Life, Travels, and Labours of the Rev. Daniel H. Peterson (1854)." In *Liberian Dreams: Back-to-Africa Narratives from the 1850s,* edited by Wilson Jeremiah Moses, 1–78. University Park: Pennsylvania State University Press.

Peterson, Harold L., ed. 1964. *Encyclopedia of Firearms.* New York: E. P. Dutton and Company.

Phelps, J. W. 1873. "Road to Musadu." *AR* 49, 8:255–256.

Philips, John Edward. 1983. "African Smoking and Pipes." *JAH* 24, no. 3:303–319.

Pitman, Charles. 1877. "Into the Heart of Africa." *The Christian Advocate* 51 (21 June): 1–19.

———. 1878. "Mohammedanism in West Africa." *AR* 54:17–18.

———. 1881. "The Platform of the Republican Party." *Observer* (Monrovia) 4, no. 4 (24 February).

Population Schedules of the Sixth Census of the United States. 1840. Roll 107, Kentucky, 2:138–256. Carroll, Casey, Christian, and Carter Counties. National Archives, National Archives Microfilm Publications, microcopy no. 704, nos. 193, 205.

Porter, Philip W. 1956. "Population Distribution and Land Use in Liberia." Ph.D. thesis, University of London, London School of Economics and Political Science.

Portères, Roland. 1965. "Les noms des riz en Guinée." *Journal d'Agriculture Tropicale et Botanique Appliqué* 7, no. 9–10:370–402.

"Presidential Appointments." 1873. *AR* 49, no. 6:185.

"Progress in Liberia." 1873. *AR* 49, no. 10:311–312.

"Progress in Liberia." 1889. *AR* 60, no. 10:115–117.

"Proposed Settlement on the New Jersey Purchase." 1860. *AR* 35, no. 4:125–127.

"Propositions to the Republic of Liberia for Concessions of Land." 1874. Monrovia: Government Printing Office. In Despatches from United States Ministers to Liberia 1863–1906, no. 170, microfilm 4391, roll 4.

Prost, George E. 1869. "Arabic-Speaking Negro Mohammedans in Africa." *AR* 45, no. 5:129–133.

Prussin, Labelle. 1986. *Hatumere: Islamic Design in West Africa.* Berkeley and Los Angeles: University of California Press.

———. 1995. "Faces of Islam in the Futa-Djallon." In *Islamic Art and Culture in Sub-Saharan Africa,* edited by Karin Adahl and Berit Sahlstrom, 21–56. Fugura Nova Series, 27. Uppsala, Sweden: Acta Universitatis Upsaliensis.

"Pure Native Iron." 1855. *MCJ* 8, no. 4 (September): 63. From the *Philadelphia North American.*

"Railroads in Liberia." 1869. *AR* 45, no. 7 (July): 209.

"The Railway Scheme." 1878. *Observer* (Monrovia) 1, no. 7 (24 October).

"The Railway Scheme." 1879. *Observer* (Monrovia) 2, no. 11 (11 September).

Rambo, J. 1849. Rambo to Rt. Rev. and Dear Sir [recipient not identified], 13 April. *AR* 25, no. 10:304–307.

Rawlinson, H. C. 1875. "Sir H. C. Rawlonson's Address." *The Journal of the Royal Geographical Society* 54 (1875).

Reade, Winwood. 1870. Winwood to Momoru, King of the Condo Country. In *Narrative of a Journey to Musadu, the Capital of the Western Mandingoes,* by Benjamin J. K. Anderson. New York: S. W. Green, Printer.

———. 1873. *The African Sketch-Book.* Vol. 2. London: Smith, Elder and Company.

Réclus, Elisée. 1887. *Nouvelle géographie universelle. La terre et les hommes. XII l'Afrique occidentale, archipels Atlantiques, Sénégambie et Soudan occidental.* Paris: Hachette.

Reeve, Henry Fenwick. [1923] 1969. *The Black Republic: Liberia—Its Political and Social Conditions To-day.* New York: Negro Universities Press.

"The Regions Beyond." 1875. *Fifty-eighth ARACS,* 13–15. Also in the *AR* 51, no. 4 (1875): 41–43.

Reno, W. 1997. "African Weak States and Commercial Alliances." *African Affairs* 96, no. 383:165–186.

Report of the Special Committee of the House of Representatives on the Public Accounts. Adopted February 19, 1864. 1864. Monrovia, Liberia: G. Killian, Printer. In U.S. Consulate Despatches 1863–1906, no. 170, microfilm 4391, roll 1.

"Resolution for the Relief of Benjamin Anderson, Chief Commissioner to the Interior of Montserrado County." 1875. *ATL* (1874–1875), 33. Monrovia, Liberia: T. W. Howard, Printer, Government Printing Office.

Rhodes, Christopher. 1978. *The Gun.* Paulton, England, and London: Purnell and Sons and British Broadcasting Corporation.

Richards, Paul. 1986. *Coping with Hunger: Hazard and Experiment in a West African Farming System.* London: Allen and Unwin.

———. 1996. *Fighting for the Rainforest: War, Youth and Resources in Sierra Leone.* Oxford and Portsmouth, N.H.: International African Institute in association with James Currey.

Richards, W. A. 1980. "The Import of Firearms into West Africa in the Eighteenth Century." *JAH* 21:43–59.

Richardson, Nathaniel R. 1959. *Liberia's Past and Present.* London: Diplomatic Press and Publishing Company.

Rivière, Claude. 1969. "Bilan de l'Islamisation en Guinée." *Afrique Documents* 105–106:319–359.

"Roads to the Interior." 1873. *AR* 49, no. 7 (July): 216–217.

Roberts, Joseph Jenkins. 1845. Roberts to W. McLain, 10 February. *AR* 22, no. 5:154.

———. 1874. "Reply of the President to the Senate," In U.S. Consulate Despatches 1863–1906, no. 170, microfilm 4391, roll 4.

———. 1875. "Message of President Roberts." *AR* 51, no. 7 (July): 71–81.

Robertson, Claire C., and Martin A. Klein. 1983. "Women's Importance in African Slave Systems." In *Women and Slavery in Africa,* edited by Claire C. Robertson and Martin A. Klein, 3–28. Madison: University of Wisconsin Press.

Robinson, David. 1985. *The Holy War of Umar Tal: The Western Sudan in the Mid-Nineteenth Century.* Oxford: Clarendon Press.

[Robinson, Phillip T.]. 1996. "Liberia's Suspension Bridges: Their Importance in Travel and Security." *The Pepper Bird* 2:10–11.

Rockwell, Charles. 1842. "Sketches of Foreign Travel and Life." *AR* 18, no. 2: 305–312.

Roggeveen, Arent, and Jacob Robijn. [1687] 1971. *The Burning Fen.* Vol. 2. Amsterdam: Theatrvm Orbis Terrarvm.

Rouget, Fernard. 1906. *La Guinée*. Paris: Corbeil.

Rouire, Dr. 1894. "Délimitation de la République de Libéria." *Annales de Geographie* 3:489–498.

Rowe, Sir Samuel. 1886. "Sierra Leone and Liberia: Speech of Governor Sir Samuel Rowe." *AR* 62, no. 67:95–97.

Russell, Alfred F. 1888. Russell to Governor A. E. Havelock, December. In U.S. Consulate Despatches 1863–1906, no. 170, microfilm 4391, rolls 8–9.

Sabin, James Thomas. 1974. "The Making of the Americo-Liberian Community." Ph.D. diss., Columbia University.

Sadler, Wesley. 1951. *Untangled Loma: A Course of Study of the Looma Language of the Western Province of Liberia, West Africa.* Monrovia, Liberia: Published by the Board of Foreign Missions of the United Lutheran Church in America for the Evangelical Lutheran Church in Liberia.

Saha, S. C. 1985. "Trade as a Factor in Territorial Expansion in Liberia in the Nineteenth Century." In *History and Culture Study Seminar on Liberia, Sierra Leone, Senegal: A Compendium of Lecture and Round-table Discussion,* compiled and edited by James T. Tarpeh, 213–229. [Monrovia, Liberia]: U.S. Department of Education and U.S. Education and Cultural Foundation in Liberia.

Said, Edward W. 1979. *Orientalism.* New York: Vintage Books, Random House Division.

Salifu, Seku. Interviewed by Svend Holsoe in Monrovia on 12 July 1965. Translated by Boakai Yamah and Amara Cissé in Monrovia in 1992.

Sanneh, Lamin. 1989. *The Jakhanke Muslim Clerics: A Religious and Historical Study of Islam in Senegambia.* Lanham, Md., New York, and London: University Press of America.

Savage, Dr. 1839. "Dr. Savage's Journal." *AR* 15, no. 9:155–160; 15, no. 10: 166–171.

Sawyer, Amos. 1992. *The Emergence of Autocracy in Liberia: Tragedy and Challenge.* San Francisco: Institute for Contemporary Studies.

Sayers, E. F. 1927. "Notes on the Clan or Family Names Common in the Area Inhabited by Temne-Speaking People." *Sierra Leone Studies* 10:14–108.

Schaeffner, A., 1990. *Le sistre et le hochet: Musique, théâtre et danse dans les sociétés Africaines.* Paris: Hermann.

Schatzberg, M. 1988. *The Dialectics of Oppression in Zaire.* Bloomington: Indiana University Press.

Schieffelin, H[enry]. M. 1866. Schieffelin to William H. Seward, 22 March. In Notes from the Liberian Legation in the United States to the Department of State 1882–98, T-807, microfilm 4400, roll 1.

———, ed. [1871] 1974. *The People of Africa: A Series of Papers on Their Character, Condition, and Future Prospects by E. W. Blyden, D. D., Tayler Lewis, D. D., Theodore Dwight, Esq., Etc., Etc., Etc.* 2d ed. Edited by K. Mahmud. New York: Anson D. F. Randolph and Company; Ibadan: Ibadan University Press.

Schmokel, W. 1969. "Settlers and Tribes: The Origins of the Liberian Dilemma." In *Western African History,* edited by Daniel F. McCall, Norman R. Bennett, and Jeffrey Butler, 153–181. New York: Frederick A. Praeger.

Schulze, Willi. 1970–71. "Early Iron Smelting among the Northern Kpelle." *LSJ* 3:113–127.

———. 1973. *A New Geography of Liberia.* London: Longman.

Schwab, George. 1947. *Tribes of the Liberian Hinterland.* Cambridge: Harvard University Press.

Scott, Anna M. 1858. *Day Dawn in Africa, or Progress of the Protestant Episcopal Mission at Cape Palmas West Africa.* New York: Protestant Episcopal Society for the Promotion of Evangelical Knowledge.

Serle, W., G. J. Morel, and M. Hartwig. 1977. *A Field Guide to the Birds of West Africa.* London: Collins.

Servanté, H. [1805] 1857. "Letter, 12 August 1805." *Monthly Observer and New Church Record* 1 (1857): 313.

Seton, N. B. 1926. Introduction to *History of Liberia,* by Abayomi Karnga, xi–xvi. Liverpool: D. H. Tyte and Company.

"Settlement of Interior Difficulties." 1904. *LR* 6, no. 17 (6 August).

Severin, Timothy. 1973. *The African Adventure.* New York: E. P. Dutton and Company.

Seymour, George. 1842. Seymour to Anson G. Phelps, 21 December 1841. *AR* 18, no. 6:125.

———. 1843. Seymour to Anson G. Phelps, 12 October 1842. *AR* 19, no. 8: 232–233.

———. 1845. Seymour to Mrs. Pond, 8 January. *AR* 21, no. 11:342–343.

———. 1848. "Report on Agriculture." *AR* 24, no. 6:182–183. From *Africa's Luminary.*

———. 1851. Seymour to J. B. Pinney, 21 March. *AR* 27, no. 3:266–267. From the *NYCJ.*

———. 1853. Seymour to J. B. Pinney, 15 March. *AR* 29, no. 9:262–263.

———. 1855. "Journal of a Tour into the Country Interior of Grand Bassa." *LH* 5, no. 6 (1 July); 5, no. 7 (2 July). Also in *AR* 33, no. 6 (1856): 170–182.

———. 1857a. Seymour to J. B. Pinney, 4 January, in "Pessa Country." *AR* 33, no. 7 (1857): 197–198. From the *NYCJ.*

———. 1857b. Seymour to John Wolf, 23 April 1856, in "Missionary Appeal from Liberia." *AR* 32, no. 1: 14–15. From the *New Republic* (December 1856).

———. 1858a. "The Pessay or Pessa Country." *NYCJ* 8, no. 2, whole no. 86 (February).

———. 1858b. "The Pessay or Pessa Country: New Mission Station." *AR* 34, no. 1: 4–19.

———. 1858c. Seymour to R. R. Gurley, 1 February. *AR* 34, no. 6:177–178. Also in the *MCJ*9, no. 13 (June 1858): 200–201.

———. 1858d. Seymour to R. R. Gurley, 1 April. *AR* 34, no. 8:245–49. Also in the *NYCJ* 8, no. 10, whole no. 94 (1858), and the *Philadelphia Colonization Herald* (December 1858).

———. 1858e. Seymour to R. R. Gurley, 2 July 1857, in "The Pessay or Pessa Country:—New Mission Station." *AR* 34, no. 1 (1858): 5–19.

———. 1859a. Letter from Rev. G. L. Seymour, 17 December 1858. *AR* 35, no. 4:120–122. Also in the *NYCJ* 9, no. 5, whole no. 101 (1859), partly in the *Philadelphia Colonization Herald* (October 1859).

———. 1859b. Letter from Seymour, 31 December 1858. *AR* 35, no. 4:122.

———. 1859c. Letter from Seymour, 1 January. *NYCJ* 9, no. 4, whole no. 100 (1859). From the *Public Ledger* (2 March).

———. 1859d. "Liberia Interior Exploration." *NYCJ* 9, no. 9, whole no. 105 (September).

———. 1859e. Seymour to Coppinger, 2 January, in "The Liberian Explorer." *Philadelphia Colonization Herald* (March 1859). From *The National Intelligencer* 27, no. 14,531 (1 March 1859), and the *Public Ledger* (2 March 1859).

———. 1859–60. "Synopsis of Mr. Seymour's Journal of Liberia Interior Exploration." *NYCJ* 9, no. 2, whole no. 108 (December 1859); *NYCJ* 10, no. 1, whole no. 109 (January 1860); *NYCJ* 10, no. 4, whole no. 112 (April 1860).

———. 1860a. "Abstract of the Journal of Rev. G. L. Seymour of His Journey along the Interior Frontier of Liberia from Careysburg to Paynesville, between the St. Paul's and Junk Rivers." *NYCJ* 10, no. 5, whole no. 113 (May).

———. 1860b. "George L. Seymour's Journal." *LH* 7, no. 22 (4 January). Svend E. Holsoe Collection, Indiana University.

———. 1860c. Letter from Seymour, 25 January 1860. *AR* 36, no. 8:276–280. From the *Liberian Christian Advocate.*

———. 1861. Letter from Rev. George L. Seymour, 17 August 1860. *AR* 37, no. 2:60–61.

"Seymour's Travels in Western Africa." 1860. *Home and Foreign Record* 11: 302–304. Also in "Seymour's Travels." *Philadelphia Colonization Herald* (November): 494.

Seys, John. 1870. Seys to Hamilton Fish, 22 January. In U.S. Consulate Despatches 1863–1906, no. 170, microfilm 4391, roll 2.

Shakespeare, William. 1854. *The Dramatic Works of William Shakespeare with a Life of the Poet and Notes, Original and Selected.* Vol. 3. Boston: Phillips, Sampson, and Company; New York: James C. Derby.

———. 1959. *Richard III.* Edited by John Dover Wilson. Cambridge: Cambridge University Press.

———. 1966. *Henry IV.* Part 1. Oxford: Clarendon Press.

Sharp, Alfred. 1920. "The Hinterland of Liberia." *The Geographical Journal* 55: 289–305.

Sherman, M. A. B. 1975. "Some Liberian Intellectuals in the Nineteenth Century: An Appreciation." *LSJ* 6, no. 2:162–174.

Sherman, W. E. 1830. "Letter." *AR* 6, no. 4:111–117.

Sherwood, H. N. 1917. "The Formation of the American Colonization Society, 1817–1840." *Journal of Negro History* 2:209–228.

Shick, Tom W. 1980. *Behold the Promised Land: A History of Afro-American Settler Society in Nineteenth-Century Liberia.* Baltimore and London: Johns Hopkins University Press.

Shumard, Ann M. [1999]. *A Durable Memento: Portraits by Augustus Washington, African American Daguerreotypist.* Washington, D.C.: National Portrait Gallery, Smithsonian Institution.

Sibley, James L., and D. Westermann. 1928. *Liberia—Old and New: A Study of Its Social and Economic Background with Possibilities of Development.* Garden City, N.Y.: Doubleday, Doran and Company.

Siddle, D. J. 1969. "The Evolution of Rural Settlement Forms in Sierra Leone circa 1400 to 1968." *Sierra Leone Geographical Journal* 13:33–44.

Sieber, Roy. 1982. *African Textiles and Decorative Arts.* New York: Museum of Modern Art.

Siegmann, William. 1969. *Ethnographic Survey of Southeastern Liberia: Report on the Bassa.* Robertsport, Liberia: Tubman Center of African Culture.

Sims, James L. 1859. "Abstract from the Journal of a Journey in the Interior of Liberia by James L. Sims, of Monrovia." *NYCJ* 10, no. 12, whole no. 108 (December).

———. 1859–60. "Scenes in the Interior of Liberia: Being a Tour through the Countries of the Dey, Goulah, Pessah, Barlain, Kpellay, Suloang and King Boatswain's Tribes, in 1858." *MCJ* 10, no. 4 (September 1859): 65–69; *MCJ* 10, no. 5 (October 1859): 84–87; *MCJ* 10, no. 13 (June 1860): 208–213; *MCJ* 10, no. 14 (July 1860): 217–221. Also in *NYCJ* 10, no. 6, whole no. 114 (June 1860); *NYCJ* 10, no. 8, whole no. 116 (August 1860).

———. 1860a. "Travels in the Pessah and Barlain Countries." *MCJ* 10, no. 13 (June): 207–217.

———. 1860b. "The Pessah and Barlain Countries." *Philadelphia Colonization Herald* (September).

———. 1860c. "Liberia Inland Tribes." *Philadelphia Colonization Herald* (November).

———. [1860] 1996. "James Sims' Journal." *The Pepper Bird* 2, no. 10. Excerpts are from *MCJ* 10, no. 14 (1860).

Singler, John V., with J. Gbehwalahyee Mason, David K. Peewee, Lucia T. Massalee, and J. Boima Barclay Jr. 1981. *An Introduction to Liberian English.* East Lansing: Michigan State University African Studies Center.

Sixty-fifth ARACS. 1882. *AR* 58, no. 4:38–40.

Sixty-ninth ARACS. 1886. *ARACS,* 1–13.

Sixty-third ARACS. 1880. *ARACS,* 5–18.

Smith, Robert S. 1989. *Warfare and Diplomacy in Pre-colonial West Africa.* London: James Currey.

Smith, T., ed. 1995. *British Medical Association Complete Family Health Encyclopedia.* London: Dorling Kindersley.

Smyth, John H. 1879a. Smyth to William M. Evarts, 13 August, in "Message of King Blama Sissi to the Liberian Government." In U.S. Consulate Despatches 1863–1906, no. 42, roll 7.

———. 1879b. Smyth to Wm. E. Evarts, 18 November, in "Translation of Letter from President Gardner to the King of Musardu at Medina." In U.S. Consulate Despatches 1863–1906, no. 170, microfilm 4391, roll 7.

———. 1879c. Smyth to Wm. H. Evarts, 12 December. In U.S. Consulate Despatches 1863–1906, no. 170, microfilm 4391, roll 7.

———. 1880. Smyth to W. M. Evarts, 21 May, in "Report upon the Subject of the Extension of American Commerce with Liberia, and with the Nations of the Soudan." In U.S. Consulate Despatches 1863–1906, no. 170, microfilm 4391, roll 8.

———. 1882. Smyth to Eli Whitney, Jr., 28 November. In U.S. Consulate Despatches 1863–1906, no. 170, microfilm 4391, roll 4.

———. 1885. Smyth to James S. Porter, 11 May. In U.S. Consulate Despatches 1852–1906, no. 169, microfilm 4389, roll 4. In U.S. Consulate Despatches 1863–1906, no. 170, microfilm 4391, roll 7.

———. 1886. "Liberian Commerce and Agriculture." In U.S. Consulate Despatches 1852–1906, no. 169, microfilm 4389. In U.S. Consulate Despatches 1863–1906, no. 170, microfilm 4391, roll 5.

"The Spectre of an Overview of Islamic Fundamentalism in Liberia: ULIMO-K's Agenda." 1995. *New Patriot Gazette* (11 November).

Stakeman, Randolph. 1986. *The Cultural Politics of Religious Change: A Study of the Sanoyea Kpelle in Liberia.* Queenston, Ontario: Edwin Mellen Press.

Starr, Frederick, ed. 1912. *Narrative of the Expedition Despatched to Musahdu,* by Benjamin J. K. Anderson. Monrovia: College of West Africa Press.

———. 1913a. *Liberia: Description, History, Problems.* Chicago: University of Chicago Press.

———. 1913b. Starr to President Woodrow Wilson, 20 March. Frederick Starr Research Collection at the Department of Special Collections, Joseph Regenstein Library, University of Chicago, box 3, folder 7.

Starr, Frederick, Jr. 1862. "What Shall Be Done with the People of Color in the United States? A Discourse Delivered in the First Presbyterian Church of Pennsylvania, New York, November 2nd, 1862." Albany: Weed, Parsons and Company, Printers.

Statute Laws of the Republic of Liberia. 1856 [1857?]. Monrovia: G. Killian, Printer.

Steingass, R. [1898] 1969. *The Assemblies of Al Hariri, Translated from the Arabic, with Historical and Grammatical Notes.* Vol. 2. Westmead, Farnborough, Hants, England: Gregg International Publishers.

Steuart, Bradley W. 1989. *Philadelphia, PA, 1870 Census Index.* Vol. 2. Bountiful, Utah: Precision Indexing.

Stevens, A. B. 1910. "A Bird's Eye View of the Political Horizon in Maryland County, Liberia." *African League* 12, no. 4 (October): 1–2.

Stockwell. G. S. 1868. *The Republic of Liberia: Its Geography, Climate, Soil, and Productions, with a History of Its Early Settlement.* New York: A. S. Barnes and Company.

Stone, Jeffrey C. 1995. *A Short History of the Cartography of Africa.* Lewiston, New York, Queenston, Ontario, Lampeter: Edwin Mellen Press.

Strong, James. 1890. *The Exhaustive Concordance of the Bible.* New York and Nashville: Abingdon Press.

Strong, Richard P., ed. 1930. *The African Republic of Liberia and the Belgian Congo.* Vols. 1 and 2. Cambridge: Harvard University Press.

Sumawolo. 1984. Interviewed by Martin Ford in Gban, Liberia. Translated by Faliku Sanoe.

Sundström, Lars. [1965] 1974. *The Exchange Economy of Pre-colonial Tropical Africa.* London: C. Hurst and Company.

Sundiata, I. K. 1980. *Black Scandal: America and the Liberia Labor Crisis.* Philadelphia: Institute for the Study of Human Issues.

Supplementary Act to the Act Providing for the Establishment of an Interior Settlement. 1858. *ATL:* 33–34.

"Survey for a Rail Road." 1880. *Sixty-third ARACS,* 14–16.

Syfert, Dwight N. 1975. "The Origins of Privilege: Liberian Merchants, 1822–1847." *LSJ* 6, no. 2:109–128.

———. 1977a. "A History of the Liberian Coastal Trade, 1821–1900." Ph.D. diss., Indiana University.

———. 1977b. "The Liberian Coastal Trade, 1822–1900." *JAH* 18, no. 2:217–235.

T., J. "Railroads in Liberia." 1871. *AR* 47, no. 1:6–9.

Taryor, Nya Kwiawon, Sr. 1989. "Religions in Liberia." *Liberia-Forum* 5, no. 8:3–17.

Thach, Sharon V., with David J. Dwyer. 1981. *A Reference Handbook of Kpelle.* East Lansing: Michigan State University African Studies Center.

Tham, Percy. 1972–74. "Liberian Gunpowder." *LSJ* 5, no. 2:107–111.

"That Celebrated Election Case." 1927. *The Agricultural World* 36, no. 11:8.

Thomas, Lamont D. 1986. *Paul Cuffe: Black Entrepreneur and Pan-Africanist.* Urbana and Chicago: University of Illinois Press.

Thomasson, Gordon Conrad. 1987. "Indigenous Knowledge Systems, Sciences, and Technologies: Ethnographic and Ethnohistorical Perspectives on the Educational Foundations for Development in Kpelle Culture." Ph.D. diss., Cornell University.

———. 1991. "Liberia's Seeds of Knowledge." *Cultural Survival Quarterly* (Summer): 23–28.

Thompson, George. 1852. *Thompson in Africa, or An Account of the Missionary Labours . . . of George Thompson in Western Africa at the Mendi Station.* Cleveland: D. M. Ide.

———. 1856. "Rev. George Thompson." *NYCJ* 7.

Thompson, H. 1911. "The Forests of Southern Nigeria." *Journal of the African Society* 10, no. 38:120–145.

Todson, G. P. 1840. "Africa and the Africans: With the Resources of the Colonists of Liberia,—Productions, Animal and Vegetable." *AR* 16, no. 6: 81–84.

Tonkin, Elizabeth. 1981. "Model and Ideology: Dimensions of Being Civilized in Liberia." In *The Structure of Folk Models,* edited by Ladislav Holy and Milan Stuchlik. London: Academic Press.

Toupou. 1989. "L'histoire du pays Toma à travers les Toponymes." In "Memoire de fin d'étude supérieures." Université Jules Nyerere, Kankan, Republique de Guinée.

"Tour among West-African Mahommedans." 1869. *AR* 45, no. 4:126–127.

"Tour into the Interior." 1852. *NYCJ* 3, no. 2 (March).

Tracy, Joseph. 1869. "Muhammedanism in Central Africa." *AR* 45, no. 8:237–241.

"Trade in Montserrado County." 1881. *Observer* (Monrovia) 4, no. 16 (8 September).

The Tribes of the Western Province and the Denwoin People. 1955. Monrovia, Liberia: Bureau of Folkways, Interior Department.

Tuchscherer, Konrad. 1996. "The Kikakai (Mendi) Syllabary and Number Writing System: Descriptive, Historical and Ethnographical Accounts of a West African Tradition of Writing." Ph.D. diss., University of London.

———. 1999. "The Lost Script of Bagam." *African Affairs* 98:55–77.

United Kingdom. House of Commons. 1865. "Report of the Select Committee on West Africa." *Parliamentary Papers,* 5 question 3962.

Untitled article. 1921. *The Liberian Patriot* (20 August): first page missing.

Viator. 1870. "Excursion to Kaipo's Creek." *AR* 46, no. 12:354–357.

Vikør, Knut S. 2000. "Sufi Brotherhoods in Africa." In *The History of Islam in Africa,* edited by Nehemia Levtzion and Randall L. Pouwells, 441–476. Athens, Oxford, and Cape Town: Ohio University Press and James Currey.

Voigt, K. H. 1997. *Biographisch Bibliographisches Kirchenlexicon,* s.v. "Treviranus," 12:474–479.

Voorhees, P. F. 1834. "Letter from Captain Voorhees, of the United States Navy." *AR* 10, no. 2:20–22.

"Voyage du Capitaine Binger, 1887–1889." 1890. *Journal le Temps (Le Soudan Français)*, supplement (March): 1–4.

"Voyage to Liberia—Continued: The Emigrants." 1857. *MCJ*, n.s., 9, no. 3:33–39.

"Voyages of the Ship *M.C. Stevens*." 1857. *MCJ*, n.s., 9, no. 6 (November): 81–82.

Vydrine, Valentin F. 1987. *Iazyk Looma* [Loma Dictionary]. Akademiia nauk SSSR, Ordena Trudovogo Krasnogo Znameni Institut vostokovedeniia. Moskva: Izd-vo "Nauka," Glav. red vostochnoi lit-ry.

———. 1999. *Manding-English Dictionary (Maninka, Bamana)*. Vol. 1. St. Petersburg: Dimitry Bulanin Publishing House.

W., R. 1870. "Interior Trade of West Africa." *AR* 56, no. 12:370–372.

Walls, Andrew F. 1999. "Africa as the Theatre of Christian Engagement with Islam in the Nineteenth Century." *Journal of Religion in Africa* 29, no. 2: 155–174.

Wallis, Braithwaite. 1910. "A Tour in the Liberian Hinterland." *The Geographical Journal* 35:285–295.

Washington, Augustus. 1851. "African Colonization." *AR* 27, no. 9:259–265. From the *New York Tribune*. Reprinted in Moses 1998a, 194–197.

———. 1851–1863. "Five Letters on Liberian Colonization (1851–1863)." In *Liberian Dreams: Back-to-Africa Narratives from the 1850s*, edited by Wilson Jeremiah Moses, 179–224. University Park: Pennsylvania State University Press.

———. 1854. Augustus Washington to John Orcutt, 8 February. *AR* 30, no. 6: 185–188. Reprinted in Moses 1998a, 198–201.

———. 1855a. Letter from Augustus Washington. *AR* 31, no. 10:296–297. From the *Philadelphia Colonization Herald*.

———. 1855b. "A Message from A. Washington." *AR* 31, no. 6:178.

———. 1859. Augustus Washington to Mrs. L. H. Sigourney, 8 July. *AR* 35, no. 11:331–340.

———. 1864. "Six Thousand Dollars Better." *AR* 40, no. 3:90–91. Reprinted in Moses 1998a, 222–224.

Watt, J. [1794] 1994. *Journal of James Watt: Expedition to Timbo, Capital of the Futa Empire in 1794*. Edited and introduced by B. L. Mouser. Madison: University of Wisconsin, Madison, African Studies Program.

Wauwermans, Colonel. 1885. *Liberia: Historie de la fondation d'un état negre libre*. Brussels: Institut National de Géographie.

"We Are Compelled to Hold." 1903. *West African Mail* 1, no. 29 (16 October): 773.

"We Have Busied Ourselves." 1903. *Liberia Recorder* 6, no. 2 (28 November): 7.

Webb, James L. A. 1993. "The Horse and Slave Trade between the Western Sahara and Senegambia." *JAH* 34, no. 2:221–246.

———. 1995. *Desert Frontier: Ecological and Economic Change among the Western Sahel, 1600–1850.* Madison: University of Wisconsin Press.

Weir, H. T. 1953. *Shorter Encyclopedia of Islam,* s.v. "Sadaka," 483–484. Ithaca, N.Y.: Cornell University Press.

Weisswange, Karin I. S. 1976. "Mutual Relations between Loma and Mandingo in Liberia According to Oral Historical Tradition." Paper presented at the Eighth Annual Liberian Studies Conference, Bloomington.

Welmers, William E. 1949. "Secret Medicines, Magic, and Rites of the Kpelle Tribe in Liberia." *Southwestern Journal of Anthropology* 5:208–243.

———. 1958. "The Mande Languages." In *Report on the Ninth Annual Round Table Meeting on Linguistics and Language Studies,* 9–24. Washington, D.C.: Georgetown University Press.

———. 1974. "Manya." Unpublished manuscript. Monrovia: Institute for Liberian Languages.

"West Africa." 1872. *Times* (London), 21 October.

"West African Exploration." 1873. *AR* 49, no. 11:345–346.

"West African Mails." 1873. *AR* 49, no. 1:30–31.

Whatley, Richard. 1867. *Historic Doubts Relative to Napoleon Bonaparte, and Historic Certainties Respecting the Early History of America.* New York: R. Carter and Brothers.

Whetstone, Harold. 1955. *Lutheran Mission in Liberia.* Board of Foreign Missions of the United Lutheran Church in America.

White, Gavin. 1971. "Firearms in Africa: An Introduction." *JAH* 7, no. 2:173–184.

White, Susan L. 1974. "Iron Production and Iron Trade in Northern and Central Liberia: History of a Major Indigenous Technology." Paper read at the Sixth Annual Liberian Studies Conference, Madison, Wisconsin, April.

Whitehurst, A. D. 1936. "Mr. Whitehurst's Journal." *AR* 12, no. 4 (April 1836): 105–111; 12, no. 5 (May 1836): 144–150; 12, no. 6 (June 1836): 177–184; 12, no. 7 (July 1836): 208–216; 12, no. 8 (August 1836): 241–246; 12, no. 9 (September 1836): 273–281; 12, no. 10 (October 1836): 307–315.

Wiley, Bell I. 1980. *Slaves No More: Letters from Liberia, 1833–1869.* Lexington: University Press of Kentucky.

Wilkeson, Samuel. 1839. "Concise History of the Commencement, Progress and Present Condition of the American Colonies in Liberia." Washington, D.C.: Madisonian Office located at the Library of Congress.

Wilkinson, Frederick. 1981. *A Source Book of Small Arms.* London: Ward Lock.

Wilkinson, James John Garth. 1892. *The African and the True Christian Religion: His Magna Charta—A Study in the Writings of Emanuel Swedenborg.* London: J. Speirs.

Wilks, Ivor. 2000. "The Juula and the Expansion of Islam into the Forest." In *The History of Islam in Africa,* edited by Nehemia Levtzion and Randall L.

Pouwels, 93–116. Athens, Oxford, and Cape Town: Ohio University Press and James Currey.

Williams, Samuel. [1857] 1998. "Four Years in Liberia: A Sketch of the Life of the Rev. Samuel Williams, with Remarks on the Missions, Manners and Customs of the Natives of Western Africa. Together with an Answer to Nesbit's Book." In *Liberian Dreams: Back-to-Africa Narratives from the 1850s,* edited by Wilson Jeremiah Moses, 127–178. University Park: Pennsylvania State University Press.

Wilson, D. A. 1869. "Reminiscences of Sierra Leone." *AR* 45:327–333.

Wilson, J. Leighton. 1836. "Extracts from the Journal of Mr. Wilson." *Missionary Herald* (May): 193–197; (June): 242–248; (July): 387.

———. 1856. *Western Africa: Its History, Condition, and Prospects.* New York: Harper and Brothers.

Winterbottom, T. [1803] 1969. *An Account of the Native Africans in the Neighbourhood of Sierra Leone.* London: Frank Cass.

Wondj, C. 1992. "The States and Cultures of the Upper Guinea Coast." In *The General History of Africa.* Vol. 5, *Africa from the Sixteenth to the Eighteenth Century,* edited by B. A. Ogot, 168–398. Berkeley and Los Angeles: University of California Press.

Wylie, Kenneth C. 1989. "From the Fountainheads of the Niger: Researching a Multiethnic Regional History." In *Studies in the African Diaspora: A Memorial to James R. Hooker (1929–1976),* edited by John P. Henderson and Harry A. Reed, 67–86. Dover, Mass.: Majority Press.

Zahan, Dominique. 1974. *The Bambara.* Leiden: E. J. Brill.

Zahniser, Clarence Howard. 1957. *Earnest Christian: Life and Works of Benjamin Titus Robert.* Winona Lake, Ind.: Free Methodist Publishing House.

Zetterström, Kjell. 1980. "Poro of the Yameni Mano, Liberia." *Ethnologische Zeitschrift Zürich* 1:41–55.

Index

General Headings

(*) indicates a substantial discussion of the entry.
Numbers in italics refer to illustrations.

Geographic Locations

Groups: Kinship, Social, Political and National

Individuals

JAMES FAIRHEAD is Professor of Social Anthropology at the University of Sussex. He has written extensively on agricultural, environmental, and historical issues in the Republic of Guinea and the Democratic Republic of Congo.

TIM GEYSBEEK has taught at ELWA Academy in Monrovia, Liberia, and is Visiting Assistant Professor of History at Grand Valley State University. He has published some of his work in *History in Africa* and the *Liberian Studies Journal.*

SVEND E. HOLSOE is Professor Emeritus of Anthropology at the University of Delaware. He has done extensive research on Liberia and is the founding editor of the *Liberian Studies Journal.*

MELISSA LEACH is Professorial Fellow at the Institute of Development Studies at the University of Sussex. She has researched and published extensively on issues of gender, environment, science, and history in West Africa.